# New Hampshire

Kim Grant

AN EXPLORER'S GUIDE

# New Hampshire

Christina Tree & Christine Hamm

FIFTH EDITION

The Countryman Press * Woodstock, Vermont

We welcome your comments and suggestions. Please contact Explorer's Guide Editor, The Countryman Press, P.O. Box 748, Woodstock, Vermont 05091, or e-mail countrymanpress@wwnorton.com.



Fifth Edition



ISBN 0-88150-515-3
ISSN 1538-8409

Maps by XNR Productions, © 2002 The Countryman Press
Book design by Bodenweber Design
Text composition by PerfecType, Nashville, TN
Cover photograph of Stark, NH, by Robert J. Kozlow

Published by The Countryman Press, P.O. Box 748, Woodstock, Vermont 05091

Distributed by W. W. Norton & Company, Inc., 500 Fifth Avenue, New York, NY 10110

Printed in the United States of America

10 9 8 7 6 5 4 3 2

# EXPLORE WITH US!

Welcome to the most widely used and comprehensive travel guide to the Granite State. As we have expanded our guide in response to the increase in ways to explore New Hampshire, we have also been increasingly selective, making recommendations based on years of conscientious research. All inclusions—attractions, inns, and restaurants—are chosen on the basis of personal experience, not paid advertising.

We hope you'll find our new design attractive and easy to read. Although we've kept the organization simple, the following points will help to get you started on your way.

## WHAT'S WHERE

In the beginning of the book you'll find an alphabetical listing of highlights and important information that you may want to reference quickly.

## LODGING

**Prices:** Please don't hold us or the respective innkeepers responsible for the rates listed as of press time in 2002. Some changes are inevitable. The state rooms and meals tax is 8 percent as of this writing, but that also may change. The following codes are used to specify: **EP:** lodging only; **MAP:** lodging, breakfast, and dinner; **B&B:** lodging and breakfast; **AP:** lodging and three meals.

## RESTAURANTS

In most sections, please note a distinction between *Dining Out* and *Eating Out*. In the *Dining Out* section, prices not listed specifically range from:
**Moderate:** \$12–18. **Expensive:** \$18–25. **Very Expensive:** over \$25.
Restaurants in the *Eating Out* group are generally inexpensive.

## KEY TO SYMBOLS

- The special value symbol appears next to lodging and restaurants that combine quality and moderate prices.
- The kids alert symbol appears next to lodgings, restaurants, activities, and shops of special appeal to youngsters.
- ♿ The wheelchair symbol appears next to lodgings, restaurants, and attractions that are partially or completely handicapped accessible.
- The pet symbol appears next to lodgings that accept pets (usually with prior notice).
- The wedding ring symbol denotes properties that specialize in weddings.

We would appreciate your comments and corrections about places you visit or know well in the state. Please address your correspondence to Explorer's Guide Editor, The Countryman Press, P.O. Box 748, Woodstock, VT 05091. You can also e-mail Chris Tree: ctree@traveltree.net.

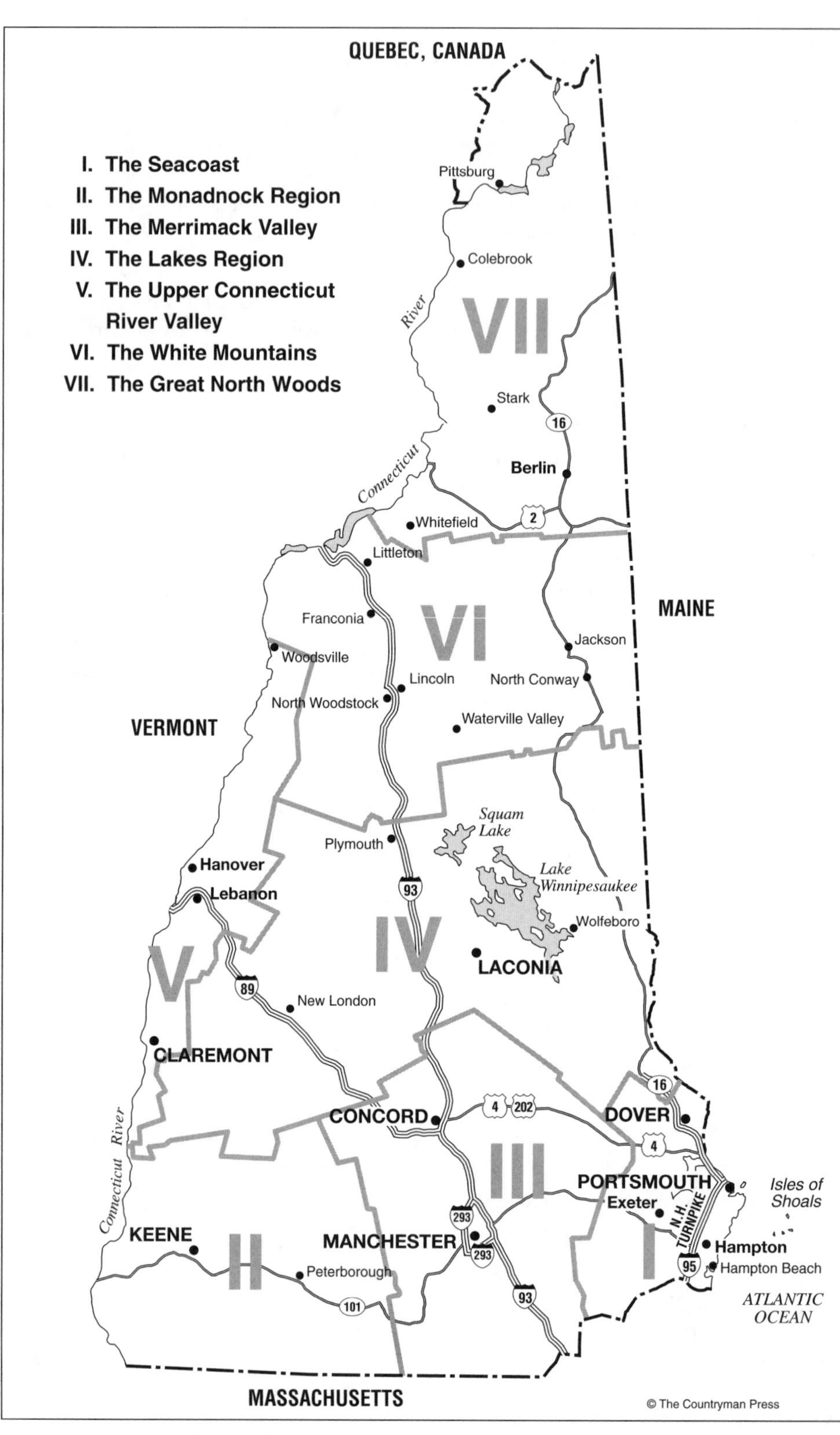

QUEBEC, CANADA
I. The Seacoast
II. The Monadnock Region
III. The Merrimack Valley
IV. The Lakes Region
V. The Upper Connecticut River Valley
VI. The White Mountains
VII. The Great North Woods
Pittsburg
Colebrook
River
VII
Stark
16
Connecticut
Berlin
Whitefield
2
Littleton
Franconia
VI
MAINE
Jackson
Woodsville
Lincoln
North Conway
North Woodstock
Waterville Valley
VERMONT
Squam Lake
Plymouth
Hanover
Lake Winnipesaukee
Lebanon
93
IV
Wolfeboro
V
LACONIA
89
New London
CLAREMONT
16
4
202
CONCORD
DOVER
4
Connecticut River
III
PORTSMOUTH
Isles of Shoals
Exeter
N.H. TURNPIKE
KEENE
II
293
MANCHESTER
293
I
Hampton
95
Hampton Beach
Peterborough
101
93
ATLANTIC OCEAN
MASSACHUSETTS
© The Countryman Press

# CONTENTS

# INTRODUCTION

In the 19th century fine scenery, fresh air, and a flourishing work ethic brought thousands of tourists to New Hampshire. Ever since artist Thomas Cole first visited the Granite State in 1827, his pictures and those of a host of followers brought the landscape that Cole called "a union of the picturesque, the sublime, and the magnificent" to the attention of the world. Mark Twain, who summered in the Monadnock region, reported that "the atmosphere of the New Hampshire highlands is exceptionally bracing and stimulating, and a fine aid to hard and continuous work." Visitors came to see for themselves.

With the improvement of roads and the coming of the railroads, the fame of the region spread. As the eastern seaboard became more and more urbanized, the country atmosphere of New Hampshire's farms and villages offered a step back in time that was only a short train ride away.

At the same time that small country households throughout the state were opening their doors to guests, major entrepreneurs were investing in the new business of tourism. By the turn of the 20th century, the Granite State had become the most heavily touristed spot in New England, with a greater concentration of grand resort hotels in New Hampshire's White Mountains than anywhere else in America. Travelers flocked to hundreds of these wooden hotels, built to accommodate city dwellers who wanted a sanitized version of the wilderness, a kind of eastern dude ranch in which families could ride in the relative comfort of a stagecoach to view the Flume, Echo Lake, and the Old Man of the Mountain. In late afternoon parents and grandparents could retire to a rocking chair, sip a glass of claret, and view the peaks of the Presidentials from the cloister of a sweeping, colonnaded porch. This curious mix of wilderness and civility made the area an ideal destination. Most tourists stayed at one hotel for a week, a month, or for the entire summer season. Far enough away but not so dangerously distant as the still wild-seeming West, the towering waterfalls, emerald hills, and placid ponds of New Hampshire offered an escape to another world.

In the early part of the 20th century, the automobile changed this vacation pattern. As travelers gained more mobility, the large establishments with all their amenities for a full "season" closed. Many of the big, wooden hotels were destroyed by fire, while others were razed, unable to compete with the more economical cabin colonies and, later, motels. For New Hampshire there was a real decline in the number of accommodations available for visitors. This situation changed dramatically during the 1980s and '90s, however, when the state experienced an explosion of new lodgings. The proliferation of inviting places to stay—all around the state, not just along tried-and-true tourist routes—inspired us to present an accurate picture of attractions and facilities throughout the state.

This book is intended for New Hampshire residents and visitors alike. No other portrait of the state gathers so much practical information between two covers. All listings in this book are free; there is no paid advertising.

Each chapter focuses on a different region. It begins with a verbal snapshot of the landscape and historical background. Sources of information, how to get around, and descriptions of everything to see and do, from winter sports to places to swim and picnic, follow. Then come capsule descriptions of places to stay. Our focus is on inns and bed & breakfasts because we feel that the Mobil and AAA guides do a fine job with motels. We have personally visited more than 90 percent of the lodgings included (that other 10 percent have been highly recommended). We include prices for lodging, because categories like "moderate" and "expensive" can be misleading, depending on what they include. Please allow for inflation. Most lodging places add the 8 percent New Hampshire room and meals tax (a small percentage include it in the price), and some also add a service charge; be sure to inquire. After lodging come critiques of local upscale restaurants *(Dining Out)* and more casual options *(Eating Out).* We also describe shops worth seeking out and the special events of that area.

In recent decades lodging options have widened throughout the state. This trend is particularly noticeable along New Hampshire's seacoast, where visitors can now linger long enough in and around historic Portsmouth to sample the region's many fine restaurants, theater, museums, boat excursions, and beaches. It's equally noteworthy in the Monadnock region, which remains pristine ironically because it's too near Boston to be generally viewed as a place to stay the night. So it happens that despite its exceptional beauty, great hiking and biking, and the quality of its inns and B&Bs (which give guests access to the swimming holes that are off-limits to day-trippers), it remains low-key and relatively pristine.

Lake Winnipesaukee, the state's largest lake, remains the popular tourist destination that it's been for more than a century. Still, it harbors a surprising number of quiet corners, especially along its northern and western shores, around Squam Lake and in the hills around Center Sandwich.

In the region we call the Western Lakes—because it harbors so many lakes, not just Sunapee—myriad widely scattered lodging places offer access to swimming, sailing, summer theater, fine dining, and hiking up such mountains as Sunapee, Kearsarge, and Cardigan.

The Upper Valley region includes towns scattered along both the Vermont and New Hampshire banks of the Connecticut River for some 20 miles north and south of Dartmouth College. Here you can enjoy a picnic and chamber music concert on the lawns of the Saint-Gaudens National Site in Cornish, New Hampshire, overlooking Mount Ascutney (in Vermont). The country's longest covered bridge links the two. Esssentially rural, this is also one of New England's most sophisticated corners, with outstanding museums, dining, and lodging.

The White Mountains form a ragged line, beginning near the Connecticut River with Mount Moosilauke and marching diagonally northeast across New Hampshire. We begin by describing the Western Whites, a rugged region largely within the White Mountain National Forest. It includes Loon Mountain and Waterville Valley, both founded as ski areas but now full-fledged year-round resorts, especially good bets for families, offering varied activities and condo-based lodging. This region also includes dramatic Franconia Notch and the old resort communities of Franconia, Sugar Hill, and Bethlehem.

Mount Washington, literally the high point of New England, has been New Hampshire's top tourist attraction for more than 150 years. Accessible by cog railway and car or "Stage" as well as by spectacular hiking trails from all directions, it remains magnificent and untamed. This region has loomed large on the national ski map since the birth of alpine skiing. It presently offers a choice of half a dozen varied ski resorts and hundreds of miles of outstanding cross-country trails. During summer and fall it is a mecca for hikers and technical climbers as well as a great family destination, offering an easy entrée both to natural and human-made attractions. It also represents New Hampshire's largest concentration of lodging places, complemented by a wide range of dining spots and an enormous variety of outlet shopping. We call the foothills of the White Mountains, just south of this area, the Mount Washington Gateway region. It's spotted with small lakes, inviting country roads and villages, and some exceptional places to stay.

The least touristed section of the state is the Great North Woods, the vast forested area that includes the northern White Mountains, the headwaters of the Connecticut River, and the mighty Androscoggin. Here moose graze beside the roads, and you can find wilderness campsites and fall asleep to the call of loons. You can also stay in The Balsams and the newly reopened Mountain View, two surviving grand hotels or in a surprisingly wide choice of sporting camps and lodges.

Most visitors scoot on by the urban communities along the Merrimack Valley in southern New Hampshire, but several well-marked sights are well worth the short detours off I-93. Manchester offers the superb Currier Gallery of Art and a fascinating walking tour of what was once the world's largest mill community. Concord's state capitol building is the oldest in the nation still in use, and the Museum of New Hampshire History across the street offers a superb introduction to the state. The city also boasts the state-of-the-art Christa McAuliffe Planetarium and the recently renovated Capitol Center for the Arts, featuring big-name entertainers. In contrast, a quick dip off the highway reveals that many of the surrounding towns are as picturesque as any in New England.

One author of this book is a "visitor," the other a longtime resident. Chris Tree has explored the Granite State for more than 30 years as a travel writer whose New England stories appear regularly in the *Boston Globe* Sunday travel section. She is the author of *How New England Happened* (a historical guide to the region) and coauthor of *Best Places to Stay in New England* and the Explorer's Guides to Maine, Massachusetts, and Vermont.

Christine Hamm first moved to Hopkinton, New Hampshire, in 1972. She recently exchanged her circa-1790 farmhouse at the end of an old dirt road for a "new" home of the same vintage in Hopkinton's much-admired white clapboard village. In addition to her weekly contributions to the *Concord Monitor*'s arts and entertainment pages, Christine has written for several other New Hampshire publications, including *New Hampshire Home, New Hampshire Images,* and *New Hampshire Legacy,* and is a feature writer for the New Hampshire Humanities Council. Her "Editor's Picks" for New Hampshire appear in *Yankee Magazine's* Annual Guide to New England. Chronicles of her frequent adventures outside the state have appeared in the travel section of the *New York Post.*

The authors wish to thank Peter Randall, original coauthor of the book, who contributed hugely to its first two editions, and Martha Coombs, who assisted in updating this edition. We also owe thanks to numerous local chambers of commerce, innkeepers, and friends who helped provide and check information for the book. Chris could not have written the "Great North Woods" chapter without help from Dick Mallion of Whitefield; she also wants to thank Annie Bartlett of Lancaster, Stan Judge, and the Philbrook family of Shelburne. For help with the Lakes region, thanks to the Carpenter family and to Susan Cerutti of Meredith, to Susan and John Davies of Sandwich, to Mary DeVries of Wolfeboro, and to Lorie McClory of the Greater New London Chamber of Commerce. For the Mount Washington Valleys we are indebted to Karen Erickson of Tamworth, Marti Mayne of the chamber, Rob Burbank of the AMC, and Fritz Koeppel of Jackson. For the Monadnock region thanks go to Janet Reilly and Karen Bannister of the Greater Peterborough Chamber of Commerce, to Carol Bickhart and Brenda Woods of the Greater Keene Chamber of Commerce, to Freda Haupt of Fitzwilliam, and to Ann and John Keefe of Peterborough. More thanks go to Carolyn O'Brien of the Greater Concord Chamber of Commerce and to Meredith B. Nickerson of the Greater Manchester Chamber of Commerce for their help with the Merrimack Valley Region. For help with the Upper Valley we are indebted to Kay and Peter Shumway. We would also like to thank the state of New Hampshire's Division of Travel and Tourism's Lauri Ostrander Klefos and Terry Rayno, and publicist Jayme Simoes. Thanks especially to our editors, Ann Kraybill and Kermit Hummel at The Countryman Press, for their support and patience.

# WHAT'S WHERE IN NEW HAMPSHIRE

**AREA CODE 603** covers all of New Hampshire.

**AGRICULTURAL FAIRS** New Hampshire boasts a baker's dozen summer and fall country fairs. Part of the social fabric of the 19th century, and still popular today, the country fair is the place where farm families meet their friends and exhibit their best home-canned and fresh vegetables, livestock, and handwork such as quilts, baked goods, and needlework. Horse and cattle pulling, 4-H competitions, horse shows, and woodsmen's competitions are joined by midways, food stalls, and exhibits of farm implements, home furnishings, and a host of other items. The *New Hampshire's Rural Heritage* pamphlet from the **New Hampshire Department of Agriculture** (603-271-3551; www.nhfarms.com) lists the dates and locations of all fairs. These events are also mentioned in the *Special Events* sections of this book. The largest fair is Deerfield, held annually in fall, but other popular fairs include Hopkinton and Lancaster, both held on Labor Day weekend; Cheshire Fair in Swanzey, held in early August; and Sandwich, on Columbus Day weekend. Additionally, many local towns and organizations hold annual 1-day fairs. Check with local chambers of commerce for exact dates.

**AIR SERVICE Manchester Airport** (603-624-6539; www.flymanchester.com) has recently expanded to become a major New England gateway. It's served by United Airlines and United Express (1-800-241-6522), USAirways and USAirways Express (1-800-428-4322), Con-tinental Express (1-800-525-0280), Air Canada (1-888-247-2262), Delta Air Lines (1-800-221-1212), Delta Connection Comair (1-800-354-9822), Northwest Airlines (1-800-225-2525), and Southwest Airlines (1-800-435-9792), and by national rental car companies. **Lebanon Municipal Airport** (603-298-8878), just off I-89 in West Lebanon, is served by USAirways Express to Boston, New York, and Philadelphia. Boston's **Logan**

**International Airport** (617-488-2800) and **Portland (Maine) International Jetport** (207-775-5809) are also major gateways for New Hampshire. In addition, the state offers 20 airfields without scheduled service. Flying schools are located at Berlin, Claremont, Concord, Hampton, Jaffrey, Keene, Laconia, Lebanon, Manchester, Nashua, Rochester, Whitefield, and Wolfeboro. For details contact the **New Hampshire Division of Aeronautics** (603-271-2551), 65 Airport Road, Concord 03301.

**AMTRAK** After many years without service, New Hampshire now has daily service to New York and Montreal, albeit on the **Vermonter** (1-800-872-7245; www.Amtrak.com), which stops at Claremont and White River Junction, Vermont.

**ANTIQUARIAN BOOKSHOPS** It's hard to resist a good old book, and New Hampshire has enough dealers in used, rare, and antiquarian books to keep any bibliophile busy just looking for bargains, to say nothing of actually sitting down and reading newly found treasures. Among the specialty dealers are shops selling first editions and books related to espionage, gardening, the White Mountains, hot-air ballooning, and women's studies. One shop has only 750 volumes, while several others approach 100,000 titles to search. Members of the **New Hampshire Antiquarian Booksellers Association** are listed on their web site (www.conknet.com-bksbylaake/nh-aba.html) or at most antiquarian bookstores.

**ANTIQUES** The **New Hampshire Antiques Dealers Association** (P.O. Box 2033, Hampton 03843; www.nhada.org) lists some 170 dealers and nearly 20 group shops in the state, more than enough to keep the antiques buff happy. From the seacoast to the mountains and from the Lakes region to the Monadnock region, there are dealers in nearly every community, and the diversity of items offered equals any to be found in New England. Perhaps the largest concentration of shops is along Route 4 in Northwood and Epsom, but nearby Concord, Hopkinton, and Contoocook have nearly as many shops. Meredith, Center Harbor, and Center Sandwich also have many shops, as do Hillsboro, Peterborough, Fitzwilliam, and Route 1 in the seacoast area. The association's annual show is held in early August in Manchester, but several other annual shows are listed elsewhere in this book.

**APPALACHIAN MOUNTAIN CLUB** Founded in 1876 to blaze and map hiking trails through the White Mountains, the AMC was a crucial lobbying group for the passage of the Weeks Act. Today it continues to support environmental causes and cater to hikers, maintaining hundreds of miles of trails and feeding and sheltering hikers in a chain of eight "high huts" (see *High Huts of the White Mountains* and *Hiking*) in the Presidential Range, each a day's hike apart. **Pinkham Notch Camp** (603-466-2727; www.outdoors.org), Box 298, Gorham 03581, a comfortable complex at the eastern base of Mount Washington, serves as headquarters for the high huts and as a year-round center for a wide variety of workshops in subjects ranging from nature drawing to North Country literature as well as camping and cross-country skiing. The AMC also maintains a hostel-like

Rob Burbank/AMC

camping and lodging facility at Mount Cardigan, runs shuttle buses for hikers around Mount Washington, and much more. Their guidebooks (see *Canoeing and Kayaking* and *Hiking*) remain the best of their kind. For more information contact AMC headquarters at 5 Joy Street, Boston, MA 02108 (617-536-0636).

**APPLE AND FRUIT PICKING** New Hampshire has many orchards and farms where you can pick your own apples, pears, peaches, and berries, and press cider. The vegetable- and fruit-picking season begins in early summer, while apples and other tree fruits ripen as fall begins. Many orchards have weekend festivals with fresh-baked apple pies, doughnuts and cider, pumpkins, tractor-pulled wagon rides, music, and other activities aimed at making a perfect family outing. Don't forget to visit the orchards in spring when the trees are blossoming. From the **New Hampshire Department of Agriculture** (603-271-3788; www.nhfarms.com), request the *Experience Rural New Hampshire* and *Harvest New Hampshire* pamphlets.

**ART MUSEUMS AND GALLERIES** New Hampshire's two major art museums are the **Currier Gallery of Art** (currier.org) in Manchester and the **Hood Museum of Art** at Dartmouth College. The Currier's collection includes some outstanding 19th- and 20th-century European and American works, and the museum is a departure point for tours to the Zimmerman House, designed by Frank Lloyd Wright. The Hood Museum's permanent collection ranges from some outstanding ancient Assyrian bas-reliefs to Picasso and Frank Stella. Both museums stage changing exhibits. (See "The Manchester/Nashua Area" and "Upper Valley Towns" for descriptions of each museum.)

**BANDS** Town bands are still popular in New Hampshire, and many hold summer concerts in outdoor bandstands. Schedules change yearly, so check with local chambers of commerce. Conway, North Conway, Alton, Wolfeboro, Exeter, and Hampton Beach are among the places with regular band concerts. The Temple Band claims to be the oldest town band in the country.

**BED & BREAKFASTS** B&Bs appear under their own listing within the *Lodging* section of each chapter. We don't list every one, but we checked out every B&B we could find. Our selection ranges from working farms to historic mansions and from two-guest-room, private homes to larger places with a score or more of rooms. B&B rates in this book are for two people (unless otherwise specified); single rates are somewhat lower.

**BICYCLING** The Monadnock region is particularly popular with touring bikes (see Peterborough for rentals). For mountain biking check Waterville Valley and Loon Mountain in "The Western Whites"; Mount Sunapee and Gunstock in "The Lakes Region"; Great Glen Trails; and Attitash Bear Peak in Bartlett. Other popular venues include **Bear Brook State Park** in Allentown (603-485-9874), **Pawtuckaway State Park** in Raymond (603-895-3031), and **Pisgah State Park** in Winchester (603-239-8153). Maps for the White Mountain National Forest can be obtained by calling 603-528-8721. The **Granite State Wheelmen** schedules frequent rides throughout the state for resident bicycling enthusiasts. Write to 215 South Broadway #216, Salem 03079-3309.

**BIRDING** Our favorite venues include coastal Route 1A from Seabrook to New Castle, which provides numerous ocean, harbor, and salt-marsh vantage points for observing shorebirds and sea fowl of all types, as well as various ducks and larger wading birds, especially in summer when snowy egrets, great and little blue herons, glossy ibis, and black-crowned night herons are common. Umbagog Lakes, described in "Northern White Mountains," has nesting eagles and ospreys, loons, and other freshwater birds. In the course of the book we have described many of the more than 40 properties maintained by the Audubon Society of New Hampshire (603-224-9909; www.nhaudubon.org). Regional Audubon chapters offer bird walks throughout the year. Audubon House, the society's headquarters (3 Silk Road, Concord, just off I-89, Exit 2), includes an information center and Audubon Nature Store (open Monday through Saturday, 9 AM–5 PM; Sunday noon–5 PM) and walking trails around Great Turkey Pond.

**BOATING** New Hampshire law requires all boats used in fresh water to be registered, a formality that most marinas can provide. Otherwise contact the **New Hampshire Department of Safety, Motor Vehicle Division** (603-271-2251), Hazen Drive, Concord 03301, or the **Division of Safety Services** (603-271-3336). In the Lake Winnipesaukee area, contact the **Safety Services Marine Division** (603-293-2037), Route 11, Glendale. Boats used in tidal waters must be registered with the U.S. Coast Guard. Contact the **USCG Portsmouth Harbor Station** (603-436-0171), New Castle 03854; the **New Hampshire Port Authority** (603-436-8500), Box 506, 555 Market Street, Portsmouth 03802; or the **New Hampshire Department of Safety, Marine Services Division** (603-431-1170), Portsmouth State Fish Pier, Box 1355, Portsmouth 03802. (Also see *Canoeing and Kayaking.*) Request the excellent *New Hampshire Boating & Fishing Public Access Map* from the **New Hampshire Fish and Game Department** (603-271-2224; www.wildlife.state.nh.us).

**BOOKS** Many New Hampshire books are mentioned throughout this guide. The **Mountain Wanderer Map & Book Store** in Lincoln (1-800-745-2707; www.mountainwanderer.com) is

Kim Grant

devoted to New Hampshire maps and guidebooks; author-owner Steve Smith is himself an authority on the state's history, hiking, and snowshoeing. For a general history of the state, try *New Hampshire* by Elting and Elizabeth Morison, Jere Daniell's *Colonial New Hampshire: A History*, and *New Hampshire: Portrait of the Land and Its People.* Although these three long-time standards are currently out of print, they are likely to be available at your local library or through interlibrary loan. Peter Randall's *New Hampshire: A Living Landscape* (University Press of New England) is a collection of panoramic photographs. The *New Hampshire Atlas & Gazetteer* (DeLorme) has topographic maps that cover the entire state, plus detailed maps of all major communities. The Appalachian Mountain Club publishes the definitive guidebooks to outdoor recreation in New Hampshire (1-800-262-4455; www.outdoors.org). Also be sure to check with independent bookstores, most of which have strong local book sections and may carry titles that are not available elsewhere.

**BUS SERVICE** New Hampshire enjoys better bus service than any other New England state. **Concord Trailways** (603-228-3300; 1-800-639-3317) serves Manchester and Concord; Laconia, Meredith, and Center Harbor in the Lake Winnipesaukee region; Franconia, North Conway, and Jackson in the White Mountains. **Greyhound Bus Lines** (1-800-231-2222) stops daily in Portsmouth's Market Square, connecting the seacoast with nationwide bus service. **Vermont Transit** (1-800-451-3292) or **Greyhound** (1-800-231-2222) stops in Nashua, Manchester, Concord, New London, and Hanover en route from White River Junction (Vermont) to Boston. It also stops in Keene and Fitzwilliam en route from Brattleboro (Vermont) to Boston; another route includes stops in Charlestown and Walpole.

**CAMPGROUNDS** New Hampshire camping opportunities range from primitive sites with few amenities to full-service areas with water and sewer hook-ups, electricity, TV, stores, recreation buildings, playgrounds, swimming pools, and boat launching. The most complete information is available from the **New Hampshire Campground Owners' Association** (603-846-5511; www.ucampnh.com), Box 320, Twin Mountain 03595. Its free 80-page directory lists private and state campgrounds. Most private areas take reservations, and some are completely booked by the end of one summer for the next. The state-owned campgrounds operate on a first-come, first-served basis only and offer few amenities, but many are on lakes with sandy beaches. Reservations (and payment) are accepted at least 1 week in advance for a minimum 2-night stay (3 nights on major weekends) between mid-May and Columbus Day by calling 603-271-3628 January through October, weekdays 9 AM–4 PM (see www.nhstateparks.us). Most **White Mountain National Forest** sites are also available on a first-come, first-served basis; however, a toll-free reservation system (1-800-280-2267) operates for some sites in the following campgrounds: White Ledge (Conway); Covered Bridge (Kancamagus); Sugarloaf I and II (Twin Mountain); Basin, Cold River, and Hastings (Evans Notch); Dolly Copp (Pinkham Notch); and Campton, Russell Pond, and Waterville (near I-93). The reservation service operates March through September, Monday through Friday noon–9 PM, weekends noon–5 PM. Reservations may be made up to 120 days before arrival, but 10 days before arrival is the minimum time.

**CANOEING AND KAYAKING** New Hampshire offers many miles of flatwater and white-water canoeing opportunities. The Androscoggin, Connecticut, Saco, and Merrimack Rivers are perhaps the most popular waters for canoeing, but there are many other smaller rivers as well. Many folks also like to paddle the numerous lakes and ponds of New Hampshire. Since spring runoffs have an impact on the degree of paddling difficulty to be found on a river, make sure you know what your river offers before heading downstream. The best source of information is the *AMC River Guide: New Hampshire and Vermont,* published by the Appalachian Mountain Club, 5 Joy Street, Boston, MA 02108. Also see *Canoe Camping Vermont and New Hampshire Rivers* (Backcountry Publications). Contact the **Merrimack River Watershed Council** (603-224-8322) in Concord for information on the Merrimack River. Canoe and kayak rentals have, happily, become too numerous to list here. Check every chapter.

**CHILDREN, ESPECIALLY FOR** Throughout the book, the ✐ symbol indicates restaurants, lodgings, and attractions that are particularly appropriate for children and families. Children's museums are described in the Portsmouth, Peterborough, Manchester, and Concord chapters. Although it is technically a science museum in Vermont (just across the bridge from Hanover, New Hampshire), the **Montshire Museum of Science** (www.montshire.org) in Norwich (see "Upper Valley Towns") gets our vote for the most stimulating museum in this category, both inside and out. The **White Mountain Attractions** add up to the state's single largest family-geared magnet. With members ranging from the excursion vessel M/S *Mount Washington* on Lake Winnipesaukee to the gondola at Wildcat Mountain, from natural phenomena like Lost River (in North Woodstock) to theme parks like Story Land (in Glen) and Six Gun City and Santa's Village (both in Jefferson), this is a highly organized promotional association with a helpful visitors center just off Exit 32, I-93, in North Woodstock. Phone 603-745-8720 or 1-800-FIND-MTS, or e-mail them at info@whitemountains.com. Other attractions with child appeal range from **Friendly Farm** in Dublin to New England's biggest video center, in Weirs Beach. All are described as they appear, region by region.

**CHILDREN'S SUMMER CAMPS** More than 100 summer camps are located in New Hampshire. For a free brochure contact the **New Hampshire Camp Directors' Association** (1-800-549-2267; www.nhcamps.org), P.O. Box 501, Farmington 03835.

**CHRISTMAS TREES** Plantation-grown New Hampshire Christmas trees are perfect for the holidays. The trees are grown to be harvested at about 10 years of age. Some growers allow you to come early in the season to tag your own tree, which you can cut at a later time; others allow choose-and-cut only in December. Contact the **New Hampshire Christmas Trees Promotional Board** (www.nhchristmastree.com) or the **Department of**

**Agriculture** (603-271-3551; www.farms.com).

COLLEGES AND UNIVERSITIES Higher education opportunities range from 2-year schools to the highly regarded University of New Hampshire and Dartmouth College. For information contact the **New Hampshire College and University Council** (603-669-3432), 2321 Elm Street, Manchester 03104.

CONSERVATION GROUPS Elsewhere in this section, see the Appalachian Mountain Club, the Society for the Protection of New Hampshire Forests (SPNHF), and the Audubon Society of New Hampshire (under *Birding*). The Nature Conservancy (603-224-5853; www.nature.org\nh), a national organization with state holdings, publishes its own list.

COVERED BRIDGES New Hampshire harbors 64 covered bridges. These are marked on the official state highway map, and we have tried to describe them within each chapter. The country's longest covered bridge connects Cornish with Windsor, Vermont (technically the New Hampshire line runs to the Vermont shore, so it's all in New Hampshire). The state's oldest authenticated covered bridge (1827) links Haverhill and Bath. The Swanzey area near Keene (see "Peterborough, Keene, and Surrounding Villages") boasts the state's greatest concentration of covered bridges: five within little more than a dozen miles.

CRAFTS The **League of New Hampshire Craftsmen** (603-224-3375), with headquarters at 205 North Main Street, Concord 03301, is one of the country's oldest, most effective statewide crafts groups. It maintains half a dozen shops displaying work by members, and sponsors the outstanding annual **Craftsmen's Fair** in early August at Mount Sunapee State Park in Newbury. In the Monadnock region the **Sharon Arts Center** in Peterborough offers destination crafts shopping.

Robert Kozlow

CRUISES Few summer activities are as relaxing as a boat ride, and New Hampshire has many trips available, from the ocean to the lakes. The two most popular cruises are the M/V *Thomas Laighton* (Isles of Shoals Steamship Company), which sails several times daily from Portsmouth to the offshore Isles of Shoals, and the M/S *Mount Washington* on Lake Winnipesaukee. Squam Lake has two small boat cruises, and Lake Sunapee has several also. For details see *To Do—Boat Excursions* in the relevant chapters.

Robert Kozlow

**EMERGENCIES** The statewide emergency number is 1-800-525-5555; from a car phone, dial ∗77 New Hampshire's telephone books have full listings of local emergency numbers inside the front cover. **911** also now covers the state.

**EVENTS** The *Official New Hampshire Guidebook* (see *Information*) lists current events, and in each chapter we have listed special events that occur year after year (see *Special Events*). May through mid-September phone 1-800-258-3608 for a recording of upcoming events. Special events are also listed on the state's visitors information web site (www.visitnh.gov); agricultural fairs and festivals are listed at www.nhfarms.com.

**FACTORY OUTLETS** Several areas of New Hampshire have become destination shopping centers. The best-known region is **North Conway,** where some 200 shops, discount stores, and factory outlets have given the term *shopping trip* a new meaning. If you can't find what you want to buy there, you probably don't need it. North Hampton also has a large outlet shopping complex, but seacoast shoppers often drive across the Piscataqua River to Kittery, Maine, where outlets are nearly as numerous as in North Conway. Remember, Maine has a sales tax, New Hampshire does not. In the Winnipesaukee area more than 50 outlets are grouped in the **Lakes Region Factory Stores** just off I-93, Exit 20 at Tilton.

**FARMERS' MARKETS** Many farms used to have roadside stands where they sold their produce, and many still operate in New Hampshire, but the current trend is to sell through farmers' markets—once-a-week gatherings of many farmers. Open mainly from late June through Columbus Day, markets operate in Concord, Conway, Dover, Exeter, Hampton, Portsmouth, Laconia, Manchester, Milford, and Warner. Fresh fruits and vegetables, baked goods, honey, and crafts are among the items for sale. Many of the state's organic farmers sell their produce at these markets. The pamphlet *New Hampshire's Rural Heritage* lists farmers' market locations and hours and is available from the **New Hampshire Department of Agriculture** (603-271-3551; www.nhfarms.com).

**FISHING** Freshwater fishing requires a license for anyone age 12 and older. Some 450 sporting goods and country stores sell licenses, or you can contact the **New Hampshire Fish and Game Department** (603-271-3421; www.wildlife.state.nh.us), 2 Hazen Drive, Concord 03301. Request a copy of the *New Hampshire Boating and Fishing Public Access Map*. The White Mountain National Forest issues a special brochure on trout fishing in the forest. No license is required for saltwater fishing. Party boats leave several times daily from April until October from docks at Rye, Hampton, and Seabrook harbors. Most of these boats have full tackle for rent.

Robert Kozlow

**FOLIAGE** Color first appears on hillsides in the North Country in mid-September, and by the end of that month Franconia, Crawford, and Pinkham Notches are usually spectacular. The colors spread south and through lower elevations during the first 2 weeks in October. Columbus Day weekend is traditionally the time New England residents come "leaf-peeping," and it's the period we suggest you avoid, if possible. At least avoid the traditional foliage routes—the Kancamagus Highway, Route 3 through Franconia Notch, and Route 16 to North Conway—on those 3 days. Come a week earlier instead and try to get off the road entirely. This is prime hiking weather—no bugs. The state maintains a **Fall Foliage Hotline** (1-800-258-3608) with "conditions" updated regularly; their web site keeps a visual tab on what's going on: www.visitnh.gov. The wise traveler will make reservations for overnight accommodations well in advance for the foliage season, since even such areas as Lincoln or North Conway, with hundreds of rooms, are fully booked on key weekends.

**GOLF** We describe golf courses as they appear region by region. They are also listed in the *Official New Hampshire Guidebook* (see *Information*).

**HANDICAPPED ACCESS** Throughout this book, the wheelchair symbol ♿ indicates restaurants, lodgings, and attractions that are handicapped accessible.

**HIGH HUTS OF THE WHITE MOUNTAINS** The most unusual lodging opportunities in the state are found in the White Mountains, where the

Kim Grant

Appalachian Mountain Club operates eight full-service high mountain huts. Generally the huts are open from June through Labor Day, but several welcome hikers through September and two are open all year on a self-serve, caretaker basis. Guests hike to the huts, most of which are located a day's walk apart so that you can walk for several days and stay in a different hut each night. You sleep in coed bunk rooms equipped with mattresses and blankets. Meals are huge and varied. Reservations are required. A shuttle service allows you to park at the trailhead for one hut, then ride back to your vehicle after your hike. Contact the **Appalachian Mountain Club Pinkham Notch Camp** (603-466-2727 for overnight or workshop reservations; www.outdoors.org). See "Mount Washington and Its Valleys—Mount Washington."

**HIKING** New Hampshire offers the most diverse hiking in New England. The **White Mountain National Forest** alone has some 1,200 miles of hiking trails, and there are additional miles in state parks. A long, difficult section of the **Appalachian Trail** cuts through New Hampshire, entering the state near Hanover, crossing the highest peaks, including Mount Washington, and exiting along the rugged Mahoosuc Range on the Maine border. The White Mountains is the most popular hiking area, and the many trails offer easy to challenging routes. The most spectacular climbs are on the Franconia Ridge and over the Presidential Range, which includes **Mount Washington,** at 6,288 feet the highest peak in the Northeast. Although relatively low compared to the Rockies, for example, Mount Washington records the worst weather for any surface station outside of the polar regions. Hikers are urged to use caution and to consult weather forecasts before venturing onto the exposed areas above tree line. More than 110 people have died on Mount Washington, some of them in summer when caught unprepared by sudden, extreme changes in weather conditions. White Mountain hiking information is available from the **Appalachian Mountain Club Pinkham Notch Camp** (603-466-2725 for weather, trail, or general information; 603-466-2727 for overnight or workshop reservations), Route 16, Box 298, Gorham 03518, or from the White Mountain National Forest. Daily weather updates are posted on the AMC's web site: www.outdoors.org. (For details, see "Mount Washington and Its Valleys.") There is plenty of hiking elsewhere in New Hampshire as well. **Mount Monadnock** in southern New Hampshire is one of the most climbed peaks in the world, and **Kearsarge** in central New Hampshire offers a relatively easy walk to its summit and nice views. Several lower mountains in the Lake Winnipesaukee area are easily climbed. **Mount Major,** in particular, is easy and has a fine view across the

Robert Kozlow

lake. These hikes are described elsewhere in this book, but for more details one of the following books is recommended. The *AMC White Mountain Guide* has the most comprehensive trail information available for hiking anywhere in New Hampshire, but also see *50 Hikes in the White Mountains, 50 More Hikes in New Hampshire, Waterfalls of the White Mountains*, and *Ponds and Lakes of the White Mountains* (all Backcountry Publications); the *Monadnock–Sunapee Greenway Trail Guide* (Society for the Protection of New Hampshire Forests, Concord); and a trail guide of the Squam Range available through Squam Lakes Association in Holderness. An exciting hiking project now under way is the creation of the **Heritage Trail,** which will run the length of the state following the banks of the Merrimack, Pemigewasset, and Connecticut Rivers. Many segments of the trail are in place, and new sections are added annually. For details call 603-271-3627.

Robert Kozlow

**HISTORIC HOMES AND SITES** New Hampshire residents have a strong appreciation for the state's history. Most communities have historical societies, and throughout the state many historic buildings and sites are open to the public; most are listed in this guide. A complete booklet guide to these town museums can be obtained by joining the **Association of Historical Societies of New Hampshire.** Send $4 plus $1 for mailing to Mildred Isley, AHSNH, 14 Ironwood Lane, Atkinson 03811-2706. The largest concentration of historical houses is in Portsmouth, home of the large **Strawbery Banke** restoration and eight other houses open to the public. Along New Hampshire highways roadside markers recount short tidbits of local history. A copy of the roadside marker guide is available from the **New Hampshire Preservation Office** (603-271-3483). *New Hampshire Architecture* (University Press of New England) is a fine guide to historical and significant buildings. The Hampshire Historical Society's **Museum of New Hampshire History** (603-226-3189; www.nhhistory.org) in Concord (see "The Merrimack Valley") is well worth checking out. The state's other major historical museum is **Canterbury Shaker Village** (www.shakers.org) in the same chapter. Many more are described as they appear regionally.

**HONEY** More than 200 members of the New Hampshire Beekeepers Association have hives throughout the state, and their honey is usually for sale at farmers' markets, some country stores, and at roadside stands.

**HORSEBACK RIDING** Rising insurance costs are narrowing trail riding options, but you can still ride a horse through the woods at **Chebacco Dude Ranch** in South Effingham (see "The Lake Winnipesaukee Area"). If you just want the sense of being on a horse (no experience necessary), contact **Castle in the Clouds** and **Gunstock** (see *To See* in "The Lake Winnipesaukee Area"), **Waterville Valley** and **Loon Mountain** in the Western Whites, and the **Mount Washington Hotel** and **Farm by the River** (see "Mount Washington and Its Valleys").

**HUNTING** New Hampshire has long been a popular state for hunting. Licenses are required and are available from some 450 sporting goods and country stores, or contact the **New Hampshire Fish and Game Department** (603-271-3421; www.wildlife.state.nh.us), 2 Hazen Drive, Concord 03301.

**ICE CREAM** It's hard to beat **Annabelle's Ice Cream,** located on Ceres Street in Portsmouth, open from spring through late fall. Former president George Bush liked their flavors so much that he had them make and serve red, white, and blueberry ice cream at the White House for the Fourth of July. Another popular homemade brand of ice cream is served at **Lagos' Lone Oak Dairy Bars** on old Route 16 in Rochester and Route 1 in Rye. In the Lake Winnipesaukee region **Kellerhaus** is the big name, while **Sandwich Creamery** is the insider's pick. **Beech Hill Farm,** just off Routes 9, 202, and 103 between Concord and Hopkinton, has been owned by the Kimball family since 1776. The old dairy farm remains the place to go for a scoop of history along with make-your-own sundaes.

**INFORMATION** We describe regional information sources at the head of each chapter. The **New Hampshire Office of Travel & Tourism Development** maintains a toll-free hot line (1-800-258-3608) with recorded info, varying with the season; or check their web site at www.visitnh.gov. You can also call (603-271-2343; 1-800-386-4664) or write to the office for a copy of the *Official New Hampshire Guidebook* and a highway map. The guidebook includes year-round listings of the basics: golf courses, alpine and cross-country ski areas, covered bridges, scenic drives, events, fish and game rules, state parks, and state liquor stores. It also includes paid dining and lodging listings. Maps and pamphlets are also available in the state's full-service rest areas (see *Rest Areas*).

**LAKES** Central New Hampshire is open, rolling country, spotted with lakes. **Winnipesaukee** is by far the state's largest, most visitor-oriented lake, and it is surrounded by smaller lakes: **Winnisquam, Squam, Wentworth, Ossipee.** Traditionally this has been New Hampshire's Lakes region, but we've added the Western Lakes because there are so many west of I-93 as well: **Sunapee** and **Newfound** for starters; **Little Sunapee, Massasecum, Pleasant, Highland,** and **Webster** when you start looking for places to swim. Outdoorsmen are also well aware of the grand expanses of **Umbagog Lake** in Errol and of the **Connecticut Lakes** in New Hampshire's Great North Woods. *Ponds and Lakes of the White Mountains* by Steve B. Smith (Backcountry Publications) describes more than 100 lakes and ponds, "from wayside to wilderness," including many bodies of water hidden

Robert Kozlow

deep in the woods (with detailed directions on finding them).

**LIBRARIES** Every New Hampshire city and town has a public library, and there are many college and private libraries as well. On the seacoast, the **Portsmouth Public Library** and the **Portsmouth Athenaeum** and the **Exeter Public Library** and **Exeter Historical Society** are centers for regional history and genealogical research. The **University of New Hampshire's Dimond Library** has an extensive New Hampshire special collections section and all of the resources you would expect to find in a major educational institution. In Concord, the **State Library** and the **New Hampshire Historical Society,** located side by side on Park Street, are centers for New Hampshire research. **Peterborough's public library** was the first in New Hampshire, and it and the nearby **Peterborough Historical Society library** have important regional collections. In Keene, the **Historical Society of Cheshire County Archive Center** and the **Keene State Library** are the best sources for local research. **Baker Library at Dartmouth College** is one of the finest institutions in the East. Among its many resources is an extensive White Mountains collection.

**LOTTERY** New Hampshire's is the oldest legal lottery in the country. Since 1964 it has funded more than $186 million to local education. For details from out of state, phone 603-271-2825; from in state, 603-271-3391. The web site is www.state.nh.us/lottery/nhlotto.htm.

**MAGAZINES AND NEWSPAPERS** For such a small state, New Hampshire has an abundance of periodicals. The *Manchester Union-Leader* (Box 780, Manchester 03105) is the largest daily, and its strong conservative editorial policy has made it well known throughout the country. It is the best source of statewide news, but there are also dailies in Portsmouth, Dover, Laconia, Conway, Claremont, Lebanon, Keene, Nashua, and Concord. Many of the larger towns also have weekly newspapers. These and several regional, free, tourist-oriented periodicals are good sources of information about local events and activities.

**MAPLE SUGARING** When cool nights and warm days during late February through April start the sap running in

Robert Kozlow

maple trees, maple syrup producers fire up their evaporators to begin making the sweet natural treat. Most producers welcome visitors and many offer tours, sugar-on-snow parties, and breakfast (pancakes with maple syrup, of course). For a list of maple syrup producers, contact the **New Hampshire Maple Producers** (603-225-3757; www.nhmapleproducers.com). During Maple Weekend, usually the last weekend in March, more than 50 sugarhouses hold open house and stage special events.

**MOOSE** The state's largest animal is becoming more common and is often seen along roadsides, especially in the mountainous northern half of the state. Stay very alert when driving, since moose may unexpectedly walk into the road without looking. The state has recorded nearly 200 vehicle–moose collisions. A colorful annual **North Country Moose Festival,** based in the town of Colebrook, is staged annually the last weekend in August. See the "Great North Woods" introduction for a full description of this noble beast. The state's most popular organized moose tours are based in Gorham, described in "Northern White Mountains."

Robert Kozlow

**MOUNTAINTOPS** The summits of some New Hampshire mountains are more popular than others mainly because they offer better views, great hiking trails, or ways to ride to the top. The most popular, of course, is Mount Washington, at 6,288 feet the highest peak in the Northeast. The **Mount Washington Auto Road** is an 8-mile graded road on which you can drive your own car or ride in a chauffeured van. The **Mount Washington Cog Railway** offers an unusual steam-powered ride to the summit. Across Route 16 from Mount Washington, the **Wildcat Mountain gondolas** whisk you to the top of that wooded peak for a spectacular view of the Presidential Range, and the **Loon Mountain "Skyride"** (via gondolas) is to a summit complete with cafeteria, cave walk, and hiking trails. Both here and at **Mount Sunapee** (where a chairlift hoists you to the summit) cookout-style suppers are offered throughout the summer. The **Cannon Mountain Tramway** in Franconia offers its riders a view of the Franconia Range, the state's second highest group of mountains. Although it is not a mountaintop, **Castle in the Clouds** (Route 109, Moultonborough) gives nonhikers the best view of Lake Winnipesaukee. For purist hikers **Mount Lafayette** is the favored summit in Franconia Notch. **Mount Moosilauke,** westernmost of the White Mountains, is also a spectacular summit. Lower mountains can nonetheless provide worthy views: **Mount Chocorua** rises beside Route 16 in Tamworth; although only 3,400 feet high, it is a challenging hike with a great vista from its summit. **Mount Major** (Route 11, Alton) has an easy walk to its open summit. **Mount Monadnock** dominates the view throughout southwestern New Hampshire, but if you are not up to the hike, drive to the top of nearby **Pack Monadnock** (Miller State Park), Route 101, Peterborough. For those who like a challenge, the **Appalachian Mountain Club** has an informal Four Thousand Footer Club; become a member by climbing all 48 New Hampshire mountains higher than 4,000 feet in elevation. The peaks are listed in the *AMC White Mountain Guide*. Some rugged folks have climbed all 48 in winter; others have done them all twice, or with their dogs, or some other unique way.

**MUSEUMS** Aside from art museums and children's museums (see *Art Museums and Galleries* and *Children, Especially for*), New Hampshire offers historical museums and houses (described here region by region). **Canterbury Shaker Village** in Canterbury (see "The Concord Area") is an outstanding museum village. The **New Hampshire Farm Museum** in Milton tells the history of farming in the state. The **Montshire Museum of Science** in Norwich, Vermont (just across the river from Hanover, New Hampshire, where it began), is the most highly regarded science museum in northern New England, worth a stop for inquiring minds of all ages. The **Mount Kearsarge Indian Museum** in Warner is also well worth checking out.

**MUSIC** Music festivals are described under *Entertainment* and/or *Special Events* in each chapter. Check out the **New Hampshire Music Festival** in Center Harbor (see "The Lake Winnipesaukee Area"), year-round performances at the **North Country Center for the Arts** in Lincoln, summer concerts at the **Lake Winnipesaukee Music Festival** in Wolfeboro, the **Prescott Park Festival** in Portsmouth, the **Mount Washington Valley Arts Festival,** and the **Cochecho Arts Festival** in Dover. The Monadnock region is a traditional center for outstanding music; **Monadnock Music** is a series of two dozen summer concerts, operas, and orchestra performances staged in town halls, churches, and schools, and the **Apple Hill Chamber Players** in Nelson offers free faculty concerts. Band music is another sound of summer in New Hampshire. The **Temple Band,** also based in the Monadnock region, claims to be the oldest town band in the country.

**NATIONAL PUBLIC RADIO** Public radio addicts will find the (FM) commercial-free news and music station at 89.1 in central and southern New Hampshire, at 90.3 in Nashua, 104.3 in Dover, 91.3 in the Upper Valley, and 90.7 in the Monadnock region. You can also pick up Vermont Public Radio at 89.5 in the western part of the state.

**PARKS** New Hampshire has one of the oldest and best state park systems in the country. High mountains; lake, ocean, and river shores; unique stands of flowering shrubs and trees; historic buildings; and geological and archaeological sites comprise the diverse locations of the nearly 50 parks. Swimming, fishing, picnicking, camping, and hiking are among the many activities enjoyed in these parks. See *Campgrounds* for camping information or contact the **New Hampshire Division of Parks** (603-271-3556; www.nhparks.state.us), 172 Pembroke Road, Concord 03301. Also see *White Mountain National Forest* in this section. Almost all cities and towns have parks, many of which include tennis courts open to the public.

**PETS, TRAVELING WITH** The dog paw symbol 🐾 indicates lodgings that accept pets as of press time in 2002. Most require prior notice and a reservation; many also require an additional fee. But don't take our word for it; always call ahead to confirm an establishment's policy when traveling with your pet.

**PICK-YOUR-OWN** See *Apple and Fruit Picking.*

**RAIL EXCURSIONS** The **Mount Washington Cog Railway,** the country's oldest railroad excursion, takes nonhikers on a steam locomotive trip to the top of the highest mountain in the Northeast (see "Mount Washington and Its Valleys—Crawford Notch and Bretton Woods"). Less hair-raising but just as appealing is the **Conway Scenic Railroad,** which journeys through historic Crawford Notch (see "Mount Washington and Its Valleys—North Conway Area"). Also see the **Hobo Railroad** in Lincoln and its **Winnipesaukee Railroad** based in Meredith.

**RENTAL COTTAGES, CONDOMINIUMS** Cottages are particularly plentiful and available in the **Lake Winnipesaukee** and **Western Lakes** areas (contact the local chambers). Condominiums at the state's self-contained ski resorts like Waterville Valley, Loon Mountain, Cranmore, and Attitash Bear Peak are good-value family summer rentals, with golf, horseback riding, hiking, and a variety of other activities making them increasingly attractive. **The Mount Washington Valley Chamber of Commerce** (603-356-3171; 1-800-367-3364) also keeps year-round tabs on condominiums and other family lodging. In the seacoast region, contact the **Hampton Beach Chamber of Commerce** (603-926-8718; 1-800-GET-A-TAN) for information about condo and cottage rentals.

Kim Grant

**REST AREAS** The state operates 17 highway rest areas. Three are open 24 hours a day: Hooksett (I-93 northbound and southbound) and Seabrook (northbound on I-95). The complete list of rest areas is printed on the official New Hampshire highway map, which is available at any information center or from the **New Hampshire Office of Travel and Tourism Development** (603-271-2343), Box 1856, Concord 03302.

**ROCKHOUNDING** **Ruggles Mine** in Grafton (see "The Western Lakes") is said to offer 150 kinds of minerals and gemstones. Commercial production of mica began here in 1803, and it's an eerie, interesting place that has gotten many a rockhound hooked.

**SALES TAX** New Hampshire has no sales tax, making it a destination for shoppers from throughout the Northeast.

**SKIING, CROSS-COUNTRY** New Hampshire offers more than 1,300 km of trails. The **Jackson Ski Touring Foundation** is the state's largest, with

Rob Burbank, AMC

150 km of varied trails including a run down the backside of Wildcat Mountain (accessible from the alpine summit via a single ride on its gondola). **Bretton Woods Ski Touring Center** offers a similar run from the top of its alpine area and a total of 88 km of trails. The **Mount Washington Valley Ski Touring Foundation** offers another 60 km, and the Appalachian Mountain Club in Pinkham Notch offers cross-country workshops and guided tours on national forest trails, too. **Great Glen Trails at Mount Washington** is a new area offering backcountry trails and the unique 8-mile run down the auto road. Farther south both **Loon Mountain** and **Waterville Valley** offer major cross-country centers that tie into national forest trails. **Norsk** in New London is the outstanding cross-country center in central New Hampshire (in terms of size, elevation, and grooming), and **Windblown Ski Touring Center** in New Ipswich is favored by Bostonians; it's high, handy, and quite beautiful. The New Hampshire **cross-country snow report** line is 1-800-887-5464. The centers are described region by region within this book. Also look for the free ***New Hampshire Ski Map*** (see *Skiing, Downhill*), available from the state's Office of Travel and Tourism (see *Information*). Information about 17 of the larger ski-touring centers is available from **Ski New Hampshire:** 1-800-258-3608 or 1-800-262-6660. The Internet address is www.skinh.com.

**SKIING, DOWNHILL** New Hampshire boasts 17 major downhill ski areas. It's worth noting that on weekends their proximity to Boston puts their lifts (and lift tickets) at a real premium, but on weekdays they tend to be relatively empty. This pattern is beginning to alter as several "areas" become full-fledged "resorts." **Loon Mountain** in Lincoln, **Waterville Valley** (see "The Western Whites"), **Cranmore, Attitash Bear Peak** (see "Mount Washington and Its Valleys"), and **Mount Sunapee Ski Resort** (see "The Western Lakes")—the state's largest areas—now offer a variety of activities to attract "ski weekers" as well as day-trippers and weekenders. New Hampshire's areas may just also represent

Robert Kozlow

the world's largest concentration of snowmaking. The quality of the snowmaking itself varies, but most of New Hampshire's alpine slopes are now dependably white from Christmas through Easter. There's some discussion between Vermont and New Hampshire about whether alpine skiing was introduced to this country in Woodstock (Vermont) or in Jackson (New Hampshire); the **New England Ski Museum** in Franconia Notch favors the New Hampshire version of regional ski history. We have described each ski area as it appears, region by region. Request a copy of the free ***New Hampshire Ski Map;*** it profiles the ski areas and includes winter events and attractions. Call **Ski New Hampshire** at 1-800-258-3608 or 1-800-262-6660 for general information (lift-ticket prices, facilities, etc.) on all ski areas. The Internet address is www.skinh.com.

**SLED DOG RACES** The world championships are in **Laconia** in February, but earlier in the winter there are local races in **Colebrook-Pittsburg** and **Sandwich.** Snow conditions often determine whether or not races are held. For details contact the **New England Sled Dog Club** (603-483-2677), 42 North Road, Candia 03034.

**SLEIGH RIDES** A number of New Hampshire inns and farms offer sleigh rides and hayrides in-season. Several are listed in this guide, and others are found in *New Hampshire's Rural Heritage,* a pamphlet from the **New Hampshire Department of Agriculture** (603-271-3788; www.nhfarms.com).

**SNOWMOBILING** With some 6,000 miles of trails, New Hampshire offers the snowmobiler vast opportunities for winter fun. *Note:* Large portions of the White Mountain National Forest are off-limits to snowmobiling, trail bikes, or off-road vehicles, but most state parks do permit off-road vehicles on marked trails. For maps and regulations, contact the **Bureau of Off-Road Vehicles** (603-271-3254), Box 1856, Concord 03302; the **New Hampshire Snowmobile Association** (603-224-8906; www.nhsa.com), 722 Route 3A, Bow 03304; or chambers of commerce in Twin Mountain, Colebrook, Lincoln–North Woodstock, or North Conway. For snowmobile **snow conditions,** call 603-226-6699.

**SOCIETY FOR THE PROTECTION OF NEW HAMPSHIRE FORESTS (SPNHF)** Founded in 1901 to fight the systematic leveling of the state's forests by lumber firms, SPNHF was instrumental in securing passage of the 1911 Weeks Act, authorizing (for the first time) the federal purchase of lands to create national forests. One direct result is the 729,353-acre White Mountain National Forest. The group is also largely responsible for Mount Monadnock's current public status, and it now holds more than 60 properties for public use that total more than 20,000 acres. Many are described within this

Robert Kozlow

book, especially within the Monadnock region, which harbors a large percentage. Stop by SPNHF headquarters (603-224-9945; www.spnhf.org) in East Concord (just off I-93, Exit 15) or write SPNHF, 54 Portsmouth Street, East Concord 03301, to obtain a copy of the society's *Lands Map & Guide* to its properties. If you are a hiker, angler, or cross-country skier, this is a valuable key to real treasure.

**SUMMER THEATER** New Hampshire offers some outstanding summer theater. The **Barnstormers** in Tamworth, the **Peterborough Players** in Peterborough, and the **New London Barn Playhouse** in New London all rank among New England's oldest, best-respected "strawhat" theaters. The **Weathervane Theater** in Whitefield, the **American Stage Festival** in Milford, the **Lakes Region Theater** in Meredith, the **Hopkins Center** at Dartmouth College in Hanover, the **Arts Center at Brickyard Pond** in Keene, and the **Prescott Art Festival** in Portsmouth also stage lively summer productions. See *Entertainment* for each region.

**TRAILS, LONG-DISTANCE** New Hampshire from the road is beautiful, but unless you see its panoramas from a high hiking trail, you miss its real magnificence. Long-distance hiking trails now crisscross the state. The longest, most spectacular, and most famous, the **Appalachian Trail,** cuts diagonally across the White Mountains, entering the state in Hanover on the west and traversing Franconia Notch, Mount Washington, and Pinkham Notch on its way into Maine. Detailed maps and guides as well as a free pamphlet guide, *The Appalachian Trail in New Hampshire and the White Mountains,* are available from the **Appalachian Mountain Club** (www.outdoors.org). The **Metacomet Trail,** running 14 miles south from Little Monadnock; the **Wapack Trail,** which heads south along ridges from North Pack Monadnock; and the **Monadnock-Sunapee Trail,** a 47-mile footpath, are also well mapped. (Also see *Hiking* within each region.) The newest long-distance trail links exisiting paths, railbeds, and logging roads into one continuous trail from Bartelett down in the Mount Washington Valley to the Canadian border in Pittsburg. See www.cohostrail.org for details.

**WATERFALLS** The White Mountains have the best waterfalls to view. All are described in *Waterfalls of the White Mountains* (Backcountry Guides), which lists 30 trips to some 100 waterfalls.

**WHITE MOUNTAIN NATIONAL FOREST (WMNF)** The 778,000-acre **White Mountain National Forest** runs through the middle of New Hampshire from east to west. The largest national forest in the East, it is managed for multiple-use activities including lumbering as well as recreation. Several ranger stations are located along major highways to provide infor-

Robert Kozlow

mation and assistance for forest users. For information contact **WMNF headquarters** (603-528-8721), Box 638, 719 Main Street, Laconia 03247. The **Saco Ranger Station** (603-447-5448), at the Conway exit off the Kancamagus Highway, is open 7 days a week, 8 AM–4:30 PM; other stations include the **Ammonoosuc Ranger Station** in Bethlehem (603-869-2626); **Androscoggin Ranger Station** in Gorham (603-466-2713); **Pemigewassett Ranger Station** in Plymouth (603-536-1310); and **Evans Notch Ranger Station** in Bethel, Maine (207-824-2134). The web site is www.fs.fed.us/r9/white. Also see the map and introduction to the WMNF at the beginning of "The White Mountains."

# The Seacoast

PORTSMOUTH AND VICINITY

HAMPTON, HAMPTON BEACH, EXETER, AND VICINITY

DOVER, DURHAM, AND VICINITY

Robert Kozlow

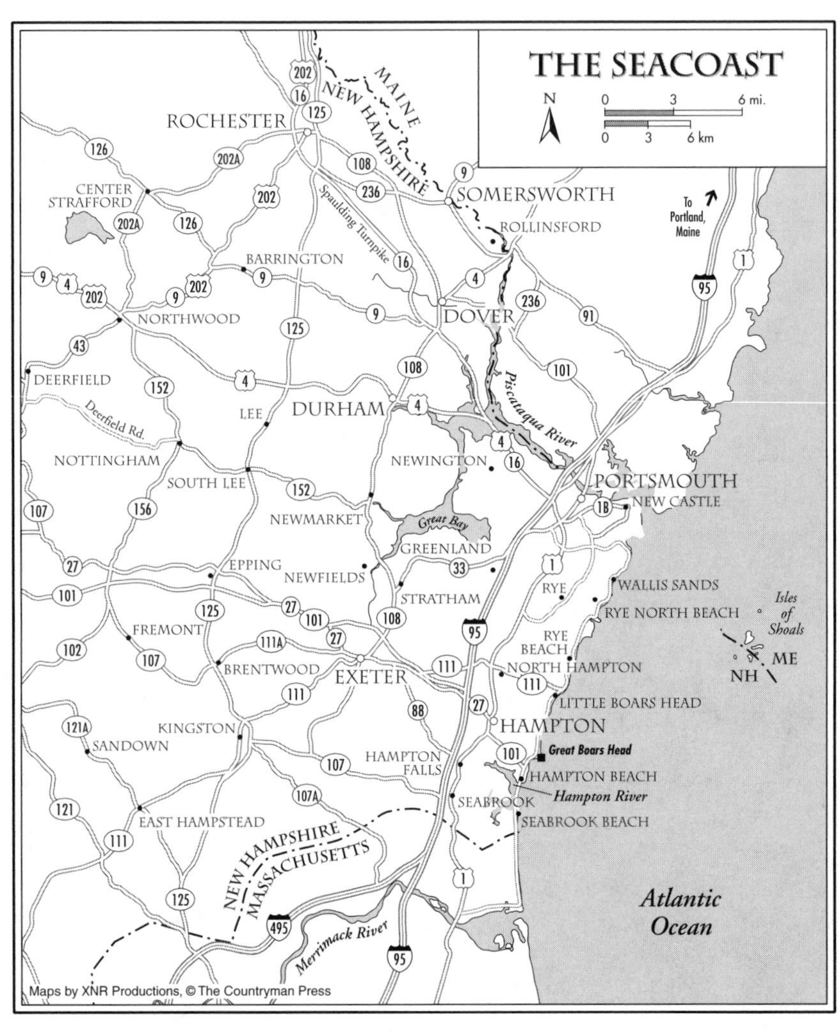
THE SEACOAST
N
0 3 6 mi.
0 3 6 km
MAINE
NEW HAMPSHIRE
ROCHESTER
SOMERSWORTH
ROLLINSFORD
To Portland, Maine
CENTER STRAFFORD
Spaulding Turnpike
BARRINGTON
NORTHWOOD
DOVER
DEERFIELD
Deerfield Rd.
LEE
DURHAM
Piscataqua River
NOTTINGHAM
NEWINGTON
SOUTH LEE
PORTSMOUTH
NEW CASTLE
NEWMARKET
Great Bay
GREENLAND
EPPING
NEWFIELDS
WALLIS SANDS
RYE
STRATHAM
RYE NORTH BEACH
Isles of Shoals
FREMONT
RYE BEACH
ME
NH
BRENTWOOD
EXETER
NORTH HAMPTON
LITTLE BOARS HEAD
KINGSTON
HAMPTON
SANDOWN
Great Boars Head
HAMPTON FALLS
HAMPTON BEACH
Hampton River
SEABROOK
SEABROOK BEACH
EAST HAMPSTEAD
NEW HAMPSHIRE
MASSACHUSETTS
Atlantic Ocean
Merrimack River
Maps by XNR Productions, © The Countryman Press

# INTRODUCTION

With only 18 miles of oceanfront, New Hampshire's seacoast is often overlooked by visitors, who are more impressed with neighboring Maine's more than 2,500 miles of coastline. In its small coastal area, however, New Hampshire has more than enough historical sites, beaches, restaurants, and events and attractions to keep her guests busy for many days and returning again and again for more.

At opposite ends of the seacoast are Portsmouth and Hampton Beach, near to each other in mileage but much farther apart in ambience and style.

Settled in 1630, Portsmouth was the colonial capital and an important seaport during the Georgian and Federal eras, periods that have given the city its distinctive architectural character. With fine inns and restaurants, a number of original and restored historical houses open to the public, theater, dance, music, and a superb waterfront park, Portsmouth is New Hampshire's most delightful and interesting city, loved and appreciated by its residents and visitors alike.

Hampton Beach has been one of New England's most popular seaside resorts since the development of the electric trolley at the turn of the 20th century. Too bad the trolleys don't operate anymore, since the automobile traffic, especially on weekends, is one long snarl. Sand and sun, pizza and fried dough, and lively entertainment characterize Hampton Beach, where more than 200,000 people can be found on a summer holiday weekend. For many people, a week at Hampton Beach has been an annual family tradition for half a century or more.

Between these two extremes are mostly small towns (less than 1,000 to 12,000 population) with white churches, town commons, Colonial architecture, and an ambience that is attracting many new residents and straining the capacity of these towns to manage the growth that has characterized this area since the end of World War II. The recent closure of Pease Air Force Base and conversion of its property to industrial development and to a public airport with daily service bodes well for the future and might ultimately offset the decline in activity at the Portsmouth Naval Shipyard, a facility that in 1995 again escaped closure. The seacoast's superb location and abundant educational, cultural, physical, and human resources seem to be more than adequate to continue the region's reputation as one of the top places in the country to live and work (and vacation).

**GUIDANCE** Greater Portsmouth Chamber of Commerce (603-436-1118; www.portsmouthnh.com), 500 Market Street, Box 239, Portsmouth 03802-0239, publishes the region's most comprehensive, year-round visitors guide and stocks a wealth of information on local history, attractions, accommodations, dining, and shopping.

Also see *Guidance* under sectional listings.

**GETTING THERE** *By plane:* **Boston's Logan Airport, Portland's Jetport,** and the **Manchester Airport** are each an hour's drive from the seacoast.

*By car:* I-95, the state's first superhighway, built in the 1950s, bisects the seacoast, connecting New Hampshire to the seacoast regions of Massachusetts and Maine. From the west, Routes 4 and 101 connect the seacoast with the central regions of the state, while Route 16 is the road from the mountains.

*By bus:* **Greyhound Bus Lines** (603-436-0163; www.greyhound.com) stops daily in Portsmouth's Market Square, connecting the seacoast with nationwide bus service. **Coach Company** (603-431-0163; 1-800-874-3377; www.coachco.com) has twice-daily trips to Boston. **C&J Trailways** (603-431-2424; 603-742-2990; www.cjtrailways.com) provides many trips daily, connecting Logan Airport and downtown Boston with Dover, Durham, and Portsmouth (Pease), New Hampshire; Newburyport, Massachusetts; and Portland, Maine. **Hampton Shuttle** (603-659-9853; outside New Hampshire, 1-800-225-6426), a reservation-only shuttle service, makes eight trips daily from Hampton, Exeter, and Seabrook to Logan Airport.

*By train:* **Amtrak** (www.thedowneaster.com). Slide down the Maine and New Hampshire coasts with ease on the Downeaster, a commuter train that heads to Boston. The train runs year-round; one-way fares run about $4–21. On the seacoast the train stops at Dover, Durham, and Exeter.

# PORTSMOUTH AND VICINITY

For more than 300 years, the seacoast's largest community has been influenced by its maritime location. "We came to fish," announced Portsmouth's first residents in 1630, but shortly the community (first called Strawbery Banke) became a center for the mast trade, supplying long, straight timbers for the Royal Navy. Portsmouth's captains and crews soon roamed the entire world in locally built vessels, hauling cargoes to and from New England, the Caribbean, Europe, and the Far East. In the years before and after the Revolutionary War, wealthy captains and merchants built many of the fine homes and commercial buildings that characterize Portsmouth today.

Unhappy with the demands of the British government, Portsmouth residents were quick to voice opposition to the Crown. Before Paul Revere rode to Lexington and Concord, he first galloped to Portsmouth, warning the patriots to raid nearby Fort William and Mary (now Fort Constitution) and to remove the gunpowder before the British came from Boston to strengthen the undermanned fort. John Paul Jones lived in Portsmouth while overseeing the construction of two major warships during the Revolution. Built on the banks of the Piscataqua River were 28 clippers, unrivaled in construction, beauty, and speed as they hauled passengers and merchandise around the world.

The Portsmouth Naval Shipyard, founded in 1800, has long been associated with submarines, turning out 100 vessels to aid the Allied cause in World War II. Portsmouth's red and green tugboats symbolize the city's current maritime activity. Oil tankers and bulk cargo vessels continue to ply the river, halting traffic as they pass through bridges, creating a bustle of activity now missing from so many other old New England seaports, which have lost their commercial ship traffic.

The result of this 300-year maritime heritage is present in the city's architecture; in its active waterfront, which is used for international, commercial, and recreational boating; and in the many cultural activities that involve its riverfront location. Once an old swabbie town, complete with rundown bars and a decaying city center and surrounding neighborhoods, Portsmouth has been transformed into an exciting city as its residents have begun to appreciate its historical traditions and classic architecture. Portsmouth's renaissance continues, fueled by fine restaurants (the best north of Boston, and some would say "including" Boston), inns, music, dance, theater, and, seemingly, a festival every month of the year.

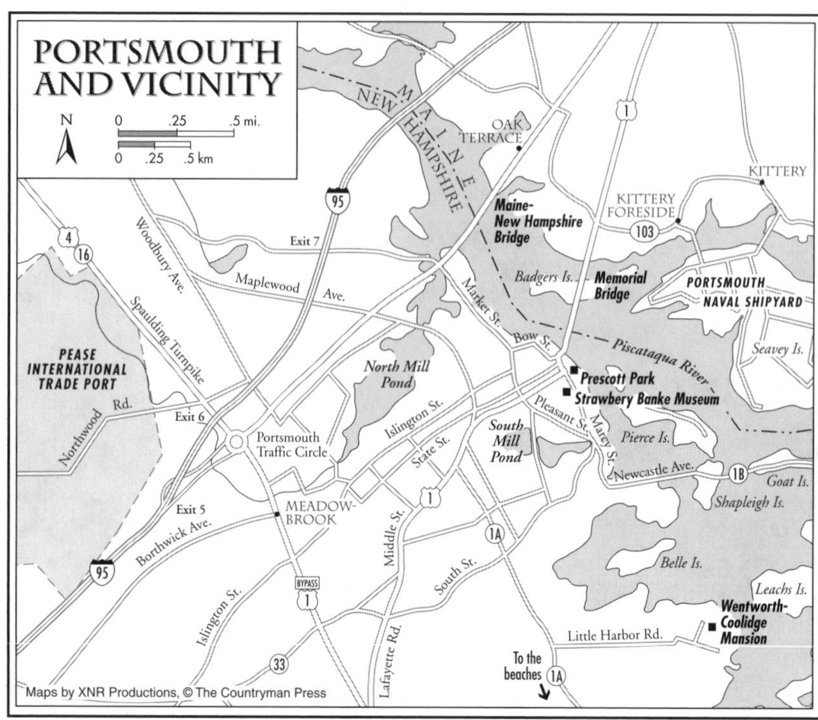


The Piscataqua River, one of the fastest-flowing navigable rivers in the world, separates New Castle, Portsmouth, and Newington, New Hampshire, from Kittery and Eliot, Maine. It is crossed by three main bridges. The lowest is Memorial Bridge, near the center of town, which raises its draw many times daily for commercial and recreational vessels. Residents and visitors alike usually stop to watch as the little tugs shepherd huge oceangoing vessels past this bridge. Next upstream is the Sarah Mildred Long Bridge, once the busiest bridge for motor vehicles but no longer now that the I-95 bridge just upriver carries most of the through traffic. The Piscataqua drains Great Bay, a large, relatively shallow tidal bay known for its wildlife and winter ice fishing (see *Green Space* in "Dover, Durham, and Vicinity").

GUIDANCE **Greater Portsmouth Chamber of Commerce** (603-436-1118; www.portsmouthnh.com), 500 Market Street, Box 239, Portsmouth 03802-0239. A busy and active promoter of local tourism, the chamber has a year-round information center on Market Street, a short walk west of downtown. It serves Portsmouth and adjacent communities on both sides of the Piscataqua River. There is also a summer information kiosk in Market Square.

GETTING AROUND *By taxi:* **Portsmouth Taxi** (603-430-1222) is available by phone.

*By bus:* **COAST** (Cooperative Alliance for Seacoast Transportation) (603-743-5777; www.coastbus.org), the local bus transportation, connects Portsmouth and major outlying shopping centers with Durham, Dover, Newmarket, Rochester, and Somersworth, New Hampshire, and Berwick, Maine. A main stop is in Market Square. Fares range from 75 cents to $1.75; children under 5 ride free.

*By car:* When traveling on I-95, take Exit 7, Market Street, which leads directly downtown, past the Chamber of Commerce Information Center to Market Square.

**PARKING** Although Portsmouth's traffic is no worse than any other city's, it does have limited on-street parking, and its meter attendants will often issue a ticket within moments of your parking meter's expiration. Metered parking (daily except Sunday) is limited to 2 hours, so seek out the parking garage, situated just off Market Square in the middle of town, or the large lot off Pleasant Street, adjacent to the South Mill Pond. All of Portsmouth's points of interest and finest restaurants are within an easy walk of both places. Portsmouth is best enjoyed on foot, anyway.

**MEDICAL EMERGENCY** **Portsmouth Regional Hospital** (603-436-5110; 1-800-685-8282), 333 Borthwick Avenue, Portsmouth. The hospital offers 24-hour emergency walk-in service.

**Careplus Ambulance Service** (1-800-633-3590).

## ✷ Villages

Portsmouth is surrounded by four small towns: Newington, Greenland, New Castle, and Rye. **Newington,** upriver from Portsmouth, is the commercial and industrial center of the region. It has two major shopping malls and many other shops, plus a large power plant, oil storage tanks, and other industries. Most of this commercial-industrial complex is located between the river and the Spaulding Turnpike (Route 4/16). The residential area and village are south of the turnpike, by Pease Air Force Base, whose construction in the 1950s cut the town of Newington in half. **Greenland** is south of Newington, another residential town with a picturesque village green. East along the Piscataqua is the small island village of **New Castle.** Winding, narrow streets lined with 18th- and 19th-century homes combine to give New Castle the appearance of a town unchanged since the turn of the 20th century. The historic Wentworth-by-the-Sea Hotel has been closed for a number of years, but the adjacent large marina keeps the town's tourist image alive. Next to New Castle is the largest of the four towns, **Rye,** once a popular summer retreat when it had several large hotels. Those old structures are gone now, and its summer residents live in oceanfront cottages. Several of the finest residential developments have been built in Rye, and it is a popular address for many seacoast executives. Route 1A along the coast of Rye is a fine bike route, passing several state parks, restaurants, and a few motels.

Also not to be missed is the **Isles of Shoals,** a historic, nine-island group about 10 miles off the coast and visible from Route 1A. Summer ferry service provides tours around the islands and a 3-hour stopover on **Star Island.**

Robert Kozlow

THE CIRCA-1800 GOSPORT CHURCH AND NEWER STONE BUILDINGS ARE PART OF THE STAR ISLAND CONFERENCE CENTER ON THE ISLES OF SHOALS.

## ✷ To See

**St. John's Episcopal Church** (603-436-8283; www.stjohnsnh.org), 101 Chapel Street, Portsmouth. Open Sunday and other times by applying at the church office in the adjacent building. Built in 1732, this church is a prominent city landmark located beside the river. Its classic interior has wall paintings, religious objects, and interesting plaques. Its adjacent 1754 graveyard is the resting place of many of the city's colonial leaders, including Benning Wentworth, royal governor 1741–1766.

**Newington Historical Society** (603-649-7420), Nimble Hill Road, Newington. Open Thursday 2–4 PM in July and August. The Old Parsonage, built in 1710, has local artifacts and a special children's room with antique toys. Across the street is the 1712 Old Meetinghouse, in continuous use since that time but structurally altered, and nearby is the Langdon Library, with an extensive genealogical collection.

**Port of Portsmouth Maritime Museum and Albacore Park** (603-436-3680), 600 Market Street, Portsmouth. Take Exit 7 off I-95, drive 0.2 mile east, and turn right off Market Street. Open daily 9:30–5:30. Tour the USS *Albacore,* an important experimental submarine built in the 1950s at the nearby Portsmouth Naval Shipyard. Once the world's fastest submarine, this 55-person vessel was used for 20 years as the design model for the contemporary U.S. nuclear fleet. The tour includes a memorial park and gardens, a short film, a picnic area, a gift shop, and the submarine. Adults $4; seniors over 60 $3; children 7–17 $2, under 7 free; family rate $10 for a group of four.

**Portsmouth Athenaeum** (603-431-2538), 9 Market Square, Portsmouth. Research library open Tuesday and Thursday 1–4 PM, Saturday 10 AM–4 PM, and by appointment. Reading Room open to the public for tours Thursday 1–4 PM. This three-story brick Federal building, with its four white pilasters, is the architectural anchor for Market Square. Built in 1805, after one of Portsmouth's disastrous fires, the building has, since 1823, been the home of the Athenaeum, a private library and museum. Genealogy, maritime history, biographies, and Civil War memorabilia are among its important holdings. Throughout the building are fully rigged ship models, half models, and paintings. Free.

**Strawbery Banke** (603-433-1100; www.strawberybanke.org), ticket office off Marcy Street, Portsmouth. Open May through October and the first two weekends in December; special winter and off-season group tours are also available. In the early 1960s the 10-acre site that is now this nationally known and respected restoration was supposed to be razed for an urban renewal project. Local protests stopped the demolition, saving more than 30 historically significant buildings. The museum now has 42 buildings, including several moved to this site to protect them from demolition elsewhere in the city. Most of the buildings are on their original foundations, which makes this a unique project when compared to other historical restorations composed of new re-creations or buildings assembled from many places. As the location of Portsmouth's first settlement in 1630 and a residential area until the early 1960s, Strawbery Banke reflects the living 300-year history of this neighborhood, not just one era. Furnished houses have rooms reflecting life from the 17th through the mid–20th centuries, depicting a variety of lifestyles, from wealthy merchants and professional people to sea captains, poor widows, and ordinary working families. Other houses have exhibits, displays, and craftspeople who offer their work for sale. The December candlelight stroll is a popular holiday attraction, and there are other special events throughout the year, including militia musters, horticulture and fabric workshops, and small-craft displays—the latter complementing the institution's wooden boat shop. Extensive 18th- and 19th-century gardens enhance the grounds. The **Café on the Banke** (603-436-

STRAWBERY BANKE IN PORTSMOUTH

Robert Kozlow

8803), one of the city's best spots for gourmet sandwiches, soups, and light meals, is on the grounds. Picnic area and gift shop.

Also see *Green Space*.

**HISTORIC HOMES** Beginning at the kiosk in Market Square, knowledgeable **Portsmouth Harbor trail guides** (603-436-1118) offer a wealth of background about the city's early settlers, patriots, ship captains, and industrialists on regularly scheduled tours Monday and Thursday through Saturday at 10:30 AM and 5:30 PM, Sunday at 1:30 PM June through mid-October. Adults $8; children 8–14 $5. There is also a trail guide and map, available for $2 from many area shops and hotels, which highlights three different routes through the city's waterfront and downtown.

**John Paul Jones House** (603-436-8420), Middle and State Streets, Portsmouth. Open May 15 through October 15, Monday through Saturday 10 AM–4 PM, Sunday noon–4 PM. The museum house of the Portsmouth Historical Society, this home was the residence of Capt. John Paul Jones when he lived in Portsmouth overseeing the construction of two Revolutionary War frigates, the *Ranger* and the *America*. A traditional Georgian house, built in 1758, it has furnished period rooms and a small museum. Adults $5; children 6–14 $2.50.

**Governor John Langdon Memorial** (603-436-3205; www.spnea.org/visit/homes/landon.htm), 143 Pleasant Street, Portsmouth. Open June through mid-October. Tours on the hour Wednesday through Sunday 11 AM–5 PM (last tour one hour before closing). One of New England's finest Georgian mansions, this house was built in 1784 by John Langdon, a wealthy merchant who was an important figure in the Revolution and later a U.S. senator and governor of New Hampshire. George Washington was entertained in this house, which is now owned by the Society for the Preservation of New England Antiquities. Extensive gardens are behind the house. Adults $5; seniors over 65 $4.50; children 6–12 $2.50.

THE JOHN PAUL JONES HOUSE IN PORTSMOUTH

Robert Kozlow

**Moffat-Ladd House** (603-436-8221; www.whipple.org), 154 Market Street, Portsmouth. Open mid-June through September, Monday through Saturday 11 AM–5 PM, Sunday 1–5 PM. Built in 1763, this house was the residence of wealthy 18th-century shipowners and merchants and is furnished in that period to reflect the family's lifestyle. William Whipple, a signer of the Declaration of Independence, lived here. Its great hall is a masterpiece of detailed woodworking. Internationally famous gardens fill the backyard, and don't miss the summerlong book sale in the carriage house. Owned by the Society of Colonial Dames. Adults $5; children 7–12 $2.

**Rundlet-May House** (603-436-3205; www.spnea.org), Middle Street, Portsmouth. Open June through mid-October, Saturday and Sunday 11 AM–5 PM; last tour an hour before closing. Built in 1807, this Federal mansion remained in the builder's family until just a few years ago, when it was acquired by the Society for the Preservation of New England Antiquities. Although it has many fine Federal pieces built especially for the house, it does reflect the continuous ownership of successive generations of a family who valued the original features of the house and adapted their lifestyle with an appreciation for the past. The stable is impressive, as are the extensive gardens and grounds, which retain much of their original layout. Adults $5; children 7–12 $2.

**Warner House** (603-436-5909), 150 Daniel Street, Portsmouth. Open June through mid-October, Tuesday through Saturday 10 AM–4 PM, Sunday 1–4 PM. The finest New England example of an 18th-century, urban brick dwelling, this house was built in 1716 and, during its early years, was the home of leading merchants and officials of the royal provincial government. It has outstanding murals painted on the staircase walls, splendid paneling, and period furnishings. Benjamin Franklin is said to have installed the lightning rod on the west wall. Owned by the Warner House Association. Fee charged.

**Wentworth-Gardner and Tobias Lear Houses** (603-436-4406; www.seacoastnh.com), Gardner and Mechanic Streets, Portsmouth. The Wentworth-Gardner House is open June through mid-October, Tuesday through Sunday 1–4 PM; the Lear House is only open June through August, Wednesday 1–4 PM and by appointment. Built in 1760, the Wentworth-Gardner House is one of the perfect examples of Georgian architecture found in America. Built by Madam Mark Hunking as a gift to her son Thomas (brother of the last royal governor), its exquisite carving took 14 months to complete. It has been beautifully restored and furnished. Adjacent is the Tobias Lear House, built in 1740, the childhood home of George Washington's private secretary. The president enjoyed tea in the parlor in 1789. Not completely restored, the Lear House is occasionally open to the public. Both houses are owned by the Wentworth-Gardner and Tobias Lear Houses Association. Adults $4; children 6–14 $2.

**Richard Jackson House** (603-436-3205), 76 Northwest Street, Portsmouth. Open the first Saturday of every month from June through October. Tours on the hour noon–4 PM. This is New Hampshire's oldest house, built in 1664 with later additions. It has few furnishings and is of interest primarily for its 17th-century architectural details. It is most picturesque in May when its apple orchard is in bloom. Owned by the Society for the Preservation of New England Antiquities. Admission $4.

**Wentworth-Coolidge Mansion Historic Site** (603-436-6607), Little Harbor Road (off Route 1A), Portsmouth. Open mid-June through September, Monday through Saturday 11 AM–5 PM, Sunday 1–5 PM. Owned by the state, this rambling 40-room mansion is one of the most interesting and historic buildings in New Hampshire. It was the home of Royal Gov. Benning Wentworth, whose term from 1741 until 1766 was the longest of any royal governor in America. Council meetings were held in an ornately paneled room overlooking the channel between Portsmouth and Little Harbors. Its lilacs, which bloom in late May, are said to be

Kim Grant

THE WENTWORTH-COOLIDGE MANSION

the first planted in America. Although the house is not furnished, its extensive woodwork is an exquisite display of the prowess of Portsmouth craftsmen of the period. Admission $5.

**FOR FAMILIES** ✐ **Water Country** (603-436-3556; www.watercountry.com), Route 1, 1 mile south of town, Portsmouth. Open weekends Memorial Day through mid-June, then daily through Labor Day. June and September, 11 AM–6 PM; July and August, 9:30 AM–8 PM. Called New England's largest water park, this complex has seven large water slides, a huge wave pool, a Raging Rapids ride, plus an Adventure River ride, bumper boats, fountains, and a kiddie pool. One admission covers all day for all rides; tube and boat rentals are additional. Discount admission after 4:30 PM.

✐ **The Children's Museum of Portsmouth** (603-436-3853; www.childrensmuseum.org), 280 Marcy Street, Portsmouth. Open from mid-June through August and during public school vacations, Monday through Saturday 10 AM–5 PM, Sunday 1–5 PM. Housed in an old meetinghouse in the city's historic South End, this colorful museum is exciting for children of all ages. Many of its exhibits reflect the area's maritime heritage. Kids can explore the yellow submarine or ride in the lobster fishing boat, and there are many other hands-on exhibits, changing displays, and organized activities. Adults and children $5; senior citizens $4; children under 1 free. Children under 9 must be accompanied by someone age 12 or older. Memberships also available.

✐ **Seacoast Science Center** (603-436-8043; www.seacntr.org), Route 1A at Odiorne State Park, Rye. Open all year, 10 AM–5 PM. A facility of the Audubon Society of New Hampshire, this environmental center is right on the rocky shore and offers marine exhibits and aquariums, a museum shop, children's workshops, tidepooling and marsh walks, and occasional lectures. Small fee charged; free to members.

**Prescott Park** (603-436-2848), Marcy Street, Portsmouth. Located directly across from Strawbery Banke, this city park offers an annual arts festival with a full schedule of attractions from late May through mid-October. Locals and tourists alike fill the lawn with blankets and picnics to enjoy jazz concerts, Broadway musicals, and Shakespeare under the stars. Admission is free, although a $3 donation is suggested. (Also see *Green Space.*)

HISTORIC CEMETERIES **North Cemetery,** Maplewood Avenue, Portsmouth. Dating from 1753, this cemetery holds the remains of prominent people from the Revolutionary War to the War of 1812. Diverse headstones reveal the skill of early stonecutters.

**Point of Graves Cemetery,** off Marcy Street, Portsmouth. Adjacent to Prescott Park, this old cemetery was established in 1671. Although most of the oldest stones have sunk from sight, many old and uniquely carved stones remain.

## ✳ To Do

BOAT EXCURSIONS **Isles of Shoals Steamship Company** (603-431-5500; 1-800-441-4620; www.islesofshoals.com), Barker Wharf, 315 Market Street, Box 311, Portsmouth 03802. Open daily mid-June through Labor Day and Memorial Day weekend; special fall schedule until September 28. Whale-watch cruises begin in mid-April, and there are also fall foliage cruises. This is the Isles of Shoals ferry, hauling passengers and freight to Star Island and providing one of New England's finest narrated tours. The 90-foot *Thomas Laighton* is a replica of a turn-of-the-20th-century steamship, the type of vessel used when the islands were the leading New England summer colony, attracting the era's most famous artists, writers, poets, and musicians. The boat docks at Star Island, home of the Star Island Conference Center, a summer religious institution meeting here since the turn of the 20th century. On the 11 AM ferry trip, a maximum of 100 visitors can leave the *Laighton* for a 3-hour stopover, returning to the mainland on the 3 PM boat, which docks in Portsmouth at 4:30 PM. Buy tickets early for this cruise—it often sells out. Bring your picnic lunch and plenty of film for the camera. Since the *Laighton* is the supply line for the conference center, delivering food, drinking water, supplies, mail, and oil for the island's generators, it operates rain or shine. The trip to the islands takes about an hour; the round trip, about 3 hours. In addition to the daily Isles of Shoals cruises, the *Laighton* is used for dinner cruises, including clambakes and big-band dance cruises. The 71-foot *Oceanic* is used for whale-watching (an all-day, offshore trip), special lighthouse cruises, the nightly sunset cruise to the islands, and weekend cocktail and dance cruises.

**Portsmouth Harbor Cruises** (603-436-8084; 1-800-776-0915), 64 Ceres Street, Oar House Dock, Portsmouth 03801. Open early June through Labor Day, with a reduced schedule until late October. The 49-passenger *Heritage* offers a variety of daily narrated cruises, which, depending on the tide, tour the harbor and wend down the Piscataqua, past the two lighthouses, around New Castle Island, through Little Harbor, and back to the dock. Several trips circle the Isles of Shoals, and fall foliage trips travel the winding rivers and expanse of Great Bay. Our favorite is the 5:30 sunset cruise—no narration, just a cool drink and a quiet ride after a hot summer day. Several trips regularly sell out, so buy tickets early. Also available is a large sailboat for single-day or overnight charters.

**Granite State Whale Watch** (603-964-5545; 603-382-6743; www.whales-rye.com), Rye Harbor State Marina, Route 1A, Box 232, Rye 03870. Open daily mid-June through Labor Day; weekend whale-watches May, June, September, and October. Ride the 150-person-capacity *Granite State* for a 6-hour whale-watch or a 2-hour cruise around the Isles of Shoals.

**Atlantic Fishing and Whalewatching** (603-964-5220), Rye Harbor Marina, Route 1A, Box 678, Rye 03870. Open Wednesday and weekends in April for all-day fishing, two half-day trips daily Memorial Day through Labor Day and weekends through early October, and night fishing in-season. The speedy, 70-foot *Atlantic Queen II* is designed for all-weather ocean fishing. Offshore trips seek cod, cusk, pollack, and haddock. Rods for rent.

BUGGY RIDES **The Portsmouth Livery Company** (603-427-0044), 319 Lincoln Avenue, Portsmouth. Open daily May through October; November through April open Friday through Sunday and Monday holidays, weather permitting. You will find Ray Parker and his horses and buggies in Market Square next to the North Church. Day and evening sight-seeing tours are offered, ranging in length from 15 to 35 minutes. The latter includes a ride through historic Strawbery Banke. A gourmet picnic ride for two with lunch served at a scenic picnic area, then a return ride, is also offered.

FARMERS' MARKET **Farmers' Market** (603-778-3702), Parrott Avenue, Portsmouth. Saturday 9 AM–1 PM, June through mid-October. Fresh, locally grown veggies and fruits in-season, home-baked goods, and crafts. Seacoast Growers' Association.

GOLF **Pease Golf Club** (603-433-1331), Country Club Road, Portsmouth. An 18-hole course open to the public daily from spring through November. Tee times must be reserved and can be set up 3 days in advance. Pro shop, cafeteria, car rentals, driving and practice ranges.

**Portsmouth Country Club** (603-436-9719), Country Club Drive (off Route 101 south of Portsmouth), Greenland. Open mid-April to mid-November. Designed by Robert Trent Jones; 18 holes, the longest course in New Hampshire, with several holes sited on the shores of Great Bay. Cart rentals, full bar and food service, and pro shop. Call for starting times.

## * Green Space

PARKS **Prescott Park,** Marcy Street, Portsmouth. Open year-round. Marcy Street was once an area of bawdy houses, bars, and run-down businesses. The Prescott sisters, who were born in this section of the city, inherited millions of dollars and sought to clean up the waterfront by creating a park, which they gave to the city. Supported by a substantial trust fund, the park is famous for its beautiful gardens, but it also includes boat wharves, an amphitheater, picnic areas, sculpture, fountains, and the historic 1705 Sheafe Warehouse with exhibits. During the summer it is the location of the daily Prescott Park Arts Festival (donation requested), offering outdoor summer theater, varied musical performances, an art exhibit, and children's theater and art programs (see *To See—For Families* and *Special Events*). At the eastern end of the park, cross the bridge to adjacent Pierce Island, home of the state's commercial fishing pier, and walk out to Four Tree Island, a picnic ground nearly in the middle of the river.

Robert Kozlow

PRESCOTT PARK

**Urban Forestry Center** (603-431-6774), Elywn Road, off Route 1 south of Portsmouth. Open year-round; summer 8 AM–8 PM, winter 8 AM–4 PM; office hours Monday through Friday 8 AM–4 PM. Bordering tidal Sagamore Creek, this site has nature trails, herb gardens, hiking, cross-country skiing, and snowshoeing, and offers environmental programs throughout the year. Free.

**Fort Constitution,** off Route 1A, New Castle. Open year-round 10–5. Turn in at the U.S. Coast Guard Station and park where indicated. This historic site was first used for fortifications in the early 1600s, but today it reflects the Revolutionary and Civil War periods. In December 1774, after being alerted by Paul Revere, local patriots raided what was then called Fort William and Mary, overwhelmed its few defenders, and removed its powder and some weapons before British warships from Boston could reinforce the garrison. This is considered to be the first overt act against the king and predated the war's outbreak by some four months. The powder was used against the British at the battle of Bunker Hill. The last royal governor, John Wentworth, and his family fled their home in the city and remained in the fort before leaving the rebellious province. Restored and maintained by the state, the fort's entrance portcullis reflects the colonial period, while the fortifications along the water date from the Civil War, although there were no battles here. Adjacent to the fort is the picturesque and still-important Fort Point lighthouse, and just offshore is the Whaleback lighthouse. Ten miles at sea the Isles of Shoals are visible. Free.

**Fort Stark,** Wild Rose Lane, off Route 1A, New Castle. Open weekends and holidays, May through October, 10 AM–5 PM. To protect the important Portsmouth Naval Shipyard during World War II, the military occupied several points at the mouth of the river. One was Fort Foster, across the river from Fort Constitution, and Fort Stark was another. Although used as a fort from 1746, the site today reflects its World War II service. Free.

**New Castle Great Common,** Route 1A, New Castle. Open year-round; a small fee is charged to nonresidents during the summer. Another World War II site, this was Camp Langdon, an army base. It was acquired by the town of New Castle as a recreation area and the site for a new office complex. There are rest rooms, picnic tables, a small beach, and a pier for fishing. Overlooking the mouth of the river and its two lighthouses, this area is one of the scenic highlights along the coast.

♿ **Odiorne Point State Park** (603-436-7406), Route 1A, Rye. Open year-round; a park fee is charged in the main season, June through September. This 137-acre oceanfront park is the site of the first settlement in New Hampshire in 1623. Later, fine mansions were built here; then the site was taken over during World War II and named Fort Dearborn, with huge guns placed in concrete bunkers. As a park it has handicapped-accessible nature trails, a boat-launching ramp, picnic tables, and a fine nature center—open late June through late August—operated by the University of New Hampshire. The center has exhibits and offers varied daily nature programs using the park, its nearby marsh, and the ocean's intertidal zone. No swimming.

**Rye Harbor State Park and Marina** (603-436-5294), Route 1A, Rye. Open year-round; a fee is charged in the summer season for the park and boat launching. New Hampshire's smallest state park, this jewel occupies an ocean point just south of Rye Harbor. It has picnic tables, a playground, a jetty for fishing, a view of the picturesque harbor, and cooling ocean breezes on hot summer days.

RYE HARBOR

Robert Kozlow

Around the corner is the Rye Harbor State Marina with a launching ramp and wharves, where you can buy tickets for deep-sea fishing, whale-watches, or sightseeing boat rides.

**BEACHES** **Wallis Sands State Park** (603-436-9404), Route 1A, Rye. Open weekends mid-May through late June, then daily until Labor Day. A large, sandy beach with lifeguards, rest rooms, parking, and a snack bar. Fee charged.
**Jenness State Beach,** Route 1A, Rye. Another large, sandy beach with lifeguards, rest rooms, and parking meters. A snack bar is across the street.

## ✱ Lodging

**BED & BREAKFASTS** **Bow Street Inn** (603-431-7760; www.bowstreetinn.com), 121 Bow Street, Portsmouth 03801. Open all year. Overlooking the waterfront, this converted brick brewery has a cosmopolitan feel with the **Seacoast Repertory Theatre** on the main floor (see *Entertainment*); the inn is an elevator's ride above. Only 2 of the 10 rooms have river views, but all have a queen-sized brass bed, private bath, phone, and cable TV. The harbor-view rooms are mini suites. Just a short walk to all of the city's sights and fine dining. Continental breakfast with fresh-baked items. $119–175, depending on season and accommodations.

**The Inn at Christian Shore** (603-431-6770), 335 Maplewood Avenue, Portsmouth 03801. Open year-round. An interesting mix of art and antiques furnishes this lovely, in-town Federal house, restored and operated as a B&B since 1979. There are five rooms, all with private bath, air-conditioning, and TV. Innkeeper Mariaelena Koopman serves full New England breakfasts and afternoon tea in a charming dining room with a roaring fire, brass candelabra, and exposed old beams. Rates are $100–115 high season, $90–95 low season.

**The Inn at Strawbery Banke** (603-436-7242; 1-800-428-3933), 314 Court Street, Portsmouth 03801. Around the corner from Strawbery Banke and two blocks from Market Square, Sarah Glover O'Donnell's homey B&B has location, location, location! It also boasts seven bright, comfortable rooms that meander through the circa-1800 home and a more recent addition. All have updated private bath. Some rooms have queen-sized beds; others, a queen and a single. Upstairs and down, common rooms offer TV and travel books. A skylit breakfast room overlooks gardens, a strawberry patch, and bird feeders, assuring a sunny start to your day. Full breakfast. Rates are $145–150 high season, $100–105 off-season.

**Martin Hill Inn** (603-436-2287), 404 Islington Street, Portsmouth 03801. Open year-round. Super-friendly innkeepers Jane and Paul Harnden have invested the city's first B&B with their love of antiques and their talent for gardening. From the street, this yellow-clapboard inn with its white picket fence looks cheery and chic. Inside, the elegance of early Portsmouth comes alive. Adjacent 1820 and 1850 houses are joined by a brick garden path overlooking a courtyard and water garden. The main inn has three guest rooms with period furnishings and canopy or four-poster beds. The Guest House has four rooms, three of which are suites, one with an attached solarium. All rooms have private bath, air-conditioning, writing tables, sofas, or separate sitting areas. A no-smoking inn. Full breakfast is served in the elegant, mahogany-furnished dining room. Rates are $90–130, depending on the room and season.

**Sise Inn** (603-433-1200; 1-800-267-0525), 40 Court Street, Portsmouth 03801. Open year-round. An easy walk from Portsmouth's "happening" Market Square, the Sise Inn offers hotel amenities in a handsomely restored Victorian stick-style home and addition. The 34 rooms, including several suites, have private baths, mostly queen-sized beds, TVs, VCRs, telephones, alarm clocks, radios, tables, and comfortable chairs. Many rooms also have CD players and whirlpool baths; one has a fireplace, and another, a skylight and a private staircase. With several meeting rooms, the inn was designed for the business traveler, but vacationers are welcome to share the Victorian luxury as well. A light breakfast is served. Rates are $125–210.

**Great Islander B&B** (603-436-8536), 62 Main Street, New Castle 03854. Open all year. With Wentworth-by-the-Sea Hotel closed, this is the only place to stay in one of the prettiest villages in New Hampshire. This B&B offers both a central location—across from the town hall and the Congregational church in front—and a river view from the back deck. Each of the three rooms is brightly furnished with antiques and quilts. One has a private bath with Jacuzzi; the other two rooms share a bath. Innkeepers Fred and Greselda Pitts encourage use of their lap pool, and offer suggestions for birding and boating excursions. Breakfast is expanded continental. Rates are $100–125.

**Rock Ledge Manor** (603-431-1413; www.rockledgemanor.com), 1413 Ocean Boulevard (Route 1A), Rye 03870. Open all year, reservations requested. On the ocean with views from each room to the Isles of Shoals, this white-shingled Victorian "cottage" has four rooms, two with private bath, two with half bath and a shared shower. Have a full breakfast, then relax on the veranda overlooking the sea. Convenient to Portsmouth and a short walk to the beach. There's good biking from the door. A nonsmoking inn. $125–225, depending on the room and season. Stan and Sarah Smith, owners.

**Downtown on Market Street** (Exit 7 off I-95) is the full-service Sheraton Harborside Portsmouth Hotel and Conference Center (603-431-2300) with 205 rooms, restaurant, and lounge, within walking distance of everything.

**MOTELS** Portsmouth is well supplied with motels, most of which are located on Route 1 south of the city and at the traffic circle intersection of I-95, Route 1 bypass, and Route 4/16 (Spaulding Turnpike). Among these are the **Anchorage Inn** (603-431-8111), **Comfort Inn** (603-433-3338), **Courtyard by Marriott** (603-436-2121), **Hampton Inn** (603-431-6111), **Holiday Inn** (603-431-8000), and **Howard Johnson Hotel** (603-436-7600).

## ✷ Where to Eat

Portsmouth is famous for its numerous quality restaurants, the best collection of fine dining north of Boston. Several of the top restaurants are located in the Old Harbor area where Bow, Ceres, and Market Streets intersect. Here six-story warehouses, the largest structures north of Boston when built in the early 1800s, have been remodeled as restaurants and shops. A treat for summer and early-fall visitors are the five outdoor decks located here on the waterfront, open for lunch and late into the evening (until the legal closing for serving liquor). Everything from snacks to sandwiches and full dinners is available on the decks. View the tugboats and watch large oceangoing ships pass, seemingly within an arm's length.

DINING OUT ♿ **43° North Kitchen and Wine Bar** (603-430-0225; www.fortythreenorth.com), 75 Pleasant Street, Portsmouth. Open Monday through Saturday for dinner at 5 PM. Reservations strongly encouraged. A European ambience, stellar wine selection (served by the glass and half bottle, too), and ambitious menu combine to attract an upscale crowd to this small, well-proportioned bistro just a short block off bustling Market Square. The star of the attractive room is the wine bar tucked in a corner, which you can see from most tables. The menu here changes frequently; expect to find dishes borrowing from Asian, Italian, and French cuisines. Appetizers are served tapas-style and include small plates of duck spring rolls drizzled in tamari, pan-seared rock shrimp, and blue point oysters topped with creamy Gorgonzola and crispy pancetta. The main-course selection usually features meats, seafood, and pasta such as tuna, quail, wild mushroom ravioli (for vegetarians), elk, and flatiron steak. Vintages are carefully chosen, and you can be assured of a perfect match—these folks know their food and wine. Entrées $17–27; appetizers $6.50–10.

**Anthony Alberto's Ristorante Italiano** (603-436-4000; www.anthonyalbertos.com), 59 Penhallow Street, Portsmouth. Dinner daily from 5 PM; closed Sunday in summer. Tucked along a picturesque side street, this romantic basement restaurant features elegantly prepared northern and southern Italian cuisine in a grottolike setting. The pastas ($15.95–19.95) are homemade, with interesting selections such as pappardelle with braised rabbit, fettuccine with shrimp, or cappellini topped with scallops and prosciutto; the antipasti and entrées are a mix of creative and classic specialties. Olive-marinated filet mignon, grilled rack of lamb, and seared salmon with beet-encrusted scallops are among the good choices. Fresh seafood specials change daily. Entrées $19.95–29.95.

**Blue Mermaid** (603-427-2583; www.bluemermaid.com), The Hill, Portsmouth. Open all year daily at 11:30 AM for lunch and dinner. This eclectic and lively restaurant offers a diverse, flavorful menu that covers the globe. The kitchen pays homage to its coastal proximity with appetizers such as lobster and corn chowder or a Caesar salad topped with grilled shrimp; this trend carries over to the main dishes, where you can take your pick from a variety of seafood and have it tossed on the wood grill. Land-based dishes are easy to come by, too: Barbecued ribs, lamb on a skewer, and pad Thai make ordering a challenge for the daring diner. Light eaters can order from the small tapas-style menu—it features the likes of yucca fritta with cilantro adobo or a lobster quesadilla—and interesting side dishes such as plantains also pop up here and there. Eating here is definitely a unique adventure, and you may also be treated to an evening of live music if you visit on the weekend. Entrées $11.95–21.95.

**Café Mirabelle and La Crêperie** (603-430-9301; www.portsmouthnh.com), 64 Bridge Street, Portsmouth. Open Wednesday through Saturday for lunch 11:30 AM–2 PM; for dinner Wednesday through Sunday 5:15–9 PM. A cozy place with many plants and large windows, this restaurant offers authentic country French dining on the second floor and crêpes on the first floor. Lunch features a variety of crêpes like the forestière (mushrooms) and the Riviera (shrimp and tiny bay scallops) as well as bistro classics like coq au vin and cassoulet. Dinner promises coquilles Saint-Jacques studded with local scallops and mushrooms baked in a champagne shallot cream sauce topped with garlic-herb bread crumbs; or you might try the beef Zachary—tenderloin pan-sautéed with shrimp, sun-dried tomatoes, and herbed goat cheese in a red Zinfandel demiglaze. Choose from the more formal dinner menu or the lighthearted brasserie menu. Lunch $3.95–8.95; dinner $11.95–23.95.

**The Carriage House** (603-964-8251; www.carriagehouserye.com), 2263 Ocean Boulevard, Rye Beach. Open daily at 5 PM, Sunday brunch 11 AM–3 PM. Built as a restaurant in the 1920s, the Carriage House has been a favorite gourmet eatery for two decades, offering quality Continental cuisine at reasonable prices. Specialties might include an Indian curry of the day; a *navarin* (stew) of lobster pan-roasted with big juicy sea scallops and vegetables and flamed with Pernod; or the *frutti di mare* fra diavolo, which features shrimp, scallops, mussels, squid, and fish all sautéed in Chablis, garlic, and lemon and tossed with spicy marinara sauce—then served over linguine! There are seven pasta entrées, salmon poached with Chablis in parchment, sole Oscar, roast duckling, and several steaks. Appetizers, salads, and desserts to match. Entrées $8.95–15.50.

**Chiangmai Thai Restaurant** (603-433-1289), 128 Penhallow Street, Portsmouth. Lunch Tuesday through Saturday 11:30 AM–2:30 PM; dinner Tuesday through Thursday and Sunday 5–9 PM, until 10 PM Friday and Saturday. An extensive menu of authentic Thai cooking with curries and both hot and spicy dishes. Chicken, seafood, and vegetarian entrées are featured; some entrées allow you to create your own meal. Tasty Thai spring rolls and hot and sour soups highlight the appetizers. Lunch specials, appetizers from $3.25, entrées $8.95–15.50.

**The Dolphin Striker** (603-431-5222; www.dolphinstriker.com), 15 Bow Street, Portsmouth. Lunch 11:30 AM–2 PM; dinner 5–9:30 PM, until 10 PM on Friday and Saturday. On the waterfront in a restored warehouse, this is an old favorite with a new menu that features creatively prepared seafood and such innovative specialties as grilled andouille sausage with apple-braised red cabbage, and grilled beef tenderloin topped with a roasted chili, balsamic syrup, and chipotle sauce. On the lower level is the **Spring Hill Tavern,** offering entertainment amid a collection of memorabilia that celebrates the city's maritime heritage. Moderate.

**Dunfey's Aboard the *John Wanamaker*** (603-433-3111; www.portsmouthnh.com), 1 Harbor Place, just west of the old Route 1 bridge. Open daily 11:30 AM–2:30 PM and 5–10 PM; Sunday brunch 10:30 AM–3 PM. New Hampshire's only floating restaurant, this well-appointed 125-foot, circa-1920s tugboat is now one of Portsmouth's most unique eateries, specializing in fresh, local, and seasonal cuisine. Lunch $7–10; dinner $20–24.

**The Library** (603-431-5202; www.libraryrestaurant.com), 401 State Street, Portsmouth. Open for lunch Monday through Saturday 11:30 AM–3 PM; dinner Sunday through Thursday 5–9:30 PM, Friday and Saturday until 10 PM. Sunday brunch 11:30 AM–3 PM. The dark paneled walls and ceilings of the old Rockingham Hotel, once Portsmouth's finest hostelry, give this restaurant its name. The menu features traditional favorites with contemporary flair. Salmon Benedict is a Sunday brunch favorite. In the English-style pub, the hotel's original front desk makes an impressive backdrop for a nightcap or cigar. Lunch entrées $8–15; dinner $18–28; brunch $8–13.

♿ **The Metro** (603-436-0521; www.themetrorestaurant.com), 20 Old High Street, Portsmouth. Open for lunch and dinner Monday through Saturday, closed Sunday. Located just off Market Square, this is one of the city's most elegant restaurants, with rich paneling and a brass rail in the bar. An updated menu features Maine crabcakes and smoked salmon carpaccio for appetizers; pan-seared diver scallops with a champagne tarragon sauce served with black tobika caviar, rack of lamb à la Provençal with ratatouille, fresh seafood with a rouille swimming in a leek, fennel, and tomato broth, and choice beef or lobster specials as entrées. Handicapped accessible, parking adjacent. Lunch inexpensive, dinner moderate to expensive.

**Oar House** (603-436-4025; www.portsmouthnh.com), 55 Ceres Street, Portsmouth. Lunch Monday through Saturday 11:30 AM–3 PM; Sunday brunch until 3:30 PM; dinner Monday through Saturday 5–9:30 PM, until 9 PM on Sunday. Valet parking. Located in a remodeled warehouse, this is another longtime favorite on the waterfront and our choice for chowder. Seafood is featured and varies from bouillabaisse and baked stuffed lobster to broiled scallops and Oar House Delight, a sautéed combination of shrimp, scallops, and fresh fish topped with sour cream and crumbs baked in the oven. Sirloin with peppercorn sauce, rack of lamb, and a chef's chicken, varied daily, are also offered. The Oar House deck, open Memorial Day through early autumn, is our favorite for picturesque riverside relaxing and dining. Entrées $19–30.

**Porto Bello Ristorante Italiano** (603-431-2928; www.portsmouthnh.com), upstairs at 67 Bow Street, Portsmouth. Open Tuesday through Saturday 4:30–9:30 PM; reservations appreciated. No smoking. This small, second-floor restaurant specializes in traditional Italian cuisine representing many regions of the country. The four-course menu offers the chance to sample a variety of dishes. Begin with antipasto, then try a pasta dish, followed by meat or seafood, and a rich dessert. Pasta dishes $11.95–20, mains $14.95–22.

**Sakura** (603-431-2721; www.portsmouthnh.com), 40 Pleasant Street, Portsmouth. Lunch Tuesday through Saturday 11:30 AM–2:30 PM; dinner weekdays and Sunday 5–9 PM, Friday and Saturday until 10:30 PM. Fine

Japanese dining with a long sushi bar where you can watch the chefs prepare creative and tasty portions of sushi and sashimi. We like the dinner box (the meal is actually served in a portioned box) with miso soup, rice, salad, and a choice of two portions of sushi, sashimi, tempura, teriyaki, and other specialties. Although fish is featured, there is beef and chicken teriyaki and sukiyaki (slices of beef and vegetables with soup and rice). For a special occasion, try "Heaven"—12 pieces of sushi and two rolls with 10 pieces of sashimi. Japanese beer, sake, and plum wine also served. Entrées $10–22, dinner box $13.50, sushi $13–20.

**Saunders at Rye Harbor** (603-964-6466; www.saundersatryeharbor.com), off Route 1A at Rye Harbor, Rye. Open all year. Luncheon 11:30 AM–3 PM, dinner 5–10 PM, Sunday noon–9 PM. This well-known restaurant has offered harborside dining for almost a century. The specialty is lobster (boiled, baked, or broiled stuffed) served fresh from saltwater tanks, but the diverse menu also includes chicken with lemon and herbs, Saunders jambalaya (lobster, crab, scallops, shrimp, sausage, vegetables, and Creole sauce over rice), a variety of fresh fish, and land 'n' sea (prime rib with shrimp, scallops, or sautéed lobster). Saunders's deck overlooking picturesque Rye Harbor is one of the best spots on the seacoast for a relaxing lunch or beverage. Live music on the deck on Sunday afternoons in July and August. On Friday nights from January to April the dining room is a supper club with live entertainment. Dinner prices $14.95–19.95, lobster dishes at market price.

EATING OUT ✐ **A. D.'s Barbeque House** (603-433-6330), 107 State Street, Portsmouth. Open Tuesday 3–9 PM; Wednesday and Thursday 11 AM–10 PM summer (until 9 PM in winter); Friday and Saturday 11 AM–11 PM summer (until 10 PM in winter); and Sunday noon–9 PM all year. Since 1991 local resident Andre DeGraffe has served up mighty good barbecue in a down-and-dirty joint implausibly placed just off prim and proper Strawbery Banke. But you won't walk away hungry after a plate of A. D.'s choice ribs, chicken, beef, or spicy sausage links. The room is kitschy—all picnic tables, with a big-screen TV tuned to local sports broadcasts—and draws all sorts of people, from bemused tourists to bikers. Some afternoons you'll even be treated to an all-you-can-eat spread that includes side dishes like collard greens, dirty rice, and macaroni and cheese (currently Tuesday 3–8 PM and Wednesday noon–8 PM, but check ahead). Smoked-food fans may be slightly disappointed to learn that the meat is cooked on gas, not wood, but this is still the town's most down-home eating experience. Prices are all over the map and reflect the number of side dishes chosen; also, some items, such as fish or ribs, cost more. Expect to pay at least $10 per person.

**Celebrity Sandwich** (603-433-7009; hot line for daily specials, 603-433-2277; www.portsmouthnh.com), 171 Islington Street, Portsmouth. Open Monday through Friday 10 AM–6 PM; Saturday 11 AM–4 PM. More than 100 sandwiches, each named for a different celebrity, served in an art deco dining room. Box lunches, soups, salads, and desserts, too. Eat in or take out.

**The Ferry Landing** (603-431-5510), Ceres Street, Portsmouth. Open April

15 through September, 11:30 AM–9 PM; the bar is open until 11 PM. Light seafood dishes of many varieties, sandwiches, chowder, and burgers are served in this 100-year-old building, which was the original ferry landing before the bridges were built. Hanging out over the river, right beside the tugboats, the place is mostly a deck. It is always busy (especially the bar on weekends) during its summer season. Prices range from inexpensive to moderate.

**Friendly Toast** (603-430-2154), 121 Congress Street, Portsmouth. Open Monday through Thursday 7 AM–11 PM; Friday and Saturday open 24 hours; Sunday 7 AM–9 PM. This popular kitsch-a-thon features great breakfasts and lunches that scream *diversity.* Pick from unusual combinations like orange French toast, green eggs and ham, Almond Joy pancakes (buttermilk pancakes with chocolate chips, coconut, and almonds), omelets, egg scrambles, and a whopping list of sides including Cuban beans, vegetarian "soysage," and homefries. Lunch is slightly tamer, and you can get old-time faves like BLTs, club sandwiches, and grilled cheese sandwiches along with late-20th-century newcomers such as hummus or nachos. Be prepared for waitstaff sporting unique tattoos, piercings, and a doin'-my-own-thing attitude. The room appears to have been furnished by a *Leave It to Beaver* set decorator gone bad, with Formica tables and clown paintings clashing with folk-art touches. Most items $3.25–7.

**Poco's Bow Street Cantina** (603-431-5967; www.portsmouthnh.com), 37 Bow Street, Portsmouth. Open daily 11:30 AM–9 PM, Friday and Saturday until 11 PM. A popular Mexican restaurant with big bay windows overlooking the tugboats and the river; local art covers the walls. Almost any Mexican item you can imagine is here (sizzling fajitas a specialty), plus Mexican beer, sangria, Cuban drinks, and the best margaritas in the city. The riverside deck opens as early as April and closes when it's too cool to use it (usually mid-October). Sunday brunch served when the deck is closed. Prices range from $4.50 to $19. Lighter menus served in the downstairs bar and on the deck.

**The Portsmouth Brewery** (603-431-1115), 56 Market Street, Portsmouth. Open daily 11:30 AM–12:30 AM, dinner 5–11 PM, Sunday brunch 11 AM–2 PM. A lively spot best known for its microbrewery, which produces six varieties of beer including Old Brown Dog, Pale Ale, Amber Lager, and Black Cat Stout, along with seasonal special ales. A downstairs lounge features comfortable seating with a pool table, shuffleboard, and a jukebox. The menu is varied and includes soups, salads, chili, pizza, hot and cold super sandwiches, and nine dinner entrées. Special dishes, changing monthly, might include spicy poached salmon or Thai curry chicken. Lunch is inexpensive; dinners $8.95–16.95.

**The Press Room** (603-431-5186), 77 Daniel Street, Portsmouth. Open Tuesday through Saturday 11:30 AM–1 AM, Sunday 5–11 PM. Inexpensive, light meals, nachos, pizza, salads, soups, and sandwiches. The food is good and served with draft beer, but the music is the best in the city. This Irish-style pub has live music most of the time; see *Entertainment*.

**Ray's Seafood Restaurant** (603-436-2280), 1677 Ocean Boulevard, Rye. Open daily from 11:30 AM to closing.

For more than 30 years a seacoast favorite specializing in fresh fried seafood, lobsters, and steamers. Dinners and lobsters cooked to go. Moderate.

**The Stockpot** (603-431-1851), 53 Bow Street, Portsmouth. Open daily 11 AM–11:30 PM. This is a popular spot on the waterfront for lunch and dinner. Homemade soups and desserts, a variety of salads and sandwiches, fresh seafood, and paella (a Spanish dish with chicken, mussels, shrimp, chorizo, and veggies served over rice). Full bar. A small deck, open whenever it's warm enough to use it, offers relaxing dining with views past the tugboats and up the river. Most dinners are under $14.

**Yoken's Thar She Blows Restaurant and Gift Shop** (603-436-8224; 1-800-552-8484), Route 1, Portsmouth. Open daily 11 AM–8 PM, summer until 9 PM. Closed Thanksgiving and Christmas. The state's largest and best-known family restaurant, Yoken's, with its spouting-whale neon sign, has been a landmark since it first opened with a 20-stool counter and 99-cent dinners in 1947. Today it seats 750 and serves more than 2 million meals a year. *Reasonable price for a complete dinner* has been the trademark here since it first opened. Lobster; fried, baked, and broiled seafood; entrée salads; and roast beef, roast turkey, liver and onions, and a few Italian dishes provide something for everyone. The 20-entrée luncheon menu, served until 4 PM, offers a choice of appetizer, dinner, beverage, and dessert, all for under $6. The Whale Gift Shop, open at 10 AM, with 20,000 square feet of space, is the largest in New England, selling everything from tourist mementos to fine china, collectible glass and figurines, handbags, cards, T-shirts, and more. There is a 121-room Comfort Inn next to the restaurant. Menu prices inexpensive to moderate.

**Zaatar Café** (603-436-9705), 100 Market Street, Portsmouth. Open daily for breakfast and lunch; buffets on weekends. This ambitious little place is hidden downstairs in a bland-looking office building of art galleries and clothing stores, so you might expect to find average fare. However, the professionally trained chefs (one from Marseilles, France) cook up such favorites as beef bourguignon along with paninis, wraps, soups, and Middle Eastern items. Plus they lay out what might be Portsmouth's best salad bar for lunch each day—though it's small, so come early—all in a cute, tiled room that reminds us of a European café. It's also popular in the morning for its pastries, smoothies, espressos, and upscale bottled beverages. On Friday night music and dance performances take over the interesting room. (As we said, these café chairs seem plucked straight out of Paris.) Under $10.

**LOBSTER** Lobsters are a seacoast specialty, and almost every restaurant has a lobster dish. Live or cooked lobsters to go are available at several places. **Sanders Lobster Pound** is the largest local dealer. Their main lobster pound is at 54 Pray Street (603-436-3716; www.sanderslobster.com), open Monday through Saturday 8 AM–5 PM; Sunday 9 AM–12 PM; and they own the **Olde Mill Fish Market** (603-436-4568) nearby at 367 Marcy Street, open daily 9–6. The latter shop has all kinds of fresh fish in addition to live or cooked-to-order lobsters. Sanders can ship a mini clambake anywhere in the country.

**ICE CREAM AND SNACKS** **Ceres Bakery** (603-436-6518), 51 Penhallow Street, Portsmouth. Open 6 AM–5:30 PM, Saturday 7 am–4 PM, closed Sunday. Our favorite bakery. Has the best bran muffins anywhere but also brioches, croissants, cookies, and a host of breads, cakes, and other diet busters. A few mostly vegetarian soups, quiches, and salads are served for lunch;, special breakfast and lunch items on Saturday. Many local restaurants serve Ceres Bakery breads.

**Café Brioche** (603-430-9225; www.cafebrioche.com), 14 Market Square, Portsmouth. Open Monday- through Friday 6:30 am–5 pm; Saturday 6:30 AM–9 PM and; Sunday 6:30 AM–6 PM. A French-style bakery and café with breads and sweets, serving homemade soups, salads, and a variety of sandwiches plus espresso and cappuccino. Especially popular in warm weather, when the outside tables lend a European-plaza atmosphere. Live jazz on weekends makes this the center of bustling Market Square.

**Annabelle's** (603-436-3400), 49 Ceres Street, Portsmouth. Open for lunch until late in the evening; closed in winter. Imaginative and tasty handmade ice cream comes from this popular local landmark. Their red, white, and blueberry ice cream even made the White House menu one year for the Fourth of July. Sandwiches and soups are secondary to the sundaes, sodas, banana splits, and hand-scooped cones.

**Lagos' Lone Oak Restaurant** (603-964-9880), Route 1, Rye Beach. Open from spring through early fall. They have a long list of ice cream flavors (and huge portions) and also serve fried foods and sandwiches.

## ✷ Entertainment

Portsmouth's busiest performance season is September through May—except for the Prescott Park Arts Festival, which features theater and music outdoors July through mid-August. The night scene is active all year with nearly a dozen restaurants and lounges offering live music on weekends and several other nights: jazz, blues, big-band, folk, and country music.

**Seacoast Repertory Theatre** (603-433-4472; 1-800-639-7650; www.seacoastrep.org), 125 Bow Street, Portsmouth. Professional theater in the former Theatre-by-the-Sea building. Several different plays are performed September through early June. Also presents youth theater.

**The Music Hall** (603-436-2400; www.themusichall.org), 28 Chestnut Street, Portsmouth. Built in 1878 as a stage theater and, more recently, revised as a movie theater, this restored hall has been acquired by a nonprofit group and offers a variety of dance, theater, and musical performances throughout the year. International classical music, Sesame Street, magic shows, bluegrass, and jazz are among the regular offerings. Three to four events are held each month September through May.

**Pontine Movement Theatre** (603-436-6660; www.pontine.org), 135 McDonough Street, Portsmouth. This nationally known company with guest performers offers four productions between fall and spring but no summer performances.

**The Players' Ring** (603-436-8123; www.playersring.org), 105 Marcy Street, Portsmouth. Attend a variety of theatrical and musical performances at this attractive and historic venue.

**The Press Room** (603-431-5186), 77 Daniel Street, Portsmouth. Open Tuesday through Saturday 11:30 AM–1 AM, Sunday 5–11 PM. This Irish-style pub has lots of live music. Acoustic guitar, folk, Irish, blues, and country sounds in an informal atmosphere make this a popular spot with the locals. Friday 5–8 PM is a country jam session, the only thing like it in the state, when an ever-changing group of amateurs and professionals joins a group of regulars playing country tunes, sea chanties, and music from the British Isles. Sunday night features jazz, with many nationally known performers sitting in with the best house combo in the region.

## ✷ Selective Shopping

Portsmouth is filled with small shops, especially in the waterfront area bounded by Market, Bow, and Ceres Streets. Here rows of mostly Federal-era brick buildings have been remodeled and restored and now offer the shopper everything from upscale clothing and antiques to natural foods, candles, secondhand clothing, jewelry, a fine children's shop, and even a Christmas shop. With several of the city's best restaurants and five waterfront decks, this is a busy and lively place until late in the evening—several shops are open until 11.

**ART GALLERIES** **New Hampshire Art Association–Robert Levy Gallery** (603-431-4230), 136 State Street, Portsmouth. Open all year, Wednesday through Sunday 11 AM–5 PM. Members exhibit oils, watercolors, acrylics, photographs, prints, and sculpture.

**BOOKSTORES** Two great antiquarian bookshops are located in downtown Portsmouth:

**The Book Guild of Portsmouth** (603-436-1758), 58 State Street, near Strawbery Banke, specializes in maritime and local books.

**The Portsmouth Book Shop** (603-433-4406), 1 Islington Street, is located in a historic house and offers local history, travel, literature, maps, and prints.

## ✷ Special Events

Summer on the seacoast offers a nearly unlimited number of special events and activities for people of all ages. Check with local chambers of commerce, the Portsmouth Children's Museum, and Strawbery Banke for varied activities.

*February:* **Annual African-American Heritage Festival** (603-929-0654), seacoast-wide. Various organizations sponsor a variety of musical, art, theater, and other events in several seacoast locations. Coordinated by the Blues Bank Collective.

*April:* **New England Blues Conference** (603-929-0654), Portsmouth. Blues workshops, conferences, and concerts.

*Early June:* **Prescott Park Chowder Festival** (www.artfest.org). For $7 adults or $5 children, sample the city's best restaurant chowders.

*Second Saturday in June:* **Market Square Day** (603-436-5388; www.proportsmouth.org). The center of Portsmouth is closed to traffic, and the streets are lined with booths selling food, crafts, and more; as many as four stages provide continuous entertainment. More than 30,000 people jam the city for this free event. A popular clambake is held the night before at the Port Authority; purchase tickets in advance.

*Mid-June:* **Blessing of the Fleet,** Prescott Park. The Piscataqua River's commercial fishing fleet, with all boats decorated, converges for a water parade and traditional blessing for safety at sea.

*Early July:* **Seacoast Jazz Festival** (www.artfest.org), Prescott Park. The show runs from noon to 6 PM. Top jazz artists from across the country join local musicians for a musical blast. A $5 donation is requested.

*Early July through late August:* **Prescott Park Arts Festival** (www.artfest.org), on the waterfront, Portsmouth. A daily variety of outdoor theater and musical events beginning late in the afternoon. Come early, bring a picnic basket, and spend a few enjoyable hours at one of New England's most popular summer festivals. A $5 donation is requested. There are also art shows and art classes for kids.

*Mid-July:* **Bow Street Fair** (603-433-4793). A colorful weekend street fair with music and booths selling food and crafts. Affiliated with the Seacoast Repertory Theater.

*Mid-August:* **Candlelight house tour** (603-436-1118). An evening tour of Portsmouth's historic houses, all lit by candles. **Blues Festival** (603-929-0654; www.bluesbankcollective.org), Harbor Place, Portsmouth. Blues on an outdoor, waterfront stage, and in several bars, along with a gospel blues church service. Starts at 11 AM and runs until sunset.

*Late August:* **Prescott Park Folk and Acoustic Festival** (603-436-2848). Seacoast folkies congregate in this spacious and attractive park from 3 to 9 PM to appreciate a variety of folk and world music—Celtic and African drumming among the offerings.

*Late September:* **Grand Old Portsmouth Brewers' Festival.** This annual Strawbery Banke event celebrates the history of brewing in Portsmouth. **Chili Cook-Off** (www.artfest.org), Prescott Park. Sample the culinary skills of the city's best chili cooks. A $7 donation is requested.

*Columbus Day weekend:* **Piscataqua Faire** (www.artfest.org), Prescott Park. A Renaissance weekend on the waterfront with food, crafts, and entertainment from a time when knights ruled the day. The first day of the faire runs 10 AM–5 PM, the second 11 AM–4 PM. Admission: adults $6, children $4. **Building the Sukkah,** a Strawbery Banke Jewish harvest celebration.

*Late November and early December:* **Candlelight Stroll** (603-433-1100), Strawbery Banke. See Strawbery Banke's historic houses by candlelight.

*December 31:* **First Night** (603-436-5388). A nonalcoholic, family-oriented New Year's Eve celebration held annually in Portsmouth, late afternoon to midnight, with a wide variety of musical performances and other entertainment. Most events are held in downtown churches.

# HAMPTON, HAMPTON BEACH, EXETER, AND VICINITY

The two large towns of Hampton and Exeter were founded in 1638, but while Hampton has retained little of its architectural heritage, Exeter's streets are lined with old houses and buildings.

**Hampton** was mostly a farming town with a small, beachside tourist community until the beginning of the 20th century, when trolley lines connected the town and its beach with the large cities of the Merrimack Valley and cities in Massachusetts and central New Hampshire. The low-cost trolley transportation made the beach an inexpensive and accessible place for urban workers to bring their families for a day or a week. A large casino was built to provide these visitors with games to play, lunches, and ballroom dancing, though not on Sunday. Hampton is now a fast-growing residential community. After World War II the population was about 2,300; now it is 12,000 people, and much of its open space has been developed except for large family holdings west of I-95. Hampton has a small shopping district, a movie complex, and several good restaurants.

Though Hampton village was small, **Hampton Beach** boomed and became one of the leading family vacation centers in New England. Now, during peak summer weekends, more than 200,000 people jam the beach, nearly covering the long, sandy oceanfront from one end to the other with blankets. Young people seem to predominate, but there are plenty of older folks who would not consider any other place to spend their summer free time. The center of the beach is still the 90-year-old Casino, complete with restaurants, shops, penny arcades, and a nightclub offering nationally known entertainment.

Often overlooked by residents and visitors alike is the **Hampton River.** Here three family-owned fishing-party businesses have been serving the public for more than 50 years, recently expanding to include whale-watches and some sight-seeing cruises. Surrounding the harbor is the state's largest salt marsh, once thought of as a swamp and earmarked to be dredged and filled to create a lagoon-style seasonal home development. Although Hampton Beach development has pushed into the fringes of this 1,300-acre marsh, people now know the importance of the tidal wetlands as a source of nutrients for a wide variety of marine life, and the marshes are protected from development by state and local laws. As a green space, the marsh is used by anglers, boaters, and bird-watchers; it is perhaps the only piece of ground left on the seacoast that still looks today about the way it did when settlers arrived in the 1600s. South of the Hampton River bridge in Seabrook, bordering the marsh, is a recently protected sand dunes natural area.

West of Hampton is **Exeter,** with a much larger commercial area and one of the country's premier prep schools. Its marvelous architectural diversity reflects its past as a center of government and education as well as the economic success of its residents, especially when Exeter had a small industrial center. Exeter also has about 12,000 people, although its growth has been slower than Hampton's. During the Revolution, Exeter was the center of government, and many of its citizens were prominent participants in the rebellion. Several historic houses open to the public date from those times. The falls on the Squamscott River helped power textile mills, giving the community an important economic base.

**Phillips Exeter Academy,** one of America's leading preparatory schools, has a list of alumni who have achieved the highest levels of prominence in literature, business, and government service. Distinguished visiting lecturers in all fields, who often speak or perform for the public, and a fine art gallery contribute to the cultural and educational atmosphere of the town and the area. Many students from surrounding towns attend the academy as day students. The academy's buildings reflect nearly three centuries of architectural design, contributing to the great diversity of Exeter's cityscape. The academy is in the center of the **Front Street Historic District,** where the wide variety of architectural styles ranges from Colonial residences of the 1700s to 20th-century institutional buildings. Notable are the First Parish Meetinghouse, a variety of Victorian buildings, and the contemporary Phillips Exeter Academy Library designed by Louis Kahn.

**Historic Route 1** bisects the seacoast from south to north. On the Massachusetts border is **Seabrook,** home of the controversial nuclear power plant, a huge facility that pays most of the town's taxes, giving Seabrook one of the lowest property tax rates in the state. The low property tax, combined with the state's lack of a sales tax, has fueled commercial development in Seabrook; most of the retail shoppers come from heavily taxed Massachusetts. **Seabrook Beach** is a heavily developed residential area with little public access to the ocean since parking is limited, but many summer homes here are available for weekly rentals.

Seabrook's unplanned growth is in contrast to neighboring **Hampton Falls,** a residential community whose many farms are now being subdivided into exclusive home developments. North of Hampton along Route 1 is **North Hampton,** also primarily a residential community but with a large colony of summer mansions along the coast in the section called Little Boars Head.

Adjacent to Exeter, and extending west to the Merrimack Valley, are mostly small towns, once farming communities, now being heavily developed with residential subdivisions. Among these towns are **Stratham, Kensington, Epping, Newfields, Brentwood, Fremont, Danville, Hampstead, the Kingstons,** and **Nottingham.** Since New Hampshire has no sales or income taxes, and once had low property taxes, the seacoast-area towns have been rapidly growing into popular bedroom communities for people who work in the Boston area, many of whom grew up in Massachusetts but moved north to escape the congestion of urban life for the peaceful countryside. The attractions of the seacoast and its proximity to metropolitan Boston are certain to make the area a magnet for new residents and for visiting tourists.

**GUIDANCE** **Hampton Beach Area Chamber of Commerce** (603-926-8717; outside New Hampshire, 1-800-GET-A-TAN; www.hamptonbeach.org), 180 Ocean Boulevard (winter and business office: 490 Lafayette Road, Box 790), Hampton 03842. A seasonal information center is open daily at the state park complex in the middle of Hampton Beach. The chamber runs daily summer events at the beach and seasonal programs in Hampton village, and publishes a free accommodations and things-to-do guide.

**Exeter Area Chamber of Commerce** (603-772-2411; www.exeterarea.org), 120 Water Street, Exeter 03833.

**GETTING AROUND** *By car:* Route 1 (Lafayette Road) between Seabrook and Portsmouth is lined with strip development and on summer weekends is especially snarled with traffic. If you want to go to Hampton Beach just to see the sights and the latest bathing suits, we do not recommend the weekend, when traffic entering the beach from I-95 or Route 1A south may be backed up for several miles.

*By taxi:* **Exeter Taxi** (603-778-7778) serves Exeter and offers Logan Airport service.

*By trolley:* A seasonal trolley service serves Hampton Beach, running the length of Ocean Boulevard, with stops in Hampton village and the North Hampton Factory Outlet Center.

**PARKING** Municipal and private parking lots behind Hampton's main beach, just a short walk to the sand, are the best places to park if you are not staying at beach lodgings. The parking meters are part of the state park and are closely monitored, so keep them filled with quarters to avoid an expensive ticket.

**MEDICAL EMERGENCY** **Exeter Hospital** (603-778-7311), 10 Buzzell Avenue, Exeter, offers 24-hour emergency walk-in service. **Exeter ambulance:** 603-772-1212. **Hampton ambulance:** 603-926-3315.

## ✷ To See

**Fuller Gardens** (603-964-5414; www.fullergardens.org), 10 Willow Avenue, Little Boars Head, North Hampton. Open early May through mid-October, 10 AM–6 PM. One of the few remaining estate gardens of the early 20th century, this beautiful spot was designed in the 1920s for Massachusetts Governor Alvin T. Fuller, whose family members still live in many of the surrounding mansions. There is an ever-changing display here as flowers bloom throughout the season. Among the highlights are 1,500 rosebushes, extensive annuals, a Japanese garden, and a conservatory of tropical and desert plants. Nominal fee charged.

**The Science and Nature Center at New Hampshire Yankee** (1-800-338-7482), Route 1, Seabrook. Open 10 AM–4 PM, Monday through Saturday, March through Thanksgiving; Monday through Friday the rest of the year. The Seabrook Nuclear Power Plant has been a continual controversy since it was proposed more than a quarter century ago. The best off-site view of the plant is from Route 1A at

Robert Kozlow

A DAIRY FARM IN STRATHAM

the Hampton River, where it rises above the marsh on the western shore of the estuary. After demonstrations, construction delays, lengthy and complex legal proceedings, and the bankruptcy of its prime owner, the plant finally began producing power in 1990. The center is its educational facility and has a variety of exhibits about electricity, nuclear power, and the environment, especially the nearby marsh habitat, which you can view on a mile-long nature trail. Free admission.

✐ **Tuck Memorial Museum** (603-929-0781; www.nh.ultranet.com/~hhs/HHSHome.htm), 40 Park Avenue, Hampton 03842. Open mid-June through mid-September, Tuesday, Friday, and Sunday 1–4 PM. The museum of the Hampton Historical Society has local memorabilia, especially related to early families, the trolley era, and Hampton Beach. Adjacent is the **Hampton Firefighter's Museum** with a hand engine, other equipment, and a district schoolhouse, all restored. Free admission.

**Atkinson Historical Society** (603-362-4760), 3 Academy Avenue, Atkinson 03811. Open Wednesday 2–4 PM. The Kimball-Peabody Mansion houses a collection of local artifacts plus extensive genealogical materials.

**Exeter Historical Society** (603-778-2335; www.exeternh.org), 47 Front Street, Exeter 03833. Open Tuesday, Thursday, and Saturday 2–5 PM, April through November; 2–4:30 PM, the rest of the year. Located in the former 1894 town library, this society has research materials for local history and genealogy, artifacts, photographs, maps, and changing exhibits.

**Fremont Historical Society** (603-895-4032), 225 South Road, Route 107, Fremont 03044. Open by appointment. The museum was the town library, built in 1894 and measuring only 20 feet by 14 feet. From 1965 until 1981 it was a first-aid society, lending its rural residents hospital equipment.

♿ **Sandown Historical Society and Museum** (603-887-6100; www.sandownnh.org), Depot Road, Box 300, Sandown 03873. Open May through October, Saturday and Sunday 1–5 PM. Local history and railroad artifacts; wheelchair access plus rest rooms, picnic tables, and a nearby public swimming beach.

**Stratham Historical Society** (603-778-0434; www.strathamhistoricalsociety.org), corner of Portsmouth Avenue and Winnicutt Road, Stratham 03885. Open Tuesday 9–11:30 AM, Thursday 2–4 PM, and the first Sunday of each month 2–4 PM. The former Wiggin Library has recently been acquired by the historical society. Local artifacts and some genealogical materials.

**HISTORIC HOMES** ✐ **American Independence Museum** (603-772-2622; www.independencemuseum.org), 1 Governor's Lane, Exeter. Open May through the end of October, Wednesday through Saturday 10 AM–4 PM. Also known as Cincinnati Hall, and one of New Hampshire's most historic buildings, part of this place was constructed in 1721. It served as the state treasury from 1775 to 1789 and as governor's mansion during the 14-year term of John Taylor Gilman. The Gilman family members were political and military leaders during the Revolutionary War, when Exeter served as the revolutionary capital. The house has recently been restored, and its diverse exhibits revitalized. Admission: adults $5; children over 6 $3; children under 6 free.

**Gilman Garrison House** (603-436-3205; www.independencemuseum.org), Water Street, Exeter. Open June through October, Tuesday, Thursday, Saturday, and Sunday noon–5 PM. A portion of this house was constructed of logs in 1660 as a garrison, but most of the building reflects the 18th century with fine paneling, especially in the governor's council meeting room. Owned by the Society for the Preservation of New England Antiquities. Fee charged.

**Moses-Kent House** (603-772-2044; www.independencemuseum.org), corner of Pine and Linden Streets, Exeter. Open June through September; call for times. Built in 1868, this is the finest of three mansard-style houses in the historic district. The continuous occupation by one family is responsible for the remarkable state of preservation in the house. In the museum rooms are original furnishings from 1903.

**HISTORIC SITES** **Fremont Meetinghouse and Hearse House,** Route 107, Fremont. Open May 30 and the third Sunday in August or by appointment; inquire locally. Built in 1800, this unique meetinghouse, unaltered since it was built, contains an early choir stall, slave pews, and twin porches. The Hearse House, built in 1849, has a hand engine built in that same year.

**Sandown Meeting House** (603-887-3946), Fremont Road, Sandown. Owned by the Old Meeting House Association, this is the finest meetinghouse of its type in New Hampshire, unaltered since it was built in 1774. Its craftsmanship and architectural details are nationally recognized. You can easily imagine our colonial ancestors listening to a fire-and-brimstone sermon from the preacher standing in the wineglass pulpit. Service at 11 AM, second Sunday in August. Open by appointment; inquire locally for the caretaker.

**Old South Meetinghouse** (Route 1) and **Boyd School** (Washington Street), Seabrook. School opens the third Sunday in August. The old school has exhibits and local artifacts relating to salt-hay farming, shoemaking, and decoys used for bird hunting. The church is open by appointment only; inquire locally. Built in 1758, it has been altered inside.

**SCENIC DRIVE** Follow Route 1B through New Castle, then connect with Route 1A through Rye, North Hampton, and the north end of Hampton Beach. The ocean is in view most of the way, and there are several restaurants and beaches. This route is also popular with bicyclists.

## ✷ To Do

**Hampton Beach** is an attraction by itself. The center of activity is the Casino, a historic, rambling complex with arcades, gifts, specialty shops, and a nightclub. Adjacent is the Casino Cascade Water Slide. Nearby, along the half-mile business district, is the first seasonal McDonald's plus other fast-food take-outs, more arcades, shops, gift and clothing stores, miniature golf, and bike rentals. Across the street from the Casino are the ocean and the state park complex with the chamber of commerce information center, rest rooms, a first-aid room, and the bandstand, which offers free concerts and talent shows throughout the summer. There are fireworks on the Fourth of July and every Wednesday night during July and August, the heart of the season; but many places are open weekends beginning in April, then open daily in June. A few of the newer, larger hotels are open year-round, and some have restaurants and lounges.

**BOAT EXCURSIONS** **Smith and Gilmore Fishing Parties** (603-926-3503), Route 1A, Hampton Harbor, Hampton 03842. All-day fishing on Wednesday and weekends April through Columbus Day; daily half-day trips May through September; night fishing June through August; weekend evening whale-watches July and August; fireworks cruises on Wednesday July through August. Three modern vessels provide a variety of fishing experiences for this longtime family-operated business. A specialty is a 24-hour overnight fishing trip, 50 to 90 miles offshore to New England's famed fishing banks; limited to 40 people. A great trip for seeing offshore birds. The business also has a bait-and-tackle shop, rowboats to rent for Hampton Harbor flounder fishing, and a restaurant.

**Al Gauron Deep Sea Fishing** (603-926-2469), State Pier, Hampton Harbor, Hampton 03842. All-day fishing, spring through Columbus Day; two half-day trips daily; bluefish trips; night fishing; fireworks cruises on Wednesday night; evening whale-watches. Four vessels including the 90-foot *Northern Star.* Family owned and operated for half a century.

**Eastman's Fishing Parties** (603-474-3461), Seabrook Harbor, Route 1A, Seabrook 03874. Open April through October. All-day fishing, half-day and evening fishing, morning and afternoon whale-watch trips. The oldest of the family-operated fishing businesses on the seacoast. The Lucky Lady fleet has three modern vessels. Tackle-and-bait shops plus a full restaurant and pub with patio dining overlooking the harbor.

**GOLF** **Apple Hill Country Club** (603-642-4414), Route 107, East Kingston. Open whenever weather conditions permit; 18 holes, cart rentals, snack bar.

**Exeter Country Club** (603-772-4752), Jady Hill Road (off Portsmouth Avenue), Exeter. Open May through October; 18 holes, cart rentals, full bar, and food service.

**Sagamore-Hampton Golf Course** (603-964-8322), North Road (off Route 1), North Hampton. Open mid-April to mid-December; 18 holes, no motorized carts allowed, pro shop, light food, and beverages. A busy recreational course, inexpensive.

ORCHARDS, PICK-YOUR-OWN, FARMERS' MARKETS ✐ **Applecrest Farm Orchards** (603-926-3721), Route 88, Hampton Falls. Open year-round, but the best times to visit are in May when apple blossoms cover the hillsides and in late summer through fall when apples are harvested. Pick your own apples and enjoy weekend festivals in-season. Also pick your own strawberries, raspberries, and blueberries. Cross-country ski in winter. The Apple Mart and gift shop are open year-round.

**Raspberry Farm** (603-926-6604), Route 84, Hampton Falls. Open the first week in July through October. The state's largest grower, with 6.5 miles of rows in which to pick your own blackberries, black raspberries, and raspberries, plus a farm stand with vegetables and baked goods.

**Farmers' markets** are open Tuesday afternoons June through October at Sacred Heart School, Route 1, in Hampton, and Thursday afternoons at Swasey Parkway in Exeter. Local homegrown vegetables, herbs, flowers, fruits, and plants plus baked goods and crafts.

## ✷ Green Space

✐ **North Hampton State Beach,** Route 1A, North Hampton. A long, sandy beach with lifeguards, parking meters, and rest rooms. A small take-out food stand

HAMPTON BEACH

Robert Kozlow

is across the street. For one of the area's most scenic walks, park here, then proceed north past the old fish houses, which are now summer cottages, and a beautiful garden maintained by the Little Boars Head Garden Club. A sidewalk follows the coast for about 2 miles to the Rye Beach Club.

**Hampton Central Beach,** Route 1A, Hampton. From the intersection of High Street and Route 1A, south through the main section of Hampton Beach, is a state park with lifeguards, metered parking, and rest rooms. North of Hampton's Great Boars Head the beach is much less crowded but at high tides has limited sand area. South of Great Boars Head the beach is opposite the business and touristy area. At the main beach are an information center, a first-aid room, and rest rooms. Opposite the Ashworth Hotel is the **New Hampshire Marine Memorial,** a large statue and plaque dedicated to state residents in the merchant marine service who were lost at sea during World War II.

**Hampton Beach State Park and Harbor** (603-925-3784), Route 1A, Hampton. Fees charged for the beach and boat launching in-season. At the mouth of the Hampton River is this long, sandy beach with some of the state's last oceanfront sand dunes. There is a bathhouse with dressing rooms, rest rooms, and snack bar. Twenty RV sites with full hook-ups are available on a first-come, first-served basis. Across Route 1A is the harbor, with a boat-launching ramp and the state pier.

**Swasey Parkway,** off Water Street, Exeter. A small park beside the Squamscott River in downtown Exeter. Picnic area and playground.

**Sandy Point Discovery Center** (603-778-0015), 89 Depot Road, just off Route 101, Stratham. Part of the Great Bay National Estuarine Research Reserve (see *Green Space* in "Dover, Durham, and Vicinity"), this new education center is set up primarily for school groups, but it offers great bird-watching on self-guided nature trails through wooded uplands and over a 1,600-foot boardwalk on the tidal marsh. The grounds are available all year during daylight hours. The building, with interpretive exhibits on the ecology of an estuary, is open on weekends in May, and Wednesday through Sunday 10–4, June through October. There is a launch ramp for car-top boats.

**Kingston State Beach,** off Route 125, Kingston. Open weekends beginning Memorial Day, daily late June through Labor Day. A small state facility on Great Pond, this park has a long, sandy beach, picnic groves, and a bathhouse. Fee charged.

## Lodging

Hampton and Hampton Beach offer a nearly unlimited number of rooms for tourists, especially at the beach and along Route 1 between Hampton Falls and North Hampton. The **Hampton Beach Area Chamber of Commerce** (see *Guidance*) provides a guide to most of the motels, but we have listed a few lodgings below. Both Hampton and Seabrook Beaches have numerous cottages to rent by the week, and Hampton also has many condo units. Seabrook Beach is just residential and thus quieter than Hampton, and its beach is uncrowded. For information try **Harris Real Estate** (603-926-3400), **Preston Real Estate** (603-474-3453; 603-926-2604), or **Oceanside Real Estate** (603-926-3542).

BED & BREAKFASTS **Around the Corner B&B** (603-778-0058; 1-800-443-0344; day4@mediaone.net), 72 High Street, Exeter 03833. Open all year. "Around the corner" from Exeter's main drag, this home is located in a quiet residential neighborhood, a short walk from the historic downtown. The three guest rooms (one with private bath; the other two share a bath) are named for and inspired by the innkeepers' favorite artists: Claude Monet, Winslow Homer, and three generations of Wyeths. All of the rooms have books about artists and are filled with the artwork of their namesakes. Full breakfast. Donna and Dick Herrmann and Evelyn Shields, innkeepers. $60–85 double, $145 suite with two bedrooms.

**The Governor Jeremiah Smith House Inn** (603-778-7770), 41 Front Street, Exeter 03833. Open all year. Once the residence of former New Hampshire governor Jeremiah Smith, who delivered the eulogy at George Washington's funeral, this centrally located, circa-1730 home has recently been converted into a B&B. Innkeepers Richard and Joan Poutenis have fashioned eight guest rooms, each featuring unique architectural details, period antiques, private bath, remote color television, and air-conditioning. Local calls are free, and some rooms feature fireplaces or daybeds. $99–149, breakfast included, for two.

**The Inn at Kinney Hill** (603-394-0200; 1-888-OUR-HILL), 96 Woodman Road, South Hampton 03827. Open May 1 through October 31. Innkeepers Dotti Ann and George O'Connor bought this brick hillside mansion at auction in 1992 and 5 years later opened it as an upscale B&B. Three luxury rooms and a suite offer top-drawer accommodations plus such on-site amenities as a billiard room, heated indoor pool, hot tub, and exercise room. You can bring your own horse—experienced riders can hire one at the adjacent Kinney Hill equestrian facility—to enjoy 120 acres of woods and seacoast views. Full breakfast, and fireside afternoon tea with hors d'oeuvres and sherry. $95–160 for two.

**The Inn by the Bandstand** (603-772-3652; www.innbythebandstand.com), 4 Front Street, Exeter 03833. Open all year. This stylish 1809 town house, run by Susan Henderson and her amiable golden retriever, Zachariah, is in downtown Exeter overlooking the historic bandstand and close to movies, restaurants, and shopping. There are nine cleverly decorated rooms, including one honeymoon suite with a Jacuzzi, CD player, kitchenette, and living room, and two other family-style suites. All rooms are furnished with pizzazz, and all have phones with a dataport for laptop computers. Working fireplaces and antique canopy or four-poster queen beds (one room with twins) reside harmoniously with more contemporary amenities such as air-conditioning, cable TV, and refrigerator. Coffee, tea, and sherry are available; a breakfast buffet with fresh-baked pastries is served in the morning parlor. There's also a fax and copier machine on site, and active types can rent kayaks, canoes, or bikes. $100–175 for two; suites $195.

**Stillmeadow B&B** (603-329-8381; www.stillmeadmeadowbandb.com; lori@stillmeadowbandb.com), 545 Main Street, Hampstead 03841. Open all year. This 1850 Greek Revival, Italianate village inn has five chimneys and three staircases. Each of four and a half rooms (one includes a sitting room with a trundle bed) has a private bath. The family suite has two queen beds, a TV, and a refrigerator. There are formal living and dining rooms, and the cookie jar's always kept full. Not far away is the **Robert Frost Farm** and several rather kitschy attractions. Expanded continental breakfast. $65–100 for a family of four. Lori Offord, host.

**The Victoria Inn** (603-929-1437), 430 High Street, Hampton 03842. Open year-round. This renovated former carriage house has six rooms, three with private bath. Beds are doubles, queens, and kings; all rooms have air-conditioning and overhead fan, cable TV, and telephone. There are two sitting rooms, one with TV, and a glassed-in porch where a full gourmet breakfast is served. Lovely grounds with a Victorian gazebo, half a mile from the beach. Nicholas and Tara DiTullio, innkeepers. Rates are $75–115; off-season discounts available.

**HOTELS** ♿ **Ashworth by the Sea** (603-926-6762; 1-800-345-6736; www.ashworthhotel.com), 295 Ocean Boulevard, Hampton 03842. The only full-service oceanfront hotel has been a beach landmark and the finest beach lodging since the early 1900s. With the addition of a modern new wing and remodeling of the original hotel, it is now open year-round. Most of its 105 rooms have queen- or king-sized beds; others have two doubles. Five handicapped-accessible rooms. There is a lounge with nightly entertainment, three restaurants (see *Dining Out*), an indoor pool, and private sun decks overlooking the ocean. Summer rates are $120–275; off-season October through March is $85–145; discounts for multinight stays.

**Hampton House** (603-926-1033; 1-800-458-7058), 333 Ocean Boulevard, Hampton 03842. Open year-round. Fifty-one spacious, modern, oceanfront rooms. All rooms have two doubles or a king-sized bed, air-conditioning, TV, telephone, private balcony, and refrigerator. On-site parking, elevator. Coffee shop. Summer rates are $105–155; off-season is $50–80.

♿ **The Inn of Exeter** (603-772-5901; 1-800-782-8444), 90 Front Street, Exeter 03833-0508. Open year-round. On the campus of Phillips Exeter Academy but no longer owned by the private school, this three-story, Georgian-style inn and restaurant was originally intended to accommodate visiting dignitaries and the families of students. The inn serves a wide clientele of tourist and business travelers. The 50 rooms include family suites, all with TV, radio, and telephone, with traditional antique and reproduction furnishings. Some are on the small and simple side, while others are larger and include fireplaces; those with views of the back lawn are doubly blessed. The two plush Senior Executive rooms have a Jacuzzi as well as queen beds, a pull-out sofa, and plenty of space to stretch out. Handicapped accessible. The fine restaurant serves three meals daily and an award-winning Sunday brunch (see *Dining Out*). Lounge, living room fireplaces. Rates for two: $130–245.

**D. W.'s Oceanside Inn** (603-926-3542; 1-866-OCEAN-SI; info@oceansideinn.com), 365 Ocean Boulevard, Hampton Beach 03842. Open mid-

May through mid-October. This turn-of-the-20th-century summer home, located across the street from the ocean, has undergone many changes, but its interior has been maintained and tastefully furnished to reflect its Victorian beginnings. Innkeepers Duane "Skip" and Debbie Windemiller have fulfilled their dream of providing a luxurious and restful oceanside escape; returning guests tell them it's a place they dream of the rest of the year. This is not typical Hampton Beach lodging. There are 10 rooms, all with private bath, all distinctively decorated, many with antiques and period pieces, including two with canopy beds; a lovely Victorian common room; and two porches. Midsummer rates (late June through Labor Day) are $150–190; off-season, $120–155. Discounts for multinight stays. Breakfast included. No smoking.

HOUSEKEEPING UNITS **Seaside Village Resort** (603-964-8204), 1 Ocean Boulevard, North Hampton 03862. Open May through September, weather permitting. This is the only motel in New Hampshire with lodging right on the beach, with no street to cross. There are 19 units, 13 of which are full housekeeping, and 6 motel units for two to four people. Housekeeping guests bring towels and linens and rent Saturday to Saturday. Eight new housekeeping units have a private master bedroom and a loft for the kids; the motel units are rustic but are air conditioned and have refrigerators and access to a galley, grills, and picnic tables. Many of the units are rented by the end of one season for the season to come. Housekeeping units are $750–1,295 per week; motel units are $89–109 per night for two to three people.

## ✷ Where to Eat

DINING OUT **Breakers at Ashworth by the Sea** (603-926-6762; 1-800-345-6736; www.ashworthhotel.com), 295 Ocean Boulevard, Hampton. Open year-round. Breakfast from 6:30 AM; lunch and pub 11:45 AM–2:30 PM; dinner 5–10 PM. A full-service, oceanfront hotel, the Ashworth is a beach landmark, and its restaurant is the best on the main beach. Seven lobster entrées, baked and broiled seafood, and steaks are menu features (dinners range from $9.95). An all-you-can-eat buffet ($14.50 adults; $9.50 children; $5.50 children under 6) is offered Tuesday through Saturday evenings in July and August, the peak beach season.

**The Inn of Exeter** (603-772-5901; 1-800-782-8444), 90 Front Street, Exeter. Open year-round. Breakfast, lunch, and dinner served. The moderate to expensive Continental menu changes four times a year and ranges from lobster ravioli, veal Oscar, and salmon to daily specialties. Award-winning Sunday brunch, 10 AM–2 PM, is a local favorite.

**The Old Salt Eating & Drinking Place at Lamie's Inn and Tavern** (603-926-0330; www.oldsaltnh.com), 490 Lafayette Road, Hampton. Open all year. Breakfast, lunch, then dinner served until 9 PM Monday through Thursday, until 10 PM Friday and Saturday; noon–8 PM on Sunday. Founded in 1931, this is one of the oldest restaurants in the area, and when Route 1 was the main road between Boston and Portland, the place was open 24 hours a day on major weekends. With huge beams, pine paneling, tavern tables, and a large fireplace, Lamie's has a Colonial atmosphere, but its menu adds a Continental accent to the mostly New England fare. Try fried clams or scallops *en brochette* (placed on a skewer with scallions and bacon), baked lobster pie or beef *au poivre* with creamy peppercorn sauce, or Shoal's baked seafood delight (clams casino, scallops, scrod, and stuffed shrimp). Also several veal and pasta dishes, plus lamb, dinner sandwiches, a variety of soups and salads. Lunch, complete dinner, or à la carte are all inexpensive to moderate. A 32-room motor inn with Colonial decor is attached. Entrées $7.99–14.99.

**Ship to Shore Food and Spirits** (603-778-7898; www.ship-to-shore.com), Route 108, Newfields. Open Thursday through Saturday for dinner at 5 PM, lunch Thursday and Friday September through May. Constructed by a local shipbuilder in 1792, this half barn (built shorter than it is wide) has been restored and turned into an intriguing, antiques-filled restaurant. The menu ranges from baked shrimp and haddock to roast duckling, barbecued baby back ribs, and broiled seafood. Daily chicken, veal, seafood, and pasta specials. Average price $18.95.

**The Widow Fletcher's Tavern** (603-926-8800), 401 Lafayette Road, Hampton. Open Monday through Thursday 11 AM–9 PM, Friday and Saturday until 9:30 PM (half an hour later during the summer); Sunday brunch 11 AM–3 PM. This remodeled in-town home is decorated with eclectic folk art and antiques; it has a popular lounge and a diverse menu. Caesar salad supreme is a meal in itself. Try open-flame Thai shrimp as an appetizer; for an entrée, select shrimp and cheese tortellini, swordfish prepared differently daily, English-cut prime rib, roast duck, or grilled pesto chicken. There are many other seafood, beef, and chicken choices. Inexpensive to moderate.

**EATING OUT** **Abercrombie & Finch** (603-964-9774), 219 Lafayette Road, North Hampton. Open daily 11:30 AM–9 PM, Sunday brunch 9 AM–1 PM. Locally popular restaurant and lounge with a large menu ranging from salads, soups, and sandwiches to full dinners. Vegetarian entrées, plus steaks, quiche of the day, lobster pie, baked scrod, stir fries, and fried seafoods. Dinner $5.95–12.95; New England Sunday brunch buffet (eggs and omelets cooked to order) $6.95.

**Blue Moon Natural Foods & Green Earth Café** (603-778-6850), 8 Clifford Street, Exeter. Monday through Friday 9 AM–6 PM; Saturday 9 AM–4 PM; Sunday noon–4 PM. Café open for lunch only Monday through Saturday 11 AM–2:30 PM. Vegetarians and others rejoice at this healthy place offering sandwiches and salads featuring tofu, tuna, egg salads, and salad specials such as white bean, couscous, and hummus. There are also daily soup specials. From 4 to 5 PM on weekdays the store offers heat-your-own meals like lentil loaf and lasagna to go. Inexpensive.

♿ **Galley Hatch** (603-926-6152), Route 1, Hampton. Open daily 11 AM–10 PM, Friday and Saturday until 11 PM. A large and popular seacoast restaurant with a diverse and reasonably priced menu. Fish, chicken, steaks, pastas, and vegetarian entrées plus pizza, salads, and sandwiches. Breads and pastries are made in the Galley's own bakery, which is open to the public. Two lounges; light meals, special coffees, and desserts served in the lounge until closing. Weekend entertainment. Handicapped accessible. Next door is the Hampton Cinema complex. Prices are moderate.

**Penang and Tokyo Restaurant** (603-778-8388) 97 Water Street, Exeter. Open Sunday to Thursday 11:30 AM–10 PM, Friday and Saturday until 11 PM. Following the odd trend of seacoast-area combination restaurants featuring Malaysian, Chinese, and Japanese (there may even be some Thai in there), this bustling eatery in the heart of Exeter plays host to Phillips Exeter parents, students, families with children, and local business types who don't feel it's a day unless they consume sushi. And us. Don't expect super-friendly service, but do come for the unique Malaysian food, like coconut scallops encrusted with sesame seeds or spicy apple chicken. Everything's well flavored, portions are huge, and the sushi laid out at the sushi bar is nothing if not artful. Prices top out at $25 and usually run $9–15. Look for luncheon specials.

LOBSTER AND SEAFOOD Fried seafood, chowder, steamed clams, and lobster in the rough are seacoast specialties. Local favorites include the following places:

**Brown's Seabrook Lobster Pound** (603-474-3331), Route 286, Seabrook Beach. Open year-round (weekends from mid-November through mid-April). Its screened dining room is on the marsh beside the Blackwater River.

**Little Jack's Seafood** (603-926-0444), 539 Ocean Boulevard, Hampton Beach. Open late spring through Labor Day.

**Newick's Fisherman's Landing** (603-926-7646; 1-800-649-7646; www.newicks.com), 845 Lafayette Road, Hampton. Open winter and spring, Wednesday through Sunday 11:30 AM–8 or 9 PM; open daily in summer and early fall. Fish, clams, scallops, shrimp served deep-fried, broiled, or baked, plus lobsters cooked any way you want them. (Also see Newick's in "Dover, Durham, and Vicinity.") Fresh fish market and lobsters packed to travel. Seniors' and children's menus.

Lobsters are a seacoast trademark. For live or cooked lobsters, try the **New Hampshire Lobster Company** (603-926-3424), located at the Smith and Gilmore Pier at Hampton Harbor, open daily 9 AM–5 PM, summer until 6 PM; or **Al's Seafood** (603-946-9591), Route 1, Lafayette Road, North Hampton, open daily. Al's is a lobster pound and fish market with a small seafood restaurant offering mainly fried seafood, but in warm weather they serve lobster in the rough on a porch.

## Entertainment

**Act One** (603-329-6025), Winnacunnet Road, Hampton. Replacing the razed Hampton Playhouse, this theater company performs musicals and dramas in the local high school under the direction of the spirited Stephanie Voss-Nugent.

## Selective Shopping

**North Hampton Factory Outlet Center,** Route 1, North Hampton. More than 35 stores offer bargains in clothing, books, records, luggage, footwear, housewares, and gifts.

**League of New Hampshire Craftsmen** (603-778-8282), 61 Water Street, Exeter 03833. Open Monday through Saturday 10 AM–5 PM. More than 200 craftsworkers are members of the league, supplying a wide variety of distinctive handmade items.

**Exeter Handkerchief Fabrics and Custom Draperies Co.** (603-778-8564), 48 Lincoln Street, Exeter 03833. Open Monday through Saturday 9 AM–5 PM. A huge selection of yard goods and patterns makes this place a must-stop for the sewers in the family.

## ✷ Special Events

Summer on the seacoast offers a nearly unlimited number of special events and activities for people of all ages. Check with local chambers of commerce for varied activities.

*Mid-May:* **New Hampshire Towing Association Wrecker Rodeo** (603-926-8717), Hampton Beach State Park. Scores of wreckers parade and compete for prizes. Parade 9 AM on Sunday.

*Mid-June:* **Hobie Cat Regatta** (603-926-8717), Hampton Beach. A weekend of racing just off Hampton Beach makes a colorful spectacle.

*Mid- to late June:* **Master Sand Sculpting Competition** (603-926-8717). Seven thousand dollars in prize money goes to one of the 12 master sand sculptors who spend a week working and are judged. Past winning sculptures have included a depiction of carpenters building a house and frogs playing at the beach. Each year 250 tons of sand is dumped on the beach for contestants' use.

*Late June through early August:* **Concerts in the Park** (603-778-0595), Swasey Park, Exeter, every Thursday.

*July and August:* **Hampton Beach fireworks,** every Wednesday at 9:30 PM. **Hampton Beach concerts,** every night at 7 and 9:30 PM.

*Fourth of July weekend:* **Kingston Fair,** Route 125, Kingston. A Fourth of July weekend country fair. **Exeter Revolutionary War Festival,** Exeter. Historic demonstrations, militia encampments, battle reenactments, road race, canoe rally, and lots of family fun.

*Mid-July:* **Stratham Fair,** Route 101, Stratham. A weekend, agricultural country fair with horse and cattle pulling, midway, children's events, fireworks.

*Late July:* **Miss Hampton Beach Pageant.** A serious beauty pageant with evening gown and swimsuit competitions; 2 PM.

*Mid-August:* **Annual Children's Festival** (603-926-8717), Hampton Beach.

*September:* **Seacoast Seafood Festival** (603-926-8717), Hampton Beach. Sample a variety of seafoods prepared by area restaurants.

# DOVER, DURHAM, AND VICINITY

**Durham** is the home of the University of New Hampshire, whose beautiful campus dominates the center of the town. The Paul Creative Arts Center with its galleries, music, dance, theater, and intercollegiate athletics has the most to offer visitors, though these activities tend to happen during the school year, September through May. **Dover,** long an important mill town and the oldest permanent settlement in the state, is beginning to attract its share of tourists with its summer arts festival, theater, museum, and several fine restaurants and shops.

GUIDANCE **Greater Dover Chamber of Commerce** (603-742-2218; www.dovernh.org), 299 Central Avenue, Dover 03820.

**University of New Hampshire** main switchboard (603-862-1234) can provide details of various events or direct your questions to the proper office.

GETTING THERE *By car:* From Portsmouth, follow the Spaulding Turnpike (Route 4/16) north, then Route 4 west for Durham, or remain on the turnpike and take one of the three Dover exits.

*By bus:* **C&J Trailways** (603-431-2424; 603-742-2990; www.cjtrailways.com) provides many trips daily connecting Logan Airport and downtown Boston with Dover, Durham, and Portsmouth, New Hampshire; Newburyport, Massachusetts; and Portland, Maine.

*By train:* **Amtrak** (www.thedowneaster.com). Slide down the Maine and New Hampshire coasts with ease on this short train that heads to Boston. The train runs year-round; one-way fares run about $4–21. On the seacoast the train stops at Dover, Durham, and Exeter.

GETTING AROUND *By bus:* **COAST** (Cooperative Alliance for Seacoast Transportation) (603-862-1931; www.coastbus.org), a local bus transportation network, connects Portsmouth and major outlying shopping centers with Durham, Dover, Newmarket, Rochester, and Somersworth, New Hampshire; and Berwick, Maine. **Wildcat Transit** (603-862-2328) makes frequent trips among Dover, Portsmouth, and the University of New Hampshire in Durham.

**MEDICAL EMERGENCY Wentworth-Douglas Hospital** (603-742-5252; www.wdhospital.com), 789 Central Avenue, Dover, has 24-hour emergency walk-in service. **Dover ambulance:** 911. **Durham ambulance:** 603-862-1212.

## ✱ To See

**GAME FARM Little Bay Buffalo Company** (603-868-3300), 50 Langley Road, Durham. Open daily 9 AM–6 PM from April 1 through October 31, 10 AM–sunset the rest of the year. A family-owned and -operated wildlife estate, Little Bay Buffalo Company offers specially designed tours focusing on the American bison. A vintage Farmall tractor pulls a large covered wagon across the rolling landscape, where you can view bison as they breed and calve. Bison meat and various other bison by-products are available for sale at the Drowned Valley Trading Post. Special arrangements can be made with the **Isles of Shoals Steamship Company** (1-800-441-4620; see *To Do* in "Portsmouth and Vicinity") to arrive at the ranch by boat.

**HISTORICAL SOCIETIES Durham Historical Museum** (603-868-5436), corner of Main Street and Newmarket Road, Durham 03824. Open September through May, Tuesday and Thursday 1–3 PM; June through August, by appointment only.

**Lee Historical Society** (603-659-5925), Mast Road, Lee 03824. Open on Lee Fair Day (the Saturday after Labor Day) and June through August Saturday 9 AM–2 PM. Local artifacts, including farm tools, household items, and antique photographs, are housed in an old railroad freight station, moved to this site between the town library and the police station.

**Newmarket Historical Society** (603-659-7420), Granite Street, Newmarket 03857-0175. Open by appointment and June through August, Thursday 2–4 PM. The old Granite School Museum has old tools and local artifacts plus photographs of Newmarket mills and shoe shops.

**Woodman Institute Museum** (603-742-1038), 182 Central Avenue, Dover. Open April through November, Sunday through Wednesday 12:30–4:30 PM. This three-building complex is Dover's historical museum. The Woodman House (1818) is a research library that has galleries and natural history and war-related museum rooms. The 1813 Hale House is a historical museum with period furniture. The Damm Garrison, built in 1675, is a unique building that was used as a home and fortress by early settlers. Adults $3; children 14–18 $1.

## ✱ To Do

**GOLF Hickory Pond** (603-659-2227), Route 108, Durham. Open spring through early fall. This is a nine-hole, par-3 course. Pro shop. Inexpensive.

**Nippo Lake Golf Course** (603-664-7616), Province Road (off Route 126), Barrington. Open April through November. Nine holes, cart rentals, full bar and food service year-round; call for starting times on weekends.

**Rochester Country Club** (603-332-0985), Route 125, Gonic. Open mid-April through mid-November. Eighteen holes, cart rentals, full bar and food service, and pro shop; call for starting times on weekends.

**Rockingham Country Club** (603-659-9956), Route 108, Newmarket. Open mid-April through mid-November. Nine holes, cart rentals, pro shop, full bar and food service; call for starting times on weekends and holidays.

**Sunningdale Golf Course** (603-742-0172), 301 Green Street, Somersworth. Open mid-April through mid-November. Nine holes, cart rentals, full bar and light food.

WALKING TOURS **Dover's Heritage Trails** (603-742-2218), 299 Central Avenue, Dover. The chamber of commerce offers a brochure with a series of walking tours exploring Dover's long history.

## ✻ Green Space

**Great Bay National Estuarine Research Reserve** (603-868-1095; www.greatbay.org), 37 Concord Road, Durham. Great Bay, with some 4,500 acres of tidal waters and tidal wetlands and 800 surrounding upland acres, has been designated part of the national estuarine research system. Famous for winter smelt fishing, oystering, and waterfowl, the bay is a unique resource in the midst of the rapidly growing towns of the seacoast. Some 23 rare or endangered species, including bald eagles in winter, depend on the shallow bay as a refuge. It is an important stop for migrating birds of all species. Its status as a research reserve will help continue the scientific studies conducted since 1970 by the University of New Hampshire's Jackson Estuarine Lab on **Adams Point.** From Route 108 in Durham, follow Bay Road to Adams Point, where there is a launch ramp and a self-guiding nature trail. Return to Bay Road and follow it south to Newmarket, an especially scenic drive with views across the bay. Just across the bay from Adams Point is the **Great Bay National Wildlife Refuge** (603-431-7511), part of the Pease International Tradeport. The public is welcome at the **Sandy Point Discovery Center** on Depot Road, just off Route 101 in Stratham. It's open to the public May through September (plus weekends in October), Wednesday through Sunday 10 AM–4 PM. Nearby on Route 108 in Stratham is **Chapmans Landing,** a launching site with rest room facilities. There is another launch ramp in the middle of **Newmarket** on Route 108. Although the bay has a large surface area, its average depth is only 8 feet, making navigation in larger boats a challenge. Some of the Portsmouth tour boats offer fall foliage cruises on the bay and its tributaries. The bay drains through the Piscataqua River, the boundary between Maine and New Hampshire.

**Hilton Park** is located on Dover Point, bisected by the Spaulding Turnpike. It has a boat-launching ramp, picnic tables, outdoor grills, and play area.

**Cochecho River Trail** (603-749-4445), Strafford County Farm at County Farm Road and County Farm Cross Road, Dover. An easy 1-mile loop trail that crosses an old floodplain with scenic river vistas and through forests rich with tall pines and ancient oaks. Trail maps and interpretive materials are available at the trailhead.

UNH's Department of Campus Recreation publishes an excellent little booklet of self-guiding hikes on and around the university's sprawling, wooded campus. Call UNH's main switchboard (603-862-1234) or drop by the New England Conference Center (see *Lodging,* below) to pick up a copy of *Running and Walking Routes.*

## ✱ Lodging

HOTELS ✐ **The New England Conference Center and Hotel** (603-862-2712; 1-800-590-4334; www.newenglandcenter.com), 15 Strafford Avenue, UNH, Durham 03824. Located on the University of New Hampshire campus, this contemporary conference center (also open to the public) has 115 guest rooms, 61 of which are located in the newest of the two green, ceramic brick towers that make up the complex. The building isn't much to look at, but the rooms all have wall-to-wall carpet, air-conditioning, TV, hair dryer, iron and ironing board, and phone. The newer wing has two queen-sized beds in each room. All rooms have dramatic views across the campus or into the treetops of this heavily wooded site, and there is daily bus service to Boston's Logan Airport, about an hour away. **The Acorns Restaurant and Lounge** serves breakfast, lunch, and dinner daily (see *Dining Out*). Rates vary seasonally $72–120. Children stay free.

BED & BREAKFASTS **Hickory Pond Inn and Golf Course** (603-659-2227; 1-800-658-0065; www.hickorypondinn.com), Route 108 and Stagecoach Road, Durham 03824. Open all year. In a country location midway between Durham and Newmarket, this inn has 18 rooms, 14 of which have private bath, cable TV, and air-conditioning. A continental breakfast is served in one of two large common areas. Floor-to-ceiling windows overlook a challenging par-3, nine-hole golf course, open to guests and the public. Doug Baxter, Libby Baxter, and Chris John, innkeepers. $69–99.

**Highland Farm** (603-743-3399; www.highlandfarmbandb.com), 148 County Farm Road, Dover 03820. Open year-round. This interesting brick Victorian country house is on the outskirts of the city in a unique pastoral setting. There are nature trails for walking or cross-country skiing along the nearby Cocheco River. Four guest rooms, two with private bath; the other rooms share two baths. Beds include a queen-sized with a canopy. Most rooms have a queen-sized bed or two twin beds. Common rooms include a living room, wood-paneled library, sun room, and dining room. Furnishings are antiques, enhanced by the unusual woodwork and architectural design of this house. Full breakfast. Rates are $90–120 for two. Noreen Bowers and Michael Sherman are your gracious hosts.

**Three Chimneys Inn** (603-868-7800; 1-888-399-9777; www.threechimneys-inn.com; chimney3@threechimneysinn.com), 17 Newmarket Road, Durham 03824. Open all year. Seemingly, no expense has been spared restoring Durham's oldest home, now the town's newest inn. This circa-1649 house and carriage house, perched on a little hill an easy walk from the University of New Hampshire campus and 5 miles from Portsmouth, overlooks formal gardens, the Oyster River, and Old Mill Falls, as well as a small cemetery of old gravestones. The 23 guest rooms—all with private bath with two-person shower or Jacuzzi, many with fireplace or woodstove—are poshly furnished with four-poster canopy beds, Edwardian bed drapes, tapestries, and Oriental rugs. Added comforts include two-line telephones with dataports and full-sized desks. Concierge service and conference facilities for up to 100 are available. Rates include a full breakfast served in one of the three restaurants on the property (see *Dining Out*). $119–229 high season, $109–189 off-season.

♿ **The Silver Street Inn** (603-743-3000), 103 Silver Street, Dover 03820. Open year-round. Located on a residential street, this gray, mansard-roofed B&B was built in the 1880s by a wealthy industrialist who spared nothing in the way of Gilded Age elegance. Many of the architectural details, including mahogany, crystal, slate, and Caen stone, were imported from Western Europe, and the craftsmanship of the molded plaster ceilings and hand-painted dining room walls reflects the sumptuousness of the age. Ten rooms (all but one with private bath) have air-conditioning, cable TV, and telephone. One downstairs room is handicapped accessible and has double and queen-sized beds. The dining and living rooms and the ornate library are comfortable and have fireplaces. Full breakfast, served in your room by request. Rates are $79–119.

## ✷ Where to Eat

**DINING OUT Maples** (603-868-7800; 1-888-399-9777; www.threechimneysinn.com), 17 Newmarket Road, Durham. Open year-round. Nightly dining from 5 PM until closing; Sunday brunch 11 AM–2 PM. This is the Three Chimneys Inn's most formal restaurant. With four fireplaces and Georgian furnishings, it offers fine dining in a candlelit atmosphere. The varied menu features such appetizers as butternut squash bisque with cinnamon crème fraîche, and oysters steeped in white wine served with potato finished with julienne of leek. Entrées, which range $15–26, include pan-seared sea bass napped with spicy Thai ginger sauce on lo mein noodles, free-range chicken breast with wild mushroom risotto, tenderloin of beef with creamy polenta and seasonal vegetables, and grilled polenta in a coconut-lime marinade.

**ffrost Sawyer Tavern** (603-868-7800; 1-888-399-9777; www.threechimneysinn.com), 17 Newmarket Road, Durham. Open year-round, Monday through Saturday 11:30 AM–closing; Sunday from 5 PM. Great ffood. Lunch and dinner are served with style next to a roaring fireplace in this granite-walled tavern, the midlevel entry in Three Chimneys Inn's trifecta of eateries. By inn standards this is casual dining, but it's still pretty classy; figure on spending anywhere between $8 and $23 for entrées, which range from beef tenderloin to lobster to, yes, ostrich. Big sandwiches (including local bison) at lunch only. Good soups, salads, and moderately priced entrées all day.

**The Conservatory** (603-868-7800; 1-888-399-9777; www.threechimneysinn.com), 17 Newmarket Road, Durham. Open seasonally. The Three Chimneys Inn offers outdoor dining on the terrace under an old English grape arbor as weather permits. Selections from both the Maples and the ffrost Sawyer Tavern menus are available, with entrées such as pot roast, chicken potpie, and fish-and-chips priced $8–15.

**The Acorns Restaurant and Lounge** (603-862-2815), 15 Strafford Avenue, Durham. Open year-round for breakfast, lunch, and dinner. Dinner is 5–10 PM, Sunday brunch 11 AM–1:30 PM. Part of the New England Conference Center and Hotel, this is one of the most popular restaurants in the region. It's as well known for its fine food as for its distinctive architecture, which features angled walls and huge windows that place diners seemingly in the midst of the surrounding forest. Veal, Maine lobster, roast stuffed leg of lamb, salmon, and filet mignon are among the specialties, which are matched by varied appetizers and rich desserts. There are also early-bird specials—light meals of fish or pasta served for just $9.95 plus tax, Sunday through Thursday 4–5:30 PM. The Sunday brunch, with jazz to accompany, has been called the best in New Hampshire by a statewide magazine. Prices are moderate.

**Firehouse 1** (603-742-2220; www.firehouseone.com), 1 Orchard Street (adjacent to the municipal parking off the lower square), Dover. Open Monday through Friday 11:30 AM–5 PM for lunch, 5–9 PM for dinner; Sunday buffet 10 AM–2 PM. Reservations recommended. Housed in a remodeled 1830s firehouse, this is Dover's best restaurant. The dinner menu is quite diverse, featuring steaks, haddock, veal, barbecued ribs, fresh pasta dishes, and seafood scampi. Appetizers include corn and seafood chowders, grilled focaccia with pesto, roasted red peppers and fruit, and grilled stuffed portobello mushrooms. Children's menu. The bar is open until legal closing. Lunch $6–12, dinner $12.95–22.95.

**Alexander's Italian Restaurant** (603-742-2650), 489 Portland Avenue (Route 4), Rollinsford. Tuesday through Thursday 11:30 AM–9 PM, Friday until 10 PM, Saturday 4–10 PM, Sunday noon–8 PM. This popular restaurant is located just west of downtown Dover. For antipasti select red peppers and anchovies or eggplant parmigiana, then try calamari with linguine in red sauce, octopus with linguine, or shrimp with garlic and butter on linguine. Meat entrées range from veal parmigiana and roast veal to chicken cacciatore, pork chops, and New York strip steak. Also pizza (white with Fontina cheese), lasagna, and fettuccine carbonara. Entrées $6–17.

EATING OUT **Café on the Corner** (603-742-0314), 478 Central Avenue, Dover. Open for breakfast, lunch, and coffee until midnight. A cozy spot that draws most of its clientele from nearby UNH, Café on the Corner features great coffee, sandwiches, soups, and salads as well as Internet access (there's a minimum charge even if you're just quickly checking your e-mail), board games, books, and comfortable seating. It's very friendly, and even if the crowd is younger than you might like, it's open for a bite or a coffee far later than almost anything else in the seacoast area. As a bonus, the friendly owners are planning to expand the space soon to incorporate more seats and possibly a performance space. Inexpensive.

**Newick's Lobster House and Restaurant** (603-742-3205; www.newicks.com), Dover Point Road, Dover. Open daily 11:30 AM–8 PM, Friday and Saturday until 9 PM, closed Monday from after Columbus Day until the Memorial Day weekend. Fresh fish and lobster right off the boat are the specialties at this large, very popular restaurant overlooking Great Bay. Not fancy dining, but you can have deep-fried (in cholesterol-free vegetable oil) fish of all kinds with combinations of scallops, oysters, haddock, clams, and shrimp. Portions are huge. For those with lighter tastes, try boiled lobsters, steamers, or broiled, baked, or stuffed fish dinners. Also chicken, sandwiches, chowders, and lobster stew. Expect a wait at weekend dinnertimes. (**Newick's Fisherman's Landing** in Hampton is also operated by Jack Newick.) Prices range from $4.50 to $21.

**Strafford Farms Restaurant** (603-743-3045), Route 108, Dover. Open Sunday through Thursday 6 AM–9 PM; Friday and Saturday 6 AM–10 PM. Sixty years ago Leo Allen and the Rollins families opened a milk-processing plant, which soon expanded to sell ice cream, and eventually became a full-fledged restaurant serving breakfast, lunch, and dinner. Today, despite its location on a busy strip of fast-food restaurants and chain stores, Strafford Farms continues to offer such homemade, back-on-the-farm specialties as Yankee pot roast, meat loaf, and turkey croquettes. The full menu also includes hot and cold sandwiches, seafood entrées, Black Angus beef, homemade soups, salads, and several Italian dishes. Most are priced under $10. A 20-ounce grand prime rib with all the trimmings is $15.50.

## ✷ Entertainment

**Cochecho Arts Festival** (603-742-2218), Cochecho Falls Millworks Courtyard, Dover. Open June through early September. In the center of Dover beside the Cochecho River is a huge textile mill complex, recently remodeled into a business center. The courtyard is the location for Friday-night, Wednesday-noon, and occasional Sunday-evening concerts featuring a variety of regional music groups. Children's concerts and programs are held Tuesday at noon at nearby Henry Law Park.

**Mill Pond Center for the Arts** (603-868-2068; www.millpondcenter.org), 50 Newmarket Road, Durham. You'll be amazed at the bounty of performing arts housed in this historic former inn set in the woods. You'll find chamber music, dance, and theater performances year-round. Call for schedules and pricing information.

## ✷ Selective Shopping

**Calef's Country Store** (603-664-2231), Routes 9 and 125, Barrington. Open daily. Since 1869, five generations of Calefs have operated this old-fashioned country store. Penny candy, cheddar cheese, maple syrup, Barbados molasses, jams and jellies, pickles and crackers in the barrel, dried beans for baking, hand-dipped candles, pumpkins in fall, gifts, and more.

**The Christmas Dove** (1-800-550-3683), junction of Routes 125 and 9 in Dover. Open daily 10 AM–5 PM. This Dover establishment, which has sister stores in New York, Boston, and Ogunquit, Maine, has been around for more than a quarter century. Trimmings, lights, nutcrackers, candles, and nativities turn the complex into a southerly North Pole, allowing organized shoppers to ho-ho-ho all year and get a leg up on those who wait until after Thanksgiving to prepare for the holidays.

**Farmers' Market,** Henry Law Park, Dover. Wednesday afternoons, June through October. Locally grown veggies and fruits, home-baked goods, and crafts.

**Salmon Falls Stoneware** (603-749-1467), the Oak Street Engine House, Dover. Open Monday through Saturday 8 AM–5 PM, Sunday from 9 AM. Salmon Falls Stoneware has gained a following for its line of cobalt-blue country designs on salt-glazed pottery. The casserole dishes, crocks, dinnerware, mugs, and pie plates are ovenproof, and microwave and dishwasher safe. There's a shop that sells both first-quality items and selected seconds, as well as a studio where you can watch potters at work.

**Tuttle's Red Barn** (603-742-4313), Dover Point Road, Dover. Open daily 10 AM–6 PM. Tuttles have lived on this site since 1632, making this the oldest continuously operating family farm in America. Once just a seasonal farm stand operating from the large, old red barn, it has been expanded as a market and garden center. In-season much of the produce, especially sweet corn, comes from the surrounding fields, but they also have plenty of fresh vegetables and fruit, breads, and cheeses.

## ✷ Special Events

*June:* **Somersworth International Children's Day,** an all-day event with four entertainment stages including one for children, a crafts fair, food booths, a hands-on crafts tent for children, and an activities section for children.

*June:* **Great Cocheco Boat Race** (603-868-1494). Sponsored by the Strafford Rivers Conservancy, this canoe race proves a challenge to all participants and is great fun to watch.

*July–August:* **Cochecho Arts Festival** (603-742-2218), Dover. Music and children's programs, several times weekly.

*Early September:* **Lee Fair Day,** Mast Road, Lee. A community fair with exhibits, games, and food.

*Mid-September:* **Rochester Fair,** 72 Lafayette Street, Rochester. A 10-day fair with a midway, agricultural exhibits, and pari-mutuel harness racing.

*First Saturday in October:* **Apple Harvest Day** (603-742-2218), Dover. An all-day crafts fair with entertainment, food, petting zoo, children's activities, and more.

# The Monadnock Region

PETERBOROUGH, KEENE, AND SURROUNDING VILLAGES

Robert Kozlow

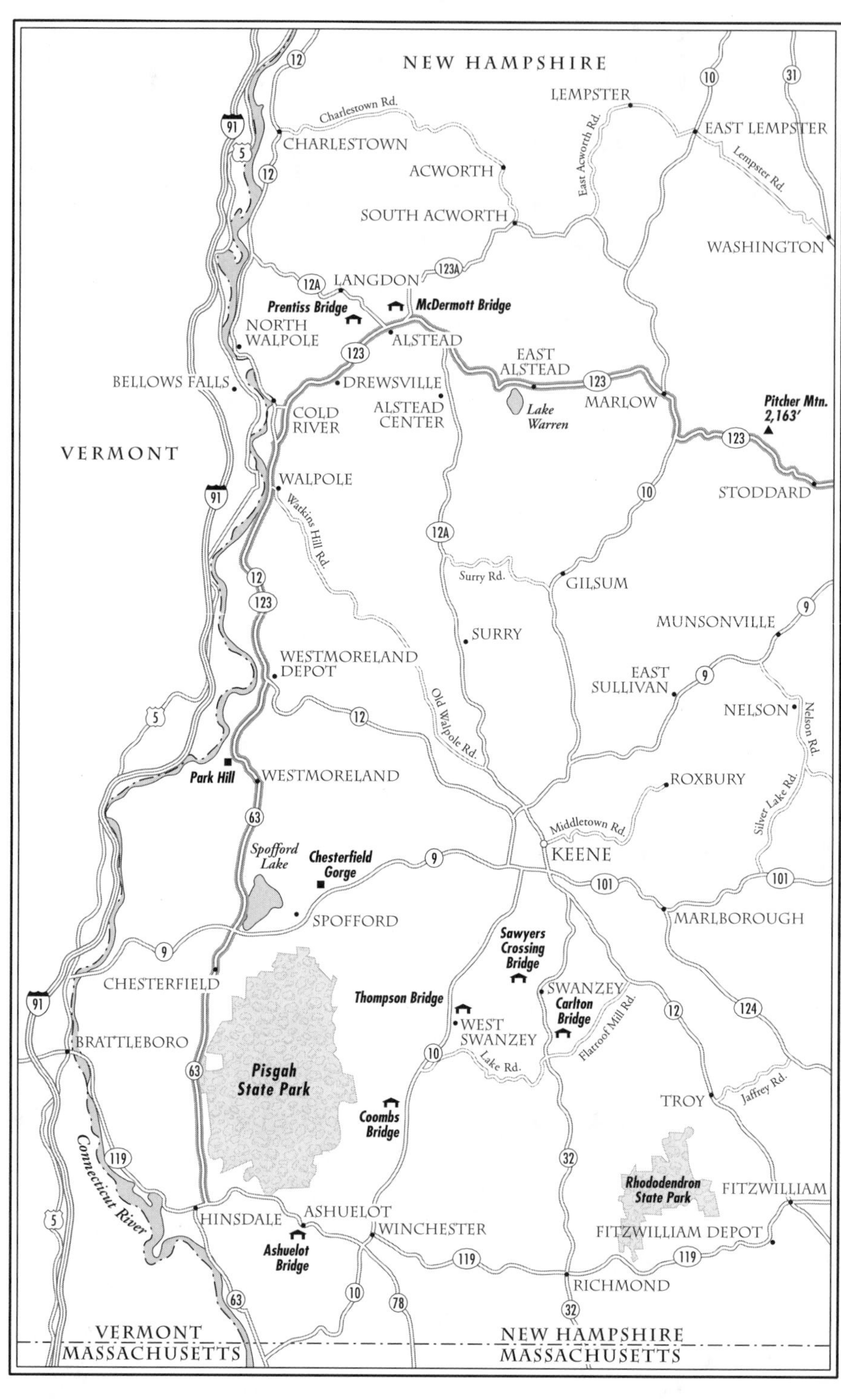

NEW HAMPSHIRE
VERMONT
LEMPSTER
EAST LEMPSTER
Lempster Rd.
East Acworth Rd.
Charlestown Rd.
CHARLESTOWN
ACWORTH
SOUTH ACWORTH
WASHINGTON
LANGDON
Prentiss Bridge
McDermott Bridge
NORTH WALPOLE
ALSTEAD
EAST ALSTEAD
BELLOWS FALLS
DREWSVILLE
ALSTEAD CENTER
Lake Warren
MARLOW
Pitcher Mtn. 2,163′
COLD RIVER
WALPOLE
STODDARD
Watkins Hill Rd.
Surry Rd.
GILSUM
MUNSONVILLE
SURRY
WESTMORELAND DEPOT
EAST SULLIVAN
NELSON
Nelson Rd.
Old Walpole Rd.
Park Hill
WESTMORELAND
ROXBURY
Silver Lake Rd.
Middletown Rd.
Spofford Lake
Chesterfield Gorge
KEENE
SPOFFORD
MARLBOROUGH
Sawyers Crossing Bridge
CHESTERFIELD
SWANZEY
Thompson Bridge
Carlton Bridge
WEST SWANZEY
Flatroof Mill Rd.
BRATTLEBORO
Lake Rd.
Pisgah State Park
Coombs Bridge
TROY
Jaffrey Rd.
Connecticut River
Rhododendron State Park
FITZWILLIAM
HINSDALE
ASHUELOT
WINCHESTER
FITZWILLIAM DEPOT
Ashuelot Bridge
RICHMOND
VERMONT
MASSACHUSETTS
NEW HAMPSHIRE
MASSACHUSETTS

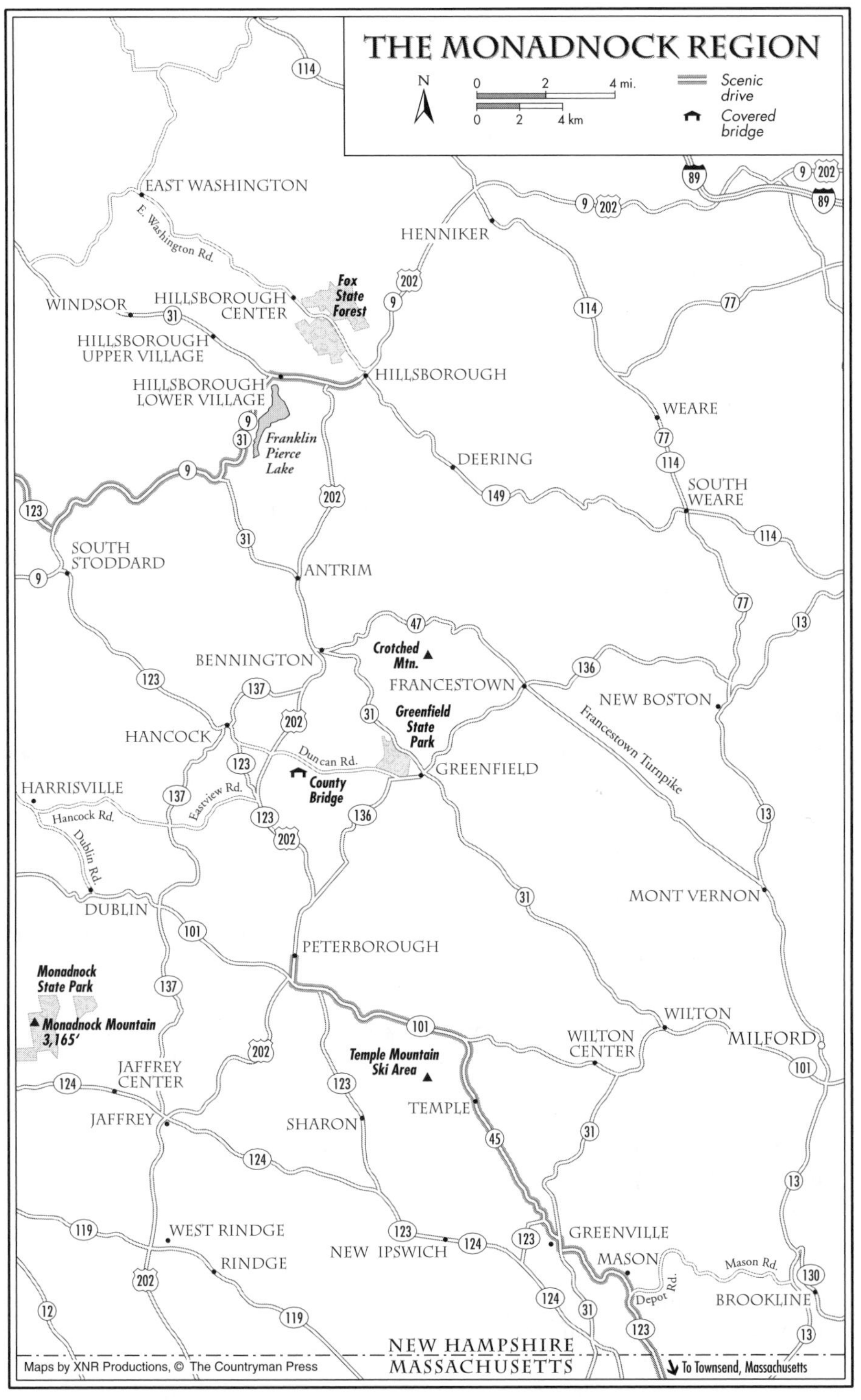
THE MONADNOCK REGION
N
0 2 4 mi.
0 2 4 km
Scenic drive
Covered bridge
EAST WASHINGTON
E. Washington Rd.
HENNIKER
WINDSOR
HILLSBOROUGH CENTER
Fox State Forest
HILLSBOROUGH UPPER VILLAGE
HILLSBOROUGH
HILLSBOROUGH LOWER VILLAGE
Franklin Pierce Lake
WEARE
DEERING
SOUTH WEARE
SOUTH STODDARD
ANTRIM
Crotched Mtn.
BENNINGTON
FRANCESTOWN
NEW BOSTON
Francestown Turnpike
HANCOCK
Greenfield State Park
Duncan Rd.
County Bridge
GREENFIELD
HARRISVILLE
Eastview Rd.
Hancock Rd.
Dublin Rd.
DUBLIN
MONT VERNON
PETERBOROUGH
Monadnock State Park
Monadnock Mountain 3,165′
WILTON
WILTON CENTER
MILFORD
Temple Mountain Ski Area
JAFFREY CENTER
JAFFREY
SHARON
TEMPLE
WEST RINDGE
GREENVILLE
RINDGE
NEW IPSWICH
MASON
Mason Rd.
Depot Rd.
BROOKLINE
NEW HAMPSHIRE
MASSACHUSETTS
To Townsend, Massachusetts
Maps by XNR Productions, © The Countryman Press

# PETERBOROUGH, KEENE, AND SURROUNDING VILLAGES

Mount Monadnock towers a dramatic 2,000 feet above the surrounding roll of southwestern New Hampshire. Not only is the mountain visible from up to 50 miles in every direction, but it's also as much a part of the dozens of surrounding towns as the steeples on their meetinghouses. Uplands around the mountain, in turn, rise like a granite island 1,000 feet above the rest of southern New Hampshire. Hardy spruce, fir, and birch are the dominant trees, and the rugged terrain has deflected both developers and interstate highways.

Depending on where you draw the line, the Monadnock region as a whole encompasses some 40 towns, all characterized by narrow roads, quintessential New England villages, and mountain vistas. A region of rushing streams, this entire area was once spotted with small 19th-century mills, and many of these buildings survive. Harrisville, with its two cupola-topped mills graceful as churches, is said to be the country's most perfectly preserved early-19th-century mill village. Larger brick mill buildings in South Peterborough and in Keene now house shops and restaurants, and half a dozen old mills are still producing a wide variety of products: paper, lightbulbs, and matchbooks, for starters.

Mount Monadnock itself spawned the region's tourism industry early in the 19th century. Early settlers had trimmed its lower beard of hardwood and spruce, planting orchards and pasturing sheep between tidy stone walls right up its rocky shoulders. Then they took to burning the summit. The idea was to kill off the wolves, but the effect was to expose the mountain's bald pate. Once this bare spot was created, alpine flora (usually found only on mountains twice as high) took root, and hikers could enjoy not only the high-altitude landscape but also the spectacular view.

"Grand Monadnock" quickly became a famous freak. By 1823 a shed, the Grand Monadnock Hotel, was selling refreshments just below the summit, and a rival, Dinsmore's Comfortable Shantee, opened high on the mountain a few years later. By the 1850s local farmers and innkeepers had blazed trails up every side of Monadnock, and from 100 to 400 people could be found hiking them on any good day.

In the 1850s the mountain inspired works by Henry David Thoreau and Ralph Waldo Emerson, and around the turn of the century Dublin became known as a literary and art colony—writers included Samuel Clemens and Willa Cather; artists included Abbot Thayer, Frank Benson, and Rockwell Kent. In 1908 the MacDowell Colony in Peterborough became one of the country's first formal retreats for musicians, artists, and writers. The region's cultural climate remains rich, expressed through the unusual number of art galleries and musical and theatrical productions.

Most of the 19th-century summer hotels around Mount Monadnock are long gone, but half a dozen of the region's earlier stagecoach taverns survive, and over the past decades a couple of dozen attractive bed & breakfasts have opened. The Monadnock region is thus once more a destination area. But even innkeepers will tell you that a resort area it isn't. Residents take pride in the fact that Mount Monadnock is the world's second most heavily hiked mountain (after Mount Fuji in Japan), but everyone wants to keep the region's roads as delightfully traffic-free as they are.

Mount Monadnock itself is unquestionably the region's spiritual and physical hub—but mountains, after all, divide. There's some rivalry between Keene and Peterborough for recognition as the commercial center of the region. In fact, Mount Monadnock divides the area in two; all roads west of the mountain seem to converge in Keene, while in the hillier area to the east they run to Peterborough.

Keene is the shire town of Cheshire County, home of Keene State College and the place most residents of southwestern New Hampshire come to go to the movies or the hospital or to shop seriously. Far smaller Peterborough prides itself on having "the first tax-supported Free Public Library in the world," on having inspired Thornton Wilder to write *Our Town,* and on serving as home for one of New England's oldest summer theaters. It also offers some unexpectedly fine shopping and dining.

The Monadnock region remains pristine in part because of its location: too near Boston to be generally viewed as a place to spend the night, too far from Manhattan to draw the New Yorkers, who tend to get no farther east than Vermont. So it happens that, despite the region's beauty, its ski and hiking trails, biking routes, and wealth of antiques shops, and the quality of its lodging and dining, prices are relatively and refreshingly low. The only way to truly experience and explore the region, moreover, is to stay at least overnight.

**GUIDANCE** **Greater Peterborough Chamber of Commerce** (603-924-7234; www.peterboroughchamber.com), P.O. Box 401, Peterborough 03458. Open weekdays 9 AM–5 PM; Saturdays in summer and fall, 10 AM–3 PM. The chamber publishes a beautiful 100-page guide to the 20 central and eastern towns in the region, and the walk-in information center at the junction of Routes 101 and 202 is unusually friendly and helpful.

**Greater Keene Chamber of Commerce** (603-352-1303; www.keenechamber.com), 48 Central Square, Keene 03431. Open weekdays 9 AM–5 PM. The Keene chamber's easy-to-find, walk-in office is also a source of brochures and detailed information about the western and Connecticut River Valley sides of the region.

**GETTING THERE** *By air:* **Manchester Airport** (603-624-6539) offers connecting service to the world; see *Air Service* under "What's Where." **Silver Ranch Airpark** (603-532-8870) accommodates private planes.

*By bus:* **Vermont Transit Lines** (1-800-451-3292; in Keene 603-352-1331) stops in Keene (Gilbo Avenue), Troy, and Fitzwilliam en route from Boston to Montreal.

**GETTING AROUND** *By car:* Although the beauty of this region is its winding country roads, it's also worth noting the straightest, quickest routes: **Route 101,** which becomes Route 9 west of Keene, bisects the region from east to west, linking with Boston via Routes 101A and 3; by the same token, **Route 202** serves as a north–south spine linking I-89 north of Hillsborough with Route 2 (via Route 140) in Massachusetts. These two high roads cross at the lights in Peterborough, site of the region's prime information center (see *Guidance*). Route 12 also links with Route 140 to form an obvious route (the one the bus takes) from Boston via Fitzwilliam and Keene to southern Vermont.

**WHEN TO GO** Occasionally this high and hilly corner of New Hampshire gets the kind of old-fashioned winter on which its ski areas once thrived. In recent years, however, the snowline has moved north and the alpine areas are gone. More than ever, this is a summer and fall destination.

**MEDICAL EMERGENCY** **911** now covers the entire region**. Cheshire Medical Center** (603-352-4111), 580 Court Street, Keene. **Monadnock Community Hospital** (603-924-7191), Old Street Road, Peterborough, has a 24-hour emergency department.

## ✷ Villages

No other area in New England is as thickly studded with picture-perfect villages—clusters of clapboard and brick buildings around common centers that have changed hardly at all since the mid–19th century. Each has a town clerk, listed with directory assistance, who can furnish further information. See *To See—Scenic Drives* for suggestions on ways to thread these villages together.

**Alstead.** There are actually three Alsteads (pronounced "aal-sted"), a grouping of quiet hill towns in the northwestern corner of the region not far from the Connecticut River. From the handsome old white houses and the Congregational church in **East Alstead,** Route 123 dips down by Lake Warren and into Mill Hollow, by 18th-century water-powered **Chase's Mill,** and by **Vilas Pool**—an unusual dammed swimming area with an elaborate island picnic spot, complete with carillon (see *To Do—Swimming*). The center of **Alstead** includes a general store and the **Shedd-Porter Memorial Library** (inquire here for the hours of the historical society), a domed, Neoclassical Revival building given by native son John Shedd. Shedd was an associate of Marshall Field, who gave an almost identical library to his hometown of Conway. Turn left at the library and follow Hill Road up into **Alstead Center,** another hilltop cluster of old homes. The town also boasts two covered bridges. (Also see **Darby Brook Farm** under *Lodging—Bed and Breakfasts.*)

**Dublin.** The flagpole in the middle of the village sits 1,493 feet above sea level, placed in New Hampshire's highest village center. But the best views (a mile or so west on Route 101) are of Mount Monadnock rising above **Dublin Lake.** Large old summer homes are sequestered in the greenery around the lake and on wooded heights that enjoy this view. The original offices of *Yankee Magazine* and *The Old Farmer's Almanac* are in the middle of the village, as is the "oldest public library in the United States supported by private funds."

**Fitzwilliam.** The buildings gathered around this handsome green include an elegantly steepled town hall, an inviting, double-porched inn, and a number of pillared and Federal-style homes. One of the latter is now a library, and another is a friendly historical society called the **Amos J. Blake House** (603-585-7742), open Memorial Day through mid-October, Saturday 1–4 PM or by appointment. Exhibits include a law office, old-time schoolroom, military room, and a vintage-1779 fire engine.

The **town hall** was first built as a Congregational church in 1816 and then totally rebuilt after lightning struck it the following year. The spire is four tiered: a belfry above the clock tower, then two octagonal lanterns topped by a steeple and a weather vane. The facade below is graced by a Palladian window and slender Ionic pillars set in granite blocks quarried right in town. Of course, the bell was cast by Paul Revere. **Laurel Lake** on the western fringe of town is a favorite local swimming hole, and **Pinnacle Mountain,** just down the street from the Fitzwilliam Inn, offers inviting walks in summer and cross-country skiing in winter. For a description of **Rhododendron State Park** on the edge of town, see *Green Space*. (Also see *Lodging, Dining Out, Eating Out,* and *Selective Shopping.*)

**Francestown.** Named for Governor Wentworth's wife, Francestown has an almost feminine grace. The white-pillared, 1801 meetinghouse stands across from the old meetinghouse at the head of a street lined on both sides by graceful Federal-era houses. One of these is now the **George Homens Bixby Memorial Library** (603-547-2730; closed Monday) with wing chairs, Oriental rugs, and a children's story corner that many a passing adult would like an excuse to curl up in; inquire about the historical collection upstairs. Pick up a guide to local antiques shops in the **Francestown General Store.** Contra dances are held the second Saturday of every month in the town hall. **Crotched Mountain** is just up the road (see *To Do—Hiking*).

**Greenfield** is best known for its state park, with **Otter Lake** as its centerpiece, and for the **Crotched Mountain Rehabilitation Center,** which sits high on the shoulder of the mountain and has spectacular views. The village itself is appealing. The vintage-1795 **Congregational church** is the oldest meetinghouse in New Hampshire, serving as both a church and a town hall. It stands tall with maples in front and a graveyard curving up the hill behind. The heart of the village is **Carbee's Corner,** a store that's been in the same family since 1952, housed in the mansard-roofed complex across from the church and a source of penny candy and assorted gifts. The parakeets are a nice touch, and **Latham's** (see *Eating Out*) is a find.

**Hancock.** The Hancock Inn, one of the oldest continuously operating inns in New England, forms the centerpiece of this village, and **Norway Pond** shimmers on the edge. There's also a green with a bandstand. A number of the aristocratic old homes have been occupied by "summer people" since the mid–19th century. The

Robert Kozlow

ONE OF THE COUNTRY'S OLDEST CONTINUOUSLY OPERATING INNS FORMS A CENTERPIECE FOR HANCOCK VILLAGE.

**Harris Center for Conservation Education** (see *To Do—Hiking*) offers guided and unguided walks and workshops (also see *Lodging, Dining Out,* and *Eating Out*).

**Harrisville.** What excites historians about this pioneer mill village is the uncanny way in which it echoes New England's earliest villages. Here life revolved around the mills instead of the meetinghouse: The mill owner's mansion supplanted the parsonage, and the millpond was the common. What excites most other people about Harrisville is its beauty. This little community of brick and granite and white-trimmed buildings clusters around a millpond and along the steep **Goose Creek Ravine** below. The two mills have cupolas, and the string of wooden workers' houses, "Peanut Row," is tidy. Decades ago when the looms ceased weaving, townspeople worried that the village would become an industrial version of Old Sturbridge Village. Instead, new commercial uses have been found for the old buildings, a few of them appropriately filled by **Harrisville Designs** (see *To Do—Special Programs* and *Selective Shopping—Crafts*), founded by John Colony III the year after his family's mill closed. "Wool has been spun here every year since 1790," he notes. (Also see *Lodging*.)

**The Hillsboroughs.** This town is one of the region's more confusing areas, but it is rewarding once you figure out how it fits together. The oldest part of town, **Hillsborough Center,** is an incredibly photogenic grouping of more than a dozen late-18th- and early-19th-century houses with a church, graveyard, pond, and several open studios. It's up School Street beyond the **Fox State Forest** (see *Green Space*) from **Bridge Village,** a funky mill town with an unusual number of surviving wooden mills along the Contoocook River. Note the "Dutton Twins," two Greek Revival 1850s mansions on Main Street. The **Franklin Pierce Homestead** (see *To See—Historic Houses*) is in **Hillsboro Lower Village** (continue west on West Main Street, which is also Route 9, past the Sylvania bulb plant, and turn north on Route 31). On the banks of the Contoocook River, **Kemps Truck Museum** is said to hold the biggest collection of Mack trucks in the world. There are also two local swimming holes (see *To Do—Swimming*).

**Jaffrey Center.** Jaffrey itself is a workaday town, but Jaffrey Center, west on Route 124 just east of Mount Monadnock, is a gem. Its centerpiece is a white, steepled meetinghouse built in 1773, the site of the summer lecture series known as the **Amos Fortune Forum Series** (see *Entertainment*). Willa Cather, who spent many summers in attic rooms at the Shattuck Inn writing two of her best-known books—*My Antonia* and *Death Comes to the Archbishop*—is buried in the cemetery here. So are Amos Fortune (1710–1801), an African-born slave who bought his freedom, established a tannery, and left funds for the Jaffrey church and schools, and "Aunt" Hannah Davis (1784–1863), a beloved spinster who made, trademarked, and sold this country's first wooden bandboxes. The **Melville Academy Museum,** Thorndike Pond Road, Jaffrey Center, a Greek Revival schoolhouse built in 1833, houses an eclectic collection of Jaffrey artifacts and documents (open July and August, weekends 2–4 PM). The **Inn at Jaffrey Center** marks the middle of the village. The **Jaffrey Chamber of Commerce** (603-532-4549) offers local guidance. In Jaffrey itself, check out the **Jaffrey Civic Center** (603-532-6527), 40 Main Street (Route 124 west); open year-round, Tuesday 10 AM–6 PM, Wednesday 1–5 PM, Saturday 10 AM–2 PM. Here you'll find a historical society collection with information about past Jaffrey personalities—including Willa Cather, Amos Fortune, and Hannah Davis—and changing exhibits by local artists. Note *Buddies,* the World War I monument outside, carved from a single block of granite.

THE HARRISVILLE LIBRARY ON THE MILLPOND

Robert Kozlow

**Mason.** Another picture-perfect cluster of Georgian- and Federal-style homes around a classic Congregational church, complete with horse sheds and linked by stone walls. A historic marker outside one modest old house explains that this was the boyhood home of Samuel Wilson (1766–1844), generally known as "Uncle Sam" because the beef he supplied to the army during the War of 1812 was branded "U.S." We were lucky enough to first visit Mason with Elizabeth Orton Jones, illustrator of the Golden Book *Little Red Riding Hood.* Today the house that served as a basis for "Grandmother's House" is **Pickity Place,** an herb farm and restaurant (see *Dining Out*).

**Nelson.** This quiet gathering of buildings includes 1841 Greek Revival and Gothic Revival churches and an early, plain-faced but acoustically fine town hall that's the site of contra dancing every Monday night (see *Entertainment*).

**Stoddard.** Sited on a height-of-land that's said to divide the Connecticut and Merrimack River watersheds, Stoddard is known for the fine glass produced in three (long-gone) 19th-century factories. The **Stoddard Historical Society** is open Sunday 2–4 PM in July and August. **Pitcher Mountain,** with a picnic area and trailhead on Route 123, is a short hike yielding a spectacular view.

**Temple.** The common, framed by handsome old homes and a tavern (now the **Birchwood Inn;** see *Lodging* and *Dining Out*), is classic. Known for its glasswork in the 18th century, Temple is now known chiefly for its band, founded in 1799 (see *Entertainment*).

**Walpole.** A particularly handsome village of large, white-clapboard houses, some dating from the 1790s and more from the early and mid–19th century when Walpole was a popular summer haven with three large inns. Louisa May Alcott sum-

JAFFREY CENTER

Robert Kozlow

mered here, and Emily Dickinson visited; current residents include filmmaker Ken Burns. It's now off the beaten tourist track but offers pleasant lodging, dining, and golf. Summer band concerts are staged on the common. The **Walpole Historical Society** (603-756-3308), displaying a significant collection of paintings, photographs, furniture, and other local memorabilia, is housed on three floors of the old tower-topped academy building in the middle of the village and includes a large research library. It's open May through October, Wednesday and Saturday 2–4 PM and by special request. The village is set high above Route 12, with long views off across the Connecticut River to southern Vermont. Search out the common with its fine Congregational church, then take sustenance in the way of some of the world's best chocolate at **Burdick's** (see *Dining Out*).

**Wilton Center.** Just off Route 101, but seemingly many miles away, is a ridgeline of grand old houses ranging from 18th-century to late-19th-century summer homes. Continue through the center of town, and follow signs to the **Frye's Measure Mill** (603-654-6581), a shingled, 19th-century mill, its works still water-powered, that turns out Shaker-style boxes (also see *Selective Shopping*). The old grange hall houses **Andy's Summer Playhouse** (603-654-2613), a performance camp for children ages 8–18, who stage productions in July and August (see *Entertainment*).

## ✷ To See

*Must see:* In contrast to most regions, this one offers no significant "sights" beyond Mount Monadnock itself. The beauty of the villages (see above), the roads that connect them (see *To See—Scenic Drives*), and the surprises that you'll find along the way—swimming holes, antiques shops, art galleries, summer music, and small-town celebrations—are what this area is about. Peterborough is the most visitor-friendly town, good for dining and shopping.

### *In Keene*

A small city (population 22,500), Keene serves as shopping hub for a tristate area that includes southeastern Vermont and much of upcountry Massachusetts. The most interesting shopping is to be found in the **Colony Mill Marketplace** (see *Selective Shopping*), but Keene's long **Main Street,** the widest in New England, is well worth exploring. It includes the historic houses described below as well as **Keene State College** buildings like Elliot Hall, worth stepping inside to see the Barry Faulkner mural depicting Keene's **Central Square.** Some first-rate restaurants are clustered around the square itself, site of the high-steepled **United Church of Christ** (built in 1786), the town hall, and the chamber of commerce (see *Guidance*).

**Thorne-Sagendorph Gallery at Keene State College** (603-358-2720), Wyman Way off Main Street at Keene State College, Keene. Open during the academic year daily noon–4 PM, until 7 PM Thursday and Friday; in summer open Wednesday through Sunday noon–4 PM. A handsome, modern gallery. The permanent collection includes many 19th-century landscapes; there are also changing exhibits.

**Historical Society of Cheshire County** (603-352-1895), 246 Main Street,

Robert Kozlow

THE UNITED CHURCH OF CHRIST (1786) AND KEENE'S CENTRAL SQUARE

Keene 03431. Open Monday through Friday 9 AM–4 PM, Wednesday evening until 9, Saturday 9 AM–noon. An archival center for much of New England that features products once made in the area, including Keene and Stoddard glass. Changing exhibits are often worth checking.

**Horatio Colony House Museum** (603-352-0460), 199 Main Street, Keene. Open June through mid-October, Tuesday through Saturday 11 AM–4 PM and Saturday year-round; free. A Federal-era home filled with elegant family furnishings and souvenirs collected by Horatio and Mary Colony from their extensive travels throughout the world. Special collections include cribbage boards, walking sticks, Buddhas, beer steins, paperweights, and thousands of books.

**The Wyman Tavern** (603-352-1895), 339 Main Street, Keene. Open June through Labor Day, Thursday through Saturday 11 AM–4 PM. Maintained to represent the period between 1770 and 1820, this was the scene of the first meeting of the trustees of Dartmouth College under President Eleazar Wheelock in 1770. It was also from this site that 29 of Keene's Minutemen set out for Lexington in April 1775.

### *Elsewhere*

HISTORIC HOUSES **The Barrett Mansion** (603-878-2517), 79 Main Street (Route 123), New Ipswich. Open June through mid-October, Saturday and Sunday tours at 11 AM, noon, and 1, 2, 3, and 4 PM; admission $5, senior citizens $4, children $2.50. One of New England's finest Federal-style, rural mansions, built in 1800 as a wedding gift. The bride's father is said to have boasted that he would furnish as large a house as the groom's father could build. Both fathers outdid themselves, and it remained in the family until 1948. The rich furnishings are mainly Empire and Victorian, and they offer a sense of the surprisingly early sophistication of this area. Inquire about teas and other frequent special events.

**Franklin Pierce Homestead** (603-464-5858), 3 miles west of town near the junction of Routes 9 and 31, Hillsborough. Open daily in July and August, 10 AM–4 PM, Sunday 1–4 PM; otherwise weekends only from Memorial Day through Columbus

**IN PETERBOROUGH**

Far smaller than Keene, Peterborough (population 5,883) serves as the dining, shopping, and entertainment hub of the eastern half of the Monadnock region. Its walkable core is **Depot Square,** a gathering of galleries, shops, and restaurants that also offers parking and riverside picnicking. The former depot itself is now a popular restaurant; the old A&P is a bookstore and café, and the *Sharon Arts Center's* crafts and art gallery is a destination in itself. See *Dining Out, Entertainment,* and *Selective Shopping.* The **Peterborough Historical Society, Museum and Archives** (603-924-3235), 19 Grove Street. Open year-round Monday through Friday 10 AM–4 PM; donations accepted. An unusually large and handsome facility with an intriguing upstairs exhibit of the town's past products—from thermometers to soapstone stoves. Even a quick visit will help fill in the obviously missing buildings along Grove and Main Streets. Note the photos of the big old Tavern Hotel that stood at the head of Grove Street and in the middle of Main Street until 1965, of the depot, and of the Phoenix Cotton Mill that used to stand near the middle of town. A circa-1800 mill house has been preserved behind the museum, as well as well as an 1824 one-room schoolhouse, open by appointment only. A colonial kitchen can be seen in the museum, and the research library is extensive. Also check out the new **Mariposa Museum of World Culture** in the former Baptist Meeting House, 26 Main Street, open in summer and fall, daily noon–4 PM. Exhibits feature folk art, local and worldwide, with many special events.

Day; admission $3 adults. This is the restored, vintage-1804 home of the 14th president of the United States (1853–1857), the only one from New Hampshire. The hip-roofed, twin-chimney house was built in 1804 (2004 means a major celebration) by Benjamin Pierce, Franklin's father, two-time New Hampshire governor. It is beautifully restored to illustrate the gracious home Franklin knew as a boy.

FOR FAMILIES ✐ **Friendly Farm** (603-563-8444; www.friendlyfarm.com), Route 101, Dublin. Open daily 10 AM–5 PM (weather permitting), mid-May through mid-October, then weekends through mid-October. $5 per adult; $4.25 per child. Operated since 1965 by Allan and Bruce Fox, this 7-acre preserve is filled with barnyard animals: cows, horses, pigs, goats, sheep, donkeys, chickens, geese, turkeys, rabbits, and a working beehive. Feeding and cuddling welcome. Don't forget your camera. (We treasure photos of our presently 6-foot, 3-inch son feeding a Friendly Farm goat when he was still small enough to heft.)

✐ **Stonewall Farm** (603-357-7278; www.stonewallfarm.org), 242 Chesterfield Road, Keene. This working farm welcomes visitors on weekdays, 8:30 am–4:30 PM;

## COVERED BRIDGES

The Swanzey area, just south of Keene, boasts one of the densest concentrations of covered bridges east of Madison County. Our favorite is the white, red-roofed **Winchester–Ashuelot,** built in 1864 across the Ashuelot River just off Route 119 in Ashuelot. The 1830s **Winchester–Coombs bridge** across the Ashuelot is west of Route 10, half a mile southwest of Westport. The 1860s **Swanzey–Slate bridge** across the Ashuelot is east of Route 10 at Westport. The 1830s, 155-foot **Swanzey–West Swanzey bridge** across the Ashuelot is east of Route 10 at West Swanzey. **Swanzey–Sawyer's Crossing,** rebuilt in 1859, bridges the Ashuelot 1 mile north of Route 32 at Swanzey village. The **Swanzey–Carlton bridge** across the South Branch of the Ashuelot River is east of Route 32, half a mile south of Swanzey village. **The Swanzey Historical Museum,** Route 10 in West Swanzey (open June through foliage season, weekdays 10 AM–5 PM, weekends and holidays 10 AM–6 PM), dispenses maps locating the covered bridges and displays a Concord Coach, an Amoskeag steam fire pumper, and much more. Off by itself 1 mile east of Route 202 or 3.5 miles west of Greenfield is the **Hancock–Greenfield bridge,** built in 1937, which spans the Contoocook.

WINCHESTER–ASHUELOT COVERED BRIDGE

Robert Kozlow

call for weekend hours and special programs. Cows are milked at 4:30 daily, and there are hiking trails, a wetlands boardwalk, and a learning center. No admission fee.

Also see **Eccardt Farm** (603-495-3157), described under *To See—Scenic Drive* in "The Western Lakes." Phone the farm for directions from Antrim or Hillsborough.

**SCENIC DRIVES** **From the Boston area to Peterborough:** Take Route 119 to West Townsend and turn right over the bridge up Route 123, but at the first fork bear right on the unnumbered road to **Mason** (see *Villages*). Then take Route 123 into **Greenville,** a classic mill village (see the **Red Brick Inn** under *Eating Out*); Route 45 to Temple; and Route 101 into Peterborough.

**Hinsdale to Walpole:** Take Route 63, a high, rural road, past the entrance to **Pisgah State Park** (see *Green Space*) and on up to the hilltop village of **Chesterfield.** Drive across Route 9 (careful: it's a major east–west highway) on up Route 63 past **Spofford Lake** (see *To Do—Swimming*) and through Westmoreland, another vintage village, then on to **Park Hill,** a showstopper even by Monadnock village standards. Its meetinghouse was built in 1762 and a Paul Revere bell was installed in 1827; handsome early homes frame the hilltop common. At Westmoreland Depot continue north on Route 12 until you reach the yellow blinking lights, then go left up the hill into Walpole Village.

**Walpole to Hillsborough:** Take Route 12 to Route 123 and drive through **Drewsville** (another village you can fit in a photograph) to **Alstead** (see *Villages*), then on through East Alstead (unless you want to check out the **two covered bridges** on the way to Acworth) to **Marlow,** a pretty village by a lake. Be sure to stop at the trailhead for **Pitcher Mountain,** because it's a quick hike to the fire tower for a panoramic view. From here the road plunges down to Stoddard and on to its Mill Village (see *Villages*) where two adjacent general stores divide the town. Continue on along Route 23 to Route 9.

## ✷ To Do

**AIR RIDES** **SOAR** (603-672-5272), based in Mount Vernon, offers hang-gliding lessons.

Hot-air balloon rides are available in Hillsborough, home of the mid-July Hot Air Balloon Fest, from **Bellanger's** (603-464-3262) and **Ed Lappis** (603-478-5666).

**BICYCLING** The Monadnock region's many miles of back roads and widely scattered lodging places endear it to bicyclists of all abilities.

**Eclectic Bicycle** (603-924-9797), 109 Grove Street, Peterborough, offers full service, rentals, and routing maps.

**BOATING** **Boat rentals** are available at **Greenfield State Park** (603-547-3497), which also offers a boat launch on Otter Lake and at **Eastern Mountain Sports** (603-924-7231; see *Selective Shopping*) north of Peterborough on Route 202, handy to access points on ponds, lakes, and rivers. **Monadnock Outdoors** (603-

924-9832), based at Peterborough Manor (see *Lodging*) offers guided kayaking and canoeing half- and full-day paddles on local waters.

**Public boat landings** can also be found (ask locally to find them) in Antrim on Franklin Pierce Lake, Gregg Lake, and Willard Pond; in Bennington on Whittemore Lake; in Dublin on Dublin Lake; in Francestown on Pleasant Pond and Scobie Lake; in Hancock on Norway Pond; in Jaffrey on Frost Pond; and in Rindge on the Contoocook River, Emerson Pond, Grassy Pond, and Pool Pond. A popular canoe route begins in Peterborough, where the Contoocook River crosses under Route 202, with a takeout at Powder Mill Pond in Bennington. The Audubon Society of New Hampshire's Willard Pond is rich in water wildlife.

**CARRIAGE RIDES, SLEIGH RIDES, HAYRIDES** **Inn at East Hill Farm** (603-242-6495), Jaffrey Road, Troy. Sleigh rides along with cross-country skiing are offered to nonguests; also horseback riding.

**Silver Ranch** (603-532-7363), Route 124, Jaffrey. Carriage rides, hayrides, and sleigh rides are a tradition.

**Sleeper Hill Farm** (603-478-1100), Hillsborough. Carriage, hay, and sleigh rides; horseback riding.

**Stonewall Farm** (603-357-7278), 243 Chesterfield Road, Keene. Specializes in groups of 15 or more; hayrides, sleigh rides.

**Mount Monadnock** (603-532-8862), Monadnock State Park. Marked from Route 124, just west of Jaffrey Center. *Monadnock* is reportedly Algonquian for "mountain that stands alone," and in the early 19th century the name spread from this mountain to designate every solitary prominence in the world that rises above its surroundings. To distinguish it from all others, purists now call this mountain "Grand" Monadnock. It acquired its bald summit in the 1820s (see the introduction to this chapter) and has been one of the country's most popular hiking mountains ever since. In 1885 the town of Jaffrey managed to acquire 200 summit acres, and, with the help of the Society for the Protection of New Hampshire Forests (SPNHF), which still owns 3,672 acres, much of the rest of the mountain was gradually acquired. The state park on the western side of the mountain is 900 acres. There are 40 miles of trails and half a dozen varied routes up to the 3,165-foot summit. First-timers, however, are advised to follow either the White Dot or the White Cross Trail from the state park in Jaffrey. Detailed information about the mountain is available at a small museum, the Ecocenter. There are also rest rooms, a snack bar, and picnic grounds. The park and its 21-tent campground (see *Lodging—Campgrounds*) are open year-round, and 12 miles of marked, cross-country trails are maintained. Admission is $3 for visitors over age 11. Dogs are not permitted on the trails.

**FISHING** Anglers have discovered the Contoocook River as a source of cold-water species, especially above Hillsborough and the stretch along Route 202 north of Peterborough. The North Branch is stocked with trout.

**Hillsborough Trout Farm** (603-464-3026), 154 Old Henniker Road, Hillsborough. Three ponds are stocked with rainbow trout; no license needed, and you can rent a rod or buy bait.

**GOLF** **Angus Lea** (603-464-5405), Routes 9 and 202, Hillsboro. **Bretwood Golf Course** (603-352-7626), East Surry Road, Keene. Twenty-seven holes, par 72; driving range, pro shop, golf carts, snack bar. **Keene Country Club** (603-352-0135). Eighteen holes, par 72. **Monadnock Country Club** (603-924-7769), Peterborough. A nine-hole course with back tees for the second nine. **Tory Pines Resort** (603-588-2923), Route 47, Francestown. Eighteen holes, Donald Ross design, par 72. Full pro shop, packages including dining, lodging, and golf school. (Also see *Other Lodging*.) **Hooper Golf Club** (603-756-4020), Prospect Hill, Walpole. Nine holes. **Woodbound Inn Golf Club** (603-532-8341), Woodbound Road, Jaffrey. Nine holes, rental clubs, par-3 course.

**GREYHOUND RACING** **Hinsdale Greyhound Park** (603-336-5382; 1-800-NH-TRACK), Route 119, Hinsdale. Year-round racing, dining room, club room.

**HIKING** (Also see *Green Space*.)

**Crotched Mountain.** Three trails lead to this 2,055-foot summit. The start of the Bennington Trail is marked 3 miles north of Greenfield on Route 31. The Greenfield Trail starts just beyond the entrance to Crotched Mountain Rehabilitation Center (also on Route 31). The Francestown Trail starts beyond the entrance to the former Crotched Mountain Ski Area on Route 47.**Harris Center for Conservation Education** (603-525-3394); follow signs from Hancock village. A nonprofit land trust and education center with 7 miles of hiking trails, including two mountains with summit views; guided hikes and snowshoeing treks offered on weekends.

**Long-distance trails.** Hikers are advised to pick up trail maps to the following trails from the Monadnock State Park Ecocenter (see Mount Monadnock, above).

**Metacomet Trail**—the northernmost 14 miles of a trail that theoretically leads to Meriden, Connecticut. The two most popular sections are Little Monadnock, accessible from the parking lot at Rhododendron State Park in Fitzwilliam, and Gap Mountain, accessible from trailheads on Route 124 west of Jaffrey Center from a spot just east of the Troy town dump. The trail is marked with white rectangles and is famed for its abundance of wild blueberries in July.

**Monadnock–Sunapee Trail.** The 47-mile, northern continuation of the Metacomet Trail, originally blazed in the 1920s by the SPNHF, was reblazed in the early 1970s by Appalachian Mountain Club volunteers. It descends Mount Monadnock on the Dublin Trail, then cuts across Harrisville, through Nelson village, up and down Dakin and Hodgeman Hills in Stoddard, up Pitcher Mountain (a rewarding stretch to hike from Route 123 in Stoddard), and up Hubbard Hill (prime blueberry picking). It then goes up 2,061-foot Jackson Hill, through Washington, and up through successive, high ridges in Pillsbury State Park to Sunapee. Sounds great to us, but since we've never done it, be sure to pick up a detailed trail map from the Ecocenter, which displays a topographic relief map of the entire trail.

**Wapack Trail.** A 21-mile ridgeline trail with many spectacular views from North Pack Monadnock in Greenfield to Mount Watatic in Massachusetts. The trail crosses roads about every 4 miles. Just west of Miller State Park on Route 101, turn right onto Mountain Road, continue until the road makes a T, then turn right. After the road turns to gravel, look for a trail to your right. You will see a parking area. A 45-minute climb here yields great views.

**Willard Pond,** Hancock Village, is a wildlife sanctuary with Bald Mountain on the north, surrounded by large glacial boulders. You can walk around the northern side of the pond and hike to the top of Bald Mountain, from which there is a spectacular view.

SPA **The Grand View Inn & Resort** (603-532-9880; www.thegrandviewinn.com), Route 124, 4.5 miles west of Jaffrey, open daily 7 AM–10 PM. Housed in a converted stable, this attractive day spa offers a full menu of services: a variety of massages, herbal, mud, and parafango wraps, as well as a steam room and sauna, great for the day after hiking.

SPECIAL PROGRAMS **Harrisville Designs** (603-827-3996; www.Harrisville.com), Harrisville 03450. Open Tuesday through Saturday, 10 AM–5 PM. Weekend and multiday weaving workshops, as well as sessions featuring knitting, felting, and other skills, are held throughout the year; some are simply introductions to weaving, others are specialized and advanced courses. The workshops are held in the Weaving Center overlooking the millpond, and lodging is available in nearby B&Bs and in the Cheshire Mills Boardinghouse, built in 1850 for transient weavers. Daylong workshops are also offered; request a schedule.

**Sharon Arts Center** (603-924-7256; www.sharonarts.org), Route 123, Sharon. This newly rebuilt facility is a venue for year-round day, weekend, and multiday courses in drawing and painting, glass, basketmaking, photography, weaving, jewelry, ceramics, and more.

**Great River Arts** (603-756-3638; www.greatriverarts.org), 47 Main Street, Walpole. A variety of literary and visual arts workshops and programs are offered by this relatively new nonprofit institute. The Granary, a historic barn, is slated to house all programs, but at present most are held at Alyson's Apple Orchard (see *Other Lodging* and Walpole under *Villages*).

**The Old School** (603-878-1758), 23 Hadley Highway, Temple 03084. A former brick schoolhouse with long windows now houses this yoga retreat center (founder Robert Moses is widely known in ashtanga yoga circles), just off the common of a classic Monadnock village. Facilities include the Yoga Hall, a meditation hall in a separate building, and accommodations for 16 guests in dorm-style rooms with a separate bathhouse. The center is also handy to several B&Bs. See Temple under *Villages*.

**SWIMMING** Although the region is spotted with clear lakes and ponds, public beaches are jealously held by towns—understandably, given their proximity to Boston. Guests at local inns and B&Bs, of course, have access to local sand and water.

*In Alstead:* **Vilas Pool,** just off Route 123. Open in summer Wednesday through Sunday. A dammed pool in the Cold River with bathhouse and picnic area. **Lake Warren** has swimming from the public landing.

*In Greenfield:* **Greenfield State Park** (603-547-3497), off Route 136, offers a beach that's mobbed on summer Sundays but not midweek. $2.50 per person.

*In Hillsborough:* Options include **Franklin Pierce Lake** (Manhattan Park is just off Route 9) and **Beard Brook** (along Beard Road), both at the shaded public beach and at the Glean Falls bridge.

*In Jaffrey:* **Contoocook Lake Beach,** a small but lovely strip of soft sand along Quantum Road east of the junction of Routes 124 and 202 (take Stratton Road to Quantum), and **Sciatic Park Beach** on Thorndike Pond near the main entrance to Monadnock State Park are both open to nonresidents; weekend fee.

*In Rindge:* **Pearly Pond** adjacent to the Franklin Pierce College campus is good for swimming and picnicking.

*In Roxbury:* **Otter Brook Recreation Area,** Route 9, northwest of Keene. A human-made lake with lawns and sandy beach that can fit the bill on a hot day. Fee.

*In Spofford:* **Spofford Lake,** Route 9. Town-run beach.

*In Surry:* **Surry Mountain Dam and Lake,** Route 12A not far north of Keene, offers a sand beach, as well as picnicking. Free.

*In Swanzey:* Swanzey Lake and Wilson Pond.

## ✷ Winter Sports

**SLEIGH RIDES** See *Carriage Rides, Sleigh Rides, Hayrides,* under *To Do,* above.

**CROSS-COUNTRY SKIING** Also see *Green Space.* **Windblown** (603-878-2869), Route 124 west of the village, New Ipswich. Open Thursday through Sunday and holidays. Since 1972 Al Jenks has been constantly expanding and improving his high, wooded spread that straddles the Wapack Trail. Thanks to the elevation and northerly exposure, this 40 km network frequently has snow when the ground is bare just 10 miles away. There's an unusual variety to the trails: easy loops from the ski shop and around Wildlife Pond; wooded, more difficult trails up on the Wapack; backcountry trails, including a climb to Mount Watatic (1,800 feet high); and a long, 75-foot-wide, open slope for practicing telemarking. Hot soups, sandwiches, and home-baked munchies are served at the shop; there's a warming hut and a couple of cabins. Rentals, instruction. Trail fee.

**The Inn at East Hill Farm** (603-242-6495), Jaffrey Road, Troy. Some 13 miles of trails meander gently around this property with its great view of Mount Monadnock. Rentals and instruction are offered, and informal meals are available at the inn. A warming hut on the trail, with fireplace and woodstove, serves hot drinks on weekends. Trail fee.

**Sargent Center** (603-525-3311), Windy Row, Peterborough. A dozen miles of cross-country trails web this 850-acre property maintained by Boston University.

**Woodbound Inn** (603-532-8341), Jaffrey. Fourteen km of wooded trails; rental equipment. Trail fee.

**Mount Monadnock State Park** (603-532-8862), Dublin Road from Route 124, Jaffrey Center. A 12-mile, well-marked but ungroomed system of trails webs the base of the mountain; loops from 1 mile to more than 7 miles. Winter camping is also available. Entrance fee: $3 over age 11. No dogs allowed.

## ✷ Green Space

*Also see* Hiking *and* Swimming *under To Do.*

### *In the Keene area*

**Bear Den Geological Park,** Route 10, Gilsum. Look for a large pull-off area on the right (heading north). This is a geologically fascinating area, with glacial potholes and caves.

**Cathedral of the Pines** (603-899-3300; www.cathedralpines.com), marked from Route 119, a few miles east of Route 202, Rindge. Open for an Easter sunrise service, then May through mid-October, 9 AM to dusk. Tall pine trees shelter simple wooden benches, and the backdrop of the ridgetop stone altar is Mount Monadnock, rising grandly beyond intervening, heavily wooded hills. The roadside farmhouse and its 400 acres had been the summer home of Douglas and Sibyl Sloane for quite some time before the 1938 hurricane exposed this magnificent view, and their son Sandy picked the site for his future home. When Sandy was shot down over Germany in 1944, his parents dedicated the hilltop "cathedral" to his memory. In 1956 the U.S. Congress recognized it as a national memorial to all American war dead. It's used for frequent nondenominational services and for weddings (performed in the nearby stone Hilltop House in case of rain). On the stone Memorial Bell Tower at the entrance to the pine grove, four bronze bas-reliefs, designed by Norman Rockwell, honor American women. A museum in the basement of the Hilltop House is a mix of religious and military pictures and artifacts, thousands of items donated by visitors from throughout the country. Visitors are welcome to stroll the extensive grounds. Please: No dogs, no smoking, no picnicking (the Annett Wayside Area is a mile up the road). The **Cathedral House Bed & Breakfast** (603-899-6790) caters wedding receptions and is otherwise geared to the many weddings in the adjoining "cathedral." Ecumenical services are every Sunday, May through October, 9:15 AM; an Easter sunrise service usually begins at 5:45 AM.

**Charles L. Pierce Wildlife and Forest Reservation,** Stoddard. From Route 9 in Stoddard, follow Route 123 north approximately 2 miles; turn right at the fire station; cross the bridge. At the junction go straight on a dirt road approximately 1 mile; park in the lot 300 feet beyond the woods road, on the left. The 5-mile Trout-n-Bacon Trail, beginning at a small brook to the left of the road, offers outstanding views from Bacon Ledge and leads to Trout Pond. This is a 3,461-acre preserve with more than 10 miles of hiking trails and woods roads that wind over ridges, through deep forest, and around beaver dams. The Society for the Protection of New Hampshire Forests (SPNHF) also owns the 379-acre Thurston V. Williams Forest and the 157-acre Daniel Upton Forest in Stoddard.

**Chesterfield Gorge,** Route 9, Chesterfield. Open weekends from Memorial Day, daily from late June through mid-October. Footpaths along the gorge were carved by a stream that cut deep into ledges. The 0.5-mile trail crosses the stream several times, and there are plenty of picnic tables within sound and sight of the rushing water. Nominal fee on weekends and holidays.

**Horatio Colony Trust,** off Daniels Road (take a left 0.5 mile west of the blinking light on Route 9), Keene. A 450-acre bird and animal preserve with marked trails through the woods.

**Piper Memorial Forest,** off Route 9, East Sullivan. A 199-acre wooded SPNHF property traversed by a loop trail to the top of Boynton Hill.

**Pisgah State Park** (603-239-8153), Routes 63 and 119, 2 miles east of Chesterfield. A 13,500-acre, largely undeveloped area with pit toilets and old logging trails (good for hiking and cross-country skiing), plus ponds to satisfy the adventurous angler.

**Rhododendron State Park** (603-239-8153), Route 119 west of the village, Fitzwilliam. The wild rhododendrons grow up to 30 feet high and are salted along paths above wildflowers and ferns and under pine trees. It is one of those deeply still and beautiful places. These *Rhododendron maximum* bloom in mid-July. A great place for a picnic. $3 day-use fee.

### *In the Peterborough and eastern Monadnock area*

**Fox State Forest** (603-464-3453), Center Road, Hillsborough. Twenty miles of trails within 1,445 acres of woodland. A detailed booklet guide is available from the state's Division of Forests Office in Concord.

**Gap Mountain Reservation,** Jaffrey. From Troy, follow Route 12 south 0.4 mile; turn left onto Quarry Road; continue past transmission lines. At a sharp left in the road, a woods road continues straight uphill. Park and hike up the hill. Near the top, trail markers bear left through the woods. Gap Mountain is a favorite with berriers and picnickers. The 1,107-acre preserve includes three peaks, two bays, and a rich variety of plants and wildlife.

**Greenfield State Park** (603-547-3497), Route 136, 1 mile west of Greenfield. A 401-acre preserve with a half-mile frontage on Otter Lake; 252 tent sites access their own beach. (Also see *To Do—Boating* and *Swimming*.)

**The Heald Tract,** off Route 31 in Wilton. A Society for the Protection of New Hampshire Forests (SPNHF) preserve with fairly flat trails, pond views.

**MacDowell Reservoir** (603-924-3431), Peterborough. Good for picnicking, boating, fishing. Maintained by the U.S. Army Corps of Engineers.

**McCabe Forest,** Antrim. Take Route 202 north from Antrim for 0.2 mile; turn right onto Elm Street Extension; turn right to the parking area. This former 192-acre farm has 2 miles of trails, including a fine self-guided interpretive trail, and a variety of wildlife.

**Monadnock State Park** (603-532-3672), off Route 124 or Dublin Road, west of

Jaffrey. In addition to 40 miles of New England's most popular trails (see *To Do—Hiking*), the park includes 21 tent sites, picnic grounds, a visitors center, a park store, and ski-touring trails.

**Pack Monadnock Mountain** in Miller State Park (603-924-7433), Route 101, 3 miles east of Peterborough. For those who don't feel up to climbing Mount Monadnock, this 2,300-foot-high summit is a must. A 1.5-mile winding, steep, but paved road leads to the top, where there are walking trails, picnic sites, and views of Vermont to the west and (on a good day) Boston skyscrapers to the south. Opened in 1891, this was New Hampshire's first state park.

🐾 **Shieling Forest,** off Old Street Road, Peterborough (marked from Route 202 north of town). This is one place you can walk your dog. There are 45 acres of tree-covered ridges and valleys, and a forestry learning center.

## ✱ Lodging

### INNS

### *In and around Keene*

🐾 **Chesterfield Inn** (603-256-3211; 1-800-365-5515; www.chesterfield-inn.com), Route 9, West Chesterfield 03466. The original house served as a tavern from 1798 to 1811, but the present facility is a contemporary country inn with a large, attractive dining room overlooking Vermont hills, a spacious parlor, and 15 guest rooms scattered between the main house and the Guest House. All rooms have a sitting area, phone, controlled heat or air-conditioning, and optional TV and wet bar; some have working fireplace or Jacuzzi. Innkeepers Phil and Judy Hueber have created a popular dining room (see *Dining Out*) and a comfortable, romantic getaway spot that's well positioned for exploring much of southern Vermont as well as the Monadnock region and Connecticut River Valley. The inn is set back from busy Route 9, much closer to Brattleboro, Vermont, than to Keene. $150–275 double includes breakfast; inquire about MAP rates. Pets are accepted with advance permission.

♿ **E. F. Lane Hotel** (603-357-7070; 1-888-300-5056; www.someplacesdifferent.com), 30 Main Street, Keene 03431. Shop till you drop in downtown Keene, then mosey on into what was once Goodnow's, known for a century as the area's finest department store. The newest member of the Someplace(s) Different hotel chain, this stately 1890 brick and granite structure is now doing a star turn as the city's most luxurious "inn" spot. Its 40 rooms vary in size from large to two-story Chairman Suites suitable for a small household. Although no two are alike, each is furnished in elegant period style and is equipped with high-speed Internet access, compuer/fax modems, and individual temperature control. Many suites offer whirlpool tub and separate sitting room. The **Salmon Chase Bistro** (see *Dining Out*) offers a light breakfast buffet, included in the $129–285 room rate. Check for corporate and group rates.

**The Walpole Inn** (603-756-3320; www.walpoleinn.com), R.R. 1, Box 762, 297 Main Street, Walpole 03608. Originally, this distinguished Colonial was home to Col. Benjamin Bellows, commander of Fort Number Three, a strategic garrison along the Connecticut River during the French and Indian War. Now, in another life, it offers a restaurant that's among the best in the area (see *Dining Out*) and eight quietly elegant guest rooms, each furnished in chic understatement with a pencil-post, queen-sized bed and simple, tailored linens. Four have walk-in shower; the others feature luxurious soaking tub with shower. You can choose among chess in the paneled parlor, tennis on the grounds, or golf at the nearby Hooper Golf Course. A full breakfast comes with an artist's view of meadows and hills, and is included in the $130–160 rate.

🐾 ✐ **Inn at East Hill Farm** (603-242-6495; 1-800-242-6495; www.east-hill-farm.com), Troy 03465. This isn't a fancy place, but over the years (since 1973) David and Sally Adams have created a lively, friendly family resort. The core of the complex is an 1830s inn with a fireplace in its living room and a large dining room in which meals are served at long tables; it's frequently cleared for square dances and other events. In all there are now 70 guest rooms and family units, all with private bath. Facilities include an indoor and two outdoor pools, a lake beach, tennis, shuffleboard, and boats. Waterskiing, horseback riding, and a children's program are also available, and the barn is filled with animals. $78–88 per person plus 15 percent gratuity; children's rates; all three meals are included and weekly rates available. Credit cards accepted but not for gratuities.

**The Wright Mansion Inn & Conference Center** (603-355-2288; 1-800-352-5890; www.wrightmansioninn.com), 695 Court Street, Keene 03431. Guests will feel to the manor born in this redbrick, Georgian-style mansion, built in 1930 for the grandson of the Wright Silver Polish Company. Although the original 15 acres is now mostly developed into condominiums, the home still evokes memories of another era. The linen finger towels and chinoisserie wallpaper in the entry powder room are typical of the decor. Upstairs, there are six tastefully furnished guest rooms, two with working fireplace, four with private tiled bath. All have phone, cable TV, and air-conditioning. Rates are $80–175, depending on season; $15 lower for additional nights. Arrange ahead if you want to have dinner in the sumptuous dining room (see *Dining Out*).

*Note*: At this writing the landmark **Fitzwilliam Inn** in Fitzwilliam is closed, awaiting new ownership.

### *In and around Peterborough*

♿ **The Hancock Inn** (603-525-3318; 1-800-525-1789; www.hancockinn.com), 33 Main Street, Hancock 03449. Built in 1789 and the state's oldest, this inn has a late-19th-century look, thanks to two-story pillars and a mansard roof. It sits in the center of a picture-perfect village, with Norway Pond shimmering at one end of the street. Innkeeper Robert Short offers 13 guest rooms (all with private bath), with elegantly classic country inn decor: canopy and four-poster beds, handmade quilts, braided and hooked rugs, rockers, and wingback chairs. One room is decorated with genuine Rufus Porter stencils, and authentic 1830s stencil patterns decorate many of the other rooms as well. The tavern room serves light meals in the evening, and the dining room, which has been sponge-painted a deep cranberry (see *Dining Out*), is open to the public. $120–250 double plus 10 percent service charge; no smoking, no children under 12. See Hancock under *Villages*.

**Inn at Jaffrey Center** (603-532-7800; 1-877-510-7019; www.theinnatjaffreycenter.com). Under ownership by Noel and Stephen Pierce and his brother Max Mitchell, this fine old landmark (formerly the Monadnock Inn) has blossomed. The 11 rooms, all upstairs, have been deftly, tastefully decorated in soft, pleasing colors, each different and varying widely in size but all with private bath. The old plumbing has been retained: Claw-foot tubs have been glazed and sinks refitted. Furnishings are a mix of antiques and reproductions. The food is superb, too (see *Dining Out*), but we lament the loss of the parlor, now another dining room. While families are welcome and some guest rooms are quite large (there's also a two-room suite), shared space is limited to the tavern and dining areas. See Jaffrey Center under *Villages*.

NELSON, ONE OF THE MANY PICTURESQUE MONADNOCK REGION TOWNS

Robert Kozlow

ꝏ **The Grand View Inn & Resort** (603-532-9880; www.thegrandviewinn.com), 580 Mountain Road, Jaffrey 03452. The inn itself is a white brick mansion set off in its own 330 acres at the base of Mount Monadnock. The former stables, just below the inn, have been transformed into a spa facility, with a full menu of treatments (see *To Do*), and **Churchill's,** a restaurant, open to the public (see *Dining Out*). Common space includes formal living and dining rooms, a large screened porch, and a breakfast room. Guest rooms, divided between the mansion and the neighboring "Tom Thumb cottage," are pleasant but we think a bit high for what they are at $100–125 for the three smallest rooms (two with shared bath), $170–175 for the remaining five, and $250 for a suite with a sitting room, fireplace, and a bath with Jacuzzi and steam shower. Facilities include a pool, outdoor hot tub, game and smoking rooms. Weddings are a specialty. Horses can be boarded in the stables across the road.

**The Birchwood Inn** (603-878-3285), Route 45, Temple 03084. Henry Thoreau is counted among past guests at this small brick inn, built around 1800 in the center of a tiny back road village. Since 1980 Bill and Judy Wolfe have taken personal pride in both the kitchen and the seven guest rooms (five with private bath), each decorated around a theme and each very different. There's a cheerful BYOB bar and a fine little dining room with 1820s murals by Rufus Porter (see *Dining Out*). $69–79 double, breakfast included; single rates also offered. See Temple under *Villages*.

**Woodbound Inn** (603-532-8341; 1-800-688-7770; www.woodbound.com), 62 Woodbound Road, Rindge

03461. A rambling old inn complex set in 200 wooded acres on Contoocook Lake. Owned now by the Kohlmorgan family, it caters to groups and families. More than half of the 47 units are motel-style in a newer annex (preferable to rooms in the main inn), and there are six lakeside cabins with fireplaces. Facilities include a nine-hole golf course, cross-country ski trails and rentals, and a private beach. Pets permitted in cabins. $89–135 per couple for bed & breakfast; EP and MAP rates also available.

## BED & BREAKFASTS

### *In and around Keene*

**Hannah Davis House** (603-585-3344), 106 Route 119, Fitzwilliam 03447. Kaye and Mike Terpstra have turned an 1820s Federal-style house into an outstanding bed & breakfast. Guests enter through a cheery, light- and flower-filled country kitchen and gather in the sitting and breakfast rooms or on the deck overlooking a beaver pond. All three of the upstairs bedrooms have been nicely furnished. Our favorite is Chauncey's Room, with bold colors, a queen-sized, antique iron bed, and a working fireplace. There is also a downstairs suite with a king bed and working wood-burning fireplace. The most sumptuous accommodation (great for a family) is, however, upstairs in the old carriage house. Named Popovers, it has a private entrance, deck, cathedral ceiling, and wall of windows overlooking the beaver pond, also a wood-burning fireplace, antique cannonball bed (a queen), and a sleeper sofa. Downstairs in the carriage house is the Loft, a romantic hideaway with its own entrance, a sitting room with fireplace and a bath downstairs, and a loft-style sleeping area. $70–140 per room includes an extravagant breakfast. See Fitzwilliam under *Villages*.

**The Inn at Valley Farms** (603-756-2855; 1-877-327-2855; www.innatvalleyfarms.com), R.R. 1, Box 280, Wentworth Road, Walpole 03608. As if the bucolic setting (105 acres bordering an apple orchard) weren't enough, this circa-1774 treasure, hidden up the hill from Walpole village, also offers exceptionally handsome, antiques-filled guest rooms along with lovely common rooms, including a formal parlor and dining room, and a sun room overlooking the garden. Upstairs in the main house there is a two-bedroom suite with bath, along with two other bedrooms, each with four-poster bed, private bath, phone, and dataport. Niceties include fresh flowers, plush robes, and Burdick chocolate good-night treats. Family travelers can choose one of two, three-bedroom cottages, each with kitchen and living area. Innkeepers Jacqueline and Dane Badders are serious about organic gardening and cooking, which makes breakfast a truly farm-fresh treat. Rates for the inn are $125–160 with full breakfast. Cottages, which sleep six, are $160 for two, plus $15 per person under 12; $25 per person over 12.

**The Carriage Barn Guest House** (603-357-3812; www.carriagebarn.com), 358 Main Street, Keene 03431. Dave Rouillard, a retired fifth-grade teacher, is the enthusiastic host of this B&B attached to the back of a large home just past the college on the southern end of Keene's Main Street. His librarian wife, Marilee, knows the area well and can direct you to downtown shops, movies, restaurants, and a host of nearby activities. Behind their large home, a converted Civil War–era barn now holds four guest rooms, each with private bath, a large sitting room with TV and phone, and a sunny breakfast room. $65–100 double includes tax as well as a continental "plus" breakfast. Children over 5 are welcome.

**Darby Brook Farm** (603-835-6624; www.howard@darbybrookfarm.com), Alstead 03602. Open May through October. Alstead is in the little-touristed northwestern corner of the region, handy to canoeing on the Connecticut River; there's also a choice of swimming holes in town. Howard Weeks has summered all his life in this Federal-style house that's been changed little by the three families who have owned it since the 1790s. Weeks has devoted his retirement to maintaining the house and its 10-acre hay field, the apple orchard above the field, and the berry bushes and sizable vegetable garden just behind the house. He also takes care of a few chickens. The two large front rooms share a bath but have working fireplaces, set in their original paneling, and the $40 per-person rate includes tax as well as a full breakfast, served in the elegant old dining room.

**Goose Pond Guest House** (603-357-4787; www.goosepondguesthouse.com), East Surry Road (2 miles north of Central Square, past the hospital off Court Street, and 0.6 mile past Bretwood Golf Course), Keene 03431. Set on a knoll along a pretty country road, this vintage, 15-room 1790 Colonial is a classic. There are three guest rooms, each furnished stylishly in period antiques. One is a suite with its own entrance, fridge, woodstove, and private terrace. Depending on the season, you can hike, swim, or skate at nearby Goose Pond; golf at the 27-hole course next door; or simply amble the surrounding 13 acres. The $90–140 rate for two ($20 for a third person) includes continental breakfast in the formal dining room. Nonsmoking.

♿ **Green Meadow Nature Escape** (603-835-6580; www.tamarackfarm.com), Route 123A, Acworth; mailing address Box 215, Alstead 03602. Six generations have owned and operated this family farm. Now Tim and Clare Gowen have decided to "share the beautiful land with others" by opening a bed & breakfast for folks with a hankering to get back to nature. In early spring that means boiling maple syrup; in late summer, harvesting hay. The newly renovated house offers five guest rooms, each with private bath (some with whirlpool) and views of the hills and meadows. For the best view of all, enjoy an afternoon on the deck in the hot tub or, for the more adventuresome, a tube ride down Cold River. The pool is up the hill. Rates, $95–170, include a farm-fresh breakfast—naturally. A fixed-price dinner ($22.95) is served Friday and Saturday nights. (See Tamarack Farm under *Dining Out*.)

♿ **Inn of the Tartan Fox** (1-877-836-4319; 603-357-9308; www.tartanfox.com), 350 Old Homestead Highway, Swanzey 03446. Once known as Meademere, this Arts & Crafts-style stone cottage, with its mahogany woodwork and and cobblestone fireplace, is an unexpected architectural surprise. Owners Meg and Wayne Miller offer four recently-renovated guest rooms, each furnished with Eastlake-era antiques and a signature tartan plaid. Private bathrooms boast heated marble floors. One, which opens onto a patio, has a shower wide enough for a wheelchair. The four-course breakfast, included in the $80–120 rate (for two), is an elegant affair.

**Stonewall Farm** (603-478-1947), 235 Windsor Road, Hillsborough 03244. Halfway between Concord and Keene, this imposing farmhouse is two minutes off Route 9 and two centuries off the beaten track. Built in 1785, the house crowns a quiet ridge, looking much the same as it probably did when neighbors Franklin Pierce (the only New Hampshire native to serve as president) and his father Benjamin used to come to call. (See *To See* for information about the **Pierce Homestead.**) Current owners Skip and Meg Curtis have researched the home's history. Nearly every room has a framed document or photo relating to the past. One summer day when we visited, the house was cool. It was equally inviting in February when the Glenwood stove in the big country kitchen was the obvious congregating spot. The five guest rooms, each with private bath, are pleasant, furnished with antiques and feature antique linens and quilts. The 6 acres of grounds include walking paths, raspberry bushes, and the possibility of a game of croquet, horseshoes, or volleyball. Meg is a serious cook who throws her all into breakfast, included in $85–135 double. Crated, trained dogs are welcome.

**The Maples of Poocham** (603-399-8457; 1-800-659-6810; www.themaplesofpoocham.com), 283 Poocham Road, Westmoreland 03467. Where's Waldo? Find Larry McFarland's furry golden retriever friend and you'll have found this cozy retreat located on a back road off Route 63. When we visited one cold day in February, Waldo beckoned along with a group of hanging lanterns on the porch. In summer you might find an upturned canoe and hanging planters. Inside, bright colors and books continue the genial atmosphere. Two upstairs bedrooms share a bath across the hall. Weekdays, there's cereal, muffins, fruit, and coffee laid out in the dining room; on weekends, owner Larry is around to cook pancakes, eggs, or French toast. He'll also give directions to hiking trails and the nearby heron rookery. Rates range $50–70, depending on season. Pets are welcome with advance notice and deposit.

**Post and Beam B&B** (603-847-3339; 1-888-3-ROMANCE; www.postandbeambb.com), Box 18, Centre Street, Sullivan 03445. From Keene Route 9 is the fast, not the scenic, route northwest to Hillsborough, and it's easy to whiz by some glorious backcountry to which this hospitable B&B is the key. The house itself dates in part back to 1797, and its open kitchen/gathering place is indeed open-beamed. The seven rooms are furnished with what its genial hosts call "friendly furniture," and the whole place exudes informal hospitality and helpfulness when it comes to making the most of the area's hiking, biking, and shopping. We happened by on a particularly hot day and were quickly issued towels and directed to the **Otter River Recreation Area** (see *To Do—Swimming*) just down the road. Your hosts are Darcy Bacall and Priscilla Hardy; rates are $100–125 during the mid-September through October foliage season, otherwise $75–95, and include a very full breakfast. Inquire about the rental cottage in Harrisville, accommodating 13.

**The Amos A. Parker House** (603-585-6540; www.amosparkerhouse.com), Fitzwilliam 03447. Serious gardeners will be particularly pleased by this elegant 18th-century retreat that is, sadly, up for sale. Bordering a beaver pond, the garden harbors a couple thousand plants in a dozen distinct beds, including many species we have never seen elsewhere. Common space included a book-lined den as well as a formal front parlor. All guest rooms have private bath and are furnished with carefully chosen antiques; three have working fireplace. There's also a downstairs suite with garden view and a small kitchen. Candlelight breakfasts are full and elaborate. $95–110 double.

**Ashburn House** (603-585-7198), 20 Upper Troy Road, Fitzwilliam 03447. Tina and David Ashton settled in Fitzwilliam in 1996, not only buying an antique village house and filling it with English antiques but also opening **Old England Enterprises Antiques** on the common. Tina added stenciling throughout the B&B. Three guest rooms all have private bath (we like the Rose Bedroom with its antique pine, roses, and cherubs). Smokers will feel comfortable here; common space includes both smoking and nonsmoking "lounges." The dining room is particularly attractive. $80–90 per night, taxes included.

### *In and around Peterborough*

**Apple Gate B&B** (603-924-6543), 199 Upland Road, Peterborough 03458. Ken and Dianne Legenhausen's 1832 house sits beside an apple orchard not far from the Sharon Arts Center. It's all very tasteful yet cozy—the double parlor, fireplace, and piano in the living room, and the low-beamed dining room. All four guest rooms, ranging from an inviting single in the back to spacious doubles (one with twin beds), have private bath. Rooms are named for apples (we particularly like the sunny Cortland Room), which also figure in breakfast dishes—like baked apple with spinach pie or baked apple pancakes. Many small touches, like the fridge under the stairs, make guests feel welcome. $70–85 double includes a full candlelit breakfast. No children under 12 and no smoking, please.

**Auk's Nest** (603-878-3443; auksnest@cs.com), 204 East Road, Temple 03084. Anne Lunt's 1770s Cape sits at the edge of an apple orchard. It's filled with books and antiques, and offers a low-beamed living room with a Rumford fireplace and three guest rooms. A country breakfast is served in a sunny, stenciled dining room looking out on gardens and an orchard or, in summer, on the screened-in porch overlooking a meadow. Walks, tennis, swimming, and skiing are all within minutes. Both pets and children are welcome by prior arrangement. From $40 single to $50 double, full breakfast included.

**Peterborough Manor Bed & Breakfast** (603-924-9832; www.peterboroughmanor.com), 50 Summer Street, Peterborough 03458. Over the years Ann and Peter Harrison have restored this 1890s Victorian mansion, creating a reasonably priced B&B catering to outdoorspeople. The seven rooms are unusually large and comfortable, most with both a double and a single bed and phone, six with private bath. Two rooms have twin beds and a half bath; some have cable TV. The kitchen is available for those who want to make their own meals, but Peterborough's many dining options are just down the street. Ann comes from an old local innkeeping family, and Peter is from Australia via New Zealand. Both are avid hikers (on our last visit Peter had just climbed Mount Kilimanjaro) and knowledgeable about local trails and biking routes, to which

Ann has authored a guide. Under the name **Monadnock Outdoors,** she offers guided half- and full-day kayak trips. Continental breakfast is included in $60 single, $65 double; $10 per extra person. Children and small dogs (no cats) accepted.

**Three Maples B&B** (603-924-3503; www.threemaples.com), Route 123, Sharon. Directly across from the Sharon Art Center, a fine old country home dating in part to 1795, set behind three, century-old sugar maples. Linda and Dan Claff have created an appealing haven with three guest rooms. One downstairs, furnished in white cottage furniture and a brightly quilted bed, has a two-person sauna as well as a bath. Upstairs are two more nicely furnished rooms, one with a four-poster canopy queen and an extra-deep jet tub. The living room and two of the guest rooms feature gas fireplaces. A full breakfast is included in the $75–95 rates.

**The Benjamin Prescott Inn** (603-532-6637; www.benjaminprescottinn.com), Route 124, East Jaffrey 03452. This stately, 1850s Greek Revival farmhouse has been meticulously restored. Each of the 10 guest rooms has a private bath and charm of its own, and a few of the rooms, especially the upstairs suite with views out across the fields, are ideal for honeymooners. A downstairs suite with two bedrooms and a sitting room is ideal for families. A full breakfast is served in the large, attractive combination dining room/sitting room. Current hosts are Dan and Mimi Atwood, but the place is up for sale. $75–160 double.

### *Eastern Monadnock region*

**The Inn at Crotched Mountain** (603-588-6840; www.virtualcities.com), Mountain Road, off Route 47, Francestown 03043. The 1822 brick farmhouse is now a centerpiece for wooden wings, but it still contains a gracious parlor and two dining rooms. The Pine Room also serves as a small gathering space for guests. The real beauty of this place, aside from the warmth of its longtime innkeepers, John and Rose Perry (who celebrated their 25th year here in 2001), is its setting at 1,300 feet, high on a ridge with sweeping views. Three of the 13 rooms have working fireplace, and 8 have private bath. Amenities include a pool, sited to take advantage of the view, tennis courts, and cross-country skiing. $70–140 double, including full breakfast; holidays and foliage season, $20 more. Pets $5. Closed April and November.

**Stepping Stones Bed & Breakfast** (603-654-9048; 1-888-654-9048; www.steppingstonesbb.com), Bennington Battle Trail, Wilton Center 03086. This remarkable house—flower and sun filled, at once unusually cozy and airy—is hidden away in a bend off a back road that leads to a picture-perfect old village. Guests enter through a skylit kitchen/sitting room that is one of the most pleasant we know. The three upstairs guest rooms are small but cheerful, one with a queen, one with a double, and one with twin beds, all with handwoven rugs and throws and down comforters; all with private bath. A full breakfast is served in the solar garden room, with its many books and plants. There's a fireplace and a weaving room. The gardens are inviting and extensive, reflecting Ann Carlsmith's training and skill in landscape design. "There's no soil so I use a lot of weavers," she explains about the intensity of the front of the house; the back is terraced, graced with several unusual trees, and usually filled with birds. Breakfast is served on the porch or terrace, weather permitting. $45 single, $65–70 double; full, imaginative breakfast included. Inquire about the nearby waterfall.

**The Greenfield Inn** (603-547-6327; www.greenfieldinn.com), Greenfield 03047. Vic and Barbara Mangini have turned this Victorian village mansion into a romantic bed & breakfast. There's a woodstove and organ in the parlor, and each of the 12 guest rooms has its own name and lacy decor; all rooms are furnished with antiques and 1890s touches. If the Casanova Room with its delicate pink lace spread isn't your style, you can opt for the smaller, less frilly rooms, which are perfectly comfortable (we like Sweet Violet's). All rooms have TV, and there's a "guest pantry" with sodas and munchies. Two suites and a three-bedroom cottage are also available; a glass-walled deckhouse lends itself to retreats and receptions. Breakfast is a party, with crystal, china, and Mozart. Rates are $49–79 per room, $149 for the suite with a hot tub and Jacuzzi; breakfast is included. Ask about special packages.

**OTHER LODGING** **Crestwood Chapel & Pavilion** (603-239-6393; www.crestwood-e.com), 400 Scofield Mountain Road, Ashuelot 03441. Location, location—and not just one but many. The entry allée of maples could be in France; the out-of-sight accommodations suggest a tropical paradise, and the view is pure New England. That much, at least, is no surprise, considering that this 200-acre estate sits in the absolute southwest corner of New Hampshire. Owner Gary O'Neal describes the spot atop Scofield Mountain as 1 mile straight up from the covered bridge in the mill village of Ashuelot (pronounced "ash-wool-it"). Because there are no other mountains immediately around, the summit commands a view west across the Connecticut Valley to the Green Mountains of Vermont and south down the Pioneer Valley to the Holyoke Range in Massachusetts. The chapel, occupying the center of the formal grounds, was built by Cyrus Ingersol Scofield, who was the personal chaplain to famous 19th-century evangelist Dwight Moody, founded the schools that are now Northfield Mount Hermon, and built a big (long-vanished) summer hotel in nearby Northfield, Massachusetts. For more than 20 years O'Neal, owner of a mill in Ashuelot, an avid cook, and also a justice of the peace, has been gradually transforming the estate into a retreat geared to weddings and small meetings. His own house includes handsome common spaces and guest rooms; the Pavilion, a marble-floored cottage in the gardens, is its own luxurious retreat, with a vast living room, Jacuzzi, and full kitchen. The chapel has also been expanded to include guest rooms but continues to be a venue for weddings, as are the gardens. The entire compound accommodates just 12. Rates start at $225 per night for the Pavilion, breakfast included. Inquire about rates for groups and for individual rooms.

**Naulakha** (802-254-6868 for information), c/o The Landmark Trust, 707 Kipling Road, Dummerston, VT 05301. Just across the river in Brattleboro, with views east across the hills to Mount Monadnock, this house is the one English novelist Rudyard Kipling built in 1893. It is 90 feet long but just 22 feet wide, designed to resemble a ship riding the hillside like a wave. At 26 years old, Kipling was already one of the world's best-known writers, and the two following years that he spent here were among the happiest in his life. Here he wrote *The Jungle Books.* Here the local doctor, James Conland, a former fisherman, inspired him to write *Captains Courageous* and also delivered his two daughters. Kipling's guests included Sir Conan Doyle, who brought with him a pair of Nordic skis, said to be the first in Vermont. The home been painstakingly restored by the nonprofit Landmark Trust and is available for rent by the week or, sometimes, the night (3-night minimum). More than half the furnishings—including a third-floor pool table—actually belonged to the Kiplings. There are four bedrooms, ample baths (old fixtures, new plumbing), a full kitchen, and 55 acres. $1,200–2,600 per week.

ꝏ **Rochambeau Lodge at Alyson's Orchard** (603-756-9800; 1-800-756-0549; www.alysonsorchard.com), P.O. Box 562, Wentworth Road, Walpole 03608. Rustic paneling and a sauna give this renovated barn, set amid acres of working apple orchard, a casual European feel. Eight bedrooms, four with twin beds, two with bunks, and two with double beds, share two and a half baths. A large common area with laundry, fully equipped kitchen, living room, and a long, inviting dining table make this the ideal setting for a reunion of family or friends. The **Caleb Foster Farmhouse** next door adds three more bedrooms and additional kitchen and common areas. Along with pumpkin fields and 30,000 apple trees, the property features miles of trails for cross-country skiing or hiking, and there are several spring-fed ponds suitable for swimming, canoeing, and fishing. The Orchard Room across the road is available for wedding receptions and conferences. To rent the lodge for a minimum 2-night stay is $800–1,000, depending on season. Weekly, it's $1,300–1,500. The house is $500–700 for 2 nights; $1,000–1,200 for a week. Meals, prepared by a prizewinning chef, can be provided with advance notice.

ꝏ **Tory Pines Resort** (603-588-2000; www.torypinesresort.com), Route 47, Francestown 03043. Open in winter for cross-country skiing but primarily a golf resort, Tory Pines offers 32 contemporary guest rooms in a condo-style complex, all with efficiency kitchenette, phone, cable TV, patio, working fireplace, and private bath. All three meals are served at the venerable **Gibson Tavern** on the property (see *Dining Out*). $89–119 per room per night. Less off-season.

**The Jack Daniels Motor Inn** (603-924-7548; www.jackdanielsmotorinn.com), Route 202 North, Peterborough 03458. An attractive 17-room motel, nicely furnished in cherry with all the comforts: climate control, remote control cable, and web access. It's just north of town on busy Route 202 but positioned with its side to the road to minimize noise. $73–98 single, $88–98 double, depending on season. No pets.

**CAMPGROUNDS** **Monadnock State Park** (603-532-8862) offers 21 sites. See *Green Space*.

**Greenfield State Park** (603-547-3497) offers 252 tent sites, handy to a public beach and nature trails.

*Note:* Private campground listings are available from the sources listed under *Guidance*.

## ✻ Where to Eat

### DINING OUT

### *In and around Keene*

♿ **Luca's Mediterranean Café** (603-358-3335), 10 Central Square, Keene. Open for lunch (11:30 AM–2 PM) and dinner (5–9 PM) Monday through Friday; Friday and Saturday 5–10. Be prepared for a culinary journey with this menu that translates the flavors of the Mediterranean from simple Italian to elegant French to hearty Moroccan fare. Entrées range from $11.95 to $16.95. Their signature pasta is rigatoni *à la segreta* with grapes, artichoke hearts, roasted peppers, and Gorgonzola for $13.95; tilapia with yellow peppers, grape tomatoes, champagne, and cilantro served over Israeli couscous is $16.95. Dine alfresco when weather permits.

♿ **Nicola's Trattoria** (603-355-5242), 39 Central Square, Keene. Open for dinner Tuesday through Sunday 5–9 PM; Friday and Saturday until 10 PM. Friends rave about chef Nicola Bencivenga's cheerful trattoria with its open kitchen and reasonably priced dinner menu that's studded with pasta dishes like ziti della casa (chicken sautéed in olive oil with broccoli rabe, arugula, and portobello mushrooms) or osso buco (thick veal shank simmered with onions, tomato, carrots, celery, and fresh Italian herbs). Everything is made to order with fresh ingredients, and you can taste it. Reservations are recommended, but walk-ins can usually be accommodated.

♿ **Burdick's Bistro and Café** (603-756-2882; www.burdickchocolate.com), 47 Main Street (next to the post office), Walpole. Open Monday through Friday noon–2:30 PM for lunch; Tuesday through Saturday 5:30–9 PM for dinner. Also chocolate bar open daily 7–9 PM, Sunday until 5 PM. (See *Snacks*.) Chocolatier extraordinaire Larry Burdick and his friend, filmmaker Ken Burns, have transformed the town's former IGA into a *très chic* dining spot. Like the decor, the menu, much of which changes daily, is understated but close to perfect. Lunch features soups, pâtés, gravlax, salads, and omelets. Dinner might be pan-roasted chicken garnished with lemon and olive oil and served with straw potatoes; or maybe a slow-roasted pork loin served with fennel over white beans. The bread is crusty; the wine list, top-notch; the chocolate desserts, to die for. Dinner entrées are $14–19; for two, figure $50 with wine.

**One Seventy-Six Main** (603-357-3100), 176 Main Street, Keene. Open 11:30 AM–11 PM daily; until midnight Saturday, 10 PM Sunday. Brunch Saturday and Sunday 11 AM–4 PM. Casual gourmet dining, friendly, warm ambience, walls hung with works by local artists, 16 beers on tap (plus 50 bottled beers). Features Mexican food on Monday and Tuesday, Italian on Wednesday, seafood on Thursday and Friday, something special every day. Dinner entrées range from $9.95 for fish-and-chips to $18.95 for New York sirloin.

**Sakura** (603-358-9902), 601 South Main Street, Keene. Open Tuesday through Saturday for lunch (11:30 AM–3 PM) and dinner (4:30–9:30 PM); Sunday noon–9:30 PM. First-rate Japanese fare: sushi, tempura, donburi, and udon (Japanese noodles). Entrées $8.95–12.95, less at lunch.

♿ **Salmon Chase Bistro and Lounge** (603-357-7070; www.someplacesdifferent.com), 30 Main Street, Keene. Located in the **E. F. Lane Hotel,** this attractive dining room features traditional and contemporary American cuisine, and is open to the public for lunch (Monday through Friday 11:30 AM–2 PM) and dinner (Monday through Saturday 5–9 PM). In addition to soups and salads, lunch entrées range from $5.95 for a spinach phyllo triangle with salad to $8.95 for beef Burgundy. The dinner menu ranges from vegetarian pasta at $12.95 to a 7-ounce filet mignon served on a Parmesan crouton for $19.95.

**Tamarack Farm** (603-835-6580; www.tamarackfarm.com), Route 123A, Acworth. Open Friday and Saturday for one serving only at 7:15 PM. Much of the food served here was also raised here on the Gowens' 400-acre farm. Actually, even the wood in the tables is part of the property's harvest. Prime rib is the specialty. The five-course dinner is $22.95. Reservations.

♿ **Thai Garden** (603-357-4567), 118 Main Street, Keene 03431. Open daily 11:30 AM–3 PM and 5–10 PM for lunch and dinner. An attractive restaurant that, like its sisters in Boston and the Berkshires, offers a menu that invites exploration. All the traditional Thai soups and noodle dishes are here. Dinner entrées range from $7.95 for ground chicken mixed with peanut sauce on a bed of lettuce to $13.95 for seafood curry. Luncheon specials are $5.75–6.50. Reservations accepted.

♿ **Tony Clamato's** (603-357-4345), 15 Court Square, Keene. Closed Monday, otherwise open for dinner and beyond, 4:30 PM–1 AM. Italian trattoria decor and menu with pasta specialties like fettuccine alla Siciliana (egg noodles with prosciutto, mushrooms, and peas) and pollo Gamberi Francese (chicken and shrimp in egg batter, sautéed with lemon, butter, and wine sauce). Moderate.

♿ **The Walpole Inn** (603-756-3320), Main Street, Walpole. Open Tuesday through Sunday for dinner 5–9 PM, until 9:30 PM on Friday and Saturday. Bar and lounge open from 4 PM. The menu changes weekly. The dining room, overlooking a painterly scene of rolling meadows, is simple but elegant with celery-toned paneling, exposed brick, white linen, and appealing art. Favorite menu items include pan-seared sea scallops with spinach risotto and mushroom ragout ($22), and a grilled Black Angus strip steak with caramelized onions, melted Gorgonzola cheese, and whipped red potatoes for the same price. Dinner is frequently accompanied by jazz on weekend nights. Reservations recommended.

**Chesterfield Inn** (603-256-3211), Route 9, West Chesterfield. Open for dinner every night except Christmas Eve and Christmas Day. Chef Glenn Gonyea has an enviable reputation for imaginative dishes, and the setting is an 18th-century tavern expanded to create one of the most attractive dining areas in the region, with views of Vermont hills. Entrées on a winter menu here might include pork loin braised in beer with apple cider sauce ($18), salmon roulade with spinach and mascarpone cheese ($19), and veal saltimbocca over white bean stew ($21). There is a nightly vegetarian entrée as well.

**The Wright Mansion Inn** (603-355-2288; 1-800-352-5890; www.wrightmansioninn.com), 695 Court Street, Keene. Open Tuesday through Saturday for one 6 PM seating. A reservations-only deal designed to make a big deal of a birthday or anniversary. The dining room of this 1930s Georgian Revival mansion is mahogany paneled with French doors to the terrace. Gilded frames, white linens, candles, and a fireplace add to the somewhat dated allure. The $30 fixed-price menu includes a choice of two appetizers, several entrées, a salad course, dessert, and beverage.

### *In and around Peterborough*

**Acqua Bistro** (603-924-9905), 18 Depot Square, Peterborough. Dinner Tuesday through Sunday 5–9 PM, until 10 PM on the weekends. Reservations advised. Rave reviews for this attractive restaurant with views of the brook. Fully licensed. Dinner entrées might include braised veal ragout with roasted garlic and mirepoix over housemade pappardelle with herbed ricotta; thyme-roasted boneless half chicken over apple-fennel mashed potatoes with lemon-infused pan sauce; and pepper-crusted seared rare sushi-grade tuna with gingered vegetable stir fry and Himalayan red rice. Entrées $17–24. Pizzas ($11–15) in the bar.

**Inn at Jaffrey Center** (603-532-7800; 1-877-510-7019), 379 Main Street, Jaffrey Center. Open for lunch and dinner Monday through Saturday, and for brunch Sunday 10 AM–2 PM. Sunday dinner is seasonal. Known for more than a century as the Monadnock Inn, this classic country hostelry sits at the center of one of the Monadnock region's prettiest villages, minutes from the entrance to Monadnock State Park. Under new ownership, its dining rooms have been expanded and its reputation for fine dining has soared. We certainly can't complain about the lamb shanks, slow braised with garlic and rosemary. Choices range from vegetarian pastas and fish dishes to a mixed grill of rack of lamb and coconut-grilled shrimp with Hunan sauce. Entrées $10–22. There's also an informal tavern.

**The Hancock Inn** (603-525-3318), Main Street, Hancock village. Open for dinner nightly. An 18th-century inn with a candlelit, cranberry-colored dining room and a far-ranging menu that usually features grilled rack of lamb and filet mignon and might also include Asian five-spice pomegranate-glazed salmon, and grilled chicken and portobellos stacked with Boursin and served on a twist of angelhair pasta tossed with fresh basil and tomatoes. Entrées are $20–26. A tavern menu that includes brick-oven-baked thin-crust pizza ($10–16) as well as sandwiches and burgers is available, along with the regular menu, in the genuine old tavern.

**Del Rossi's Trattoria** (603-563-7195; www.delrossi.com), Route 137, Dublin. Open Thursday through Monday for dinner. Inquire about scheduled music and poetry readings. David and Elaina Del Rossi have created a genuine Italian trattoria in a pleasant old house just north of Route 101. Homemade pastas are a specialty, as are Italian classics like bisteca and scaloppine with penne pasta Alfredo. The menu might also include fresh Wellfleet littleneck clams steamed in a homemade fish broth with chopped shrimp, served on homemade spaghetti. Entrées $10.95–17.95.

**Lilly's on the Pond** (603-899-3322), Route 202, Rindge. Open Tuesday through Saturday for lunch and dinner, Sunday 10 AM–8 PM. A restaurant under various names since 1952, this former sawmill turned gristmill and forge only hit the culinary map in 1994 when current owners Susanne and Luis Ygleisas and Lee Kendall renamed it for the mermaid said to live on the shores of this pond in the 1700s. Dinner might be Tequila Lime Chicken (if you like margaritas, you'll love this dish)—a boneless breast of chicken sautéed with fresh lime, tequila, cilantro, and cream—or veggie phyllo, artichoke hearts in a spinach-ricotta sauce wrapped in phyllo pastry. Entrées $9–16.

**The Birchwood Inn** (603-878-3285), Route 45, Temple. Open to the public for breakfast weekends and for dinner Tuesday through Sunday, summer and fall. BYOB. Innkeeper Bill Wolfe is the chef and with the help of his wife, Judy, makes everything from scratch on the premises—the reason for the low prices and strong local following. The dining room is small (so be sure to reserve ahead), candlelit, and decorated with murals painted in the 1820s by itinerant artist Rufus Porter. The blackboard menu always lists a choice of chicken, duckling (a specialty), red meat, or fish. Homemade breads, soups (try the She Crab Soup on Saturday night), and delectable desserts like fresh fruit cobblers and pie in-season are made daily from scratch. The inn's reasonably priced breakfasts (featuring homemade jams) are also worth noting for those Mount Monadnock–bound hikers who like getting up and out, eating an hour or so later. Complete dinners are $18.95–23.95.

**Churchhill's at the Grand View Inn and Resort** (603-532-9898), 580 Mountain Road (Route 124), west of Jaffrey Center. Open Thursday through Saturday for dinner; Sunday brunch 10:30 AM–2 PM. Reservations required. There's a prix fixe menu at $52 per person and a limited à la carte menu featuring dishes like oven-roasted pheasant breast with a wild mushroom sage ragout, fingerling potato, and crispy parsnip. The post-and-beam dining room is designed to maximize the view and to serve as a space for wedding receptions and other special occasions.

**Monadnock Mountain View Restaurant** (603-242-3300), Gathering Mall, Route 12, Troy. Open weekdays 11:30 AM–9 PM, Saturday 4–9 PM, Sunday 10 AM–2 PM. Chef-owner Mark Starrett has upscaled this longtime way stop, which really does offer the best Mount Monadnock view of any area restaurant. Dinner entrées run from pastas to prime rib, $12–20.

### *Eastern Monadnock region*

**The Gibson Tavern at Tory Pines Resort** (603-588-2000), Route 47, Francestown. Open for lunch and dinner in summer; off-season, open for dinner on weekends, and inquire about other hours. The centerpiece 1790 mansion of a golf-resort development has a handsome dining room and a reputation for fine dining. Dinner entrées range from vegetarian delight to filet mignon. Moderate.

**The Maplehurst Inn** (603-588-8000), Main Street, Antrim. Open for Wednesday lunch, noon–2 PM; dinner Wednesday through Saturday 5 PM–close; and for Sunday brunch 10 AM–2 PM. An old-fashioned dining room and an à la carte menu featuring changeable specials such as London broil ($15.95), maple-glazed salmon ($13.95), and Caribbean jerk chicken ($12.95).

♿ **Rynborn Restaurant** (603-588-6162; www.rynborn.com; info@rynborn.com), Main Street, Antrim. Open 5–9 nightly, until 10 PM Thursday through Saturday. Just across the street from the Maplehurst Inn in the middle of Antrim, an informal, chef-owned restaurant with a series of small dining rooms—the nicest overlooking a pond in back—a friendly pub, and a major reputation as New England's premier **blues club.** (Check the web site for who's coming when.) The dinner menu is large and varied with entrées ranging from hand-cured turkey and prime rib au jus to chili, ribs, and sweet potato fries as well as other interesting Cajun and southwestern dishes. Children's menu. (Also see *Eating Out*.)

**Pickity Place** (603-878-1151; www.pickityplace.com), Nutting Hill Road, Mason (see *Villages*). Open year-round daily for three lunch sittings: 11:30 AM, plus 12:45 and 2 PM. Reserve ahead because there are just 15 tables in this 200-year-old house. Homegrown herbs are the draw here, and you come for "herbal lunches." The set menu changes each month. When we stopped by, it included roasted garlic-herb soup; wild mushroom strudel with grilled trout over julienned vegetables with cranberry vin blanc; or Mediterranean spinach fettuccine, along with home-baked breads and dessert. Children can have a Little Red Riding Hood basket of sandwiches and fruit; they come to see "Grandmother's bed" in the Red Riding Hood Museum. A five-course luncheon is $14.95 plus tax.

## EATING OUT

### *In and around Keene*

**The Stage Restaurant** (603-357-8339), 30 Central Square, across from the County Courthouse, Keene. Open Monday through Saturday 11:30 AM–11:30 PM, Sunday 8 AM–4 PM. A trendy, family-owned café with a playbill decor and a large menu: burgers, sandwiches, pasta, steaks, and salads. Full bar. Entrées $7.95–14.95.

**Timoleon's Restaurant** (603-357-4230), 27 Main Street, Keene. Open daily 6 AM–9 PM. This is the kind of place every town once had: a long counter and booths with better-than-average service, deli and club sandwiches, hot sandwiches, salads, fried haddock, and ham steak with a pineapple ring, served with salad, a roll, and potato for $6.95. Like all Keene restaurants, it's now smoke-free, and we're told business has picked up as a result.

**Elm City Brewing Co.** (603-355-3335), 222 West Street, Keene. Open daily for lunch and until 11 PM Monday through Wednesday, until 1 AM Thursday through Saturday; Sunday 1:30–9 PM. In the Colony Mill, a large, attractive brew pub with its own ales, draft, and a large, varied, and reasonably priced menu.

**Lindy's Diner** (603-352-4273), Gilbo Avenue just off Main Street across from the bus station, Keene. Open daily 6 AM–9 PM, until 10 PM on Saturday. George and Arietta Rigopoulos take particular pride in their chowders and chicken pies.

**Murray's,** Walpole village. Open daily 6 AM–3 PM. Walpole's longtime local hangout, this is the kind of place where everyone looks up when a stranger walks in. But that's okay; the food is great. On a summer day the pepper pot soup and fresh fruit cocktail were splendid.

♿ **Walpole Village Tavern Restaurant & Bar** (603-756-3703), 10 Westminster Street, Walpole village. Open Tuesday through Saturday 11 AM–9 PM. Closed Sunday and Monday. The menu offers the usual suspects—soups, salads, sandwiches, burgers, and fish-and-chip baskets—along with such newcomers as quesadillas and flavored tortilla wraps. There's also a kid's menu and full bar.

Christina Tree

THE MT. PISGAH DINER IN WINCHESTER

**Casey J's** (603-585-2229), junction of Routes 12 and 119, Fitzwilliam. Open for all three meals, closed for dinner Monday through Wednesday off-season. The kind of family restaurant every town should have. The rolls, cakes, pies, soups, and lasagna are all homemade, and the hams, turkeys, and roasts are home baked.

**Gap Mountain Bakery Café** (603-242-3284), on the common, Route 12, Troy. Open 8 AM–7 PM Monday through Wednesday, until 8:30 PM Thursday through Saturday. We find it impossible to pass through Troy without stopping at Diane Kenner's cheerful bakery-café. It's a source of outstanding morning muffins (made with honey), sundry breads, and oatmeal cookies; also distinctly less healthy but addictive chocolate whoopee pies. Subs, great pizzas by the slice, soups, and salads are served at lunch, and gourmet coffees are on tap.

**Mt. Pisgah Diner** (603-239-4101), 18 Main Street, Winchester. Open Monday through Friday 5 AM–2 PM, Saturday 5–11 AM. An authentic 1930 Worcester diner (#769) that's sparkling clean and pridefully maintained by Joni Otto. The food's not bad, either! We went for the kielbasa omelet but might have sampled sausage gravy over biscuits with two eggs and homefries.

### *In and around Peterborough*

**The Café at Noon Falls** (603-924-6818). Route 202 south, Peterborough. Open 8:30 AM–3 PM. The premier space in a former mill building, right by the falls. Pleasant any time of year, it's superb in warm-weather months when you can eat on the deck. The food is now above average: soups and sandwiches with freshly made bread, also Thai and Indian specialties. Under the same management as la Bonne Table, a respected local catering service and culinary arts school.

**R. S. Gatto's** (603-924-5000), 6 School Street, Peterborough. Open Tuesday through Saturday for lunch and dinner. This attractive space in a former movie house (designed for the original Latacarta) is now a popular spot for lunch and dinner, specializing in seafood, pasta, homemade desserts. The dinner menu ranges from eggplant Parmesan to grilled swordfish and New York sirloin.

**Aesops Tables at the Toadstool Bookstore** (603-924-1612), 12 Depot Square, Peterborough. Open 8:30 AM–4 PM weekdays, 10 AM–3 PM Saturday. An inviting corner of this outsized bookstore, a former A&P. The blackboard menu lists sandwiches and café fare like bagels, raspberry squares, and Brazilian chocolate cake. There's a play corner for small fry and a choice of gourmet coffees on tap.

**Fiddleheads Café** (603-525-4432), 28 Main Street, Hancock. Open breakfast through early evening. In the middle of Hancock village, this attractive café offers a separate sitting room designed for patrons to simply read and relax. Bettee and Steve Zakon-Anderson offer several daily soups as well as scones and muffins, pizzas and calzones, coffees and teas. Local art on the walls is for sale.

**Brady's American Grill** (603-924-9322), Route 202 north, Peterborough. Open daily for lunch and dinner. A friendly place with good food: burgers, sandwiches, salads, pasta, and a surprising choice of dinner entrées. Beer and wine served.

**Nonies** (603-924-3451), 28 Grove Street, Peterborough. Open early morning to 2 PM. Doughnuts made daily, full breakfasts, soups, sandwiches, local gossip.

**The Peterborough Diner** (603-924-6202), Depot Street, Peterborough. Open daily 6 AM–9 PM. A 1950s green-and-yellow diner featuring dependable diner food including homemade soups, pies, daily and nightly specials, beer. Choose the counter or wooden booth.

**Twelve Pine** (603-924-6140), Depot Square, Peterborough. Open Monday through Friday 11 AM–6 PM, Saturday 11 AM–3 PM. The aroma is a mix of coffee, spices, and baking, which—combined with the array of salads, quiches, calzones, and soups—is something to savor before deciding on any one thing. This former train depot is now filled with delectable deli and baked items, cheeses, also specialty foods, flowers, and fruit. Small tables (too small!) are scattered throughout; better to get something delicious to go and walk over to the banks of the Contoocook River or head for one of the spots described under *Green Space*.

**Uncle Don's Kitchen at The Harrisville General Store** (603-827-3138), Harrisville. Open 7 AM–7 PM except Sunday, when closing time is 3 PM. Very much a part of this historic mill village (see Harrisville under *Villages*), recently reopened with a few staples and more specialty foods, a first-rate deli with soups, salads, and a wide range of "create-your-own-sandwich" ingredients. There are tables and picnic sites by the neighboring millpond.

**Latham's Meetinghouse Depot** (603-547-3491), 1 Slip Road, Greenfield. Open for breakfast and lunch daily, dinner Thursday and Friday. There's always been a coffee shop in Carbee's Corner (see Greenfield under *Villages*), but new owner-chef Jacob Latham is creating something more—specialty omelets, four different kinds of eggs Benedict, and French toast stuffed with sweet orange mascarpone at breakfast; soups, salads, and vegetable panini as well as burgers and subs at lunch; dinner specials ranging from pasta to prime rib.

### *Eastern Monadnock region*

**Alberto's** (603-588-6512). Route 31,

Bennington. Open daily at 5 PM. A red-sauce Italian place with a big menu that includes 11 kinds of pizza, garlic bread, and 19 Italian dishes like manicotti, lasagna, and chicken cacciatore.

**A Common Place Eatery** (603-588-6888), Main Street, Bennington. Open Monday through Wednesday 6 AM–2 PM, until 9 PM Thursday through Saturday; Sunday 7–11 AM. No pretensions, but a dependable stop in a rural corner of the region where you might need one.

**The Melting Pot** (603-654-5150), Main Street, Wilton (across from town hall). Open Wednesday 11 AM–2 PM, Thursday through Saturday 7 AM–2 PM, Sunday 8 AM–1 PM. "Same, same but different" is the way Karen Anderson, who has traveled widely in Southeast Asia, South America, and the Mediterranean, describes the fare in this storefront restaurant with batik tablecloths and photos of Anderson's travels. It's good for omelets, meat loaf, daily-baked bread, burgers, and BLTs—but also Thai soup and daily specials like spinach and cheese quiche or asparagus on homemade bread with cheese sauce.

**Red Brick Inn** (603-878-4028), 3 High Street, Greenville. Open Monday through Friday, 5 AM–9 PM weekends and most nights; Sunday breakfast buffet 8 AM–noon. The mill village of Greenville was built in the early 19th century by investors from Lowell, Massachusetts, and this boardinghouse on a knoll in the middle of the village dates from 1856. For many years it was the "Greenville Inn" with a dubious reputation, but Dave Barry got it back on track. A mural on the dining room wall depicts all the old mills along the river (several now house thriving companies). Fare is standard and reasonably priced, and there are nightly specials, like "all you can eat" prime rib on Saturday night ($15.95) and a similar Friday-night fish entrée for $9.95. The inn also offers small but attractive upstairs rooms; $81 includes breakfast.

**Rynborn Restaurant** (see *Dining Out*) in Antrim is a good lunch and Sunday-breakfast bet for soups and salads, burgers, or an open-faced Reuben. Children's menu.

**Caron's Diner** (603-464-3575), Hillsborough. Open 5 AM–2 PM for breakfast and lunch, 5–8 PM for dinner; Sunday 7 AM–noon. One of those places that has obviously forgotten what it looks like from the outside—a chrome diner tacked onto a brick extension with a door that looks like it never opens but does, onto the town's gossip center (your coffee cup never gets empty). It's spanking clean and always full, good for freshly made minestrone, meat loaf, or liver and onions; blackboard specials.

**High Tide** (603-464-4202), Route 9, Hillsborough. Open for lunch through dinner in warm weather. A seasonal fried-fish place with soft serve and a great screened-in dining area.

**Sampan Chinese Restaurant and Lounge** (603-464-3663), Route 9, Hillsborough. Open daily for lunch and dinner. The attractive decor suggests the quality of this place, one of the better spots to eat in the area. Dishes are all cooked to order, no MSG.

**Tooky Mills Pub** (603-464-6700; www.tookymillspub.baweb.com), 9 Depot Street, Hillsborough. Named for the mills that used to border the Contoocook River in these parts, this restaurant right on the main drag is open for lunch and dinner daily. Sunday through Thursday 11:30 AM–9 PM; Friday and Saturday until 10 PM.

SNACKS ♿ **Burdick's Bistro and Café** (603-756-2882; www.burdick-chocolate.com), 47 Main Street (next to the post office), Walpole. Aside from making and selling some of the world's best chocolates, Burdick operates a café (his others are in New York and Cambridge) good for teas, coffees, and varied sinful snacks. (Also see *Selective Shopping.*)

**German John's Bakery** (603-464-5079), West Main Street, Hillsborough. Try the soft sweet almond or raisin pretzels, or a slice of kuchen or streusel, and bring home a loaf of bread.

**Kimball Farm Ice Cream,** Route 124 at Silver Ranch, Jaffrey. Open April through October, 10 AM–9 PM. A Massachusetts import, but that doesn't make this ice cream any less delicious in every conceivable flavor.

## ✱ Entertainment

DANCE **Nelson Town Hall** (603-827-3455; 603-827-3732), Nelson. Show up any Monday at 8 PM at this elegantly simple old building, one of the region's longtime centers for traditional contra dancing. Young or old, with or without a partner, you'll soon be tapping your toes and caught up in a reel. Several Nelson musicians have gained national reputations. Call or check www.ultranet.com/harts/nhdances for information about events throughout the area.

FILM **The Colonial Theater** (603-352-2033), 95 Main Street, Keene. A majestic, magical old theater featuring both current and classic films and live performances.

LECTURE AND PERFORMANCE SERIES **Amos Fortune Forum Series.** Ongoing since 1947, Friday evenings in July and August at the Jaffrey Center Meeting House.

**Monadnock Summer Lyceum** (603-924-6245), Unitarian church, Main Street, Peterborough. Every Sunday in July and August at 11 AM. Originally established in 1828, programs by well-known speakers.

MUSIC ♿ **Apple Hill Chamber Players** (603-847-3371), Apple Hill Center for Chamber Music, Apple Hill Road, East Sullivan 03445. The Apple Hill Summer Chamber Music School attracts 275 participants of all ages; inquire about free weekly concerts by faculty (Tuesday at 8 PM) and students (check current calendar) in June, July, and August; all concerts are in the hilltop Apple Hill Concert Barn. This noted group also performs throughout the country and the world.

**Monadnock Music** (603-924-7610; 1-800-868-9613), Box 255, Peterborough 03458. This is a prestigious summer series of some three dozen concerts, operas, and orchestra performances, many of them free, staged by highly professional artists in churches and meetinghouses throughout the region, from the Walpole Unitarian church to Marlow's Jones Hall, the Unitarian church in Wilton Center, and the Jaffrey Center Meeting House. A subscription series is available for those performed at the Town House in Peterborough. Call or send for the current calendar, or check local listings.

**The Peterborough Folk Music Society** (603-827-2905) features performances by well-known artists throughout the year at one of several venues around Peterborough. Watch for listings or phone.

**Live jazz** is performed regularly at **Rynborn Restaurant and Blues Club** (603-588-6162) in Antrim.

**Temple Band** (603-878-2829), said to be the oldest town band in the country, performs at the Sharon Arts Center, the Jaffrey Bandstand, and a number of scheduled festivities throughout the summer. Past masters of oompah-pah.

**Jaffrey Bandstand.** Performances Wednesday evenings in summer.

Also see **Del Rossi's Trattoria** under *Dining Out*.

THEATER **American Stage Festival** (603-673-7515), Milford. Summer productions usually include a classic, like Shakespeare or Molière, and new plays. The Young Company stages children's matinees. Tickets $16–20.

**Andy's Summer Playhouse** (603-654-2613), Wilton. A summer theater program for children 8–18 with frequent performances in July and August in the old grange hall in Wilton Center.

**The Arts Center** on Brickyard Pond at Keene State College in Keene and Franklin Pierce College in Rindge. Both stage musical, theatrical, and dance performances. Check local listings.

**Peterborough Players** (603-924-7585), Middle Hancock Road, Peterborough. Since 1933 this professional group has performed everything from Will Shakespeare to Tom Stoppard. One of New England's better-known summer theaters, presenting five to seven plays each summer in a renovated, air-conditioned 19th-century barn.

## Selective Shopping

Few corners of New England are as conducive to finding just what you want while winding around back roads. The area is studded with genuine finds, ranging from unusual crafted items and antiques to exceptional chocolates and cheeses.

ANTIQUARIAN BOOKSHOPS **Eagle Books** (603-357-8721), 19 West Street, just off Central Square, Keene. Open daily except Sunday and holidays; 12,000 volumes specializing in WPA writers' project books.

**Homestead Bookshop** (603-876-4213), Route 101 just east of Marlborough village next to Wilber Brothers Supermarket, Marlborough. Open daily; 45,000 volumes specializing in juvenile series, town histories, older fiction.

**Hurley Books** (603-399-4342), east side of Route 12 (just north of Route 63), Westmoreland. Open by appointment or chance; 35,000 volumes specializing in religion, farming, and gardening.

**Bequaert Old Books** (603-585-3448), Fitzwilliam. Open April through November, 11 AM–5 PM except Wednesday. In the vintage barn beside their house near the Fitzwilliam village green, the Bequaerts stock some 35,000 tittles, including books on mountaineering, fiber arts, cookbooks.

**Stone House Antiques & Books** (603-363-4866; www.stonehouseantiques.com), junction of Routes 9 and 63, Chesterfield. This granite house was once a stagecoach stop. Now the double parlors are divided by pocket doors and fitted with shelves offering a variety of used, antiquarian, and rare books.

**ANTIQUES** Listing the more than 50 antiques stores in the Monadnock region would simply be confusing. Be it said that antiquing is *big* but composed of many small shops, thickest in the Francestown and Fitzwilliam areas. Free, frequently updated flyers describing these shops and their whereabouts are available locally. **Fitzwilliam Antiques** at the junction of Routes 12 and 19 houses the merchandise of 40 dealers, and there are half a dozen more dealers in Fitzwilliam (pick up a pamphlet guide). **Antiques at Colony Mill** (603-358-6343) represents more than 100 dealers. With 300 dealers, **Knotty Pine, Inc.** (603-352-5252), on Route 10W in West Swanzey claims to be the state's oldest and largest group shop. *The Directory of New Hampshire Antiques Dealers,* available from most chambers of commerce and antiques shops, lists dozens of dealers in this area.

**ART GALLERIES** **Sharon Arts Center** (603-924-7878), 30 Grove Street, Peterborough. Open Monday through Saturday 10 AM–5 PM, Sunday noon–5 PM. Truly the "center" and showcase for the best current art and craft work in this creative corner of the state. The combination art and crafts gallery, running a block through from Grove Street to Depot Square, displays a wide variety of original art in many media. This is also a great place to shop for quality gifts ranging from toys to jewelry. Workshops and studio space are at the center's original locale in Sharon (see *To Do—Special Programs*).

**Peterborough Fine Art** (603-924-7558), Depot Square, Peterborough. Open year-round, Tuesday through Saturday noon–5 PM. A serious gallery specializing in 19th- and early-20th-century landscape paintings, especially those of the Dublin Art Colony, also some contemporary work.

**Peterborough Art Academy and Gallery** (603-924-4488), Depot Square, Peterborough. Regional artists' gallery, children's and adult classes, summer art camp and art supplies.

**Spheris Gallery of Fine Art** (603-756-9617; www.sperisgallery.com), Walpole village. Sited just below the historical society (see Walpole under *Villages*), this is a standout gallery. Owner Cynthia Reeves was also instrumental in founding **Great River Arts** (see *To Do—Special Programs*).

**AUCTIONS** **Ed's Country Auction House** (603-899-6654), Rindge (behind Lilly's on the Pond Restaurant; see *Dining Out*), auctions every Saturday year-round.

**Richard Withington** (603-464-3232), Hillsborough Center, holds auctions every week, June through Columbus Day. A legend in his own time, Withington has gaveled more auctions than anyone in the state.

**The Cobb's Auctioneers** (603-924-6316), 50 Jaffrey Road (Route 202), Peterborough. Attractive showrooms in the same former mill that houses the café at Noone Falls, a major local auction house.

**BOOKSTORES** **The Toadstool Bookshops** (603-924-3543), 12 Depot Square, Peterborough, and in the Colony Mill (603-352-8815), Keene. Outstanding bookstores with a wide range of general titles, including many regional and art books. Under *Eating Out* note **Aesops Tables,** a café in the immense Peterborough store (a former A&P).

Also see *Antiquarian Bookshops.*

**CRAFTS** **Country Artisans** (603-352-6980), Colony Mill Marketplace, Keene. Offers a wide selection of crafts produced in New England and beyond.

**Five Wings Studio** (603-585-6682), East Lake Road, Fitzwilliam. Susan Link makes and sells her attractive dinnerware—porcelain with an Oriental look—and two stoneware lines. All pieces are formed on a potter's wheel or hand built then bisque fired in a gas kiln and coated with a clear glaze, then fired again. Hand-cut painted tiles are also a specialty. The way to the studio is west from Fitzwiliam village on Route 119 to the four corners, then keep on straight through. Route 119 angles off to the right at that point; beyond this turn is **The Pottery Works,** in which Terry Silverman (Susan's husband) creates distinctive pottery flameware.

**Frye's Measure Mill** (603-654-6581), Wilton Center. Open April through December 21, Tuesday through Saturday 10 AM–5 PM, Sunday noon–5 PM. The store is housed in part of a 19th-century mill that retains its original machinery, some still water-powered to make Shaker boxes and woodenware. Quilts and coverlets, salt-glaze pottery, and other country folk art items are also sold.

**Harrisville Designs** (603-827-3996; www.Harrisville.com), Harrisville. Open Tuesday through Saturday 10 AM–5 PM. Handweaving looms are designed and made here, priced from $700 to $5,000. Check out the new children's weaving looms and kits. A variety of yarns and weaving accessories is also sold in the Weaving Center, housed in an 1850 brick storehouse by the millpond. (Also see *To Do—Special Programs*.) Inquire about used looms.

**North Gallery at Tewksbury's** (603-924-3224), junction of Routes 101 and 123, Peterborough. Open daily 10 AM–6 PM. The floor and gallery of a former barn are filled with a wide assortment of things you never before thought you wanted—cookbooks, mugs, puzzles, toys, and some well-chosen crafted items ranging from jewelry to place mats, furnishings, and throws.

**Granite Lake Pottery** (603-847-9908), Route 9, Munsonville. Open year-round, daily except Sunday. Hand-thrown dinnerware and accessories from mugs to lamps and bathroom sinks (the sinks are a specialty).

**Hannah Grimes Marketplace** (603-352-6862), 46 Main Street, Keene. Open daily 10 AM–6 PM, selling locally made crafts and farm products.

**Sharon Arts Center** (603-924-7256), Depot Square, Peterborough. (See also *Art Galleries*.) This is the region's leading crafts shop.

**Parkside Gallery** (603-464-3322), Route 9 west of Hillsborough. Open daily. A funky, fabulous mix of antiques, crafts, and gifts.

**FARMS, PICK-YOUR-OWN AND CUT-YOUR-OWN** Cut your own Christmas tree at **Butterfield Hill Farm** (603-399-4886) and at **Farmstead Acres** (603-352-8730), both in Westmoreland; or at **Grassy Pond House** (603-899-5166) and **Wright's Tree Farm** (603-352-4033) in Keene.

**High Hopes Orchard** (603-399-4305), 582 Glebe Road, Westmoreland. Raspberries in July, blueberries in July and August, apples in September and October, and pumpkins (wagon rides) in September and October; gift shop, cider, homemade pies, apples, doughnuts, and apple gift packs August through December.

**Maple Lane Farm** (603-352-2329), Gunn Road, Keene. PYO apples—dwarf trees make it easy.

**Rosaly's Farmstand,** Route 123 just south of Route 101, Peterborough. Thanks to reader Alexandra Kelly for her recommendation of Rosaly Bass's you-pick flower and herb gardens and farm stand featuring organic vegetables, most grown on the property. Rosaly also sells hand-painted T-shirts, maple syrup, and muffins, cakes, and bean salads on which you can picnic with a view of the fields and Mount Monadnock.

**Upland Farm** (603-914-3163), Route 123 south, Peterborough. A great place to pick apples, also good for cider and pumpkins.

FARM STANDS **Alyson's Orchard** (603-756-9800; 1-800-856-0549; www.alysonsorchard.com), Wentworth Road, Walpole. Some 28,000 trees cover this beautiful hilltop overlooking the Connecticut River Valley. Heritage variety apples, peaches, pears, blueberries, raspberries, hops, and firewood are available at the farm stand in-season.

**Boggy Meadow Farm** (603-756-3300), location marked from Route 12, Walpole. The 620-acre Boggy Meadow Farm has been in the Cabot family since 1822, but Powell Cabot has been producing Fanny Mason Farmstead Swiss Cheese for only the past few years. Call ahead to make sure the cheese plant and retail shop are open. The drive along the river to the shop is a treat in itself, and the Fanny Mason cheese—baby Swiss or smoked Swiss—is excellent.

**Davis Family Farm** (603-835-2403), Acworth. A horse-powered, family-run farm, selling vegetables, raspberries, blueberries, strawberries, honey, maple syrup, flowers, and herbs.

**Ellis Farm** (603-357-0334), 149 Hurricane Road, Keene. In the same family since 1868, selling flowers, vegetables, herbs, perennials, cut flowers, vegetables; also pick-your-own strawberries, blueberries, raspberries.

HERBS **Harvest Thyme Herbs** (603-563-7032), Dode Road, Dublin. Herbal baskets and dips.

**Herb Barn** (603-532-8486), 80 Main Street, Jaffrey. Open weekends 10 AM–4 PM. Extensive gardens and selection of herb products. Guided garden viewing with plant identification and folklore, followed by a "garden tea," is available by reservation.

**Lambs & Thyme** (603-239-8621), 240 Bullock Road, Richmond. A vintage-1855 schoolhouse on a back road houses an interesting gift shop featuring herbs grown and processed on the property. Judith Graves also publishes a catalog with some 300 herbal products, gives cooking classes and an early-November open house at Randallane, her 18th-century home.

**Pickity Place** (603-878-1151), Nutting Hill Road, Mason. A large herb garden and gift shop, catalog. (Also see *Dining Out* and *Villages*.)

**Red Oak Farm** (603-585-9052), Royalston Road, Fitzwilliam. Herb and perennial plants, dried herbs and flowers, wreaths.

**Sage Knoll** (603-478-5461), 955 East Washington Road, Hillsborough. Open Memorial Day through Labor Day, Tuesday through Saturday 10 AM–4 PM. Herbs and perennials, spe-

## SUGARING

Maple sugaring season in the Monadnock region is March through mid-April, but farmers may not be "boiling" (40 gallons of sap boil down to 1 gallon of syrup) every day, so phone ahead to make sure there's something to see—and something to eat. Most maple producers offer "sugar parties": sugar-on-snow (usually crushed ice these days) and maybe the traditional accompaniment (a pickle). Most sell a variety of maple products year-round.

**Bacon's Sugar House** (603-532-8836), Dublin Road, just south of Monadnock State Park entrance, Jaffrey Center. The familiar plastic jug now used by 75 percent of the country's maple producers was invented in 1973 by Charles Bacon, who welcomes visitors on March weekends. Adjacent to cross-country ski trails in the state park, this vintage-1910 sugarhouse stands on a farm that's been in the family since 1780.

**Bascom's Sugar House** (603-835-6361), between Alstead and Acworth off Route 123A. One of the largest maple producers in New England, a huge sugarhouse and warehouse set high on Mount Kingsbury. Visitors are welcome to tour the plant, which uses unusual reverse-osmosis evaporators. Monday through Friday 7:30 AM–5 PM, Saturday 8 AM–noon.

**Clark's Sugar House** (603-835-6863), Alstead. Award-winning syrup boiled over a wood fire. Will ship.

**Fisk's Little Sugar House** (603-654-9784), Dale Street just off Route 31, Wilton. Specializes in maple candy.

**Jack Niland's Sugar House** (603-399-7712), a visitor-friendly sugarhouse, ships anywhere in the world.

**Parker's Maple Barn and Sugar House** (603-878-2308), Mason (follow signs from Route 13 in Brookline). Big dining barn.

**Stuart & John's Sugar House and Pancake Restaurant** (603-399-4486), junction of Routes 12 and 63, Westmoreland. Open weekends in spring and fall; syrup available year-round.

cializing in hardy, farm-grown plants, old-fashioned and colonial varieties.

SHOPPING COMPLEXES **Colony Mill Marketplace** (603-357-1240), 222 West Street, Keene. Open daily 10 AM–9 PM, Sunday 11 AM–6 PM. This 19th-century, brick woolen mill now houses 33 shops and a food court. Many interesting clothing shops along with the **Country Artisans,** a large, handsome crafts gallery displaying batik, kites, quilts, pottery, weaving, ironwork, lamps and shades, toys, and more, and the **Toadstool Bookshop** (see *Bookstores*).

SPECIAL STORES ♿ **Burdick's Bistro and Café** (603-756-2882; www.burdickchocolate.com), 47 Main Street (next to the post office), Walpole. Exquisite, hand-cut chocolates made from French Valrhona chocolate without extracts or flavorings are crafted in the small shop and shipped to the best Manhattan restaurants and customers throughout the country. We can attest to the quality of the mocha square and white pepper truffle. Burdick's signature is a chocolate mouse, handmade with toasted almond ears. Seconds and a brand-new bistro (see *Dining Out*) make this a must-stop.

**Eastern Mountain Sports** (603-924-7231; www.ems.com), Vose Farm Road, off Route 202 north, Peterborough. Open Monday through Thurday and Saturday 9 AM–6 PM, Friday 9 AM–8 PM, Sunday 11 AM–5 PM. Founded in 1967 and specializing in quality and hard-to-find equipment and clothing for backpacking and climbing enthusiasts, EMS now has 50 stores across the country. This is the corporate headquarters and one of the largest stores, one with a discount corner. Pick up a pamphlet guide to hiking and other outdoor sports possibilities in the Monadnock region.

**Peterborough Basket Co.** (603-924-3861), 130 Grove Street (south of Route 101). Open daily 10 AM–5 PM; Sunday 1–5 PM. The showroom is impressive and prices are reasonable, but the real fun of this place is the seconds room with its bins of baskets and major markdowns on large items like woven hampers. Basketmaking has been an important industry in Peterborough since the 1850s, and this company traces its origins to 1875.

**Ashwood Basket Corp.** (603-924-0000), 350 Union Street, Peterborough. Classic picnic baskets, hampers, even bassinets; a variety of sturdy products made on the premises and sold throughout the country.

**Joseph's Coat** (603-924-6683), 15 Depot Square, Peterborough. Colorful clothing, jewelry, shawls, sloth, alpaca yarn, quilts, puppets, and gifts.

**Miranda's Verandah** (603-352-0681), 1 Main Street, Keene. Lots of flair in this shop with clothes that run the gamut from funky to fine.

**Steele's,** 40 Main Street, Peterborough. In business since 1860, the nicest kind of stationery, card, and generally useful supply store.

**Wood'n'Things** (603-925-6381), Route 124, New Ipswich. Open daily 9 AM–6 PM. Doe and Dottie Apa and son Bob claim to offer more than 7,000 items, mostly wood: pie safes, quilt racks, tables, Adirondcak and rocking chairs, et cetera, et cetera.

## ✷ Special Events

*February*: Keene's annual **Ice and Snow Fest** features ice sculptures and a carving contest.

*May:* **Spring concert,** Monadnock Chorus and Orchestra.

*Mid-May:* Children and the Arts Festival, Peterborough.

*June–September:* **Peterborough Players Summer Theater.**

*Late June:* The annual **Rock Swap** in Gilsum (behind the elementary school on Route 10) attracts 8,000 to 10,000 mineral buffs.

*July:* See *Entertainment* for music, theater, and lecture series in July and August. **July Fourth celebrations,** the most unusual of which is held July 3 in **Greenville:** At midnight all the bells and sirens in town ring and residents parade down Main Street banging pots and pans, leading a parade that includes fire engines, floats, and baby carriages. In Peterborough the Fourth is also a gala celebration with a crafts fair, music, food, and children's entertainment at the Peterborough Historical Society 10 AM–4 PM.

*July–August:* **TGIF Summer Music Series** in Depot Park, Peterborough.

*July–September:* **Monadnock Music Concert Series** (see *Entertainment*).

*Third week of July:* **Fitzwilliam Antiques Fair,** more than 40 dealers.

*Third weekend of July:* ***The Old Homestead,*** a pageant/play, is performed in the Potash Bowl, a natural amphitheater in Swanzey. **Balloon Fest and Fair,** Hillsborough. **Monadnock Festival of the Arts,** Peterborough.

*August:* **Oak Park Festival,** Greenfield. **Medal Day,** MacDowell Colony, Peterborough (a public picnic and open house). **Old Home Days,** Hancock.

*September:* **Labor Day Festival,** Francestown. Annual **Balloon Festival,** Monadnock Travel Council. Annual **Music Festival** in Keene.

*October:* Keene's **Pumpkin Festival** has made national news in recent years: Two 40-foot-high scaffold pyramids are erected on Main Street to display more than a thousand lighted, hand-carved jack-o'-lanterns. **Foliage Festivals** are also held in Francestown and Greenfield. **Antique Auto Show** and **Octoberfest** at Crotched Mountain Foundation. German music, food, and classic cars. Annual **Book Fair,** MacDowell Colony. Biannual **Monadnock Festival of Quilts,** Monadnock Quilters Guild. **Wool Arts Tour** of farms and crafts studios in the Francestown-Antrim-Hillsborough area.

*November:* **Monadnock Music Christmas Fair,** South Meadow School, Peterborough.

*December:* **Christmas teas** at the Sharon Arts Center. **Messiah Festival** at Franklin Pierce College. **Monadnock Chorus Christmas Concert** at Peterborough Town House.

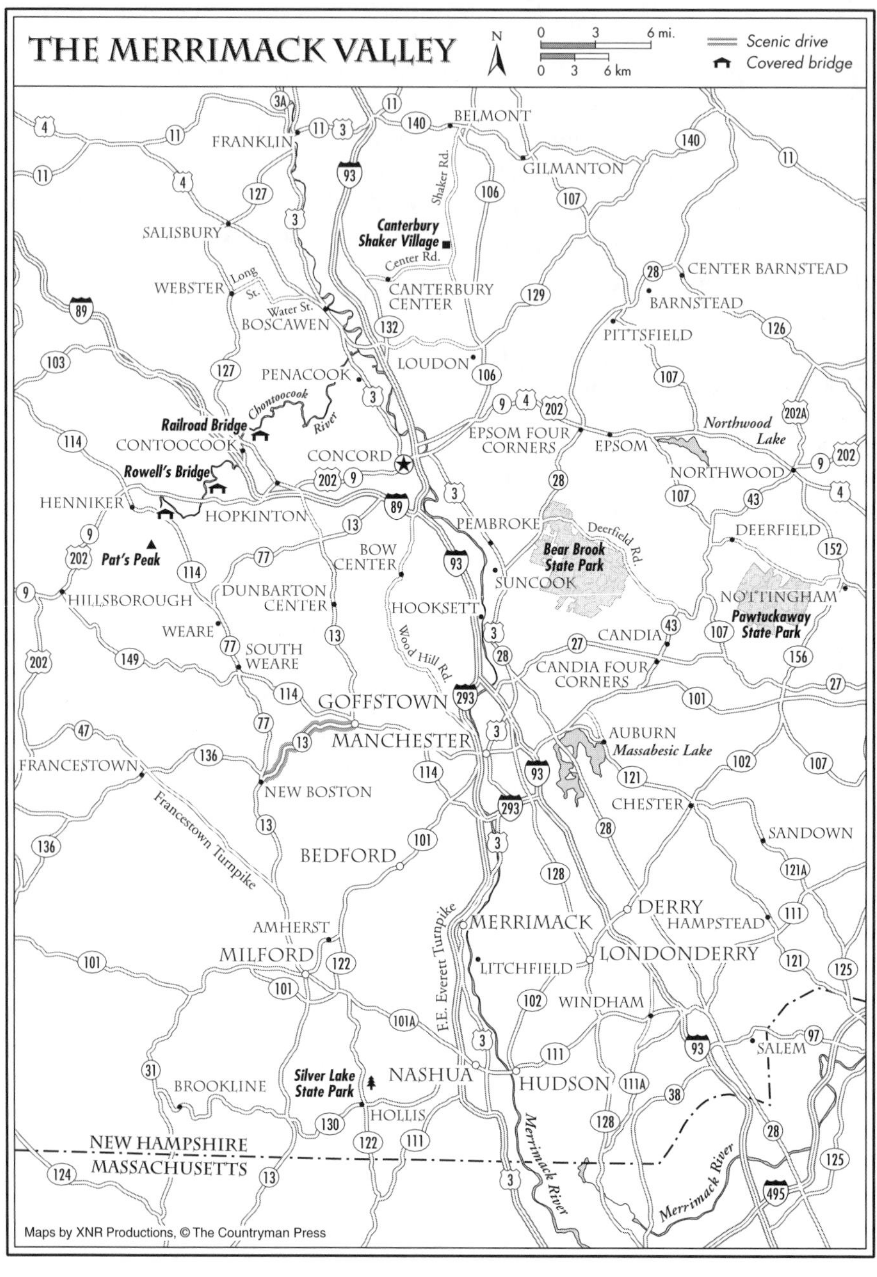
THE MERRIMACK VALLEY
N
0 3 6 mi.
0 3 6 km
Scenic drive
Covered bridge
FRANKLIN
BELMONT
GILMANTON
SALISBURY
Canterbury Shaker Village
WEBSTER
BOSCAWEN
CANTERBURY CENTER
CENTER BARNSTEAD
BARNSTEAD
PITTSFIELD
PENACOOK
LOUDON
Railroad Bridge
CONTOOCOOK
Rowell's Bridge
CONCORD
EPSOM FOUR CORNERS
EPSOM
Northwood Lake
NORTHWOOD
HENNIKER
HOPKINTON
PEMBROKE
Bear Brook State Park
DEERFIELD
Pat's Peak
BOW CENTER
SUNCOOK
DUNBARTON CENTER
HILLSBOROUGH
HOOKSETT
NOTTINGHAM
Pawtuckaway State Park
WEARE
SOUTH WEARE
CANDIA
CANDIA FOUR CORNERS
GOFFSTOWN
MANCHESTER
AUBURN
Massabesic Lake
FRANCESTOWN
NEW BOSTON
CHESTER
SANDOWN
Francestown Turnpike
BEDFORD
DERRY
HAMPSTEAD
AMHERST
MERRIMACK
MILFORD
LONDONDERRY
LITCHFIELD
WINDHAM
SALEM
F.E. Everett Turnpike
NASHUA
HUDSON
Silver Lake State Park
BROOKLINE
HOLLIS
NEW HAMPSHIRE
MASSACHUSETTS
Merrimack River
Maps by XNR Productions, © The Countryman Press

# The Merrimack Valley

THE MANCHESTER/NASHUA AREA

THE CONCORD AREA

Kim Grant

# INTRODUCTION

The Merrimack, New England's second longest river, was an early New Hampshire highway, and today it's paralleled by I-93, New Hampshire's north–south transportation spine. One of the state's first settled corridors, the Merrimack Valley has recently been enjoying another migrational rush from hundreds of companies and thousands of families moving north from Massachusetts to take advantage of New Hampshire's tax breaks (no sales or income tax).

Relatively few visitors, however, venture farther into this area than the fast-food chains just off I-93. The very way the highways slice through and around both Manchester and Concord does little to encourage exploration. Manchester's proud, old, brick shopping streets, its Currier Gallery of Art, and its Amoskeag Mills—once the world's largest textile "manufactury"—are rewarding stops. So are Concord's state capitol building, the Museum of New Hampshire History, and the Christa McAuliffe Planetarium. The headquarters for the New Hampshire Audubon Society (just off I-89) and the Society for the Protection of New Hampshire Forests (just off I-93) are also well worth the small detours they require.

Other genuine finds are salted around this little-touristed central New Hampshire corridor. Canterbury Shaker Village, just 15 miles north of Concord, remains a working Shaker community in addition to being one of New England's most interesting museums. "America's Stonehenge" is at Mystery Hill in North Salem. The town of Henniker offers skiing and some fine lodging, dining, and shopping, while Hopkinton village's Main Street, a simple loop between two exits off I-89, presents a picture-perfect slice of early American architecture. There are also numerous state parks with sandy beaches.

# THE MANCHESTER/NASHUA AREA

Manchester is by far New Hampshire's largest city (just over 100,000 people). It's also arguably New England's most interesting "mill city," an image the city has recently begun to re-embrace.

When white men first traveled up the Merrimack, they found a large Native American village at Amoskeag Falls. In 1650 the English missionary John Eliot set up one of his "Praying Indian" communities and called it Derryfield. The Native Americans were later displaced by a white settlement early in the 18th century. By 1810 local judge Samuel Blodgett foretold the community's future, suggesting that its name be changed from Derryfield to Manchester, then the world's biggest manufacturing city (in England).

This early American Manchester population was just 615, but Judge Blodgett raised money to build a canal around Amoskeag Falls to enable flat-bottomed boats to glide downstream and onward, via the Middlesex Canal, into Boston. Both the canal and the town's first cotton mill opened in 1809.

It was a group of Boston entrepreneurs, however, who put Manchester on the map. By the 1830s these "Boston Associates" had purchased waterpower rights for the entire length of the Merrimack River and had begun developing a city full of mills in Lowell, Massachusetts, 32 miles downriver from Manchester. Incorporating themselves as the Amoskeag Manufacturing Company, they then bought 15,000 acres around Amoskeag Falls and drew up a master plan for the city of Manchester, complete with tree-lined streets, housing, churches, and parks.

Like Lowell, Manchester enjoyed an early utopian period during which "mill girls" lived in well-regulated boardinghouses. It was followed by successive periods of expansion, fueled by waves of foreign immigration. With direct rail connections to Quebec, Manchester attracted predominantly French Canadian workers, but Polish, Greek, and Irish communities were (and are) also substantial.

At its height in the early 20th century, the Amoskeag Manufacturing Company employed 17,000 workers, encompassed 64 mill buildings lining both sides of the Merrimack River for a mile and a half, and contained the world's largest single mill yard. Imagine this space filled with the noise and movement of nearly 700,000 spindles and 23,000 looms!

Life for workers was unquestionably hard. The tower bells rang each morning at 4:30, and the first call for breakfast was 5:30; the workday began at 6:30, lasting

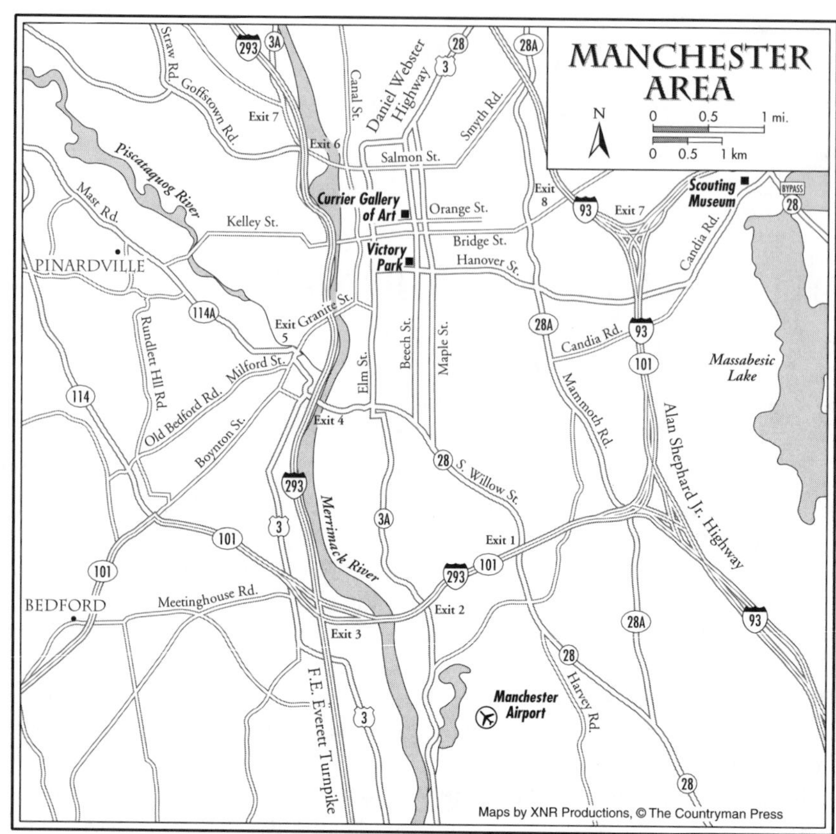


until 7:30 in the evening. But it's a way of life that many workers remember fondly in the oral histories recorded in *Amoskeag: Life and Work in an American Factory-City* by anthropologist Tamara Hareven and photographer Randolph Langenbach. Based on interviews with thousands of former Amoskeag employees, this interesting book, published in 1978, vividly conveys what it was like to live within Manchester's tightly knit ethnic circles, reinforced by a sense of belonging to a full city of workers united like one family by a single boss.

The Amoskeag Manufacturing Company went bankrupt in 1935, and the following year the mills were shut down. In desperation a group of local businessmen formed Amoskeag Industries, Inc., purchased all the mills for $5 million, and managed to lease and sell mill space to diversified businesses.

"Diversify" has been the city's slogan ever since. Having once experienced complete dependency on one economic source, Manchester now prides itself on the number and variety of its industries and service businesses as well as on its current status as a financial and insurance center. New business and residential buildings rise high above the old mill towers.

Loosely circled by hills and with buildings that rise in tiers above the mills on the eastern bank of the Merrimack, Manchester is an attractive city with a Gothic Revival town hall, handsome 19th-century commercial blocks, the gemlike Palace Theater, and the brand-new 10,000-seat Verizon Wireless Arena featuring such top acts as Bob Dylan and Elton John, as well as the city's own American Ice Hockey League team, the Manchester Monarchs. The Currier Gallery of Art, one of the country's outstanding small art museums, is also located here.

GUIDANCE **Greater Manchester Chamber of Commerce** (603-666-6600), 889 Elm Street, Manchester 03101. The chamber office stocks a first-rate *Visitors Guide to Greater Manchester.*

**Greater Nashua Chamber of Commerce** (603-891-2471), 146 Main Street, Nashua 03060.

GETTING THERE *By bus:* From the **Manchester Transportation Center** (603-668-6133), 119 Canal Street, you can get anywhere in the country; Concord Trailways, Vermont Transit Lines, and Peter Pan all stop regularly.

*By air:* The **Manchester Airport** (603-624-6539) is not only the largest in the state, it's also one of the fastest growing in the country. Carriers include United Airlines (1-800-241-6522), USAirways (1-800-428-4322), Continental Express (1-800-525-0280), Delta (1-800-221-1212), Comair Delta (1-800-354-9822), Northwest (1-800-225-2525), Southwest (1-800-435-9792), and Air Canada (1-888-247-2262). There are nonstop flights to Albany, Atlanta, Baltimore, Boston, Chicago, Cincinnati, Cleveland, Detroit, Kansas City, Nashville, New York, Orlando, Philadelphia, Pittsburgh, and Washington. Hertz, Budget, Avis, and Thrifty Car Rental are all here and offer free airport transfers. For parking information call 603-641-5444.

*By car:* The biggest problem with Manchester is finding your way in. It's moated by interstate highways 93 and 293 more effectively than it ever was by canals and mill walls. The simplest access points to downtown are marked from I-293. A handy map, available from the chamber of commerce (see *Guidance*), pinpoints parking garages, and there are reasonably priced (*warning:* and well-monitored) meters.

GETTING AROUND **Hudson Bus Lines** (424-2446), 22 Pond Street, Nashua, offers limousine service between pickup points in Concord, Manchester, Nashua, downtown Boston, and Logan International Airport. City dispatch services are offered by **Town and Country** (603-668-3434), **Yellow Cab** (603-622-0008), and **Executive Airport Service** (603-625-2999).

MEDICAL EMERGENCY **Catholic Medical Center** (603-668-3545), 100 MacGregor Street, Manchester.
**Elliot Hospital** (603-669-5300), 1 Elliot Way, Manchester.

## * To See

MUSEUMS ♿ **Currier Gallery of Art** (603-669-6144), 192 Orange Street, Manchester. Open Wednesday through Monday 11 AM–5 PM, Friday until 8 PM, Sunday 10 AM–5 PM. Admission: $5 per adult, $4 per senior or student with ID; under 18, free. Free admission Saturday until 1 PM. This excellent regional museum, already one of New England's finest, received a major bequest in 2001. It offers

*AMOSKEAG CANAL*, 1948, BY CHARLES SHEELER

Currier Gallery of Art

unexpected treasures: a lovely landscape by Claude Monet; a spooky 1935 Edward Hopper Maine coastal scene titled *The Bootleggers;* a 1940s painting by Sheeler of the Amoskeag mills; and a recently acquired abstract by Mark Rothko. Paintings range from a 13th-century Tuscan Madonna and Child to 20th-century works by Rouault, Picasso, Wyeth, Matisse, and Maxfield Parrish. Silver, pewter, art, glass, textiles, and an extensive collection of early furniture are also displayed. Special exhibits are frequently outstanding. The café and museum shop have been recently expanded; inquire about frequent lectures and concerts.

**The Zimmerman House** (603-669-6144), 201 Myrtle Way. This Usonian home designed in 1950 by Frank Lloyd Wright—his only house open to the public in New England—is also maintained by the Currier. Guided tours are offered from the museum Thursday through Monday for most of the year, with special in-depth weekend tours. Standard tour is $9 per adult; $6 for seniors, students, and those under 18; this price includes museum admission (no children under age 7, please). Call ahead for handicapped accessibility. The Currier is in a residential neighborhood on the site of the Victorian home of Moody and Hannah Currier, the couple who donated the property and who specified in their will that their house be torn down to make way for the museum. The trick to finding it is to begin at either highway exit from which it's marked (the Amoskeag Bridge exit on Route 293 and the Wellington Street exit on I-93), then follow the trail of signs.

THE CURRIER GALLERY OF ART

Currier Gallery of Art

**Franco-American Centre** (603-669-4045), 52 Concord Street. Open Monday through Friday, 9 AM–4:45 PM. Handy to Elm Street and other downtown museums, the gallery here mounts changing exhibits by Franco-American artists and is a leading source of information about French culture, heritage, and history in North America.

**New Hampshire Institute of Art** (603-623-0313), 148 Concord Street, Manchester. Open Monday, Friday, and Saturday 9 AM–5 PM. Just across Victory Park from the Historical Association, New Hampshire's only independent college of art features changing exhibits of regional and national importance in six galleries. The center also offers lectures and theatrical performances. A gift and art supply shop features handcrafted items.

HISTORICAL MUSEUMS AND SITES **Manchester Historic Association Research Library** (603-622-7531), 129 Amherst Street, Manchester 03101. Open Tuesday through Saturday 10 AM–4 PM. Closes at 3 PM in July and August. Free. The library contains Amoskeag Manufacturing Company records, city records, and family papers. Inquire about frequent lectures and workshops, as well as walking tours of the Amoskeag mills (see below) and residential neighborhoods in the city.

✐ ♿ **Mill Yard Museum** (603-622-7531), corner of Commercial and Pleasant Streets, Manchester. Open Tuesday through Saturday 10 AM–4 PM, Sunday noon–4 PM. Adults $5; students and seniors $4; children 6–18 $2, under 6 free. A branch of the Manchester Historic Association, this new museum in former Mill 3 offers a glimpse into what was once the world's largest textile enterprise. Originally conceived as a planned industrial center, the buildings of the former Amoskeag Manufacturing Company still represent one of the country's leading examples of 19th- and early-20th-century industrial architecture. The four- and five-story-high mills stand in two rows along the eastern bank of the river. Built variously from the 1830s to 1910, they look fairly uniform because, as the older mills were expanded, their early distinctive features were blurred. The adjoining blocks lined with tidy, brick mill housing, however, reflect a progression of styles from the 1830s to 1920. The two large mills on the western side of the river were once connected to these by tunnels and bridges. The museum documents the area's history, beginning with a permanent exhibit about the Native Americans who used to catch salmon at Amoskeag Falls. Multimedia exhibits and programs and guided walking tours of the mill yard offer more insights into the social and architectural history of the area.

**Nashua,** New Hampshire's second largest city, has its share of monumental mill buildings along Water and Factory Streets, built by the Nashua Manufacturing Company, which was

**NASHUA CENTER FOR THE ARTS**

✐ (603-883-1506), 14 Court Street, Nashua. Displays contemporary art, including photography and sculpture, in its gallery. It also sponsors a January-to-May "Downtown Live" performance series and a Saturday program of children's entertainment. In summer it sponsors outdoor performances in Holman Stadium.

Currier Gallery of Art

THE DINING ROOM OF THE FRANK LLOYD WRIGHT-DESIGNED ZIMMERMAN HOUSE

chartered in 1823 to produce cotton fabric.

**Robert Frost Farm** (603-432-3091), 2 miles south of Derry on Route 28. Open daily 10 AM–5 PM June 23 through Labor Day; weekends from Memorial Day until Columbus Day. Adults $3; children under 18 and New Hampshire residents over 65, free. Grounds open free at all times. This 1880s clapboard house in which the poet lived between 1901 and 1909 is filled with original furnishings. An interpretive nature trail runs through surrounding fields and woods, past the "mending wall." Frost did the bulk of his writing here.

**Taylor Up and Down Saw Mill,** Island Pond Road, Derry. A water-powered up-and-down sawmill that processed logs into boards; open usually in spring when the water level is high enough to power it and on Saturday in July and August. For precise operating times call the Department of Resources and Economic Development (603-271-3456).

**Old Sandown Railroad Museum** (603-887-3259; 603-887-4611), Route 121A, Sandown. Open June through October, Saturday and Sunday 1–5 PM. Railroad memorabilia, telegraph equipment, old magazines, posters, photographs, and Civil War letters are among the exhibits.

**NASHUA HISTORICAL SOCIETY** (603-883-0015) exhibits its collections in the Florence Speare Memorial Museum, 5 Abbott Street, just off Route 101A. Open March through November, Tuesday through Thursday 10 AM–4 PM, Saturday 1–4 PM. Changing exhibits. The neighboring Abbot-Spalding House, a Federal-era mansion built by Daniel Abbot, "Father of Nashua," is an extension of the museum open the third Saturday of the month March through November.

**FOR FAMILIES** ✐ **Amoskeag Fishways** (603-626-3474), Amoskeag Dam, 6 Fletcher Street (Exit 6 off I-293), Manchester. Open Monday through Saturday 9:30 AM–5 PM. There's a fish ladder where you can watch fish returning to spawn in the Merrimack River during May and June. Year-round educational exhibits highlighting the natural history of the Merrimack River watershed, include a historic diorama and waterpower displays.

✐ **Canobie Lake** (603-893-3506), Exit 2, I-93, Salem. Open Memorial Day through Labor Day, daily noon–10 PM; mid-April through

Memorial Day, weekends noon–6 PM. One of New England's biggest amusement parks: more than 40 rides, including a big roller coaster, extensive Kiddieland, swimming pool, wild log flume ride, antique carousel, and excursion boat and mini train ride around the park.

**Charmingfare Farm** (603-483-5623), Route 27, Candia. Open mid-May through October, Wednesday through Sunday 10 AM–4 PM. $7.50 admission (kids under 1 are free) includes petting zoo and hayride.

**The Children's Metamorphosis** (603-425-2560), 217 Rockingham Road, Londonderry. Take Exit 5 off I-93, then go 1 mile north on Route 28. Open Tuesday through Saturday 9:30 AM–5 PM, Sunday 1–5 PM, Friday evening until 8. Adults $5 ($10 per family with children under 1 free). Geared to kids 2–8, there are 13 exhibit areas including a nature center, water-play area, construction site, grocery store, hospital emergency room, and many hands-on exhibits.

**The Lawrence L. Lee Scouting Museum** (603-669-8919), Bodwell Road, Manchester. Open July and August, daily 10 AM–4 PM; September through June, Saturday 10 AM–4 PM. Considered the finest collection of Scouting memorabilia and books in the world; exhibits include original drawings and letters of Scouting founder Lord Robert Baden-Powell. The library of 3,000 books and bound periodicals also relates to Scouting.

**Mystery Hill** (603-893-8300), off Route 111, North Salem. Take I-93 Exit 3 and follow Route 111 for 5 miles east to Island Pond Road, then take Haverhill Road to the entrance. Open daily except Thanksgiving and Christmas; hours vary by season. Check for current rates. Billed as "America's Stonehenge, one of the largest and possibly the oldest megalithic . . . sites in North America." How and why these

THE ROBERT FROST FARM IN DERRY

Robert Kozlow

intriguing stone formations originated is a mystery, whether built by Native Americans or migrant Europeans, but what's known for sure is that they remain an amazing example of prehistoric astronomical and architectural prowess.

♂ ♿ **SEE Science Center** (603-669-0400), 200 Bedford Street, fourth floor, Manchester. Open Monday through Friday 10 AM–3 PM, Saturday and Sunday noon–5 PM. Housed in a mill building, this hands-on science discovery center allows children to experience weightlessness on a moon walk, and to experiment with an electricity and a momentum exhibit, giant bubbles, gyroscopes, and more. $4 per person.

SCENIC DRIVES **Goffstown to New Boston.** With its bandstand and country stores, New Boston is an unusually handsome town, and the ride between it and Goffstown is one of the most pleasant around. The road follows the winding Piscataquog River, a good stream for fishing and canoeing. Take Route 114 west from Manchester and Route 13 to New Boston.

**Londonderry.** For a glimpse of southern New Hampshire's agricultural past, call 603-432-1100, ext. 134, to obtain a map for a tour of country roads through blossoms in spring and apples in fall.

## ✷ To Do

BASEBALL **Holman Stadium** (603-883-3355), Nashua. The Nashua Pride may be a minor-league team (it's part of the Atlantic League of Professional Baseball), but around here it's major summertime fun.

BOATING There's public access to the Merrimack River's kayak course from Arms Park in downtown Manchester. Lake Massabessic offers two public launches for sailing, powerboating, and canoeing. Detailed boating maps of the Merrimack River are available from the **Merrimack River Watershed Council,** 56 Island Street, Lawrence, MA 01840. For information about local rentals and events, try the council's headquarters at 508-681-5777.

FACTORY TOURS **Anheuser-Busch Brewery** (603-595-1202), 221 Daniel Webster Highway, Merrimack (between Manchester and Nashua). Tours of the brewery with complimentary tastings are offered daily 10 AM–4 PM May through December (9:30 AM–5 PM June through August), and Thursday through Monday 10 AM–4 PM the rest of the year. The shop where you can buy Budweiser logoed merchandise stays open an hour later.

**Stonyfield Farm Yogurt Museum** (603-437-4040, ext. 2252), 10 Burton Drive, Londonderry. Open Monday through Saturday, 9:30 AM–5 PM. Tours on the hour from 10 until 4. Stonyfield Farm is known for good yogurt and good sense with its environmentally friendly operation. Follow the milk from its arrival at the farm to the end of the line when it emerges as a cup of yogurt. $1.50 per person; children 4 and under free.

GOLF **Bedford Golfland** (603-624-0503), 549 Donald Street, Bedford. Year-round driving range and 18-hole miniature golf course.

**Candia Woods Golf Links** (603-483-2307; 1-800-564-4344), Exit 3, Route 101, High Street, Candia. Eighteen holes, open to the public.

**Derryfield Country Club** (603-669-0235), 625 Mammoth Road, Manchester.

**Legends Golf & Family Recreation** (603-627-0099), 18 Legends Drive (behind Wal-Mart), Hooksett. Miniature golf and lighted driving range, along with lessons by a PGA professional and free tips on Wednesday night. Also batting cages for baseball and softball.

**Stonebridge Country Club** (603-497-8633), 161 Gorham Pond Road, Goffstown. Eighteen holes, open to the public.

**Tory Pines Resort** (603-588-2000), Route 47, Francestown.

**Valley View Golf Club** (603-774-5031), Dunbarton. Nine holes.

♿ **Victorian Park Mini-Golf & Family Entertainment Center** (603-898-1803), 350 North Broadway, Salem. Victorian-motif ice cream parlor, arcade, and challenging 18-hole mini golf course.

HOCKEY **Verizon Wireless Arena** (603-644-5000; 603-626-PUCK, or -7825), 832 Elm Street, Manchester. Premiering in fall 2001, the Manchester Monarchs, an affiliate of the Los Angeles Kings, have fielded this American Hockey League team at New Hampshire's newest and largest sports and entertainment facility. The season lasts from mid-November through the first week in April.

HORSE RACING **Rockingham Park** (603-898-2311), Route 28 and I-93, Salem. Open spring through fall for major-league thoroughbred racing; year-round day and night simulcasting from the country's best thoroughbred racetracks. Dining at the Sports Club.

**Splash & Dash Hot Air Ballooning** (603-483-5503), 25 Maple Farm Road, Auburn. Balloon rides offered over the Merrimack Valley.

WALKING TOURS **Heritage Walking Tours** (603-625-4827), P.O. Box 3402, Manchester. Enthusiastic and knowledgeable local historians offer regularly scheduled and specially tailored tours of the Amoskeag Mill Yard, workers' housing, the Franco-American West Side and other ethnic neighborhoods of Manchester. Scheduled tours last 1½–2 hours.

## ✻ Green Space

**Bear Brook State Park** (603-485-9874), off Route 28 in Allenstown. Open mid-May through mid-October. Take the Hooksett exit off I-93. The park has 9,600 heavily forested acres with six lakes, swimming, rental boats, picnicking for up to 1,500 visitors under tall pines, a physical fitness course, nature trails, fishing (Archery Pond is reserved for fly-fishing), and camping with 81 tent sites on Beaver Pond (where the swimming beach is reserved for campers). The Bear Brook Nature Center also has programs, two nature trails, and more than 30 miles of hiking trails in the park with separate routes for ski tourers and snowmobilers in winter. Very crowded on summer weekends but not too bad midweek. Fee.

**Massabesic Audubon Center** (603-668-2045), Auburn. Open daily, Monday through Saturday 9 AM–5 PM; Sunday 1–5 PM. Free. Miles of scenic trails for hiking, snowshoeing, and skiing. Live animals, osprey viewing, and large Nature Store with snowshoe and binocular rentals.

**Pawtuckaway State Park** (603-895-3031), off Route 156, Nottingham. Open mid-May through mid-October. At Raymond, 3.5 miles north of the junction of Routes 101 and 156. The attraction is a small beach on 803-acre Lake Pawtuckaway, with good swimming, a bathhouse, a 25-acre picnic area, and hiking trails. Rental boats are available; outboard motors are permitted; and the lake is stocked for fishing. Horse Island and Big Island, both accessible to cars, have a total of 170 tent sites, many right on the water; campers have their own boat launch. Trails lead up into the Pawtuckaway Mountains. Both cross-country skiing and snowmobiling are popular here in winter.

**Silver Lake State Park** (603-465-2342), Route 122, Hollis. A great beach with a bathhouse, a concession stand, picnic tables, and a diving raft. More than 100 picnic sites are scattered through the pine groves. Summer weekend crowds come from Nashua, but midweek is pleasant. Fee.

**Clough State Park** (603-529-7112), between Routes 114 and 13, about 5 miles east of Weare. Open daily late June through Labor Day. The focus here is 150-acre Everett Lake, created by the U.S. Army Corps of Engineers as a flood-control project. The 50-acre park includes a sandy beach and bathhouses, a picnic grove, and a playground. Motorized boats are not permitted, but there is a boat launch and rental boats are available. Fee.

## ✷ Lodging

HOTELS ✐ ♿ **The Center of New Hampshire Holiday Inn** (603-625-1000), 700 Elm Street, Manchester 03101. Located in the center of downtown near the new Verizon Wireless Arena, this is Manchester's major convention center. Two restaurants, 250 guest rooms, garage parking, all under one roof. $145–160; group rates available.

✐ ♿ **The Highlander Inn** (603-625-6426; 1-800-548-9248), 2 Highlander Way, Manchester 03103. A very nice 65-room hotel in a well-landscaped setting just 2 minutes from the airport. $99–129 with 24-hour shuttle and discounted airport parking.

✐ ♿ **Wayfarer Inn** (603-622-3766; 1-877-489-3658), 121 South River Road, Bedford 03110. A Manchester landmark since the 1960s, this full-service hotel and conference center offers 194 rooms, a health and fitness center with an indoor and outdoor pool, and a restaurant surrounded by pretty landscaping that includes waterfalls and a covered bridge. Free shuttle to Manchester Airport, 4 miles away. $115–169 with variable special rates.

INN ✐ ♿ **Bedford Village Inn** (603-472-2001; 1-800-852-1166), 2 Village Inn Lane, Bedford 03110. This is the inn the big-name media folk prefer when they're in town to cover New Hampshire's first-in-the-nation presidential primary. Once a working farm, the circa-1810 dairy barn now offers 12 elegant guest rooms and two apartments. All the rooms are spacious, equipped with large-screen TV and Jacuzzi, and are handsomely decorated with period antiques, custom fabrics, paintings, and Oriental rugs. The complex also includes a patrician-looking Federal home that now houses a restaurant with eight intimate dining rooms and a tap room tavern (see *Dining Out*). Plans are in the works to expand this four-diamond inn with 36 additional guest suites, an upscale spa facility with a café featuring spa cuisine, and a Northern Italian restaurant, all due to open by summer 2003. Rates, which include breakfast, start at $225 per couple.

BED & BREAKFASTS **Derryfield Bed & Breakfast** (603-627-2082), 1081 Bridge Street Extension, Manchester 03103. A friendly, gracious B&B in a quiet neighborhood, handy to I-93. The three rooms include an attractive single ($75 per night); a full breakfast is served in the sunny dining room, and guests also have access to the living room (with fireplace and cable TV) and to the pool. $85 per couple.

**Ash Street Inn** (603-668-9908), 118 Ash Street, Manchester 03104-4345. One of Manchester's rambling old Queen Anne houses, this one (circa 1885) is the setting for the Queen City's newest and poshest B&B. In addition to plush queen-sized beds, private bath, and cable TV, the five rooms offer air-conditioning, computer dataports, and voice-mail phones. There's a full breakfast in the dining room, a fireplace in the parlor, and a Rolls-Royce to shuttle you to and from the airport. $129 with breakfast and complimentary shuttle. Nonsmoking; no children or pets.

**Breezy Hill Bed & Breakfast** (603-432-0122), 119 Adams Road, Londonderry 03053. This 1850s farmhouse is neighbor to a large local orchard. Choose from two rooms with private bath on the second floor ($85) or two rooms with shared bath on the first ($55 single, $75 double). A full breakfast recalls the area's agricultural past, with eggs from the Foley family's hens and honey from their apiary.

For **camping sites,** see Bear Brook State Park and Pawtuckaway State Park under *Green Space.*

## ✷ Where to Eat

DINING OUT **Bedford Village Inn** (603-472-2001; 1-800-852-2001), 2 Village Inn Lane, Bedford. Open for breakfast, lunch, and dinner daily; Sunday brunch. This beautifully restored 18th-century house is now a four-diamond restaurant with a variety of elegant dining rooms. The glassed-in porch has off-white furniture and mint-green carpeting with floral design; another room boasts mahogany paneling. There's also a cheery tavern with its own less expensive menu. Breakfast is a production—specialty omelets and crêpes, plus treats like deep-fried fruit fritters. The dinner menu might include pan-seared jumbo sea scallops served with chive risotto and butternut-apple salad ($27) or veal porterhouse with red wine demiglaze, shallot mashed potatoes, and wilted greens ($29).

**Baldwin's on Elm** (603-622-5975), 1105 Elm Street, Manchester. Open weekdays for lunch 11:30 AM–2 PM; nightly for dinner 5–9:30, Friday and Saturday until 10 PM. Closed Sunday. The talk of the town since the Verizon Wireless Arena has brought new buzz to Elm Street, this restaurant opened in October 2001 with Nathan Baldwin, the former executive chef at the Bedford Village Inn, at the helm. There's a three-course wine-tasting dinner on Monday for $35. The regular menu includes such unusual but delicious combinations as goat cheese and dates on baby greens in the appetizer column; caramelized scallops with celery root and truffle puree as an entrée. Expensive.

♿ **Cotton** (603-622-5488), 75 Arms Park Drive, Manchester. Open Sunday through Thursday 5–9 PM, weekends until 10 PM. Lunch is served Monday through Friday 11:30 AM–3 PM, with a bar menu 3–5 PM. Located below Canal Street, the bold font and tilted martini glass on the marquee herald the casually sophisticated, slightly 1950s retro look of this trendy eatery in Manchester's historic old mill complex. Jeffrey Paige, once the chef at Canterbury's Shaker Village, is well known for his innovative dishes using fresh seasonal ingredients. Now he's earning a name for his presentations as well. Asian-style tuna stacked on a sesame rice cake and topped with warm crab salad is typical of his style. Entrées range $13–20.

**C. R. Sparks** (603-647-7275), 18 Kilton Road, Bedford. For roast beef and steak, this is the best stop in town. Casual dining in a new facility with the feel of an updated hunting lodge. Moderate to expensive.

**Fratello's** (603-624-2022), 155 Dow Street, Manchester. One more entry on the city's Italian dining scene, Fratello's offers a good, moderately priced menu with steaks, seafood, Italian specialties, and major desserts.

**Richard's Bistro** (603-644-1180), 36 Lowell Street, Manchester. Open daily 11:30 AM–10 PM. Just off Elm Street in downtown Manchester, this attractive restaurant, good for unusual soups and salads at lunch and for Sunday brunch dishes like salmon hash and poached eggs topped with horseradish dill cream or a frittata of fresh vegetables baked with feta. Dinner entrées might include pecan-dusted chicken breast with kiwi, mango, and sweet potato garnished with raspberries, and charbroiled filet mignon with shiitake mushrooms and focaccia potatoes. For dessert try the raspberry trifle. A number of wines are available by the glass, and the wine list is respectable.

**Tiya's Restaurant** (603-669-4365), 8 Hanover Street, Manchester. A clean, attractive Thai eatery right downtown at the corner of Elm and Hanover. You can get a tuna salad or Reuben, but stir-fried dishes like shrimp, scallops, sea legs, broccoli, pepper, and mushrooms are the same price. House specialty is pad Thai: stir-fried egg, chicken, bean sprouts, and spicy sauces garnished with crushed peanuts. Moderate.

EATING OUT **The Athens** (603-623-9317), 31 Central Street, Manchester. Open daily for lunch and dinner. Standard Greek dishes, generous portions, moderately priced.

**Chez Vachon** (603-625-9660), 136 Kelly Street, West Manchester (minutes from I-293). Open Monday through Saturday 6 AM–2 PM, Sunday 7 AM–1 PM. A small Franco-American eatery with a big following for its salmon pie, pork pie, French crêpes, and the like.

**Down 'n Dirty Bar B.Q.** (603-624-2224), 168 Amory Street, Manchester. Open Tuesday through Thursday 11:30 AM–8 PM, Friday and Saturday until 9 PM; Sunday 1–8 PM. Closed Monday. Eat in or take out, but don't bother if you don't like real southern pit barbecue. Pulled pork, ribs, chicken, beef, catfish and shrimp, all cooked lovingly over hickory wood. Hush puppies and pecan-topped sweet potato pie, with a little blues music for background, will have you whistling "Dixie."

**Red Arrow Diner** (603-626-1118), 61 Lowell Street, Manchester. Open 24 hours. A city landmark since 1922, this small, friendly diner was voted one of the top 10 diners in the country by *USA Today*. It's the kind of place with a brass hanger for your coat and a mug of coffee that's brought the moment you sit down. Specialties like meat loaf, chicken potpie, and hot sandwiches.

**Shorty's Mexican Roadhouse** (603-472-3656), 230 Route 101 west, Bedford, and (603-625-1730) 1050 Bicentennial Drive, Manchester. Open daily from 11:30 AM, Sunday from 1 PM. This is a local favorite: a 1940s roadhouse atmosphere with Mexican reliables like tacos, fajitas, and enchiladas; also dinner specials like chicken mole and grilled fish with salsa. Same menu all day.

**Venetian Canal Espresso Caffé** (603-627-9200), 805 Canal Street, Manchester. Open Monday through Thursday 7 AM–4 PM, Friday until 3 PM; Saturday 8 AM–1 PM. Soups, salads, sandwiches, pastry, and enough yummy coffee, tea, and chai drinks to float a gondola.

## ✷ Entertainment

♿ **The Palace Theater** (603-668-5588), www.palacetheatre.org, 80 Hanover Street, Manchester 03101. Opened in 1915, reopened and restored in 1974, this 883-seat theater is a beauty—with small, glittering chandeliers, bright local art, and an intimate feel. Its own resident company mounts six productions a year, and during the summer there is children's programming and a July summer camp. Phone for the current program.

**Stage One Productions** (603-669-5511), 132 Bridge Street, Manchester. Dinner theater during winter months.

**American Stage Festival Theater,** Milford, stages a series of summer productions, mid-July through early August.

♿ **Verizon Wireless Arena** (603-644-5000), 832 Elm Street, Manchester. The state's new 10,000-seat venue for big-time concerts, wrestling, dirt shows, figure skating, hockey, basketball, arena football, and political forums.

## ✷ Selective Shopping

ART GALLERY **Art 3 Gallery** (603-668-6650), 44 West Brook Street (off Canal), Manchester. Contemporary and traditional work by a range of artists.

SPECIAL STORE **McQuades** (603-625-5451), 844 Elm Street, Manchester. Open Monday through Saturday 9:30 AM–5:30 PM, until 9 PM Thursday and Friday; Sunday noon–5 PM. The nicest kind of family-owned clothing store. Coffee is always hot for shoppers. The bargains in the basement range from coats to comforters with plenty for both adults and children. In this store, the largest of the three McQuades (there's one on Concord's Main Street, another in Nashua's Simoneau Plaza), cash and checks are still shunted from cash registers through tubes.

**Vintage Vending** (1-888-242-6633), 288 North Broadway, Salem. Open daily except major holidays, Monday through Friday 10 AM–6 PM, Saturday until 5 PM; Sunday 11 AM–4 PM. Nostalgia's a way of life in this 3,000-square-foot flash from the past. Fully restored jukeboxes, diner furniture, soda machines, automobilia—you name it—bring back the birth of the cool.

**MALLS** Reluctantly we include directions to malls along Manchester's "strip," because that's what many out-of-staters are here for; New Hampshire's lack of sales tax has its appeal.

**The Mall of New Hampshire,** 1500 South Willow Street, is the state's largest, with the usual suspects including J. C. Penney, Filene's, and Sears. **Willow Tree Mall,** 575 Willow Street, and **TJ Maxx Plaza,** 933 South Willow Street, are also large.

## ✷ Special Events

*May:* **Hillsborough County Annual Sheep and Wool Festival,** New Boston.

*July:* **Family Outdoor Discovery Day,** Bear Brook State Park Campground (see *Green Space*).

*August:* **Annual Antique Dealers Show,** Manchester.

*September:* **Riverfest,** Manchester. Three days with fireworks, live entertainment, canoe competitions, country fair exhibits. **Hillsborough County Agricultural Fair** (603-674-2510), New Boston. **Hanover Street Fine Arts Fair,** Manchester. **Deerfield Fair** (603-463-7421), Deerfield.

*October:* **Annual Weare Craft Bazaar,** Weare. **Head of the Merrimack Regatta** (603-888-2875), Nashua.

# THE CONCORD AREA

The golden dome of the state capitol building still towers above downtown Concord. Since 1819, when it was built out of local granite by convict labor, this building has been the forum for the state's legislature—now numbering 400 members—said to be the third largest deliberative body in the English-speaking world.

The Native Americans called this site Penacook, or "crooked place," for the snakelike turns the Merrimack makes here. Concord's compact downtown clusters along the western bank of the river, and it's encircled by the concrete wall of I-93 along the opposite bank.

Concord owes its prominence to two forgotten phenomena: the Middlesex Canal—opened in 1815 to connect it with Boston—and the steam railroad from Boston, completed in 1842. Today Concord remains an important transportation hub—the point at which I-89 forks off from I-93 to head northwest across New Hampshire and Vermont, ultimately linking Boston with Montreal.

Concord is really just a medium-sized town of just over 40,000 residents, and you are quickly out of it and into the countryside of East Concord at the Society for the Protection of New Hampshire Forests headquarters, or into the western countryside at Silk Farm, New Hampshire's Audubon Society.

While still very much in the Merrimack Valley, Concord, in contrast to Manchester, is just beyond southern New Hampshire's old industrial belt with its ethnic mix. Some of Concord's surrounding towns are as Yankee, and as picturesque, as any in New England.

Canterbury Shaker Village, a striking old hilltop community, is a gathering of white wooden buildings surrounded by spreading fields. Hopkinton, a proud, early-19th-century town, offers a different kind of serenity and some good antiquing; and Henniker is a mill town turned college town, with more to offer visitors than many resorts.

**GUIDANCE** **The Greater Concord Chamber of Commerce** (603-224-2508), 40 Commercial Street (just off Exit 15W, I-93), Concord 03301. Open year-round, Monday through Friday 8 AM–5 PM. Plenty of parking by the new Concord Courtyard Marriott & Grappone Conference Center. Friendly and helpful once you get inside. The chamber also maintains an information kiosk downtown on State House Plaza, open weekends June through Columbus Day, depending on the availability of volunteers.

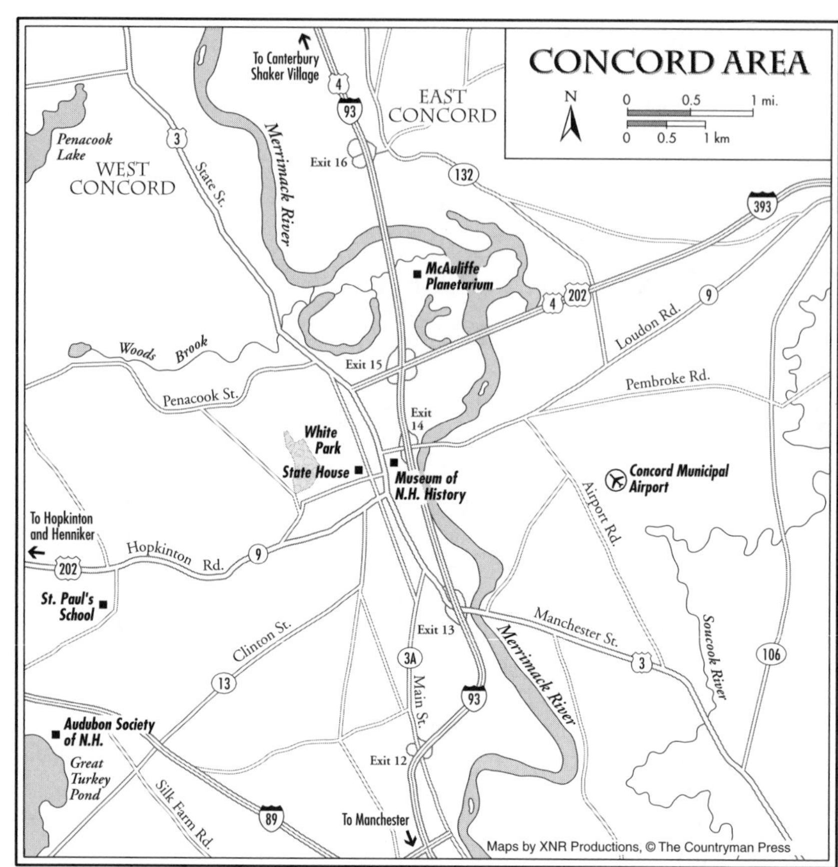


**GETTING THERE** *By bus:* **The Concord Bus Terminal** (603-228-3300), Stickney Avenue, is served by Concord Trailways, Peter Pan Bus Lines, and Vermont Transit.

**GETTING AROUND** *By taxi:* **A&P Taxi** (603-224-6573), **Central Taxi** (603-224-4077). **Concord Cab Company** (603-225-4222), **Main Street Taxi** (603-226-8888). **Celebrity Express Limousine** (603-776-5775) and **Grace Limousine** (603-226-0002) offer limousine service between pickup points in Concord, Manchester, downtown Boston, and Logan International Airport.

**MEDICAL EMERGENCY** **Concord Hospital** (603-225-2711), 250 Pleasant Street, Concord.

## ✷ Villages

**Henniker.** West of Concord at the junction of Routes 9/202 and 114 (take Exit 5 off I-89), the "only Henniker on earth" is a delightful college town with an outstanding small ski area, a cross-country ski center, and a number of interesting shops and restaurants. Well into the 20th century Henniker was a bustling crossroads town with a thriving inn, a number of farms, and three mills on the Contoocook River—one mill making bicycle rims; another, handles; and the third, leatherboard for shoes. Several mills, however, were destroyed by a 1936 flood, and in the 1940s **New England College** was established. With a combined student and faculty population of 1,000, the college now forms the heart of the town. The former Henniker Inn is the administration office, the art gallery next door showcases New England art, and shops and restaurants line a green strip along the Contoocook River across the street. A winery, two outstanding inns, and a wide scattering of shops and restaurants are also part of this unusual small town.

**Hopkinton.** Just west of Concord off I-89, Hopkinton village boasts a Main Street lined with picturesque churches, early white-clapboard mansions, a traditional town hall that once served as the state capitol, and the New Hampshire Antiquarian Society, an ambitiously named but excellent local museum and gallery (see *To See—Museums*). Beyond the village center are lovely back road drives. Be sure to stop at Beech Hill Farm, still owned by the Kimball family nine generations after the king's grant, for Donna's home-baked coffee cake and make-your-own sundaes. Another old family property, Gould Hill Orchards, is located high enough to see Mount Washington on a clear day. It offers "pick-your-own" and a barn filled with seasonal gifts, homemade goodies, and fruit (see *Selective Shopping—Special Shops*). Three miles west on Route 103, Contoocook village is host to the Hopkinton Fair (Contoocook is one of three villages that form the town of Hopkinton), held annually over the Labor Day weekend. The new Hopkinton Town Library, just off Fountain Square on Pine Street, is a handsome shingle-style building set on a former 68-acre farm. Its screened reading porches overlook soccer and baseball fields, and the Local History Room features a dozen outstanding murals with area scenes painted by talented local artists.

THE HENNIKER–NEW ENGLAND BRIDGE SPANS THE CONTOOCOOK RIVER.

Robert Kozlow

Kim Grant

THE MEETING HOUSE AND DWELLING HOUSE AT CANTERBURY SHAKER VILLAGE

**CANTERBURY SHAKER VILLAGE**

(603-783-9511; www.shakers.org), Shaker Road, Canterbury 03224. Open May 1 through October, daily 10 AM–5 PM; weekends in April, November, and December, 10 AM–4 PM. Admission: $10 per adult; $5 per child 6–15.

The single most rewarding sight to see in central New Hampshire, this complex of 24 buildings set in 694 acres conjures up a unique, almost vanished way of life that produced many inventions and distinctive art, food, and music. Between the 1780s and 1990, some 2,300 Shaker men, women, and children lived in this rural community, putting their "hands to work and hearts to God." In the 1850s, when this Shaker village owned 4,000 acres with 100 buildings, it was one of 18 such American communes extending from Kentucky to Maine to Ohio. Today just six communities survive to tell their story, and Canterbury is one of just two settlements that have never been out of Shaker hands. In 1969 Eldress Bertha Lindsay (who died in 1990) had the foresight to incorporate the present buildings and property as a nonprofit museum.

The last village to assume the "Lead Ministry," Canterbury absorbed a number of brethren from other communities as they closed and so conveys a vivid sense of Shaker life from the 1880s to about the turn of the 20th century. Visitors are guided through a dozen buildings, and encouraged to lunch and on weekends to dine in the **Creamery,** generally recognized as one of the best places to eat in New Hampshire (see *Dining Out*). You can also follow the nature trail around Turning Mill Pond, one of the eight that once powered a variety of mills on a 4,000-acre spread. The vintage-1792 Meeting House now doubles as exhibit and performance space. The Laundry is immense and fascinating, and the brightly lit sewing room is furnished with exquisitely crafted tables, and hung with the "Dorothy Cloaks" invented here, popularized by Mrs. Grover Cleveland, who wore one to her husband's inauguration in 1885. The infirmary is equally fascinating, restored to trace the evolution of medical care here. Herbs in the built-in drawers are left from the last time they were used, and the tools on the dentist chair are just as Elder Henry Blinn left them. (Also known as a cartographer and geologist, Blinn began practicing dentistry here in 1860.) In the School House it's easy to assume that the pupils are just out for recess and will be rushing back in, up the graceful staircase and into the bright, wood-paneled room that is filled with books, hung with maps. The blackboard bears a reminder written there by Sister Bertha: "No one will find a spirit-real heaven, until they first create earthly heaven."

Special evening dinners and candlelight tours of the village are also offered by reservation Friday and Saturday when the village is open. The village's Creamery restaurant is open daily when the museum is open. Note the many special happenings listed at the end of this chapter under *Special Events.*

Southbound on I-93, the village is marked from Exit 18. Northbound, use Exit 15E and follow I-393 east for 5 miles; then take Route 106 north for 7 miles and turn at the sign for Shaker Road.

## ✷ To See

**MUSEUMS** ✐ **Christa McAuliffe Planetarium** (603-271-STAR), 2 Institute Drive, Concord. Take I-93 Exit 15E, drive east on I-393 to Exit 1, and follow signs. Open Tuesday through Saturday 10 AM–5 PM, Sunday noon–5 PM. McAuliffe was a teacher at Concord High School when she was chosen from among 11,000 to be the first teacher in space. Dedicated to her memory (she died in the *Challenger* tragedy of 1986), this facility, with its dramatic rendition of the universe, has the most sophisticated electronics system of any planetarium. Although geared primarily to schoolchildren, it has a variety of programs. There are several shows daily, but the general public should reserve in advance since seating is limited to 92 people. $8 per adult; $5 for children, college students, and seniors. Inquire about special programs and workshops.

**Museum of New Hampshire History** (603-226-3189), 6 Eagle Square, off Main Street, Concord. Follow directions to parking from I-93 Exit 14. Open Tuesday through Saturday 9:30 AM–5 PM, until 8:30 PM Thursday and Friday; Sunday noon–5 PM. Admission $5 per adult ($4 if over age 55), $2.50 per student 6–18, under 6 free; $15 family maximum. Opened in 1995 by the New Hampshire Historical Society. Exhibits fill two floors of a 19th-century stone warehouse with one floor devoted to the densely packed permanent exhibit, *New Hampshire through Many Eyes.* Chronological displays draw you through the state's history, from the Native Americans (in addition to an ancient dugout canoe and Indian artifacts, there is a wigwam in which youngsters can sit and hear an old Abenaki tale) to 20th-century industry. The exhibit captions tell some fascinating stories, like that of an exquisite porcupine quill belt (woven in 1763 by a young girl who had been captured by Native Americans) and of a piece of linen made by Henniker's "Oceanborn Mary" (who was such a captivating baby that she charmed pirates out of capturing a ship). The collection includes the predictable Portsmouth-made highboy, Revolutionary War muskets, and, of course, a Concord Coach (3,000 were made in this town), but what's most interesting about the exhibit is its chronicle of past New Hampshire residents. You can hear Eldress Bertha Lindsay of Canterbury Shaker Village (thanks to the sound tape from Walpole resident Ken Burns's Shaker documentary) and ponder the fact that Christian Science founder Mary Baker Eddy (born in Bow, New Hampshire), poet Robert Frost, Pres. Franklin Pierce, and *Peyton Place* author Grace Metalious are all in the same corner. The top floor, accessed through a staircase that suggests the look and view (through murals) of a White Mountains fire tower, is devoted to changing exhibits. There's no need to pay admission to access the extensive gift shop, featuring New Hampshire books. The historical society's headquarters, in its original neoclassical building enhanced by Daniel Chester French's frontispiece, is nearby at 30 Park Street, and contains changing exhibits and an extensive library.

THE CHRISTA MCAULIFFE PLANETARIUM

**The New Hampshire Antiquarian Society** (603-746-3825), Main Street, Hopkinton 03229. Open year-round, Thursday and Friday 10 AM–5 PM, and Saturday 10 AM–2 PM. On a street full of white-clapboard Colonials, this redbrick Palladian-windowed building is notable for its 1890s architecture, as well as for its genealogical materials, research library, local memorabilia, and paintings. There is a small shop and changing exhibits, including a popular autumn art show of exceptional regional talent. Ask for a brochure that includes a driving tour of local attractions.

**HISTORIC HOMES AND SITES** A leaflet describing a self-guided walking tour of Concord, *Concord on Foot,* is available from the chamber of commerce's Capital Region Visitor Center (see *Guidance*). It includes some of the following:

**Benjamin Kimball House and Capitol Center for the Arts** (603-225-1111), 44 South Main Street, Concord. This Romanesque Revival house was built around 1885 by Benjamin Kimball, but later became the state headquarters of the Masonic Order. Now the house and adjoining 1920s-era theater are the core of the Capitol Center for the Arts, a recently renovated regional cultural arts center that hosts internationally known theater troupes, dance companies, and musical acts.

**The Eagle Hotel,** North Main Street, Concord. For more than 135 years the Eagle Hotel was the center of Concord's social and political happenings. Andrew Jackson, Benjamin Harrison, Jefferson Davis, Charles Lindbergh, and Eleanor Roosevelt were all guests. The hotel, now handsomely renovated as the Eagle Square Marketplace, houses mostly offices with a few shops and a restaurant.

**First Church of Christ, Scientist,** North State and School Streets, Concord. Mary Baker Eddy, born in nearby Bow in 1821, formulated the spiritual framework of the Christian Science faith. She contributed $100,000 toward the construction of this Concord granite building, whose steeple makes it the tallest in the city.

**Kimball-Jenkins Estate** (603-225-3932), 276 North Main Street, Concord. Built in 1882, this high Victorian brick and granite mansion has hand-carved oak woodwork, frescoed ceilings, Oriental rugs, and many original furnishings. Inspired by a directive in the late Carolyn Jenkins's will, the estate now houses a thriving community art school.

**New Hampshire State House and The State House Plaza** (603-271-2154), 107 North Main Street, Concord. Open year-round, weekdays for guided and self-guided tours 8 AM–4:30 PM. A handsome 1819 building, this is the oldest state capitol in which a legislature still meets in its original chambers. A visitors center contains dioramas and changing exhibits. More than 150 portraits of past political figures are displayed, and the plaza boasts statues of several New Hampshire notables.

**The Pierce Manse** (603-224-9620), 14 Penacook Street, Concord. Open mid-June through Labor Day, Monday through Friday 11 AM–3 PM, or by appointment. Closed holidays. Built in 1838 and moved to its present site in 1971, this Greek Revival structure was home for Franklin and Jane Pierce from 1842 to 1848, between the time Franklin served in the U.S. Senate and was elected 14th president of the United States. Exhibits include many items owned by the Pierce family prior to 1869.

**St. Paul's School** (603-225-3341), 325 Pleasant Street, Concord. Founded in 1855 by Dr. George Shattuck, St. Paul's is one of the country's premier preparatory schools, a 4-year boarding school with more than 500 students and 100 faculty members. Although the 2,000-acre campus is private, many of the lectures and theater and dance performances are open to the public. Exhibitions in the Tudor-style Hargate Art Center are scheduled throughout the school year, and feature a variety of works by well-known and up-and-coming professional artists and student artists, as well as occasional highlights from the school's collection of works. Past exhibitions have featured works by artists such as Robert Motherwell, Jacob Lawrence, Andrew Wyeth, Milton Avery, Arthur Dove, Eugene Atget, Thomas Buechner, Joyce Tenneson, and others. The school's Ohrstrom Library is also of particular interest. Designed by postmodern architect Robert Stern and opened in 1991, the building references a variety of features from other buildings on campus and offers an outstanding view of Turkey Pond from the reading room.

**Upham-Walker House,** 18 Park Street, Concord. One of the best examples of late Federal architecture in the area, this building is open to the public and offers a glimpse into the lifestyle of successive generations of a prominent Concord family.

COVERED BRIDGES **Henniker–New England College bridge.** A single-span, 150-foot bridge across the Contoocook River on the New England College campus.

**Hopkinton–Rowell bridge,** West Hopkinton. Built in 1853 across the Contoocook River; rebuilt in 1997.

**Hopkinton bridge,** Contoocook village. No longer operating, the bridge spans the Contoocook River at Fountain Square and is said to be the oldest railroad covered bridge in the United States. The nearby depot is in the process of being restored.

FOR FAMILIES ✐ **New Hampshire Fish & Game Department Discovery Room** (603-271-3421), 2 Hazen Drive, Concord. Open year-round Monday through Friday. In the Wild New Hampshire nature center, visitors can try hands-on exhibits, view fish close up in the aquarium, create an animal-track story, and learn about the role of the state in managing wildlife.

## ✷ To Do

CANOEING See *To Do—Boating* in "The Manchester/Nashua Area" for the Merrimack River Watershed Council.

**Hannah's Paddles** (603-753-6695), I-93, Exit 17, Route 4 west, 15 Hannah Duston Road, Penacook. Offers canoe and kayak rentals and a livery service for the Merrimack and Contoocook Rivers.

Note that the Contoocook between West Hopkinton and Henniker is a popular white-water canoeing and kayaking stretch in spring.

CAR RACING **New Hampshire International Speedway** (603-783-4931), Route 106, Loudon. Billed as "the country's newest auto racing facility," the

90,000-seat complex annually attracts an estimated 400,000-plus motor-sport enthusiasts from throughout the nation to the only super-speedway in New England. Races include the world-class NASCAR Winston Cup series, the NASCAR Busch series, and many more. Call for current schedule.

FISHING **The New Hampshire Fish and Game Department** (603-271-3211; 603-271-3421), 2 Hazen Drive, Concord. A source of information about where to fish as well as how to obtain licenses. Trout fishing is particularly good in this area.

GOLF **Beaver Meadow Golf Course** (603-228-8954), Concord, 18 holes on the oldest course (1896) in the state. **Dustin Country Club** (603-746-4234), Hopkinton, nine holes. **Loudon Country Club** (603-783-3372), Loudon, 18 holes. **Plausawa Valley Country Club** (603-224-6267), Pembroke, 18 holes.

DOWNHILL SKIING ✐ **Pat's Peak** (603-428-3245; snow phone, 1-800-258-3218), Route 114, Henniker. The mountain rises steeply right behind the base lodge. It's an isolated, 1,400-foot-high hump, its face streaked with expert trails and a choice of intermediate and beginner runs meandering down one shoulder, half a dozen beginner runs—served by their own lifts—down the other. Big, old fir trees are salted around the base area, and the summit and some of the intermediate trails—certainly Zephyr, the quarter-mile-long beginner's trail off the top—convey the sense of skimming through the woods. When it comes to expert runs, Tornado and Hurricane are wide and straight, but Twister is an old-timer—narrow, twisty, and wooded. This is a family-owned, -run, and -geared ski area that's a great place to learn to ski. *Lifts:* Six, including a double chair and a triple chair to the summit. *Trails:* 20. *Snowmaking:* 90 percent. *Night skiing:* 15 trails, six lifts. *Services:* Ski school, rentals, ski shop, lounge, cafeteria, child care, snowboarding. *Rates:* $33; $25 for juniors on weekends; $25 for all skiers midweek; $19 for everyone for night skiing.

## ✷ Green Space

**Elm Brook Park and Wildlife Management Area,** off Route 127, West Hopkinton. Swimming and picnic areas; built and managed by the U.S. Army Corps of Engineers.

**Hannah Duston Memorial,** west of I-93, Exit 17 (4 miles north of Concord), Boscawen. The monument is on an island at the confluence of the Contoocook and Merrimack Rivers. It commemorates the courage of Hannah Duston, a woman taken prisoner from Haverhill, Massachusetts, during a 1696 Indian raid. She later made her escape, killing and scalping 10 of her captors (including women and children) at this spot on the river. The 35-foot-high monument, erected in 1874, depicts a busty lady with a tomahawk in one hand and what look like scalps in the other. Open all year, but the trail from the parking lot is not plowed in winter.

**Silk Farm Wildlife Sanctuary** (603-224-9909), 3 Silk Farm Road (follow Audubon signs from I-89 Exit 2), Concord. Open year-round, Monday through Saturday 9 AM–5 PM, Sunday 1–5 PM. This is the headquarters of the Audubon Society of New Hampshire, offering an overview of Audubon centers and programs in the state, a Discovery Room with a "touch table," a research wildlife library, an aerie for spotting passing birds, and a gift shop. Trails thread forests and wetlands around Great Turkey Pond, and traverse orchards and fields with a variety of flora and fauna.

**Society for the Protection of New Hampshire Forests Conservation Center** (603-224-9945), Portsmouth Street, Concord. Bring a picnic and hike along the Merrimack River on 90 acres of nature trails, or enjoy exhibits in the recently expanded, award-winning passive solar building.

**White's Park,** Liberty and School Streets, Concord. In summer feed the ducks or swing on the playground; in winter sled or ice skate, just as Concord residents have done for generations. This well-kept park is located in a residential area a few blocks west of downtown.

## ✷ Lodging

**INNS** ♿ **Centennial Inn** (603-225-7102; 1-800-267-0525), 96 Pleasant Street, Concord 03301. Built in 1892 as a home for the aged, this impressively turreted brick building now boasts the city's most luxurious accommodations. Converted to a hotel by Someplace(s) Different in 1997, the inn offers six individually decorated suites featuring a mix of reproduction furnishings and antiques. All have private bath; four provide whirlpool tub and private porch. Rooms include modem jack, VCR, remote-control television, and independent climate control. On the main floor, the **Franklin Pierce Dining Room** serves three meals (see *Dining Out*). There are also function rooms and a paneled lounge. Single rates range $139–250. Corporate and group rates are also available.

**Colby Hill Inn** (603-428-3281; 1-800-531-0330), just west of the village center, The Oaks, P.O. Box 779, Henniker 03242. Cindi and Mason Cobb's rambling 1795 farmhouse offers yesteryear charm and comfort on 6 acres just half a mile from downtown Henniker. Despite the popular public dining room (see *Dining Out*), there's privacy for inn guests: a comfortable living room with hearth off by itself and a game room. There are 10 rooms in the inn itself, 6 more in the neighboring Carriage House, all with private bath, phone, and air-conditioning, 4 with working fireplace. Rooms are wallpapered in flowers and furnished with antiques, with beds ranging from twins to king-sized. Facilities include a pool that's sequestered behind the barn, as well as croquet and badminton; tennis is across the street. A full breakfast is served in the glass-walled dining room, overlooking birds feeding in the barnyard. It's included in the rates: $110–200.

**The Meeting House Inn and Restaurant** (603-428-3228), 35 Flanders Road, Henniker 03242. Mathew and Michele Mitnitsky, the new owners of this well-established inn, have created a most hospitable haven in this 200-year-old farmhouse located up a hill and right across from the entrance to Pat's Peak. Guests can expect to be pampered. Braided rugs, pretty linens, and a smattering of family heirlooms personalize the six air-conditioned guest rooms, all with private bath. (There is also a private hot tub and sauna available for rent.) Breakfast, a changeable daily feast, is delivered to your room in a basket. Dinner is served in the barn next door, one of the area's most popular dining spots (see *Dining Out*). Rates, which include a full, hot breakfast, are $65–115 per couple. No smoking.

**BED & BREAKFASTS** **The Farmhouse** (603-796-2155), 433 High Street, Boscawen (mailing address: P.O. Box 243, Salisbury 03268). This pale gold restored 1826 Cape Cod home offers a sunshiny welcome throughout the year. Two pretty guest rooms, each with private bath, share access to a screened porch overlooking fields and gardens in summer; a cozy parlor with board games, good books, and an open fire the rest of the year. $50 per single, $60 per double, includes a full country breakfast. Children over 6 welcome; extra cot, if needed, $10.

**H. K. McDevitt Bed and Breakfast** (603-746-4254), 1077 South Road, Hopkinton 03229. Down a country road off the main street of Hopkinton village, this B&B features neighborly hospitality in an attractive reproduction saltbox home. Four guest rooms (two with private bath) offer a variety of accommodations. Innkeeper Helen McDevitt is also an accomplished craftswoman; her homemade hooked rugs and quilts are featured throughout. Rates ($60–70) include a scrumptious country breakfast.

**Horse Haven Bed and Breakfast** (603-648-2101), 462 Raccoon Hill Road, Salisbury 03268. Open year-round. Bring the dog, the kids, even the horse to this working farm where thoroughbred foals frolic on 35 acres surrounded by mountains and quiet unpaved roads and trails. Rooms in the 1805 farmhouse are "country comfortable," with shared baths. Most have a woodstove or fireplace. Rates—$75 first night, $65 after that—include a large continental breakfast served on the deck or in the immense, woodstoved kitchen. Pets, $10 per stay, can take advantage of the nearby river to swim.

**Lovejoy Farm** (603-783-4007), 268 Lovejoy Road, Loudon 03301. A new B&B in a 1790s white-clapboard Georgian house that Art Monty has sensitively and superbly renovated over the past two decades. Sequestered up a back road (10 minutes' drive from I-93), this classic, four-square mansion looks truly grand with its attached carriage barn set against landscaped grounds and surrounding woods and fields. Both the formal dining room and parlor retain their original, richly colored woodwork and the parlor, its extensive 1810 stenciling. There's also an informal TV room/library and a large country kitchen in which the only stove is a vintage wood-and-gas Kalamazoo. Our favorite guest room is upstairs, with a working fireplace, four-poster bed, cottage furniture, and wing chairs, but there are two other smaller rooms in the main house and five more open-beamed rooms that Monty has created from scratch upstairs in the barn. All rooms have private bath. The host speaks fluent French and Spanish and prides himself on the quality of the full breakfasts included in $89–99 double, $69 single. Art Monty is also an avid cyclist and welcomes bicylists interested in exploring local country roads. Call ahead to arrange to bring pets or children.

**Temperance Tavern** (603-267-7349), Gilmanton Four Corners, P.O. Box 369, Gilmanton 03237. You'll find all the modern amenities in this longtime stagecoach stop; otherwise, a weekend here smack in the center of Gilmanton's charming historic district is truly a trip back in time. Step into the inn's old Tap Room with its Moses Eaton stenciling and 18th-century bar, and you'll think you're in *Early American Life*. Actually, the magazine did feature several full-color pages on the inn a few years back. This very special place has been lovingly and knowledgeably preserved. Enjoy tea in front of an open-hearth fireplace, then climb the steep staircase (no elevator) to five well-appointed period guest rooms. All have private bath and feature antique canopy or brass beds. Two have working fireplaces; others boast vaulted ceilings and fascinating histories. Breakfasts are health-conscious but delicious; gourmet picnic baskets are an option. Rates range $65–125, depending on season and accommodations.

❀ **Wyman Farm** (603-783-4467), Wyman Road, Loudon 03301. Open year-round. Despite its location just a few minutes east of Concord and a 5-minute drive from Canterbury Shaker Village, the remote, storybook setting of this hilltop farm makes it feel like one of those places you could search for forever and never find. The 200-year-old "extended" Cape rambles along the very top of a hill, with lawns and fields that seem to roll away indefinitely. Expect to be greeted by Dunklee, who's the inn's model dog—literally: The golden retriever was pictured lounging around his home turf in the Nordstrom catalog. With small-paned windows and original woodwork, the living room exudes age and comfort, and each of the three air-conditioned guest rooms has its own bath and sitting room, all furnished with carefully selected antiques. (In some cases, innkeeper Judith Merrow has equipped even the bathrooms with vintage furnishings; in addition to a shower stall, one has a wooden, copper-lined tub she picked up years ago at an antiques show.) The farm has been in Merrow's family for many generations, and accommodating guests has been a tradition since 1902 when this was "Sunset Lodge" and the going rate for room and board was $5 a week. Today, with room rates ranging $55–90 (including tax), Wyman Farm remains a bargain for the genuine luxury it offers. Merrow provides a tea tray in the afternoon, and breakfast, which includes homemade breads, is cooked to order from the menu guests receive when they check in.

## ✱ Where to Eat

**DINING OUT** ♿ **Angelina's Ristorante Italiano** (603-228-3313), 11 Depot Street, Concord. Open Monday through Friday 5–9 PM, Saturday until 10 PM. Exposed brick, soft pink walls, and white tablecloths make this one of the prettiest restaurants in town. Well-prepared regional Italian cuisine and decadent desserts complete the experience. Moderate.

♿ **Bao Bao Restaurant** (603-228-0600), 520 South Street, Exit 2 just off I-89 in Bow. Open Sunday through Thursday 11:30 AM–10 PM, Friday and Saturday until 11 PM. Extended hours in the bar. New owners have brought new style to this handy way stop built on an old mill site next to the Hampton Inn. The extensive menu features American classics and Asian specialties, including sushi, in a fine-dining atmosphere.

♿ **The Barley House** (603-224-6363), 128 North Main Street, Concord. Open Monday through Saturday 11 AM–1 AM. Directly across Main Street from the capitol building, this destination offers billiards, darts, and a dozen micro beers on tap, plus a full menu of hearty cuisine in both the pub and more sedate dining room.

♿ **Brianas' Bistro** (603-224-6940), 90 Low Avenue (on the south end of Eagle Square off North Main Street), Concord. Open Monday through Friday 11:30 AM–2:30 PM for lunch; nightly for dinner from 5 PM. Probably the city's most glamorous digs, this onetime warehouse features an eclectic assortment of accessories on bare brick walls. The menu is equally chic, with dinners ranging from pan-seared tuna carbonara-style with prosciutto, garlicky spinach, and sliced mushrooms in a corn sweet broth of herbs and ginger ($15.95) to a grilled Tuscan rib eye finished with a lemon-thyme butter sauce and served with braised vegetables ($18.95).

♿ **Candlelight Evening at the Creamery** (603-783-9511), 288 Shaker Road, Canterbury. Family-style dining in the old tin-ceilinged creamery makes this a memorable experience. Chef Leo Cuthbertson uses Shaker-inspired recipes and fresh produce from the village garden to create such dishes as sherried pumpkin-apple soup, corn and blueberry salad, and baked sole with salmon stuffing. The candlelight evening meals are by reservation only, Friday and Saturday at 6:45 PM, April through December, with candlelight tours offered 5:30–6:30 preceding dinner from June through September. Prix fixe. (Also see *Eating Out.*)

♿ **Capitol Grille** (603-228-6608), 1 Eagle Square, Concord. Open for lunch and dinner daily, Saturday and Sunday breakfast/brunch 7 AM–2 PM. Located in the handsome Eagle Square shopping and office complex, this restaurant offers soft lighting and a moderately priced menu with everything from burgers to pasta, filet mignon, and swordfish. All-you-can-eat $7.95 lunch buffet Tuesday through Thursday, 11 AM–2 PM.

♿ **Centennial Inn** (603-225-7102; 1-800-360-4839), 96 Pleasant Street, Concord. Open for lunch Monday through Friday; dinner 5–9 PM; Sunday brunch 11 AM–2 PM. Quiet and sedate with oak paneling and a fireplace, this inn's historic Franklin Pierce Dining Room offers a changing but always up-to-date, health-conscious menu in a late-Victorian setting. The Hannah Duston Lounge, with its ornate "staircase bar," is particularly handsome.

♿ **Colby Hill Inn** (603-428-3281), off Western Avenue, Henniker. Open Monday through Saturday 5:30–8:30 PM, Sunday 4:30–7:30 PM. Candlelight makes the paneling and furniture glow, and the view of fields adds to the romantic, old-country-tavern feel of this dining room. The chef's signature dish is chicken breast stuffed with lobster, leeks, and Boursin cheese, served with a Supreme sauce. Leave room for dessert. Expensive.

♿ **The Common Man** (603-228-3463), Exit 13 just off I-93, Concord. Open Monday through Thursday 11 AM–9 PM, Friday and Saturday until 9:30 PM; Sunday 10 AM–9 PM. What looks like a large green Colonial home that somehow survived the surrounding commercialization of Concord's South Main Street is actually a brand-new restaurant. Post-and-beam construction provides two spacious, high-ceilinged dining rooms plus four function areas. Fireplaces and a mix of Yankee artifacts lend a cozy atmosphere. Lobster corn chowder and a deli board to make your own sandwich are among the lunch specialties; dinner entrées, including thick-cut roast prime rib at $15.95, range $10.95–18.95.

♿ **Country Spirit** (603-428-7007), junction of Routes 202/9 and 114, Henniker. Open daily 11 AM–9 PM, Friday and Saturday until 10 PM; closed Christmas and Thanksgiving. Walls are festooned with memorabilia from "the only Henniker on earth": old tools, signs, and photos. Specialties include the restaurant's own smoked meats, aged Angus sirloin, fresh seafood, and vegetarian dishes.

**Crystal Quail Restaurant** (603-269-4151; www.crystalquail.com), Pitman Road, Center Barnstead. Open Wednesday through Sunday 5–9 PM. Reservations only. Dining in this old 18th-century post house is an experience. Service is limited to a dozen patrons per night. Three entrées are offered, usually including chefs Harold and Cynthia Huckaby's specialty quail or pheasant. Vegetables are picked from the extensive organic garden, and vegetarian dishes can be prepared with advance notice. Needless to say, everything is made from scratch, and the desserts (Belgian *gâteau au chocolat* or crème caramel, for example) are exquisite. Be sure to ask for directions—there is no sign outside, and Barnstead is one of those towns webbed with back roads; even the owners admit to not knowing them all. The five-course dinner is $55 prix fixe. BYOB. No credit cards.

**Daniel's** (603-428-7621), Main Street, Henniker. Open for lunch Monday through Saturday, dinner nightly, Sunday brunch. An unusually attractive dining space that overlooks the Contoocook River; there's also a brick-walled lounge. Lunch can be a Mediterranean salad (fresh greens, roast turkey, smoked ham, and imported cheeses garnished with marinated vegetables) or simply a Cajun burger. For dinner you might try chicken Contoocook—a breast of chicken baked with an apple, walnut, and sausage stuffing and glazed with maple cider sauce. Moderate.

♿ **Ginger Garden** (603-226-8866), 161 Loudon Road, Concord. Open Sunday through Thursday 11:30 AM–9:30 PM; Friday and Saturday until 10:30 PM. A very hospitable restaurant with luncheon bargains from the sushi bar and a full menu of Chinese and Japanese specials.

**The Green Martini** (603-223-6672), 6 Pleasant Street Extension, Concord. Restaurant open for lunch and dinner from 11:30 AM Monday through Friday; Saturday 5–10 PM. Lounge open until 12:30 AM. Definitely green in the nonsmoking dining room; definitely funky in the smoke-filled bar, this place bills itself as "not your average hole in the wall." Choose Carol's down-home meat loaf for $8.95 or Mark's "Spin-Em" chicken with creamy Dijon sauce, shrimp, and asparagus for $12.95. Also pasta, sandwiches, salads, burgers, and a range of appetizers served on both sides of the building.

♿ **Hermanos Cocina Mexicana** (603-224-5669), 11 Hills Avenue, Concord. Open daily for dinner; lunch Monday through Saturday 11:30 AM–2:30 PM. This Mexican restaurant has gotten high ratings for its authenticity and incredible margaritas for years. Several dining rooms on two floors are nearly always full. Frequent musical entertainment adds to the festive atmosphere.

♿ **Makris Lobster & Steak House** (603-225-7665), Route 106, Concord. Open daily 11 AM–9 PM, Friday and Saturday until 10 PM; closed Monday in fall and winter. The Makris family has been in the food business for 90 years, operating half a dozen restaurants around the city. This one, now 10 years old, is still a success. Dozens of entrées with lobster are perennial favorites. Summer dining on the back porch patio; weekend entertainment in the lounge.

**Margarita's** (603-224-2821), 1 Bicentennial Square, Concord. Open nightly from 4 PM. This former city jail is now a favorite (and very festive) gathering spot for locals and travelers alike. Ask for a table in one of the old cells for an intimate dining experience. The menu is typical Mexican fare, with fajitas and margaritas as good as they get.

**The Meeting House Inn and Restaurant** (603-428-3228), 35 Flanders Road (off Route 114, across from Pat's Peak), Henniker. Open for dinner Wednesday through Saturday 6–9 PM; Sunday brunch, 11 AM–2 PM. An attractive dining area fills this 200-year-old barn. Chef Mathew Mitnitsky is a Culinary Institute graduate and former corporate chef with an interest in eclectic foods featuring local ingredients. Brandied rabbit with vegetable and potato of the day is $23; Mediterranean-style swordfish, $26.

♿ **Moritomo** (603-224-8363), Fort Eddy Plaza (Exit 14 off I-93), Concord. Open for lunch and dinner Monday through Saturday; Sunday 2–9:30 PM. Concord's newest eating adventure offers several attractive choices: a Benihana-style grill, cushioned chambers for up to six, or regular tables in the main dining room. There's a sushi bar and extensive menu with a variety of tempura, teriyaki, noodles, soups, and salads.

**The Pasta House** (603-226-4723), 11 Depot Street, Concord. Open Monday through Saturday 11 AM–9 PM, Sunday 4–9 PM. "Great Food, Great Prices" is the logo, and it's true. Traditional pasta specialties with nothing over $9.95. Comfortable, attractive seating, or you can take out.

**Siam Orchid** (603-228-1529), 158 North Main Street, Concord. Open for lunch Monday through Friday 11:30 AM–3 PM; dinner daily 5–10:30 PM. Concord's first Thai restaurant continues to draw a well-satisfied clientele. Excellent specialties and service in an attractive, well-located setting.

**EATING OUT** ♿ **Bread and Chocolate** (603-228-3330), 29 South Main Street, Concord. Open Monday through Friday 7:30 AM–6 PM, 8–4 on Saturday. Concord's own konditorei, operated by Franz and Linda Andlinger. This European-style bakery offers the best selection of breads and pastries in town, as well as gemüttlich atmosphere for lunch or tea. Great sandwiches and superlative pastries, plus browsing privileges and inside access to **Gibson's Book Store** (see *Selective Shopping*).

♿ **The Creamery** (603-783-9511), 288 Shaker Road, Canterbury. Lunch on weekends in April, November, December; daily, May through October. Closed January through March. The soups and breads are outstanding, and all the Shaker-inspired dishes are imaginative and nicely herbed and spiced.

♿ **In a Pinch Café** (603-226-2272), 146 Pleasant Street, Concord. Open

Monday through Thursday 6:30 AM–5 PM, Friday until 4; Saturday 7 AM–2 PM. A cheerful, informal café locally known for its gourmet sandwiches, soups, salads, and an assortment of luscious pastries. Take out or picnic inside on a snazzy, wicker-filled sun porch. No table service.

**Intervale Farms Pancake House** (603-428-7196), Route 114 and Flanders Road (bottom of Pat's Peak access road), Henniker. Open daily 5:30 AM–noon, until 1:30 PM on weekends. Shaped like a giant red sugar shack, this spacious, friendly, family-run restaurant is one of the very best places for breakfast in the state, featuring the farm's own homemade syrup.

♿ **Washington Street Cafe** (603-228-2000; 603-226-2699), 88 Washington Street, Concord. Open Monday through Saturday from 7 AM to 5 PM. Deli sandwich shop that also offers outstanding Middle Eastern fare.

## ✷ Selective Shopping

ANTIQUES Route 4 between the Epson Circle and the Lee Rotary, especially in **Northwood,** is widely known as **Antique Alley.** More than two dozen shops here represent up to 400 dealers; the primary customers are antiques-store owners and other dealers from throughout the country. This area is just far enough off the beaten tourist path to make for exceptional pickings. Along Route 4 in Northwood, **Tavern Antiques** (603-942-7630) represents 50 dealers, **Hayloft Antique Center** (603-942-5153) has 120 dealer spaces, the **Parker-French Antique Center** (603-942-8852) represents 130 dealers, and half a dozen more shops in town represent a full range of antiques, from country furniture to quilts, folk art, china, and jewelry.

**The Brick House** (603-267-1190), intersection of Routes 107 and 140 in the historic district of Gilmanton. Open daily 10 AM–5 PM. What appear to be museum-quality furnishings and an ever-changing inventory of Americana are actually antique reproductions, all for sale, from the rooms of Doug Towle's imposing home.

**Henniker Kennel Company Antiques** (603-428-7136), 2 Old Ireland Road, Henniker. Deals only with antique and collectible canines.

ART GALLERIES **McGowan Fine Art Inc.** (603-225-2515), 10 Hills Avenue, Concord. Open Monday through Wednesday 9 AM–5 PM, Thursday and Friday 9 AM–7 PM, Saturday 10 AM–2 PM. Perhaps the state's premier outlet for contemporary art, this gallery features changing exhibits by the region's best-known artists.

**The Art Center in Hargate,** St. Paul's School (603-229-4644), 325 Pleasant Street, Concord. Exhibits vary throughout the school year, from student work to private collections to traveling shows by well-known contemporary artists and photographers. Gallery hours are Tuesday through Saturday 10 AM–4:30 PM.

**Mill Brook Gallery & Sculpture Garden** (603-226-2046), 236 Hopkinton Road, Route 202/9, Concord. Open daily 11 AM–5:30 PM or by appointment. Sculpture, fountains, and birdbaths displayed in seasonal gardens; paintings exhibited in a distinctive contemporary gallery on a country estate.

**New England College Gallery** (603-428-2329), Preston Barn, Main Street, Henniker. Frequently changing shows always look good in this high-ceilinged exhibit space. The gallery is open Monday 9:30 AM–4 PM, Tuesday through Thursday 9:30 AM–6 PM, Friday through Sunday 1–5 PM when school is open.

BOOKSTORES **Blue Sky Used Books** (603-225-8113), 1 Depot Street, Concord. Open Monday through Saturday 10 AM–6 PM. Used, out-of-print, and antiquarian books bought and sold.

**Book Farm** (603-428-3429), 2 Old West Hopkinton Road (just off Route 202/9), Henniker. An inviting browsing spot with a woodstove and 30,000 titles of general interest and those reflecting owner Walter Robinson's special interests: history, literary criticism, and biography.

**Bookland** (603-224-7277), 30 North Main Street, Concord. Lots of magazines, newspapers, and books.

♿ **Borders Books, Music & Café** (603-224-1255), 76 Fort Eddy Road, Exit 14 off I-93, Concord. Open Monday through Saturday 9 AM–11 PM, Sunday 10 AM–8 PM. Always busy and nearly always open, this is a great place to browse and buy. Their calendar includes frequent author visits, concerts, and special events.

**Gibson's Book Store** (603-224-0562), 27 South Main Street, Concord. Open Monday through Thursday 9 AM–6 PM, Friday 9 AM–8:30 PM, Saturday 9 AM–5:30 PM, plus expanded holiday hours. Nourish both body and soul in Michael Herrmann's friendly, well-stocked bookstore linked to a European-style bakery and café. There's a cosmopolitan selection of poetry, literary fiction, memoirs, travel, gardening, and cookbooks, plus children's story hours, book discussion groups, and frequent author signings.

**Old Number Six Book Depot** (603-428-3334), 26 Depot Hill Road, Henniker (up the hill from the town hall). Open daily 10 AM–5 PM. General and scholarly stock in all fields.

**34 Churchillbooks** (603-746-5605), 181 Burrage Road, Hopkinton. The world's largest stock of books by and about Sir Winston Churchill.

CRAFTS **Canterbury Shaker Village** (603-783-9511), Shaker Road, Canterbury. The museum shop features Shaker crafts (see *Villages*).

**The Capitol Craftsman** (603-224-6166), 16 North Main Street, Concord. Fine jewelry and handcrafts.

**The Elegant Ewe** (603-226-0066), 71 South Main Street, Concord. Designer yarns, rug hooking and spinning supplies, Tuesday night knitting clinics, quality handcrafted gifts, and the area's best selection of recorded Celtic music.

**The Fiber Studio** (603-428-7830), 9 Foster Hill Road (off Route 202/9), Henniker. Open year-round, Tuesday through Saturday 10 AM–4 PM; Sunday by chance. Wide selection of natural knitting and weaving yarns and spinning fibers; looms, spinning wheels, knitting machines, handwoven and knit items, workshops.

**Heritage Herbs and Baskets** (603-753-9005), Hannah Duston Road, Canterbury. Open May through October, daily 11 AM–6 PM. Herb garden, a country barn stocked with herbs, handcrafted baskets, wreaths, books.

**The League of New Hampshire Craftsmen** (603-224-1471) has its state headquarters/gallery at 205 North Main Street (a beige Colonial just off I-93, Exit 15) in Concord. The gallery is open weekdays and has changing shows. The league's downtown shop in Phoenix Hall, 36 North Main Street (603-228-8171), is open Monday through Saturday and has works by juried craftspeople in a range of media and prices.

**Mark Knipe Goldsmiths** (603-224-2920), 2 Capital Plaza, Main Street, Concord. Studio and gallery with beautifully designed, custom-made jewelry.

SPECIAL SHOPS ✐ **Beech Hill Farmstand** (603-224-7655), 107 Beech Hill Road, Hopkinton. Open daily 11 AM–9 PM from May through October. A direct descendant of the first white child born in Hopkinton, Bob Kimball and his wife, Donna, have converted their ninth-generation dairy farm into a showplace for New Hampshire products and agricultural history. There are 50-plus flavors of NewHampshire–made ice cream with make-your-own sundaes, plenty of friendly animals to pet, a garden of cut-your-own flowers, and a barn filled with Donna's homemade goodies, as well as Kimball farm artifacts and regionally produced soaps, cheese, maple products, and decorative accessories. Kids and adults alike will enjoy navigating the 2-acre corn maze laid out in the shape of New Hampshire. With luck, you'll happen onto one of the occasional concerts and dances in the big red barn.

**Caring Gifts** (603-228-8496), 18 North Main Street, Concord. Specializes in personalized baskets filled with everything from toys to gourmet foods.

**David Levine Oriental Rugs** (603-225-5512), 34 Warren Street, Concord. A unique selection of rugs, plus tea, sympathy, and knowledgeable service in an inviting shop just off Main Street.

**The Golden Pineapple** (603-428-7982), off Route 202/9, Henniker. A trove of unusual gifts.

**Gondwana Imports** (603-228-1101), 86 North Main Street, Concord. Expressive clothing and decorative accessories from around the world.

**Gould Hill Orchards** (603-746-3811), 656 Gould Hill Road, Contoocook. A 200-year-old family farm located high on Gould Hill with spectacular 75-mile views to the White Mountains. A nature trail winds through the orchard, and the inviting orchard store is filled with fruit, baked goods, maple syrup, cider, and gifts of the season. The barn also houses The Little Nature Museum featuring displays of seashells, birds' nests, fossils, and stuffed animals. Open daily 9 AM–6 PM from August through November.

**Granite State Candy Shoppe** (603-225-2591), 13 Warren Street, Concord. A great old-fashioned candy shop that's been in business since 1927, making its own mints and chocolate buttercreams along with a wide assortment of chocolates, all crafted on the premises. A number of customers are also hooked on the freshly roasted cashews.

**Henniker Pharmacy** (603-428-3456), middle of Henniker. This distinctive building marks the center of Henniker in more ways than one. Pharmacist and owner Joe Clement stocks fishing gear, stationery, grocery items, wine and beer, cards, and much more. There's also a soda fountain/snack bar and, in the basement, a surprising selection of toys.

**Interior Additions** (603-224-3414), 38 North Main Street, Concord. Also (603-644-1901) 25 South River Road, Bedford. Interesting gifts and unique finishing touches for the home.

**L.L. Bean Factory Store** (603-225-6575), Fort Eddy Road, Concord. Discounted clothing and outdoor gear from the well-known Maine purveyor.

**Olde House Smoke House** (603-783-4405), 164 Briarbush Road, Canterbury. Gift baskets of home-cured and smoked cheeses and meats in an interesting old building near Canterbury's bucolic town green.

**Viking House** (603-228-1198), 19 North Main Street, Concord. A large selection of Norwegian sweaters and Scandinavian crystal, china, textiles, food, and gifts temptingly displayed.

## Special Events

*May:* **Annual Family Memory Day,** Shaker Village, Canterbury. Family picnics, traditional games, genealogy talks.

*June:* **Annual Herb and Garden Day,** Shaker Village, Canterbury. Herbal demonstrations, land management lectures, beekeeping. **New Hampshire Concord Coach & Carriage Festival** (early June), New Hampshire Technical Institute, Concord. Horse-drawn parade, rides, competitions. **Wood Day** (end of the month) with traditional folk musicians and members of the Guild of New Hampshire Furniture Makers demonstrating traditional techniques.

*July:* **Fourth Fireworks,** Memorial Field, Concord. **Strawberry Festival,** Contoocook. A 5K road race, a 5-mile canoe race, a parade, strawberries. **Fireman's Muster,** Pembroke. **Market Days,** downtown Concord. Main Street closes to traffic for 3 days; entertainment. **Canterbury Fair,** Canterbury. Chicken barbecue, auction, antiques, juried crafts, Morris dancers. **Annual Bean Hole Bash weekend,** Northwood. Food, games, raffle, auction, flea market. **Race Fever,** Concord. A downtown Concord motor-sports street festival held the Wednesday before the July Winston Cup race.

*August:* **Annual Hot Air Balloon Rally,** Drake Field, Pittsfield. Twenty balloons usually come; arts, crafts, entertainment. **Annual Northwood Community Craftsmen's Fair,** Northwood. Country fair, more than 60 craftspeople, music, food, folk dancers, flower show. **Annual New Hampshire Antiques Show,** Manchester.

*Labor Day weekend:* **Annual Hopkinton State Fair** (603-746-4191). **Annual Kiwanis Antique & Classic Car Show,** New Hampshire Technical Institute, Concord. **Annual Riverfest,** Arms Park, Manchester. **Annual Wool Day at Shaker Village,** Canterbury. Natural dyeing, rag-rug weaving, fleece-to-shawl.

*October:* **Annual Harvest Day at Shaker Village,** Canterbury. Farm stands, organically grown produce, applesauce making, music.

*December:* **Annual Contoocook Artisans Craft Show and Sale,** Hopkinton.

# The Lakes Region

THE LAKE WINNIPESAUKEE AREA

THE WESTERN LAKES

Kim Grant

# THE LAKE WINNIPESAUKEE AREA

Winnipesaukee is one of the largest natural freshwater lakes in the country, and it's by far the largest in New Hampshire. Twenty-four miles long and varying in width from 1 to 15 miles, it harbors no less than 274 habitable islands and 72 square miles of very deep, spring-fed water. Ringed by mountains, it's magnificent.

It's also convenient. Sited in the very center of New Hampshire, Lake Winnipesaukee is a 90-minute drive from Boston. Not surprisingly, its shore is lined with cottages, year-round homes, condominiums, and mansions, and every property owner seems to have at least one boat. On major holiday weekends the lake is jammed with everything from sailboards to schooners, from Jet Skis to high-speed runabouts, from canoes to luxury cabin cruisers. More than 20,000 registered vessels regularly use the lake.

The message is clear. The first thing to do here is to get out on the water, and it's easy. The M/S *Mount Washington,* New Hampshire's flagship excursion boat, offers frequent daily cruises, and many marinas and outfitters rent boats, from canoes and kayaks on up.

Where you stay along Winnipeauukee's 283 miles of shoreline makes a huge difference in what you experience. Wolfeboro and Weirs Beach are, for instance, not just at opposite corners of the lake but worlds apart.

Wolfeboro, tucked in an eastern corner of Winnepesaukee and backing on Lake Wentworth, is New Hampshire's tidiest, most compact and upscale resort town, filled with small year-round shops and restaurants as well as seasonal small museums. It offers easy access to walking and cross-country ski trails as well as to boats.

Weirs Beach, on the other hand, remains a Victorian-style boardwalk, evoking the late 1800s when it was known for religious "Grove Meetings" and the large wooden hotels and gingerbread cottages that flanked its Victorian depot and docks. Fire has destroyed many buildings here, including the elaborate Weirs Hotel and the original train station, but the present depot and docks are impressive, summer home of both the M/S *Mount Washington* and the Winnipesaukee (excursion) Railroad. This remains the amusement center for the lake, one with a public beach.

Ironically, views of and access to this lake are limited unless you are a property owner or guest at a local property. Many public beaches are restricted to local residents and guests. For more than 20 miles northwest of Wolfeboro, the lake is

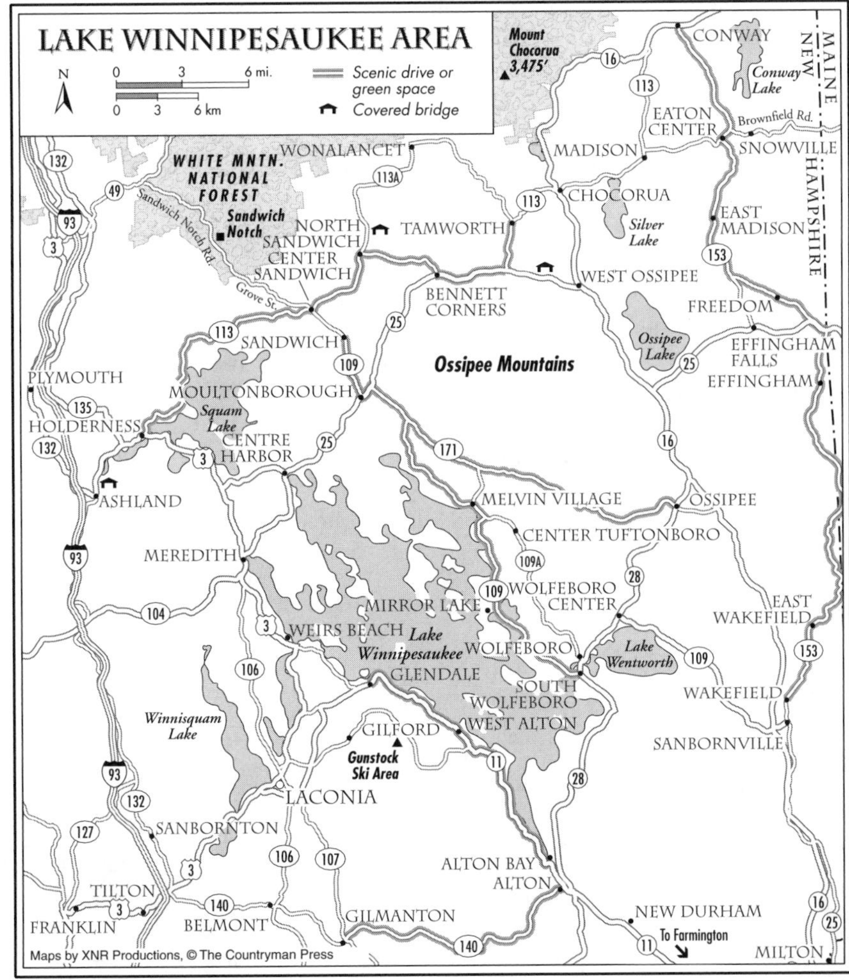


obscured by numerous "necks," lined with private homes. Happily, one of the more opulent old estates here, the more-than-5,000-acre Castle in the Clouds, set high on a hill in Moultonborough, is open to the public.

It's the western and southern shores of the lake—from Meredith in a northwestern corner, along through Weirs Beach to Gilford on the southern shore and Alton Bay in the very southeast—that offer dramatic views of the lake and its mountains. Ellacoya State Park in Gilford is the only big public beach.

In sharp contrast to Winnipesaukee's heavy summer traffic, both on and off the water, Squam Lake is the seemingly remote and quiet haven pictured in the movie *On Golden Pond.* Just northwest of Winnipesaukee, this pristine jewel has been carefully, sensibly preserved, but it's also surprisingly visitor friendly—on its own terms. Kayakers, canoeists, and naturalists of every ilk are welcome, as are members of Sunday open-air (Episcopal) services on Church Island.

The villages of Meredith and Centre Harbor, while on Winnipesaukee, double as shopping centers for nearby Squam and for Sandwich, an exceptional hill town best known for its annual agricultural fair and as birthplace of the League of New Hampshire Craftsmen. Center Sandwich still showcases fine craftsmanship; more can be found by following its numerous and heart-stoppingly beautiful byways. Several scenic drives lead to Tamworth, an equally inviting destination described in "Mount Washington and Its Valleys—Gateway Region." East of Winnipesaukee, Route 153 through Wakefield and Effingham is also described in that chapter.

In contrast to most visitors to Mount Washington's valleys, those in the Winnipesaukee area tend to be here only in summer, frequently for the entire summer, staying in their own cottages (or mansions) or renting housekeeping cottages. Many families have owned their summer places for generations, and many renters have returned to the same cottages for the same week year after year. Indeed, while there are numerous housekeeping colonies, we have not listed many, because few of them have any weeks open for newcomers.

Winter does bring skiing, snowmobiling, and ice fishing. Gunstock offers both alpine and Nordic skiing, and there are several cross-country facilities in the region. Winter has, however, been off-season around here for thousands of years. Members of the Winnipesaukee tribe who frequented this lake and named it either "smile of the Great Spirit" or "beautiful water in a high place" (no one seems sure which) wintered over on the site that's now Weirs Beach but fanned out around the lake only in warm weather.

*LAKE WINNIPESAUKEE,* 1853, BY BENJAMIN F. NUTTING

Currier Gallery of Art

The area's mill towns are, of course, true year-round, workaday communities. Laconia, "the City on the Lakes," is by far the largest (still less than 17,000 people) local community, connected to Winnipesaukee but also bordering Lake Winnisquam, Paugus and Opechee Bays. At its core stands the tower-topped brick Belknap Mill, built in 1823 and said to be the oldest unaltered textile mill in the country. It now serves as a gallery and an entrée to the city's colorful industrial history. The nearby, grandiose railroad station is now the bus stop and visitors center.

Beginning in the 1840s rail lines on this western side of Winnipesaukee also invited expansion of mills in Ashland and Tilton, two towns that served as transfer points for summer visitors just as they still do as Interstate 93 exits. Ashland (Exit 24) remains an obvious dining and shopping stop en route to Squam Lake and Centre Harbor, but the town of Tilton now tends to be equated with the outlet shopping mall and commercial strip at Exit 20. The town itself is west of I-93, worth checking for its public monuments, interesting shopping, and lodging (take Exit 19).

**MUST SEE AND DO** Cruise Lake Winnipesaukee aboard the M/S *Mount Washington* or rent your own boat. Visit Castle in the Clouds in Moultonborough and the Science Center of New Hampshire at Squam Lakes in Holderness. Sunbathe. Swim. Hike.

**GUIDANCE** **Lakes Region Association** (603-744-8664; 1-800-60-LAKES; www.lakesregion.org), P.O. Box 430, New Hampton 03256, produces *Where To in the Lakes Region,* a handy guide to towns, accommodations, and attractions, also maintains a walk-in information center on Route 104 just east of I-93, Exit 23, in the rear of a mustard-colored Colonial-style house. Open 8:30 AM–4:30 PM, later on Friday and Saturday in summer.

*Note:* The following are the most active chambers. Others are included in the *Villages* descriptions. All are good for finding summer cottage rentals.

**Wolfeboro Chamber of Commerce** (603-569-2200; 1-800-516-5324; www.wolfeborochamber.com), Box 547 (the walk-in office is at the old railroad station, 32 Central Avenue), Wolfeboro 03894.

**Meredith Chamber of Commerce** (603-279-6121; 1-877-279-6121; www.meredithcc.org), Box 732 (office on Route 3 and Mill Street), Meredith 03253-0732.

**Greater Laconia Chamber of Commerce** (603-524-5531; 1-800-531-2347; www.laconia-weirs.org), office in the old railroad station, 9 Veterans Square, Laconia 03246. A summer information booth is maintained on Route 3, just south of Weirs Beach.

**Squam Lakes Area Chamber of Commerce** (603-968-4494), Box 498, Holderness 03245, and **Squam Lakes Association** (603-968-7336), Box 204, Holderness 03245. Contact this nonprofit association for hiking, boating, and wilderness information and maps.

**GETTING THERE** *By air:* There is regular service to airports in Manchester (see "The Manchester/Nashua Area") and Lebanon (see "Upper Valley Towns"), both of which are just a short drive via rental car from the Winnipesaukee region.

## MORE HISTORY

Although land grants were made in this region as early as 1748, it was not until the 1760s, and the end of the dangers caused by the French and Indian Wars, that widespread settlement began in the Lakes region. Royal Gov. Benning Wentworth became a millionaire by granting new townships and retaining a portion of each grant for himself. It is his nephew John Wentworth, however, who deserves the credit for launching the summer vacation on Lake Winnipesaukee. In 1763 Wentworth began building a summer estate on his huge holding in present-day Wolfeboro, and in 1769 he completed a road from Portsmouth to that farm, eventually extending it to Hanover, home of the then-nascient Dartmouth College. The so-called Governors Road encouraged other wealthy seacoast families to build summer homes in the region and helped other settlers move to the area. Wentworth and his family were forced to flee the colony in 1775 as the Revolutionary War was beginning, abandoning his mansion, which burned in 1820. It is now a historic site. Although Wolfeboro remained a vacation area, the western side of Winnipesaukee developed more quickly, since it was on the main stagecoach route from the south and eventually was served by railroads pushing north toward the White Mountains.

Various types of vessels have hauled freight and passengers around the lake over the past 250 years. Steamboats at one time dominated the traffic. Train passengers stopping at Weirs, Alton Bay, or Wolfeboro could transfer to boats bound for other land ports and islands all around the lake. Some boats offered direct service to various hotels or connected with smaller vessels sent to major ports from villages or hotels in some of the bays. This convenient transportation system led to rapid development, so that by the late 1800s Winnipesaukee was a full-fledged recreation area. Although the Victorian ambience has faded, Weirs Beach retains its turn-of-the-20th-century flavor.

The relative lack of commercial development on the eastern side of Lake Winnipesaukee dates back to the days when the railroads serviced only the western shore and much of the eastern shoreline was contained within large estates. Except for Wolfeboro, other eastern-shore towns remained small, mostly farming communities with a few guest houses, even when the large estates were eventually sold and subdivided for summer cottage lots. By 1895 a single railroad spur line reached Wolfeboro from a junction in Sanbornville, a stop on the Boston & Maine Railroad route between the seacoast and North Conway. This line ensured Wolfeboro's importance to the vacation business, but it did little to boost the fortunes of the surrounding towns, many of which still appear as they did at the turn of the 20th century.

*By bus:* **Concord Trailways** (603-228-3300; 1-800-639-3317) provides scheduled service from Boston's Logan Airport to central and northern New Hampshire via Tilton, Laconia, New Hampton, Meredith, and Plymouth. Daily service varies.

MEDICAL EMERGENCY **911** covers this area.

**Lakes Regional General Hospital** (603-524-3211; 1-800-852-3311), Highland Street, Laconia. Walk-in care 9 AM–9 PM; 24-hour emergency service.
**Huggins Memorial Hospital** (603-569-2150), South Main Street, Wolfeboro.

## ✵ Villages

**Alton Bay.** One of the lake's early tourist centers, Alton Bay's waterfront area appears little changed from the turn of the 20th century, when train passengers transferred to steamboats. Concerts are held in the bandstand, and the old railroad station is the information center. Cottages around the bay shore evoke memories of the days when summer places were small houses, not condos. The **Harold S. Gilman Museum** (603-875-2161), Routes 11 and 140 in Alton (open 2–4 PM on Memorial Day as well as on Wednesday and Saturday and the first Sunday in July and August) is an eclectic collection of country antiques including furniture, dolls, guns, china, glass, pewter, toys, clocks, and a working Regina floor-model music box. **Alton–Alton Bay Chamber of Commerce,** Box 550 (summer office in the old railroad station, Route 11), Alton 03809, issues a detailed schedule of numerous summer events and maintains a seasonal information booth.

**Ashland,** the gateway town to the Squam Lakes area from I-93, is a delightfully visitor-friendly upcountry mill village. It's been this way since the 1850s, when the Boston & Montreal Railroad arrived, bringing lakes-bound visitors. The Victorian **Ashland RR Station** is now a seasonal museum (603-968-3902) open July through Labor Day, Wednesday and Saturday 1–4 PM; inquire about special excursion rides to Lakeport, Plymouth, and Lincoln. The center of town offers one of the region's most popular restaurants, **The Common Man** (see *Dining Out* and *Eating Out*), and good shopping, ranging from Bailey's 5&10 cents store to several art and crafts galleries. The Ashland Historical Society (603-968-7716) maintains the **Whipple House Museum,** 4 Pleasant Street (open same times as the railroad station), home of a Nobel laureate (1934) for medicine, Dr. George Hoyt Whipple, featuring exhibits related to his life plus local artifacts, and the neighboring **Pauline Glidden Toy Museum,** with plenty of games, toys, and books from the mid–19th century.

**Center Sandwich.** This quintessential white-clapboard, green-shuttered New England village, complete with steepled churches and general store, is exceptionally visitor friendly. You'll find an appealing café in the back of the store, fine dining and an inviting tavern in **The Corner House** up the road. Next door is the **Sandwich Historical Society** (603-284-6269), 4 Maple Street (open June through September, Tuesday through Saturday 11 AM–5 PM), displaying portraits by native Albert Gallatin Hoit as well as special annual exhibits. Across the road is **Sandwich Home Industries,** founded in 1926 to promote traditional crafts, a project that evolved into the present League of New Hampshire Arts & Crafts . See *Selective Shopping* for several more shopping possibilites scattered along the back roads that web this mountainous, 100-square-mile town. Note Route 113A to Tamworth, described under *To See—Scenic Drives* in "Mount Washington and Its Valleys—Gateway Region." Also see Sandwich Notch Road in *To Do—Hiking.* A century ago there were two hotels in the village itself and some 40 "guest farms" that took in summer boarders (see *Lodging—B&Bs*). The **Sandwich Fair,** held the 3 days of Columbus Day weekend, is the last one of the year, famed for its old-fashioned feel and for the traffic it attracts to the fairgrounds (south of the village on Route 109).

**Center Harbor.** At the head (northwestern corner) of Lake Winnipesaukee, this is the winter home of the M/S *Mount Washington.* The village is bisected by Route 25, but it still retains its 19th-century character. The town was named for the Senter family, but the *S* became a *C* somewhere along the way. Whether it's *Centre* or *Center* is still debated. The original name is preserved in its core shopping complex, Senter's Marketplace, best known for **Keepsake Quilting,** a mecca for quilters from the world over (see *Selective Shopping—Special Stores*). Unfortunately, the village's big old 19th-century summer hotels, Senter House and the Colonial Hotel, are long gone but the dock and a small beach survive. Note the bronze goose that's a fountain, sculpted by S. R. G. Cook, a student of Augustus Saint-Gaudens. The **Centre Harbor Historical Society** (603-253-7892), Plymouth Street (Route 25B), maintains its collection in an 1886 schoolhouse, open Saturday 2–4 PM in July and August.

**Melvin Village.** The antiques center of the eastern Winnipesaukee region, the little town of Melvin Village still looks as it did in the 19th century, when many of the houses lining the Main Street were built. Some of these homes now host antiques shops, and one business repairs antique motorboats. The **Tuftonboro Historical Society** (603-544-2400), Main Street (Route 109), Melvin Village, open in July and August, Monday, Wednesday, and Friday 2–4 PM and Saturday 10 AM–1 PM, displays photographs and literature relating to Lake Winnipesaukee.

**Meredith.** North–south Route 3 now runs along Meredith's waterfront, meeting Routes 104 east and 25 at a busy junction. The village, with its shops, restaurants, and B&Bs, is actually up above, bordering Lake Waukewan. In 1818 a canal was built from the site that is now John Bond Swase Park down to Lake Winnipesaukee, a 40-foot drop that eventually powered a number of mills. Despite disastrous fires, one four-story wooden 1820s textile mill survived, functioning off and on until the 1960s, but it was largely hidden by cinder-block industrial buildings. Thanks to local developer Rusty McLear, the mill and falls have been resurrected as a centerpiece for a shops, restaurants, and three large inns, with a fourth planned at this writing, replacing the lakeside Catholic church. The **Meredith Historical Society** (603-279-4655), 45 Main Street, is open Memorial Day through the Columbus Day weekend, Wednes-

TAMWORTH

Robert Kozlow

day through Saturday 11 AM–4 PM. Formerly the Oak Hill Church, the museum exhibits tools, costumes, photographs, "made-in-Meredith" items, and local historical information. **The Meredith Chamber of Commerce** (see *Guidance*) maintains a major information center in a white cottage at 272 Daniel Webster Highway (Route 3).

**Tilton** is now better known for its chain stores and discount malls than its village atmosphere, but the part of town west of I-93 does boast more statues than any other American town of its size. From the interstate, you first notice the 55-foot-high, granite Tilton (actually in Northfield) arch, an exact copy of a Roman memorial built in A.D. 79. Beneath it is a Numidian lion carved from Scottish granite, a tribute to Charles E. Tilton, the town's wealthiest mid-19th-century citizen and a descendant of the first settler. He persuaded the town of Sanbornton Bridge to change its name to Tilton in 1869, a decision no doubt made easier by his gift of statuary. Such allegorical figures as America, Asia, and Europe can still be found around town, along with Tilton's mansion, now the library of the private preparatory Tilton School, founded in 1845. The town offers unexpectedly good lodging and shopping.

**Wakefield.** The sprawling town of Wakefield is composed of several villages: **Union, Brookfield, Sanbornville,** and **Wakefield Corners,** the latter now a historic district of more than two dozen mostly white-painted, 18th- and 19th-century houses and public buildings, well worth finding (it's just off Route 16). Stop by the **Museum of Childhood** on Mount Laurel Road (603-522-8073), open Memorial Day week through Labor Day, daily except Tuesday 11 AM–4 PM, Sunday 1–4 PM. Adults $3; children under 9 years $1.25. Town historian Elizabeth Banks MacRury and her late sister Marjorie Banks accumulated some 5,000 dolls and teddy bears—plus music boxes, puppets, stuffed animals, model trains, and dollhouses—in their lifetimes of collecting. When this collection outgrew their home, they bought the house next door, and eventually opened this museum with 12 rooms full of exhibits. The garage has been converted into Miss Mariah Plum's 1890 schoolroom, complete with old-fashioned desks, books, chalkboards, and the teacher herself. Sanbornville, several miles south, is the commercial center (see *Eating Out*). **The Greater Wakefield Chamber of Commerce** (603-522-6106; wakefieldnh.org) furnishes maps and brochures.

**Weirs Beach,** at the junction of Routes 3 and 11B, is the attractions center of the region—the place to go for many folks, and the place to avoid for others. It is difficult to be ambivalent about two water slides, miniature golf, a go-cart track, the country's largest arcade, and a strip of pizza parlors, fast-food spots, gift shops, and penny arcades. Right beside all of this activity is a summer religious conference center dating back to the turn of the 20th century, the wharf for the M/S *Mount Washington,* and the **Winnipesaukee Railroad.** There is also a fine public beach beside the **Endicott Rock Historical Site,** a large boulder found in 1652, when a surveying party claimed this region for the Massachusetts Bay Colony, said to be the second oldest historic landmark in the country.

**Wolfeboro.** Billed as "America's oldest summer resort" (see the chapter introduction), Wolfeboro remains a lively but low-key, old-fashioned resort village with some outstanding shops, restaurants, and museums as well as entrées to the lake and surrounding countryside. The campus of **Brewster Academy,** a private prep school, is the venue for summer music. **The Wolfeboro Historical Society** (603-569-4997), 337 South Main Street, maintains three buildings open July through Labor Day, Monday through Friday 10 AM–4 PM, and Saturday 10 AM–2 PM. $4 admission adults; free for children under 12. The complex includes the restored and furnished 1778 Clark House, an 1820 one-room schoolhouse, and the replica 1862 Monitor Engine Company, complete with a restored 1872 horse-drawn, Amoskeag steam-pumper fire engine and an 1842 Monitor hand engine. **Wright Museum** (603-569-1212; www.wrightmuseum.org), 77 Center Street, Wolfeboro. Open April through October, daily 10 AM–5 PM, Thursday until 7 PM, then weekends and by appointment the rest of the year. This facility is devoted to the spirit of American enterprise as it was expressed during the war years of 1939 through 1945. The collection includes memorabilia, artifacts, vehicles (fully operating jeeps, tanks, command cars, and half-tracks), and films from the period. Gift shop and snack bar. A 200-yard walking path connects the museum with downtown Wolfeboro. ♿ **Libby Museum** (603-569-1035), Route 109, 4 miles north of Wolfeboro village, is open Memorial Day through Labor Day, daily except Monday 10 AM–4 PM. This natural history museum was built by a Wolfeboro native in 1912 and is now operated by the town. It has a varied collection of mounted bird, fish, and animal specimens; Native American relics, including a dugout canoe; old maps and photographs; and 18th- and 19th-century country-living artifacts. Programs include nature walks, lectures, concerts, children's programs, and art exhibits. Small fee. The **New Hampshire Antique and Classic Boat Museum** (603-596-4554), a fine collection of antique boats and related artifacts, is at 397 Center Street (Route 28 north). Also note the **Governor Wentworth Historic Site,** Route 109, the site of Royal Gov. John Wentworth's summer estate. During July and August daily tours aboard **Molly the Trolley** (603-569-1080) depart regularly from the town docks. An all-day pass is $3 for adults, $1 for children 4–12; under 4 free. The exceptionally helpful **Wolfeboro Chamber of Commerce** (see *Guidance*) maintains an information center in the former depot at 32 Central Avenue in the middle of the village.

## ✷ To See

**Castle in the Clouds** (1-800-729-2468; www.castlesprings.com), Route 171, Moultonborough. Open weekends early May through June, then daily until mid-October. Built in 1913 at a cost of $7 million, this stone mansion is high on the side of the Ossipee Mountains, overlooking Lake Winnipesaukee. Part of a 5,200-acre estate constructed by eccentric multimillionaire T. G. Plant, the castle has become a family recreation area and the source of Castle Springs water. Tour the mansion, picnic, or take a guided horseback trip (it's a good idea to reserve a ride) on part of the 85 miles of graded carriage trails. $12 adults, $8 students.

**Squam Lakes Natural Science Center** (603-968-7194;www.nhnature.org), junction of Routes 25 and 113, Holderness. The Science Center is open May through November 1, daily 9:30 AM–4:30 PM. This nonprofit organization expanded its Welcome Center and gift shop in 2002 but the emphasis remains on its quarter-mile walking trail with displays of live bears, deer, bobcats, foxes, owls, bald eagles (and other birds of prey), and other native wildlife. Hike through 200 acres of meadow and forest, past streams and brooks. Inquire about special summer family activities, which include live animal programs every hour daily during July and August, when admission is $9 adults, $6 children, free 4 and under; less in shoulder months. The Science Center's pontoon is used for Golden Pond Tours (see *To Do—Boat Excursions*); on Sunday you can reserve a spot on the shuttle to Church Island, site of open-air services (weather permitting) for almost a century. On rainy days the service is held at the Playhouse at Rockywold-Deephaven Camps, another long-standing institution.

Blink and you are through the village of Holderness (see **Walt's Basin** in *Dining Out*), but don't miss the **Squam Lakes Association** (see *Guidance*), housed in a former motel west of the village on Route 3, source of information about local hikes, kayak and canoe rentals, and lakeside tenting. Also see Squam Lake Tours under *To Do—Boat Excursions.*

✐ **New Hampshire Farm Museum** (603-652-7840; www.farmmuseum.org), 1305 White Mountain Highway (Route 16, Exit 18 off Spaulding Turnpike), Milton. Open June through late October, Wednesday through Sunday 10 AM–4 PM. New Hampshire's rural agricultural heritage is maintained in this unusual collection of buildings, situated about midway between the Lakes region and the seacoast. The three-story Great Barn is filled with wagons and a host of other farm artifacts. The Jones Farmhouse is furnished to reflect its ownership by the Jones family from 1780 to 1900; you'll also find the adjoining Plummer Homestead, blacksmith and cobbler shops, a well-stocked country store (good for historical books, reproduction toys, and much more), and 50 acres with picnic areas and a self-guiding trail. Themed Saturday programs highlight specific traditional crafts or aspects of farming. These range from quilting and blacksmithing to rock-wall building and demonstrations of horse- and mulepower. Special days are devoted to sheep, dairy animals, goats, and even llamas and alpacas. Children's Day, the second Saturday in July, is geared to young children. The second Saturday in August is an annual Old-time Farm Day, with many farmers, artists, and craftspeople gathered to demonstrate their skills. Admission: $5 adults; $1.50 children 3–12. See the web site for a detailed program of events. Also see *Villages* for more museums.

**COVERED BRIDGES** The **Grafton covered bridge** just off Route 3 in Ashland was built for the town by resident Milton Graton, a renowned builder and restorer of covered bridges throughout the Northeast. The **Whittier bridge** crosses the Bearcamp River, just off Route 16 and north of Route 25, in West Ossipee. The **Cold River bridge** is a little difficult to find but well worth the effort. It is located off Route 113A just north of North Sandwich.

AN EXHIBIT AT THE SQUAM LAKES NATURAL SCIENCE CENTER IN HOLDERNESS

Squam Lake Natural Science Center

**SCENIC DRIVES** To the east of Lake Winnipesaukee **Route 153** from Sanbornville to Conway (see *Scenic Drives* "Mount Washington and Its Valleys—Gateway Region") is a wandering alternative to busy Route 16. Another rewarding drive is **Route 113** east from Route 3 in Holderness, or **Route 109** north from Route 25 in Moultonborough. Either way you reach Sandwich Center (see *Villages*) and can opt—assuming you have a high, rugged car—for the **Sandwich Notch Road** (see *To Do—Hiking*) or **Route 113A** to North Sandwich, Whiteface, and Wonalancet (also see *Scenic Drives* in "Mount Washington and Its Valleys—Gateway Region"), then on to Tamworth. **Route 171** from Center Ossipee to Moultonborough, **Route 11** from Alton Bay to Glendale, and **Route 140** from Alton to Gilmanton are all great scenic drives.

## ✷ To Do

**AIRPLANE RIDES** **Laconia Airport** (603-524-5003), Route 11, Laconia, is an all-weather, paved runway facility with air-taxi operators available for charter.

**Moultonboro Airport** (603-476-8801), Route 25, Moultonborough. Sight-seeing rides.

**AMUSEMENT AREA** ✐ **Weirs Beach,** at the junction of Routes 3 and 11B, is the attractions center of the region, with two water slides, miniature golf, a go-cart track, the country's largest arcade, and a strip of pizza parlors, fast-food spots, gift shops, and penny arcades. The attractions, most open weekends Memorial Day through mid-June, then daily until Labor Day, include **Surf Coaster** (603-366-4991; www.surfcoaster.com), the largest water-slide complex in the region, with seven slides, changing rooms, and lifeguards. Pay once and slide all day. Also, two 18-hole miniature golf courses (additional fee). **Weirs Beach Water Slide & Volcano Mini Golf** (603-366-5161) is a complex with a mini golf course and a variety of slides for beginners through experts. The Super Slide for experts is the longest in New England. **Funspot** (603-366-4377; www.funspotnh.com), Route 3, 1 mile north of Weirs Beach. Open all year and 24 hours a day, July through Labor Day: 550 games, billed as the largest complex of its type in the country. From pinball to video and driving games, this has something for people of all ages, including both candlepin (a mostly New England game) and 10-pin bowling, a driving range, and miniature golf.

**BICYCLING** **The Cotton Valley Trail** is an evolving 12-mile rec path that begins at the Wolfeboro Depot and follows the old rail line toward Wakefield.

**Mountain Sports** (603-279-5540), Routes 3 and 106, Meredith, rents mountain bikes and supplies area maps. Also see Gunstock under Sports Park for mountain biking.

**BOAT EXCURSIONS** **M/V *Sophie C*** (603-366-5531), Lakeside Avenue, Weirs Beach. Mid-June through the week after Labor Day, Monday through Saturday 11 AM and 2 PM. This is a floating U.S. post office, and her cruises wind around the islands, into coves and channels, delivering mail to residents on five islands. Some of the 2-hour cruises are with mail stops, some without. Light refreshments, available. Adults $12, children 4–12 $8, children under 4 free.

Robert Kozlow

WEIRS BEACH

**M/V *Doris E*** (603-366-5531), Lakeside Avenue, Weirs Beach 03246. Departs Meredith and Weirs Beach. From June through Labor Day there are three daytime cruises and one sunset cruise (BYOB, complimentary snacks). Discover Meredith Bay and many islands on these 1- or 2-hour trips. Adults $10, children 5–12 $5; under 4 free.

**M/V *Winnipesaukee Belle*** (603-569-3016; 1-800-451-2389). Owned by the Wolfeboro Inn, based at the Wolfeboro Town Docks, this 65-foot side paddlewheeler makes several 1½-hour narrated cruises daily from the Memorial Day weekend through Columbus Day. Snacks and beverages are available. Inquire about Thursday-night dinner dance cruises.

***Millie B*** (603-569-1080). Half-hour boat rides in a classic 1920s motor launch departing from the Wolfeboro Town Dock; operated by the Wolfeboro Trolley Company. Daily late June through Labor Day, 10 AM–sunset, weather permitting.

**Squam Lake Tours** (603-968-7577; www.squamlaketours.com), Route 3, Holderness. May through October, daily scheduled tours at 10 AM as well as 2 and 4 PM; also June through August, 2-hour cruises at 6:30 and 9 PM daily. Reservations suggested. See this pristine lake, the second largest in New Hampshire, aboard Capt. Joe Nasser's 28-foot, canopy-top pontoon boat. He'll show you loons, Church Island, and the spot where *On Golden Pond* was filmed. Available for charters. Joe also runs a fishing-guide service.

**Golden Pond Tour** (603-968-7194) departs from the bridge at Walt's Basin, but passengers gather 15 minutes before departure at Squam Lakes Natural Science Center (see To See). Cruises are Memorial Day through foliage season at 11 AM, 1 PM, and 3 PM. Ninety-minute cruises led by naturalists, $12 per person, in an all-weather boat to see loons, the islands, and the movie-filming location. Reservations suggested. Inquire about nature, sunset, and full-moon cruises.

**M/S *MOUNT WASHINGTON***

(603-366-5531; 1-800-THE-MOUNT; www.cruisenh.com), Lakeside Avenue, Weirs Beach. Two cruises daily late May through June 30; three daily July 1 through Labor Day, then two cruises daily until late October. Special theme cruises and dinner and moonlight dancing cruises (two floors and two bands). For a first-time Lakes region visitor, a ride on this famous vessel is a great introduction to Lake Winnipesaukee. Her namesake vessel was a wooden side-wheeler in service from 1872 until she was destroyed by an off-season fire in December 1939. She was replaced by the present, steel-hulled *Mount Washington II* a year later but remained in port for most of World War II, when her engines were commandeered for the war effort. In 1946 she returned to service as the M/V *Mount Washington.* Lengthened in 1983 and changed to M/S (motor ship) status, she continues today as the queen of the lake and a New Hampshire landmark. Some 230 feet long with space for 1,250 passengers, the *Mount* cruises at 14 knots on a 2.5-hour, 50-mile route beginning at the Weirs, with stops at Wolfeboro and, on alternate days, Center Harbor and Alton Bay. Round trips are available from all four ports. Depending on the schedule, dinner cruises depart from and return to Weirs Beach or Wolfeboro. Breakfast, luncheon buffet, snacks, and cocktails are served. Adults $19, children 4–12 $9; under 4 free. Reduced fares and special family package fares on 2.25-hour cruises from Wolfeboro and Weirs. Inquire about dinner dance and theme cruises: $34–44, reservations required, under age 21 not admitted unless with parent, guardian, or spouse over 21.

THE M/S *MOUNT WASHINGTON* PLIES THE WATERS OF LAKE WINNIPESAUKEE.

Robert Kozlow

**BOAT RENTALS** No driver's license is required to operate a boat, but you must be 16 years old to operate one with more than 25 horsepower. There are, of course, marine patrol officers, speed limits at certain congested areas, and a number of accidents each summer. For boating regulations and education contact the New Hampshire Department of Safety's Marine Patrol Division in Gilford (603-293-2037). Also, keep an eye on the weather, because high winds, sudden squalls, and thunderstorms can quickly whip the lake surface into waves as rough as the ocean, an especially dangerous situation for those in small boats who have no experience in such conditions. Most towns provide public launching sites, and boat rentals are so numerous that we have given up listing them all. In Wolfeboro they include **Goodhue Hawkins Navy Yard** (603-569-2371), **Back Bay Boat'n Sled** (603-569-3200), **Wet Wolfe Rentals** (603-569-1503), and **Wolfeboro Corinthian Yacht Club** (603-569-1234), North Main Street, Wolfeboro. In Melvin Village: **KRB Marine** (603-544-3231) and **Melvin Village Marina** (603-544-3583). In Alton Bay: **Castle Marine** (603-875-2777). In Gilford **Fay's Boat Yard** (603-293-8000; www.faysboatyard.com) rents sailboats, pontoons, fishing boats, and canoes. In Weirs Beach **Anchor Marine** (603-366-4311; 1-800-366-8110; www.anchormarine.net) and **Thurston's Marina** (603-366-4811; www.thurstonsmarina.com) both offer rentals. In Meredith **Meredith Marina** (603-279-7921) offers rentals and **Sports & Marine Parafunalia** (603-279-8077) also rents Walden kayaks and waterskiing gear. **The Sailing Center on Squam Lake** (603-968-3654) in Holderness rents sailboats, sailboards, motorboats, and canoes by the half day, day, or week. Also sailing instruction.

**CANOEING AND KAYAKING** **Wild Meadow Canoes & Kayaks** (603-253-7536; 1-800-427-7536; www.wildmeadow.com) in Center Harbor offers instruction and guided tours. Canoes and kayaks are also available from several of the sources listed in *Boat Rentals*, above.

**Winnipesukee Kayak** (603-569-9926; www.winnikayak.com), 17 Bay Street, Wolfeboro (at Back Bay Marina), offers intruction, rentals, and guided excursions.

**FISHING** **Gadabout Golder Guide Service** (603-569-6426; www.gadaboutgolder.com), based in Wolfeboro, offers guided fly-fishing trips on Winnipesaukee and nearby lakes and rivers.

**Sumner Brook Fish Farm** (603-539-7232), Route 16, Ossipee. A former state fish hatchery, this is now a private business welcoming visitors to feed the fish, to catch fish (rod rentals available, also fly-fishing), or to purchase fresh or smoked fish. Fee charged, inexpensive.

*Note:* For advice on local fishing contact the New Hampton office of the **New Hampshire Fish and Game Department** (603-744-5470).

**GOLF** Most courses in this region operate from mid-April through October, weather permitting, and all offer cart rentals. **Den Brae Golf Course** (603-934-9818), Prescott Road, off Route 127, Sanbornton. Nine holes, driving range, full bar, and light food. **Indian Mound Golf Course** (603-539-7733), off Route 16, Center Ossipee. Nine holes, full bar and food service. **Kingswood Golf Course** (603-

569-3569), Route 28, Wolfeboro. Eighteen holes, full bar and food service. This is a busy summer place, so call for tee times. **Laconia Country Club** (603-524-1273), off Elm Street, Laconia. Eighteen holes, full bar and food service. Call for tee times; none available to the public on weekend mornings. **Lakeview Golf Course** (603-524-2220), Ladd Hill Road, opposite Belknap Mall, Belmont. Nine holes, sandwiches, and bar service. Great views of the lake from this hilltop course. **Mojalaki Country Club** (603-934-3033), Prospect Street, off Route 3, Franklin. Challenging nine-hole course, food and bar service; tee times needed, especially on weekends. **Oak Hill Golf Course** (603-279-4438), Pease Road, off Route 104, Meredith. Nine holes, full bar and food service. No tee times. **Pheasant Ridge Country Club** (603-524-7808), Route 11A, Gilford. 18 holes, light food and bar service, tennis. **Province Lake Country Club** (207-793-9577), Route 153, East Wakefield. Eighteen holes, full bar and food service; tee-time reservations available 7 days in advance. The Maine–New Hampshire state line cuts through the course, and several holes line picturesque Province Lake. **Waukewan Golf Course** (603-279-6661), off Route 3/25, Center Harbor. Eighteen holes, full bar and food service. No tee times, so plan ahead for busy weekend play. **White Mountain Country Club** (603-536-2227), off Route 3, Ashland. Eighteen holes, full bar and food service, tee times suggested on weekends.

**HIKING** Most people head for the White Mountains to hike, but the Winnipesaukee region offers a variety of trails with fewer hikers and splendid mountaintop lake views (although the peaks are not as high as those farther north). The **Squam Lakes Association,** which maintains many trails in this region, has a

THE BALD SUMMIT OF MOUNT CHOCORUA AFFORDS SPECTACULAR VIEWS OF THE WHITE MOUNTAINS.

Robert Kozlow

guidebook (see *Guidance*). We have listed only a few of the many possible trails in the region. We recommend using a guidebook, because many of these trails are traveled less and marked less than the more famous trails farther north. All times shown are for the ascent only. Hikers should carry their own water. (Also see *Green Space*.)

**Sandwich Notch,** from Center Sandwich to Route 49 in Campton. This ancient Indian trail was an important 18th- and early-19th-century route from the western White Mountains down to the lakes, and it's lined with stone walls that once marked open meadows. Once more wooded and now part of the White Mountain National Forest, this haunting, 11-mile road has been preserved as is (to widen and pave it would inevitably turn it into a heavily traveled shortcut between Winnipesaukee and Waterville Valley). Closed in winter, it remains popular with cross-country skiers and snowmobilers; in summer it's steep, rough, and slow-going but passable for all but low-slung cars. It's also a popular walk, at least the 3.5 miles from Center Sandwich to **Beede Falls** (a town park). The **Wentworth Trail** to the summit of **Mount Israel** (elevation 2,620 feet), which offers fine views of the Lakes region, begins 2.6 miles from Center Sandwich. Watch for signs to Mead Base, a Boy Scout camp. The 1.6-mile-long trail usually takes 2 hours to hike. Park in the field below the camp buildings and enter the woods at a sign at the left rear of the main building. Farther along the Notch Road (about 3.7 miles south of the junction with Route 49), the 4.5-mile-long **Algonquin Trail** ascends **Sandwich Dome** (elevation 3,993 feet). It's rough but offers fine views from its rocky ledges. Hiking time is 3½ hours.

**Rattlesnake** is a popular short hike on Squam Lake. From Holderness go 5.7 miles north on Route 113, past the Rockywold-Deephaven Road sign. Park on the left at the base of the Mount Morgan Trail but follow the old **Bridle Trail** (across the road). It bears left at the end of a row of maples and up a wide, gradual path to the summit of **West Rattlesnake** (0.9 mile). There's an excellent view to the southwest just below the summit.

**Red Hill.** A fine view of Lake Winnipesaukee is the prize at the end of the **Red Hill Trail.** In Center Harbor, at the junction of Routes 25 and 25A, take Bean Road for 1.4 miles, then follow Sibley Road (look for the fire-tower sign) to a parking lot with a gate. Past the gate is a jeep road that becomes the trail. The hike is 1.7 miles and requires just over an hour. A famous Bartlett lithograph, often found in local antiques shops, shows a gathering of Native Americans on Red Hill.

**Belknap Range.** On the western side of the lake is a low ridge of mountains with many trails. A good starting point is the Gunstock Recreation Area on Route 11A in Gilford (see *Green Space*). Several trails ascend beside the ski slopes. Ask for a map at the camping area office.

**Mount Major.** Located just north of Alton on Route 11, this is everybody's favorite climb. The **Mount Major Trail** is only 1.5 miles long and requires about 1 hour 20 minutes; views across the lake are impressive. Hike on the right day and watch the M/S *Mount Washington* as she cuts through the waters of Alton Bay. Also look for Knight's Pond Conservation Area in Alton, Rines Road off Route 28 south. You'll find more than 300 acres good for fishing as well as hiking.

In the Wolfeboro area several short hiking trails are rewarding.

✐ **Abenaki Tower,** Route 109 in Tuftonboro. A 5-minute walk from the parking area to an 80-foot tower overlooking Lake Winnipesaukee and the Ossipee Mountains; great for short legs. In Wolfeboro itself the **Russell C. Chase Bridge Falls Path** behind the railroad station leads half a mile to Wolfeboro Falls, and the **Cotton Valley Trail** stretches from the station 12 miles along the old railbed to the railroad turntable in Sanbornville. It traverses trestles and three lakes as well as woods and fields.

HORSEBACK RIDING ✐ **Chebacco Dude Ranch** (603-522-3211; www.chebaccoduderanch.com), Route 153, South Effingham. Open all year. A 170-acre farm has access to hundreds of miles of trail, quarter horses, geared to all ages and ability levels.

**Castle in the Clouds** (1-800-729-2468). Trail rides (see *To See*).

**Gunstock** (603-293-4318; 1-800-486-7861; www.gunstock.com), Route 11A, Gilford, is the venue for frequent trail rides.

RAILROAD EXCURSION ✐ **Winnipesaukee Railroad** (603-279-5253; 603-745-2135; www.hoborr.com), South Main Street, Meredith. Open weekends (except Father's Day) from Memorial Day through late June, then daily until mid-October. Board from Meredith or Weirs Beach. Ride beside the lake on historic coaches of the 1920s and 1930s or connect with the M/S *Mount Washington* for a boat ride (see *Boat Excursions*). Inquire about dinner trains featuring a Hart's hot roast turkey dinner and other special excursion rides.

SAILING **Winni Sailboard School** (603-528-4110), 687 Union Avenue, Lake Opechee, Laconia. Rentals of sailboards, rowboats, canoes, and paddleboats. (Also see *Boat Rentals.*)

SCUBA DIVING **Dive Winnipesaukee** (603-569-8080), 4 North Main Street, Wolfeboro. Open all year. Lake and ocean diving, scuba certification programs, rentals, guided dives, charter trips.

SPORTS PARK **Gunstock** (603-293-4318; 1-800-486-7861; www.gunstock.com), Route 11A, Gilford. This county-owned, 2,000-acre ski area is now a summer sports park offering mountain boarding, skating, mountain biking, and horseback riding, plus a swim pond, hiking, and camping. (Also see *Green Space.*)

## ✱ Winter Sports

CROSS-COUNTRY SKIING **The Nordic Skier** (603-569-3151), North Main Street, Wolfeboro. Open daily 9 AM–5:30 PM. Sales, rentals, and instruction for cross-country and telemark skiing, also sales and rentals of toboggans, ski skates, and snowshoes. They also schedule moonlight tours and races and maintain a 20 km trail network. Visit the shop for directions to **Abenaki Trails** (10 challenging km) or the **Sewall Woods Trails** (10 km of easy, family-geared trails); also maps or suggestions for backcountry skiing.

**Gunstock Ski Area** (603-293-4345; www.gunstock.com), Route 11A, Gilford.

This county-operated area has both downhill and cross-country facilities plus ski jumping.

**DOWNHILL SKIING** **Gunstock Ski Area** (603-293-4345; 603-293-4341; 1-800-GUNSTOCK; www.gunstock.com), Route 11A, Gilford. The original trails in this county-operated area were designed by Pres. Franklin D. Roosevelt's WPA in the 1930s. From the beginning it included cross-country as well as alpine trails (since then it's been almost entirely redesigned). Since 1937 it has been drawing families with intermediate-level terrain and a magnificent lake and mountain view. *Lifts:* 1 quad, 2 triples, 2 doubles, and 3 surface lifts. *Trails:* 45 trails, 72.5 percent intermediate. *Vertical drop:* 1,400 feet. *Snowmaking:* 80 percent coverage. *Snowboarding:* All trails, terrain park, half-pipe. *Night skiing:* 15 trails, 4 lifts, Thrill Hill Tubing Park and lift. *Services:* Rentals, nursery, ski school, cross-country facilities. *Rates:* $45 adult weekends, $36 midweek; $36/28 for teens; $25/16 per child. Special night and half-day rates.

**SLEIGH RIDES** **Belgian Acres Farm** (603-286-2362), 91 Clark Road, Tilton, offers sleigh rides on 33 secluded acres. $10 per adult, $5 per child.

## ✱ Green Space

**BEACHES** ♿ **Ellacoya State Beach,** Route 11, Gilford. Open weekends from Memorial Day, daily mid-June through Labor Day. The only state beach on Lake Winnipesaukee. A 600-foot beach with refreshment stand and changing rooms; handicapped accessible. The view across the lake to the Ossipee Mountains is one of the best in the region. Fee charged.

**Wentworth State Park and Clow Beach** (603-569-3699), Route 109 east, Wolfeboro. Open daily mid-June through Labor Day. This small park on Lake Wentworth has a bathing beach, play field, changing rooms, and shaded picnic area. Fee charged. **Albee Beach,** Route 28 north on Lake Wentworth, is open mid-June through Labor Day, 9 AM–dusk. Also in Wolfeboro but on Lake Winnipesaukee, **Brewster Beach** on Clark Road and **Carry Beach** on Forest Road are both open mid-June through Labor Day, 9 AM–dusk.

**OTHER** **Cate Park,** Wolfeboro, on the waterfront by the town wharf. Occasional concerts and art exhibits in summer, a delightful place to relax anytime.

🖍 **The Loon Center and Markus Wildlife Sanctuary** (603-476-5666), Lees Mills Road (Box 604), Moultonborough. The center is operated by the Loon Preservation Committee of the Audubon Society of New Hampshire. This 200-acre site has 2 miles of walking trails through the woods and down to the shore of Lake Winnipesaukee, where a loon nest can be observed. There is also a gift shop and exhibit space, but the main purpose of the facility is to research the American loon, the large waterbird whose eerie calls symbolize wilderness. Overdevelopment of New Hampshire's lakes once appeared to doom the bird, but this organization has been influential in protecting nesting sites and building public awareness of the loon's plight. The organization has accumulated some 20 years of data on the loons, which currently number about 550 birds in New Hampshire.

There are programs for adults and children, and self-contained loon education kits that can be sent to schools.

**Chamberlain-Reynolds Forest,** College Road, off Route 3, 2 miles north of Meredith village. Owned by the New England Forestry Foundation, this 150-acre managed woodland is on the shore of Squam Lake. With beaches, trails, and picnic tables, it is a quiet spot to enjoy the country.

**Ragged Island on Lake Winnipesaukee.** Docking is available at the southern end of the island. Shuttle service and programs on the island are offered by the Squam Lakes Natural Science Center (see *To See*).

**Stonedam Island Wildlife Preserve** (603-279-3246), operated by the Lakes Region Conservation Trust, Box 1097, Meredith 03253. Open weekends from July 4 through Labor Day, Saturday and holidays 10 AM–5 PM, Sunday noon–5 PM. Stonedam Island is an undeveloped, 112-acre preserve in Lake Winnipesaukee. A variety of family-oriented nature programs are offered to the public on weekends, but visitors are also welcome to walk the trails, relax under a tree on the shoreline, or pursue their own nature study. Private boats may dock at the 60-foot pier on the northeastern side of the island. Bring water, as none is available on the island; no pets, audio equipment, smoking, fires, or glass containers. Inquire about public transport to the island on weekends.

**Leonard Boyd Chapman Wildbird Sanctuary,** Mount Isreal Road, Sandwich. A very special 150 acres, open year-round but you would be well advised to have four-wheel drive in winter because it's up a steep road (off Grove Street out of Center Sandwich). There's a trail network groomed for cross-country skiing and snowshoeing, along with picnic tables. A trail leads to Eacup Lake, and in winter the ice that forms on this small pond is cleared for family skating (no hockey sticks, please).

**Unsworth Wildlife Area at the Squam Lakes Conservation Society** (see *To See*), Holderness. These 159 acres are webbed with trails, rich in wildlife. A canoe awaits, but you have to bring your own paddle.

**Gunstock Recreation Area** (603-293-4341), Route 11A, Gilford. Operated by Belknap County, this 2,000-acre facility includes the Gunstock Ski Area and a large campground with related facilities. The 420-site campground has swimming, fishing, horseback riding, a store, and a playground. Extensive hiking trails lead to the summits of the Belknap Mountains, one of which is Gunstock. Trail maps are available. Warm-weather events include dances, crafts and woodsmen's festivals, and Oktoberfest.

Also see **Sandwich Notch Road** under *To Do—Hiking.*

## ✷ Lodging

### INNS

#### *On Lake Winnipesaukee*

**The Wolfeboro Inn** (603-569-3016; 1-800-451-2389; www.wolfeboroinn.com), 44 North Main Street, Wolfeboro 03894. Open all year. This inn dates back to 1812 but now offers some the region's finest rooms and one of its better restaurants. Nine guest rooms are in the original front portion of the inn, while the modern addition, built with a contemporary design to resemble an old barn, brings the room count to 44, including some suites with four-poster beds. The country-style rooms have private bath and king, queen, double, or twin beds, with phone, TV, and individually controlled heat and air-conditioning. The deluxe water-view rooms in the addition have decks where you can watch lake activities or catch cooling breezes. Two rooms are handicapped accessible. The center sections of the three-story addition have open areas with chairs and reading nooks. The inn has a private beach on the lake, and it's just steps to the village shops and to the dock to board the M/S *Mount Washington.* In-season, guests are invited on a free morning lake cruise aboard the *Winnipesaukee Belle* (see *To Do—Boat Excursions*). The inn has conference facilities, a large dining room (see *Dining Out*), and **Wolfe's Tavern,** which is located in the old portion of the inn. From $89 in winter to $285 for a suite on holiday weekends in summer. Rates include continental breakfast. Children over the age of 1 year are $10 extra. Inquire about the many packages, including spring fishing and summer water sports.

**The Inns at Mill Falls** are three separate nicely designed inns, totaling more than 100 rooms, built over the past decade or so along the lake in Meredith (see *Villages*). All share the same ownership, phone numbers (603-279-7006; 1-800-622-MILL), web site (www.millfalls.com), and address: Route 3, Meredith 03253. Rates range $199–279, and package plans are available for all three inns. The original **Inn at Mill Falls** is built around a tumbling waterfall and adjoins the old linen mill that's now a shopping complex. Each of the 54 rooms has New Hampshire–made maple or Shaker pine furnishings with easy chairs and desks, air-conditioning, TV, and telephone. Beds are queens, twins, or a queen and a twin, and half the rooms

*MOUNT CHOCORUA, NEW HAMPSHIRE,* 1856, BY SOPHIA TOWNE DARRAH

Currier Gallery of Art

have views out to Meredith Bay. There is an indoor pool, a spa, a sauna, and two restaurants. The neighboring **Chase House at Mill Falls** offers 23 rooms and 3 one-bedroom suites Most rooms feature fireplace, whirlpool spa, and private balcony overlooking the lake. There is also a function room with fireplace, patio, and panoramic view. **Camp,** the inn's restaurant, offers great grub and a woodsy decor (see *Dining Out*). The 24-room gleaming, white-clapboard **Inn at Bay Point,** across Route 3 from its sister inns, extends into Lake Winnipesaukee, resembling a ship that's just pulled into port. Amenities include a beach, private dock, sauna, and whirlpool spa area. Many rooms have lakeside balcony, fireplace, and whirlpool. All feature New Hampshire–made furnishings, including king or queen beds (some with pullout sofas) and easy chairs, desks, air-conditioning, TV, and telephone. Dine directly on the water in the **Boathouse Grille** (see *Dining Out*), or opt for a dinner for two on your balcony.

**The Lakeview Inn** (603-569-1335), 120 North Main Street, Box 713, Wolfeboro 03894. Open all year. Situated on a hill on the edge of the village, this is a combination restored old inn and adjacent two-level motel. All rooms have private bath, TV, and phone; a few have a kitchenette. Beds are doubles and queens (two beds in motel units). The inn houses a good restaurant (see *Dining Out*). $55–95 for two depending on the season.

ↀ **Kona Mansion** (603-253-4900; www.konamansion.com), off Moultonborough Neck Road (turn at the blinker on Route 25 and follow the signs; mailing address: Box 458, Center Harbor 03226). Open daily Memorial Day through Columbus Day and weekends earlier and later. No expense was spared when this Tudor-style mansion was built in 1900 by Herbert Dumaresq, a onetime partner in Boston's famed Jordan Marsh department store. There's an elaborate painted ceiling and a sumptuous tiled fireplace in the dining room, and the property retains the aura of another time. Since 1971, the Crowley family has operated the inn, which includes 100 acres of private woodland, a nine-hole, par-3 golf course, tennis courts, extensive lawns, a private beach, and its own lakeside boat dock, and borders the Kona Wildlife Preserve with 100 acres of private woodland and 15 miles of hiking trails. The inn has 10 rooms with twin or one or two double beds and private bath. On the lakefront are four housekeeping cottages with 1 or 2 bedrooms and two 3-bedroom chalets. Relax in the lounge with a view across the lake to the Belknap Mountains. Breakfast and dinner are served to guests and the public. EP $69–165; MAP for two (weekly only), two-bedroom cottages are $560 per week and A-frame chalets with two bedrooms are $795 per week. Inquire about weekly MAP rates.

### *On Squam Lake*

**The Manor on Golden Pond** (603-968-3348; 1-800-545-2141; www.manorongoldenpond.com), Shepard Hill Road and Route 3 (Box T), Holderness 03245. This golden stucco mansion overlooking Squam Lake ("Golden Pond"), now owned by Brian and Mary Ellen Shields, was originally built in 1907 as a summer estate for a wealthy Englishman and his new bride. Three of the inn's 13 hillside acres overlook the water and surrounding mountains. Inside, the rooms are a combination of old and new, with turn-of-the-20th-century leaded-glass windows and ornate woodwork partnered with whirlpool baths and updated decor. No two of the 25 guest rooms are alike, but all are furnished mostly with antiques (four-poster beds) and have private bath, telephone, and television; most have a fireplace. Eight of the rooms also have a whirlpool. Most rooms are large. Deluxe rooms have king, queen, or twin beds, ceiling fan, air-conditioning, and lake views; some have balcony. Two large common rooms have fireplaces, and there is a second-floor library. Several detached housekeeping cottages sleep two to six people. One right on the lake has a fireplace. Four housekeeping cottages suggest romantic getaways with king-sized beds, fireplaces, double Jacuzzis, and porches with lake views. You'll also find tennis courts and a private, 300-foot beach with a boat dock that offers paddleboats and canoes. Breakfast and dinner are served daily (see *Dining Out*). Rates with breakfast for two: $165 for a "classic" room, $260–280 for a room with fireplace, and $350–375 for a room with fireplace and whirlpool bath. B&B. Inquire about the cottages.

### *Elsewhere*

**The Patriots Tavern** (603-286-7774; www.1875inn.com), 255 Main Street, Tilton. This old mill town isn't the obvious place to find a tastefully restored old inn—one that was obviously a labor of love for Joanne Oliver (owner of popular Oliver's Restaurant) and Rob Ciampa. Built in 1875 in the middle of Main Street, the three-story wooden hotel has been totally renovated. Each of the 11 guest rooms is a different creation, an uncluttered mix of country antiques, folk art, and comfort, all with private bath. A second-floor library serves as common space; the street-level Patriots Tavern is open for all three meals, an attractive space with tables by the long, small-paned windows and by the big fieldstone fireplace. $60–80 off-season, $100-210 in-season.

## BED & BREAKFASTS

### *Center Harbor/Meredith Area*

♿ **The Meredith Inn** (603-279-0000; www.meredithinn.com), corner of Main and Waukewan Streets, Meredith 03253. Open all year. Innkeeper Janet Carpenter clearly knows her business, one she grew up with in Rangeley, Maine, where her parents Ed and Fay (who live next door and frequently assist) owned the Rangeley Inn. This rambling Victorian "painted lady," the home of Meredith's leading physician for several decades, has been transformed into a charming B&B. The eight unusually spacious rooms offer a choice of twin, queen-, and king-sized beds. Each is different, but all combine real comfort and charm. They are furnished in antiques and feature luxurious linens and large, well-equipped private baths; five of the rooms have a whirlpool tub. The living room has a fireplace and is well stocked with local menus and information. The hosts are delighted help guests plan itineraries. It's just over a quarter mile in one direction to downtown shopping and restaurants; half a mile the other way to Lake Waukewan. Full breakfast. Nonsmoking. Children 6 and older are welcome. Rates range $89–149 in low season, $109–159 in summer and fall.

**The Nutmeg Inn** (603-279-8811; www.bbhost.com/nutmeginn), 80 Pease Road, Meredith 03253. This 230-year-old inn looks as crisp as the day it was built, but the huge maple in front lets you know that this white-clapboard home has deep roots. There are eight air-conditioned bedrooms, all with private bath. Two have a working fireplace. There is an outdoor pool screened from the road by pines; also billiards and an exercise room, plus 24-hour access to a refrigerator, ice machine, and coffeemaker. Full gourmet breakfast included in the $90–110 room rate.

**Olde Orchard Inn** (603-476-5004; 1-800-598-5845; www.oldeorchardinn.com), 108 Lee Road (R.R. Box 256), Moultonborough 03254. Open all year. A country location with a surrounding apple orchard makes this restored brick farmhouse a find. Nine guest rooms are decorated with quilts, stenciling, antiques, and many eclectic items gathered by the Senner family during 26 years in the foreign service. All rooms have air-conditioning and private bath, and three have a fireplace. Two keeping rooms also have fireplaces, and one has a TV; the other is for reading and conversation. Within walking distance are **The Woodshed** restaurant (see *Dining Out*) and the **Loon Center** (see *Green Space*). $75–140 for two with full breakfast.

**Tuckernuck Inn** (603-279-5521; 1-888-858-5521; www.thetuckernuckinn.com), 25 Red Gate Lane, Meredith 03253. Open all year. Up the hill from Main Street, this five-room inn is within walking distance of shops, restaurants, and Lake Winnipesaukee. Owners Donna and Kim Weiland have added baths (all five guest rooms now have them) as well as stenciled walls, handcrafted quilts, and period furniture; one room has a gas fireplace. The living room has a fireplace and a huge shelf of books and games to play. $95–135 for two includes a full breakfast.

### *In Sandwich*

**John Beede House** (603-284-7413; www.jonathanbeedehouse.com), 711 Mount Israel House, Center Sandwich 03227. High up on a back road, this 1787 farmhouse offers three comfortable guest rooms furnished with family antiques. Built by one of Sandwich's early settlers, it has been lovingly restored by owners Susan and John Davies. The three upstairs guest rooms share two baths and range from a big corner room to a cozy double. All have small, white-curtained, small-paned windows (no shades), heirloom quilts, and intriguing books. Downstairs, the formal parlor and less formal keeping room feature similar books and inviting places to read. There is also a big screened porch/sun room overlooking the meadows; next door the **Chapman Wildbird Sanctuary** beckons you to walk, snowshoe, or cross-country ski. The house is filled with a sense of history (before the Civil War it served as a stop on the Underground Railroad) and with a warm sense of hospitality. $75–90 includes a full breakfast served in the dining room with its 18th-century fireplace and Indian shutters.

🐾 ✎ **Strathaven** (603-284-7785), Route 113, North Sandwich 03259. Open all year. Twenty years ago Betsy and Tony Leiper started taking in overflow guests from a local inn, and they've never stopped: Guests became friends who returned annually. Picture windows overlook beautiful grounds with extensive gardens, a trout pond for swimming or skating, and an English croquet court. Betsy is an embroidery teacher and has a flair for color. Her favorite, blue, shows up in her extensive collection of blue-and-white

Meissen china in the dining room cabinet. There are four lovely rooms; two large rooms each have two double beds and a private bath, and two rooms share a bath. Many feature antiques as well as Betsy's embroidery. Tony Leiper prepares a full country breakfast, serves as town treasurer, and leads guests on cross-country ski trails that connect the inn with Sandwich Notch. From $80 for two with full breakfast. These grandparents insist there be no extra charge for children.

**Overlook Farm** (603-284-6485), 14 Mountain Road (off Route 250), Sandwich 03227. Open June through mid-October. This white, 1780 Colonial sits above a broad expanse of lawn in a quiet setting minutes from Route 25. Windows face north, with views of Mount Israel and Sandwich Dome. Four rooms (two with private bath and two that share) feature homemade quilts, lots of antiques, and painted-pine woodwork and floors. Innkeeper Phyllis Olafsen has a canoe for guests and a Squam Lake beach pass. In summer the former woodshed, with exposed beams and floor-to-ceiling screens, is a fabulous retreat, offering sweeping views of fields and flowers. $85–95 for two with full breakfast.

### *On Squam Lakes*

**The Inn on Golden Pond** (603-968-7269; www.innongoldenpond.com), Route 3, Box 680, Holderness 03245. Open all year. Bill and Bonnie Webb have been operating this large, cheerful, friendly B&B since 1984. While this 1870s house doesn't overlook the lake, huge picture windows in the breakfast room and living room do frame meadows and woodland, a sampling of the inn's 50 wooded acres. Most of the eight rooms have queen-sized maple beds, and all have private bath. All the rooms are furnished tastefully and comfortably "country"-style and have one or two easy chairs, a nice touch. Amenities include table tennis or darts in the separate sports shed. The living room has a fireplace, and a second common room has cable TV; there's also a small room set up for computer use. $105–140 off-season, $130–165 per couple in summer and fall, includes breakfast. Children over 12 welcome.

**Pressed Petals Inn** (603-968-3661; 1-800-839-6205; www.pressedpetalsinn.com), Shepard Hill Road, P.O. Box 695, Holderness 03245. Open all year. Innkeeper Ellie Dewey has used a pastel palette to breathe new life into this century-old farmhouse. She also has indulged her penchant for pressed flowers. Each of the eight guest rooms (all with private bath) is named for the framed blossom on its door, and the color cue continues inside. You can choose your favorite: green or blue hydrangea, azalea, wisteria, and more. Rooms come equipped with hair dryers, robes, and fancy soaps. Breakfast and Saturday-evening hors d'oeuvres are served by candlelight; afternoon tea comes with dessert. Nonsmoking except on porches and grounds. Rates are $120–150 mid-May through October; lower in winter and spring.

**The Mary Chase Inn** (603-968-9454; www.marchaseinn.com), Route 3, P.O. Box 94, Holderness 03245. Built atop a granite outcropping that rises above Route 3, this Victorian B&B has lovely views over Little Squam Lake. Four guest rooms, each with antique double beds, share two baths with tubs and showers. There is also a suite with a queen bed, private bath, balcony, and fireplace. Innkeepers John and Phyllis Chase. $95–135 with full gourmet breakfast.

**The Glynn House Inn** (603-968-3775; 1-800-637-9599; www.glynnhouse.com), 59 Highland Street, Ashland 03217. Jim and Gay Dunlop are the new owners of the 1890 Queen Anne–style home and neighboring carriage house that make up this impressive B&B, set above the village. The house retains all of its handsome, original woodwork and Oriental wallpaper. Each of the 13 rooms (11 with fireplace) is furnished to the period, and all have private bath; nine with whirlpool. A family suite shares a bath and has a sitting room. Full breakfast included. B&B $99–239 double.

### *In Wolfeboro and vicinity*

**Tuc' Me Inn** (603-569-5702; www.tucmeinn.com), 118 North Main Street, Wolfeboro 03894. Open all year. This 19th-century inn, with screened porches, a large common room with a fireplace, TV, and guest telephone, is just two blocks from village shops and restaurants. There are seven rooms, three with private bath (the others share two full baths) with a choice of queen, double, and twin beds. New innkeepers Wes and Linda Matchett also offer a choice of three full breakfasts. $95–105 with private bath, $85-98 with shared.

**The Little Farm** (603-569-8641), 75 North Line Road. Norm and Ann Hammond offer two comfortable guest rooms in their immaculate Cape-style house set in its meadows with a pond and nature trail and a barn full of animals (we met a miniature pony, goats, and chickens). $95 per couple includes a full breakfast; children 12 and under are free.

### *On the south shore*

**The Inn at Smith Cove** (603-293-1111; www.innat.smithcove.com), 19 Roberts Road, Gilford 03246. This 1890s home with a third-floor tower suite and wraparound porch is right on one of Lake Winnipesaukee's many sheltered coves. There are nine guest rooms in the inn itself, most with a water view, all with private bath (the tower suite has a Jacuzzi tub). The Light House in the garden is a two-level suite with a Jacuzzi, and the Little House is a cottage with a porch on the cove. Handy in winter to skiing at Gunstock. $95–130 per couple includes a full breakfast.

### *On Winnisquam Lake*

**Ferry Point House** (603-524-0087; www.ferrypointhouse.com), off Route 3 in Winnisquam (mailing address: 100 Lower Bay Road, Sanbornton 03269). Open May 1 through November 1. Built in the 19th century as a summer retreat, this bracketed Victorian, with its wide parlor windows and veranda overlooking Lake Winnisquam, still fits the bill. This area is quieter than bigger Lake Winnipesaukee, with simpler pleasures such as the grassy point, across the road from the house, with a gazebo and hammock. Guests also have use of a paddleboat and rowboat. The six rooms, all with private bath (one with a Jacuzzi), have antique high-backed beds and lovely views. Breathe deep and you can smell the lake air. Since the Damato family has published its own breakfast cookbook, be prepared for a gourmet start to your day. Try stuffed French toast, crêpes, cheese-baked apples, stuffed pears, and fresh breads and muffins. Make sure to get directions to this country location. $110–145 for two.

### *Elsewhere*

♿ **Black Swan Inn** (603-286-4524), 354 Main Street, Tilton 03276. Open all year. Sheryl and George

Regan offer nine guest rooms in this 1880s mill owner's mansion with its stained glass and ornate woodwork in parlors and guest rooms alike. There's a spacious, other-era feel throughout the house, which the Regans have furnished with their own collection of European antiques. It's a comfortable, interesting place to stay. Two suites (handicapped accessible) in the carriage house have a sitting area, bedroom, and porch with TV, air-conditioning, and a coffeemaker. In the main house rooms vary widely, with an assortment of bed arrangements. Our favorite is actually up on the third floor with skylights and an amazing bird's-eye maple vanity. Children over 10 please. Full breakfast. $90–115 for two.

✐ **Belgian Acres Farm** (603-286-2362), 91 Clark Road, Tilton 03276. Out in the country but just a few miles from downtown, this 1812 house has been nicely, comfortably restored. The floors are wide pine and the original wainscoting has survived, along with the granite hearth. The big front guest rooms upstairs are both attractive; one comes with a smaller room (great for parents with a student shopping the local prep schools). There is also a downstairs guest room and plenty of inviting common space. Children are welcome and will love the barn with its Belgian horses, goats, miniature donkeys, and other assorted animals. Hay- and sleigh rides are a house specialty. $75–150 includes a full breakfast.

**The Wakefield Inn** (603-522-8272; 1-800-245-0841), 2723 Wakefield Road, Wakefield 03872. Open all year. A centerpiece of the historic district (see *Villages*), this handsome, three-story 1804 Federal inn has been open to travelers in one form or another for more than a century. Now operated as a B&B by Lou and Harry Sisson, it features Indian shutters, a wraparound porch, and a three-sided fireplace in the sitting room. The seven guest rooms are reached by an unusual old spiral staircase. All the rooms, two of which are two-bedroom suites, have private bath, and the attractive furnishings feature Lou's homemade quilts. During the winter Lou runs 3-day quilt-making workshops. There is a large common room with a fireplace. $75–85 for two, B&B.

**COTTAGES** Consult the chambers of commerce listed under *Guidance* for cottage rentals—but we just had to mention the following:

**Ames Farm Inn** (603-293-4321; 603-742-3962; www.amesfarminn@worldpath.com), 2800 Lake Shore Road (Route 11), Gilford 03246. Open April (for fishermen) though October. Tradition! This 300-acre inn and cottage community has been here since 1890, having been operated by five generations of the Ames family. Needless to say, book early for the short peak season of July and August. Nineteen fully equipped housekeeping cottages are spread out on the lakefront. Each has one or two bedrooms, kitchenette, living room, and screened porch. The view across Lake Winnipesaukee stretches across the Broads for miles to the Ossipee Mountains and Mount Washington. Away from the shore are buildings with housekeeping apartments and 12 modern guest rooms with private bath. No charge to guests to launch and dock a boat. Some rental boats are available. The inn restaurant is open from late June through Labor Day, daily 7:30 AM–2 PM. Weekly rates: apartments and small cabin, $535;

housekeeping cottages, $925 peak season, $515 off-season. $70 per day for the private rooms.

**DUDE RANCH** **Chebacco Dude Ranch** (603-522-3211; www.chebaccoduderanch.com), Route 153, South Effingham 03882. Open all year. New Hampshire's only dude ranch, this 170-acre farm has access to hundreds of miles of trails. Merlyn and Jim Rutherford keep quarter horses and offer package programs throughout the year, limited only by good riding conditions. Since they only have five rooms, the atmosphere is quiet, with plenty of individual attention. They like to have at least four riders. A large, remodeled, three-story barn with two of the rooms (each with two doubles and a twin, perfect for families) is also an entertainment center with games and TV and an adjoining hot tub. The other three rooms, all with private bath, are in the main house. Three-hour trail rides are also offered to the public, and guests are not far from King Pine ski area and North Conway. Rooms are $69 for two with meals extra; inquire about riding packages.

**MOTELS AND CAMPING** Check the AAA and Mobil guides' motel listings if it's a motel you're after; we frankly have a hard enough time personally checking all the inns and B&Bs. Ditto for campgrounds, of which the area offers plenty.

## ✱ Where to Eat

### DINING OUT

#### *In Wolfeboro and vicinity*

**The Bittersweet Restaurant** (603-569-3636), Route 28 north and Allen Road, Wolfeboro. Open all year; in summer, Sunday through Thursday 5–9 PM, Friday through Saturday until 10; closed Tuesday, Wednesday off-season. Reservations recommended. Here's an 1823 barn, furnished with antiques, that has been recycled as a fine restaurant. Specialties include steak Diane, lobster pie, roast duck, and roast stuffed pork tenderloin. The Friday all-you-can-eat fish fry is $8.95, and there's a children's menu.

**The Wolfeboro Inn** (603-569-3016), 44 North Main Street, Wolfeboro. Open all year, Wolfe's Tavern 7 AM–11 PM, the dining room from 5 PM. Located in the old section of the inn, the tavern serves a wide variety of lighter fare, from hot and cold sandwiches and salads to soups, pasta, munchies, and dinners. More than 50 brands of beer, too. The 1812 Dining Room features New England–style cuisine (prime rib and seafood) as well as northern Italian specialities. It changes nightly; the more than a dozen choices the night we visited ranged from spinach ravioli with root vegetables and spinach cream sauce ($16) to rack of lamb with a sweet potato tart, carrots, and string beans ($20). There are lovely views of Wolfeboro Bay and gardens.

**Garwoods** (603-569-7788), 6 North Main Street, Wolfeboro. Open daily for lunch and dinner in summer, closed Wednesday in winter. This deep, lakeside storefront that began life as a lady's clothing store in 1899 is now an attractive new restaurant overlooking Wolfeboro Bay. The best seats are of course way in the back, beyond the bar (an inverted racing scull hangs above), with water views. Lunch runs from burgers to salads and pastas; dinner features seafood, from beer-battered fish-and-chips ($9.95) to lobster baked in a sherry cream sauce ($21.95). Inquire about live music.

**The Cider Press** (603-569-2028), 30 Middleton Road, South Wolfeboro. Nightly, except Monday, 5–9 PM; Sunday until 8 PM. Winter hours may vary. Since 1982, this has been a popular rustic spot with barnboard walls, fireplaces, antiques, candlelight dining, and a varied menu. Baby back ribs, grilled salmon, lamb chops, tempura shrimp, plus nightly blackboard specials. Entrées $10.95–17.95.

**East of Suez** (603-569-1648), Route 28, South Wolfeboro. Open daily except Monday, late June through early September, for dinner. Representative Asian food of all descriptions is prepared by the Powell family. Japanese, Chinese, Philippine, Thai, Indian, and Korean specialties (all prepared with authentic ingredients and condiments), huge portions, and moderate prices make this place a dining adventure. Here for more than 30 years, yet still something of a secret. Sushi, daily grilled seafood, and homegrown organic vegetables are featured. No alcohol is served, but you may bring your own bottle.

**The Lakeview Inn** (603-569-1335), 200 North Main Street, Wolfeboro. Serving dinner 7 days from 5 PM. Dining is in the restored rooms of this old inn. Highly regarded locally, this restaurant has a diverse menu of American and Continental entrées, including shrimp scampi, bouillabaisse, and well-prepared veal, steaks, and prime rib. Fresh-baked breads and pastries, homemade soups. The adjacent lounge serves sandwiches, soups, salads, and lighter fare. Reservations suggested. Entrées $9.95–26.95, with nightly specials.

**Loves' Quay** (603-569-3335), 51 Mill Street, Wolfeboro. Open for lunch and dinner 11:30 AM–10 PM. Arrive by land or lake; it's right on the water. Ten specials are served nightly, including sev-

CENTER SANDWICH

Robert Kozlow

eral varieties of fish and sirloin of lamb. Pastas are a regular feature. The fettuccine jambalaya, with sautéed chicken, scallops, andouille sausage, garlic, sherry, onions, peppers, tomato, and Cajun spices, is a humdinger. Dinner entrées $9.95–19.95.

**The Foxy Johnnie Restaurant and Firehouse Lounge** (603-859-3381), off Route 11, New Durham (south of Alton). Open daily 5–9 PM, Friday and Saturday until 10 PM, Sunday noon–9 PM. Reservations advised on weekends. Part of this popular, rambling place was built in 1764, and many old elements remain, including the massive fireplace, hand-hewn beams, and wide floorboards. Roast beef and steaks broiled over live coals are the specialties. Several entrées, including tenderloin and baked seafood such as haddock, shrimp, scallops, and mixed casserole. All steaks are served with sautéed mushrooms or pan-fried onions. Other entrées include sautéed lobster, fried seafoods, and veal parmigiana. $9.95–15.58. The lounge menu is very reasonably priced.

**The William Tell Inn** (603-293-8803), Route 11, West Alton. Open for dinner daily except Monday, spring through fall; Sunday brunch starting at noon. Call for winter hours. With a name from Switzerland and housed in a chalet, expect Swiss cuisine. One of the region's better restaurants, with a variety of Continental favorites served by owner-chef Peter Bossert and his wife, Susan. Wiener schnitzel, sauerbraten, venison, and cheese fondue share the menu with more conventional favorites such as filet mignon, New York sirloin, salmon, lamb, and seafood grill. The desserts feature dark Tobler chocolate imported from Switzerland. Early-bird specials from $7.50; entrées $12–17.95.

### *On the west shore and northward*

**The Woodshed** (603-476-2311; www.woodshedrestaurant.com), Lees Mill Road, off Route 109, Moultonborough. Open Tuesday through Sunday all year for dinner. To operate a successful restaurant in the countryside, on a side road, off a less-than-major route, in a small, spread-out town, you must have atmosphere and good food. This place has both in abundance. What began as a small restaurant in an old farmhouse a decade or so ago has grown into a large operation using the barn, its loft, and even a screened-in patio. The barn is exquisite, retaining its old hand-hewn features and decorated with antiques and collectibles. An evening could begin at the raw bar for clams and oysters or peel-and-eat shrimp and escargots. Prime rib is the specialty, but how about a combination with king crab or lobster? After Cajun roast pork tenderloin, shrimp kabob, lamb chops, or chicken gourmet, no wonder the dessert menu begins with "We dare you." Cheesecake, a one-scoop hot chocolate sundae, or Indian pudding can complete the repast. Entrées $15.95–22.95.

**The Boathouse Grille** (603-279-2253), Routes 3 and 25, Meredith. Open all year, daily 11:30 AM–3 PM for lunch, 5–9 PM for dinner Sunday through Thursday, until 9:30 PM Friday and Saturday. First come, first served. Located at the **Inn at Bay Point,** this restaurant (a member of the Common Man family) has a great deck that could make you believe you own the water. The food is varied and well prepared. Dinner entrées range from $12.95 for a Tuscan vegetable medley to $25. Try the venison roulades ($17.95).

**Café Lafayette Dinner Train** (603-745-3500; 1-800-699-3501; nhdinnertrain.com). Open weekends after Mother's Day until late June, then more frequently through early September. Call for times and reservations. For a movable feast, board at Meredith Station and ride in a 1924 Pullman dining car along the shore of Lake Winnipesaukee to Paugus Bay. The $55 fare (children 3–11, $32) includes a five-course meal served with linen, fine china, and appropriate aplomb.

**Corner House Inn** (603-284-6219), Route 109, Center Sandwich. Open daily year-round at 4:30 PM, lunch too June through October. An inn for 150 years and owned by Don and Jane Brown for 20, during which they established a reputation for good food in the traditional low-beamed dining room. Better still is what they've done recently: converting the upstairs (formerly lodging rooms) into one of the area's most inviting pubs. The same menu is available upstairs and down. You might begin with a lobster and mushroom bisque and dine on veal Oscar or grilled venison with a wild mushroom and Marsala wine sauce. In the pub, which features scattered couches and informal seating as well as regular tables and a semicircular bar, you can also dine (as we did) an impossibly huge grilled chicken Caesar salad or flatbread pizza. Storytellers hold forth on Thursday evenings off-season. Dinner entrées $14.95–21.95

**The Coe House** (603-253-8617), Route 3, Center Harbor. Open April through December, daily for dinner from 4:30 PM. A distinctive early-19th-century mansion with many windows and a cupola from which New Hampshire native Franklin Pierce watched Harvard and Yale compete in a rowing race on August 3, 1853. Reservations suggested on weekends. The food is good. Entrées range from a medley of fresh vegetables tempura ($12.95) to wood-grilled western elk steak ($21.95).

**Camp at Mill Falls** (603-279-3003), Route 3, in the Chase House at Mill Falls, Meredith. Dinner nightly 5–9:30 PM. The decor is summer camp, appropriate in this kids'-camp-studded corner of the world. Like other members of the Common Man restaurant chain, it's a dependable bet. Entrées range from "camp cakes" ($13.95) to a 20-ounce porterhouse steak ($19.95)—not your standard camp fare. Try the "Firecracker Dip."

**The Common Man** (603-536-4536; www.theCman.com), North Main Street, Ashland. Open daily for lunch and dinner; no lunch Sunday. Opened in 1971, this is the original, and still popular, star of a New Hampshire success story. The Great American Dining Company now operates eight restaurants that run north to south off I-93 from Windham to Lincoln. Here, the country decor features old posters, books, tools, and art, a comfortable feeling for relaxed dining. There is also a brick patio and lounge deck, as well as a new menu featuring 'Sconset pie, grilled shrimp, mixed grill, hazelnut-crusted chicken, and three cuts of prime rib. Dinners include cheese, crackers, and dips; salad; fresh-baked bread; veggies; potato; and white chocolate. They range $12.95–18.95.

**Mame's** (603-279-4631), 8 Plymouth Street, Meredith. Open daily for lunch 11:30 AM–3 PM, dinner 5:30–9 PM, and Sunday brunch 11 AM–2 PM. An 1825 brick house with barn, now with six dining rooms, Mame's offers varied and reasonably priced dining. Chicken baked in white wine with lemon and mushrooms, vegetables Alfredo, baked haddock, and roast prime rib are offered, along with nightly early-bird specials. Dinner entrées range from baked Boston scrod ($12.95) to lobster-scallop Divan ($18.95), with surf 'n' turf at $21.95. Mud pie, liqueur parfaits, cheesecake, and more for dessert. There's also a tavern menu. Nightmare—a casserole of turkey, ham, broccoli, bacon, tomato, and mushrooms, topped with Swiss—has been a house specialty for more than 20 years ($7.50 at lunch, $10.95 at dinner).

**Walt's Basin,** Route 3, Holderness. Open daily all year, except Tuesday off-season, 11:30 AM–3 PM for lunch, 5–9 PM for dinner. Come by land or water. A popular restaurant overlooking Little Squam Lake, at the bridge in the middle of Holderness. Casual but polished decor in dark greens and natural wood. Specialties include panfried rainbow trout, seafood fra diavolo, pesto steak pizziola, prime rib, and "chowda." We lunched on the best of turkey and bacon sandwiches with salad. Dinner entrées run from meat loaf ($11.95) to beef and shrimp ($24.95).

**The Manor on Golden Pond** (603-968-3348; 1-800-545-2141), Shepard Hill Road and Route 3, Holderness. Open daily for breakfast, and dinner 6–9 PM. Dining is a big deal here, as well it should be in the Manor's elegant Edwardian dining rooms. But while the surroundings take you back in time, the food is up to the minute. The menu, which changes daily, features such innovative offerings as wild mushroom bisque with toasted crouton and tomato relish, macadamia-encrusted chicken breast with maple beurre blanc and house-blend rice, or citrus-roasted salmon with wild rice. For dessert, their apple pie has been judged the best in New England, but it's hard to pass up chocolate decadence torte or Kahlúa custard with caramel sauce and fresh fruit. The wine list received the *Wine Spectator* award of excellence. The $46 prix fixe does not include dessert, beverage, tax, or gratuity.

### *On Lake Winnipesaukee south*

**Hickory Stick Farm** (603-524-3333), 60 Bean Hill Road, Belmont. Open at 5 PM every day but Monday, Memorial Day through Columbus Day; Sunday brunch 10 AM–2 PM, dinner 4–8 PM. After Columbus Day the days of operation vary but always include weekends. Reservations, please, and ask for directions. Although less than 4 miles from Laconia, this restaurant is well off the beaten path. In business since 1950, it is now owned and managed by Brian and Irene Mackes and nationally known for its duck dishes. The main dining room has early American decor, but the large screened gazebo overlooking the gardens is our favorite summer spot. For an appetizer, among other items, try duck-liver pâté, fried duck livers, or duck soup. Roast duck is prepared for one, or a whole duck can be carved at the table. Slow-roasted to remove the fatty layer under the skin, these 4- to 5-pound Wisconsin-bred ducks have crisp skin with moist, fork-tender meat beneath. Frozen, cooked duck with a packet of orange sherry sauce is available in the gift shop or by mail. Casseroles of seafood, scallops, or vegetables; baked chicken with apple-pecan stuffing; prime rib; and rack of lamb are among other menu specialties. Dinners include orange curl rolls, a molded pineapple salad, or country green salad. Entrées $13.95–25.95.

**Oliver's** (603-286-7379; www.oliverscountrydinng.com), Route 3 at I-93, left off Exit 20, Tilton (handy to the outlet mall). Open daily for lunch and dinner 11 AM–9 PM weekdays, 11 AM–10 PM Friday and Saturday; Sunday brunch 11–2. Reservations suggested. Locals voted this popular restaurant the most romantic in the area. There's candlelight dining in five cozy rooms, two with fireplaces. Dinner offerings include steak *au poivre*, veal du jour, and salmon *en croute*. The **Fox and Hounds Pub** serves a lighter menu until closing. Dinner entrées $15.95–22.95.

## EATING OUT

### *In the Wolfeboro area and on Lake Winnipesaukee east*

**Bailey's** (603-569-3662), 298 South Main Street, Wolfeboro. Open mid-May through Columbus Day for all three meals. An old favorite known for its ice cream. The Bailey family has offered casual dining in the Wolfeboro area for 65 years. A full menu, from breakfast omelets and blueberry muffins to homemade clam chowder, baked Virginia ham, and barbecued stuffed chicken, keeps families happy year after year.

**Wolfetrap Grill and Raw Bar** (603-569-1047), 19 Bay Street, Wolfeboro. Open daily 4–11 PM. Wolfecatch is the fish market; Wolfetrap is the grill and raw bar that goes with it. Even the most FINicky can rest assured this fish is fresh. Quahog chowder and spicy crab soup; steamers, cherrystones, littlenecks, softshell crab, New England clam boil, plus lobsters and shrimp boiled, in a salad, on a roll, or boxed to go. Burgers and steak, desserts and coffee, are also on the menu. Moderate.

**Maddie's By the Bay** (603-569-8888), 11 Dockside, Wolfeboro. Seasonal dockside dining, good for breakfast and lunch.

**Strawberry Patch** (603-569-5523), 50 North Street, Wolfeboro. Open Monday through Saturday for breakfast and lunch, Sunday breakfast only (7:30 AM–1 PM). Strawberry pancakes, shortcake, and sundaes, not to mention fresh strawberries rolled in brown sugar and sour cream. Quiche and salads, too.

**Poor People's Pub** (603-522-8378), Route 109, Sanbornville. Open for lunch and dinner. A local gathering spot with good roadfood: burgers, pizzas, daily specials, and subs. We can vouch for "Tramp's Treat": fresh chicken salad on a grilled roll ($3). Beer and wine are served.

### *On Lake Winnipesaukee west*

**Hart's Turkey Farm Restaurant** (603-279-6212), junction of Routes 3 and 104, Meredith. Open all year at 11:15 AM for lunch and dinner. A big barn of a place serving turkey in every conceivable form, but there are also steaks, seafood, and sandwiches in this large, popular restaurant, family owned since 1954. Gift shop. Moderate.

**Sam & Rosie's Café and Bakery** (603-253-6606), Route 25, Center Harbor. Open 6 AM–3 PM except Sunday. Sam and Rose Blake run a first-rate breakfast and lunch place, with fresh baked goods.

**George's Diner** (603-279-8723; www.georgesdiner.com), Plymouth Street, Meredith. Open 6 AM–8 PM daily. Nothing fancy, just dependably good food.

**Kellerhaus** (603-366-4466), Route 3,

just north of Weirs Beach. Known for the ice cream made here for 90 years with a view of the lake, sundaes with a dozen different toppings, waffle breakfasts, and an old-fashioned candy store.

**Tilt'n Diner** (603-286-2204), Route 3 at I-93, left off Exit 20, Tilton. Another member of the Common Man family, this diner is a takeoff on the 1950s, with period menu, music, and memorabilia. Open until 9 PM for breakfast, lunch, and dinner. Nothing's expensive; everything's filling. For quick food and lots of fun, this place is just swell!

### *Sandwich/Squam Lakes*

**The Corner House** (see *Dining Out*). It's hard to beat the upstairs pub for an informal night out. Mid-day fare (June through October) features soups, salads, and the crêpe of the day.

**The Endeavor Café in the Sandwich Store,** Center Sandwich. Open for breakfast 6–10 AM, lunch 11:30 AM–2:30 PM, Sunday brunch 1–2:30 PM. The back of the store is a truly pleasant space with a woodstove and easy chairs as well as tables draped in checked cloths. Order the soup you can see simmering on the stove; sandwiches, salads, and daily specials. The store also houses the Sandwich Baker (the ovens are in the back) and is a source of Sandwich Creamery (see *Selective Shopping—Farms)* ice cream. Try ginger.

See **Walt's Basin** a good bet for lunch, and **The Common Man** in Ashland under *Dining Out*,

## ✷ Entertainment

**Belknap Mill Society** (603-524-8813), Mill Plaza, Laconia 03246. Open all year, weekdays 9 AM–5 PM, Saturday 9 AM–1 PM. Built in 1823, this is the oldest unaltered textile mill in the country. It's now a year-round arts center with art exhibits, music, lectures, and children's programs as well as many special events.

MUSIC **Lake Winnipesaukee Music Festival** (603-569-1440; 1-800-505-2612; lwmf.org). Frequent performances from mid-July into August in the Wolfeboro area.

**New Hampshire Music Festival** (603-253-4331; www.nhmf.org). For 50 years, this regional music institution has brought big-time classical musicians to the small towns of the New Hampshire's Lakes region. The 6-week season begins in early July. Performances are three times weekly at the Silver Cultural Arts Center at Plymouth State College and at Memorial Middle High School Auditorium in Gilford. Stay tuned as the festival's new venue evolves on a 700-acre estate in Center Harbor, formerly the Red Hill Inn.

**Meadowbrook Farm Summer Concert Series** (603-293-4700; www.meadowbrookfarm.net). A July and August series of concerts; in 2001 performers ranged from Peter, Paul and Mary to the Boston Pops.

**Great Waters Music Festival** (603-569-7710; www.greatwaters.org), on the Brewster Academy campus, Wolfeboro. July through September, a series of concerts held in an acoustically designed tent.

**Wolfeboro Friends of Music** (603-569-3657) sponsor a series of 10 summer concerts held in local churches and auditoriums.

SUMMER THEATER **The Lakes Region Theater** (603-279-9933),

Route 25, Box 1607, Meredith. Professional summer-stock productions of Broadway plays presented in Inter-Lakes High School. Late June through August.

Also see the **Barnstormers** in Tamworth under *Entertainment* in "Mount Washington and Its Valleys—Gateway Region." It's New Hampshire's oldest professional theater, staging outstanding plays with Equity casts.

## ✷ Selective Shopping

ANTIQUES **Burlwood Antique Center** (603-279-6387), junction of Routes 3 and 104, Meredith. The largest collection of antiques in the Lakes region—175 selected dealers. Open daily May 1 through October 31, 10 AM–5 PM. Furniture, jewelry, china, glass, books, the works.

**Alexandria Lamp Shop** (603-279-4234), 62 Main Street, Meredith. Several rooms full of antique (kerosene, gas, and electric) as well as unusual fixtures and chandeliers. Also hard-to-find lamp shades, parts, and repairs.

**Gordon's Antiques and Auctions** (603-297-5458), Route 3, Meredith. Open daily. Quality antiques with plenty of Victoriana.

**New Hampton Antique Center** (603-744-5652), Route 104 east, Exit 23, New Hampton. Open daily but closed Tuesday and Wednesday January through March. Antiques, collectibles.

ART AND CRAFTS **Sandwich Home Industries** (603-284-6831; open mid-May to mid-October) in Center Sandwich was founded in 1926 to promote traditional crafts, eventually spawning the current League of New Hampshire Craftsmen with its stores throughout the state and its big annual August Craftsmen's Fair at Mount Sunapee. The present shop dates from 1934. For many years a signature item in this particular shop has been the locally made botanical lampshades. You can still buy them here or, better still, find them in the studio by Teacup Lake where they are made by Suzanne Rowan and Sarah Zuccarelli (phone for directions: 603-284-7003; www.botanicallampshades.com). Just up Route 113 from Home Industries, **The Designery** (603-284-6915; open year-round, Thursday through Saturday 10 AM–2:30 PM; mid-June through Labor Day, Tuesday through Saturday 10 AM–5 PM; and by appointment) is a working studio and shop offering limited-edition apparel and handwoven household accessories. Knitters, weavers, and spinners come for the hand-dyed yarns and fibers, as well as the kits and extensive book selection. The shop also offers locally made tartans and other craft items.

**League of New Hampshire Craftsmen.** Shops in **Meredith** (603-279-7920), Route 3, and in **Wolfeboro** (603-569-3309), 64 Center Street, are open year-round, displaying superb New Hampshire–made, juried crafts of all types including lamps, furniture, prints, carvings, textiles, pottery, and much more. Demonstration programs in July and August.

**Cornish Hill Pottery** (603-569-5626; 1-800-497-2556), 39 North Main Street, Wolfeboro, is a combination studio and showcase for Gogi Millner Adler's stunning functional and decorative pieces, all hand-thrown and decorated.

Also in Wolfeboro: **The Art Place** (603-569-6159), 9 North Main Street, showcases regional, original art and limited-edition prints, as does the

**Blue Shutter Gallery** (603-569-3372), 19 Lehner Street. **Made on Earth** (603-569-9100), North Main Street, showcases artisans from around the earth. **Hampshire Pewter** (603-569-4944), 9 Mill Street (just off the Main Street), open year-round daily except Sunday, 9 AM–5 PM. A factory store showcasing pieces made here; factory tours are offered spring through fall.

**Yikes American Craft Gallery** (603-253-4966), Route 25 and Main Street, Center Harbor. Open except January through April, daily 10 AM–6 PM, Sunday 10 AM–5 PM. A zany mix of well-chosen items representing more than 500 American craftspeople, from metals and clothing to toys and sculpture.

**The Old Print Barn** (603-279-6479), Winona Road, off Route 104, Meredith. Open year-round except Thanksgiving and Christmas, 10 AM–5 PM. One of the largest displays of original prints in New England, some 2,000 original antique and contemporary works from 1600 to the present, housed in a Civil War–era barn. We especially like the old New Hampshire views of the lakes and White Mountains, but you can find etchings, lithographs, and engravings covering virtually any subject from any continent as well as work by locally prominent and world-famous artists. The huge restored barn, with its detailed, 19th-century craftsmanship, is impressive, too. Free, but it will be hard to resist buying a print!

**Oglethorpe** (603-279-9909), at Mill Falls Marketplace, Route 3 in Meredith, a gallery representing some 300 craftspeople, featuring hand-forged ironwork and handcrafted jewelry. Also in Meredith**: Pottery by Meredith Bay** (603-279-7419), Route 3 across from the dock, open daily except Monday: a working studio showcasing regional pottery and fine arts.

**Village Artists & Gallery** (603-968-4445), 51 Main Street, Ashland, is a new nonprofit cooperative representing 40 local artists, well worth checking.

**Laconia Pottery Gallery** (603-528-4997), 45 Court Street, Laconia. A showcase for New England potters, much of it handcrafted on site.

**Lambert Folk Art Gallery** (603-286-4882; www.jimlambertfolkart.com), 271 Main Street, Tilton. Not the kind of shop you might expect to find in the middle of Tilton, but Jim Lambert points out that his whimsical creations perpetuate the town's tradition of striking sculptures (see *Villages*). His own folk sculptures are the real finds here, but many other outstanding craftspeople, most of them regional, are represented.

**BOOKS** ✐ **Bayswater Book Co.** (603-253-8858), Route 25 and Main Street, Center Harbor. A well-stocked bookstore offering volumes of extra service including kids' story hours, a young adults' discussion group, arts-and-crafts workshops, journal-writing courses, frequent author signings, and coffee by the pound or cup.

**Innisfree Bookshop** (603-279-3905), Mill Falls Marketplace, Meredith. A big, full-service bookstore also carrying music, toys, and cards.

**The Country Bookseller** (603-569-6030; 1-800-877-READ), Railroad Avenue, Wolfeboro. An inviting, well-stocked independent bookstore in the middle of the village.

Also in Wolfeboro, see Camelot under *Special Stores.*

**FARMS** **Moulton Farm** (603-279-3915), Quarry Road, just off Route 25 east of Meredith. A simply outstanding farm stand in a great setting.

**The Sandwich Creamery** (603-284-6675), Hannah Road off 113A, North Sandwich. A source of ice cream (ginger is the standout flavor); also Brie and cheddar cheeses. Also available at the general store in Center Sandwich.

**Booty Farm** (603-284-7163), 610 Mount Israel Road. Open year-round. The sugarhouse was billowing sweet steam when we passed. Syrup is sold year-round, along with organic produce.

**Belknap Mill Plaza,** Laconia. An outdoor farmers' market located in the parking lot between the mill and town hall. Open mid-July through October, Saturday 9 AM–noon.

**SPECIAL STORES** **Keepsake Quilting and Country Pleasures** (603-253-4026; 1-800-865-9458; www.keepsakequilting.com), Route 25, Senter's Marketplace, Center Harbor. Open daily. Billed as America's largest quilt shop, this is a destination for quilters from throughout the country and even the world. Many are members, paying a nominal annual fee to display their own work here (on consignment); thousands also subscribe to the catalog, which features—as does the store—everything and anything a quilter could desire. There is nothing, however, like actually seeing and fingering the 10,000 bolts of cotton cloth in a heady range of colors and patterns. Mannequins greet patrons by the door, proffering white gloves, the better to examine both fabrics and finished quilts. Stencils, patterns, and kits are also sold.

**The Old Country Store,** Route 25, Moultonborough. Open daily. Built as a stagecoach stop in 1781, this rambling old building has a small museum to go along with gifts, books, New Hampshire–made products, and typical country store items.

**Annalee Dolls** (603-279-6542; 1-800-433-6557; www.annalee.com), off Route 3 or Route 104, Meredith. Open all year. Dolls are for kids, of course, but these dolls are also among the more collectible items you can purchase today, so probably more golden agers stop here than children. Annalee Thorndike began making her felt dolls in 1934; now she runs a major local industry employing more than 450 people, and her dolls are sold and collected nationally. For collectors, the best inventory is maintained here, including more than 1,000 different early dolls. You can see the finished pieces in the gift shop, the doll museum (open Memorial Day through Labor Day), and the Annalee Doll Antique and Collectible Doll Shoppe. Join the Annalee Doll Society and receive a free doll, membership pin, newsletter, and an invitation to the annual barbecue and doll auction held on the last Sunday of June.

✐ **Camelot** (603-569-1771), 16 North Main Street, Wolfeboro. Open daily except Wednesday off-season. Over more than 37 years Al Pierce has created an eclectic mix of good things that jam-pack his shop. Locals are addicted to his special cream cheddar mix, and youngsters know this as a peerless place for the kind of toys (educational and otherwise) you won't find everywhere. Cards, many books, and assorted gifts fill every inch of space remaining.

**Basket World** (603-366-5585), Route 3, Weirs Beach. Leave the kids across the street at the Funspot while you shop through this huge display of woven baskets, furniture, and other items.

**chi-lin** (603-527-1115; 603-279-8663), corner of Lake and Main Streets, Meredith. Terry and Suzanne Lee have filled their shop with a selection of imported and custom-made cabinets, furniture, and accessories with an Asian sensibility. They have also created an oasis off this busy shopping area, with pocket gardens for occasional tea parties. You can consult with them to implement your own design ideas.

**Pepi Herrmann Crystal** (603-528-1020), Lily Pond Road, Gilford. Monday through Saturday 9:30 AM–5 PM. Showroom and museum. Fine-quality, hand-cut crystal and giftware. Watch crystal cutters at work.

**Country Braid House** (603-286-4511), 462 Main Street, Tilton. Open Monday through Saturday 9 AM–5 PM. Pure wool rugs in many patterns.

**Ye Olde Sale Shoppe,** Route 153 at Taylor City, South Effingham. Open May through Christmas 10 AM–5 PM, weekends until 6. Antiques, gifts, and collectibles in this jam-packed old barn. Penny candy, fabrics, dolls, toys, and a Christmas room. See Route 153 under *To See—Scenic Drives* in "Mount Washington and Its Valleys—Gateway Region."

SHOPPING COMPLEXES **Lakes Region Factory Stores** (603-286-7880), Route 3 at I-93, left off Exit 20, Tilton. Open May through December 10 AM–9 PM, Sunday 10 AM–6 PM; off-season closing at 6 PM, except Friday and Saturday when it's 8 PM. More than 50 tax-free factory outlets include Brooks Brothers, J. Crew, Polo/Ralph Lauren, and Black & Decker.

**Mill Falls Marketplace Shops** (www.millfalls.com), Route 3, Meredith. Open daily year-round, weekdays 10 AM–9 PM, Sunday until 5:30 PM. This remarkable restoration of an 1820s mill beside its 40-foot falls now houses 15 shops, also rest rooms and an ATM.

## ✷ Special Events

Dozens of events are held each summer in the Winnipesaukee region, too many to list here in detail. Check with such organizations as the **Lakes Region Association** (603-744-8664), **New Hampshire Farm Museum** (603-652-7840), **Belknap Mill Society** (603-524-8813), and **Gunstock Recreation Area** (603-293-4341).

*Early February:* **World Championship Sled Dog Derby,** Opechee Park, Laconia. Three days of racing by colorful teams of sled dogs.

*Mid-February:* **Winter Carnival** (603-569-2758), Wolfeboro Lion's Club. A week of events. **Sandwich Notch Sled Dog Races.** Annual 60-mile races from Tamworth to Sandwich.

*Mid-May:* **Annual Winni Fishing Derby** (603-253-8689), Lake Winnipesaukee. A weekend fishing contest with cash prizes for the largest landlocked salmon or lake trout.

*Early June:* **Laconia Race Week** is huge, the biggest annual event in New Hampshire. In 2001 it drew some 375,000 motorcyclists over 9 days, a tradition dating back to 1916. The races are held at the New Hampshire Speedway in Loudon 10 miles away, but parades and rallies are held at

Gunstock and in the Lake City itself. Two-wheeled visitors from throughout the country fills every bed for miles around. For a full schedule of events log onto www.laconiaMCweek.com or call 603-366-2000. **Annual Barn Sale and Auction** (603-652-7840), New Hampshire Farm Museum, Milton. Call for a detailed schedule of many summer events.

*July and August:* **Alton Bay band concerts.** Several free concerts are held weekly during July and August, plus a week of events during Old Home Week in mid-August. Write the chamber of commerce for a full schedule of summer activities (see *Guidance*).

*Early July:* **New Hampshire Music Festival** (603-524-1000). A 6-week regional tradition, with world-class performers playing chamber and orchestral music at various venues.

*Fourth of July:* Regionwide celebrations with parades and fireworks, some special events, some events held the night before. Alton, Ashland, Center Harbor, Laconia, Meredith, Wolfeboro.

*Mid-July:* **Arts and Crafts Street Fair,** downtown Laconia.

*Late July:* **Annual Antiques Fair and Show** (603-539-5126), Kingswood High School, Wolfeboro. **Antique and Classic Boat Show,** Weirs Beach. **Annual Flea Market and Chicken Barbecue,** East Alton.

*Early August:* **Huggins Hospital Street Fair** (603-569-1043), Brewster Field, Wolfeboro. **Sandwich Old Home Days,** an entire week of very special events.

*Mid-August:* **Old Home Week** (603-539-6323), Freedom and Alton. **Miss Winnipesaukee Pageant** (603-366-4377), Funspot, Weirs Beach.

*Late August:* **Annual Lakes Region Fine Arts and Crafts Festival** (603-279-6121), Meredith. A major, juried outdoor exhibit with music, entertainment, and food.

*Mid-September:* **Annual Winnipesaukee Relay Race** (603-524-5531). Teams of runners circle the lake, beginning in the Gunstock Recreation Area. **Altrusa Antique Show and Sale** at the Inter-Lakes High School, Meredith (603-279-6121).

*Early October:* **Annual Quilter Show** (603-524-8813), Belknap Mill Society, Laconia.

*Columbus Day weekend:* **Sandwich Fair** (603-284-7062; www.sandwichfairnh.com), 3 days: an old-fashioned fair with tractor pulls, ox, mule, and draft horse pulls, clogging, an antique auto parade, 4-H exhibits, fleece-to-shawl spinning, stage shows, a grand street parade, and much more.

*First weekend in December:* **Annual Christmas in the Village,** Center Sandwich. Crafts, bake, and book sale with the historical society decorated for Christmas.

# THE WESTERN LAKES

From Lake Sunapee to Newfound Lake, this region is spotted with lakes big and small, all set in open, rolling countryside, each with a view of one of the area's three mighty mountains: Sunapee, Kearsarge, and Cardigan.

All three summits make rewarding hikes, and all the lakes offer attractive shoreline lodging as well as swimming, fishing, and boating. But this entire area is far less well known than the Winnipesaukee region, because the old hotels here were replaced with second homes instead of with the cottage colonies and motels that sprang up around Winnipesaukee. Still, these "summer people" continued to patronize summer theater, shops, ski areas, and restaurants. When lodging places began proliferating again, as they have over the past couple of decades, these amenities were all in place.

The activity is very low-key, however. The year-round hub of the area is the handsome old college town of New London, with a rambling, 18th-century inn and Colby-Sawyer College at its center and two small lakes (Little Sunapee and Pleasant) on its arms.

The region's most famous lake is Sunapee. Unusually clear (it is still a source of drinking water) and unusually high (1,100 feet), Lake Sunapee sits midway between the Connecticut River Valley and the Merrimack River Valley. Ten miles long and 3 miles wide, still sheathed almost entirely in green, it's unquestionably a special place.

Lake Sunapee, however, is a tease. Stand on the summit of Mount Sunapee (accessible by chairlift) and its 10-mile-long expanse shimmers below, seemingly inviting you to jump in. Back on level ground, though, reaching the water is elusive. You can swim at the beach in Lake Sunapee State Park, choose from two excursion boats, or rent almost any kind of boat; but no road circles the lake because, from the 1850s until the 1920s, everyone came and went by train and got around the lake itself by steamboat. The largest cluster of hotels and busiest steamboat landing was Sunapee Harbor, still the summer focal point of the lake.

Newfound Lake (8 miles west of I-93), with 22 miles of shoreline, is even more low-key than Sunapee; and Mount Cardigan looms above its western shore as Mount Sunapee does above Lake Sunapee. Both Sunapee and Newfound offer sandy state beaches, as does smaller Kezar Lake in North Sutton, off I-89, Exit 10 (see *To Do—Swimming*). Other lakes accessible to guests at local inns include

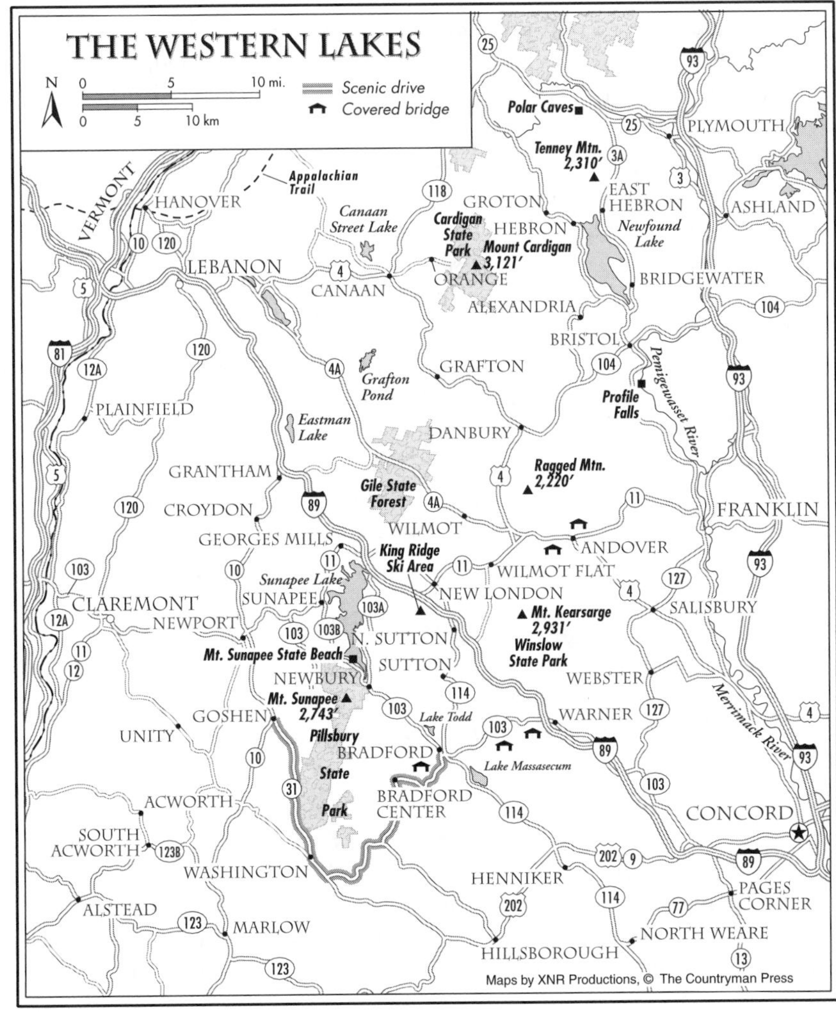


Little Sunapee and Pleasant Lakes, both in New London; Lake Todd and Lake Massasecum in Bradford; Highland Lake in East Andover; and Webster Lake in Franklin.

Since its opening in 1968, I-89 has put New London and Sunapee less than 2 hours from Boston, but the increase in tourist traffic has not been dramatic. In winter, skiers tend to day-trip from Boston as well as Concord; and in summer, innkeepers complain, they whiz right on through to Vermont. Lodging prices are relatively low, even lower in the northern part of this region, which was bypassed when I-89 replaced Route 4 as the region's major east–west route.

In New Hampshire state promotional literature you'll find this area under "Dartmouth/Lake Sunapee," but we believe that these "Western Lakes" (west of I-93) deserve more recognition. While it is handy to the cultural happenings around the Dartmouth green, the area is equally handy to attractions in the White Mountains, the Merrimack Valley, and the Monadnock region. These Western Lakes are great spots to explore from or to just stay put.

**GUIDANCE** **The New London Lake Sunapee Region Chamber of Commerce** maintains a helpful, walk-in information booth in the middle of New London's Main Street, June through Labor Day, and another seasonal information booth for Sunapee in Sunapee Lower Village.

**The Newport Chamber of Commerce** (603-863-1510; www.chambernewport.nh.us) maintains a seasonal information booth in the center of town.

**The Newfound Region Chamber of Commerce** (603-744-2150; www.newfoundchamber.com) maintains a seasonal information booth on Route 3A at the foot of the lake.

**GETTING THERE** *By bus:* **Vermont Transit** (1-800-451-3292; www.greyhound.com) stops at the Gourmet Garden, 127 Main Street, New London, once a day en route from Boston to White River Junction; direct service from Boston's Logan Airport.

*By car:* I-89 cuts diagonally across the heart of this region, putting it within 1½ hours of Boston; via I-91 it's also 2½ hours from Hartford.

*By air*: See *Getting There* in "Upper Valley Towns" and "The Manchester/Nashua Area."

**MEDICAL EMERGENCY** Dial **911.**

**New London Hospital** (603-526-2911), County Road, New London, has a 24-hour walk-in clinic. (Also see *Medical Emergency* in "Upper Valley Towns.")

## * Villages

**Andover.** This is an unusually proud town, with Proctor Academy, established in 1848 (actually it moved to Wolfeboro in 1865, then back in 1875), at its core; hence the B&Bs and unusually good dining and shopping. The **Andover Historical Society Museum,** housed in a vintage-1874, Victorian-style railroad station on Route 4 in the tiny village of Potter Place (open weekends from Memorial Day through Columbus Day, Saturday 10 AM–3 PM, Sunday 1–3 PM), is worth a stop. According to a historical marker in the nearby Route 11 rest area, Potter Place takes its name from Richard Potter, a 19th-century magician known throughout America. **Highland Lake** is in East Andover.

**Bradford Center.** Just off the main drag (Route 103), but it feels like a million miles away. Coming north, the turn for River Road is a left just beyond the junction of Routes 103 and 114. You go through the *Bement covered bridge* (see *To See—Covered Bridges*), built in 1854. Continue up the hill, up and up until you come to the old hill-town crossroads. Turn left, and you will find the old schoolhouse and vintage-1838 meetinghouse with its two doors and Gothic-style tower topped with decorative wooden spikes (peculiar to New Hampshire), resembling upside-down icicles. The old graveyard is here, too. The present town hall was moved from this village down to what is now the business center of Bradford when the train arrived in the 1860s.

**Hebron** is a classic gathering of white-clapboard houses around a common at the northwestern corner of Newfound Lake. The handsome, two-story meetinghouse was completed in 1803, and the Hebron Village School is housed in a churchlike building with a Gothic Revival steeple (upside-down wooden icicles again).

**New London.** Sited on a ridge, good for summer views and winter skiing, New London is the home of **Colby-Sawyer College** (603-526-2010), a 4-year, coed college founded as a Baptist academy in 1837. The 80-acre campus includes the Marion G. Mugar Art Gallery, with changing exhibits by recognized artists and by college faculty and students. The **New London Historical Society Museum and Library** (see *To See—Historic Homes*) on Little Sunapee Road is an ambitious gathering of restored buildings, including an 1835 Cape with an attached ell and barn; also a schoolhouse, country store, and blacksmith shop on 5 acres. In 2001 the society opened a newly constructed Transportation Building to house an outstanding collection of old carriages and sleighs, including an original Concord Coach. New London is also home to the Barn Playhouse (see *Entertainment*), one of New England's oldest and best summer theaters. The town's hidden gems are **Cricenti's Bog** (see *Green Space*) and **Little Sunapee Lake,** site of Twin Lake Village, one of New England's most authentic and low-profile 19th-century family resorts.

**Newport** is an old mill town and commercial center with some elaborate 19th-century buildings like the circa-1886 **Newport Opera House** (603-863-2412) on Main Street, the scene of frequent concerts, plays, and dances. It's also the scene of the annual presentation of the Sarah Josepha Hale Medal to the likes of Arthur Miller and Arthur Schlesinger. (Hale, the town's best-known citizen, was the author of the famous children's poem "Mary Had a Little Lamb" and was instrumental in promoting Thanksgiving as a national holiday.) **The Richards Library**

HEBRON MEETINGHOUSE

Robert Kozlow

**Arts Center** (603-863-3040), 58 North Main Street, hosts continuous exhibits by local artists, including an open studio the last Thursday of the month when visitors can view and discuss weaver Patryc Wiggins's long-term Mill Tapestry Project. The handsome brick **South Congregational Church** at the other end of Main Street (it's diagonally across from the Mobil station), completed in 1823, is almost identical to the Unitarian church (1824) in Deerfield, Massachusetts. No longer an outlet for the woolen mill across the street, the **Dorr Mill Store** (see *Selective Shopping*) has become a destination for rug hookers and quilters looking for supplies. The recently opened **Sargent Museum Center for Connecticut River Archaeology** (see *To See—Museums*), temporarily located in the restored Nettleton House on Central Street, contains the late Howard Sargent's 7,000-volume library and thousands of archaeological finds from the region.

**Sunapee Harbor.** In the **Sunapee Historical Society Museum** (see *To See—Museums*), you browse through scrapbooks filled with pictures of the village's half a dozen vanished hotels, most notably the four-story, 100-room Ben-Mere, which sat until the 1960s on a knoll in the middle of "the Harbor." Local residents worry that most of the lakeshore is now privately owned, and therefore, the Sunapee Harbor Riverway Corporation has been formed to revitalize the Harbor's adjacent waterway, which once fueled a tannery, a pulp mill, and clothespin and wooden hame (part of a harness) factories. To date the corporation has restored several buildings in Sunapee Harbor, and worked to bring in restaurants, shops, and summer entertainment.

**Sutton,** off I-89, Exit 10, and south on Route 114. **South Sutton** is a 19th-century mill-village center with a 1790s meetinghouse and a former general store—now the **Old Store Museum,** exhibiting (we're told) no fewer than 4,000 items—along with the 1863 schoolhouse, open to visitors in July and August, Sunday 1–4 PM or by appointment (603-927-4183; 603-938-5005). **North Sutton** is also an appealing village with a meetinghouse, general store, and historic marker noting the several large summer hotels that used to stand here by **Kezar Lake.** Only the annex of one (now the Follansbee Inn) survives, but Wadleigh State Beach offers access to the lake. **Muster Field Farm** (see *To See—Museums*) conveys a sense of both the beauty and the history of the area.

**Washington.** A tiny gem of a village with a cluster of imposing buildings, a meetinghouse completed in 1789 (the Asher Benjamin–style steeple was added later), an 1840s Gothic-style Congregational church, and a two-story, 1830s schoolhouse—all huddled together on the northern side of the common. According to a historical marker, this is the birthplace of the Seventh-Day Adventist Church (April 1842) and also the first town in the country incorporated (December 13, 1776) as "Washington."

## ✱ To See

**MUSEUMS** Also see *Villages*.

**Andover Historical Society Museum** (603-735-5694), Routes 4 and 11, Potter Place. Classic, authentically furnished 1874 railroad station houses local history exhibits.

**Claremont Historical Society and Museum** (603-542-1400), 26 Mulberry Street, Claremont. Exhibits of local and state interest. Free admission. A walking tour of 37 sites in the area's historic mill district is available from the Claremont Chamber of Commerce (603-543-1296), 24 Tremont Square.

♿ **Marion G. Mugar Art Gallery** (603-526-3000; 603-526-3661), Colby-Sawyer College, 100 Main Street, New London. Open during the school year Monday through Friday 9 AM–5 PM; weekends and summer by appointment or chance. Excellent changing exhibits by recognized artists.

**Mount Kearsarge Indian Museum** (603-456-2600; www.indianmuseum.org), Kearsarge Mountain Road, Warner. Open May through October, Monday through Saturday 10 AM–5 PM, Sunday noon–5 PM. Doors open at 10 AM for Special Events Days. Open Saturday and Sunday from November to the weekend before Christmas. Guided tours on the hour. $5 per adult; $3 for children 6–12. This is one of the most impressive displays of Native American artifacts in the Northeast. Frankly, we weren't prepared for the quantity or quality of this collection, amassed by one man, Bud Thompson, over more than 40 years. With the skill of a professional curator (he was formerly with Canterbury Shaker Village), Thompson has transformed a former riding arena into a showcase for hundreds of priceless and evocative pieces: dozens of intricate sweet-grass baskets from the Penobscot, carved ash baskets from the Passamaquoddy, intricate quillwork from the Micmac, Seneca corn-husk masks, Anasazi pottery from Chaco Canyon in New Mexico (dating from somewhere between A.D. 800 and 1200), Navajo Yei rugs, elaborate saddlebags beaded by the Plains Indians, cradleboards from Idaho, and much, much more.

"I don't want people bending and squinting over labels," Bud Thompson observes. Instead, guides elaborate on the various Native American pieces as well as the cultures they represent. One of the few modern pieces in this museum is an imposing, bigger-than-life statue of a Native American in full regalia, which Thompson bought many years ago at the annual League of New Hampshire Craftsmen's Fair at Mount Sunapee State Park.

"It wasn't until after I had settled on this site for the museum and positioned the statue at the entrance that its sculptor told me it was carved from a single tree he had cut from the slopes of Mount Kearsarge," Thompson relates. The museum stands at the base of Mount Kearsarge, near the entrance to Rollins State Park and its trails to the mountain's bald summit. (Also see *To Do—Hiking* and *Green Space*.)

**Sunapee Historical Society Museum** (603-763-4418), Sunapee Harbor. Open mid-June through Labor Day; call for hours. A former livery stable filled with photos of Sunapee's grand old hotels and steamboats. You discover that visitors began summering on Lake Sunapee as soon as the railroad reached Newbury in 1849 and that the lake's resort development was sparked by the three Woodsum brothers from Harrison, Maine (another lake resort), who began running steamboats to meet the trains. Soon there were two competing ferry lines (one boat carried 650 passengers) serving dozens of small landings on the shore and islands.

**Muster Field Farm Museum** (603-927-4276), Harvey Road, off Keyser Street, which runs along Kezar Lake from North Sutton village. Open daily. These 250 hilltop acres have been farmed since the 18th century. The original Matthew Harvey Homestead remains remarkably intact; it changed ownership only once—in the 1940s—before acquiring its current status as a nonprofit trust. On any given day visitors are welcome to stroll around, inspect a dozen and a half outbuildings like the 1881 springhouse from a long-vanished hotel in Bradford, buy vegetables and fruit in-season, and tour the main house, an excellent example of rural Georgian architecture. During the course of the year, the farm hosts several special events—Ice Day, Harvest Day, and Farm Days, among others—designed to highlight New Hampshire's agricultural traditions. The Annual Muster Field Farm Days, the weekend before Labor Day weekend, involves more than 100 exhibitors demonstrating crafts and traditional farming methods (see *Special Events*).

**Sargent Museum Center for Connecticut River Archaeology** (603-863-1944), Central Street, Newport. Open Sunday 10 AM–4 PM, Tuesday and Thursday 10 AM–2 PM, and Wednesday 9 AM–5 PM. The late Howard R. Sargent, a revered anthropology professor, spent a lifetime collecting Native American and European artifacts from all over the country. His influence ranged far and wide; at the museum's opening in 2001, Steven Tyler, lead singer of Aerosmith, reminisced about finding an arrowhead when he was a kid digging in one of Sargent's excavations. In addition to housing Sargent's collection of artifacts and his 7,000-volume library, the museum serves as a center for field studies, workshops, and lectures focusing on the heritage of the Connecticut River Valley.

**HISTORIC HOMES** **Daniel Webster Homestead** (603-934-5057 in summer; 603-271-3254 off-season), Flaghole Road, marked (badly) from Routes 11 and 127 in Franklin. You might want to call for directions and hours. This is a small, clapboard, 18th-century cabin filled with replicated furnishings. Webster (1782–1852), Dartmouth class of 1801, represented New Hampshire in Congress from 1813 to 1817 and Massachusetts in the Senate from 1827 to 1841. He was a legendary orator, involved in many of the major issues of his day.

**The Fells State Historic Site at the John Hay National Wildlife Refuge** (603-763-4789; www.thefells.org), Route 103A between Newbury and Blodgett Landing. Open year-round from dawn to dusk. House tours on weekends and holidays, Memorial Day through Columbus Day ($3 adults; $1 children 6–15). Call for a schedule of programs and workshops. The former estate of writer and diplomat John Hay, The Fells sits high above the eastern shore of Lake Sunapee. Although the 42-room mansion is unfurnished (Teddy Roosevelt once slept here), the 800-acre property provides an example of one of New England's finest early-20th-century gardens—a delightful mix of rugged landscape, cultivated perennials, and formal terraces. Walk from the exquisite Alpine Garden half a mile down along meadowlike lawn to the water. In spring the half-mile walk from the parking area is magnificent with century-old stands of rhododendron and mountain laurel. In all, there are more than 5 miles of hiking paths.

**The New London Historical Society** (603-526-6564; 603-763-9782), Little Sunapee Road, New London. The society owns and maintains a village of 19th-century buildings, including a farmhouse, two barns, a schoolhouse, meeting-house, hearse house, violin shop, blacksmith shop, and a recently constructed Transportation Building that houses the group's outstanding collection of wagons, carriages, and sleighs, including an original Concord Coach. Most of the buildings have been moved to the site, which is open for self-tours at any time. When we went to press, guided tours were available on several occasions throughout the year, including Tuesday and Sunday noon–3 PM during July and August—but call to see if the schedule has changed.

COVERED BRIDGES **The Keniston bridge,** built in 1882, spans the Blackwater River, south of Route 4, 1 mile west of Andover village.

**The Cilleyville bridge,** now open to foot traffic only, was built across Pleasant Stream in 1887; it's now at the junction of Routes 11 and 4A in Andover.

**The Bement bridge,** built in 1854, is on River Road in Bradford Center.

**The Corbin covered bridge,** rebuilt by a group of Newport citizens after being destroyed by arson in 1993, crosses the Sugar River west of Route 10 in North Newport.

**The Warner–Dalton bridge,** originally built in 1800 and rebuilt in 1963, crosses over the Warner River, south of Route 103 in Warner village (multiple kingpost truss).

**The Warner–Waterloo bridge,** rebuilt in 1972, is 2 miles west of Warner village, south of Route 103 (Town lattice truss).

FOR FAMILIES **Ruggles Mine** (603-523-4275; www.rugglesmine.com), off Route 4, Grafton. Open mid-June through mid-October, daily 9 AM–5 PM; until 6 PM in July and August; weekends only mid-May through mid-June. Admission $15 per adult, $7 per child 4–11. Children of all ages will love this place; you don't have to be a mineral buff. The eerie shape of the caves high up on Isinglass Mountain is worth the drive up the access road, and the view includes Cardigan, Kearsarge, and Ragged Mountains. Commercial production of mica in this country began here in 1803. The story goes that Sam Ruggles set his large family to work mining and hauling the mica (it was used for lamp chimneys and stove windows) to Portsmouth; from there it was shipped to relatives in England to be sold. When the demand for his product grew, these trips were made in the dead of night to protect the secrecy of the mine's location. The mine has yielded some $30 million over the years. It was last actively mined by the Bon Ami Company for feldspar, mica, and beryl from 1932 to 1959. An estimated 150 different minerals can still be found. There's a snack bar, picnic area, and a gift shop with minerals so visitors can take home a piece of the rock. Collecting is permitted.

SCENIC DRIVE **Bradford Center to Washington to Sunapee.** The most difficult part of this tour is finding the starting point, just west of the stoplight at the junction of Routes 104 and 114 in Bradford. The road immediately threads a covered bridge, then climbs 2.4 miles to Bradford Center (see *Villages*). Stop to see the original town buildings (just out of view on your left), but turn right and follow that road 1.8 miles until a sign on a tree points the way to East Washington. The

Kim Grant

THE FULL MOON RISES OVER THE TOWN GREEN IN NEW LONDON.

route leads through the Eccardt Farm barnyard; visitors are welcome to stroll through the operating dairy farm, and to see the collection of live birds and antique farm equipment. You might also want to park your car at Island Pond and walk up the hill to the Baptist church grounds and cemetery. The old schoolhouse here, with its desks, foot organ, and vintage textbooks, is open on summer Sundays 1–3 PM. Turn north (right) on Route 31 into Washington (see *Villages*), a photographer's delight with its 1787 meetinghouse, school, and Congregational church all conveniently arranged to fit into one picture. Continue north on Route 31 to Pillsbury State Park (see *Green Space*). Just north of Goshen village, a right brings you back to Route 103 and Mount Sunapee. Be sure to stop at Audrey Nelson's Used Books along the way (see *Selective Shopping*).

## ✷ To Do

BICYCLING **The Sunapee Off-Road Bicycle Association** (603-763-2303) sponsors Wednesday-evening rides.

**Blackwater Ski Shop** (603-735-5437), 207 Main Street, Andover. For bicycle rentals and expert overnight service and repair.

**Bob Skinner's Ski & Sports** (603-763-2303), Route 103, Newbury, rents mountain bikes. Inquire about the many mapped local routes.

**Outspokin Bicycle & Sport Shop** (603-763-9500), junction of Routes 103 and 103A, Newbury. Another good spot for biking gear, rentals, and information.

**Village Sports** (603-526-4948), 140 Main Street, New London. All-season rental for bikes, kayaks, and snowshoes.

BOATING **Lake Sunapee State Park Water Sports Rentals** (603-763-4531). Single and double kayak, canoe, paddleboat, and Windsurfer rentals.

**Sargents Marine** (603-763-5036), Cooper Street, Sunapee. Rents canoes, boats, and motors. A great source of advice on where to fish.

**Canoe put-ins** can be found on Lake Sunapee; Pleasant Lake; Otter Pond in Georges Mills; Rand Pond in Goshen; Lake Todd, Blaisdell Lake, and Lake Massasecum in the Bradford area; Little Sunapee in New London; Kezar Lake in North Sutton; and Kolelemook Lake in Springfield.

**Public boat launches** are found in Sunapee Harbor, at Blodgett's Landing (shallow), at Sargents in Georges Mills, and at Sunapee State Park Beach (see *Swimming*).

BOAT EXCURSIONS ✐ **M/V *Mount Sunapee II*** (603-763-4030; www.sunapeecruises.com), Sunapee Harbor. From weekends in mid-May through foliage season, twice daily from late June through Labor Day: 1½-hour narrated cruises of the lake. This is unquestionably the best way to see Lake Sunapee, complete with the captain's retelling of its history and major sights. New London's long swath of eastern shore is entirely green, with rustic cottages hidden in woods above occasional docks. In Newbury on the south, you see Blodgett's Landing, a tight cluster of gingerbread cottages descended from the tents of the 1890s Sunapee Lake Spiritualist Camp Meeting Association. All children aboard are invited to take a turn at the helm.

**M/V *Kearsarge*** (603-763-5477), Sunapee Harbor. Summer months. A re-creation of a 19th-century steamer offers 1¼-hour cruises twice daily and a single dinner cruise.

FARMS, PICK-YOUR-OWN **Bartletts Blueberry Farm** (603-863-2583), Bradford Road, Newport. Blueberries.

**Beaver Pond Farm** (603-542-7339), Routes 103 and 11, Claremont. Raspberries.

**Elton's Uphill Vegetable Farm** (603-543-0410), Route 103, Claremont. Sixteen varieties of vegetables.

**Grandview Farm** (603-456-3822), Walden Hill, Warner. Strawberries, blueberries, apples, peaches, plums.

**King Blossom Farm** (603-863-6125), Dunbar Hill Road, Grantham. Apples and raspberries.

**Lavalley Orchard** (603-863-6710), Newport. Apples.

**Page Hill Farm** (603-863-2356), Page Hill, Newport. Raspberries, apples.

**StoneField Bison Ranch** (603-456-3743), 490 Pumpkin Hill Road, Warner. Open Friday through Sunday 9 AM–5 PM. This ranch boasts the first and only certified and accredited buffalo herd in New England. Call first for a group tour or stop in to buy it from the source—bison steaks, burgers, and sausage.

**Windy Hill Farm** (603-863-1136), Bascom Road, Newport. Raspberries.

BIKERS ON THE SLOPES OF MOUNT SUNAPEE CATCH GLIMPSES OF THE LAKE BELOW.

Robert Kozlow

**FISHING** **Dickie's** (603-938-5393; www.dickiesoutdoorsports.com), Route 103 in South Newbury, is a source of fishing tackle and advice. Ditto for **Sargents Marine** in Georges Mills (see *Boating*).

Lake Sunapee is good for salmon, lake trout, brook trout, smallmouth bass, pickerel, perch, sunfish, hornpout, and cusk. Otter Pond, Perkins Pond, and Baptist Pond yield bass, pickerel, and perch. Rand Pond, Croydon Pond, Long and Lempster Ponds, and Sugar River are good for trout. Pleasant Lake has salmon, trout, and bass. Inquire locally about what other lakes offer.

**GOLF** **Country Club of New Hampshire** (603-927-4246), New London. $29 weekdays, $36 weekends for 18 holes; cart rentals; reservations required.

**Eastman** (603-863-4500; 603-863-4240), Grantham. Public greens fee, $48 for 18 holes; $28 for 19. Cart rentals. Advance reservations required.

**Newport Golf Club** (603-863-7787), 112 Unity Road, Newport. 18 holes. Reservations required on weekends.

**Ragged Mt. Golf Club** (603-768-3600; 1-800-400-3911, www.ragged-mt.com), 620 Ragged Mountain Road, Danbury. A full-service golf resort featuring a Jeff Julian par-72, 18-hole course and PGA pros. Lodging packages available.

**Twin Lake Village Golf Course** (603-526-2034), Twin Lake Village Road, New London. Nine-hole, par-3 course by the lake.

**HIKING** **Mount Cardigan.** From Mount Cardigan State Park (see *Green Space*) on the western side of the mountain, the **West Ridge Trail** takes you to the summit in just 1.3 miles. From Old Baldy, the principal peak, the view is of Mount Sunapee and of Mount Ascutney in Vermont. A ridge trail runs north to Firescrew Peak and south to South Peak. In all, a network of 50 miles of trails accesses the summit from various directions. Although this western ascent is the shortest and easiest, many hikers prefer the eastern climbs. You might ascend by the **Cathedral Spruce** and **Clark Trails** (2.5 miles to the summit; average time 2 hours 10 minutes, not including stops) or by the more difficult **Holt Trail** (1.9 miles to the summit, *not* to be attempted in wet or icy weather), and return on the **Mowglis** and **Mannin Trails** (3 miles from the summit). The Appalachian Mountain Club lodge, high on the mountain's eastern flank (posted from the village of Alexandria), is the departure point for these and other year-round ascents (see *Other Lodging*).

**Mount Kearsarge.** Despite controversy about the cell phone tower that sprouted recently on top of this peak, the view remains one of the most spectacular in New England, especially for people familiar enough with the landscape to know what they're looking at. The sweep is from Mount Sunapee on the southwest to Moosilauke (the westernmost of the White Mountain peaks), to the Sandwich and Ossipee Ranges and Mount Washington. Serious hikers prefer the 2-mile ascent from Winslow State Park on the northern side of the mountain to the mere 0.5-mile saunter up from Rollins State Park (see *Green Space*). The **Northside Trail** to the summit begins in the southeastern corner of the picnic area, climbs through birch and spruce into fir, and emerges onto smooth ledges, then barren rocks. Round-trip time on the Northside Trail averages 1½ hours, or you can do it in 20 minutes from the other side. Either way, it's a lot of bang for the buck and a favorite hang-gliding spot.

**Mount Sunapee.** In winter, you can opt for the chairlift, but the most popular hiking trail up is the **Andrew Brook Trail** (1.8 miles to Lake Solitude) from a marked trailhead 1.2 miles up Mountain Road, which is off Route 103 roughly 1 mile south of Newbury. The most ambitious approach to Mount Sunapee is along the 47-mile **Monadnock–Sunapee Trail,** which begins atop Mount Monadnock (see *To Do—Hiking* in "Peterborough, Keene, and Surrounding Villages"). The last and perhaps the most rewarding stretch of this trail is from Pillsbury State Park (see *Green Space*), which offers primitive camping and its own 20-mile system of trails.

SKINDIVING **LaPorte's Skindiving Shop** (603-763-5353), Route 103, Newbury. Lessons, rentals, and light salvage work.

SWIMMING **Sunapee State Park Beach** (603-263-4642), Route 103, 3 miles west of Newbury. Open weekends mid-May through mid-June and Labor Day through mid-October, daily in between. A 900-foot stretch of smooth sand backed by shaded grass, picnic tables, a snack bar, bathhouse. Fee.

**Wellington State Park** (603-744-2197), Route 3A, 4 miles north of Bristol. Open weekends from Memorial Day, daily mid-June through Labor Day. This is a beauty: a sandy, half-mile-long beach on a peninsula jutting into Newfound Lake. Picnic tables are scattered along the shore, away from the bathhouse and snack bar, under pine trees. Fee.

**Wadleigh State Beach** (603-927-4724), on Kezar Lake, Sutton. Marked from Route 114. Open weekends from Memorial Day, daily mid-June through Labor Day. Smaller, less well known, and less crowded than nearby Sunapee; a pleasant beach sloping gradually to the water. Facilities include a shaded picnic area, a bathhouse, and a large playing field. Fee.

**Town beaches.** Many more local beaches can be accessed by guests at local inns.

TENNIS **Mountainside Racquet and Fitness Club** (603-526-9293), King Ridge Road, New London. **Colby-Sawyer College** (603-526-2010), New London. Courts (and the Sports Center with indoor swimming) are open to the public. **Newport Athletic Complex** courts (603-863-1510) are open to the public.

## ✱ Winter Sports

CROSS-COUNTRY SKIING **Norsk** (1-800-426-6775; www.skinorsk.com), Country Club Lane off Route 11 (2 miles east of I-89, Exit 11), New London. Open in-season 9 AM–4:30 PM. One of New England's most ambitious and successful cross-country centers. John Schlosser discovered the sport while attending the University of Oslo in 1972 and with his wife, Nancy, opened Norsk at the Lake Sunapee Country Club in 1976. Thanks to its unusual elevation (1,300 feet) and regular grooming, Norsk's 70 km of looped trails frequently offer the best snow conditions south of the White Mountains. A favorite 6-mile loop is to Robb's Hut, though ambitious types may prefer the 10.9 km Roller Coaster. Trails begin on the golf course, but it's possible to get quickly into the woods and stay there. Better skiers can actually access the system from the Outback parking area, 2 miles east on Route 11. The center itself was expanded and rebuilt in 1990, and the adjacent country-club restaurant caters to skiers. Trail fee: $14 weekends, $10 weekdays for adults; $12 and $10 for seniors; $10 and $8 for juniors. Lessons; ski and snowshoe rentals.

**Eastman Cross Country Ski Center** (603-863-4500), turn right off I-89 (you can't miss the sign), Grantham. Offers 30 km of groomed trails.

**DOWNHILL SKIING** ♿ **Mount Sunapee** (603-763-2356, snow phone 603-763-4020; www.mtsunapee.com), Route 103, Newbury. With 60 trails and a vertical drop of 1,510 feet, this is a major ski area that until 1998 was operated by the state. Over the past 4 years, the Muellers, who also own Mount Okemo in Vermont, have leased the ski area and spent more than $12 million, adding such amenities as a new Goosefeathers Pub in the main lodge, a PipeDragon grooming machine, and a Stimilon Approved Halfpipe and Terrain Park snowboarding facility. Nine lifts include a high-speed detachable quad, plus two other quads, as well as two triple and one double lift, and three surface lifts. The Summit Triple Chair accesses half a dozen swooping, intermediate to expert runs, each at least a mile long. Off the North Peak Triple Chair, our favorite is Flying Goose—a quick, steep, and addictive run. The smaller North Peak Lodge (at the opposite end of the parking lot) and the summit cafeteria help disperse the crowds at lunchtime. When all trails are open, skiers can choose from exposures on three peaks. PSIA ski and snowboard school, and daycare available. The area is home to the New England Handicapped Sports Association (NEHSA) and offers lessons, racing programs, and other services to disabled skiers. *Rates:* $49 weekends, $46 midweek for adults; $43 and $37 for teens 13–18; $33 and $29 for youths 7–12, and for seniors 70 and above. Free skiing for those 6 and under. Various specials, including a midweek Super Pass to Mount Sunapee and Okemo, are available.

**Ragged Mountain Ski Area** (603-768-3475; snow phone 603-768-3971), off Route 4, Danbury. A pleasant, intermediate mountain that's been upgraded in the past few years with snowmaking, a new lift, and a red barn look-alike base lodge with a soaring, three-sided fireplace. Still, it's just enough off the beaten track and little known enough to be relatively uncrowded. *Lifts:* One six-pack, two triple chairs, two doubles, and two surface tows. *Trails:* 50. *Vertical drop:* 1,250 feet. *Snowmaking:* 98 percent. *Facilities:* Ski school, ski shop, rentals, restaurant, lounge, child care, lodging. *Rates:* $45 adults, $39 teens, $30 juniors on weekends; adults $39 midweek. A genuine family area.

Also see *Winter Sports—Downhill Skiing* in both "The Western Whites" and "The Concord Area."

## ✷ Green Space

**STATE PARKS** **Mount Cardigan State Park,** off Routes 4 and 118, 4.5 miles east of Canaan. Open mid-May to mid-October. This western approach to the mountain includes a picnic area sited among pines and rocks. For more about the West Ridge Trail, the shortest and easiest route to the 3,121-foot-high summit of Mount Cardigan itself, see *To Do—Hiking*.

**Pillsbury State Park** (603-863-2860), Route 31, 3.5 miles north of Washington. Open weekends from Memorial Day, daily from mid-June. Day-use and camping fees. What a gem! This 9,000-acre near-wilderness was once a thriving settlement with its share of mills. Today the dams are all that survive of "Cherry Valley." Camping is restricted to 20 superb primitive sites on May Pond, and there's both stream and pond fishing. Inquire about hiking trails to nearby mountains.

**Rollins State Park** (603-456-3808), off Route 103, 4 miles north of Warner. Open weekends from Memorial Day, daily from early June through October. A 3.5-mile road, built originally as a scenic toll road in 1874, leads to picnic sites roughly half a mile below the summit. A walking trail (good for the elderly, young, or lazy) accesses the bald summit of Mount Kearsarge.

**Winslow State Park** (603-526-6168), off Route 11, 3 miles south of Wilmot. Open weekends from Memorial Day, daily from early June; fee. An auto road climbs to the 1,820-foot level of 2,937-foot Mount Kearsarge. There are picnic tables and comfort facilities, and you can inspect the cellar hole of a big 19th-century resort hotel, the Winslow House. A steep, mile-long trail leads to the summit for a 360-degree panoramic view. The park is named for Adm. John A. Winslow, commander of the sloop *Kearsarge* when she sank the Confederate gunboat *Alabama* in 1864. (Also see *To Do—Hiking*.)

OTHER AREAS **Audubon Society of New Hampshire Paradise Point Nature Center and Hebron Marsh Wildlife Sanctuary** (603-744-3516), North Shore Road, East Hebron. This 43-acre preserve includes an extensive, rocky, and unspoiled stretch of shore on Newfound Lake. The property is webbed with trails and includes a nature center (open late June through Labor Day, 10 AM–5 PM daily; also some spring and fall weekends) with hands-on and wildlife exhibits, a library, and the Nature Store. During the summer a natural history day camp and a variety of workshops and special events are also staged. Hebron Marsh is another 1.4 miles down the road toward Hebron Center (drive past the red Ash Cottage and take the next left down the dirt road; park off the road on your left by the sign). The 36-acre property includes the field directly across the road from Ash Cottage down to the Cockermouth River and the field to the southwest of the cottage. The marshes are teeming with bird life; follow signs to the observation tower.
**Bradford Pines,** Route 103, Bradford. Twelve giant white pines stand on 5 acres of preserved land.

**Cricenti's Bog,** Route 11, New London. A genuine bog with a nature trail. Wooden walkways thread a pond that's been filled with sphagnum moss and rare bog flora.

**Gardner Memorial Wayside Area,** Route 4A, Wilmot. Picnic site along a scenic brook and stone foundation.

**Grafton Pond,** off Route 4A. A 935-acre Society for the Protection of New Hampshire Forests preserve. North from Wilmot take a sharp left at the Grafton–Sullivan County line; take the first left, then an immediate right, and park at the dam site. The only amenity is a public boat ramp. The pond has a 7-mile shoreline. Good boating and fishing.

**Knights Hill Nature Park,** County Road, New London. Sixty acres of fields and forest, fern gardens and a pond, a marsh, and a stream, all linked by easy trails. No dogs. Inquire at the town information booth about guided hikes.

**Profile Falls,** Route 3A, 2.5 miles south of Bristol. A popular (and dangerous) local swimming hole. This is a 40-foot falls with the profile of a man silhouetted against the water at its base.

**Sculptured Rocks,** west of Groton village on Sculptured Rocks Road. The parking area is roughly a mile in (the sign may be down off-season). With grottoes formed by waterfalls, this is mermaid/merman territory. The river has carved a deep chasm through which it tumbles from pool to pool, forming a popular local swimming spot. A path, with plenty of large rocks for picnicking, follows the water down.

Also see **The Fells State Historic Site** under *To See—Historic Homes*.

## ✱ Lodging

RESORTS 🐾 ♿ **Eastman** (603-863-4444; www.eastmanlakerealty.com), P.O. Box 1 (just off I-89, Exit 13), Grantham 03753. Developed by an improbable consortium that includes Dartmouth College and the Society for the Protection of New Hampshire Forests, this second-home and condo community is scattered in clusters throughout 3,500 acres on Eastman Lake. Winter facilities include a small ski hill and an extensive ski-touring network. Summer renters can enjoy an 18-hole golf course, tennis, swimming, and boating (Sunfish, canoes, and rowboats can be rented). A restaurant, indoor pool, and recreation barn are available year-round. Units are attractive, individually decorated condos and houses with two to four bedrooms, decks, lofts, and woodstoves. Rentals start at $460 for two bedrooms in summer, from $490 for winter weekends, from $975 for 7 days in summer, from $1,065 in winter. Weekly and monthly rentals available. Pets in houses only, at discretion of owner.

♿ **Ragged Mountain Resort** (603-768-3600; 1-800-400-3911; www.ragged-mt.com), 620 Ragged Mountain Road, Danbury 03230. Open all year. A great family getaway for skiing or golf vacations (see *To Do—Golf* and *Winter Sports—Downhill Skiing*). Eight 2-bedroom condominiums at the base of Ragged Mountain offer linens, a kitchen stocked with utensils, and televisions with VCR and cable. Midweek per-night, per-condo rates are $169.95; weekends, $209.95. No pets.

♿ **Twin Lake Village** (603-526-6460; www.twinlakevillage.com), 21 Twin Lake Villa Road, New London 03257. Open just late June through Labor Day. Nothing fancy unless you count its idyllic lakeside setting, but this 1890s resort is much beloved by those who stay here. Many families have been coming for generations. Opened by Henry Kidder in 1897, it is presently owned and managed by three generations of Kidders and accommodates 160 guests among the rambling Villa and a number of Victorian houses scattered throughout surrounding trees. Sited on Little Lake Sunapee, it has a private beach and a boathouse with canoes, rowboats, and kayaks. A nine-hole golf course stretches from the rocker-lined veranda (note the untraditional rocker colors) down to the lake. All three daily meals and old-fashioned evening entertainment—maybe a suppertime picnic on Mount Kearsarge, or bingo—are included in the weekly $380–760 per-person rates.

## INNS

### *In the Lake Sunapee Area*

**Back Side Inn** (603-863-5161; www.bsideinn.com), 1171 Brook Road, Goshen 03752. Open year-round. After graduating from hotel school, then honing their skills elsewhere (including Walt Disney World), Bruce and Mackie Hefka bought this onetime hostel off the beaten track in the land o' Goshen. Still here after 14 years, they have reason to be proud of their 10 fresh, pretty guest rooms with private baths, all set amid 120 acres of hiking trails along the back side of Mount Sunapee. No matter the season, there is plenty to do with Sunapee's mountain and lake nearby. Afterward, relax in an outdoor hot tub or warm up in the cozy living room with fieldstone fireplace. Across the road is our favorite shopping/browsing spot in the region: Nelson Crafts, Antique Collectibles, and Used Books (see *Selective Shopping*). $75–85 per double room includes a full breakfast. Weekend packages, midweek specials; dinner served. No smoking.

**Candlelite Inn** (603-938-5571; 1-888-812-5571; www.candleliteinn.com), 5 Greenhouse Lane, Bradford 03221. Built in 1897 as a guest house, this inn had different names and owners for nearly a century before Bill and Barbara Cotter took over in 1993. The Cotters have added much pampering to the late Victorian structure. Pie (plus several other courses) for breakfast, and six pretty pastel guest rooms, each with queen bed and private bath (some with claw-foot tubs). Rates range $90–125, the latter for a mini suite with access to the gazebolike porch. Contact them for a calendar of special weekend activities. Nonsmoking.

♿ **Colonial Farm Inn** (603-526-6121; 1-800-805-8504; www.colonialfarminn.com), Route 11, New London 03257. Whether you want to get away from it all or enjoy the attractions of nearby New London and the Sunapee area, innkeepers Bob and Kathryn Joseph have made their fine, 1836 center-chimney home a romantic destination. Six pretty, air-conditioned guest rooms (all with private bath, one handicapped accessible) are spiffily decorated in Waverly and Laura Ashley prints. In winter, downhill and cross-country skiing are minutes away. There's a golf course across the road; tennis and hiking nearby. An adjacent antiques shop offers a wide selection of traditional, rustic, and eccentric treasures (see *Selective Shopping*). A lovely shrimp-bisque dining room offers candlelight dining with a view of pond and gardens, Wednesday through Saturday all year (see *Dining Out*). Full breakfast is included in the $95–135 room rate.

⚭ 🐾 ✎ ♿ **Dexter's Inn** (603-763-5571; 1-800-232-5571; www.dextersnh.com), Stagecoach Road, Sunapee 03782. Open year-round. This hilltop house dates in part from 1801, but its present look is 1930s, when it became a summer home for an adviser to Herbert Hoover. In 1948 Dexter and

Robert Kozlow

A HIKER PAUSES ON THE SUMMIT OF MOUNT KEARSARGE

Janelle Richards purchased the home and transformed it into Dexter's Inn, an après-ski getaway for guests coming to the newly opened Mount Sunapee Ski Resort. Recently, New Hampshire native Emily Augustine returned from New York with her husband, John, to purchase it from longtime owners. With John's business background and Emily's experience as a caterer, wedding planner, and special-events impresario, the Augustines have found the perfect home for hosting weddings, reunions, sporting events, and business retreats. A pool is set in the extensive, beautifully landscaped backyard, which also offers croquet, lawn games, and three all-weather tennis courts. Fields across the road, in front of the house, slope toward Lake Sunapee in the distance. You can also see the lake from porch rockers and from many of the 17 guest rooms (each individually decorated, all with private bath). The best views are from the annex (there are two rooms with wheelchair access here) across the road. There's also a great view from the cozy dining room. Common spaces include a formal living room; a pubby, pine-paneled library/lounge; and a kids' playroom with videos, games, toys, and stuffed animals. Altogether, this has the look and feel of a casual, unpretentious country club. Rates per double per night range, depending on season, \$125–175 plus 15 percent service charge, and include a full breakfast. Pets are permitted in the annex at \$10 per day. The Holly Cottage, with a living room with fireplace, a kitchen, and two bedrooms, is \$300–400 plus service and tax for four people. Discounts for longer stays.

**Follansbee Inn** (603-927-4221; 1-800-626-4221; www.follansbeeinn.com), Route 114, P.O. Box 92, North Sutton 03260. Open year-round. Former Coloradoans Dave and Cathy Beard visited 40 inns across the country before settling on the purchase of this classic in 2000. Located in a small town center that time seems to have forgotten, this inn takes you back to the days of picnics, farm stands, band concerts, and idling on a porch filled with wicker and flowers. The low-beamed living room is friendly; the airy dining rooms are comfortably furnished with antiques. On the upper floors the 16 guest rooms (all with private bath) are divided by wide halls, and books are scattered around. There is plenty of lounging and reading space. The white, green-trimmed structure was built originally as an annex for the huge but long-gone Follansbee Inn that once stood across the street. The property abuts Kezar Lake, and guests can swim or boat from the inn dock; for those more comfortable with a lifeguard on duty, **Wadleigh State Beach** is just down the road (see *To Do—Swimming*). Many guests also discover the joys of the 3-mile walk, bike, or jog around the lake. In winter there's cross-country skiing out the back door, and the **Muster Field Farm Museum** (see *To See—Museums*), with its charming summertime farm stand, is just up the road. The $90–175 per-couple rate includes breakfast. No smoking and no children under age 10.

**Hide-Away Inn** (603-526-4861; 1-800-457-0589; www.hideawayinn.net), Twin Lake Villa Road, P.O. Box 1249, New London 03257. Go to the end of the country lane, then keep going to find this quiet lodge, originally built in 1901, then rebuilt in the 1930s as a retreat for author Grace Litchfield. Each of the six guest rooms (one a two-room suite) has a private bath, canopy bed, and beaded paneling. Two have fireplaces. Oregon spruce paneling and another huge stone fireplace in the lobby add to the rustic ambience. A full breakfast, beginning with a fresh fruit and pastry cart, is included in the $95–190 (depending on season) rate. Children 8 and older are welcome. Nonsmoking.

🖉 **The Inn at Pleasant Lake** (603-526-6271; 1-800-626-4907; www.innatpleasantlake.com), 125 Pleasant Street, New London 03257. Open except for parts of April and November. This was one of many farms in this area that began taking in boarders in the 1880s. Guests came from New York and Boston, and strangers were expected to bring letters of introduction. Now, new innkeepers Linda and Brian MacKenzie (Brian is a graduate of the Culinary Institute of America) are applying their talents to the place, redecorating and offering such amenities as afternoon tea and elegant gourmet dining. Each of the 10 comfortable guest rooms has a view of Mount Kearsarge, the lake, or woodlands, and all have private bath. The lake just across the road provides a place to swim and fish; the inn offers two canoes and a rowboat for boating. The dining room overlooking the lake is the setting for full breakfasts (included, along with tea, in the $110–175 room rate), and prix fixe, five-course dinners for guests and public (see *Dining Out*).

🖉 **The Inn at Sunapee** (603-763-4444; 1-800-327-2466; www.innatsunapee.com), 125 Burkehaven Hill Road, Sunapee 03782. Originally built in 1875 as a dairy farm, this sunny yellow farmhouse has been an inn since the Gardner family began taking in summer folks in the 1920s. When the Harrimans purchased the property, they added an Asian flair, thanks to 25 years in the Far East. The setting above Lake Sunapee is both lovely and convenient. It also offers tennis and swimming, bay windows to take in the view, and a lounge with a massive fieldstone fireplace. Sixteen rooms, five of them suites, all with private bath, range from $70 for a single to $160 for a family suite; $15 extra per person. Children are welcome. A full country breakfast, served in the dining room, comes with your room. Dinner (the menu has echoes of both New England and Asia—clam chowder to spring rolls) is provided for an extra charge, primarily for guests of the inn.

♿ **New London Inn** (603-526-2791; outside New Hampshire, 1-800-526-2791; www.newlondoninn.net), P.O. Box 8, Main Street, New London 03257. Built originally in 1792, this large (23 guest rooms) inn sits in the middle of New London, next to Colby-Sawyer College. It's always busy, but guests can usually find quiet space in a corner of the large, graciously furnished living room. The New London **Barn Playhouse** (see *Entertainment*) is just down Main Street, which is lined with attractive shops and eateries. Stroll around town or simply rock an hour away, watching the activity from the inn's second-story gallery porch. Since the Boston–Montreal bus stops at the pharmacy practically across the street, this is one place, theoretically at least, you can get to without a car. Rooms are attractive, freshly painted and papered, and furnished in real and reproduction antiques. All have private bath. $100–140 per room. Meals (not included) are available in the dining room (see *Dining Out*).

**Potter Place Inn** (603-735-5141), 88 Depot Street, junction of Routes 4 and 11, Andover 03216. Best known for its restaurant (see *Dining Out*), this inn offers two upstairs guest rooms with queen-sized beds and private baths for those nights when you'd rather end a good meal dreaming than driving home. The fanciful Potter Place Depot, once a bustling railway stop and now the home of the Andover Historical Society, is just down the road. A continental breakfast is included in the $85 double-occupancy room rate.

**The Rosewood Country Inn** (603-938-5253; www.rosewoodcountryinn.com), 67 Pleasant View Road, Bradford 03221. Pretty in pink—or make that rose—this inn lives up to its name, beginning with the outside shutters. Both the color and the flower continue to make their spirit felt in the decor of 11 well-kept guest rooms and baths, each furnished in a mix of old and new. Inviting common rooms and sunny porches take advantage of the inn's peaceful garden setting on a dozen stone-walled acres once walked by the likes of Gloria Swanson, Jack London, Charlie Chaplin, and Mary Pickford. Three-course "candlelight and crystal" breakfasts are included in the $109–229 room rate. Children, over 12 only, are $25 a night.

**Thistle and Shamrock Inn** (603-938-5553; www.thistleandshamrock.com), 11 West Main Street, Bradford 03221. When the Bradford Hotel was rebuilt after a fire in 1898, the rambling hostelry was in the center of a bustling downtown, a major tourist stop for travelers en route to Lake Sunapee. Things have quieted down, but although innkeepers Lynn and Jim Horigan have added such up-to-date amenities as private baths, the dozen guest rooms opening off two long hallways retain a sense of the original ambience. The Horigans have been collecting turn-of-the-20th-century furnishings for years and have scattered them throughout the inn and adjoining dining room (see *Dining Out*). A room for two with full breakfast is $85–140. Nonsmoking.

*In Danbury*

✐ **The Inn at Danbury** (603-768-3318), Route 104, Danbury 03230. Geared to skiers, great for groups and for families, children over 5. Thirteen rooms with private bath; ample, comfortable common space, a hot tub room, and (of all things) an indoor pool. Handy to Ragged Mountain. $110–140 double with breakfast; winter weekend packages.

*On Newfound Lake*

✐ **Cliff Lodge** (603-744-8660), Route 3A, Bristol 03222. Open Memorial Day through Columbus Day. Over the past few years, proprietors Rob Pinkham and Aldo Vallecillo have gained a reputation for their culinary and decorating magic when they revitalized an old restaurant on a cliff overlooking Newfound Lake (see *Dining Out*). A few years ago, they extended their creativity to retrofit seven rustic, old-style cabins that share the hillside. Bright fabrics and a mix of collectible and antique furnishings pep up these knotty-pine housekeeping units, which sleep two to seven. Each includes a stove, refrigerator, shower, and cooking utensils. Swimming is available at the sandy public beach at the bottom of the hill; boating and fishing are nearby. Rates are $350–425 per week.

**The Inn on Newfound Lake** (603-744-9111), Route 3A, Bridgewater 03222. Open year-round. Although thoroughly rehabbed, this 1840s inn still looks its age with a full veranda overlooking spectacular sunsets on the state's fourth largest lake. Across the road, there's a 300-foot sandy beach and a dock. Inside, the main inn has 19 attractive guest rooms, 11 with private bath, and the adjoining Elmwood Cottage offers 12 more rooms, each with bath. There are comfortable parlors in each facility. The dining room in the main inn is a favorite spot for tourists and locals alike (see *Dining Out*). $75–225 per room, double occupancy; continental breakfast included.

**Pleasant View Bed & Breakfast** (603-744-5547), Hemphill Road, R.R. 1, Box 498, Bristol 03222. A big old white farmhouse with a wide-open view of Mount Cardigan. The home has been in the business of putting up guests since around the turn of the last century, when two men came over the hill from Dartmouth and asked if they could stay overnight. New owner Deborah Burns resettled here from her Tribeca catering business in spring 2002. Now there are six recently renovated guest rooms, four with private bath, two that share. An amazing breakfast, complete with New York specialties, is included in the $90–120 rate.

## BED & BREAKFASTS

*In the Lake Sunapee area*

✐ **Blue Goose Inn** (603-763-5519; www.virtualcities.com), Route 103B, P.O. Box 2117, Mount Sunapee 03255-2117. A 19th-century farmhouse in the shadow of Mount Sunapee, this country B&B has a wraparound porch as well as an enclosed sun porch overlooking 3½ acres of lawn and woods. Just out the door, the old Newport-to-Claremont railroad bed is now a trail for hiking, biking, cross-country skiing, snowshoeing, and snowmobiling. Rates for the four guest rooms, each with private bath and queen-sized bed, start at $80 per double with full country breakfast; extra person (children welcome), $20. Nonsmoking.

**Maple Hill Farm** (603-526-2248; 1-

800-231-8637), 200 Newport Road, New London 03257. Just off I-89, this capacious old farmhouse takes in boarders, as it did in the 19th century. An informal, comfortable place, it has a six-person spa on the deck, and an indoor basketball court in the barn that doubles as a dance floor. There are also barnyard animals, including a sheep and chickens. Winter weekends tend to be booked by the groups lucky enough to know about this place, but there is always plenty of space midweek. Acreage extends back through meadows to Little Sunapee Lake, where a canoe and rowboat await guests. There are 10 guest rooms, 6 with private bath, in the main house where, depending on season, rates run $75–125 and include a choice of four breakfasts. Or you can book a three-bedroom, four-and-a-half-bath lakefront home of your own for $2,700 a week or $450 a night. It's fully furnished with fireplace, spa, steam shower, and wet bar. Inquire about ski-and-stay packages. Nonsmoking.

**Mountain Lake Inn** (1-800-662-6005; virtualcities.com), 2871 Route 114, P.O. Box 443, Bradford 03221. Currier and Ives ambience in a rambling combination of a 1764 Colonial and a 1930s addition on 170 acres of woods and lakefront. The inn, halfway between the Pat's Peak and Mount Sunapee ski areas, has nine guest rooms, which rent for $85 double occupancy ($70 single). Each has a private bath; all have a view either of woods or of Lake Massasecum across the road. There is also a one-bedroom, fair-weather cabin with its own living room, kitchenette, and screened porch for $600 per week. Full country breakfast included with all accommodations. Pets welcome with prior notice.

**Riverview Farms Inn** (603-526-4482; 1-800-392-9627; www.newlondon-nh.com), 96 Village Road, Wilmot Flat 03287. This vintage, village Cape has grown up, down, and sideways over the years, but its cheery exterior is a sure sign of its survival. Four bedrooms, each with private bath, plus another quiet suite with a separate entrance and sun deck, boast an eclectic assortment of antiques and take advantage of the site, which overlooks the river and a lovely old bridge. $99–169 with continental breakfast. If your stay includes a Sunday, we suggest you walk 2 minutes to the Wilmot Community Center for a huge breakfast with homemade omelets, sausage, bacon, and flapjacks. All this plus local color for just $3.50.

**Shaker Meeting House Bed and Breakfast** (603-763-3122; www.virtualcities.com), 176 King Hill Road, New London 03257. The Shaker tradition of innovation lives on in this brand-new Moses Johnson–style meetinghouse, built in 2000 as a B&B. After retiring from his job with the Defense Department in New Jersey, John Chowanski and his family moved to New London with the idea of re-creating the hospitality once espoused in the Shaker villages of nearby Enfield and Canterbury. Four guest rooms are furnished in historically correct "retiring room" style, though enhanced by the addition of private baths. Breakfast—"plain, simple, wholesome, and natural"—is served in an authentically detailed dining room with a lovely view of King Ridge Mountain. Rates are $80 for double occupancy; $70 for single. Military personnel receive a 10 percent discount. No pets or smoking. Children over 10 welcome.

**Take-It-For-Granite Farm Bed &**

**Breakfast** (603-526-6376; www.granitebb.com), Campground Road, Wilmot Flat 03287. Innkeepers Craig and Lindy Heim moved to New England from the Midwest in the mid-1990s when they found the home of their dreams on 10 rolling acres surrounded by fieldstone walls. Once they fixed it up, they decided to share the rambling 1840s farmhouse with guests. Four bedroom suites (each with its own bath) are all very separate and private. Three have air-conditioning; two, a fireplace. Common areas include a paneled library, two sitting rooms, and a handsome patio with a view of Mount Kearsarge and the Heims' own pond and resident ducks. An ample continental breakfast is included in the $75–125 room rate. Children 5 years and older are $20 more. Nonsmoking.

**Turtle Pond Farm** (603-456-2738; www.turtlepondfarm.com), 4 Bean Road, Warner 03278. Innkeepers Debbie and Walt Bury offer four private cottages on 16 acres of fields, ponds, and woods, just 3 miles from Interstate 89. Each has its own private porch, bath, and TV/VCR. Rates range $75–105, depending on season, and include a hearty country breakfast in the main house. En route you can stop by the barn to visit the Burys' llama, goat, sheep, and angora rabbits. The box and painted turtles, for which the place was named, are more likely found outside. Cross-country skiing, snowshoeing, and hiking are right out the door.

**The Village House at Sutton Mills Bed & Breakfast** (603-927-4765; www.villagehousebnb.com), 14 Grist Mill Road, Sutton Mills 03221. Outside, Marilyn and Jack Paige's 1857 Victorian house sits neat as a bandbox atop a granite-stepped slope; inside, her stenciled floorcloths and his hand-wrought iron beds add a unique touch to the three stylishly furnished guest rooms. Each has its own bath, one a claw-foot tub. Downtown Sutton Mills is both a minute and a century away, with a quaint and quiet Main Street that boasts a town hall and library. In winter guests can cross-country ski from the door. Jack has his shop open early evenings and on weekends all year. Rates are $90 for a double, $65 a single, and include a full country breakfast. Children 3 years and older welcome.

### *In the Highland Lake area*

**The Andover Arms** (603-735-5953), P.O. Box 256, Village Center, Andover 03216. Hooked and needlepoint rugs, quilts, cannonball beds, and vintage wallpapers make this sprawling 1850s guest house seem like a step back in time. In summer it caters to academics attending conferences on the nearby Proctor Academy campus. In winter it's a haven for skiers. One bedroom on the second floor has its own bath; four others share. There is a two-bedroom suite with an additional bath on the third floor. Most rooms rent for $54 and include a continental breakfast.

**Highland Lake Inn** (603-735-6426; www.highlandlakeinn.com), 32 Maple Street, East Andover 03231. Open year-round. You'll know the day's a sunny one when innkeepers Steve and Judee Hodges greet you in the yellow entrance parlor of their bright and beckoning B&B. This lovely old property, which dates from 1767, retains 7 of its original acres and abuts a nature preserve. Each of the 10 guest rooms has its own bath; 2 have fireplace. Located on a country lane, this inn is charmingly remote, yet central enough to take advantage of the area's four-season activities. A full country breakfast, overlooking the lawn and lake, is included in the $85–125 rate. Children 8 and above welcome at no charge when sharing a room with a parent.

**The Petrie House** (603-648-6494; www.bbonline.com/nh/petriehouse/), 323 Raccoon Hill Road, Salisbury 03268. The original 1815 Cape has grown over the years, large enough that it once served as the clubhouse for the former Woody Glen Ski Area. Current owner George Russo was captured by the 100-mile view when he moved here in 1999 and converted the structure into a B&B. Three guest rooms are newly decorated, each with private bath. Rates run $85–95, or you can arrange to rent the whole house. Children over 6 welcome. No smoking.

### *Elsewhere*

**The Maria Atwood Inn** (603-934-3666), 71 Hill Road, Route 3A, Franklin 03235. The first time we visited this inn, three women from Florida had just checked into a trio of rooms, each one of which drew more oohs and aahs than the last. Innkeepers Sandi and Fred Hoffmeister bought this well-preserved, elegant 1830 brick Federal home in 1997, then turned it into a charming B&B with seven romantic, antiques-filled guest rooms, each with private bath, four with working fireplace. Two years later, lightning struck, literally, topped off with hurricane floods while the roof was being repaired. But the Hoffmeisters made lemonade from their troubles, transforming their third floor into two post-and-beam family guest rooms. Depending on the season, a full breakfast is served in the library or outside on the deck or in the gardens; snacks and beverages are always available. Rates are $60–65 for a single, $80–90 double. Well-behaved children are encouraged to bring their parents; those under 12 stay free. Nonsmoking.

**Snowbound B&B** (603-744-9112; www.snowboundbandb.com), 674 Murray Hill Road, Hill 03243. Located on a state-designated scenic road, this hilltop timber-frame home is a fresh, pleasant spot to kick off your shoes and relax. Innkeepers Gayle and Gene Seip have decorated an upstairs loft and three guest rooms (each with private bath) with a collection of baskets and old sewing implements. There's a gas fireplace to enjoy even if you're not really snowbound. Ragged Mountain Ski and Golf Resort is a few minutes away. $65 single; $80 double occupancy includes full breakfast with home-baked goods and fresh fruit. Children 6 years and up welcome with additional charge.

♿ **The Victorian Bed and Breakfast** (603-744-6157), 75 Summer Street (5.6 miles from I-93, Exit 23), Bristol 03222. When it comes to decorating, no one ever accused the Victorians of restraint, and this turreted Queen Anne–style home with its rainbow-hued exterior is a good example of the period. Built solidly and elaborately as the town mill owner's mansion in 1902, it now offers unusually spacious guest rooms, two with working fireplace. There are five rooms in the house and three carriage house suites, six with private bath, all carefully decorated and named. A first-floor room is especially designed for elderly and handicapped guests. The loft rooms in the carriage house can each sleep a large family; two have kitchen. Newfound Lake is nearby, as are both Ragged and Tenney Mountains. $85 double, $70 single, including a full breakfast; carriage house suites are $100 double; also weekly rates.

**RENTAL COTTAGES** The New London and the Newfound Region Chambers of Commerce (see *Guidance*) can direct you to local realtors specializing in cottage rentals.

**OTHER LODGING** **Cardigan Mountain Lodge and Reservation** (603-744-8011; 603-466-2727), Alexandria (mailing address: R.F.D. 1, Bristol 03222). The Appalachian Mountain Club, founded in 1876 to blaze hiking trails through the White Mountains, maintains a number of no-frills, outdoors-oriented huts, lodges, and family camps in New Hampshire. This is one of the most interesting, providing full-service overnight lodging and three meals daily from May 24 through October 27, bed & breakfast year-round. Perched high on the eastern side of Mount Cardigan, it offers access to literally dozens of trails to the top. Many of the lower trails are used by cross-country skiers in winter. Rates for the lodge and two-person platform tents are per person in the $50-per-day range with special weekend rates, and include three family-style meals; rooms range from two to five bunks, with sheets and blankets provided (bring your own towels). Campsites for up to six people are available for under $20, with meals optional. Summer at Cardigan includes volunteer-led hikes, swimming, and Sunday barbecues.

**Harbor House Properties** (603-763-3323; www.theharborhouse.com), P.O. Box 765, Sunapee 03782. Your home away from home can be an 11-room Victorian with outdoor hot tub or a turreted contemporary that sleeps six and noses directly into Lake Sunapee. Three houses in all, sleeping 2 to 20, with rates ranging $200–550 per night for a 2-night minimum stay. Weekly rentals also available.

**Sunapee Harbor Cottages** (603-763-5052; www.sunapeeharborcottages.com), 4 Lake Avenue, Sunapee Harbor 03782. Times change, as these charming cottages, newly rebuilt on the site of the old Whispering Pines Cabins Resort, testify. Six cottages, stylishly decorated with work by local artisans, vary in size and price ($150–250), and sleep up to five.

## ✻ Where to Eat

### DINING OUT

#### *In the Lake Sunapee area*

**Café Andre** (603-863-1842), Route 103 just west of the Mount Sunapee traffic circle, Sunapee. Open daily except Tuesday, 4 PM–1 AM. Reservations recommended. Chef Andre Woldkowski's long history in the restaurant business dates to working at his family's establishment while he was growing up in Poland. Before opening his own place with partner Mary Stillwell in December 2001, he worked for a decade—winters at restaurants in Vermont, summers on Block Island. He describes his menus as intercontinental. One offers formal dining choices: escargots, tournedos of beef, duck, and other classics. The other is served at the more casual pub. The dining room has white tablecloths, soft lighting, and a display of local art. Moderate to expensive.

**Colonial Farm Inn** (603-526-6121; 1-800-805-8504), Route 11, New London. Dinner by reservation, Wednesday through Saturday. In summer you can opt to eat on the screened porch, but fresh flowers, candlelight, and two exceptionally attractive, intimate dining rooms with fireplaces in an 1830s house make this a special-occasion restaurant during any season. The menu is usually short but sweet with four or five entrées, all freshly prepared by the chef-owner. On the day we stopped by, the menu featured a choice of tenderloin of beef pan-sautéed with a roasted shallot and port wine sauce ($22.50), boneless breast of chicken filled with homemade Boursin cheese ($15.50), and venison medallions served with a cranberry and caramelized shallot compote ($17.75). The wild mushroom soup should win a prize; their chocolate raspberry pâté dessert did.

**The Hide-Away Inn** (603-526-4861; 1-800-457-0589; www.hideawayinn.net), Twin Lake Villa Road, New London. Open for dinner daily from July through October; closed Monday and Tuesday in winter. Rustic, Oregon-spruce-paneled getaway, just 3 minutes from Main Street. Hard to find but worth it; ask directions. Lori Freeman's the chef, her husband Michael the wine savant who has compiled one of the best cellars in the state. The menu specializes in seafood—seared scallops with seasonally changing sauces, lobster cakes, pecan-encrusted trout—but also offers interesting variations on beef and poultry standards. In summer there are special dinner and theater specials in conjunction with the New London Barn Playhouse. Entrées range $11.95–22.95.

**The Inn at Pleasant Lake** (603-526-6271; 1-800-626-4907), 125 Pleasant Street, New London. Fixed price ($46), five-course gourmet dinner nightly at 7 PM, except Monday and Tuesday. Candlelight, classical music, and fine cuisine prepared by a graduate of the Culinary Institute of America who lovingly describes the menu while serving cocktails and canapés on the glassed-in porch. Dinner too is a ceremony, including an entremezzo course of, say, fresh citrus sections with a splash of sherry. Follow that with rack of lamb with roasted garlic rosemary demiglaze or mahimahi served with an exotic mushroom salad and yellow pepper oil; then perhaps a rosette of white chocolate mousse in a lace cookie cup with a trio of sauces. Star billing is shared with a view of the lake. Reservations required.

♿ **Traditions Restaurant at Lake Sunapee Country Club** (603-526-6040), Route 11 and Country Club Lane, New London. Open every day for lunch and dinner in summer; Friday through Sunday for lunch from November through May. The attractive dining room has views of the fairway. The golf course and cross-country ski trails help you work up an appetite. Entrées $6.95–25. Certified Angus beef a specialty.

♿ **La Meridiana** (603-526-2033), Route 11, Wilmot. Open for dinner nightly, from 3 PM on Sunday. This is the favorite restaurant of local children's author Tomie dePaola, who based one of his books on an Italian legend he learned here. He's not alone in considering it the best restaurant, and the best value, in central New Hampshire. The menu, like the owner-chef, is northern Italian, and the specialties are tender scaloppine and bistecca. Pastas and pastries are outstanding, too, and everything is moderately priced, even the wine list. Fresh salmon fillet baked in parchment paper with herbs is $12.75. There are always a number of daily specials.

♿ **Millstone Restaurant** (603-526-

4201), Newport Road, New London. Open for lunch and dinner daily. A veteran of the area restaurant scene claims this is where he goes when he doesn't want to be disappointed. The chef has been around for years, and it shows. Entrées, ranging from interestingly dressed pastas to venison grilled to order with a juniper berry, coriander, and Marsala sauce, are creative and consistently good. Original art, warm colors, plants, and nice light shining through French doors and skylights lend a note of relaxed gentility. Entrées $12.95–26.95.

**Potter Place Inn** (603-735-5141), Route 4/11, Andover. Long a favorite dining-out place for Proctor Academy faculty and students, this charming restaurant has recently changed ownership and is attracting folks from around the area. Where else can you find ostrich on the menu? Other of chef-owners Melba and Giovanni Leopardi's specialties include house-cured salmon, carpaccio Cipriani, grilled veal chops, homemade pastas, and venison. Fresh fish choices change daily. Moderate to expensive.

**Thistle and Shamrock Inn & Restaurant** (1-888-938-5553), 11 West Main Street, Bradford. Open for dinner Wednesday through Sunday from 5:30 PM. The Roters Dining Room gets its name from artist Carl Roters, whose work fills the walls of this turn-of-the-century (the 20th century, not the millennium) hostelry. Ceiling fans, plate rails, and cabinets filled with antique china enhance the old-timey feel. Roters's friend, chef-owner Jim Horrigan, offers his own creations in the form of special curries and pastas, along with a breast of chicken succulently filled with local Montrachet cheese and apples, then topped with plum sauce ($14.25). A 4-ounce filet mignon with three crab-stuffed shrimp is $19.95.

**The New London Inn Dining Room** (603-526-2791; 1-800-526-2791), Main Street, New London. Open Wednesday through Sunday for lunch 11:30 AM–2 PM, dinner 5–8:30 PM. On Sunday, brunch is served 9 AM–2 PM. This 1792 farmhouse with its extended ell has long been the heart of this handsome town. In the dining room, floor-to-ceiling windows overlook the town green. What could be more New England than a cup of clam chowder followed by pork tenderloin medallions with apple-cranberry pancakes and wild mushroom gravy? The seasonally changing menu also features duckling, venison, oyster stew, fresh seafood specialties, and two sizes of prime rib ($17.95 and $19.95).

### *In the Newfound Lake area*

**Cliff Lodge** (603-744-8660), Route 3A, Bristol. Open year-round, daily in summer 5–9 PM; closed Tuesday and Wednesday, September through June. With its rock walls, perennial gardens, a stone fireplace, and birch log window treatments, this refurbished, turn-of-the-20th-century summer cottage shows Rob Pinkham's and Aldo Vallecillo's considerable flair for both food and furnishings. Whether Fourth of July or New Year's Eve, there's no better view in the area than this one high on a knoll above the lake. The menu (served in summer on a candlelit deck) is equally inviting, with moderately priced entrées ranging from Argentine churrasco served with black beans and rice to Cajun-blackened duck breast and a lightly breaded Wiener schnitzel.

♿ **The Homestead** (603-744-2022), Route 104, Bristol. Dinner daily from

4:30 PM; Sunday brunch 11 AM–2 PM. Closed Monday between January 1 and Memorial Day. This handsome old roadside mansion, now painted pale yellow with dark green shutters and awnings, offers a series of dining rooms ranging from traditional to glass to stone walled. The menu boasts a variety of American and Continental dishes, with more than 40 entrées priced $9.95–18.95. Unique specials served daily.

♿ **Pasquaney Restaurant in The Inn on Newfound Lake** (603-744-9111), Route 3A, Bridgewater. Serves dinner nightly plus Sunday brunch 10 AM–2 PM during July and August; closed Monday and Tuesday the rest of the year. The traditional old hotel dining room has been deftly brightened with flowery wallpaper, linens, and individual table lights. There's also patio dining overlooking the lake. Appetizers include portobello crostini and Caribbean coconut shrimp. Entrées such as cedar-plank rib eye, pistachio chicken, and herb-grilled swordfish range $15.95–24.95.

## EATING OUT

### *In the Lake Sunapee area*

**The Anchorage at Sunapee Harbor** (603-763-3334). Open mid-May through mid-October 11:30 AM–9 PM for lunch and dinner. Jeffrey and Rose Follansbee renovated this Lake Sunapee tradition a few years back and jazzed up what was a basic menu to include specialty sandwiches and broiled as well as fried fish and seafood. They added even more jazz with live entertainment and dancing. The spot is unbeatable.

**Bradford Junction Restaurant and Bakery** (603-938-2424), Route 114, Bradford. Open 6 AM–2:30 PM. A remnant of the area's railroad days, this dinerlike restaurant was once a depot, and is still the showcase for an elaborate model train that tracks the perimeter of the cheery dining room. Homemade bread, muffins, soups; pot roast for $4.75, baked haddock for $3.95. The village gathering place.

**Four Corner's Grille and Flying Goose Brew Pub** (603-526-6899), Routes 11 and 114, New London. Open for lunch and dinner daily, 11:30 AM–9 PM; until 8 PM on Sunday. Same ownership as the Millstone Restaurant (see *Dining Out*) but a more casual atmosphere. This 195-seat restaurant has become a venue for musicians, offering every-other-Thursday-night concerts with locally and sometimes nationally known rock, folk, blues, country, jazz, and swing stylists from September through April. It features 14 handcrafted ales and homemade root beer on tap, as well as a large menu that includes daily specials and burgers, sandwiches, ribs, superb soups, pastas, and deep fries.

**Gourmet Garden** (603-526-6656), 127 Main Street, New London. Open Monday through Saturday 6:30 AM–4 PM. Cute café with a deli and bakery attached. Fresh muffins, fabulous desserts.

**Harbor Falls Deli** (603-763-3351), Sunapee Harbor. Open daily 6 AM–late evening in summer; until 4 PM the rest of the year. Whether it's coffee and muffins in the morning, a croissant sandwich for lunch, or an ice cream cone on a summer evening, you can count on this casual grocery-store-cum-tables for fine food and friendly, personalized service.

**Jack's Coffee of New London** www.jackscoffee.com), 180 Main Street, New London (603-526-8003); 19 Main

Street, Newport (603-863-0683); Knowlton House, Sunapee Harbor. Coffee, chow, and couches plus Internet computers and a real-time stock machine caught on fast at Jack's original New London location. There and in Newport, he offers casual lunch fare, including homemade soups and fresh fruit smoothies. His latest location at the Knowlton House, a restored Victorian manse on Lake Sunapee, is opening for three meals daily as we go to press.

♿ **MacKenna's Restaurant** (603-526-9511), New London Shopping Center, New London. Open for breakfast, lunch, and dinner. Every town should have a place like this: clean, friendly, fast, and inexpensive. Homemade soups, great sandwiches on homemade bread (chicken salad is exceptional), steak dinners, and broiled or fried seafood and chicken; children's plates.

**Murphy's Grille, Mount Sunapee** (603-763-3113), 1407 Route 103, Newbury. Open daily for lunch and dinner; breakfast buffet Saturday and Sunday. Casual family-style dining with a nice deck, game room, and reasonably priced burgers, sandwiches, pasta, and entrées. The prime rib's a specialty.

**Peter Christian's Tavern** (603-526-4042), Main Street, New London. Pubby and popular. It's wise to come early or late since there's frequently a line and you can't make reservations. With the **Barn Playhouse** just down the street, there's always a crowd before a play. The menu, 11 AM–10 PM, stays the same: victuals like a cheese-and-meat board (plenty for two), or a hefty sandwich like Peter's Russian Mistress (open-faced turkey, bacon, Swiss cheese, spinach, tomato, Russian dressing). Dinner specials include white pesto lasagna and hearty beef stew, with prices generally under $10.

**Profile Coffee Company** (603-543-0068), 255 Old Newport Road (Claremont–Newport town line off John Stark Highway), Claremont. Open Wednesday and Thursday 9 AM–noon, Friday and Saturday 9 AM–5 PM. All-around coffee house and espresso bar with coffee-related gifts.

**The Waterfront** (603-763-9200), Route 103, Newbury Harbor. Open for lunch and dinner until 9 PM. The one-time Perry's Boathouse is now under new ownership but remains a friendly, popular meeting place for all sides of the lake. Good for burgers, fried seafood and chicken, or broiled pizzas, steaks, whatever. Booths and a sit-up bar, plus ice cream served from a take-out window.

**Wildberry Bagel Co.** (603-526-2244), 178 Main Street, New London. Open 6 AM–3 PM daily, until 2 PM Sunday. A bagel bar plus. Large selection of bagels, sandwiches, salads, and soups in a fresh, friendly atmosphere.

### *Elsewhere*

**The Foothills Restaurant** (603-456-2140), Main Street, Warner. Open daily except Monday, 6 AM–2 PM. For tourists, a pleasant pit stop just off I-89. For locals, the place to come to see everyone they know, even at 6 AM! Weekdays and weekends, folks from Warner and surrounding towns flock here for homemade breakfasts (huge pancake platters; great corned beef hash; toasted, buttered muffins) that are better than home since someone else does the cooking. Lace curtains, fast friendly service, daily baked specials.

## ✷ Entertainment

THEATER ✎ **New London Barn Playhouse** (603-526-6710; 603-526-4631), Main Street, New London. One of New England's oldest and best summer-stock theaters, featuring dramatic, musical, and children's productions. June through August.

MUSIC **Summer band concerts.** Springfield band concert series held weekly in Sunapee Harbor. Concerts at New London's Mary D. Haddard Memorial Bandstand on Sargent Common, New London; call the chamber of commerce for details (see *Guidance*). Concerts on Newbury Common on Thursdays at 7 PM, June through August. Newport Band concerts every Sunday evening on the common from late June through August. Held in the Opera House in case of rain. Summer music at Mount Sunapee.

## ✷ Selective Shopping

ANTIQUES **Colonial Farm Antiques** (603-526-6121), Route 11, New London. This group shop in the barn adjoining the Colonial Farm Inn offers a wide selection of traditional, rustic, and eclectic treasures.

**Prospect Hill Antiques** (603-763-9676), Prospect Hill Road, Georges Mills. The selection is immense, and the quality outstanding. If you are searching for an armoire or an end table, a desk or a stool, this barn, filled with more than 1,000 pieces of furniture and hundreds of collectibles, is worth checking.

***Antiquing in the Lake Sunapee–New London Region.*** A map and guide to local antiques dealers is available at local information booths and from the New London Chamber of Commerce (see *Guidance*).

CRAFTS **Braided Rug Shop** (603-863-1139; www.BraidedRugShop.com), P.O. Box 2154, Mount Sunapee. Braiding woolen fabric and supplies, plus rugs and novelty items made to order. Instructions for groups and individuals.

**The Dorr Mill Store** (603-863-1197), Route 11/103, Guild (between Newport and Sunapee). Open Monday through Saturday 9 AM–5 PM, Sunday 11:30 AM–4 PM. No longer an outlet for the woolen mill across the street, but a very special place that actually draws bus tours from as far away as Montreal for its line of 100 percent wool used for hooking, braiding, and quilting. Bolts of fabrics, including woolens still made at the mill, but a wider selection; also classic clothing: Woolrich, Pendleton, and others. Specializing in sweaters, woolens.

**Farm Mountain Sheep & Wool Co.** (603-526-WOOL), Route 4A, Wilmot. Open by chance. Wool comforters, 100 percent wool knitting yarns, spinning fibers, and equipment.

**Hodgepodge Handicrafts & Ransom's Furniture** (603-863-1470), 59 Belknap Avenue, Newport. Open Monday through Saturday 9 AM–5 PM. Specializing in spinning and knitting supplies, including spinning wheels, homespun yarns, and even a selection of handknit wearables.

**New England Machine Quilting** (603-735-5891), Route 11, Main Street, Andover. Makes quilts to order, or will bind and finish your own quilt top. Also sells fabrics and books.

SPECIAL SHOPS **Artisan's Workshop** (603-526-4227; 1-800-457-7242), 186 Main Street, New London. A small but full shop displaying an exceptional selection of handwrought jewelry, plus pottery, prints, paintings, woodenware, glass, cards, books, and much more in the front rooms of the old inn that now houses Peter Christian's Tavern. Frequent summer demonstrations, special exhibits, concerts.

**Audrey Nelson's Used Books** (603-863-4394), 1170 Brook Road, Goshen (Brook Road begins just a mile from the rotary at Sunapee State Park). Open May through October, Thursday through Monday 10 AM–5 PM, or by appointment or chance. "If you stick with one thing you could make a fortune, I figure," Audrey Nelson says, "but it gets boring." Nelson, an established local photographer, potter, and weaver, is explaining the almost organic evolution of her shop, which includes a wide variety of general and scholarly stock, such as 80,000 carefully selected hard- and softcover books.

**Brickstone** (603-863-6760), 82 Oak Street (a quarter mile north of the town common off Route 10), Newport. Hours vary. A 200-year-old farmhouse with seven rooms of unique gifts and collectibles.

**B. Coburn & Not Just Balloons** (603-526-6010), 135 Main Street, New London. Open daily. Not just brand-name cookware, bath accessories, or New England pottery either, this shop sells a mix of gifts and gourmet items, from children's author Tomie dePaola's collection of books (he's a local) to fresh fudge made daily.

**The 18th Century Shop** (603-543-0100; www.floorcloths.net), 1 Pleasant Street, Claremont. Open Tuesday through Saturday 10 AM–5 PM. This is an "official" Colonial Williamsburg Shop, featuring 10 rooms decorated in Colonial style. Fine period furnishings and accessories plus a large selection of standard and custom-designed floorcloths.

✐ **Main Street BookEnds** (603-456-2700), 16 East Main Street, Warner. Open daily 9 AM–6 PM, Friday until 8 PM. This combination bookstore, art gallery, and community heartbeat has a wonderful selection of books with a big children's section; also changing art exhibits and an amazing array of programs.

✐ **Morgan Hill Bookstore** (603-526-5850), 170 Main Street, New London. A spacious full-service bookstore with a unique, inviting children's area set up like a barn. Specializes in fine fiction and travel; also cards and CDs. Special programs, including signings and talks by area authors.

**Nunsuch Cheeses** (603-927-4176), Route 114, South Sutton. This 5-acre, licensed dairy welcomes visitors if they call first to make sure someone's around. Former nun Courtney Haase produces justly famous cheese: soft, aged, and smoked. She also sells goat's milk for those who want to try a hand at making their own.

**Potter Place Gallery** (603-735-5758), Route 4A, Potter Place, Andover. The specialties of the house are etchings, New England landscapes in various media, and sculpture.

**Uncorked, LLC** (603-526-6355), Scytheville Row, Newport Road, New London. Open Monday through Saturday 10 AM–6 PM. A wine enthusiast even when his college buddies were drinking beer, Scott Walters left a banking career to open up this boutique/specialty wine shop. Ask about special wine-tasting events and classes.

FACTORY OUTLETS **Mesa International Factory Outlet** (603-526-4497), 135 Elkins Road (off Route 11),

Elkins. Hours vary, so call. Bright, colorful glassware and hand-painted dinnerware designed by New Hampshire artists and manufactured around the globe. Worth checking.

**The Wudcahk Fleece Company** (603-927-4555), Shaker Street (near Exit 10 off I-89), North Sutton. Open daily 9 AM–5 PM except Sunday, May through July. Handcrafted fleece outerwear, accessories, and blankets for adults and children.

## ✷ Special Events

*Note:* The following entries represent a fraction of summer happenings in this region; check local listings.

*June:* Annual **Inn Tour** of the Sunapee region.

*July:* **New London Garden Club annual antiques show. Hebron Fair.**

*August:* **New London Hospital Fair.** Annual **League of New Hampshire Craftsmen's Fair,** Mount Sunapee State Park. The biggest event of the year by far. The country's oldest and still one of its best crafts fairs: a 9-day gathering of more than 500 juried artisans. Music, an art exhibit, a wide variety of crafts demonstrations, and workshops are included in the admissions ticket, good for 2 days—the time you need to take in the full range of exhibits, try your own hand at crafting something, and see the featured demonstrations that vary with the theme of the day. **Old Home Day,** Sutton. **Annual Lake Sunapee Antique Boat Show and Parade. Alexandria Fair. Muster Field Farm Days,** North Sutton village, offers more than 100 demonstrations of colonial skills, a Grand Parade, and a roast beef dinner the last weekend of the month, the same weekend as the decades-young **Annual Apple Pie Craft Fair** in Newport.

*September:* **Mount Sunapee Triathlon. Danbury Grange Fair.**

*Columbus Day weekend:* **Warner Fall Foliage Festival.** Major crafts show, food, entertainment.

# The Upper Connecticut River Valley

## UPPER VALLEY TOWNS

Robert Kozlow

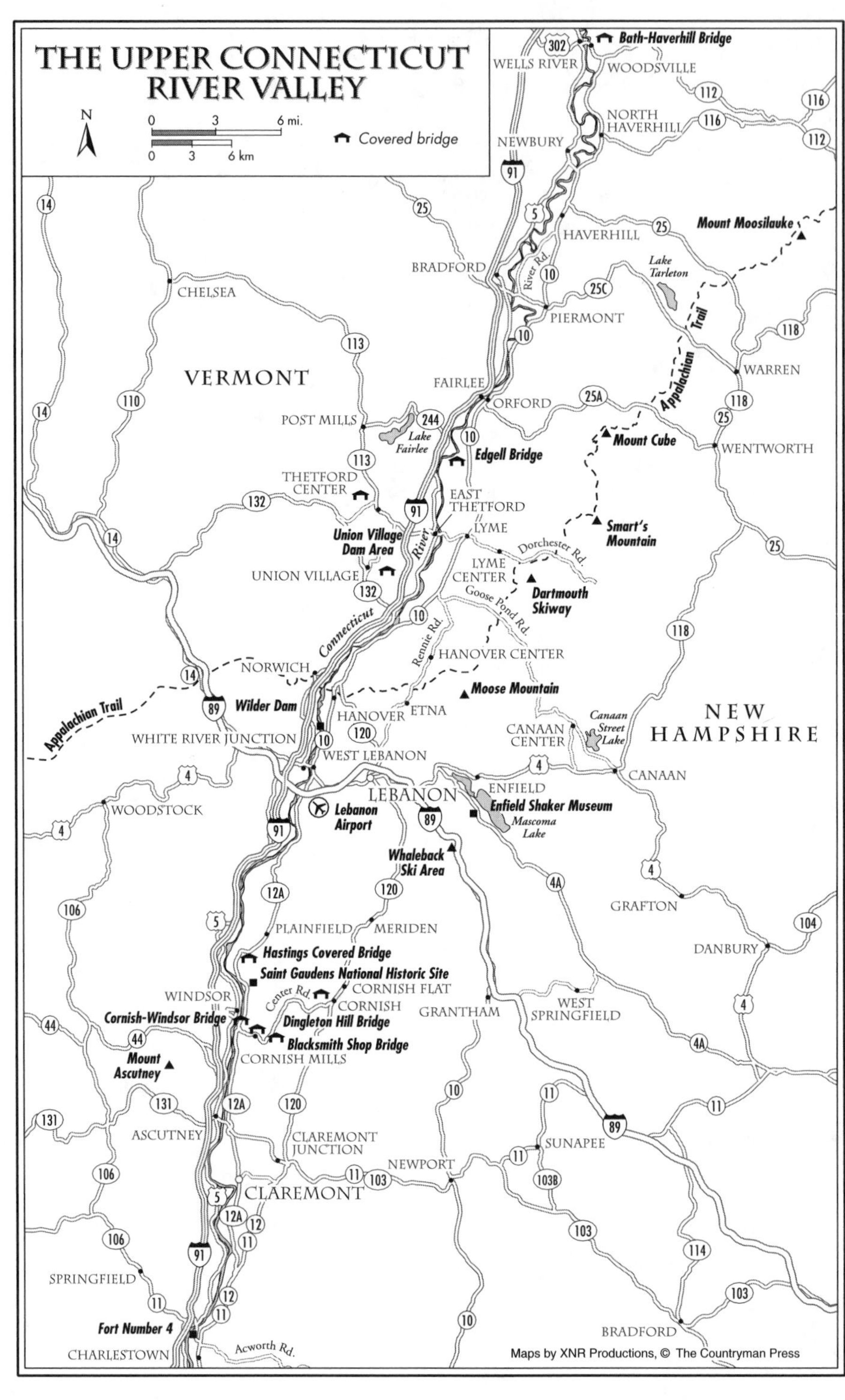
THE UPPER CONNECTICUT RIVER VALLEY
N
0 3 6 mi.
0 3 6 km
Covered bridge
Bath-Haverhill Bridge
WELLS RIVER
WOODSVILLE
NORTH HAVERHILL
NEWBURY
HAVERHILL
Mount Moosilauke
BRADFORD
Lake Tarleton
River Rd.
CHELSEA
PIERMONT
Appalachian Trail
WARREN
VERMONT
FAIRLEE
ORFORD
POST MILLS
Lake Fairlee
Mount Cube
WENTWORTH
Edgell Bridge
THETFORD CENTER
EAST THETFORD
LYME
Smart's Mountain
Union Village Dam Area
Dorchester Rd.
LYME CENTER
UNION VILLAGE
Dartmouth Skiway
Goose Pond Rd.
Connecticut River
Rennie Rd.
HANOVER CENTER
NORWICH
Moose Mountain
Wilder Dam
HANOVER
ETNA
Appalachian Trail
WHITE RIVER JUNCTION
CANAAN CENTER
Canaan Street Lake
NEW HAMPSHIRE
WEST LEBANON
CANAAN
ENFIELD
LEBANON
WOODSTOCK
Lebanon Airport
Enfield Shaker Museum
Mascoma Lake
Whaleback Ski Area
GRAFTON
PLAINFIELD
MERIDEN
DANBURY
Hastings Covered Bridge
Saint Gaudens National Historic Site
Center Rd.
CORNISH FLAT
WINDSOR
CORNISH
GRANTHAM
WEST SPRINGFIELD
Cornish-Windsor Bridge
Dingleton Hill Bridge
Blacksmith Shop Bridge
Mount Ascutney
CORNISH MILLS
ASCUTNEY
CLAREMONT JUNCTION
SUNAPEE
NEWPORT
CLAREMONT
SPRINGFIELD
Fort Number 4
BRADFORD
CHARLESTOWN
Acworth Rd.
Maps by XNR Productions, © The Countryman Press

# UPPER VALLEY TOWNS

The Upper Valley ignores state lines to form one of New England's most beautiful and distinctive regions. Its two dozen towns are scattered along both the Vermont and New Hampshire banks of the Connecticut River for some 20 miles north and south of Dartmouth College. Limitations of space prevent us from including more than a handful of attractions in Vermont that by right belong to this region; for a complete listing, see *Vermont: An Explorer's Guide* (Countryman Press).

*Upper Valley* is a name coined in the 1950s by a local daily, the *Valley News,* to define its two-state circulation area. The label has stuck, interestingly enough, to the same group of towns that back in the 1770s tried to form the state of "New Connecticut." The Dartmouth-based, pro–New Connecticut party was thwarted, however, by larger powers (namely New York and New Hampshire), along with the strident Vermont-independence faction—the Green Mountain Boys.

The valley itself prospered in the late 18th and early 19th centuries, as evidenced by the exquisite Federal-era meetinghouses and mansions still salted throughout this area. The river was the area's only highway in the 18th and early 19th centuries and was still a popular steamboat route in the years before the Civil War.

King George III's decree that the river belongs to New Hampshire still holds, which means it is responsible for maintaining the bridges. Of the dozens of bridges that once linked towns on either side of the river, only 10 survive, but they include the longest covered bridge in the United States (connecting Windsor and Cornish). The Upper Valley phone book, moreover, includes towns on both sides of the river, and Hanover's Dresden School District reaches into Vermont (this was the first bistate school district in the United States). Several Independence Day parades start in one state and finish across the bridge in the other. The Montshire Museum, founded in Hanover but now in Norwich, Vermont, combines both states in its very name.

Dartmouth College in Hanover remains the cultural center of the Upper Valley. With the nearby Dartmouth Hitchcock medical complex and West Lebanon shopping strip, this area forms the region's hub, handy to the highways radiating, the way rail lines once did, from White River Junction, Vermont.

North and south of the Hanover area, old river towns drowse and the river roads are well worth finding. Thanks to the 1970s Clean Water Act and to acquisitions, greenups, and cleanups by numerous conservation groups, the river itself is enjoying a genuine renewal, and visitors and residents alike are discovering its beauty; campsites and inns are spaced along the shore.

**GUIDANCE** **www.ctrivertravel.net,** an excellent, noncommercial web site covering the entire stretch of the Connecticut shared by Vermont and New Hampshire, is maintained by **The Connecticut River Byway Council.** Also look for "waypoint" information centers serving both sides of the river in Claremont, Windsor, White River Junction, Fairlee, and Wells River/Woodsville.

**Hanover Chamber of Commerce** (603-643-3115; www.hanoverchamber.org), 126 Nugget Building, Main Street, Hanover 03755. Open 9 AM–4:30 PM weekdays. The second-floor chamber office is stocked with flyers and brochures, as is a seasonal (early June through September) information booth (603-643-3512) on the Dartmouth green. It's staffed by helpful Dartmouth students and alums and also serves as starting point for regularly scheduled tours of the campus.

**The Upper Valley Welcome Center** (802-281-5050) in the railroad station in White River Junction, Vermont (open daily, 8 AM–7 PM) offers friendly, knowledgeable advice, rest rooms, and an evolving transportation museum. Also see www.uppervalleychamber.com.

**The Greater Lebanon Chamber of Commerce** (603-448-1203; www.lebanonchamber.com) is located just off the common and the entrance to the Mall (the city's shop-lined walking street).

**Greater Claremont Chamber of Commerce** (603-543-1296; chamber@adelphia.net), the Moody Building, 24 Tremont Square, Claremont 03743, is in the

A FARM IN THE UPPER CONNECTICUT RIVER VALLEY

Kim Grant

city's central, most distinctive building. Pick up a walking guide. No public rest rooms. Look for a new "waypoint" visitors center on North Street (Route 11/103). A seasonal **Wells River/Woodsville** information center, a log cabin just west of the bridge on Route 302, is staffed by local volunteers. This upper end of the Upper Valley is served by the **Lower Cohas Region Chamber of Commerce** (1-866-526-4273; www.cohas.org).

GETTING THERE *By car:* Interstates 91 and 89 intersect in the White River Junction (Vermont)–Lebanon (New Hampshire) area, where they also meet Route 5 north and south on the Vermont side; Route 4, the main east–west highway through central Vermont; and Route 10, the river road on the New Hampshire side.

*By bus:* White River Junction, Vermont, is a hub for **Greyhound/Vermont Transit** (802-293-3011; 1-800-321-0707) with express service to Boston.

*By air:* The **Lebanon Regional Airport** (603-298-8878), West Lebanon, has frequent service to New York and Boston via USAirways Express (1-800-428-4322), which also serves Philadelphia. Rental cars are available from Avis, Hertz, and Alamo.

*By train:* **Amtrak** (802-295-7160; 1-800-872-7245) stops in Claremont, New Hampshire, and in White River Junction, Vermont, en route to and from Washington, New York City, and St. Albans (Vermont), with connecting bus service to Montreal.

MEDICAL EMERGENCY **911** now serves this area.

**Dartmouth-Hitchcock Medical Center** (603-650-5000; 911), off Route 120 between Hanover and Lebanon. Generally considered the best hospital in northern New England.
The **Valley Regional Hospital** in Claremont (dial 911 in an emergency) also serves the southern towns of the Upper Valley.

## * Communities

### *From south to north*

**Charlestown** was a stockaded outpost during the French and Indian Wars (see the **Fort at Number 4** under *To See*). Its Main Street was laid out in 1763, 200 feet wide and a mile long, with more than five dozen structures that now comprise a national historic district; 10 buildings predate 1800. Note the 1840s Congregational church; the former Charlestown Inn (1817), now a commercial building; the vintage-1800 Stephen Hassam House, built by the great-grandfather of impressionist painter Childe Hassam; and the Foundation for Biblical Research, housed in a 1770s mansion. *Historic Charlestown Walkabout,* a nominally priced guide, is available in most town stores.

**Claremont.** Massive textile mills and machine shops line the Sugar River as it drops 300 feet from the city's compact core around Tremont Square. At this writing the mills remain vacant but Tremont Square retains some magnificent 1890s buildings, notably the massive Italian Renaissance Revival–style city hall with its magnificent and well-used second-floor **Opera House** (see *Entertainment*), and

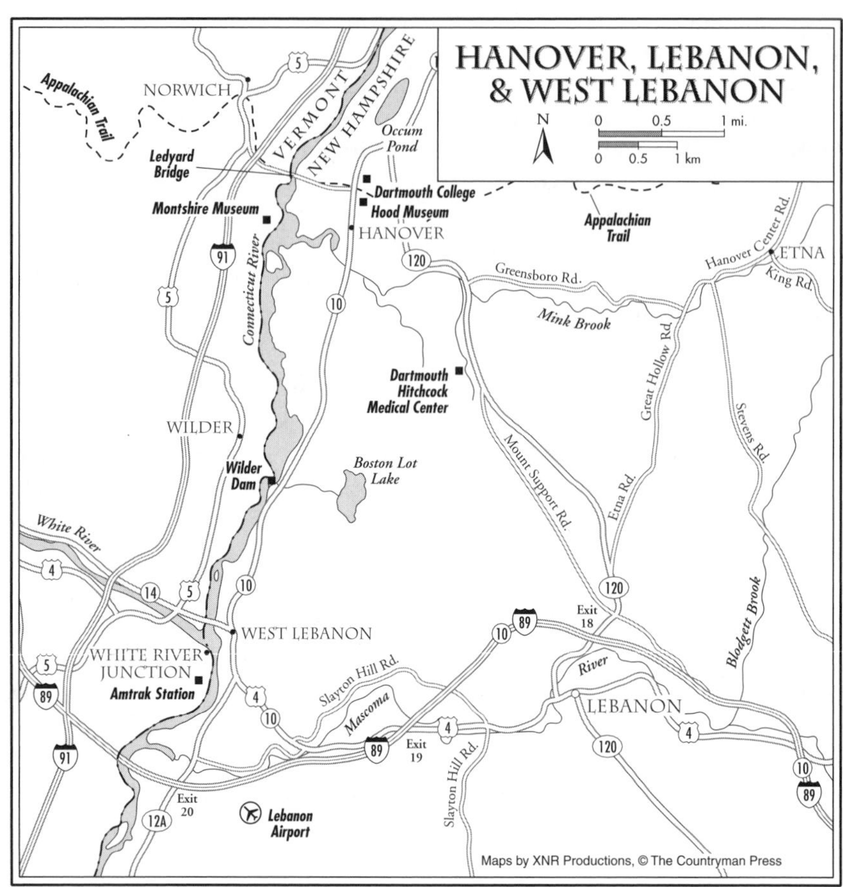


the Moody Building, built originally as a hotel in 1892. Adjoining Pleasant Street is now lined with antiques shops. The mammoth brick **Monadnock Mills** on Water Street (off Broad and Main) on the Sugar River are among the best-preserved 19th-century, small urban mills in New Hampshire; note the 1840s gambrel-roofed brick Sunapee Mill across the river and the small brick overseers' cottages (also 1840s) on Crescent Street. The railroad was an essential contributor to Claremont's industrial and cultural heyday. It remains an Amtrak stop. A sleek silver vintage-1935 Flying Yankee train has been under restoration at the rail yards here for several years; rail fans, check www.flyingyankee.com. The **Claremont Historical Society** (603-542-1400), 26 Mulberry Street, is open mid-June through September, Sunday 2–5 PM. A walking tour is available from the chamber of commerce (see *Guidance*). **West Claremont** (3 miles west on Route 103) is a vanished village graced by New Hampshire's oldest Episcopal and Catholic churches. It seems that the Catholic priest who founded St. Mary's parish in 1824 was the son of the Episcopal rector who built St. John's across the street. Both buildings are interesting architecturally. The only sign of the congregations that both men taught and served is the West Part Burying Ground adjoining the churches.

**Cornish.** In the 1880s these riverside hills were far more open, mowed by thousands of sheep, but the wool bubble had already burst and farms were selling cheap. Many were bought by artists and writers, friends of sculptor Augustus Saint-Gaudens (see *To See—Historic Sites*). By the turn of the 20th century 40 families had bought old farms or built homes in Cornish and neighboring Plainfield. This "Cornish Colony" included artists, writers, and other creative and wealthy bohemians, prominent in their own right. They also included artist Ellen Wilson, whose husband, Pres. Woodrow Wilson, spent a portion of the summers of 1914 and 1915 here at the home of writer Winston Churchill (note the historic marker near the Plainfield–Cornish line). Best remembered of the artists is Maxfield Parrish (1870–1966), whose work is featured in the **Cornish Colony Gallery and Museum** (see *To See—Historic Sites*) and in whose honor 11 miles of Route 12A in Cornish and Plainfield has recently been named the Maxfield Parrish Highway. Also see Plainfield.

**Plainfield.** A one-street village, Plainfield still clings to the memory of onetime resident Maxfield Parrish. In the 1920s Parrish painted a stage set in the **Plainfield Town Hall** picturing Mount Ascutney and the river in the deep blues for which he is famous. Stop by the vintage-1798 building to see if it's open. You might also want to follow **River Road,** where you'll find produce and bottled milk at local farms.

**Lebanon.** As near to the junction of I-91 and I-89 as it can be while still on the New Hampshire (no-sales-tax) side of the Connecticut River, "West Leb" is the shopping center of the Upper Valley. The strip of malls is a good bet for most basics, and the **Powerhouse Mall** (see *Selective Shopping*) north of I-89 offers some pleasant surprises. Positioned between the Connecticut River and Mascoma Lake, with old mills lining the Mascoma River, Lebanon itself—once you find it (east on Route 4)—is a city with a small-town feel. The common is circled by handsome buildings—a vintage-1828 church, substantial homes, and public buildings, including an opera house—and is the site of summer band concerts. Shops and restaurants are found along adjoining traffic-free streets.

**Canaan Center** is a classic hill town: a proud, old agricultural community left high and dry when the railroad came through in the 1860s and the town's business shifted to the area (now the village of Canaan) 3 miles down the road, around the depot. Like Old Deerfield Village in Massachu-

*EVENING*, 1944, BY MAXFIELD PARRISH (OIL ON BOARD)

Courtesy Alma Gilbert/Cornish Colony Museum

setts, the houses here—a few 18th-century homes and the rest built before 1850—line a single street, and over the years the community itself has become known as **Canaan Street.** Its unusual beauty—and that of its lake—was recognized early on; the train to Canaan soon began bringing summer tourists, hotels opened to accommodate them, and an elaborate pier was built. The **Canaan Historic Museum** (open July through October, Saturday 1–4 PM) displays souvenir dishes with CANAAN STREET and color pictures printed on them. Also see **The Inn on Canaan Street** under *Lodging—Bed & Breakfasts*. Canaan itself is now off the beaten track. Look closely and you may find the old depot. A second story has been added, and it's now a Laundromat.

**Hanover** is synonymous with Ivy League **Dartmouth College** (www.dartmouth.edu), chartered in 1769 and one of the most prestigious colleges in the country. Dartmouth's student population averages 4,300 undergraduate men and women and 1,000 graduate students. Its handsome buildings frame three sides of an elm- and maple-lined green, and the fourth side includes a large inn, an arts center, and an outstanding art museum. The information booth on the green (see *Guidance*) is the starting point for historical and architectural tours of the campus. **Baker Memorial Library,** a 1920s version of Philadelphia's Independence Hall, dominates the northern side of the green. Visitors are welcome to see a set of murals, *The Epic of American Civilization,* by José Clemente Orozco, painted between 1932 and 1934 while he was teaching at Dartmouth. (Some alumni once demanded these be removed or covered because of the Mexican artist's left-wing politics.) In the Treasure Room (near the western stair hall on the main floor), Daniel Webster's copies of the double elephant folio first edition of John Audubon's *Birds of America* are permanently displayed. The **Hopkins Center for the Arts** (603-646-

CANAAN

Robert Kozlow

2422) was designed by Wallace Harrison a few years before he designed New York's Lincoln Center (which it resembles). It contains three theaters, a recital hall, and art galleries for permanent and year-round programs of plays, concerts, and films. It's also home base for the **Dartmouth Symphony Orchestra** (see *Entertainment*). **Dartmouth Row,** a file of four striking, white Colonial buildings on the rise along the eastern side of the green, represents all there was to Dartmouth College until 1845. You might also want to find **Webster Cottage,** maintained as a museum by the Hanover Historical Society (see *To See—Historic Sites*), and the vintage-1843 **Shattuck Observatory** (open weekdays 8:30 AM–4:40 PM, also Tuesday and Thursday evening by reservation: 603-646-2034).

**Lyme** is known for its splendid **Congregational church,** completed in 1812, a Federal-style meetinghouse complete with Palladian window, an unusual tower (three cubical stages and an octagonal dome), and no fewer than 27 numbered horse stalls. The gathering of buildings, including the inn, fine old houses, and general stores, is one of New Hampshire's most stately. Take **River Road** north by old farms and cemeteries, through an 1880s covered bridge.

**Orford** is known for its **Ridge Houses,** a center-of-town lineup of seven houses so strikingly handsome that Charles Bulfinch has been (erroneously) credited as their architect. They were built instead by skilled local craftsmen using designs from Connecticut Valley architect Asher Benjamin's do-it-yourself guide to Federal styles, *The Country Builder's Apprentice.* These houses testify to the prosperity of this valley in the post–Revolutionary War era. Each was built by an Orford resident—with money earned in Orford—between 1773 and 1839. The best remembered of the residents is Samuel Morey. While all his neighbors were in church one Sunday morning in 1793, Morey gave the country's first little steam-powered paddle wheeler a successful test run on the river. Sam kept tinkering with the boat and in 1797 came up with a side-wheeler, but at this point Robert Fulton, who had encouraged Morey to discuss freely with him and demonstrate the invention, went into the steamboating business, using a boat clearly patterned after Morey's. It's said that an embittered Morey sank his boat across the river in the Vermont lake that now bears his name. He also heated and lighted his house with gas, and in 1826 he patented a gas-powered internal combustion engine. The **Samuel Morey House** is the oldest of the seven, a centerpiece for the others.

In **Piermont** note the **Polygonal Barn,** built in 1906, a 16-sided barn north of Piermont village on Route 10. Also see *Selective Shopping—Special Shops*.

**Haverhill** is immense, composed of seven very distinct villages, including classic examples of both Federal-era and railroad villages. Thanks to a fertile floodplain, this is an old and prosperous farming community, even with agricultural land now totaling less than 9,000 acres, and still boasts more than 20 farms. It has also been the Grafton County seat since 1773. The village of **Haverhill Corner** on Route 10 is a gem: a grouping of Federal-era and Greek Revival homes and public buildings around a double, white-fenced common (the site of all-day flea markets on the last Sunday of summer months). Just north of the village (but south of the junction of Routes 10 and 25) a sign points the way down through a cornfield and along the river to the site of the Bedell bridge. Built in 1866, this was one of the largest surviving examples of a two-span covered bridge until it was destroyed by

Robert Kozlow

THE GENERAL STORE ON THE LYME COMMON

a violent September windstorm in 1979. The site is still worth finding because it's a peaceful riverside spot, ideal for a picnic.

**Woodsville.** North of North Haverhill you come unexpectedly to a lineup of modern county buildings—the courthouse, a county home, and a jail—and then you are in downtown Woodsville, a 19th-century rail hub with an ornate 1890s brick Opera Block and three-story, mustard-colored railroad station. The **Haverhill–Bath covered bridge,** built in 1829 and billed as the oldest covered bridge in New England, is just beyond the railroad underpass (Route 135 north).

## ✷ To See

**MUSEUMS** **Hood Museum of Art** (603-646-2808), Dartmouth green. Open Tuesday through Saturday 10 AM–5 PM, until 9 PM on Wednesday; Sunday noon–5 PM. Free. Housed in a 1980s building designed by Charles W. Moore, the collection is billed as the country's oldest, begun in 1773 when the colonial governor of New Hampshire presented Dartmouth's President Wheelock with a silver monteith. It now ranges eclectically from Assyrian bas-reliefs (donated by missionary graduates in the 1850s) through Italian masters, American 18th-century portraits, and 19th-century landscapes to a huge abstract piece by Dartmouth graduate Frank Stella. On a recent visit the permanent display area included landscapes by Paul Sample (who taught at Dartmouth) and Rockwell Kent, along with works by Winslow Homer, Frederic Remington, Thomas Eakins, Frederic Frieseke, and John Sloan. A narrow flight of stairs rises dramatically to the high, skylit Lathrop Gallery, hung with modern masterpieces such as Picasso's *Guitar on the Table,* gift of Nelson Rockefeller, class of 1930. There are frequent programs and changing exhibits.

✐ **The Montshire Museum of Science** (802-649-2200; www.montshire.org), Norwich, Vermont. Take a right off I-91, Exit 13, or the first left after the bridge from Hanover (before the I-91 off-ramp). Open daily 10 AM–5 PM; $6.50 per adult, $4 children 3–17. Few cities have a science museum of this quality, and the superb exhibits, plus trails through 100 wooded acres on the Connecticut River, add up to one of New England's outstanding sights. Don't be put off by the entrance fee, and stop by whether you have children along or not. Do you really understand why night and day occur? The museum answers dozens of such questions. Its avowed goal is to demystify natural phenomena, and it does so in a way that's fun. Exhibits change but usually include an aquarium of northern New England fish, a kinetic energy machine, an elaborate colony of 25,000 leaf-cutter ants, an exhibit on "knot topography," and much more. All exhibits (except the boa constrictor) are hands-on. New in 2002: an outdoor Science Park focusing on water and understanding the ways it shapes landscapes. Also new: The Leonard M. Rieser Learning Center features the natural environment of the Upper Connecticut River Valley. The 110-acre property includes 4 miles of easy-to-walk nature trails along the Connecticut River. There's also a playground and a big gift shop; inquire about workshops, guided hikes, canoe excursions, special events, and exhibits.

**The American Precision Museum** (802-674-5781), South Main Street, Windsor, Vermont. Open May 30 through November 1, Monday through Friday 9 AM–5 PM; Saturday, Sunday, and holidays 10 AM–4 PM; $5 per adult, $3.50 seniors, $2 children over 6; $14 per family. An important, expanding collection of hand and machine tools assembled in the 1846 Robbins, Kendall & Lawrence Armory, itself a national historic landmark. The firm became world famous in 1851 because of its displays of "the American system" of manufacturing interchangeable parts, especially for what became the renowned Enfield rifle. Changing special exhibits tend to be excellent.

HISTORIC SITES **Fort at Number 4** (603-826-5700; www.fortat4.com), Route 11, 1 mile north of Charlestown village. Open Memorial Day through late October, 10 AM–4 PM. Admission: $8 per adult, $7 seniors, $4.50 per child. This living history museum, set in 20 acres on the Connecticut River, conjures an otherwise

THE HOOD MUSEUM OF ART AND THE HOPKINS CENTER ON THE CAMPUS OF DARTMOUTH COLLEGE

Stuart Bratesman

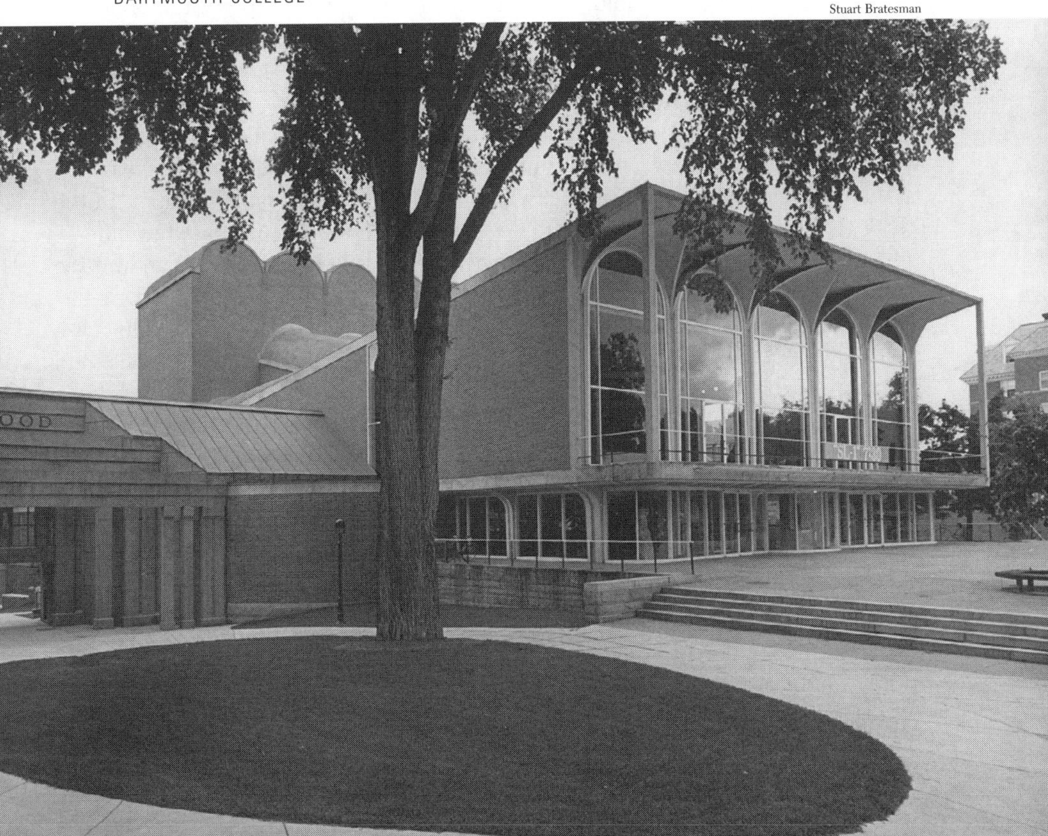

almost forgotten chapter in New England history. The stockaded village exactly replicates the way the settlement looked in the 1740s. It served first as a trading post in which Natives and newcomers lived together peaceably until the outbreak of the French and Indian War. A full 50 miles north of any other town on the Connecticut River, the original fort fell once but then withstood repeated attacks. The complex includes the Great Hall, cow barns, and furnished living quarters; there is also an audiovisual program, and costumed interpreters prepare meals, perform chores, and staff a blacksmith forge. Inquire about frequent battle reenactments and special programs for children throughout the summer. A small museum displays authentic local Native American artifacts, and the gift store carries historical books for all ages.

**Old Constitution House** (802-674-6628; www.historicvermont.org), North Main Street, Windsor, Vermont. Open mid-May through mid-October, Wednesday through Sunday 11 AM–5 PM. This is Elijah West's tavern (but not in its original location), where delegates gathered on July 2, 1777, to adopt Vermont's constitution, America's first to prohibit slavery, establish universal voting rights for all males, and authorize a public school system. Excellent first-floor displays trace the history of the formation of the Republic of Vermont; upstairs is the town's collection of antiques, prints, documents, tools and cooking utensils, tableware, toys, and early fabrics. Special exhibits vary each year. A path out the back door leads to Lake Runnemede.

**Enfield Shaker Museum** (603-632-4346; www.shakermuseum.org), Route 4A, Lower Shaker Village, Enfield, marked from I-89, Exit 17. Open Memorial Day through October, Monday through Saturday 10 AM–5 PM, Sunday noon–5 PM; November through mid-May open weekends, closing at 4 PM. Admission $7 adults, $6 seniors, $3 children 10–18. The Shaker community, founded in 1793 in this "Chosen Vale" between Mount Assurance and Mascoma Lake, prospered through the 19th century, and 13 buildings survive. In 1927 the complex was sold to the Catholic order of La Salette, which added a basilica-shaped chapel. In the 1980s the order sold the buildings to developers, and the Great Stone Dwelling—said to be the largest Shaker dwelling anywhere—has been restored as an inn (see *Lodging—Country Inns* and *Dining Out*). Surrounding buildings, including a former Catholic chapel, are now part of the evolving Shaker Museum. Exhibits are currently all in the Laundry-Dairy Building, which also houses a slide show and gift shop, and is the scene of frequent workshops in Shaker crafts: woodworking, chair taping, gardening, herbal skills, and Shaker basketmaking. Note the single stone commemorating the resting place of 330 Shakers. You might want to climb the dirt road that begins next to the stone shop; it's a steep half-mile walk to the holy Feast Ground of the Shakers of Chosen Vale. Inquire about special events. The La Salette brothers still maintain a shrine and center (603-632-4301) here. (Also see *Selective Shopping—Art Galleries and Crafts Centers*.)

**Webster Cottage** (603-646-3371), North Main Street, Hanover (two blocks north of the green). Memorial Day through Columbus Day, Wednesday, Saturday, and Sunday 2:30–4:30 PM and by appointment. Built in 1780 as the home of Abigail Wheelock (daughter of Dartmouth founder Eleazar Wheelock), it was also the senior-year (1801) residence of Daniel Webster and birthplace in 1822 of Henry

Fowle Durant, founder of Wellesley College. Maintained as a museum by the Hanover Historical Society.

**THE CORNISH ARTISTS' COLONY** **The Saint-Gaudens National Historic Site** (603-675-2175), Route 12A, Cornish. Open late May through October, daily 9 AM–4:30 PM. Admission: $4 (good for one week); under 17 free. The sculptor's summer home, Aspet, is furnished as it was when he lived here between 1885 and his death in 1907. Augustus Saint-Gaudens is remembered for such public pieces as the Shaw memorial on Boston Common, the statue of Admiral Farragut in New York's Madison Square, and the equestrian statue of General William T. Sherman on New York's Fifth Avenue near Central Park. The estate includes a barn/studio, a sculpture court, and an art gallery, set in formal gardens with Mount Ascutney across the river as a backdrop. Saint-Gaudens loved the Ravine Trail, a quarter-mile cart path now marked for visitors, and other walks laid out through the woodlands and wetlands to the Blow-Me-Down Natural Area. Visitors are invited to bring picnics before the Sunday concerts (2 PM) in July and August; also to view the changing art exhibits in the art gallery. Also see Cornish under *Communities* for more about the group that gathered around Saint-Gaudens. Works by all members of the "Cornish Colony" can now be viewed on computers at the site, which is maintained by the National Park Service. The gift store is well worth checking.

**Cornish Colony Gallery and Museum** (603-675-6000; www.almagilbert.com), Route 12A, Cornish. Open May 25 through October 20, Tuesday through Saturday 10 AM–5 PM; noon–5 PM on Sunday. Admission: $5 adult; $3 for seniors and children. A nonprofit museum said to display the country's largest exhibit of works by Maxfield Parrish. Alma Gilbert-Smith, a scholar and collector of Parrish, has transformed "Mastlands," a country mansion owned during the Cornish Colony era (see Cornish under *Communties*) by landscape architect Rose Nichols. Her gardens here have been restored. Works here by Parrish include a mammoth mural as well as paintings and prints. Current exhibits feature the women of the Cornish Colony,

ASPET, THE HOUSE AND STUDIO OF SCULPTOR AUGUSTUS SAINT-GAUDENS IN CORNISH

Saint-Gaudens National Historic Site

including paintings by Pres. Woodrow Wilson's wife, Ellen. A tearoom overlooks the gardens; the gift store sells prints and books about Parrish and the colony.

**COVERED BRIDGES** At 460 feet the **Cornish–Windsor covered bridge,** Route 12A, said to be the country's longest covered bridge, is certainly the most photographed in New England. A lattice truss design, built in 1866, it was rebuilt in 1989. There are also three more covered bridges in Cornish, all dating from the early 1880s: Two span Mill Brook—one in Cornish City and the other in Cornish Mills between Routes 12A and 120—and the third spans Blow-Me-Down Brook (off Route 12A). On the Meriden road in Plainfield another 1880s, 85-foot bridge spans Bloods Brook. Near the Lyme–Orford line the **Lyme–Edgell bridge** (154 feet long) spans Clay Brook (off Route 10), and in Haverhill what's left of the **Bedell bridge** (symbolic of dozens that once linked towns on both sides of the Connecticut) is now a riverside park.

**FOR FAMILIES** **Wilder Dam Visitors' House and Fish Ladder** (802-295-3191), Route 5, Wilder, Vermont. Open Memorial Day through Columbus Day, daily 9 AM–5 PM; free. Displays about salmon, the fish ladder, and energy. In June and part of July fish, sometimes salmon, can occasionally be seen using the ladders. In winter, when water elsewhere is iced over, a bald eagle often frequents the dam. The best viewing time is early morning.

**Pleasant Valley Recreation** (603-542-9351), Route 12, Charlestown. Open April through October, varying hours. Kid heaven: go-carts, a mini railroad, a driving range, also an 18-hole golf course.

Also see the **Montshire Museum of Science** under *Museums* and **Fort Number 4** under *Historic Sites*.

THE CORNISH–WINDSOR COVERED BRIDGE SPANS THE CONNECTICUT RIVER BETWEEN NEW HAMPSHIRE AND VERMONT.

Robert Kozlow

## ✷ To Do

**AIR RIDES** **Post Mills Airport** (802-333-9254), West Fairlee, Vermont. Brian Boland offers year-round morning and sunset balloon rides. On the summer evening we tried it, the balloon hovered above hidden pockets in the hills, and we saw a herd of what looked like brown and white goats that, on closer inspection, proved to be deer (yes, some were white!). After an hour or so we settled down gently in a farmyard and broke out the champagne. Scenic plane rides and flight instruction also offered. Ascents are also offered by **Balloons Over New England** (1-800-788-5562) and **Killington Balloon Adventures** (802-291-4887), both based in Quechee, Vermont, the site of the region's Annual Balloon Festival on Father's Day weekend.

**BICYCLING** Given its unusually flat and scenic roads and well-spaced inns, this area is beloved by bicyclists. Search out the river roads (for some reason they're not marked on the official New Hampshire highway map): from Route 12A (just north of the Saint-Gaudens site) on through Plainfield until it rejoins Route 12A; from Route 10 north of Hanover (just north of the Chieftain Motel) through Lyme, rejoining Route 10 in Orford. A classic, 36-mile loop is Hanover to Orford on Route 10 and back on the river road. The loop to Lyme and back is 22 miles. For inn-to-inn guided tours in this area, contact **Bike Vermont** (802-457-3553; 1-800-257-2226; www.bikevermont.com). The Sugar River Trail, a multiuse recreational path, follows the Sugar River east from Charlestown to Newport. Inquire about the evolving Northern Rail Trail along the Mascoma River from West Lebanon to Grafton. **Wilderness Trails** at the Quechee Inn (802-295-7620) in Quechee, Vermont, rents mountain bikes and 21-speed hybrids. **Dartmouth Outdoor Rentals** (603-646-1747), a student-run service on the green in Hanover, rents mountain bikes and helmets (see *Outdoor Adventure*).

**BOAT EXCURSION** **Peacemaker Cruises** (603-445-2371), 22 West Street, North Walpole. Bill Gallagher operates more or less daily in summer, but call to check; his canopied pontoon boat carries a maximum of 12 passengers on 2½-hour cruises upstream from the dam at Bellows Falls, Vermont. "Everybody raves about fall colors but you can get out here and see all these different shades of green, and it's pretty special," Gallagher commented the night we rode with him. Cruising upriver between green fields backed by green mountains, we spotted a blue heron perched on a log, then another one, and then swallows, soaring and swooping by the dozens around their nests in a riverbank below a cornfield.

**BOATING** With its usually placid water and scenery, the Connecticut River through much of the Upper Valley is ideal for easygoing canoeists. The Connecticut River Joint Commissions (603-826-4800; www.ctrivertravel.net) has published a useful *Boating on the Connecticut River* guide. Information on primitve campsites along this stretch of the river can be found on the web site maintained by the Upper Valley Land Trust (www.ULVT.org).

Canoeing the Connecticut can, admittedly, be a bit of a slog. The headwind is as infamous as the lack of current. So what? Why does canoeing have to be about going long distances? Study programs on and about the river are limited and locally geared, but if you are interested in guided canoe trips or workshops on the river, contact the **Montshire Museum of Science** (802-649-2200; see *To See—Museums*).

The most frequently photographed reach of the Upper Connecticut is the 3 miles above the Cornish–Windsor covered bridge, set against the dramatic lone peak of Mount Ascutney. This is part of a popular 12-mile paddle that begins just below Sumner Falls, half a mile of rolling water and jagged rock worth mentioning because it's so deceptive and so deadly.

**North Star Livery** (603-542-5802; www.kayak-canoe.com), Route 12A in Cornish, will shuttle patrons to put-ins either 3 or 12 miles above the Cornish–Windsor covered bridge (see above). Roughly half of North Star's patrons camp, either at Wilgus State Park (802-674-5422) or at another site in Windsor, Vermont. North Star itself is New England's most picturesque canoe livery: The check-in desk in the barn of a working farm, redolent of bales of hay, and owner John Hammond may well be out front shoeing horses; the canoes and kayaks are stacked behind the farmhouse. Six-person rafts are also available. Full-day, half-day, and multiday trips are offered. With over 70 boats and two buses, this is the largest and oldest commercial rental service on the Connecticut River.

**The Ledyard Canoe Club** (603-643-6709), Hanover, is billed as the oldest canoe club in America. It's named for a 1773 Dartmouth dropout who felled a pine tree, hollowed it out, and took off downriver (with a copy of Ovid), ending up at Hartford, 100 miles and several major waterfalls downstream. Hidden on the riverbank north of the Ledyard Bridge, down beyond Dartmouth's slick new rowing center, Ledyard is a mellow, friendly, student-run place. The canoeing and kayaking center for the 40 river miles above Wilder Dam, it offers kayaking clinics as well as canoe and kayak rentals. No shuttle service.

**Fairlee Marine** (802-333-9745), Route 5 in Fairlee, Vermont, rents pontoons, canoes, and rowboats, and small motors for use on the Connecticut and two local lakes.

**FISHING** You can eat the fish you catch in the Connecticut River—it yields brown and rainbow trout above Orford. There's a boat launch on the Vermont side at the Wilder Dam, another just north of Hanover, and another across the river in North Thetford, Vermont. Lake Mascoma (look for boat launches along Route 4A in Enfield) and Post Pond in Lyme are other popular angling spots.

**Lyme Angler** (603-643-6447), 8 South Main Street, Hanover. This is an Orvis outfitter and guide service offering a "Fly-Fishing School" and guided trips.

**GOLF** **Hanover Country Club** (603-646-2000), Rope Ferry Road, off Route 10, Hanover. Open May through October. Founded in 1899, an 18-hole facility with 4 practice holes, pro shop, PGA instructors. **Carter Golf Club** (603-448-4483), Route 4, Lebanon. Nine holes, par 36. **Lake Morey Country Club** (802-333-4800; 1-800-423-1211), Fairlee, Vermont. Eighteen holes, site of the Vermont Open for the past 40 years (third Sunday in June). **Windsor Country Club** (802-

674-6491), Windsor, Vermont. Nine holes, par 34, no lessons. **Fore-U Driving Range** (603-298-9702), Route 12A, West Lebanon. Buckets of balls to hit off mats or grass; 18-hole miniature golf course.

**HANG GLIDING** **Morningside Recreation Area** (603-542-4416), Route 12 in Claremont, is the site of events on weekends. Lessons in hang gliding and paragliding are offered along with a repair service, sales, swimming, and hiking.

**HEALTH CLUBS** **CCBA (Carter-Witherell Center)** (603-448-6477), 1 Taylor Street, Lebanon. Nonmembers can purchase day passes to use the facilities of this community health center: adults $8, children $4. Includes use of pool, whirlpool, and saunas; exercise and weight room; tennis and basketball courts; and child care. Call for hours.

**River Valley Club** (603-643-7720), Centerra Marketplace, Route 120, Lebanon. Open daily, 24 hours. Offers day spa services to nonmembers in its luxurious facility: massages, herbal wraps, facials, hydrotherapy, and more. Call for rates. Also included is same-day use of all facilities, including indoor and outdoor pools, whirlpool and sauna, exercise and weight room, fitness classes, and child care. A climbing wall, hair salon, and café lounge are also part of the complex.

**HIKING** **The Appalachian Trail** crosses the Connecticut River over the Ledyard Bridge and runs right through Hanover on its way to Mount Katahdin in Maine; note the marker embedded in the sidewalk in front of the Hanover Inn. Follow the white blazes down South Main Street to find where the trail reenters the woods just past the Hanover Food Coop.

CLAREMONT

Christina Tree

Short hikes in the Hanover area itself abound; a map of area trails is available from the Hanover Chamber of Commerce. Inquire locally or pick up the *Dartmouth Outing Guide*, published by the Dartmouth Outing Club. Suggested hikes include **Balch Hill Summit** north of town, the **Mink Brook Trail** off South Main Street, **Smarts Mountain** in Lyme, **Mount Cube** in Orford, and **Moose Mountain** (another section of the AT) in Etna. The westernmost peak in the White Mountains range, 4,802-foot-high Mount Moosilauke, is 50 miles north of Hanover, visible from much of the Upper Valley (see *To Do—Hiking* in "The Western Whites").

HORSEBACK RIDING **The Dartmouth Riding Center at Morton Farm** (603-646-3508) offers lessons.

OUTDOOR ADVENTURE **Dartmouth Outdoor Rentals** (603-646-1747), in the basement of Robinson Hall, on the Dartmouth green, Hanover. Open Monday through Friday, 12:30–5 PM. The country's oldest collegiate outing club rents a full line of outdoor equipment to the general public: mountain bikes and helmets, in-line skates, telemark and cross-country skis, snowshoes, rock climbing equipment, and a full line of camping gear. The scruffy, student-run rental office can be hard to reach, but keep trying.

STOCK-CAR RACING **Claremont Speedway** (603-543-3160), Bowker Street, 4 miles east of I-91, Claremont. May through September, racing Saturday 7:30 PM.

SWIMMING Ask locally about swimming holes in the Connecticut River and public swimming in Lake Mascoma.

**Canaan Street Lake** offers a small town beach on Canaan Street (see *Communities*).

**Storrs Pond Recreation Area** (603-643-2134), off Route 10 north of Hanover (Reservoir Road, then left). Open June through Labor Day, 10 AM–8 PM. Bathhouse with showers and lockers, lifeguards at both the (unheated) Olympic-sized pool, and 15-acre pond. Fee for nonmembers.

**Treasure Island** (802-333-9615), on Lake Fairlee, Thetford, Vermont. This fabulous town swimming area is on Route 244 (follow Route 113 north of town). Open late June through Labor Day, 10 AM–8 PM weekends, noon–8 PM weekdays. Sand beach, picnic tables, playground, tennis. Nominal admission.

**Union Village Dam Recreation Area** (802-649-1606), Thetford, Vermont. Open from Memorial Day through mid-September; five swimming areas along the Ompompanoosuc River. Also has walking and cross-country skiing trails, picnic tables, and grills.

**Lake Tarleton,** Piermont. See *Green Space*.

## ✱ Winter Sports

CROSS-COUNTRY SKIING **Occom Touring Center** (603-646-2440), Rope Ferry Road (off Route 10 just before the country club), Hanover. Closed Monday. Thirty-five km of trails through Storrs Pond and Oak Hill areas; rentals, lessons, waxing clinics. The center is on the lower level of the Outing Club House.

**Ascutney Mountain Resort** (802-484-7771; 1-800-243-0011), Route 44, Brownsville, Vermont. A touring center with instruction, rentals, 32 km of trails.

**Lake Morey Inn Resort** (802-333-4800; 1-800-423-1211), Fairlee, Vermont. Turns the golf course into a touring center in winter; rentals, instruction.

**Oliverian Valley Wildlife Preserve** (603-989-3351), Route 25, East Haverhill. A 2,000-acre preserve offers a total of 10 miles of trails, including a loop tour along the wooded slope of a hill (just off Route 25) with good views. You can also ski an old railroad bed in this area or ski 2.5 miles to the top of Iron Ore Mountain, with views of the valley and Mount Moosilauke. A warming hut halfway up is open on winter weekends. Camping available.

DOWNHILL SKIING **Ascutney Mountain Resort** (802-484-7771; 1-800-243-0011; www.ascutney.com), Route 44, Brownsville (I-91, Exit 8 or 9), Vermont. A family-geared, self-contained resort. Facilities include a 225-room hotel, a sports center with indoor and outdoor pools, weight and racquetball rooms, a full restaurant, and a base lodge. Owners Steve and Susan Plausteiner have increased snowmaking, added the North Peak Area, substantially increasing expert trails, served by a new mile-long quad chair. *Trails:* 56. *Lifts:* 1 quad, 3 triple chairs, 1 double chair. *Vertical drop:* 1,800 feet. *Snowmaking:* 95 percent. *For children:* Nursery/child care from 6 weeks. *Rates:* $44 adult midweek, $49 weekends and holidays; $21 juniors midweek, $38 on weekends. Sunday-morning and multiday tickets cut the price.

**Dartmouth Skiway** (603-795-2143), Lyme Center, an amenity for families as well as the college, with a snazzy new 16,000-square-foot base lodge. Open 9 AM–4 PM daily; rentals and ski school. *Trails:* 30. *Lifts:* 1 quad chair, 1 double chair, a beginners' J-bar. *Vertical drop:* 968 feet. *Snowmaking:* 54 percent. *Rates:* $34 adults, $21 juniors on weekends; $22 and $13 weekdays.

ICE SKATING **Occom Pond,** next to the country club, Hanover. Kept plowed and planed, lighted evenings until 10 unless unsafe for skating; warming hut.

**Ascutney Mountain Resort** (802-484-7771), Route 44, Brownsville, Vermont. Lighted skating rink with rental skates.

## ✷ Green Space

**Pine Park,** just north of the Dartmouth campus between the Hanover Country Club and the Connecticut River, Hanover. Take North Main Street to Rope Ferry Road and park at the trail sign above the clubhouse. These tall pines along the river are one of the beauty spots of the valley. The 125-year-old trees were saved from the Diamond Match Company in 1900 by a group of local citizens. The walk is 1.5 miles.

**Rinker Tract,** Route 10, 2.5 miles north of Hanover. This is an 18-acre knoll with a pond at the bottom of the hill below the Chieftain Motel. The loop trail is marked by blue blazes.

The city of Lebanon maintains several wooded parks for which trail maps are available from the recreation department, just inside the door of city hall (on the common). These include **Farnum Hill,** an 820-acre property with a ridge trail commanding some magnificent views. On the Connecticut River, **Chambers Park** (just off Route 10) offers trails through riverbank terrace, upland forest, and open field. The 286-acre **Boston Lot** lies between the river and the city reservoir, with trails good for hiking, biking, and cross-country skiing, and with picnic tables on the northern edge of the reservoir. **Goodwin Park,** adjoining Storrs Hill Ski Area, offers a 1.5-mile exercise trail.

**Moody Park,** Claremont. Pines, picnic benches, a summit view.

**Lake Tarleton,** Route 25C in Piermont, Warren, and Benton. More than 5,000 acres surrounding Lake Tarleton, smaller Lakes Katherine and Constance, and much of Lake Armington are now public land divided between White Mountain National Forest conservation trusts and a (currently evolving) state park featuring the sand beach on Lake Tarleton (part of a onetime resort). The property was slated for major development in 1994 when preservation forces, spearheaded by the Trust for Public Land, raised more than $7 million to preserve this magnificent woodland with its views of Mount Moosilauke. The lake is stocked with trout and also beautiful for canoeing and kayaking (public boat launch). Hiking trails are taking shape, including a connector to the Appalchian Trail, which passes through the property half a mile from the lake.

## ✷ Lodging

HOTEL 🐾 ✐ ♿ **The Hanover Inn** (603-643-4300; 1-800-443-7024; www.hanoverinn.com), Hanover 03755. This is the Ritz of the North Country. It overlooks the Dartmouth green and exudes a distinctly tweedy elegance. Guest rooms are each individually and deftly decorated, and the junior suites—with canopy beds, eiderdown quilts, armchairs, a silent valet, couch, and vanity—are pamperingly luxurious. A four-story, 92-room, neo-Georgian building owned and operated by Dartmouth College, the "inn" traces itself back to 1780 when the college's steward, Gen. Ebenezer Brewster, turned his home into a tavern. Brewster's son parlayed this enterprise into the Dartmouth Hotel, which continued to thrive until 1887, when it burned to the ground. The present building dates in part from this era but has lost its Victorian lines through successive renovations and expansions. It remains, however, the heart of Hanover. In summer the front terrace is crowded with faculty, visitors, and residents enjoying a light lunch or beer. Year-round the lobby, the porch rocking chairs, and the **Hayward Lounge** (a comfortable sitting room with clawfoot sofas and flowery armchairs, dignified portraits, and a frequently lit hearth) are popular spots for friends to meet. Roughly half the inn's guests are Dartmouth-related. Both **Zins Wine Bistro** and the more formal **Daniel Webster Room** (see *Dining Out*) draw patrons from throughout the Upper Valley. Rates range from $237 for a standard room to $297 for a junior suite, no charge for children under age 12; senior citizens' discount; honeymoon, ski, golf, and seasonal packages. Handicapped accessible and pets accepted.

**RESORTS** **Loch Lyme Lodge and Cottages** (603-795-2141; 1-800-423-2141; www.lochlyme.com), Route 10, 70 Orford Road, Lyme 03768. Main lodge open year-round; cabins, Memorial Day through Labor Day. There are four rooms in the inn and 22 brown-shingle cabins (11 with cooking facilities) spread along a wooded hillside overlooking the lake called Post Pond. The big attraction here is a private lakefront beach with a float and fleet of rowboats and canoes; also a Windsurfer. Two tennis courts, a baseball field, a basketball court, a volleyball net, and a recreation cabin are here for the using, and baby-sitting is available for parents who want time off. Lunch and dinner are served; a take-out lunch bar is open for sandwiches and cones. Loch Lyme was founded in 1917 and has been owned and managed by Paul and Judy Barker's family since the 1940s. No credit cards. Pets permitted in cabins. From $53 single to $96 double with breakfast. Housekeeping cabins are $550–800 per week. Children's rates.

**Ascutney Mountain Resort** (802-484-7711; 1-800-243-0011; www.ascutney.com), Route 44, Brownsville, Vermont 05037. A contemporary, 225-room wooden hotel and flanking condominiums at the base of Mount Ascutney. Accommodations range from standard hotel rooms to three-bedroom units with kitchen, fireplace, and deck, all nicely furnished with reproduction antiques. Facilities include the full-service **Harvest Inn Restaurant** and a sports center. In winter there are both alpine and cross-country trails (see *To Do—Skiing*); facilities include indoor and outdoor pools and an extensive summer adventure program for kids. Rooms $75–269 in summer and fall, more in winter; multiday packages.

**COUNTRY INNS** **Moose Mountain Lodge** (603-643-3529; www.moosemountainlodge.com), P.O. Box 272,

MOOSE MOUNTAIN LODGE IN ETNA

Kim Grant

Moose Mountain Highway, Etna 03750. Closed Monday and Tuesday, also November through December 25 and late March through mid-June. Just 7 miles from the Dartmouth green, the feel is remote, and the view, quite possibly the most spectacular of any inn in New England. The design is "classic lodge," built from stones and logs cleared from these hills, walled in pine. The roomy back porch (filled with flowers in summer) is like a balcony seat above the valley, commanding a view of Vermont mountains from Ascutney to Sugarbush, with Killington off across lower hills, center stage. This is also the view from the sitting room, with its window seats, baby grand piano, and massive stone fireplace. Upstairs the rooms are small but inviting (with spruce log bedsteads made by Kay Shumway herself), and the shared baths are immaculate. Kay is justly famed as a cook, and, increasingly, as a cookbook author. As she continues to prepare feasts for the groups of hikers (the inn is just off the Appalachian Trail), bikers, and cross-country skiers, her fare is evolving with many creative vegetarian dishes. Kay and Peter Shumway have been innkeepers here since 1975 and still welcome each new guest with enthusiasm and interest. The 350 acres include a deep pond, ample woods, meadows, and access to 50 miles of dependably snowy cross-country ski trails. $90 per person double occupancy MAP, $110 single; $55 children under age 14. No smoking.

**Juniper Hill Inn** (802-674-5273; 1-800-359-2541; www.juniperhillinn.com), 153 Pembroke Road, Windsor, Vermont 05069. This 28-room, turn-of-the-20th-century mansion, with a view of Mount Ascutney and the valley, has been beautifully renovated by Rob and Susanne Pearl. Teddy Roosevelt, we were told, once spent the night in the comfortable room we occupied, one of the two rooms set off in a quiet wing of the house, beyond a second living room (with TV) and above a classic "gentlemen's library" with leather chairs, an unusual hearth, plenty of books, and the only guest phone. Adults (and children over 12) can relax by the hearth in the huge main hall, in the parlors, and in a cozy library. Of the 16 guest rooms, 11 have working fireplaces. Inn guests gather for meals in the formal dining room, decorated in deep burgundy (served Tuesday through Saturday by reservation). A choice of four entrées is served by candlelight. Guests are welcome to use the inn's 18-speed bicycles to explore a mapped loop of the valley and are encouraged to canoe (**North Star Canoe Livery** is just across the covered bridge; see *To Do—Boating*). $90–180 per room, full breakfast included. Add 17.5 percent tax on meals and beverages.

ꝏ ♿ **Home Hill Country Inn** (603-675-6165; www.homehillinn.com), 703 River Road, Cornish 03745. This is one of those magnificent, four-square mansions spaced along the Connecticut River (see the introduction to this chapter); it sits at the end of a 3.5-mile road, surrounded by 25 acres. Innkeepers Victoria and Stephane de Roure have renovated all 12 guest rooms, adding three and creating a new dining room. All have private bath and some, a fireplace. The Maxfield Parrish suite in the main house, decorated in 17th-century French antiques, has a sitting room with fireplace. Rooms in the Carriage House feature French colors and fabrics. The

Shaker Inn

THE SHAKER INN AT THE GREAT STONE DWELLING, ENFIELD

grounds include a three-hole golf course, clay tennis court, a lap pool, and walking trails. The dining room is recognized as among the best in New Hampshire (see *Dining Out*). $150–325 per couple includes a continental breakfast. A seasonal cottage by the pool with a bedroom and sitting room is $235.

**Shaker Inn at the Great Stone Dwelling** (603-632-7810; 1-888-707-4257; www.theshakerinn.com), Lower Shaker Village, Route 4A, Enfield 03746. Renovated and opened as a 24-room inn and restaurant in 1997, this authentic Shaker four-and-a-half-floor granite "dwelling" was built in 1841 near Lake Mascoma. While it is not owned by the neighboring museum building (which it dwarfs), it has been meticulously restored by present owners Don Leavitt and Rick Miller. The 24 big old rooms, each with two or more Shaker-style double beds and their original built-in cabinets, now all have private bath. $105–155 double with one child free, then $15 per extra person.

**Alden Country Inn** (603-795-2222; 1-800-794-2296) on the common, Lyme 03768. Mickey Dowd offers a full dining area and 14 guest rooms on the top two floors. All have private bath, phones, and air-conditioning. There is little common space, however, because the downstairs is divided between a tavern and a dining room. This vintage-1809 tavern was long known as "The Lyme Inn." $95–155 includes tax and a full breakfast.

## BED & BREAKFASTS

### *South to north*

*Note:* See "Peterborough, Keene, and Surrounding Villages" for the **Walpole Inn** in Walpole.

**Maple Hedge** (603-826-5237; 1-800-9-MAPLE-9; www.maplehedge.com), Box 638, Charlestown 03603. Open year-round. Dick and Joan DeBrine came from California to fulfill Joan's longtime dream of running a New England B&B. This is a centrally air-conditioned beauty—a handsome, 1820s Main Street house, one in the line of old homes that form Charlestown's Main Street national historic district. Common space here includes an elegant double parlor with a hearth and a formal dining room. Each of the five guest rooms has a private bath and a theme. Our favorites are the Cobalt Room (dark mahogany twin beds with burgundy covers contrast nicely with the collection of cobalt blue glass) and the Butterfly Suite, with its iron queen-sized bed, floral wallpaper, hearth, and wicker; an adjoining single-bed room shares the big bathroom with a claw-foot tub. Joan's pride is her Buffalo Pottery collection. $100–135 includes a three-course breakfast (Dutch babies are a specialty). The garden is set up for croquet; for golf enthusiasts there is a sand trap and hole as well as a driving net. Joan is helpful about advising guests on what to do, and where to eat and shop.

**Goddard Mansion** (603-543-0603; 1-800-736-0603; www.goddard-mansion.com), 25 Hillstead Road, Claremont 03743. A grand, pillared and paneled, turn-of-the-20th-century mansion set on a knoll overlooking Mount Ascutney and tiers of smaller hills. Built in 1905 as a summer home by the president of International Shoe, it has an airy, easy elegance. Debbie Albee, with her late husband, Frank, spent two years restoring the house and decorating the 10 guest rooms. The living room has a 5½-foot fireplace, a baby grand piano, and a music system, and there's also a comfortable TV room, a splendid library (with a play corner for small children), and an attractive upstairs reading and writing room with a backgammon set on the window seat below the river view. The guest rooms vary from the traditional Bridal Suite, with its canopy bed, to the surreal third-floor Cloud Room; most have river views and three have private bath. A "natural breakfast" of homemade muffins with preserves made from homegrown fruit, fresh fruit, and whole-grain cereals is served in a formal, Tiffany-lit dining room that has some informal touches—like the completely restored 1939 Wurlitzer jukebox, complete with 78s, and the puzzle always in progress on the sideboard. Despite the grandeur of the house, small children are very welcome here (families have the run of the third floor), and babies are free if Debbie (a grandmother herself) gets a hug. Few hosts are as adept at making guests of all ages feel welcome. The rates are $75–125 depending on the room; $10 per child, $15 per extra adult. Smoke-free.

**Mary Keane House** (603-632-4241; 1-888-239-2153; www.marykeanehouse.com), Box 5, Lower Shaker Village, Enfield 03748. Built by La Salette benefactor Mary Keane in 1920, this is a sunny, spacious house overlooking Mascoma Lake. It has its own sandy beach as well as an expansive front porch from which to enjoy the view. The living room, which also overlooks the lake, has a fireplace, inviting places to sit and read, and a small self-service bar at which guests can pour themselves an early-morning coffee or keep cold drinks. The four rooms all have private bath, and two share an upstairs balcony overlooking the lake. A small, former chapel, complete with stained-glass windows and marble altar, offers a bit of uncommon common space. Sharon Carr is a warm and helpful host. $95–155; $10 for a third person in a room. Well-behaved pets accepted.

**Shaker Hill B&B** (603-632-4519; www.shakerhill.com), 259 Shaker Hill, Enfield 03748. This expanded 1793 house features a wraparound porch with a long valley view. The four rooms are decorated with taste; all have private bath, wide floorboards, and air-conditioning as well as computer access. A sitting room has a TV and is well stocked with games and books. The 24 acres, handy to Mascoma Lake, include gardens and ski/walking trails. $75–95 with a full breakfast and afternoon snacks. Innkeepers Nancy and Allen Smith are knowledgeable and helpful about the surrounding area.

**The Inn on Canaan Street** (603-523-7310), Canaan Street, Canaan 03741. This is the only place to stay on Canaan Street (see *Communities*), and it's a beauty. An early-19th-century house with five guest rooms, all with private bath, one with a canopy bed and working fireplace. Downstairs there are two parlors, both with fireplaces, and there is a piano. The breakfast room overlooks the garden, and a second-floor back porch commands the sweep of lawn and sunsets over Pico and Killington far to the west. A path leads through the woods to the lake and a view of Mount Cardigan beyond it. In all there are 14 acres. $85–110 for two includes afternoon tea as well as breakfast; a two-bedroom suite is $185. Louise Kremzner is an unusually warm and locally knowledgeable host, but at this writing the B&B is up for sale.

**The Trumbull House** (603-643-2370; 1-800-651-5141; www.trumbellhouse.com), 40 Etna Road, Hanover 03755. Four miles east of Dartmouth College, Hillary Pridgen offers four bright and spacious, tastefully decorated guest rooms in her gracious house. Amenities include private baths, down comforters, and cable TV and Internet access. The suite has a king-sized bed, a sitting area with TV/VCR, a trundle bed, and two baths, one with a Jacuzzi tub. $100–250 includes a full breakfast—guests choose from a menu that includes scrambled eggs with smoked salmon and a portobello mushroom and Brie omelet. The 16 country acres include a swimming pond, hiking trails, and cross-country ski trails. Guests enjoy access to the **River Valley Club** (see *To Do—Health Clubs*).

🏵 🐾 **Norwich Inn** (802-649-1143; www.norwichinn.com), 225 Main Street, Norwich, Vermont 05055. Just across the river from Hanover and less formal and expensive than the Hanover Inn, this is very much a gathering place for Dartmouth parents, faculty, and students. The present three-story, tower-topped inn dates from 1889 (when its predecessor burned). Since acquiring it in 1991, innkeepers Sally and Tim Wilson have steadily worked to restore its high Victorian look inside and out. The 27 rooms are divided among the main building, the Vestry, and a backyard motel. All rooms have private bath, telephone, and cable TV. Sally has redecorated with a sure touch, adding Victorian antiques but not cluttering either the guest or public rooms. A brew pub, **Jasper Murdock's Alehouse,** features 15 varieties of inn-made brew (see *Eating Out*). The dining rooms are open for breakfast, lunch, and dinner (see *Dining Out*). Rates run from $65 in the off-season in the motel to $149 for a two-bedroom suite in the Vestry. All three meals are served but not included.

Dogs are permitted in one twin-bedded room in the motel.

**Breakfast on the Connecticut** (603-353-4444; 1-888-353-4440; www.breakfastonthect.com), 651 River Road, Lyme 03768. This 1990s B&B is off on its own 23 wooded acres, right on the Connecticut River, with a private dock. Guest rooms are curiously designed, but some have whirlpool tubs, gas fireplaces, and skylights. They are divided between the main house and a 12-sided "barn," connected by an enclosed passageway, which also connects with a whirlpool tub in a gazebo. $95–195 per night includes breakfast.

ꝏ **Dowd's Country Inn** (603-795-4712; 1-800-482-4712), Lyme 03768. On Lyme's classic common, geared to groups and weddings. You'll find a large living room, a meeting space, a small dining room, a cheery breakfast room, and 23 guest rooms, including a row of upstairs rooms overlooking the spacious backyard. The presidential suite has a sitting room that can comfortably accommodate a family of five. Rooms $100 per night off-season; $145–175 in-season, double occupancy. includes breakfast and afternoon tea. Dinner by arrangement.

**White Goose Inn** (603-353-4812; 1-800-358-4267; www.whitegoosein.com), Route 10, P.O. Box 17, Orford 03777. The classic, four-chimney, green-shuttered 1766 brick house by the road is a beauty with 10 antiques-furnished guest rooms, from $85 (shared bath) to $135. Add 5 percent service charge. It's currently for sale. Guests can take advantage of **Peyton Place** (see *Dining Out*), now in the neighboring Federal-era tavern.

♿ **Piermont Inn** (603-272-4820), 1 Old Church Street, Piermont 03779. A 1790s stagecoach stop with six rooms, four in the adjacent carriage house (only the two in the inn are open year-round), all with private bath. The two in the main house are outstanding rooms, both carved from the tavern's original ballroom, high ceilinged and spacious, with writing desks and appropriate antiques. The carriage house rooms are simple but cheery; one is handicapped accessible. Common space includes a living room with a fireplace, TV, wing chairs, and a nifty grandfather clock. Breakfast is full but an extra $6 in summer (included in the winter rate). Charlie and Karen Brown are longtime Piermont residents who enjoy tuning guests in to the many ways of exploring this upper (less touristed) part of the Upper Valley, especially canoeing the river. Rooms in the main house are $95–110, $85 with breakfast in winter; in the carriage house, $60–75. Summer rates do not include breakfast. Lake Tarleton addition to the White Mountain National Forest (see *Green Space*) is nearby.

ꝏ 🐾 **The Gibson House** (603-989-3125; www.gibsonhousebb.com), R.R. 1, Box 193, Haverhill 03765. Artist Keita Colton has restored one of the Valley's finest Greek Revival homes, built in 1850 on the green in Haverhill Corners (see Haverhill under *Communities*) and at one point a stagecoach inn. The seven guest rooms, especially the four big second-floor rooms, are artistic creations, each very different from the next. Taj North is the most opulent and exotic with its faux balcony, rich colors, and glowing stained-glass moon. We enjoyed the golden, Asian-themed Bamboo Room, but our favorite is the Day at the Beach, with its quilts and colors (twin beds), overlooking the garden. While the house fronts on Route 10, the 50-foot-long sunny back porch with wicker seats and swing takes full advantage of the splendid view west across the terraced garden and the Connecticut River. The gardens are Colton's special passion. Her fanciful murals and pictures brighten the several common rooms, including a formal parlor and several dining rooms as well as a gallery. A full breakfast is served, weather permitting, on the first-floor screened porch. $150–250 (for the suite) includes breakfast, afternoon tea, wine and cheese.

## ✷ Where to Eat

**DINING OUT** **Peyton Place** (603-353-9100; www.peytonplacerestaurant.com), Route 10, Orford. Open for dinner Wednesday through Saturday 5:30–10:30 PM; Sunday brunch 10 AM–3 PM; closed Wednesday in winter. Reservations a must. A fixture for years across the river in Bradford, Vermont, this legendary restaurant (named for owners Jim, Heidi, Sophie, and Shamus Peyton) recently moved down the river a ways to a 1773 tavern. It includes a genuine old pub room (with a new pub menu) as well as more formal dining rooms. Dinner entrées might range from rack of lamb with wild mushrooms ($24; $46 for two) to vegetarian ravioli, handmade to order ($15). Ice creams and sorbets are handmade as well. Wine and spirits are served.

**Home Hill Country Inn** (603-675-6165), River Road, Plainfield. Open for dinner Wednesday through Sunday. A four-square 1820s mansion with a long, formal blue canopy proclaiming its formal dining status. The series of low-ceilinged dining rooms are dressed in white napery. A prix fixe of $37 for four courses reflects the French accent of chef-owners Victoria and Stephane de Roure. Victoria is actually English-born but has trained at the Ritz Escoffier in Paris. Stephane, from the south of France, who has owned patisseries in San Diego, carefully selects wine and oversees management of the restaurant. Dinner might include crisp duck leg confit, French bean salad, and assorted baby lettuces for starters, followed by a sorbet and then sautéed fresh Maine lobster with black truffles and champagne sauce. (Also see *Lodging—Country Inns.*)

**Hanover Inn** (603-643-4300; 1-800-443-7024), Dartmouth green, Hanover. **The Daniel Webster Room** is a large, formal dining room (open daily for all three meals), with terrace dining overlooking the Dartmouth green in summer. Executive chef Michael Gray has put this spot on New England's culinary map. Dinner might commence with baked oysters with fennel pesto or a country terrine with hearth-dried berry chutney. Entrées might include grilled venison leg with sweet potato, gnocchi, braised endive, and maple orange cream ($28) and rack and osso buco of lamb ($30), as well as grilled eggplant with roasted tomato coulis and gnocchi ($19). **Zins Wine Bistro** offers a wine-bar atmosphere and a moderately priced menu featuring pastas, flatbreads, burgers, and dinner plates ranging from salads to a grilled T-bone.

**Café Buon Gustaio** (603-643-5711), 72 South Main Street, Hanover. Lunch Tuesday through Friday, dinner Tuesday through Sunday 5:30–9:30 PM. Warm and welcoming to both fancy and funky folks. An intimate dining room with a menu that changes daily. Entrées might include serious pastas like black pepper pasta lasagna with lobster, broccoli, spinach, eggplant, and three cheeses served in roasted red pepper cream sauce, or grilled yellowfin tuna in blood-orange butter. It's possible to make a meal of appetizers like focaccia with tapenade and mussels. Many pastas are available in half size, and it's permissible to split portions. The wine list is extensive; a wide choice is available by the glass. The feeling is that of being well taken care of. Entrées $16–32.

**Three Tomatoes Trattoria** (603-448-1711), 1 Court Street, Lebanon. Open for lunch Monday through Friday 11:30 AM–2 PM, and nightly for dinner 5–9:30 PM. A trendy trattoria with a sleek decor, a wood-fired oven and grill, and a reasonably priced menu: plenty of pasta creations like penne con carciofi—sautéed mushrooms, spinach, roasted garlic, and olive oil tossed with penne ziti regate. There are also grilled dishes like pollo cacciatora alla gorgolia—boneless chicken topped with tomato basil sauce, mozzarella, and Romano cheese, and served with linguine, and no less than 16 very different pizzas from the wood-fired oven. Wine and beer are served. Entrées $14–20.

**Centerra Grill** (603-643-9227), 18 Centerra Parkway, Lebanon (off Route 120 between Lebanon and Hanover in a shopping, lodging, and dining complex). Open for lunch and dinner except Sunday. Contemporary American cuisine with an emphasis on fresh and local—and a French-Asian twist. Dinner entrées $12.95–21.95. Fish specials, daily specials, vegetarian dishes, a pub menu (fish, chips, burgers, and more).

**Norwich Inn** (802-649-1143), Main Street, Norwich. Open for breakfast, lunch, and dinner. Across the river from Hanover, the dining room in this classic inn is popular with Dartmouth faculty and local residents, good for vegetarian as well as wide variety of entrées ($15.95–19.95). **Jasper Murdock's Alehouse** (see *Eating Out*), also on the premises, is beloved for its handcrafted brews (sold only here) as well as for its atmosphere and pub food.

**Simon Pearce** (802-295-1470), The Mill, Quechee, Vermont. Open daily for lunch and dinner (reserve). Let's face it—this is the one place no visitor to the Upper Valley wants to miss. It's frequently crowded and touristy, but a special place with delicious food. Housed in a mill that once formed the centerpiece for a village, with views of the waterfall. The tableware features hand-blown, hand-finished glass designed and blown in the mill and sold in the adjoining gift shop (see *Selective Shopping*). At lunch try the shepherd's pie or coho salmon smoked here at the mill. Dinner entrées $18.50–34.50.

**The Shaker Inn at the Great Stone Dwelling** (603-632-7810; www.theshakerinn.com), 447 Route 4A, Enfield. Open daily year-round for breakfast, lunch, dinner; Sunday brunch 11 AM–2 PM. You have to wonder what former Shaker residents would have made of the bright, inviting pub that now fills a corner room or the menu in the original, now restored Shaker-style dining room. Here you might begin with baked shrimp and artichoke hearts or pan-fried meal crabcakes, then dine on roast rack of New Zealand venison ($24.95) as well as vegetable risotto flavored with Vermont cheddar, sweet cream, and Shaker herbs ($9.95). The wine list is extensive.

**Alden Country Inn** (603-795-2222; 1-800-794-2296), on the common, Lyme. Open for dinner nightly and for Sunday brunch. Ye olde New England tavern atmosphere with exposed beams, wood floors, and a fireplace. Entrées range from eggplant pirogue with tomato mushroom ragout and fettuccine ($16) to seared duck breast with orange glaze and whipped potatoes ($23).

## EATING OUT

*South to north*

**Charlestown Heritage Diner** (603-826-3110), 122 Main Street, Charlestown. Open daily 6 AM–2 PM except Sunday, when it's 8–11:30 AM, featuring a buffet. Also Friday night 4–8 PM for fresh seafood and beef specialties. This authentic 1920s Worcester diner is attached to an 1820s brick building that expands its space (there are two small dining rooms in the older building), offering a choice of atmospheres but the same blackboard menu. There's also a tavern upstairs—and the liquor license extends to the diner.

**Charlestown House of Pizza** (603-836-3700), Main Street, Charlestown. Open daily from 10:30 AM until 9 PM, Friday and Saturday until 10 PM. A cut above your usual pizza place, a variety of pastas, grinders, and a really good Greek salad.

**The Tumble-Inn Diner** (603-542-0074), Tremont Square next to the Moody Building, Claremont. Open 5:30 AM–2 PM. A genuine classic 1941 Worcester diner (#778), with blue tile, a counter, and booths, that has received a new lease on life from owner Debbie Carter. It's a local hangout: The bottomless cup of coffee is 75 cents, and the menu includes scrapple and corned beef hash. Fries are homemade. Admittedly the "turkey soup" we had here on our last visit tasted more like corned beef, but it hit the spot and the coffee was good.

**Windsor Station Restaurant** (802-674-2052), Depot Avenue, Windsor, Vermont. Open daily for lunch and dinner. Windsor's original railroad station is plusher than ever with gleaming woods and brass, velvet, and railroadiana. Lunch can be a burger, but the large dinner menu includes veal Oscar and prime rib; a children's menu is offered.

**Dan's Windsor Diner** (603-674-6555), 135 Main Street, Windsor. Open Sunday through Thursday 6 AM–2:30 PM; Friday and Saturday 6 AM–8 PM. Dan Kirby has spiffed up this 1952 classic Worcester diner, now famous up and down the river for its clam chowder. Specialties include meat loaf, liver and onions, and macaroni and cheese along with omelets, burger baskets, and pies.

**Shepherd's Pie Restaurant and Deli** (603-674-9390), 131 Main Street, Windsor. Open from 7 AM (Sunday from 8) for breakfast through lunch and dinner until 8 PM, closing Sunday at 3 PM. Every town should have a comfortable gathering spot like Sharon Shepherd's tangerine-walled storefront. The food is fine, judging from a generous chicken quesadilla one summer day and a rather unorthodox but tasty shepherd's pie on a chilly autumn evening. Specialties include soups, vegetarian dishes, and "Ralphies" (baked, breaded chicken breast, sliced and rolled into a tortilla with a choice of toppings). The deli is a sandwich source for picnicking on the river, the Mill Pond, or Lake Runnemede.

**Riverside Grill** (603-448-2571), Route 4 just off I-89 in Enfield. We finally sampled this place—with a sign that's visible from the interstate and a reputation that divides locals—and we like it. Things can get a bit greasy, but our chicken salad was great and the freshly squeezed lemonade alone is worth stopping for. It's been owned by the Laware family for 50 years, and the dining room with blue booths doesn't look like it's changed in the past 30.

**Lui, Lui** (603-298-7070), Powerhouse Mall, West Lebanon. Open daily for lunch and dinner until 9 or 10 PM. The former boiler house for the brick mill complex makes a multitiered, attractive setting for this popular, informal Italian restaurant. Pastas, salads, calzones, and specialty pizzas fill the bill of fare.

**The Seven Barrel Brewery** (603-298-5566), in the shopping center off the airport road, I-89, Exit 20. Open daily for lunch and dinner until midnight. A large, attractive brew pub with burgers and pub fare (mulligan stew, shepherd's pie, bangers and mash, and cock-a-leekie pie). Worth finding.

**West Lebanon fast-food strip,** Route 12A just south of I-89, Exit 20, is lined with representatives of every major fast-food chain in New England—a godsend to families with cars full of kids. Over the years our own carful has come to favor this Burger King, simply for its size and efficiency, but you may prefer McDonald's, Pizza Hut, Wendy's, Shorty's Mexican Roadhouse, or the Weathervane (reasonably priced seafood), among others.

**Four Aces Diner** (603-298-6827), 23 Bridge Street, West Lebanon. Open 5 AM–3 PM and 5–8 PM; Sunday 7 AM–3 PM. A classic Worcester diner is hidden beneath the unremarkable red-sided exterior. Good, reliable food, fountain drinks, and homemade pie served at booths with jukeboxes.

**Jesse's** (603-643-4111), Route 120, Hanover. Open for lunch and dinner daily, this steak and seafood tavern has long been a mainstay for Upper Valley diners. Daily fish and shellfish specials, three salad bars, burgers, and prime rib. The atmosphere varies from Victorian to Adirondack to Greenhouse but is comfortable for all ages throughout.

**Lou's Restaurant and Bakery** (603-643-3321), 30 South Main Street, Hanover. Open for breakfast weekdays from 6 AM, Saturday from 7, and Sunday from 8. Lunch Monday through Saturday until 3 PM. Since 1947 this has been a student and local hangout and it's great: a long Formica counter, tables and booths, fast, friendly service, good soups, sandwiches, and daily specials, and irresistible peanut butter cookies at the register.

**Murphy's on the Green** (603-643-4075), 11 South Main Street, Hanover. A traditional college rathskeller with a dark, pubby atmosphere and a wide-ranging beer list; burgers, soups, sandwiches, and more. Smoking is permitted in the bar/TV area; it can be crowded and noisy, but the food and service are reliable.

**Molly's** (603-643-2570), 43 Main Street, Hanover. Open daily for lunch and dinner. The greenhouse up front shelters a big, inviting bar that encourages single dining. The menu is immense and reasonably priced: big salads, enchiladas, elaborate burgers at lunch, pasta to steak at dinner.

**Mai Thai** (603-643-9980), 40 South Main Street, Hanover. Open Monday through Saturday for lunch 11:30 AM–3 PM; for dinner Monday through Thursday 5–10 PM, until 11 PM on Friday and Saturday. Traditional Thai cuisine in a pleasant atmosphere.

**Panda House** (603-643-1290), 3 Lebanon Street, Hanover. Open daily for lunch and dinner. Good Szechuan, Mandarin, Cantonese, and some Japanese dishes, plus a sushi bar.

**Rosey's Coffee and Tea** (603-643-5282), 15 Lebanon Street, Hanover. Open weekdays 7:30 AM–6 PM, from 8:30 AM Saturday; Sunday 10 AM–5 PM. This stylish café downstairs from Rosey Jeke's clothing store offers great coffee, baked goods, gourmet sandwiches, desserts, and a pleasant place to linger. A bit pricey, but good.

**Jasper Murdock's Alehouse** in the Norwich Inn (802-649-1143), Main Street, Norwich, Vermont. Open 5:30–9 PM daily. The house brew comes in 15 varieties; we favor the Whistling Pig Red Ale. A comfortable, green-walled room popular with locals, the Alehouse serves a pub menu that includes Maine crabcakes and shepherd's pie.

**The Third Rail** (802-333-9797), Route 5, Fairlee, Vermont. Open except Sunday for lunch and dinner; reservations advisable for dinner in summer. This is a roadside house with a friendly pub and several small, cheerful and informal dining rooms, under new ownership. Appetizers include "rail rolls" (blackened chicken, mushrooms, onions, and Brie wrapped in a flour tortilla and deep-fried); entrées range from vegetable strudel and roasted vegetable lasagna to pork spareribs and hand-cut grilled rib eye; they run $8.75–14.95.

**Fairlee Diner** (802-333-3569), Route 5, Fairlee. Closed Tuesday, otherwise 5:30 AM–2 PM; until 7 PM Thursday and 8 PM Friday. Turn left (north) on Route 5 if you are coming off I-91. This is a classic wooden diner built in the 1930s (across the road from where it stands), with wooden booths, worn-shiny wooden stool tops, and good food. The mashed potato doughnuts are special, and both the soup and the pie are dependably good. Daily specials.

**Colatina Exit** (802-222-9008), Main Street, Bradford, Vermont. Open daily for dinner. Casual but candlelit atmosphere (checked tablecloths, pictures of Italy), affordable wines, a great antipasto, homemade pastas, fresh seafood, poultry, and vegetarian dishes.

**P&H Truck Stop** (802-429-2141), just off I-91 Exit 17 on Route 302, Wells River, Vermont. Open 24 hours. Dozens of rigs are usually parked outside on one side, and the range of license plates on cars in the other lot is usually quite amazing. This is a classic truck stop with speedy service, friendly waitresses, and heaping portions at amazing prices.

**Central West Restaurant** (603-747-8240), 23 Central Street, Woodsville. Open for lunch 11:30 AM–3 PM and dinner, 5–9 PM. Kirk Yeaton's middle-of-town oasis features deep booths and from-scratch soups, salads with local greens. We lunched well on marinated chicken over salad, but burgers and sandwiches are also big here. A dozen dinner choices might include shrimp scampi in olive oil and garlic butter over pasta (specify garlic strength) and veal Marsala as well as liver with onions and bacon. Dinner entrées $6.95–14.95.

**New Century** (603-747-2368), 85 Central Street, Woodsville. Open daily for lunch through dinner. Locals tells us that this new Chinese (Mandarin,

Szechuan, and Cantonese) restaurant is a standout. Service is fast, prices are reasonable, and we like the look of the menu.

## ✷ Entertainment

MUSIC AND THEATER **Claremont Opera House** (603-542-4433), Tremont Square, in the city hall, Claremont. Recently restored gilded-era theater, the scene of frequent concerts, plays, and live performances of all kinds.

**Hopkins Center** (box office: 603-646-2422; www.hop.Dartmouth.edu), on the Dartmouth green, Hanover. Sponsors some 150 musical and 20 theater productions per year, plus 200 films, all open to the public.

**Lebanon Opera House** (603-448-2498), in town hall, Coburn Park. An 800-seat, turn-of-the-20th-century theater hosts frequent concerts, lectures, and summer performances by the North Country Community Players.

**Northern Stage** (802-291-9009; www.northernstage.org), Briggs Opera House, White River Junction, Vermont. Semiprofessional community theater offers high-quality productions year-round. Special children's theater classes and summer arts education classes.

**Opera North** (603-643-1946), Lebanon Opera House in August and elsewhere in the Upper Valley at other times of the year. Excellent, semiprofessional performances feature visiting soloists from major opera companies.

**Upper Valley Community Band** (603-448-9876). With many teachers among its members, the UVCB sets high standards, performing at the Lebanon Opera House and throughout the Upper Valley.

FILM **Fairlee Drive-In** (802-333-9192), Route 5, Fairlee, Vermont. Summer only; check local papers for listings.

**Dartmouth Film Society at the Hopkins Center** (603-646-2576). Frequent showings of classic, contemporary, and experimental films in two theaters.

**Nugget Theaters** (603-643-2769), South Main Strret, Hanover. Four current films nightly, surround sound.

**Sony Cinema** (603-448-6660), Lebanon. Six first-run films nightly.

## ✷ Selective Shopping

ANTIQUES Claremont has become an antiques center in recent years as empty stores along Pleasant Street have filled with dealers. **Scottish Bear's Antiques** (603-548-1978), 54 Pleasant Street, specializes in pre-1930s northern New England country furniture and paintings. **The Wing and the Wheel Antiques** (603-542-8420), 50 Pleasant Street, specializes in 19th-century furniture, china, and accessories. **Aumand's Junk-Tiques** (603-543-3808) offers a mix of everything from substantial furniture to odds and ends from Valley homes and attics.

**Colonial Antique Markets** (603-298-8132; 603-298-7712), Colonial Plaza, Route 12A, West Lebanon. Open 9 AM–5 PM daily, year-round. This looks like nothing from the outside because it's all basement level: 60 dealers with art, antiques, collectibles, jewelry, clothing, books, tools, and fun old stuff. It's easy to find once you know it's there: Exit 20 off I-89 and follow signs for the airport (it's next to the highway); as soon as you turn onto Airport Road, take a quick left into Colonial Plaza. The unpromising entrance is around the corner of the brick building on your left, across from the Seven Barrel Brewery.

**Quechee Gorge Antiques Mall** (802-295-1550), Route 4 in Quechee, Vermont, with 450 dealers, offers the largest selection on the Vermont side of the river.

**William Smith** (603-675-2549) holds antiques auctions at the Plainfield Auction Gallery, Route 12A in Plainfield, year-round.

ART GALLERIES AND CRAFTS CENTERS **AVA Gallery** (603-448-3117), 11 Bank Street (Route 4 just west of Coburn Park), Lebanon. Open Tuesday through Saturday 11 AM–5 PM. From its Hanover beginnings, the Alliance for the Visual Arts has grown to fill a sunny, former mill building. The Soho-style (and -quality) gallery mounts frequent exhibits of arts and crafts. Classes and workshops are also offered.

**Dana Robes—Wood Craftsmen, Inc.** (603-632-5385), Lower Shaker Village, Route 4A, Enfield. Showroom open weekdays 9 AM–5 PM, Sunday 10 AM–5 PM. Meticulously crafted, traditional, Shaker-design furniture, each piece signed by the craftsman who created it. Products, made on the premises, range from cherry oval boxes, trays, and towel racks to custom-designed cupboards, tables, armoires, and beds.

**League of New Hampshire Craftsmen** (603-643-5050), 13 Lebanon Street, Hanover. Closed Sunday. Next to Ben & Jerry's; a wide selection of local and regional crafts pieces.

**Long River Studios** (603-795-4909), 1 Lyme Common, Lyme. Next to the post office. Regional crafts cooperative. Nice selection.

**Simon Pearce Glass** (802-674-6280), Route 5 north of Windsor, Vermont. Open daily 9 AM–5 PM. Pearce operated his own glassworks in Ireland before moving to Vermont in 1981. Here he acquired the venerable Downer's Mill in Quechee and harnessed the dam's hydropower for the glass furnace (see *Dining Out*). In 1993 he opened this new, visitor-friendly glass factory featuring a catwalk that overlooks the gallery where glass is blown and shaped. Of course, there's a big showroom/shop featuring seconds as well as first-quality glass and pottery. There's also a small showroom in the lobby of the Hanover Inn, on Main Street in Hanover.

BOOKSTORES **Dartmouth Bookstore** (603-643-3616; 1-800-624-8800), 33 South Main Street, Hanover. Open Monday through Saturday. One of the largest bookstores in northern New England, in owner Phoebe Storrs Stebbins's family since 1884 and currently managed by her son-in-law, David Cioffi. Supplier of textbooks to the college and its graduate schools; also to local community colleges. The store stocks 130,000 different titles including medical, technical, literary criticism, and history; also general-interest titles, music, and computer and office supplies.

✐ **The Norwich Bookstore** (802-649-1114), Main Street, Norwich, Vermont, next to the post offiice. This is a light, airy store with well-selected titles and comfortable places to sit. The staff is very knowledgeable. Frequent readings, and a wonderful children's section.

**Borders Books Music & Café** (603-298-9963), Wal-Mart Plaza, West Lebanon.

**Your Idea** (603-448-0123), 160 Mechanic Street, Lebanon, is a bookstore featuring how-to and regional titles, autographed books, and a complete set of regional topographic maps. Open Monday through Saturday and most Sundays.

**Woodsville Bookstore** (603-747-3811), Main Street (Route 302), Woodsville. Dave Major's friendly, well-stocked bookstore is an unexpected find here. One room of new, one of used books.

SPECIAL SHOPPING CENTERS **Centerra Marketplace,** Route 120, Lebanon. Anchored by the co-op grocery store, this consciously upscale new complex also features a trendy restaurant (see **Centerra Grill** in *Dining Out*), a health club (see *To Do—Health Clubs*), and shops offering kitchenwares and children's clothing.

**Powerhouse Mall,** Route 10, West Lebanon. Open Monday through Friday 10 AM–9 PM; Saturday 10 AM–6 PM; Sunday noon–5 PM. A total of 40 stores are in this unusual complex, which combines an old brick electric powerhouse, a large, new but mill-style, two-story arcade, and several older buildings moved from other places, all offering a genuine variety of small specialty stores. Anchored by **Eastern Mountain Sports** (603-298-8699) featuring sporting gear, other noteworthy shops include the **Anichini Outlet Store** (603-298-8656; www.anichini.com) featuring the Tunbridge, Vermont–based company's line of antique and fine linens at substantial savings; and a surprising choice of women's clothing stores.

SPECIAL SHOPS **18th Century Shop** (603-543-0100), 1 Pleasant Street, Claremont. In a sizable shop on the corner of Tremont Square, Dennis and Sheila Belanger have created period rooms, furnished entirely with 18th-century-style reproductions: chandeliers, floor screens, mirrors, bowls, and other appropriate furnishings for "colonial" homes, including their own handmade 17th- and 18th-century floorcloths and oils.

**Enfield Granite Company** (603-523-8204), Route 4, Canaan. Monday through Saturday 9 AM–5 PM. Sure, you can buy a monument here, but you can also find a granite countertop, planter, coffee table top, clock, bookend, or candleholder.

**Dartmouth Co-op** (603-643-3100), 25 South Main Street, Hanover. Incorporated in 1919 and now owned by Dartmouth alumni, a source of sports clothes and of course an extensive line of Dartmouthiana: T-shirts, sweats, boxers, mugs, cushions.

**King Arthur Flour Baker's Store** (802-649-3361; www.kingarthurflour.com), Route 5, Norwich, Vermont. Home as well as prime outlet for the country's oldest family-owned flour company (since 1790), this store draws serious bakers and would-be bakers from throughout several time zones. The vast post-and-beam building itself is a marvel, its shelves stocked with every conceivable kind of flour, baking ingredient, and a selection of equipment and cookbooks, not to mention bread and pastries made in the adjacent bakery (with a glass connector allowing visitors to watch the hands and skills of the bakers). Next door too is the new Baking Education Center, offering baking classes ranging from beginner to expert, from making piecrust to braided breads and elegant pastries.

**Dan & Whit's General Store** (802-649-1602) Main Street, Norwich, Vermont. This quintessential Vermont country store justifies a trip across the river. Hardware, groceries, housewares, boots and clothing, farm and garden supplies, and a great community bulletin board: If they don't have it, you don't need it.

**Vermont Salvage Exchange** (802-295-7616), Railroad Row, White River Junction, Vermont. Doors, chandeliers, moldings, mantels, old bricks, and other architectural relics.

**Pompanoosuc Mills** (802-785-4851; www.pompy.com), Route 5, East Thetford, Vermont. Dartmouth graduate Dwight Sargeant began building furniture in this riverside house, a cottage industry that has evolved into a riverside factory with showrooms throughout New England. Some seconds. Open daily until 6 PM, Sunday noon–5 PM. Note the branch on Lebanon Street in Hanover.

**Copeland Furniture** (802-222-5300; www.copelandfurniture.com), 64 Main Street, Bradford, Vermont. Open Monday through Friday 10 AM–6 PM, Saturday 9 AM–5 PM. Contemporary, cleanly lined, locally made furniture in native hardwoods displayed in the handsome showroom in the converted 19th-century brick mill across from Bradford Falls. Seconds.

**Farm-Way, Inc.** (1-800-222-9316), Route 25, Bradford, Vermont. One mile east of I-91, Exit 16. Open Monday through Saturday until 8 PM. Billed as "complete outfitters for man and beast," this is a phenomenon: a family-run source of work boots and rugged clothing that now includes a stock of more than 2 million products spread over 5 acres: tack, furniture, pet supplies, syrup, whatever. Shoes and boots remain a specialty, from size 4E to 16; 10,000 shoes, boots, clogs, sandals, and sneakers in stock.

**Round Barn Shoppe** (603-272-9026), 430 Route 10, Piermont. Open May 2 through Christmas, Thursday through Monday 9 AM–5 PM; January through May 1, Friday through Sunday. This 1990s post-and-beam round barn replicates the authentic building across the road. It houses a shop selling New England products ranging from baskets and dolls to local dairy milk and fresh pies. Some 300 New England craftsmen and 100 small manufacturers are represented.

FOOD AND FARMS **Beaver Pond Farm** (603-542-7339; 1-800-750-1974), 50 McDonough Road, Claremont. Maple syrup and homemade jams and jellies are available at the farm stand on Route 11 or up at the farmhouse; they will ship anywhere.

**North Country Smokehouse** (603-543-3016; 1-800-258-4303), Claremont. Follow signs for the airport; it's across the way on a site established by Mike Satzow's grandfather in 1917. Delis throughout the Northeast carry North Country meats: hams, turkey, bacon, smoked goose and Peking duck, sausages, and more. Inquire about the catalog.

***In Plainfield on River Road***

**Edgewater Farm** (603-298-5764) offers pick-your-own strawberries and raspberries; there are also greenhouses with bedding plants, and a farm stand on Route 12A. Also on River Road, **Riverview Farms** (603-298-8519) offers apples, pumpkins, and cider pressing and hayrides in fall. **McNamara Dairy** (603-298-MOOO) sells its own glass bottled milk and eggnog.

**MAPLE SUGARING** From mid-February through early April the following local sugarhouses welcome visitors to watch them "boil off" and sample the new syrup. Most also sell their own syrup year-round. **Brokenridge Farm** (603-542-8781), Route 120, Cornish. Sap is gathered with horses on weekends; sugar-on-snow, tours.

Orford has the biggest local concentration of maple-syruping operations, including: **Gerald and Toni Pease** (603-353-9070), Pease's Scenic Highway, off Route 25A. Draft horse with wagon or sleigh. Gale and Peter Thompson (son of a former governor) operate a traditional sugarhouse and serves pancake breakfasts at **Mount Cube Farm** (603-353-4709), Route 25A. There's also **Sunday Mountain Maple Products** (603-353-4883), Route 25A.

## ✱ Special Events

For details about any of these events, phone the town clerk, listed with information.

*Mid-February:* **Dartmouth Winter Carnival,** Hanover. Thursday through Sunday. Ice sculptures, sports events, ski jumping.

*Early March:* **Meriden Wild Game Dinner,** Kimball Union Academy's Miller Student Center. Usually a Saturday. At this benefit for the Meriden Volunteer Fire Department, bear, raccoon, and boar are usually on the menu.

*Mid-May:* **Dartmouth Pow-Wow,** Hanover. A gathering of Native American craftspeople and dancers on the second Saturday of May; sponsored by Native Americans at Dartmouth (603-646-2110) and the Native American Studies Program (603-646-3530).

*Memorial Day:* **Muster Day,** Hanover Center. Recitation of the Gettysburg Address and Dr. Seuss prayer by children of the third grade on the site of Hanover's pre-Revolutionary musters.

*Mid-June:* **Bradford–Thetford Lions Club Fair,** Route 5, 1 mile north of the Orford–Fairlee bridge. Carnival rides, ox pulling, demolition derby, fiddlers' contest.

*Third weekend in June:* **Quechee Balloon Festival and Crafts Fair** (802-295-7900), Quechee, Vermont. Some 20 hot-air balloons gather, offering rides at dawn and dusk; barbecue, skydiving, crafts, food booths. **Summer Strawberry Festival,** Plainfield Historical Society Clubhouse, Route 12A, Plainfield. **Lyme Summer Suppers and Horse Sheds Crafts Festivals,** Lyme Congregational Church horse sheds, Lyme. Begin the last Wednesday in June, then every other week for four Wednesdays. The crafts festivals begin at 1 PM and the suppers, also at the church, begin at 6 PM.

*Fourth of July:* **Independence Day Open Fields Circus,** Thetford, Vermont. A takeoff on a real circus by the Parish Players. **Fourth of July celebration,** Plainfield. Community breakfast, footraces, parade, firemen's roast beef dinner. Lebanon stages the largest fireworks display in the area.

*Mid-July:* **Hanover Street Fest** (603-643-3115), Hanover. Street bazaar, hay-wagon rides, fireworks, entertainment. **Norwich (Vermont) Fair.** Mix of old-time country fair and honky-tonk carnival. Lobster dinner, parade, ox pulling. **Charlestown Yard Sale Day.** From 8 AM on the third Saturday; more than 150 yard sales in town, church breakfasts.

*Late July:* **Hanover Center Fair,** Hanover. Friday-night games, dancing, food; Saturday starts with a children's costume parade, ox pulling, food, games. **Connecticut Valley Fair,** Bradford, Vermont. Ox and horse pulling, sheep show, midway, demolition derby. **La Salette Fair** (603-632-4301), at the La Salette Shrine, Route 4A, Enfield. Usually a midway with rides, flea market, crafts booths. **Cracker-Barrel Bazaar,** Newbury, Vermont. Big old-time fiddlers' contest, antiques show, quilt show, sheepdog trials, church suppers.

*Early August:* **Canaan Old Home Day,** Canaan. Dances, parade, booths, suppers. **North Haverhill Fair.** Horse show and pulling, evening live entertainment, midway. **Thetford Hill Fair,** Thetford Hill, Vermont. Small but special: a rummage sale, food and plant booths, barbecue.

*Mid-August:* **Cornish Fair.** Horse and ox pulling, agricultural exhibits, ham and bean suppers, a Saturday woodsmen's field day.

*Late August:* **Quechee Scottish Festival,** Quechee, Vermont. Sheepdog trials, Highland dancing, piping, Highland "games," ladies' rolling-pin toss, more.

*Mid-October:* **Horse Sheds Crafts Fair,** at the Lyme Congregational Church, Lyme. Saturday of Columbus Day weekend 10 AM–4 PM; also a **Fall Festival** lunch at the church.

*Late November:* **Bradford United Church of Christ Wild Game Supper,** Bradford, Vermont. The Saturday before Thanksgiving this town nearly doubles its population as hungry visitors pour into the church to feast on 2,800 pounds of buffalo, venison, moose, pheasant, coon, rabbit, wild boar, and bear.

*Mid-December through Christmas:* **Christmas Pageants** in Norwich and Lyme. **Revels North,** in the Hopkins Center. Song and dance. **Christmas Illuminations,** at the La Salette Shrine, Route 4A, Enfield.

# The White Mountains

WHITE MOUNTAIN NATIONAL FOREST

THE WESTERN WHITES

MOUNT WASHINGTON AND ITS VALLEYS

Robert Kozlow

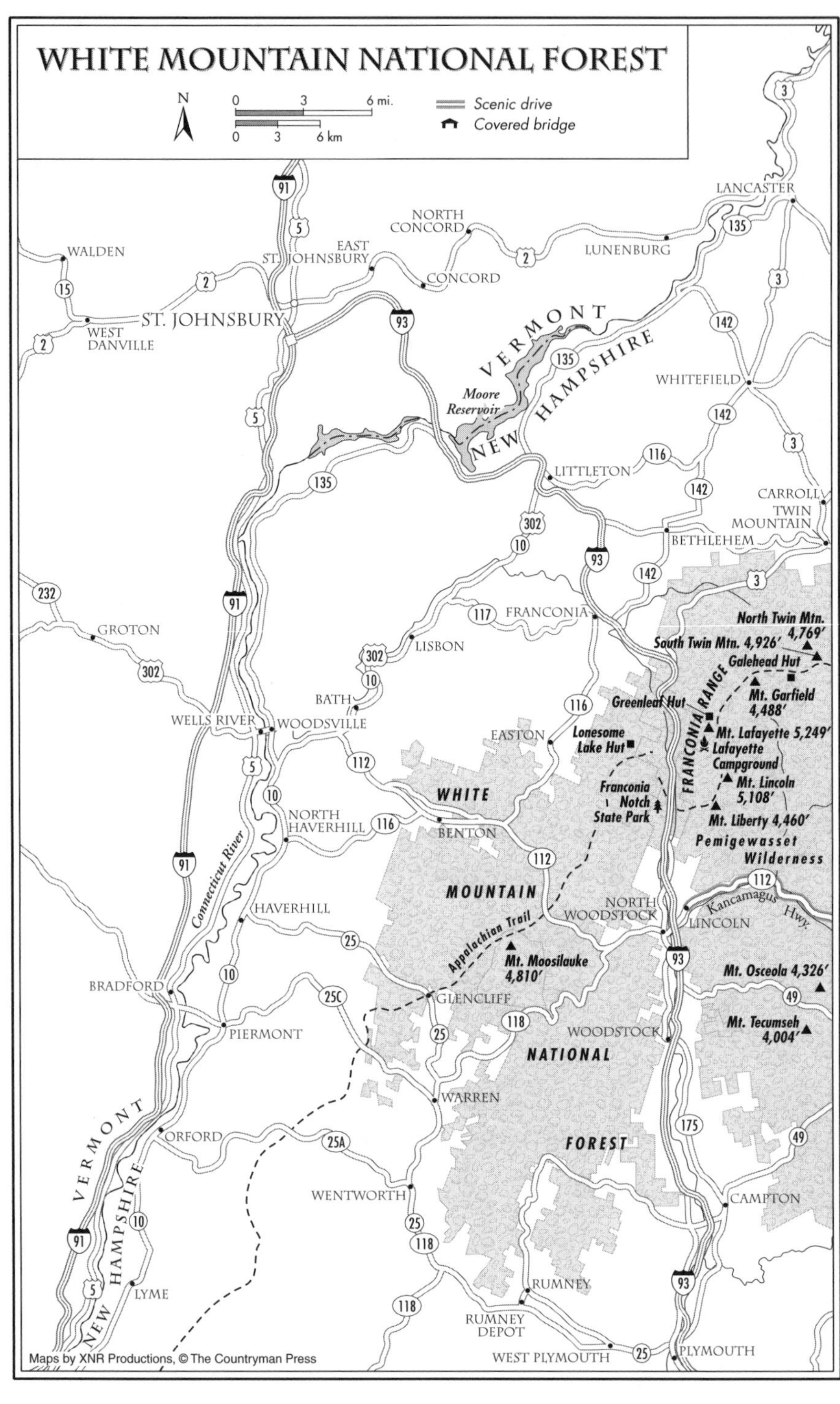

WHITE MOUNTAIN NATIONAL FOREST
N
0 3 6 mi.
0 3 6 km
Scenic drive
Covered bridge
WALDEN
WEST DANVILLE
ST. JOHNSBURY
ST. JOHNSBURY
EAST ST. JOHNSBURY
NORTH CONCORD
CONCORD
LUNENBURG
LANCASTER
VERMONT
NEW HAMPSHIRE
Moore Reservoir
WHITEFIELD
LITTLETON
CARROLL
TWIN MOUNTAIN
BETHLEHEM
GROTON
FRANCONIA
LISBON
BATH
WELLS RIVER
WOODSVILLE
EASTON
North Twin Mtn. 4,769′
South Twin Mtn. 4,926′
Galehead Hut
Greenleaf Hut
FRANCONIA RANGE
Mt. Garfield 4,488′
Mt. Lafayette 5,249′
Lonesome Lake Hut
Lafayette Campground
Franconia Notch State Park
Mt. Lincoln 5,108′
Mt. Liberty 4,460′
Pemigewasset Wilderness
WHITE
MOUNTAIN
NATIONAL
FOREST
NORTH HAVERHILL
BENTON
Connecticut River
HAVERHILL
NORTH WOODSTOCK
LINCOLN
Kancamagus Hwy.
Appalachian Trail
Mt. Moosilauke 4,810′
Mt. Osceola 4,326′
Mt. Tecumseh 4,004′
BRADFORD
GLENCLIFF
PIERMONT
WOODSTOCK
WARREN
ORFORD
WENTWORTH
CAMPTON
LYME
RUMNEY
RUMNEY DEPOT
WEST PLYMOUTH
PLYMOUTH
Maps by XNR Productions, © The Countryman Press

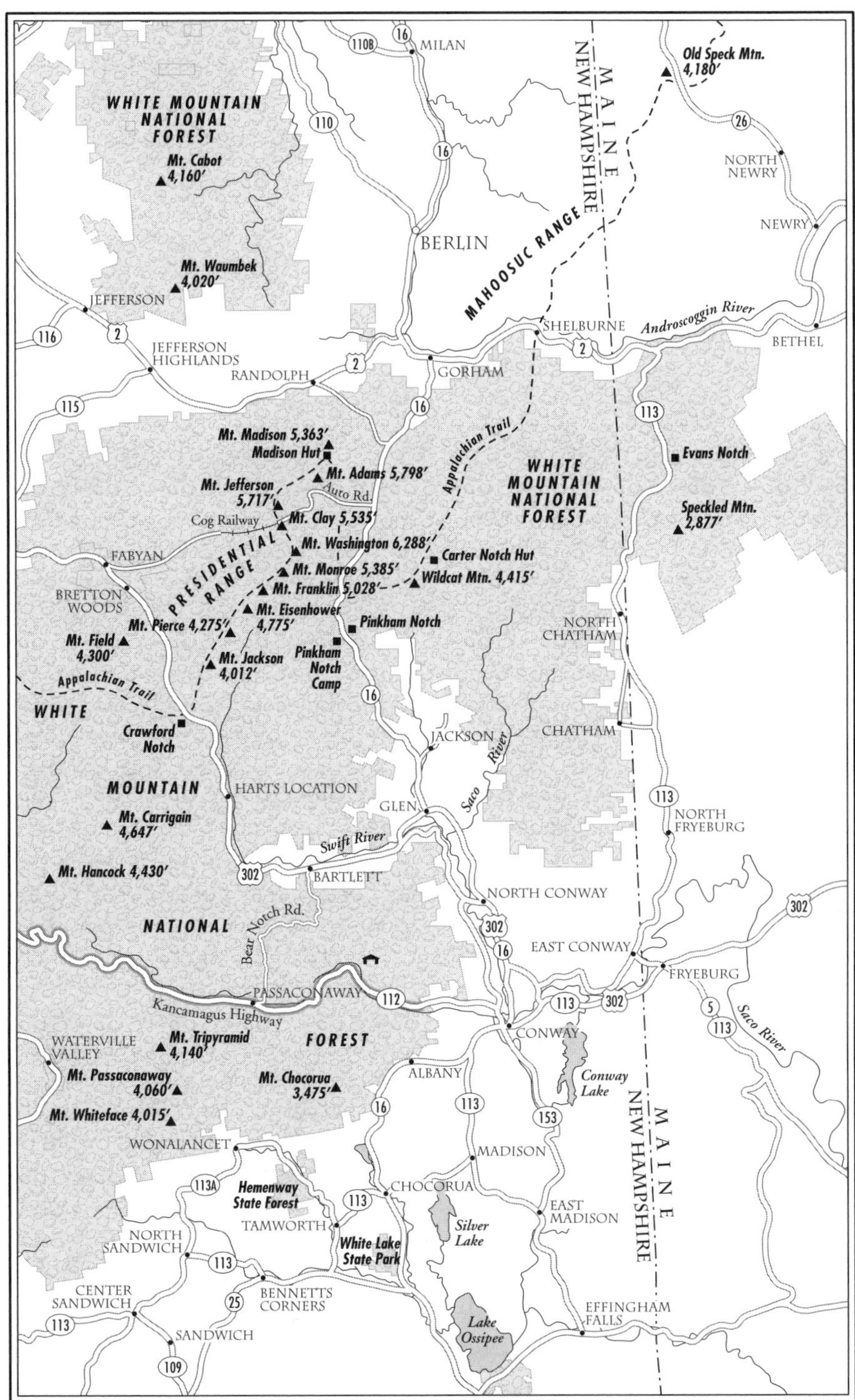

WHITE MOUNTAIN NATIONAL FOREST
Mt. Cabot 4,160′
Mt. Waumbek 4,020′
MILAN
BERLIN
MAHOOSUC RANGE
MAINE
NEW HAMPSHIRE
Old Speck Mtn. 4,180′
NORTH NEWRY
NEWRY
JEFFERSON
JEFFERSON HIGHLANDS
RANDOLPH
GORHAM
SHELBURNE
Androscoggin River
BETHEL
Mt. Madison 5,363′
Madison Hut
Mt. Adams 5,798′
Mt. Jefferson 5,717′
Auto Rd.
Cog Railway
Mt. Clay 5,535′
Mt. Washington 6,288′
Appalachian Trail
WHITE MOUNTAIN NATIONAL FOREST
Evans Notch
Speckled Mtn. 2,877′
Carter Notch Hut
Wildcat Mtn. 4,415′
Mt. Monroe 5,385′
Mt. Franklin 5,028′
Mt. Eisenhower 4,775′
PRESIDENTIAL RANGE
FABYAN
BRETTON WOODS
Mt. Pierce 4,275′
Mt. Field 4,300′
Mt. Jackson 4,012′
Pinkham Notch
Pinkham Notch Camp
NORTH CHATHAM
CHATHAM
Appalachian Trail
WHITE
Crawford Notch
JACKSON
Saco River
MOUNTAIN
HARTS LOCATION
GLEN
Mt. Carrigain 4,647′
NORTH FRYEBURG
Swift River
Mt. Hancock 4,430′
BARTLETT
NORTH CONWAY
NATIONAL
Bear Notch Rd.
EAST CONWAY
FRYEBURG
PASSACONAWAY
Kancamagus Highway
CONWAY
Saco River
WATERVILLE VALLEY
Mt. Tripyramid 4,140′
FOREST
Mt. Passaconaway 4,060′
Mt. Chocorua 3,475′
ALBANY
Conway Lake
Mt. Whiteface 4,015′
WONALANCET
MADISON
Hemenway State Forest
CHOCORUA
EAST MADISON
TAMWORTH
Silver Lake
NORTH SANDWICH
White Lake State Park
CENTER SANDWICH
BENNETTS CORNERS
EFFINGHAM FALLS
Lake Ossipee
SANDWICH
16
110B
110
26
2
116
115
113
302
112
5
153
113A
25
109

# WHITE MOUNTAIN NATIONAL FOREST

The 768,000-acre White Mountain National Forest (WMNF), the largest in the East, was created by the Weeks Act of 1911. Millions of board feet of timber were cut from these mountains in the 19th century, and a portion of the Kancamagus Scenic Byway and the Wilderness Trail were the routes of logging railroads, part of an extensive rail system built by the timber companies to harvest the dense stands of mountain trees. The clear-cutting techniques employed by the timber cutters left the steep mountain slopes denuded, leading to massive erosion and downstream flooding. The limbs and branches left behind in the woods quickly dried and fueled huge forest fires that threatened the uncut areas. It was to curtail the clear-cutting, reduce the danger of forest fires, provide for reforestation of the mountains, and prevent erosion and flooding that the national forest was created.

A ride across the Kancamagus Scenic Byway provides clear evidence of the success of the forest plan. Despite heavy use by visitors, most of the WMNF is again a wilderness. Although the U.S. Forest Service continues to harvest timber in this huge woodland, the WMNF is also managed for multiple-use activities: hiking, camping, swimming, fishing, nature study, forest research, and scenic beauty. Protection of watersheds and endangered species of plants, insects, and animals also figures into the operation of this forest. So varied is the forest, from lowland bogs to high alpine mountains, so interesting is its history, from Native Americans to settlers, loggers to scientists, that a whole guide could be written about this wild country.

The WMNF has several self-guided nature trails, is responsible for many miles of backcountry trails, and operates a number of barrier-free day-use facilities and campgrounds. Four congressionally designated wilderness areas within the forest are managed to preserve a wilderness experience. Here no timber cutting is permitted; bicycles and motorized vehicles (snowmobiles or trail bikes) are prohibited; and campsites are limited to 10 people or fewer. In addition to varied WMNF publications, the best guide to the area is the *AMC White Mountain Guide,* the hiker's 600-page handbook of trail details and also some human and natural history information.

**GUIDANCE** **WMNF headquarters** (603-528-8721; www.fs.fed.us/r9/white/), Box 638, 719 Main Street, Laconia 03247. Contact them, especially in the off-season, for details of campgrounds, fishing, hiking, or other activities.

**WMNF Saco Ranger Station** (603-447-5448; www.fs.fed.us/r9/white/), Kancamagus Highway, just off Route 16, Conway. From the end of May through mid-October, open 7 days a week 8 AM–5 PM. From mid-October through the end of May, open daily 8 AM–4:30 PM.

**WMNF Androscoggin Ranger Station** (603-466-2713; www.fs.fed.us/r9/white/), Route 16, Gorham. Open Monday through Saturday 8 AM–4:30 PM.

**WMNF Ammonoosuc Ranger Station** (603-869-2626; www.fs.fed.us/r9/white/), Trudeau Road, off Route 302, Box 239, Bethlehem 03574. Open Monday through Friday 8 AM–4:30 PM.

**WMNF Evans Notch District** (207-824-2134; www.fs.fed.us/r9/white/), Bridge Street, R.F.D. 2, Box 2270, Bethel, Maine 04217. Open daily 8 AM–4:30 PM; closed Wednesday.

**AMC Pinkham Notch Camp** (603-466-2725; www.amc-nh.org), Route 16, Pinkham Notch. (Also see *Guidance* in "Mount Washington and Its Valleys—Jackson and Pinkham Notch.")

## ✷ To See

COVERED BRIDGE **Albany covered bridge,** off Route 112 (Kancamagus Scenic Byway), 6 miles west of Conway. Built in 1858 and renovated in 1970, it is 136 feet long.

SCENIC DRIVES/EXCURSIONS **Kancamagus National Scenic Byway** (Route 112). The 34.5-mile paved highway is open all year, weather conditions permitting, but there are no motorist services on the road. More than 750,000 vehicles travel this route every year. On the eastern side of the mountains, the road begins on Route 16, just south of Conway village. One hundred yards from Route 16 is the Saco Ranger Station (see *Guidance*), a comprehensive information center open daily year-round. Adjacent to the ranger station is a 10-minute interpretive walk. After a few miles, the road closely parallels the winding, rocky Swift River, offering views across the rushing water to South Moat Mountain. There are plenty of places to stop for fishing or picnicking.

Six miles from Route 16, Dugway Road diverges right, through the Albany covered bridge to the **WMNF Covered Bridge Campground.** Near the bridge the **Boulder Loop Nature Trail** (2.5 miles; allow 2 hours) leaves Dugway Road and ascends rocky ledges, offering views up and down the river valley. An informative leaflet, keyed to numbered stations, is usually found in a box at the trailhead or at the Saco Ranger Station. Across the valley is Mount Chocorua, and to its right are Paugus and Passaconaway, named, as was the byway itself, for Native American chiefs who once lived in this region. Dugway Road can be followed east to a junction with the West Side Road, just north of Conway village. Midway along this route, the road passes the trailhead for **South Moat Mountain** (elevation 2,772 feet), one of our favorite hikes. The 2.3-mile trail (2 hours) offers magnificent views in all directions from its open, rocky summit. En route, in-season, can be seen lady's slippers and wild blueberries. This trail follows the long ridge to North Moat Mountain, then down to Diana's Baths and the River Road, a total hike of 9.1 miles requiring about 6 hours.

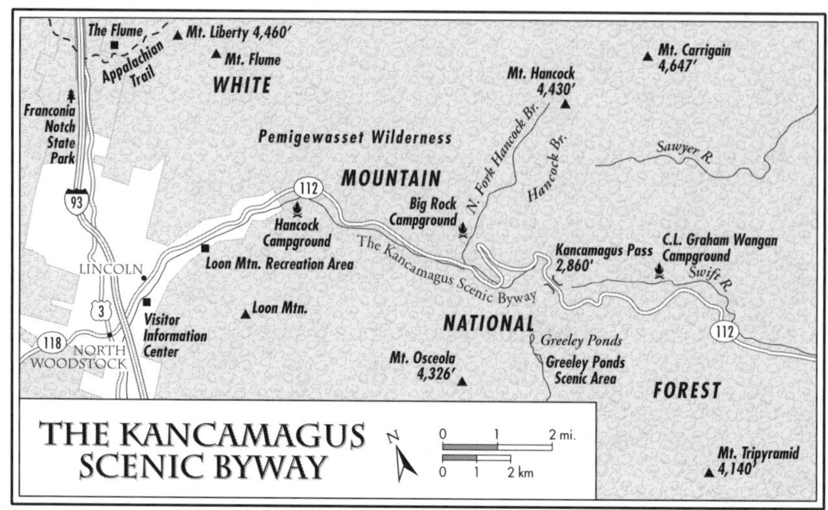


Opposite the junction of the Kancamagus Byway and Dugway Road is the **Blackberry Crossing Campground,** and half a mile west is the **Lower Falls Scenic Area,** which has rest rooms, drinking water, and picnic tables. On a summer weekend afternoon you will be amazed at how many people can squeeze onto the rocks at this popular swimming hole. This is not a wilderness experience, but what a treat for people who spend most of their lives in the city!

About 9 miles from Route 16 is the **Rocky Gorge Scenic Area,** an interesting geologic site where the rushing river has washed its way through the rocks. The footbridge leads to **Falls Pond.** Barrier-free rest rooms, drinking water, and picnic tables are found at the scenic area.

About 1.5 miles west is the **Champney Falls Trail** (3.8 miles, 3½ hours) to Mount Chocorua. The falls are an easy 3-mile round trip on the lower section of the trail. They are named for Benjamin Champney, founder of the White Mountain School of Painting, who worked in this region of the mountains for more than 60 years.

Twelve miles from Route 16, **Bear Notch Road** (not maintained in winter) diverges right for Bartlett and Route 302. This 9.3-mile gravel road has several impressive overlooks on its northern end.

At the junction with Bear Notch Road, you are entering Albany Intervale, once the township of Passaconaway. Not far beyond the junction is the **Passaconaway Historic Site.** Here the early-19th-century George House is now an information center, a remnant of the isolated farming and logging community that once prospered here (open daily mid-June through Labor Day, weekends from Memorial Day through Columbus Day). The **Rail 'n' River Trail,** a half-mile interpretive loop from this visitors center, is surprisingly varied.

About 15 miles from Conway is the turnoff for **Sabbaday Falls** (the falls are just a 10-minute hike from the highway). Resist temptation; there is no swimming allowed here.

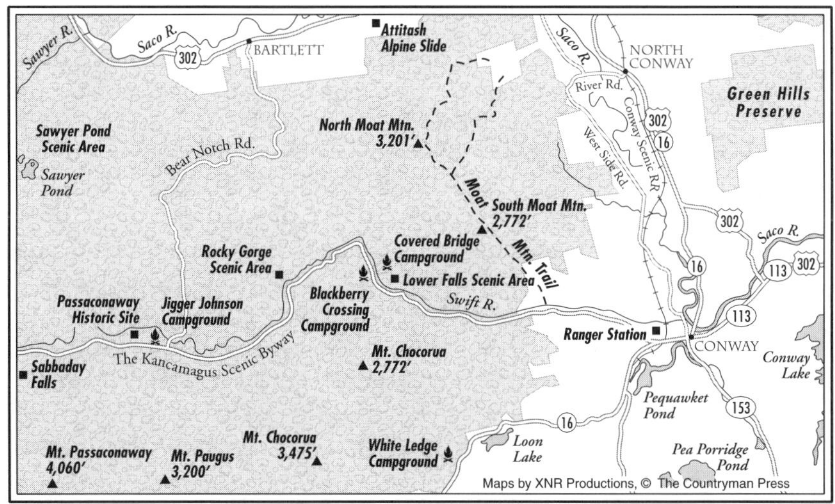


Next along the highway are the **C. L. Graham Wangan Ground**—a picnic spot (a "wangan" was a logging company store)—and picturesque **Lily Pond.** Here the highway begins a long climb to Kancamagus Pass, the highest point on this route, where there are scenic lookouts. As you traverse the pass, you leave the valley of the Swift River and cross over to the Pemigewasset River watershed.

West of the pass the highway twists down the mountainside and passes the trailhead for the **Greeley Ponds Scenic Area.** Both ponds are good trout-fishing and picnicking spots. (Hardy hikers can continue from here into Waterville Valley.) Next along the highway is the **Big Rock Campground.**

About 30 miles from Conway on your right are the large parking lot and information center (open on a limited basis year-round, daily mid-June through Labor Day) for the **Pemigewasset Wilderness Area,** one of the largest roadless areas in the eastern United States. Popular in winter with cross-country skiers, this is a prime access point for year-round backcountry hiking. Stop and walk at least as far as the middle of the suspension bridge across the Pemigewasset River, frequently a rushing torrent here. The **Wilderness Trail** follows an old logging railbed along the East Branch of the Pemi; the **Black Pond Trail** leads to a trout pond.

CROSS-COUNTRY SKIERS, SNOWSHOERS, AND SNOWMOBILERS SHARE A TRAIL OFF THE KANCAMAGUS HIGHWAY.

Kim Grant

Both the Wilderness Trail and the highway west to Lincoln follow the bed of J. E. Henry's narrow-gauge East Branch & Lincoln Railroad (see the introduction to "The Western Whites"). Next along the road is the **Hancock Campground,** and then Loon Mountain Ski Area, which is on your left just before the highway ends in the town of Lincoln.

Scenic drives through Crawford, Pinkham, and Evans Notches are described in "Mount Washington and its Valleys."

## ✷ To Do

**CAMPING** The WMNF operates 22 campgrounds. Along the Kancamagus Highway (Route 112) there are six campgrounds with a total of 267 sites and one campground on Route 16 with 28 sites; north of Crawford Notch, just south of Twin Mountain, on Route 302, are three campgrounds with 73 sites; and in Evans Notch (Route 113 south of Route 2 east of Shelburne) are five campgrounds with 77 sites. Dolly Copp Campground in Pinkham Notch has 176 sites, and adjacent to I-93 between Campton and Lincoln are five campgrounds with 214 sites. Campers should be self-sufficient, since these are not fancy campsites (no electrical, water, or sewer connections, no camp stores, no playgrounds, and so on). Toilets, water, tables, and fireplaces are provided. The sites were designed for tent camping, although trailers and RVs can be accommodated. Most of the campgrounds are open from mid-May through mid-October, with a few opening earlier and closing later; several are open all winter, though the roads are not plowed. The daily fees range from $7 to $9 per person, and many of these sites are filled every summer weekend on a first-come, first-served basis. However, a **toll-free reservation system** (1-800-280-2267) operates for some sites in the following campgrounds: White Ledge (Conway); Covered Bridge (Kancamagus); Sugarloaf I and II (Twin Mountain); Basin, Cold River, and Hastings (Evans Notch); Dolly Copp (Pinkham Notch); and Campton, Russell Pond, and Waterville (I-93). The reservation service operates March through September (Monday through Friday noon–9 PM, weekends noon–5 PM) and costs $6 in addition to the camping fee. Reservations may be made 120 days before arrival, but 10 days before arrival is the minimum time.

Backcountry camping is permitted in many areas of the WMNF but generally not within 200 feet of trails, lakes, or streams or within a quarter mile of roads, most designated campsites or huts, at certain trailheads, or along certain trails. There are also many designated backcountry camping sites, some with shelters, others with tent platforms. The WMNF promotes a carry-in, carry-out, low-impact, leave-no-trace policy for backcountry hikers and campers; fires are prohibited in many areas, and the use of portable cooking stoves is encouraged, if not required. Restricted-use areas, which help protect the backcountry from overuse, are located in many parts of the forest. For backcountry information, consult the *AMC White Mountain Guide* or contact the WMNF.

**FISHING** The WMNF publishes a comprehensive guide to trout fishing in the forest. More than 30 pond sites are listed, plus suggestions for stream fishing. A New Hampshire fishing license is required.

**HIKING** The WMNF is crisscrossed with 1,200 miles of hiking trails, some short and quite easy, others longer, and many challenging even for the most experienced backcountry traveler. A long, difficult section of the Appalachian Trail crosses the forest from the southwest to the northeast corner. The weather on the high mountains of the Presidential and Franconia Ranges can approach winter conditions in any month of the year, so hikers should be well prepared with extra food and proper clothing. Bring your own drinking water since *Giardia,* a waterborne intestinal bacterium, is found throughout the mountains. Although trails are well marked, we recommend three guidebooks to make hiking safe and enjoyable. See *50 Hikes in the White Mountains* or *50 More Hikes in New Hampshire,* both by Daniel Doan and Ruth Doan MacDougall (Backcountry Publications), and the *AMC White Mountain Guide* (Appalachian Mountain Club). *Waterfalls of the White Mountains,* by Bruce, Doreen, and Daniel Bolnick (Backcountry Publications), is a handy guide for 30 walks to 100 waterfalls. Many of the waterfall hikes are easy and perfect for families. The guide also offers interesting bits of human and natural history.

Also see South Moat Mountain, Champney Falls, Boulder Loop Nature Trail, and other trailheads reached via *Scenic Drives/Excursions.*

**SNOWMOBILING** Large portions of the WMNF are off-limits to snowmobiling, trail bikes, and off-road vehicles. For details contact the **Trails Bureau,** New Hampshire Division of Parks and Recreation (603-271-3254; www.nhtrails.org), Box 1856, Concord 03302-1856, or the **New Hampshire Snowmobile Association** (603-224-8906; www.nhsa.com), 722 Route 3A Suite 14, Bow 03304.

# THE WESTERN WHITES

New England's highest mountains march in a ragged line, heading diagonally northeast across New Hampshire, beginning near the Connecticut River with Mount Moosilauke. We've chosen to divide this spectacular mountain region into "The Western Whites" and "Mount Washington and its Valleys," which also includes the eastern peaks of the range.

The heart of the Western Whites is Franconia Notch, a high pass between the granite walls of Cannon Mountain and Mount Lafayette. Here I-93 narrows into the Franconia Notch Parkway, and visitors frequently spend a day viewing the stony profile of the Old Man of the Mountain, exploring the Flume, the Pool, and Avalanche Falls, maybe taking the aerial tram to the top of Cannon Mountain or taking a swim in Echo Lake, and ideally hiking at least up to Lonesome Lake.

A footpath from Franconia Notch to the top of Mount Lafayette is said to have been blazed as early as 1825, the year the area's first hotel opened. By the 1880s it was served by a narrow-gauge railroad, and the Profile House, the largest of several hotels here, could accommodate 500 guests. The villages of Franconia and Bethlehem, just north of the notch, and of North Woodstock, just east of Kinsman Notch as well as south of Franconia Notch, also had their share of elaborate summer hotels.

The area's steep, heavily wooded mountains were even more enticing to loggers than to tourists. While early conservationists fought to preserve the "notches" and "gorges," lumber companies built wilderness railways and employed small armies of men to clear-cut vast tracts. Legendary lumberman James E. Henry transformed the little outpost of Lincoln, with 110 residents in 1890, into a booming logging center of 1,278 by 1910. His J. E. Henry Company owned 115,000 acres of virgin timber along the East Branch of the Pemigewasset River, reducing much of it to pulp.

This Pemigewasset ("Pemi") area became part of the White Mountain National Forest in the mid-1930s. It was still being logged in 1923 when Sherman Adams came to Lincoln to work for the Parker-Young Co., J. E. Henry's successor. Over the next 20 years Adams came to know the valley intimately, and when he returned to Lincoln in the 1960s after having served as New Hampshire's governor and President Eisenhower's chief of staff, he opened Loon Mountain Ski Area.

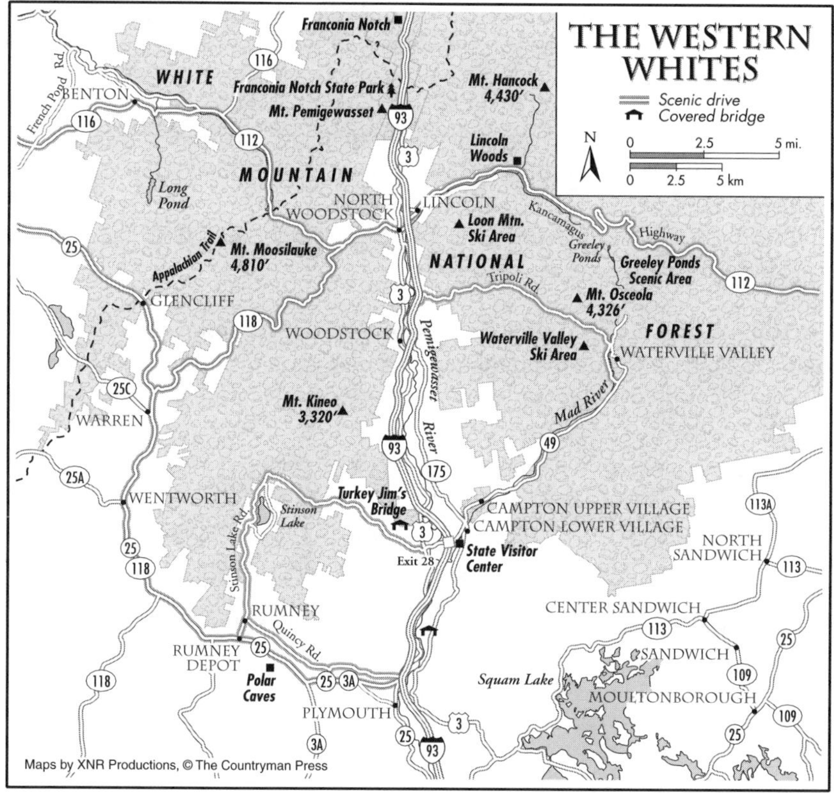


In that same month another public figure—young ex-Olympic skier Tom Corcoran—opened another ski area less than a dozen miles away (as the crow flies) in Waterville Valley. Up in Franconia Notch, state-run Cannon Mountain's aerial tramway and steep slopes had been attracting skiers since 1938, but these newcomers both represented something novel—rather than being just "ski areas," both were "ski resorts," spawning new communities.

Dictated by both the personalities of their founders and the lay of their land, Loon Mountain and Waterville Valley have, however, developed differently. Conservative Adams saw his business as running a ski area and left condominium development to others. Corcoran, fresh from Aspen, planned a self-contained, Rockies-style resort from the start. Loon's facilities, moreover, lined a narrow shelf of land above the Pemigewasset River on the edge of a mill town, whereas Waterville was in an isolated valley with two ski hills facing each other across 500 acres just waiting to be filled.

Loon Mountain and Waterville Valley are now New Hampshire's largest, liveliest ski resorts. The abundance of attractive, reasonably priced, off-season condo lodging is contributing to an interesting phenomenon: After decades as a pass-through place, this area is once more becoming as popular a summer destination as it was in the 1890s. Both resort areas cater shamelessly to families, especially in summer when organized sports programs and local attractions complement the reasonably priced, family-geared lodging.

The "beaten track" through the Western Whites remains delightfully narrow. The quiet old resort villages of Bethlehem, Franconia, and Sugar Hill have changed little in many decades thanks to the persistence of locals and new arrivals who have worked side by side to preserve the area's heritage, and the Ammonoosuc Valley retains its distinctively remote feel. Farther south, the Baker River Valley offers another little-traveled, scenic byway through the mountains.

The full magnificence of the mountains themselves can only be appreciated by climbing (or riding) to their summits, but the beauty of their high, narrow notches and hidden valleys is accessible to all.

GUIDANCE **Waterville Valley Region Chamber of Commerce** (603-726-3804; 1-800-237-2307; www.watervillevalleyregion.com), just off I-93, Exit 28, in Campton. Open daily 9 AM–5 PM. Serves as a walk-in gateway information center for the Western Whites.

**The White Mountains Visitors Center** (603-745-8720; 1-800-346-3687). Open 8:30 AM–5 PM daily, until 6 PM in summer. A walk-in facility (just off I-93, Exit 32, on the Lincoln–North Woodstock line) with rest rooms, displays, Forest Service and commercial brochures, offering information for this entire area. Also based here, the **Ski New Hampshire Association** (603-745-8101; 1-800-WE-SKI-93) is a reservation service for Cannon, Loon, Waterville Valley, and Bretton Woods ski areas.

Chambers of commerce are also listed under *Guidance* within the three sections of this chapter, "The Waterville Valley Region," "Lincoln and North Woodstock" (covering the Loon Mountain area), and "Franconia and North of the Notches."

## THE WATERVILLE VALLEY REGION

Waterville Valley itself is a 10-mile-deep cul-de-sac cut by one of New England's many Mad Rivers and circled by majestic mountains, many of them more than 4,000 feet tall.

In 1835 city folk began flocking to the town's sole lodging establishment for rest and relaxation, and by 1868 the green-shuttered inn was consistently booked. Families were attracted to the area to pursue more strenuous activities like hiking but also devoted themselves to prayer and Bible study in this inspiring wilderness. The original visitors and their progeny found the valley and its virtues addictive and, in 1919, purchased the inn when it came up for sale. So principled were they that in 1928 they donated all but a few hundred of their 26,000 acres to the White Mountain National Forest. These same families founded and filled the ski clubs that fueled the inn's winter economy, beginning in 1935 when a few trails were etched on Snow's Mountain. In 1937 the Civilian Conservation Corps (CCC) cut a precipitous 1.5-mile trail down the southern shoulder of Mount Tecumseh, across the valley from Snow's.

Tom Corcoran, a prep school student from Exeter, dreamed of skiing the treacherous Tecumseh Trail and arrived at Waterville Valley in 1949 to pursue his goal. Corcoran continued downhill racing with Dartmouth's ski team, then the U.S. Olympic ski team, and headed west to work for the Aspen Corporation, for

Kim Grant

THE GOLDEN EAGLE AT WATERVILLE VALLEY

which he conducted a feasibility study that led to the acquisition of Buttermilk Mountain. By 1965, when Corcoran was ready to buy his own ski mountain, the Waterville Valley Inn was up for sale along with 425 acres—virtually all the town that wasn't in the national forest.

Corcoran's Waterville Valley—complete with four chairlifts, a T-bar, even some snowmaking—opened for Christmas 1966. The inn burned that first season, but two new ski lodges were ready the following year, as were some condominiums, then as new to the eastern ski scene as snowmaking.

Over the years Tom Corcoran developed Mount Tecumseh into a major ski mountain, and added five condo-style lodges and more than 500 condominiums, a pond, a sports center, a nine-hole golf course, and a year-round skating rink. Finally, at the center of the resort, he built a "Town Square": three interconnected, clapboard buildings 4½ stories high with traditional saltbox lines, softened by modern touches like an occasional round window and 100 dormers. A variation on the lines of an old White Mountain hotel, this complex does something that no other New England ski-resort building has achieved: It actually heightens the beauty of its setting, a circle of majestic peaks.

In 1995 Waterville Valley Ski Area was acquired by S-K-I, New England's largest ski conglomerate, and the organization expanded the resort's snowmaking capabilities. By 1997 still another group of owners had assumed control of the resort, and year-round this area continues to be an outstanding, self-contained, family-geared resort. The quaint village of Campton offers a few refined bed & breakfasts for those seeking a more personal lodging experience, as well as some unusual restaurants—including one with a Swiss theme, perhaps owing to the Alp-like splendor of the surrounding mountains. You'll find a more youthful atmosphere in nearby Plymouth, where the industrial grit of abandoned 19th-century mills has been tempered by the calming academic presence of Plymouth State College. Though lodging is scarce, you'll be drawn to the attractive layout of the town common, which includes a sweet bandstand and an authentic 1930s diner as well a smattering of unique shops. The number and variety of hikes and scenic drives in this area keep area residents and tourists alike active throughout the year.

**GUIDANCE** **Waterville Valley Central Reservations** (603-236-8311; 1-800-468-2553).

**Waterville Valley Region Chamber of Commerce** (603-726-3804; 1-800-237-2307), just off I-93, Exit 28, in Campton. Open 9 AM–5 PM daily; closed Tuesday off-season. Rest rooms, brochures, and phones. Here you can purchase snowmobile licenses and activity-specific guidebooks from the helpful staff.

**GETTING THERE** *By bus:* **Concord Trailways** (603-228-3300; 1-800-639-3317; www.cjtrailways.com) from Boston's Logan Airport stops in Plymouth Chase Street Market at 83 Main Street. Check with lodging to arrange local transportation.

*By car:* I-93 to Exit 28, then 11 miles up Route 49.

**GETTING AROUND** **The Shuttle Connection in Lincoln** (603-745-3140; 1-800-545-3140; www.theshuttleconnection.com) provides a 24-hour service among attractions, ski areas, airports, and bus terminals.

**MEDICAL EMERGENCY** Dial **911.**

**Plymouth Regional Clinic** (603-536-4467), 258 Highland Street in Plymouth, offers limited service weekdays.

## ✷ Towns and Villages

**Plymouth.** From I-93, what you see of Plymouth are the high-rise dorms of Plymouth State College, a clue to the existence of shops and restaurants catering to the needs of 4,000 students. What you don't see from the highway is the region's appealing old commercial center. Its mills have produced mattresses, gloves, and shoe trees as well as lumber. The long-vanished Pemigewasset House, built by the president of the Boston, Concord, & Montréal Railroad, was favored by Nathaniel Hawthorne, who was living in Plymouth before his death in 1864. Today the college campus forms the centerpiece for the town, and some good restaurants can be found within walking distance.

**Rumney.** A picture-perfect village with a classic common, Rumney is in the Baker Valley, just far enough off the beaten path to preserve its tranquility. Offering the Mary Baker Eddy House, Quincy Bog, the Town Pound, and Stinson Lake, all described under *To See—Scenic Drives,* Rumney makes a good dining and shopping stop.

**Warren.** A perfectly ordinary, white-clapboard village at the base of Mount Moosilauke, Warren has had more than its share of monuments. First there was the massive Morse Museum, built in the 1920s by a Warren native who made a fortune making shoes in Lowell, Massachusetts. It displayed exotica from his travels, as well as the world's largest private shoe collection. The Morse Museum was closed several years ago (even the mummies were sold off), but the space-rocket booster with USA emblazoned on its side still towers bizarrely over the common. A local restaurant owner, we're told, brought it back from Huntsville, Alabama, and tried to give it to Derry, New Hampshire (home of astronaut Alan Shepard), which refused to take it. Warren, we understand, remains divided on whether it belongs there or not; the VFW post keeps it painted. There's also a small historical museum and a good eatery at which you can get directions to the Dartmouth Outing Club cabin. From the cabin a former carriage road (to a former summit hotel) is one among a choice of hiking trails to the summit.

**Wentworth.** Another picturesque, white wooden village with a triangular common, set above the Baker River.

## ✷ To See

COVERED BRIDGES **Blair bridge.** The easiest way to find this bridge is from I-93, Exit 27; at the bottom of the exit ramp, follow Blair Road to the blinking light, then go straight across.

**Turkey Jim's bridge.** At I-93, Exit 28, follow Route 49 west. After about 0.5 mile (as you cross over the metal bridge), look for a sign on your right for Branch Brook Campground. You must drive into the campground to see the bridge.

**Bump bridge.** At I-93, Exit 28, follow Route 49 east for about 0.5 mile. Turn right at the traffic lights and go over the dam. Turn right again onto Route 175 south. After 3 or 4 miles, you come to a sharp left turn; bear to the left and stay straight, down the dirt road. Take the first right, and the covered bridge is about 0.5 mile on your left.

FOR FAMILIES ✐ **Polar Caves** (603-536-1888; www.showcaves.com), Route 25, 4 miles west of Plymouth. Open early May through mid-October, 9 AM–5 PM. Discovered by neighborhood children around 1900 and opened as a commercial attraction in 1922, this is an extensive property with a series of caves connected by passageways and walkways, with taped commentaries at stations along the way. The name refers to the cold air rising from the first "Ice" cave, where the temperature in August averages 55 degrees. There's much here to learn about minerals and geology, much that's just fun. The complex includes picnic tables and a snack bar. $10 for adults; $6 for children 6–12; no family rate.

SCENIC DRIVES **Rumney Loop.** The easiest way to begin is from Route 25/3A west of Plymouth. Take Airport Road, then go left on Quincy Road. The sign for **Quincy Bog** (603-786-9465) should be just beyond Quincy State Forest, but if the sign is down, look for stone pillars flanking a small road to the right. One-tenth of a mile down this road look for a left leading to the bog entrance, from which to access trails and a viewing deck. This 40-acre peat bog is a place to find frogs in April and May, to see bog plant blooms in May and June, to hunt for salamanders and newts, and to bird-watch. The nature center here is open mid-June through mid-August. En route to the bog you pass the old **Rumney Town Pound,** an unusual, natural animal pen formed by gigantic boulders. Continue into Rumney (see *Towns and Villages, Eating Out,* and *Selective Shopping*), and then head out Main Street and follow it past the **Mary Baker Eddy House** (603-786-9943), home of the founder of Christian Science in the early 1860s (open May through October, Tuesday through Saturday 10 AM–5 PM). Continue along isolated **Stinson**

**Lake,** good fishing (trout, perch, pickerel) year-round. **Stinson Mountain Trail** is marked, beginning with a dirt road, then a left through the woods and a right at the brook, up through spruce and fir to the summit ledges. Great views. Continue east on this road out to West Campton and I-93, Exit 28.

**The Baker River Valley.** The Baker River charts a natural path from the base of Mount Moosilauke southeast through hilly woodland to the Pemigewasset River. It was known as the Asquamchumauke River until 1712, when a group of soldiers headed by Capt. Thomas Baker of Northampton, Massachusetts, defeated a band of local Native Americans on the site that's presently Plymouth. Today Route 25 shadows the river, beginning as a commercial strip west of Plymouth but quickly improving. You pass the Polar Caves (see *For Families*), Rumney (see *Towns and Villages* and the Rumney Loop, above), and continue on through Wentworth and Warren (see *Towns and Villages*). To return to Waterville Valley, take mountainous Route 118 east to North Woodstock (see "Lincoln and North Woodstock"), then I-93 from Exit 32 to Exit 28.

**Tripoli Road** (closed in winter). A shortcut from Waterville Valley to I-93 north: roughly 10 miles, paved and unpaved, up through Thornton Gap (a high pass between Mount Osceola and Mount Tecumseh) and over a high shoulder of 4,326-foot Mount Osceola. Begin on West Branch Road (a left before the Osceola Library); cross the one-lane bridge and turn right into the national forest. Note the Mount Osceola Trail (see *To Do—Hiking*) 3 miles up the road. Continue through the Thornton Gap. Note trailheads for the Mount Tecumseh and East Pond Trails.

**Sandwich Notch Road** (closed in winter). A steep, roughly 10-mile dirt road from Center Sandwich to Waterville, built 1 rod wide for $300 by the town of Sandwich in the late 18th century. Best attempted in a high, preferably four-wheel-drive vehicle. Be prepared to make way for any vehicle coming from the opposite direction. The road follows the Bearcamp River; stone walls tell of long-vanished farms. Center Sandwich offers a crafts center, museum, and dining (see "The Lake Winnipesaukee Area").

## * To Do

BICYCLING **The Nordic/Adventure Center at Waterville Valley** (603-236-4666), in Town Square, Waterville Valley, rents mountain bikes, tandem bikes, or bicycle buggies for toddlers. Mountain bicyclists utilize the lift and trails on Snow's Mountain, also cross-country trails and logging roads. Mountain bike clinics, special events.

**Rhino Bike Works** (603-536-3919), 95 South Main Street, Plymouth. This bike shop provides avid cyclists with reliable repair and rentals.

**Ski Fanatics** (603-726-4327), Route 49, Campton, just off Exit 28 across from the information center. Mountain bike rentals and mapped routes, also 10-mile group rides (not for beginners) scheduled twice a week in-season.

**Sugar Shack Mt. Bike Park** (603-726-3867), Route 175 north, Thornton. Rentals and trails through 240 acres of well-maintained trails, beginner through expert.

**BOATING** **Corcoran's Pond at Waterville Valley Resort** (603-236-4666). Paddleboat, canoe, and Sunfish rentals on 6 acres.

**Ski Fanatics** (603-726-4327), Route 49 in Campton, rents "funyaks," billed as "kayaks with training wheels"; guided tours on the Pemigewasset and shuttle service.

**Outback Kayak** (603-745-2002; www.outbackkayak.com), Main Street, North Woodstock. In addition to kayaks, you can find a variety of rentals including snowshoes, cross-country skis, and snowmobiles.

**CAMPING** See *Lodging* for a list of public campgrounds in the White Mountain National Forest.

**FISHING** Stream fishing was one of the first lures of visitors to this valley, and the fish are still biting in Russell Pond (Tripoli Road) and all along the Mad River, stocked with trout each spring. Campton Pond (at the lights) is a popular fishing hole.

**FITNESS CENTER** **White Mountain Athletic Club** (603-236-8303). Offers indoor tennis, racquetball, and squash courts, 25-meter indoor and outdoor swimming pools, jogging track, fitness evaluation facilities, Nautilus exercise equipment, aerobics, whirlpools, saunas and steam rooms, tanning booths, massage service, restaurant/lounge, and game room.

**GOLF** **Owl's Nest** (1-888-OWL-NEST), Route 49, 1 mile west of Exit 28 off I-93, Campton. A par-72 championship course with four sets of tees on each hole, accommodating all skill levels. The restaurant and lounge set the stage for after-round tall tales.

**Waterville Valley Resort** (603-236-4805). For those too busy pursuing other activities to play 18 full-length holes, Waterville Valley's shorter "executive" course is a good place to spend 2½hours or less; rental carts provide weary walkers some relief. There are two regulation 18-hole courses here as well, but count on paying a pretty penny to play them.

**Sugar Shack Golf Range** (603-726-8978; www.whitemountainregion.com/theshack). Grip it and rip it at this multipurpose activity center.

**Weather or Not** (603-745-3433). Practice your short game away from the elements at this indoor mini golf center and 18-hole putting green.

**HIKING** You can find detailed trail maps for short walks and information about organized longer hikes through the Waterville Valley Athletic Improvement Association in Town Square and, to a lesser extent, the Nordic/Adventure Center at Waterville Valley. Experienced local guides lead groups of all ages and abilities throughout the year. In winter, strap on cross-country skis or snowshoes for more challenging treks. Also, click on www.climbnh.com for as much information on hiking in New Hampshire you'll ever need.

**Cascades Path** begins at the base of Snow's Mountain Ski Area and follows a brook for 1.5 miles. Continue along the brook above the cascades for the best view, looking back.

**Mount Osceola.** A 7-mile, 4½ hour hike beginning on Tripoli Road (see *To See—Scenic Drives*). The Tripoli Road crests at the 2,300-foot-high Thornton Gap; the Mount Osceola Trail begins some 200 yards beyond. Follow an old tractor road up through many switchbacks and along Breadtray Ridge, then across a brook, up log steps, by another ridge to the summit ledges. This is the highest of the mountains circling Waterville Valley, and the view is spectacular.

**Greeley Ponds Trail** begins at the end of the old truck road, which is a left off Livermore Road, just past the clearing known as Depot Camp. The trail crosses a wooden footbridge and follows the course of the river to Greeley Ponds between Mounts Osceola and Kancamagus. It's a gradual grade all the way to the shelter on the upper pond and continues as a gradual ascent to the Kancamagus Highway.

**Welch Mountain.** Open ledge walking at a surprisingly low elevation overlooking the Mad River Valley. It's a challenging 4-mile, round-trip hike but well worth the sweat. According to local hiking guru Steve Smith, the broad sheets of granite offer views and blueberries in abundance. The panorama from the open summit includes Sandwich Mountain, Mount Tripyramid, Mount Tecumseh, and Mount Moosilauke. You can extend the hike into a loop by continuing over the slightly higher **Dickey Mountain** and its fine north viewpoint (the ledges on this hike may be slippery when wet). The trailhead for this loop is on Orris Road, off Upper Mad River Road between Campton and Waterville Valley.

LEARNING TO SKI AT WATERVILLE VALLEY

Kim Grant

**IN-LINE SKATING** Rentals available at **The Nordic/Adventure Center at Waterville Valley,** Town Square, Waterville Valley.

**ROCK CLIMBING** The most popular area for rock climbing is the area around Buffalo Road, accessible from I-93 by taking Exit 26 and driving about 8 miles on Route 25 until you reach Stinson Lake Road—essentially the town center of Rumney. From there, drive about a mile to a parking lot on the right. The Meadows, the name of the cliffs you'll be scaling, lie directly above this parking area. Eastern Mountain Sports, an adventure outfitter based in North Conway, offers rock climbing outings here and in the area on a regular schedule.

**SWIMMING** **White Mountain Athletic Club,** Waterville Valley, offers an indoor pool (see *Fitness Center*). Several lodges also offer indoor pools.

**Corcoran's Pond,** with a sandy beach, is Waterville Valley Resort's principal summer swimming area.

On Route 49 look for **Smart's Brook Trail**—an easy mile's hike over logging and dirt roads to a swimming hole among the pools of a mountain brook.

**TENNIS** ✐ **Waterville Valley Tennis Center** (603-236-4840). Eighteen clay, outdoor courts, two indoor courts at the White Mountain Athletic Club; clinics, round robins. A junior tennis program for children 18 and under includes private lessons, drill sessions, and round robins.

## ✷ Winter Sports

**CROSS-COUNTRY SKIING** **The Nordic/Adventure Center at Waterville Valley** (603-236-4666; 1-800-468-2553; www.waterville.com), in Town Square, Waterville Valley. Ski school, warming and waxing areas, rentals. More than 100 km through the valley and surrounding national forest; 70 km groomed for diagonal and skating; 35 additional km marked. When all else fails you can count on a 2.5-km loop covered by snowmaking. Bull Hill is now closed. The center's location in Town Square has its pros and cons: easy access but too many condos to go by before you get up into the woods. On the other hand, you can drive to the edge of the White Mountain National Forest and ski directly off into the woods. Skating as well as diagonal lessons are offered; also moonlight guided tours, weekly races, and telemark clinics. Cross-country ski rental rates for weekends and holidays run $11 for half a day or $15 a day; cross-country ski rental rates weekdays are $12 half a day or $18 a full day; rental of snowshoes is $10 half a day or $15 a full day; child trailer $20 a day. Inquire about conditions on the Greeley Ponds Trail. Open daily 8:30 AM–4 PM.

**The Sugar Shack Ski Touring Center** (603-726-3867; www.whitemountainregion.com/theshack), Route 175, Thornton. A working, third-generation sugar shack serves as the hub of a groomed cross-country trail system with gently rolling trails along the Pemigewasset River.

**DOWNHILL SKIING** ✐ **Tenney Mountain** (603-536-4125; 1-888-TENNEY2; www.tenneymtn.com), 151 Tenney Mountain Highway, Plymouth. This locally popular mountain makes a point of advertising that it offers no frills, just affordable family skiing and snowboarding.

✐ **Waterville Valley** (603-236-8311; snow report, 603-236-4144; 1-800-468-2553; www.waterville.com), 1 Ski Area Road, Waterville Valley, attracts thousands of families to a sprawling complex that features family-style lodging (including roughly 1,000 kitchens), great children's skiing, and summer programs. A limited-ticket policy ensures lift-line waits of no longer than 15 minutes. It's just a 7½-minute ride to the summit of Mount Tecumseh on the high-speed detachable quad, and the way down is via a choice of long, wide cruising trails like Upper Bobby's Run and Tippecanoe. Mogul lovers will find plenty to please them on True Grit and Ciao, and beginners have their own area served by the Lower Meadows Double Chair. *Lifts:* 2 high-speed detachable quad lifts, 2 triples, 3 doubles, 4 surface. *Trails:* 49 on Mount Tecumseh; 5 on Snow's Mountain are for snowboarding only. *Vertical drop:* 2,020 feet. *Snowmaking:* 100 percent. *Facilities:* Include the inviting Schwendi Hutte near the top of Mount Tecumseh, Sunnyside Lodge (a midmountain oasis with a hearth cafeteria, good soups, and deli sandwiches), the Base Lodge Cafeteria, and the World Cup Bar and Grill. *Ski school:* Specializes in clinics for all ages and all abilities, also private lessons for all. *For children:* There is a nursery for children from age 6 weeks. The ski area has one of the country's first and still one of its most outstanding SKIwee programs: SKIwee, ages 3–5; Mountain Cadets, ages 6–8; Mountain Scouts, ages 9–12. Small children have their own hill, with its own lift and terrain garden. Also evening children's programs.

**ICE SKATING** **Waterville Valley Ice Arena** (603-236-4813; www.watervillevalley.org). A covered, hockey-sized ice skating rink maintained throughout the year in Town Square. Complete with skate rentals, maintenance, and repairs.

**SLEIGH RIDES** Throughout the winter, horse-drawn sleigh rides depart afternoons and evenings from **Town Square,** Waterville Valley.

**SNOWBOARDING** The five lift-served trails on **Snow's Mountain** (open weekends and holidays only) are reserved for snowboarding; Mount Tecumseh, Lower Periphery and the Boneyard are also devoted to snowboarding.

## ✱ Lodging

### LODGES

### *In Waterville Valley 03215*

Central reservations numbers are 603-236-8371 and 1-800-468-2553.

**Black Bear Lodge** (603-236-4501; 1-800-349-2327; www.black-bear-lodge.com), 3 Village Road, Waterville Valley. Comfortable and well laid out for families, this lodge is a 3-minute walk from Town Square, and offers 107 one-bedroom deluxe or loft suites that sleep four to six people. Each suite has a kitchen, a dining area, a sitting area with queen-sized bed and cable TV, and a separate bedroom; indoor/outdoor pool, outdoor whirlpool, sauna, steam room, game room, and children's cinema on the lower level. From Christmas Eve through the end of April $88–209. Low season runs May through December 23 and rates are $78–128. Resort fee, additional.

**The Golden Eagle** (603-236-4551; 1-800-910-4499; www.goldeneaglelodge.com), 6 Snow's Brook Road. Cambridge architect Graham Gund's imprint is all over this resort outpost. He first designed the Waterville Valley Town Square, then added this fieldstone- and shingle-sided hotel. Both are a tribute to another era. With its sloping roofs and tall towers, the exterior of the Golden Eagle suggests a monumental, 19th-century mountain lodge, but the inside is totally in tune with today. Amenities include an indoor pool, whirlpools, and saunas.

Each of the 139 suites boasts a kitchen and eating area, a view of mountains or water, and plenty of room to sleep four to six. Low season, May-through-December rates run about $120; high season runs from $250, plus 15 percent resort fee.

**Best Western Silver Fox Inn** (603-236-3699; 1-888-236-3699; www.silverfoxinn.com), 14 Snow's Brook Road. If you're looking for a room rather than a suite, this is a lower-cost alternative. All 32 guest rooms are air-conditioned and newly decorated, with two double beds or one queen. Breakfast, afternoon wine and cheese, and free shuttle service are included. High season (third week in December to the end of April), the rates run $70–90 off-season, higher again June through foliage season.

**Snowy Owl Inn** (603-236-8383; 1-800-766-9969; www.snowyowlinn.com), 4 Village Road. An attractive lodge with a central, three-story fieldstone hearth and a surrounding atrium supported by single log posts; there's a cupola you can sit in. A case can be made that this is the most innlike and romantic of the Waterville Valley lodges, but it's also a good place for families, thanks to the lower-level game rooms adjoining a pleasant breakfast room. There are also indoor and outdoor pools. Of the 85 rooms, more than half have a wet bar, fridge, and whirlpool tub, and all have voice mail, dataports, satellite television (with five, count 'em five, HBO channels). A two-bedroom suite offers its own gas log fieldstone fireplace. Rates include a breakfast buffet, afternoon wine and cheese. $58–178 (plus resort fee) per night, depending on room and season.

**Valley Inn** (603-236-8336; 1-800-343-0969; www.valleyinn.com; info@valleyinn.com), Tecumseh Road. An attractive, 52-room lodge with an indoor/outdoor pool, whirlpool, saunas, exercise room, game room; the only valley lodging with its own dining room (see *Dining Out*). All rooms have TV and phone, and some have kitchen units, fireplaces, saunas, or whirlpool baths. From $58 for a standard room in low ski season to $279 for a suite with a deck, kitchen facilities, fireplace, and whirlpool bath. An additional meal package, including breakfast and dinner, is available.

### BED & BREAKFASTS

#### *In Campton 03223*

Note that the village of Campton is just off I-93, 10 miles west of Waterville Valley.

**The Campton Inn** (603-726-4449; 1-888-511-0790; peter@evpcreative.com), Route 175 and Owl Street. A vintage-1835 multigabled village house, this longtime inn has been nicely renovated by Robbin and Peter Adams. The large living room features a woodstove and piano, and there's a pleasant screened porch. Five guest rooms, one with private bath, some designed for families; $75–95 in high season, $45–85 low-season double occupancy includes a full breakfast. Well-behaved dogs are accepted, but management adds that families with babies should stay elsewhere—this is a small house, and the sounds of crying in the night could disturb other guests.

**The Crowe's in Campton Village** (603-726-5555; 1-877-726-5553; www.thecrowesincampton.com). Situated at the intersection of Mad River Road and Route 175 on a triangular piece of land, the Crowe's is a lovely yellow farmhouse built in 1811 that is inviting and relaxed. There are four rooms and two suites, and guests have access to the common areas that include fireplaces and gas-fired stoves. Each room has a private bath, telephone, air-conditioning, and TV/VCR combination; in addition, the suites have two-person Jacuzzi tubs. A full country breakfast is included in the rate with such yummy offerings as corn-blueberry pancakes, fish cakes, and cinnamon French toast. Golfers have the luck of being 5 minutes from **Owl's Nest Golf Club.** Rates are $85–135, and golf and ski packages are available.

**The Mountain-Fare Inn** (603-726-4283; www.mountainfareinn.com; mtnfareinn@cyberportal.net), 5 Old Waterville Road, Campton. Susan and Nick Preston run this B&B as smoothly as they do the slopes at Waterville Valley. Both high-powered coaches of competitive skiers (including U.S. ski team members), the Prestons spend their off-slope time managing one of the homiest ski lodges around. Their 1840s village home and carriage house annex offer nine sunny guest rooms, many with wide-pine floors and all furnished with bright fabrics and country antiques. All but one have a private bath. Common space includes an old-fashioned living room, a great game room with pool table, television, card tables, and woodstove, and a place to store and tune skis. There's also a brand-new sauna. Guests sit down together to breakfast in the pleasant dining room where a very full, buffet-style breakfast is set out. $85–135 high-season doubles; $75–115 low-season doubles. Susan tells us that if the kids are under 12, a family of four always pays $103!

**Osgood Inn** (603-726-3543; www.watervillevalleyregion.com/osgoodinn/; osgood@mindspring.com), 24 Osgood Road, off Route 49, Box 419. Lots of knotty pine in this village home with a comfortable living room and two large, upstairs guest rooms with shared bath. In an adjoining wing, a two-bedroom suite sleeps up to six people and has its own small sitting room and full kitchen. Room rates are based on number of nights booked and are $5–10 cheaper if you stay more than 1 night—$70–95; the two-bedroom suite is $150 with full country breakfast and tax; no charge for small children. Smoke-free.

### *Elsewhere*

**Deep River Motor Inn** (603-536-2155; 1-800-445-6809), Highland Street, Plymouth. This family-run motel is a good option for lodging in Plymouth proper, and it serves its guests well by offering a variety of accommodations including standard motel rooms with two double beds, cable TV, and air-conditioning as well as cottage units that have kitchens in summer ($390–450). You'll also have access to the in-ground pool, picnic tables, barbecue grills, and lawn games. The location is great for families since so many attractions and outdoor activities are close at hand—Polar Caves among them. Prices vary throughout the year; on weekends and holidays from May through October, rooms run $76.95 ($59–64 midweek). In low-season, November through April, rooms are $54.95 at all times.

**Hilltop Acres** (603-764-5896), East Side and Buffalo Road, Wentworth 03282. Open May through November. A pleasant old farmhouse with a large, pine-paneled rec room containing an antique piano, television, fireplace, and plenty of books. Rooms with private bath, $100 per room; also two traditional housekeeping cottages with fireplace and screened porch ($125 per night, $750 per week). Pets and children are permitted in the cottages. Room rates include breakfast.

**CONDOMINIUMS** **Village Condominiums** (603-236-8301; 1-800-532-6630; www.villagecondo.com) is the primary rental agent for most of the 500 or so condominiums ranged in clusters between the ski slopes and Town Square. Quality is uniformly high, but since these units lack the indoor pools and game rooms enjoyed by lodge guests, it's important to make sure rentals include access to the White Mountain Athletic Club. The nearer to the Sports Center and to Town Square, the better. It's worth noting that owner occupancy is unusually high at Waterville Valley and the actual number of condo units in the rental pool at prime times can be very low indeed. Rates are $125–302.50 (plus tax and a 15 percent service charge and resort fee) for a two-bedroom condo; a five-bedroom unit runs $245–600.

**CAMPGROUNDS** Some campsites in the White Mountain National Forest can be reserved up to 120 days in advance by phoning 1-800-280-2267. Public campgrounds include:

**Campton,** on Route 49, 2 miles east of I-93, Exit 28, Campton. Open mid-April through mid-October. Fifty-eight sites. Interpretive programs on weekends June through Labor Day. $16 per night; pay shower available.

**Russell Pond,** off I-93, Exit 31, 3 miles northeast on the Tripoli Road. Eighty-seven sites on a 40-acre pond, good for swimming (no lifeguard) and fishing; Saturday-evening interpretive nature programs. $14 per night.

**Waterville,** 11 miles northeast of I-93 on Route 49, Waterville. Twenty-seven sites. $14 per night; half price in winter. *Note:* Osceola Campsite is reserved for groups.

**Branch Brook Campground** in Campton (603-726-7001) and **Goose Hollow Campground** in Waterville Valley (603-726-2000) are privately owned alternatives.

## ✻ Where to Eat

### DINING OUT

### *In Waterville Valley*

**The Red Fox Dining Room at The Valley Inn** (603-236-8336; 1-800-343-0969; www.valleyinn.com). Probably the most elegant restaurant in Waterville Valley, here you can enjoy Italian dishes by candlelight. Sautéed wild mushrooms with grilled polenta is a great way to start; then choose entrées like balsamic chicken, grilled salmon on sautéed spinach with caramelized shallots and a saffron sauce, or grilled rib-eye steak on a bed of roasted red peppers. The daily dessert specials are equally tempting. Entrées run $15–22.

**Diamonds' Edge North** (603-236-2006; www.diamondsedge.com/north.html), Town Square. Open daily for dinner. Fine dining arrives in this ski town with a bang. You're treated to gourmet fare, with chicken, seafood, and meat given extra-special treatment in the form of chicken Piccata with lemon, butter, wine, and capers over pasta, pan-roasted salmon with a four-citrus caper sauce, and Tuscan sirloin steak with canelli beans and a tomato concasse. Parmigianas are also a specialty: You can choose from chicken, veal, or shrimp, served either with pasta or as a hoagie sandwich. Take-out is available, and there's a lounge menu for après-ski as well as a menu for kids and young adults with such meals as burgers, macaroni and cheese, and chicken fingers. Most entrée items $14–20.

**Wild Coyote Grill** (603-236-4919; www.wildcoyotegrill.com), Route 49. Dinner daily 5:30 PM–close. A casually elegant dining experience situated above the White Mountain Athletic Club awaits you. Sample starters like fried calamari, grilled barbecue pizza, and cod cakes ($3.95–7.95). Entrées hint at French, Italian, and Asian influences with selections like salmon *en croute* bathed in a mustard beurre blanc and layered with greens with wild mushrooms, pan-seared chicken breast with prosciutto, tomato, and mozzarella served with orzo, and ginger-soy shrimp sautéed with mushrooms, Asian veggies, cashews, and sesame seeds served over lo mein noodles—but the menu changes seasonally, so be prepared for surprises. In warm weather enjoy your meal at the Coyote Cabana by the pool. Entrées $10.95–17.95.

### *In Campton/Thornton*

**William Tell** (603-726-3618), Route 49, Thornton. The pretty stucco-and-timber exterior of this long-standing local favorite is a tip-off for the menu inside. Tried-and-true Swiss and German specialties like Wiener schnitzel and veal geschnitzeltes Zurichoise (thinly sliced veal sautéed with mushroom brandy cream sauce), prepared by Swiss native Franz Dubach. There's also a less expensive menu featuring a rich cheese fondue, steak sandwich, and curried chicken salad ($5.75–12.50), but dinner entrées run $12.50–22.95.

## EATING OUT

### *In Waterville Valley*

**Latitudes Café** (603-236-4646), Town Square. Lunch and dinner served daily 11:30 AM–9 PM. Closed April and May. Formerly known as Chile Peppers, this cheerful, reasonably priced café is now under the ownership of Mike and Janice Lambert and serves steaks, pastas, pizza, seafood, and the signature rack of lamb. Entrées $4–22.

**Jugtown Sandwich Shop and Ice Cream Parlor** (603-236-3669), the heart of Town Square. Open daily 9 AM–4 PM. A grocery store with an extensive deli (14 specialty sandwiches and a "create-your-own" menu). There are some tables, but in warm-weather months you just step outside with salads and sandwiches to the tables in the square. Fresh bagels and breads baked daily. Sandwiches are served through late afternoon; ice cream all evening.

**Waterville Valley Coffee Emporium** (603-236-4021), Town Square. Open daily 8 AM–9 PM. Enjoy cappuccinos, lattés, smoothies, chai, breakfast waffles and omelets, afternoon tea, homemade pastries, and other treats while overlooking a spectacular view of a pond and the distant mountains.

### *In Campton*

**Campton Village Café and Bakery** (603-726-4130), Route 49. Open daily for all three meals, serving until 9 PM weeknights, 10 PM on weekends. A great early or late stop on your way to or from the slopes—a bright, welcoming atmosphere and wide choice of everything from omelets and pancakes to sandwiches and burgers. Wine and beer served. Light meals $3.95–8.25; salads, pastas, and sandwiches $3.95–14.95; dinner entrées $10.95–16.95.

**Mad River Tavern & Restaurant**

(603-726-4290), Route 49 (just off I-93, Exit 28). Closed Tuesday, otherwise open from lunch through dinner. Serving until 11 PM Friday and Saturday. A homey atmosphere with an overstuffed couch, blackboard specials, and a large, varied menu. There's a wide choice of pastas and breads as well as fish. We recommend the veal Oscar, lightly breaded and topped with lobster, asparagus, and béarnaise sauce. Burgers, sandwiches, salads, beer, and wine are also served. Appetizers $2–10; pasta $7–14; entrées $11–18. Lunch $4–7.

**Mischievous Moose Deli** (603-726-1700), Route 49, Campton Corners (Exit 28 off I-93). A cute deli strategically positioned across from the local tourist information center, offering soups ($2.95), salads (chef's, tossed, and spinach, $2.95–5.95), and hefty sandwiches ($3.99) stuffed with a variety of luncheon meats, cheeses, and veggies on rye, white, and wheat bread, bulkie rolls, or tortilla wraps slathered with Boursin-style garlic-herb cheese. The horseradish cheddar spread costs an extra 75 cents but is worth it. Open for lunch.

**Sunset Grill** (603-726-3108), corner of Routes 3 and 49. Open daily from 11:30 AM to 10 PM, Sunday brunch 9 AM–2 PM. A funky, friendly roadhouse with good food: a wide selection of pastas and house specials ranging from calves' liver to buffalo steak; also burgers, chili, and a mean fried oyster po' boy. Sunday brunch is a specialty, featuring lobster omelets and crêpes Florentine. Fifty brands of bottled beer. "Kids Menu" is $4. Appetizers $3.95–6.95; entrées $8.95–17.95.

### *In Plymouth*

**Biederman's Deli and Pub** (603-536-3354), 83 Main Street, under Chase Street Market. A brick-walled, pubby oasis specializing in outstanding, create-your-own deli sandwiches; also deli salads and bag lunches.

**Jigger Johnson's** (603-536-4386), 7 Main Street. Open Monday through Saturday for lunch and dinner; Sunday dinner only. A basement pub/restaurant that is loaded with atmosphere: an inviting, three-sided bar, deep booths and dimly lit corners, walls covered with old photos and ephemera, friendly service, a wide choice of entrées—although new owners will change the menu later in 2002. Moderate.

**The Main Street Station** (603-536-7577), 105 Main Street. Open Wednesday and Thursday 7 AM–9 PM; Friday and Saturday 7 AM–9:30 PM; Sunday 8 AM–8 PM; and Monday 7 AM–3 PM. Another classic diner car (see **Littleton Diner**, below) rubbing elbows with more modern establishments along Plymouth's tightly packed Main Street. There's a huge menu sporting international dishes, fish, salads, and sandwiches—but don't look for diner standards unless you're interested in New England–style desserts like blueberry pie, strawberry shortcake, or apple crisp. Breakfasts are a gut-busting affair of eggs in all forms, pancakes, waffles, and French toast; kids are well catered to with a special menu; and at dinner you can order beer and wine with your meal. Breakfast $1.60–7; lunch $2.30–7; dinner $7–17.

**Tree House** (603-536-4084), 3 South Main Street. Open for lunch and dinner daily. A leafy atmosphere, a bar in one corner, and a big stone fireplace. The menu runs from pastas, burgers, and salads to the schnitzel du jour, steaks (aged and cut on the premises), and chicken in the tree (chicken breast stuffed with celery, herbs, and bread crumbs). Children's menu. Dinner entrées $10.95–19.95.

***In the Baker River Valley***

**Steve's Restaurant** (603-786-9788; 1-800-786-9788), just off Route 25 on Stinson Lake Road, Rumney. Open Tuesday through Thursday 11 AM–9 PM; Friday and Saturday 11 AM–9:30 PM; Sunday brunch 8 AM–2 PM; closed Monday. One of those little family restaurants that are so good they just keep growing. The menu runs from burgers and homemade meat loaf to baked scallops, prime rib, lobster, and a chicken-and-ribs barbecue. Outdoor patio and pub-style lounge. Entrées $8.95–16.95.

## ✷ Entertainment

**Plymouth Theater** (603-536-1089), 39 South Main Street, Plymouth. A 1930s movie palace that's recently been restored; screens a broad assortment of films.

Also see *Special Events* for the **New Hampshire Music Festival.**

## ✷ Selective Shopping

**ANTIQUES** In Rumney check out **Rumney Rustics** (603-786-9366), 867 Route 25; **Blue Moon Salvage** (603-786-2222), 15 Depot Street; and **Village Books** (603-786-9300) on Main Street.

**CRAFTS SHOPS** **Shanware Pottery** (603-786-9835), Route 25, Rumney. A working studio in a rustic barn features distinctive, functional stoneware pottery and porcelain: mugs, casseroles, chimes, dinnerware, lamps, and distinctive, doughnut-shaped wine casks, among many other things.

**Calico Cupboard** (603-786-9567), Main Street, Rumney, is a good place for quilts and quilters (fabrics, supplies, and classes).

**SPECIAL SHOPS**

***In Waterville Valley Town Square***

**Dreams and Visions** (603-236-2020), 6 Village Road. Books and gifts.

**Bookmonger and Toad Hall** (603-236-4544). Toys and games for children of all ages, paperbacks, games, CDs, magazines, general titles.

## ✷ Special Events

*Easter Sunday:* **Sunrise service** on Mount Tecumseh.

*Fourth of July:* **Parade and fireworks** at Waterville Valley.

*July and August:* **New Hampshire Music Festival** (603-524-1000) at Plymouth State College. Tuesday-evening chamber music concerts, Wednesday-evening concerts on the common, Thursday-evening concerts at Silver Cultural Arts Center.

*August:* **"Ugotta Regatta" and Chowder Fest** on Corcoran's Pond, Waterville Valley. **Plymouth State Fair,** Plymouth.

*September:* **Waterville Valley Labor Day Italian Festival.**

*Columbus Day weekend:* **Octoberfest** at Waterville Valley.

*November:* **Ski trails open** midmonth at Waterville Valley; **tree lighting** Thanksgiving weekend.

## LINCOLN AND NORTH WOODSTOCK

North Woodstock is a sleepy village. Lincoln, a mile east, is one of New Hampshire's liveliest resort towns. Until relatively recently, the opposite was true. Around the turn of the 20th century, Lincoln boomed into existence as a company town with a company-owned school, store, hotel, hospital, and housing for hundreds of workers, all built by the legendary lumber baron J. E. Henry. It remained a smoke-belching "mill town" well into the 1970s.

North Woodstock, set against two dramatic notches—Kinsman and Franconia—boasted half a dozen large hotels, among them the Deer Park, accommodating 250 guests. Today Deer Park is still a familiar name, but only as one of the dozen major condominium complexes that have recently become synonymous with this area. With Loon Mountain as its centerpiece, the Lincoln-Woodstock area can now accommodate 13,000 visitors.

Loon Mountain was a success from the start, opening in 1966 with a gondola, two chairlifts, an octagonal base lodge, and the then unheard-of policy of limiting lift-ticket sales. Then in 1973, I-93 reached Lincoln, depositing skiers 3 miles from the lifts. But it wasn't until the early 1980s that the town of Lincoln itself began to boom.

Three things happened at that time: All the land owned by the paper mill (see the introduction to "The Western Whites"), which had closed in 1979, suddenly became available; Loon itself had grown into a substantial ski area; and a real estate boom was sweeping New Hampshire's lakes and mountains. Positioned just south of Franconia Notch and surrounded by national forest, Lincoln was a developer's dream: relatively cheap land with no zoning.

A heady few years ensued, but now they're over. Zoning has since been imposed, and Lincoln has adjusted to its new status as a major, year-round destination—one that can accommodate as many visitors as any other resort in northern New England.

**GUIDANCE** **Lincoln-Woodstock Chamber of Commerce** (603-745-6621; 1-800-227-4191), Box 358, Lincoln 03251. A helpful, walk-in information center in the small Depot Mall on Main Street; this is also a reservation service for the area.

**GETTING THERE** *By bus:* **Concord Trailways** (603-228-3300; 1-800-639-3317; www.cjtrailways.com) provides daily service to and from Concord, Manchester, and Boston, stopping at Perry's Easy Market (603-745-3195), Lincoln.

**GETTING AROUND** Shuttle service within Lincoln makes coming by bus a viable option, especially during ski season when the Loon Mountain Shuttle serves most inns and condo complexes around town.

**The Shuttle Connection** (603-745-3140; 1-800-648-4947; www.theshuttleconnection.com) requires 24-hour advance notice but serves Manchester Airport as well as local destinations year-round.

**MEDICAL EMERGENCY** Call **911. Lin-Wood Medical Center** (603-745-2238), Lincoln.

# ✱ To See

FOR FAMILIES ✐ **Indian Head.** Like the Old Man of the Mountain, this craggy profile on Mount Pemigewasset, visible from Route 3, is an old local landmark. It is best seen from the Route 3 parking lot of the Indian Head Resort. The summit is accessible via the Mount Pemigewasset Trail, which starts off the Franconia Notch Bike Path just north of the Flume Visitors Center (see *To Do—Bicycling*).

✐ **Lost River Reservation** (603-745-8031; www.findlostriver.com), Route 112, 7 miles west of North Woodstock. July and August, 9 AM–6 PM; May and June plus September through mid-October, 9 AM–5 PM. This was the first acquisition of the Society for the Protection of New Hampshire Forests, purchased from a local timber company in 1912. The Nature Garden here is said to feature more than 300 varieties of native plants, and the glacial meltwater gorge is spectacular. Boardwalks thread a series of basins and caves, past rock formations with names like Guillotine Rock and Hall of Ships. Now maintained by the White Mountains Attractions, the complex includes a snack bar and gift shop. You can also pan for gemstones at the Lost River Mining Co. $8.50 per adult, $5 for children 6–12.

✐ **Hobo Railroad** (603-745-2135; www.hoborr.com), Hobo Junction (just east of I-93), Lincoln. Open Memorial Day through Halloween, daily July through Labor Day, otherwise weekends, and again on weekends from Thanksgiving to Christmas. A 15-mile round-trip excursion along the Pemigewasset River in "dining coaches" with velour seats and tables. Optional breakfast, picnic lunch, dinner. Café Lafayette, the deluxe dining car service on the Hobo Railroad, leaves Lincoln, Weirs Beach, and Meredith during summer months (see also *Dining Out*). Adults $8.50; children 3–11 $6.50.

✐ **Loon Mountain Park** (603-745-8111) offers a "Skyride" to mountaintop hikes and caves, also horseback riding, mountain biking, in-line skating, croquet, archery, and other activities detailed under *To Do*.

SCENIC DRIVES **The Kancamagus National Scenic Byway.** Open year-round, this 34.5-mile stretch of Route 112 runs east from Lincoln to Conway (Route 16) through the White Mountain National Forest. Officially recognized as one of the most scenic highways in the country, it climbs to 2,855 feet in elevation at the Kancamagus Pass, the ridgeline dividing two watersheds. (Streams run downhill west to the Pemigewasset and east into the Saco.) This is also the point considered the heart of the White Mountains, which, we're told, stretch for a radius of 35 miles in all directions. The highway was completed in 1959, after 25 years in the building. It offers four scenic overlooks, four picnic sites, half a dozen campgrounds (see *Lodging—Campgrounds*), several scenic areas, and access to myriad hiking trails ranging from the half-mile Rail 'n' River Trail to multiday treks into the Pemigewasset Wilderness.

Not far beyond the western entrance to the "Kanc" be sure to stop at **Lincoln Woods,** a log information center/warming hut staffed by national forest rangers. Pick up a map and guide to the highway and detailed sheets on specific trails and campgrounds.

A detailed description of the highway is offered under *To See* in "White Mountain National Forest."

For detailed descriptions of longer hikes from the "Kanc," consult the *AMC White Mountain Guide;* descriptions of individual trails are available from the **White Mountains Visitors Center** in Lincoln (see *Guidance* under "The Western Whites") and the **Saco Ranger Station** in Conway.

**Tripoli Road.** Pronounced "triple eye," this shortcut from I-93 (Exit 31, Woodstock) to Waterville Valley accesses a number of hiking trails and campsites. It is also a fine foliage-season loop, returning to Woodstock via Routes 49 and 175. (See "The Western Whites—The Waterville Valley Region.")

**Kinsman Notch.** Route 112 west from North Woodstock is less traveled but as beautiful as the Kancamagus, climbing quickly into Kinsman Notch—past Lost River (see *To See—For Families*) and Beaver Pond (see *Green Space*)—crossing the Appalachian Trail. You can continue on by the Wildwood Campground to Mount Moosilauke (see *To Do—Hiking*) or cut up Route 116 to Easton, Sugar Hill, and Franconia, and back down through Franconia Notch. Another option is to take the dirt "North–South" road off Route 116 beyond Kinsman Notch, through the national forest to Long Pond, where there is a boat launch and, we're told, good fishing; also picnic sites. You can return to Route 116 or continue on to Route 25.

**Route 118** west from North Woodstock climbs steeply through the national forest, then down into the Baker River Valley. You may want to stop at the Polar Caves in Plymouth (see *To See—For Families* in "The Western Whites—The Waterville Valley Region") and cut back up I-93; or take Route 25 to Haverhill with its handsome old village center (just south of the junction of Routes 25 and 10), returning via Routes 116 and 112 through Kinsman Notch.

## ✷ To Do

AERIAL RIDE **Loon Mountain Gondola Ride** (603-745-8111). Ride in a four-passenger, enclosed gondola to the summit, where there's an observation tower, a summit cafeteria, a summit cave walk, and hiking trails. $9.50 per adult, $5.50 per child 6–12. Under 6 free if accompanied by an adult.

Also see *Green Space* in "Franconia and North of the Notches" for **Cannon Mountain's** aerial tramway.

BICYCLING **Loon Mountain Bike Center** (603-745-8111), Lincoln. Open Memorial Day through late October. Mountain bike rentals, guided group tours, 35 km of cross-country trails along the Pemigewasset River; bikes may be hooked to the gondola and ridden down selected trails.

**The Franconia Notch Bike Path** is a favorite loop that runs 12 miles round trip from Lincoln to the Skookumchuck River.

CAMPING For a list of public campgrounds along the Kancamagus Highway see *Lodging—Campgrounds.*

THE PEMIGEWASSET RIVER

Kim Grant

**FISHING** The free *Freshwater Fishing Guide* is available at local information centers. Anglers frequent the East Branch of the Pemi, Russell Pond, and many mountain streams.

**FOR FAMILIES** **Clark's Trading Post** (603-745-8913; www.clarkstradingpost.com), Route 3, Lincoln. Open daily July through Labor Day, 9:30 AM–5 PM; weekends Memorial Day through mid-October. One of the country's oldest theme parks, begun in the 1920s as a dog ranch (Florence Clark was the first woman to reach the summit of Mount Washington by dogsled). Still owned and managed by the Clark family, known for trained bear shows (July and August); also featuring a haunted house, Avery's old-time garage and the 1890s fire station, a photo parlor, bumper boats, and Merlin's Mystical Mansion. $10 children 6 and up, $3 children 3–5; under 3 free.

**White Mountain Motorsports Park** (603-745-6727; www.whitemountainmotorsports.com), Route 3, Woodstock. Open late April through mid-October. A quarter-mile asphalt track with races every Saturday night at 6 PM. Fee charged.

**The Whale's Tale Waterpark** (603-745-8810; www.whalestalewaterpark.com), Route 3, Lincoln. Open daily late June through Labor Day 10 AM–6 PM; weekends from Memorial Day. Wave pool, speed and curvy slides, wading pool for small children, tube rentals. Rates are $20 per day, including tubes. Children under 3 and adults over 65, free.

**GOLF** **Jack O'Lantern Country Club** (603-745-3636), Route 3, Woodstock. Eighteen-hole, par-70 course, instruction, rental clubs, golf carts, and pull carts.

**HIKING** **Mount Moosilauke.** The **Benton Trail** ascends the northwest flank of Mount Moosilauke at a steady, moderate grade. The trail begins in a parking area off Tunnel Brook Road; take Route 112 west from North Woodstock about 10 miles and drive 3 miles south on Tunnel Brook Road. Other trails, the most popular being the **George Brook Trail,** begin at the Dartmouth Outing Club's **Ravine Lodge** (603-764-5858). Our favorite description of the view from the 4,802-foot summit is credited to clergyman and author Dr. Washington Gladden: "I give my preference to Moosilauke over every mountain whose top I have climbed. The view from Washington is vast, but vague; the view from Lafayette is notable, but it shows little of the sweet restfulness of the Connecticut Valley; on Moosilauke we get all forms of grandeur and all types of beauty."

**Greeley Ponds.** This easy trail is 4.5 miles round trip, beginning on the Kancamagus Highway, 9 miles east of Lincoln. As local hiking guru Steve Smith describes it: The trail climbs gradually to the high point of Mad River Notch, then dips down to Upper Greeley Pond, a deep tarn hemmed in by the cliff-studded slopes of Mount Osceola's East Peak and Mount Kancamagus. Half a mile farther you reach the south shore of boggy Lower Greeley Pond, where you can look north into the cleft of the notch.

**Lincoln Woods Trail** begins in the parking lot of the Lincoln Woods information center (warm drinks, rest rooms, trail maps) on the Kancamagus Highway just west of Lincoln. The trail crosses the East Branch of the Pemigewasset via a suspension bridge and follows the river along the bed of the old logging railroad. It accesses several other relatively short trails leading to panoramic views, connecting with the **Wilderness Trail,** which in turn accesses the trail to Zealand Ridge and Thoreau Falls.

Also see *To Do—Hiking* in "The Western Whites—The Waterville Valley Region" and "Franconia and North of the Notches" for other brief trail descriptions. Detailed descriptions of all these hikes are found in *50 Hikes in the White Mountains* by Daniel Doan and Ruth Doan MacDougall (Backcountry Publications) and in the *AMC White Mountain Guide.*

HORSEBACK RIDING **Loon Mountain** (603-745-8111). July and August. Trail rides offered; fee charged.

IN-LINE SKATING **Loon Mountain** offers a Rollerblade Arena with lessons and rentals.

MINIATURE GOLF ✐ **Hobo Hills Adventure Golf** (603-745-2125), Main Street, Lincoln. Open daily June through Labor Day, weekends in spring and fall. Eighteen holes with hills and water.

ROCK CLIMBING **Pemi Valley Rock Gym** (603-745-9800), Main Street, Route 3 at Alpine Village, North Woodstock. Twenty-foot-high indoor rock climbing wall with beginner to advanced routes. Rates are $6 juniors, $8 adults on weekdays; $8 juniors, $10 adults on weekends. Equipment extra. Also offers guided climbs and outdoor instruction.

SWIMMING **The Mountain Club Fitness Center at Loon Mountain** (603-

745-8111), Route 112, Lincoln. Open 7 AM–10 PM daily. Indoor lap pool, outdoor pool in summer.

**Swimming holes. "The Lady's Bathtub,"** in the Pemi, Lincoln. Maybe 15 feet deep, fringed with a little sand, accessible through the parking lot at Riverfront Condos. In North Woodstock the **Cascades** is a favorite dunking spot in the Pemi right behind Main Street. Other spots on the Pemi can be found along Route 175 in Woodstock. One is just across from the Tripoli Road, I-93 interchange.

Also see the **Whale's Tale Waterpark** under *To Do—For Families*.

TENNIS **Indian Head Resort** (603-745-8000). Outdoor tennis courts.

**The Mountain Club Fitness Center** (603-745-8111). Loon Mountain also offers outdoor courts.

## ✷ Winter Sports

CROSS-COUNTRY SKIING **Loon Mountain** (603-745-8111). Thirty-five km of trails, some winding partway up the mountain, others following the riverbed. Rentals, instruction, special events. Trail fee.

**Lincoln Woods Trail.** Off the Kancamagus just west of Lincoln, an inviting warming hut (warm drinks, rest rooms) staffed by national forest rangers marks the entrance to an extensive trail system; because the first 3 miles are groomed, there is a nominal trail fee .

DOWNHILL SKIING **Loon Mountain** (603-745-8111), 2 miles from I-93, Exit 32, Lincoln. With its long cruising trails and easy access, Loon attracts more skiers per year than any other New Hampshire ski area. It's a nicely designed mountain, with dozens of intermediate trails streaking its face and a choice of steeply pitched trails, served by their own high-altitude East Basin chairlift on North Peak. Beginners have the Little Sister chair and slope to themselves, then graduate to a choice of equally isolated (from hot-rod skiers) runs in the West Basin. The only hitch is that the main base area and West Basin are separated by a long, string-bean-shaped parking lot. The lay of the land dictates the strung-out shape of Loon's base facilities—along a narrow shelf above the Pemigewasset River, which in turn has cut this steep Upper Pemi Valley. The downside to skiing Loon is its popularity. Tickets are limited, and on peak winter weekends you might want to call ahead and reserve both tickets and rentals. *Lifts:* Eight, including a fast four-passenger gondola, a high-speed detachable quad, two triples, three double chairs, and one surface. *Trails:* 44 with 20 percent easiest, 64 percent more difficult, 16 percent most difficult (22 miles total). *Vertical drop:* 2,100 feet. *Snowmaking:* 99 percent. *Facilities:* Include two base lodges, three lounges, two rental shops, summit cafeteria, and midmountain lodge (Camp 3) at the base of North Peak. Slope-side lodging at the 234-room Mountain Club includes condo units, indoor pool, game rooms, and restaurants; ice skating, cross-country skiing. *Ski school:* 170 full- and part-time instructors, modified ATM system, freestyle, mountain challenge, and NASTAR terrain park. *For children:* Loon Mountain Nursery for ages 6 weeks to 6 years; Honeybears SKIwee (ages 3–5),

Bear Cubs SKIwee (ages 6–8), Mountain Explorers (ages 9–12). *Rates:* Weekends—$51 per adult, $33 juniors; $77 per adult and $48 juniors for 2 days; weekdays—$43 adults, $36 for ages 13–18, and $29 for ages 6–12; also half-day and multiday rates.

**ICE SKATING** **Loon Mountain** (603-745-8111) maintains a lighted rink near the main base lodge.

**Millfront Marketplace** (603-745-6261) maintains a lighted rink behind the complex.

**SLEIGH RIDES** **Sleigh Rides** (603-745-6261; 603-745-8766) depart regularly from the front of the Millfront Marketplace.

**SNOWMOBILING** Trail maps available locally detail the extensive local system.

## ✷ Green Space

**Beaver Pond,** Route 112 west from North Woodstock in Kinsman Notch, beyond Lost River. A beautiful pond with a rock promontory for picnicking or sunning and a view of Mount Blue.

For **Franconia Notch,** see "Franconia and North of the Notches."

Also see *Hiking* in this section and the detailed description of the **Kancamagus Scenic Byway** under *To See—Scenic Drives* in "White Mountain National Forest."

## ✷ Lodging

### RESORTS

***All resorts listed are in Lincoln 03251.***

**Lodge at Lincoln Station** (603-745-3441; 1-800-654-6188), midway between town and mountain, with studios, one-bedroom, and loft suites overlooking the river (be sure to request one) and a central "Great Room" with a hearth; also indoor and outdoor pools, a Jacuzzi, saunas, game room, and tennis courts. All units have kitchenette. Rates range $65–165, depending on season and accommodations. An optional meal plan is $25 a day per person for breakfast and dinner.

**The Millhouse Inn** (603-745-6261; 1-800-654-6183; www.millatloon.com; info@millatloon.com), Route 112 on Main Street. A 95-room hotel built from scratch but connected (a luxury in winter) to the Millfront Marketplace (see *Selective Shopping*), a complex that incorporates three of the old paper-mill buildings. It is connected to the ski area in winter by Loon's shuttle. Amenities include indoor and outdoor pools, Jacuzzis, and exercise room. Some suites have kitchen facilities but most are simply spacious one- or two-room, nicely designed spaces with phone and color cable TV. Downstairs public spaces include a library with fireplace and ample comfortable corners. Doubles are $59–119, suites (some with a separate room with bunks for children, sleeping up to six) are $60–179.

**The Mountain Club on Loon** (603-745-2244; 1-800-229-7829; www.mountainclubonloon.com). Forget the hassles of parking a mile away and lugging your gear to the slope; stay on the slope at New Hampshire's only mountainside resort hotel. Virtually within sight of the lifts at Loon Mountain, this former member of the Marriott chain offers 234 rooms, 100 of them suites with fully equipped kitchens and expansive mountain views. Park your car when you arrive, then wake up to a room-service breakfast before strapping on your skis. A complete fitness center—including indoor/outdoor pool, Jacuzzis, saunas, and steam rooms—adds to the luxury. There are also cross-country trails and a skating rink within walking distance. Rates range from $104–142 for a standard double to $199–529 for a suite that will sleep 10 during prime ski season. Packages are available throughout the year.

**Rivergreen Resort Hotel at The Mill** (603-754-2450; 1-800-654-6183; www.millatloon.com; info@millatloon.com), P.O. Box 1056, Route 112. A separate building, unattached to the Mill House Inn or the Marketplace but part of the same complex. Hotel rooms run $70–100, one-bedroom condo units are $110–179, two-bedroom, $150–250; nearly all units have in-room Jacuzzi. Weekly and package rates available.

✐ **The Village of Loon Mountain** (603-745-3401; 1-800-258-8932). Of the 650 units here, 200 are in the rental pool. Positioned directly across the road from Loon Mountain, this development is nicely designed to blend into the hillside. Amenities include two indoor pools, 12 outdoor tennis courts (2 are flooded to form a skating rink in winter), a kids' game room with arcade, and table tennis. $50–80 per person per night with a 2-night minimum in winter.

**RESORT MOTELS** **Indian Head Resort** (603-745-8000; 1-800-343-8000; www.indianheadresort.com), Lincoln 03251. First opened in the 1920s, gradually evolving to its present 90 motel rooms, 50 cabins (with fireplaces; closed in winter), as well as two bungalows. Indoor and outdoor heated pools, tennis courts, game room, coffee shop, and dining room. $48–185 per room, depending on room and season; $59–149 bungalows and cabins.

**Jack O'Lantern Resort** (603-745-3636; 1-800-227-4454; www.jack-olanternresort.com), North Woodstock 03262. Closed between foliage and ski season, open again in summer. A landmark local motel that has evolved into a resort with 25 motel rooms, 50 one- to three-room cottages and condominiums. Amenities include a pool, tennis, Jacuzzi, 18-hole golf course. $89–106 per motel room, $110–117 per suite.

**Woodward's Resort** (603-745-8141; 1-800-635-8968; www.woodwardsresort.com), Route 3, Lincoln 03251. An 85-room complex that has grown gradually over the past 48 years, this resort is now open year-round and carefully managed by the Woodward family. Rooms are clean but plain, though extras like refrigerators and coffeemakers make you feel right at home. Recreational facilities include indoor and outdoor pools, an indoor racquetball court, tennis court (you can rent racquets), and a pond that is used for winter ice skating (management provides skates). In summer there are also lawn games. The **Colonial Dining Room** serves breakfast daily, and dinner is served nightly in the **Open Hearth Dining Room;** there's also a lounge. $56–119 per room.

**INN The Woodstock Inn** (603-745-3951; 1-800-321-3985; www.woodstockinnnh.com), P.O. Box 118, Main Street (Route 3), North Woodstock 03262. Known for its microbrewery and its formal (on the glassed-in front porch) and informal dining (in Woodstock Station out back; see *Where to Eat*), this long-popular establishment also offers 21 antiques-furnished rooms (13 with private bath) in the main inn and in two additional Victorian houses, Riverside and The Deahman House. All rooms have a phone and color TV; some have Jacuzzi, fireplace, and air-conditioning. Complimentary evening beverages. $59–165 per room. Children are charged for breakfast, however.

**BED & BREAKFASTS The Red Sleigh Inn** (603-745-8517), Box 562, Pollard Road, Lincoln 03251. Located in a residential neighborhood away from the busy main drag, Lincoln's only B&B is a cozy alternative to a standard motel room or condominium. Once the home of a local lumber baron and dairy farmer, the Red Sleigh is now a home away from home with six guest rooms, four on the second and two on the top floor, with and without private bath. All are furnished with a mix of old and new. To make sure you sleep tight, innkeepers Bill and Loretta Deppe equip each bed with a teddy bear. There's television in the living room, and a full vegetarian breakfast is included in $75–110 per room depending on time of year.

**Wilderness Inn** (603-745-3890; 1-800-200-9453; www.thewildernessinn.com;wilderness@juno.com), Route 3 and Courtney Road, North Woodstock 03262. Each year innkeepers Rosanna and Michael Yarnell welcome return guests who have come back to enjoy their easy hospitality, cozy accommodations, and hard-to-beat, mountain-sized breakfasts (see *Eating Out*). Within earshot of the Lost River, this forest-green, 1912 shingled bungalow is an easy walk to town and offers eight comfortable, antiques-filled guest rooms. All rooms have private bath and TV. A separate gem of a cottage has a fireplace, sleigh bed, TV, Jacuzzi tub, and deck. Breakfasts, served most seasons on a sunny, glassed-in porch, are included in the $65–150 per room rate.

**MOTELS Franconia Notch Motel** (603-745-2229; 1-800-323-7829; www.franconianotch.com), Route 3, Lincoln 03251. The nicest kind of family-run motel: 6 two-room cottages (summer only) and 12 standard motel units, backing on the Pemigewasset River where picnic tables and grills are in place. Franconia Notch State Park is half a mile up the road. Each unit is different; most have twin beds. Board games and morning coffee are available. In-season rates are $59–79 per couple; off-season is a bargain starting at $30.

**CAMPGROUNDS** The campgrounds along the Kancamagus Highway are among the most popular in the White Mountain National Forest and are accessible only on a first-come, first-served basis.

**Covered Bridge Campground** (1-800-280-CAMP) takes reservations.

**Pemigewasset Region** (603-536-1310): **Hancock** (4 miles east of Lincoln) is open year-round with 56 sites; and **Big Rock** (6 miles east of Lincoln) is open year-round with 23 sites.

**Saco Region** (603-447-5448): **Passaconaway** has 33 sites; **Jigger Johnson** has 75 sites; **Covered Bridge** has

49 sites; and **Blackberry Crossing** has 26 sites.

**Ammonoosuc Region** (603-869-2626): **Wildwood** is open mid-April through early December. Offers 26 campsites, good fishing.

See "The Waterville Valley Region" and "Franconia and North of the Notches" for more White Mountain National Forest campsites.

## ✷ Where to Eat

DINING OUT **Café Lafayette Dinner Train** (603-745-3500), on the Hobo Railroad, Hobo Junction, Lincoln. The typical menu on this 2-hour excursion in a vintage-1924 Pullman railroad car begins with caviar or pâté and proceeds through sorbet to a choice of chicken, salmon, or pork tenderloin. Adults $42, children 4–11 $25.

**The Common Man** (603-745-3463; www.thecman.com), at the corner of Pollard Road and Main Street, Lincoln. Open nightly except Thanksgiving and Christmas. The winning formula here is a limited menu stressing simplicity and fresh ingredients, from pasta primavera ($11.95) and lobster and rock crabcakes ($15.95) to prime rib ($13.95) and filet mignon ($16.95). There's a great new grill menu to boot. This place, with its huge fireplace and the coziest lounge around, consistently rates rave reviews. Entrées range $12–20.

**Gordi's Fish and Steak House** (603-745-6635), Route 112, Lincoln. Dinner is served daily 4–10 PM. The decor is glitzy Victorian mixed with photos of ski heroes past and present (the owners include two past members of Olympic ski teams). There are nightly specials like blackened tuna, stuffed pork with apple gravy, or salmon *en papillote;* standard menu items include fish-and-chips and other seafood. Beef lovers are well served with prime rib, filet mignon, or New York sirloin. Lighter meals include chicken done up a number of ways as well as pasta dishes—and you can also make a meal of the salad bar. $7.95–18.95.

**Govoni's Italian Restaurant** (603-745-8042), Lost River Road, Route 112 west of North Woodstock. Open nightly from Memorial Day through Labor Day. No reservations. Northern Italian specialties served in a traditional New Hampshire house overlooking Agassiz Basin. House specialties range from eggplant parmigiana to scallop-stuffed scampi. Children's menu.

**The Olde Timbermill Restaurant & Pub** (603-745-3603), Millfront Marketplace, Route 112, Lincoln. Family restaurant prices but a pleasant, brick-walled, dimly lighted, multitiered place in a part of the original mill; a nightclub lounge is the liveliest place in town on ski weekends. The vast menu ranges from pastas to T-bone steak and includes a variety of stir fries. A children's menu includes a beverage with a reasonable $3.95–5.25 price; entrées range $4.95–21.95

**Seasons on Loon** (603-745-6281), in the Mountain Club on Loon Mountain. Open daily for all three meals. Formerly Rachel's, this restaurant manages to combine a relaxed ambience with a slightly upscale menu featuring memorable appetizers and entrées. Moderate to expensive.

**The Woodstock Inn** (603-745-3951; www.woodstockinnnh.com), Main Street (Route 3), North Woodstock. Open nightly 5:30–9:30 PM. The Clement Room, a glassed-in porch set crisply with white linen tablecloths and fine china, is the location for fine dining. The à la carte menu includes appetizers like ostrich quesadilla and pan-fried ravioli with red pepper pesto; entrées range from chicken dishes ($11.95 up) to fillet Barcelona: a 9-ounce center-cut fillet butterflied and stuffed with sautéed scallops and crab and topped with hollandaise sauce ($23.95).

EATING OUT **Chieng Gardens** (603-745-8612), Lincoln Square, Main Street, Lincoln. A better-than-average Chinese restaurant with a large, reasonably priced menu and the best view (upstairs, facing the mountains) of any restaurant in Lincoln.

**Elvio's Pizzeria** (603-745-8817), Lincoln Square, Lincoln. "Best pizza north of the Bronx." The best pizza in town; subs and basic Italian dinners to go or stay.

**Peg's—A Family Restaurant** (603-745-2740), Main Street, North Woodstock. Open daily for breakfast and lunch. Roll up your sleeves alongside loggers and other local denizens in this plainly furnished but friendly room for rib-sticking breakfasts of eggs and steak, omelets, pancakes, and Belgian waffles. On a budget? Keep an eye out for the 99-cent breakfast specials. New England favorites like hot meat loaf, turkey, and roast beef sandwiches—not to mention burgers, hot dogs, western *and* eastern sandwiches—are all served with a smile and words of wisdom. Look for daily specials like American chop suey (macaroni, beef, and tomato sauce baked together) or liver and onions served with mashed potatoes. Breakfast 90 cents–$5.95. Lunch $2.25–7.25.

**Truants Taverne** (603-745-2239), Main Street, North Woodstock. Open daily 11:30 AM–10 PM, until 11 PM on Friday and Saturday. Hung over the river in a back-behind kind of space, part of an old mill yard. Polished pine tables and a large menu that's fun to read: For lunch choose from a wide selection of cleverly named burgers and other dishes. At dinner the Dean's List includes veal Marsala, but you can also scrape by with that old Exchange Student or Elementary Burger. A good place.

**Woodstock Station** (603-745-3951; www.woodstockinnnh.com), at the Woodstock Inn, Main Street (Route 3), North Woodstock. This railroad station was built in the late 1800s in Lincoln and continued to serve visitors—including skiers bound for Cannon Mountain—into the 1930s and 1940s. In 1984 it was sawed in half and moved to its present location; the old freight room is now the bar, and the passenger waiting room is the lower dining room. This large, eclectically furnished space, which now includes the Woodstock Inn brewery, is one of the liveliest dining spots in the North Country, and the menu boasts—count 'em—148 items: everything from frogs' legs to Peking ravioli, quesadillas and nachos and burritos (lots of Mexican), a wide choice of original sandwiches, pastas, baked scrod, ribs, and burgers. The children's menu includes a $2 hot dog. Beverages fill four more pages of the menu and include a wide variety of imported and microbrewed beers. $6.50–16.

FOR BREAKFAST **The Country Mile** (603-745-3158), Main Street, Lincoln, across from the Millfront Marketplace. Open daily except Wednesday 7 AM–2 PM, until 1 PM on Sunday. Smoking and nonsmoking sections. The waitress greets you with, "You want coffee?" and plunks down a mug with your menu. This is a clean, cozy, friendly oasis in the middle of a commercial strip. "Breakfast all day" is the motto here, and we recommend the omelets.

**The Millaway Café & Bakery** (603-745-4771), upper level of Millfront Marketplace. Open 7 AM until early afternoon, later in July and August. Breakfast until 2 PM. Good coffee, muffins, hearty breakfasts, light lunches, and cheesecake.

**Sunny Day Diner** (603-745-4833), Route 3, Lincoln. Nothing could be finer than breakfast in a diner, especially with this selection of omelets, French toast, waffles, and bake shop specialties. Serving breakfast and lunch 6 AM–2 PM, dinner 4:30–8 PM.

**The Woodstock Inn** (603-745-3951; www.woodstockinnnh.com), Main Street (Route 3), North Woodstock. A wide range of waffles, omelets, and other memorable breakfast fare—like homemade red-flannel hash with poached egg and homefries, bagels and lox, and huevos rancheros. Breakfast is served in the Clement Room; entrées run $5.95–13.95.

**Wilderness Inn and Café** (603-745-3890), Route 3 and Courtney Road, North Woodstock. Serving 8–10 AM mid-February through mid-September. A short walk from downtown to a pleasant, hospitable guest house serving freshly ground coffee, homemade muffins, selected hot crêpes, and multiple choices of pancakes, eggs, and omelets. Reservations appreciated.

## ✷ Entertainment

**Papermill Theater at the Mill** (603-745-2141), The Mill at Loon Mountain. Shows July and August, Tuesday through Saturday, at 7:30 PM and Sunday at 2 PM; musicals, comedy, classics, children's theater on Wednesday at 11 AM.

**Lincoln Cinemas 4** (603-745-6238), Lincoln Center North, Main Street, Lincoln. Four screens.

**Summer band concerts.** Regularly on the common in North Woodstock.

**Loon Mountain Music Series** (603-745-8111). The North Country Chamber Players perform regularly at the Governor's Lodge during summer months.

## ✷ Selective Shopping

**Antiques, Crafts, and Collectibles** (603-745-8111), at Loon Mountain. Open daily late May through October. More than 50 dealers exhibiting furniture and furnishings, stained glass, pottery, crafts, and more.

**Dick's Dugout,** Main Street, North Woodstock. A baseball-card collector's oasis.

**Fadden's General Store,** Main Street, North Woodstock. Open daily. One of the few genuine, old-time general stores left in New England (now run by the third generation of Faddens), filled with genuine relics of a storekeeping past; also an amazing assortment of current stock.

**Lahout's Country Clothing and Ski Shop, Inc.,** Main Street, Lincoln. Open daily. A branch of the Littleton store opened in 1922 and was billed as "the oldest continually operated ski shop in New England." Operated by the three sons of the original Lahout and dedicated to "beating anyone's price," this is unquestionably one of *the* places in the North Country to shop for ski gear, sturdy footwear, long johns, etc., etc.

**Millfront Marketplace,** Route 12, Lincoln. Twenty shops and restaurants in a complex incorporating three turn-of-the-20th-century mill buildings. The complex includes: **The Country Carriage**—"country" gifts, reproduction furniture, tinware, collectible dolls. **Innisfree Bookshop** (603-745-6107) is the only full-service bookstore in the region, specializing in New England titles, White Mountain guides and trail maps, ski titles, field guides, and children's books and educational toys.

**Mountain Wanderer** (603-745-2594), Main Street, Lincoln. Specializing in New England maps and guides to outdoor recreation, travel, and natural history; also USGS topographic maps, compasses, and White Mountain gifts.

**Pinestead Quilts** (603-745-8640), 99 Main Street, Lincoln. An unusual selection of locally made quilts, machine-pieced but with hand-tied, traditional designs. From $65 for quilted wraps to $650 for king-sized quilts.

**Rodgers Ski Outlet,** Main Street, Lincoln. Open daily 7 AM–9 PM. "La who?" the competition may well ask if you mention Lahout's. More than 1,500 pairs of skis in stock at any time; tune-ups, rentals, repairs are the specialties. Billed as "northern New England's largest volume ski shop."

## ✷ Special Events

*January:* **Independence Day Weekend** at Loon Mountain, "celebrating Loon's independence from nature."

*March:* **Spring Fling** at Loon Mountain.

*June:* **Annual Fiddlers' Contest,** sponsored by Lincoln-Woodstock Lions Club.

*July:* **Fourth of July celebration,** Lincoln-Woodstock. **Arts and Crafts Fair** at Loon Mountain.

*September:* **Lumberjack Festival,** Labor Day weekend, at Loon Mountain. **New Hampshire Highland Games,** Loon Mountain.

*September through October:* **Royal Lipizzan Stallions** performing at the Millfront Marketplace, Lincoln.

*October:* **Fall Foliage Festival** at Loon Mountain.

*November through December:* **Holiday celebrations** at the Millfront Marketplace, Lincoln.

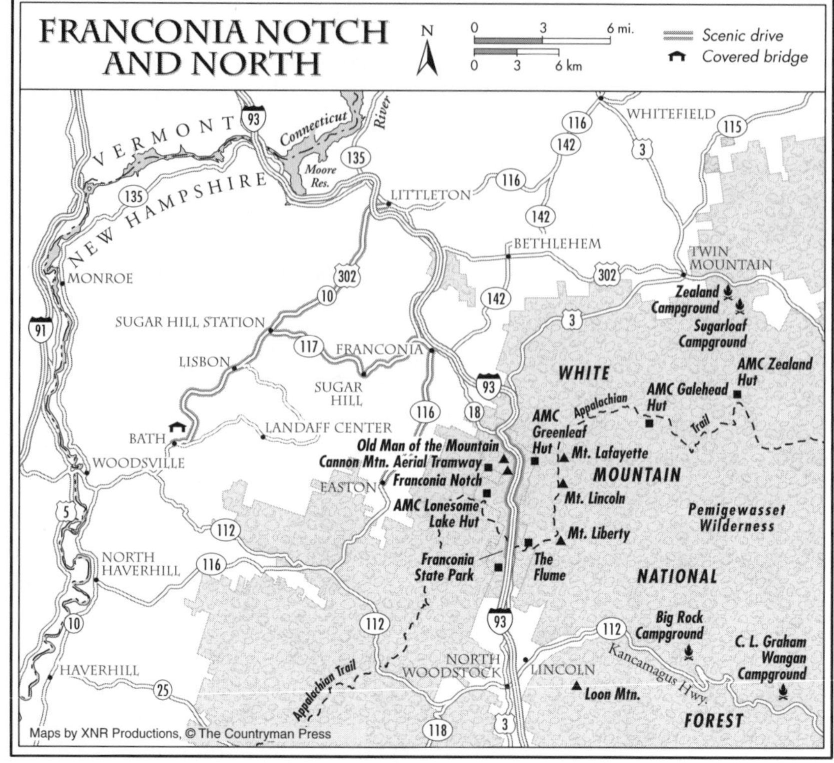


## FRANCONIA AND NORTH OF THE NOTCHES

Wrapped in forest and dominated by granite White Mountain peaks, the Franconia-Bethlehem area seems to be the distilled essence of northern New Hampshire. Northwest of this high, wooded country, the landscape changes suddenly, flattening around Littleton, the shopping town for this region. For views of both the Green Mountains and the White Mountains, follow this Ammonoosuc Valley south to Lisbon and Bath, then back up to Sugar Hill and Franconia on memorable back roads.

The town of Franconia alone packs into its 65 square miles more splendid scenic vistas and unusual natural attractions than many states or provinces can boast. Curiously, while annual visitors to Franconia Notch are said to outnumber New Hampshire residents, relatively few stray into the delightful neighboring valley, which seems happily trapped in a 1950s time warp.

Franconia and its small satellite towns of Sugar Hill and Easton have been catering to visitors of one sort or another for more than 150 years. Travelers were first attracted to Franconia Notch by its convenience as a north–south route through the mountains; but they were invariably impressed by the scenery, and their tales of natural wonders like the granite profile of the Old Man of the Mountain circulated widely.

Sightseers and health seekers began trickling into the notch after the War of Independence, and a few inns and taverns catered to them along with more conventional travelers. Then in the mid–19th century the railroad arrived, inaugurating a grand resort era. Such literary notables as Nathaniel Hawthorne, Washington

Kim Grant

A SIGHT-SEEING GONDOLA AT FRANCONIA NOTCH STATE PARK

Irving, John Greenleaf Whittier, and Henry Wadsworth Longfellow were all Franconia summer visitors whose enthusiastic accounts of the region fanned its fame. Hawthorne even wrote a story about the Old Man, "The Great Stone Face."

One of the most celebrated hotels in America in its day, and a symbol of the White Mountains' golden age, was the 400-room Profile House, which stood in the heart of Franconia Notch. Besides elegant service in a rustic setting, the hotel offered its guests a superb view of the Old Man. An institution for 70 years, Profile House burned down in 1923, just as the automobile began permanently altering America's vacation habits and the grand-hotel era was ending. The hotel site is now part of Franconia Notch State Park.

Grand hotels also appeared in Bethlehem, known for its pollen-free air. It became headquarters for the National Hay Fever Relief Association, which was founded here in the 1920s. At one time Bethlehem had 34 hotels, some large and luxurious indeed, and a 2-mile-long boardwalk for their guests to stroll along.

Although many once-famous grand hotels closed their doors in the 1920s and 1930s, a few lasted until the 1950s, when railroad service to the White Mountains ended and a resort way of life ended with it. A few traces of Bethlehem's glory days remain, such as the impressive fieldstone and shingle clubhouse (formerly The Casino) of the Maplewood Golf Course.

Summer residents and hotel guests, outraged at what unrestricted logging was doing to their beloved mountain scenery, founded the still-active Society for the Protection of New Hampshire Forests (SPNHF). The efforts of this pioneering conservation organization eventually led to the creation in 1911 of the 768,000-acre White Mountain National Forest, the first national forest in the country.

When the summer resort scene began to fade in the White Mountains, a winter one commenced, thriving as Americans discovered skiing. The Franconia area can claim a number of skiing firsts, among them the nation's first ski school (which opened at Pecketts-on-Sugar Hill in 1929) and this country's first aerial tramway (constructed in 1938), which ran to the summit of the formerly state-owned Cannon Mountain. Cannon also hosted America's first racing trail in the 1920s and its first World Cup race in the 1960s.

In 1945 a flamboyant Austrian aristocrat, Baron Hugo Von Pantz, founded Mittersill, a Tyrolean-style resort adjacent to Cannon. The baron's resort attracted high-society types from New York and Boston, and, for a time, Franconia was the New England equivalent of Aspen or St. Moritz.

Times change. The current winter hot spot is south of the notch (see "Lincoln and North Woodstock"), and the socialites have gone the way of the old hotels. An unusual number of craftspeople have settled in—graduates of Franconia College, a liberal institution of the 1960s that was housed in the old Forest Hill Hotel but died with the 1970s. Some of New Hampshire's most pleasant inns and bed & breakfasts are scattered throughout the folds of the valleys and gentler hills north and west of Franconia Notch.

GUIDANCE **Franconia–Easton–Sugar Hill Chamber of Commerce** (603-823-5661; 1-800-603-237-9007; www.franconianotch.org), Box 780, Main Street, Franconia 03580. A downtown information booth is open through the end of October; another is open at the Cannon Mountain tramway base station.

**Bethlehem Historical Museum and Information Center** (603-869-3409; www.bethlehemwhitemtns.com), P.O. Box 748, Bethlehem 03547. Year-round information booth on Route 302 near the intersection of I-93 with limited winter hours.

**Littleton Area Chamber of Commerce** (603-444-6561; www.littletonareachamber.com), 141 Main Street, Box 105, Littleton 03561. Seasonal information booth located along Main Street, but the chamber maintains an information kiosk in the Community Center behind the booth all year.

**Lisbon Chamber of Commerce** (603-838-6522), 6 South Main Street, Lisbon 03585.

**Twin Mountain Chamber of Commerce** (603-846-5407; reservations 1-800-245-8946; www.twinmountain.org), Box 194, Twin Mountain 03595, produces a brochure and operates a summer information center at the junction of Routes 3 and 302.

**WMNF Ammonoosuc Ranger Station** (603-869-2626; www.ss.fed.us/r9/white), 660 Trudeau Road, between Route 3 and Route 302, Box 239, Bethlehem 03574. Open Monday through Friday 8 AM–4:30 PM. From the north take Exit 40 to Route 302, and go through Bethlehem. From the south take Exit 35, Route 3. The helpful web site dishes out information on hiking, foliage updates, and avalanche warnings.

THE OLD MAN OF THE MOUNTAIN IS VISIBLE FROM FRANCONIA NOTCH.

Robert Kozlow

**GETTING THERE** *By bus:* **Concord Trailways** (603-228-3300; 1-800-639-3317; www.cjtrailways.com) has daily service from Boston, Manchester, Concord, Lincoln, and Littleton.

*By car:* From north or south, take I-93 to Franconia Notch Parkway (Route 3). Route 116 west leads to Franconia and the adjacent towns of Sugar Hill and Easton. Route 302 east leads into Bethlehem from the north, Route 142 east from the south.

**MEDICAL EMERGENCY** **Littleton Hospital** (603-444-7731; 1-800-464-7731), 600 St. Johnsbury Road, Littleton at Exit 43 off I-93.

**Grafton County Dispatch** (603-823-8123). Franconia-Easton rescue service.

**Bethlehem Volunteer Ambulance** (603-869-2232), 2155 Main Street.

Robert Kozlow

THE OLD BRICK STORE IN BATH IS SAID TO BE THE COUNTRY'S OLDEST GENERAL STORE.

## ✷ Villages

**Bath.** The village of Bath itself is known for its vintage-1832 covered bridge and for its 1804 Old Brick Store, billed as the country's oldest general store. Upper Bath Village, a few miles north on Route 302, is a striking cluster of Federal-era brick homes set against surrounding fields.

**Landaff Center.** Set well back into the hills east of Route 302, this is one of New Hampshire's most-photographed old hill towns. The town hall commands a superb view of the hamlet, whose population hovers around 300 souls—give or take a few summer people. You can't help wondering what it would be if Dartmouth College had been sited here the way Gov. John Wentworth suggested in 1770.

**Sugar Hill.** Once part of Lisbon, whose center was some 10 miles away, the folks of this village petitioned the legislature to become a separate town. Set high on a ridge with views to Franconia Ridge and the Presidentials, this cluster of homes, inns, and churches is one of the state's prettiest communities.

**Lisbon.** An industrial town whose growth can be owed to the many paper mills planted alongside the Ammonoosuc River.

## ✷ To See

**Mount Washington Cog Railway.** See *To See* in "Mount Washington and Its Valleys—Crawford Notch and Bretton Woods."

Also see *Green Space*.

**MUSEUMS AND HISTORIC SITES** **The Robert Frost Place** (603-823-5510; www.thefrostplace.com), Box 74, Ridge Road, off Route 116, Franconia. Open from Memorial Day through Columbus Day, Wednesday through Monday 1–5 PM. Frost's home from 1915 to 1920, now a town-run museum on a "road less traveled by," attracts international visitors. Each year a resident poet spends the summer on the property imbibing views of the same unfolding hills and fields of lupine that inspired New England's best-known poet. The 1859 farmhouse and barn are the site of frequent poetry readings and workshops. The home contains rare editions of Frost's books, photos, and memorabilia, and there is a slide presentation about his life and work in Franconia. A nature trail behind the house is posted with quotations from appropriate Frost poems. Admission $3 adults, $2.50 children 7–12.

**Franconia Iron Furnace Interpretive Center** (603-823-5000), 553 Main Street, junction of Routes 18 and 117, Franconia. Open May through October, Thursday and Saturday 1–4 PM. This is the only blast furnace left in New Hampshire, and stands as a reminder of the once-dominant iron ore industry, which enjoyed its heyday during the 19th century. The furnace is viewable only during daylight hours owing to its location on private property. You can also visit the adjacent museum of Franconia history in a 10-room 1880 house. Donation.

**New England Ski Museum** (603-823-7177; www.skimuseum.org). Next to the tramway base station at Franconia Notch Parkway Exit 2, this popular museum relates the history of New England skiing with exhibits of skis, clothing, and equipment dating from the 19th century to the present, along with vintage still photos and film. Open December through March, Friday through Tuesday noon–5 PM; every day from Memorial Day through Columbus Day. Free.

**Sugar Hill Historical Museum** (603-823-5336; www.franconianotch.org), Main Street (Route 117), Sugar Hill. Interesting, small local museum with changing exhibits about aspects of the town from its pioneer settlement in 1780 until the present. Open July through mid-October, Thursday, Friday, and Saturday 1–4 PM. Admission $2 adults, $1 seniors; children under 12 are free.

**Littleton Historical Society** (603-444-6435; 603-444-2637), 1 Cottage Street, Littleton. Open from July through September, Wednesday and Saturday 1:30–4:30 PM; Wednesday only October through June. A large collection of local items includes stereoscopic slides (unique photographs published by the famous Kilburn Brothers of Littleton). Free admission.

**Littleton Gristmill** (603-444-3971; 1-888-284-7478; www.littletongristmill.com), 18 Mill Street, Littleton. Open year-round. Powered by the Ammonoosuc River, this mill was built in 1797 and, thanks to the hard work of two local families, still runs today based on its original site, turning out organic grains for pancake, muffin, and waffle mixes on sale at the on-site gift store. Watch and learn about the grinding process while on a guided tour and from museum displays. Free admission.

**Crossroads of America** (603-869-3919; www.travel.to/cofa), corner of Trudeau Road and Route 302, Bethlehem. Open June through foliage season, 9 AM–5 PM; closed Monday. A must-stop for rail fans: the world's largest three-sixteenth-scale model railroad on public exhibit. Tours offered every hour. Admission fee.

**SCENIC DRIVES I-93,** the parkway through Franconia Notch, is perhaps too obvious since it is a destination for many visitors to New Hampshire. It's one of the state's most scenic corridors, so take your time to enjoy the views and the many roadside natural attractions. Be aware that traffic can be very slow during foliage season and on summer and ski weekends, however.

**Route 117** from Franconia village steeply uphill to Sugar Hill (take the short Sunset Hill Road for breathtaking mountain views), then continue down to Lisbon on Route 302/10, turn north beside the Ammonoosuc River to Littleton, or turn south through Lisbon village to Bath, with its old country store and covered bridge.

**Route 116** follows the valley between Franconia and Easton. Old farms and mountain scenery.

FRANCONIA RIDGE IS ONE OF THE MOST POPULAR HIKES IN THE WHITE MOUNTAINS.

Robert Kozlow

## ✱ To Do

**AIR RIDES Franconia Inn** (603-823-5542; 1-800-473-5299; www.franconiainn.com; info@franconiainn.com), 1300 Easton Road, Franconia 03580, offers glider rides.

**BICYCLING** An 8-mile-long bicycle path, used in winter as a cross-country ski trail, traverses Franconia Notch.

**GOLF Bethlehem Golf Course** (603-869-5745; www.bethlehemccnhgolf.com), Main Street (Route 302), Bethlehem. This par-70 course lies outside Bethlehem near I-93 and offers 18 pristine holes of golf for $30 per person weekends, $25 weekdays with cart and club rentals available. Check with your accommodation about package rates.

**Lisbon Village Country Club** (603-838-6004), Bishop Road, Lisbon. Nine holes.

**Maplewood Country Club and Hotel** (603-869-3335; 1-877-869-3335; www.maplewoodgolfresort.com), Main Street (Route 302), Bethlehem. Attractive, Donald Ross–designed, 18-hole layout with a grand clubhouse, this par-72 course offers a challenge to all players. There's a pro shop, driving range, and unique par-6 hole. The course is so popular on weekends that carts are required of all players to speed up play.

**Sunset Hill Golf Course** (603-823-5522), Sugar Hill. Recently rescued by townsfolk from outside developers, this short nine-hole par-33 course sits atop Sunset Hill and gives players dramatic mountain views.

THE LOWER SKI SLOPES OF CANNON MOUNTAIN RISE BEHIND MIRROR LAKE

Kim Grant

**HIKING** Hiking information is available at the Franconia–Easton–Sugar Hill Chamber of Commerce and the Bethlehem Chamber of Commerce information booths; the Franconia Notch State Park Visitors Center by the entrance to the Flume; the park's Lafayette Campground; Cannon Mountain; and the national forest's Ammonoosuc Ranger Station (see entries under *Guidance* and *Green Space*). Franconia Notch offers some of the most rewarding short hikes in the White Mountains. They include:

**Artist's Bluff and Bald Mountain.** From Route 18 in Franconia Notch State Park, 0.5 mile north of its junction with Route 3. The parking lot is across from Cannon Mountain's Peabody Ski Slopes. Favored by 19th-century guests at the notch's former hotels, Bald Mountain is an easy ascent with sweeping views. First you follow an old carriage road to a saddle between two summits, then branch left to Bald Mountain, right to Artist's Bluff. You should investigate both. The round trip is 1 or 1.8 miles.

**Basin–Cascades Trail** (3 miles). Start at the Basin, marked from Route 3 in Franconia Notch State Park, and ascend along Cascade Brook leading to the Cascade Brook Trail.

**Lonesome Lake Trail.** From Lafayette Place on Route 3 in Franconia Notch, an old bridle path leads to an 80-acre lake that sits at an elevation of 2,734 feet and is warm enough in summer for swimming. The Appalachian Mountain Club's Lonesome Lake Hut offers overnight lodging and a variety of family-geared programs. Contact the AMC Pinkham Notch Camp (603-466-2727).

**Mount Lafayette via the Old Bridle Path.** This is a full day's hike, and you should pick up a detailed map before attempting it. After 2.5 miles you reach the AMC Greenleaf Hut (for lodging, phone 603-466-2727); the summit—with magnificent views—is another 1.1 miles. If the weather is good and your energy high, continue along the **Franconia Ridge Trail** south over Mount Lincoln to Little Haystack. This narrow, rocky route is spectacular, but there are steep drops on both sides of the trail. At Little Haystack turn right (west) onto the **Falling Waters** Trail. This trail passes more waterfalls in 2.8 miles than any other trail in the mountains; it ends back at Lafayette Place.

**HORSEBACK RIDING** **Franconia Inn** (603-823-5542), Route 116, Franconia.

## Winter Sports

### CROSS-COUNTRY SKIING

#### *In the White Mountain National Forest*

Detailed maps of all these trails are available from the Franconia–Easton–Sugar Hill Chamber of Commerce, at Cannon Mountain, and from the Ammonoosuc Ranger Station (see *Guidance* and *Downhill Skiing*).

**Lafayette Trails,** Route 3, Franconia Notch. The **Notchway Trail** is the old Route 3 roadbed, accessed from Route 141 just east of I-93, Exit 36. It's identified by a metal sign with a skier symbol. The trail is 2.1 miles, and side loops include the short **Bog Trail,** the more difficult **Scarface Trail** (1.2 miles), and the **Bickford Trail** (0.3 mile).

**The Pemi Trail,** Franconia Notch. Just over 6 miles long, this trail extends from Profile Lake to the Flume parking lot and is open to cross-country skiers, snowshoers, and hikers. It can also be accessed from the Echo Lake, tramway, and Flume parking areas. Pick up a map at the information booth at the Cannon Mountain base lodge in Franconia Notch.

**Beaver Brook Cross Country Trails** begin at the Beaver Brook Wayside on Route 3 between Twin Mountain and Franconia Notch. The **Beaver Loop** is 2.3 km, Badger is a more difficult 3.1 km, and **Moose Watch** is classified as "most difficult," a total of 8.6 km with some spectacular views. These trails are ungroomed and not regularly patrolled, so be sure not to ski alone.

**Zealand Valley Trails.** See *To Do—Cross-Country Skiing* in "Mount Washington and Its Valleys—Crawford Notch and Bretton Woods."

### *Elsewhere*

**Franconia Inn** (603-823-5542; 1-800-473-5299; www.franconiainn.com), Easton Valley Road, maintains 29 miles of trails, and an additional 15 miles meander across this 1,100-foot-high valley. Rentals (skates and snowshoes, too) and lessons available.

**Sunset Hill House Touring Center** (603-823-5522; 1-800-SUN-HILL), Sunset Hill Road, Sugar Hill. Thirty km of groomed, tracked trails from this hilltop inn. No ski shop.

**DOWNHILL SKIING** During the 2002 Winter Olympics in Salt Lake City, Utah, Franconia native and noted wildman skier Bode Miller wowed his hometown and international audiences as he blew away the competition racing in downhill skiing events. Cannon Mountain is where he honed his skills.

**Cannon Mountain** (603-823-7771; 1-800-237-9007; www.cannonmt.com), Route 3, Franconia. One of New Hampshire's oldest ski mountains, Cannon has a whopping 2,146-foot vertical drop. Its aerial tram (the country's first, in the 1930s) was replaced in the 1980s, and snowmaking has since been substantially increased to cover 97 percent of the 42 trails. Lifts include one regular-speed quad chair and one high-speed quad chair, three triple chairs, and two doubles as well as the tram. While its image remains "The Mountain That'll Burn Your Boots Off!," in reality many trails here have been softened—broadened and smoothed as well as carpeted with snowmaking. In addition to runs in Franconia Notch itself, more than a dozen intermediate and beginner runs meander down the mountain's gentler northern face to the Peabody Slopes base area. The only trails still "au naturel" are Taft Slalom (a remnant of that 1920s racing trail) and the Hardscrabbles—both of which command their own followings.

**SNOWMOBILING** In Franconia Notch the bike path serves in winter as a corridor connector for the 100-mile network of snowmobile trails in this area. Twin Mountain is a popular snowmobiling center. Some winter weekends are as busy as those in summer. Many motels and lodges have trails right from the door that connect to a large trail network. For maps and other information, write **Twin Mountain Snowmobile Club,** Box 179, Twin Mountain 03595; the **Trails Bureau** (603-

271-3254, option 4), New Hampshire Division of Parks and Recreation, Box 856, Concord 03301; or the **New Hampshire Snowmobile Association** (603-224-8906), Box 38, Concord 03301. (Also see *To Do—Snowmobiling* in "Mount Washington and Its Valleys—Crawford Notch and Bretton Woods.")

## * Green Space

**Franconia Notch State Park** (603-823-5563). This 6,440-acre park runs between the Franconia and Kinsman mountain ranges and contains many of the White Mountains' most notable natural sights. As it passes through the 8 miles of the notch, I-93 is scaled down to the Franconia Notch Parkway (Route 3), built (after a 25-year controversy) to funnel traffic through with minimum scenic and environmental impact. The principal sights of the notch are all within the park and easily accessible from the parkway.

**The State Park Visitors Center** by the entrance to the Flume provides information and shows interpretive films of the area. It also has a snack bar, rest rooms, and a souvenir shop. A $10 combination ticket is available for adults, good for a round-trip tramway ride and admission to both the Flume and Echo Lake beach.

**The Flume** (www.flumegorge.com). An 800-foot-long, deep and narrow gorge—no more than 20 feet wide but up to 90 feet high—through which Flume Brook flows. A system of staircases and boardwalks takes visitors through the Flume to Ridge Path, which leads to Liberty Cascade and on to Sentinel Pine covered bridge, overlooking a clear mountain pool. The Wildwood Path loops past

FRANCONIA NOTCH PARKWAY

Kim Grant

giant boulders brought down by the glaciers and returns to the Flume entrance. Adults $8; children 6–12, $5; children 5 and under free.

**Echo Lake.** A 28-acre lake at an elevation of 1,931 feet, the mirrorlike surface of which perfectly reflects Mount Lafayette and Cannon Mountain. There are picnic tables, a swimming beach, a boat-launching area, canoe and paddleboat rentals ($10 per hour), and 10 sites for RV hook-ups. Admission is $3 ages 13 and up; children 12 and under are free.

**Cannon Mountain.** One of New Hampshire's most popular ski areas and the site of America's first aerial tramway. The present tramway, which replaced the 1938 original in 1980, carries 80 passengers to the summit of the 4,180-foot-high mountain, where there is an observation tower and the panoramic Rim Trail. Besides operating during ski season, the tram runs from late May through Columbus Day, when autumn colors are usually at or near peak. A round-trip tram ticket is $10 for adults, $6 for children 6–12 years of age, and free for children 5 and under. One-way tickets are $8 for adults, $6 for children 6–12. (Also see *Downhill Skiing*.)

**The Old Man of the Mountain.** The famous 40-foot-high rock formation—the state's official symbol—resembles the profile of a craggy-featured male. (The pioneers who discovered the profile in 1805 thought it looked like Thomas Jefferson.) The great stone face juts out from a sheer cliff above Profile Lake, and the best view and photograph are from the lakeshore.

**The Basin.** A deep glacial pothole or natural pool almost 30 feet in diameter created over eons by the churning action of water rushing down from the nearby waterfall.

**The Rocks Estate** (603-444-6228; www.therocks.org), Route 302, R.F.D. 1, Bethlehem 03574. Owned by the Society for the Protection of New Hampshire

THE BASIN

Kim Grant

Forests (SPNHF), this estate with huge barns is the northern headquarters for the state's largest and most active conservation organization. The estate's 1,200 acres are managed as a tree farm by the SPNHF; a large area is reserved as a Christmas tree plantation. Trees are sold during the annual Christmas tree celebration held in December. Several nearby inns offer special package plans for lodging, meals, and a Christmas tree. There are various conservation and family programs (see *Special Events*) held through the year, plus a self-guided nature trail and cross-country skiing.

**Bretzfelder Park** (603-444-6228; 603-869-2683; www.therocks.org), Prospect Street, Bethlehem. Owned by the SPNHF, this 77-acre site is managed as a community park, with various summer programs plus picnic tables, fishing, and a guided nature trail.

## ✱ Lodging

**INNS** **The Ammonoosuc Inn** (603-838-6118; 1-888-546-6118; www.amminn.com), 641 Bishop Road, Lisbon 03585. Open year-round. A 19th-century farmhouse perched on a knoll above the Ammonoosuc River and Route 302, the Ammonoosuc Inn provides a good base for travelers seeking an active vacation. Skiers find the short distances to Cannon Mountain and Bretton Woods a good reason to stay here, each being a 15- to 30-minute drive away. Current owners Jim and Jeni Lewis purchased the inn in 1998 and still maintain nine well-appointed rooms, each with private bath, including several with claw-foot tubs; locals flock to the **in-house restaurant.** Guests can also relax in two spacious parlor rooms; one is equipped with a television, a lounge with a full bar, and a big wraparound porch. B&B rates range $85–125; MAP rates and golf packages also available.

**The Beal House Inn** (603-444-2661; www.bealhouseinn.com), 2 West Main Street, Littleton 03561. Mrs. Beal first opened her home, built in 1833, to the public 60 years ago. In 2001 Floridians Jose and Catherine Pawelek became the innkeepers and introduced many amenities into their plush guest rooms: Some are equipped with gas fireplace, CD player, and a sitting area decked out with lovingly restored antiques and quirky decorations. All the rooms are worthy of a visit, but Mrs. Beal's suite on the first floor gives guests two rooms in which to spread out; the sitting room is decked out with a TV/VCR, a rocking chair, and a comfy couch. Two common rooms with fireplaces offer books, television, and movies—in fact, travel and lifestyle magazines are available for leisure reading throughout the inn—while the glass-enclosed front porch provides a good view of downtown Littleton. In the back, a deck overlooks a fern-filled hillside. Be aware that the inn is on a busy street, so noise from traffic may filter into your room. Rates for two are $85–135 with full breakfast.

♿ **Franconia Inn** (603-823-5542; 1-800-473-5299; www.franconiainn.com; info@franconiainn.com), 1300 Easton Road, Franconia 03580. The grande dame of the notch region, this inn makes sure you stay busy with four clay tennis courts, a heated swimming pool, guided horseback tours, bicycles, a croquet court, cross-country skiing, ice skating, sleigh rides, and a glider port, all on 107 acres in the heart of the Easton Valley. Founded just after the Civil War, the inn has 34 guest rooms (including wheelchair-accessible accommodations on the first floor), all recently renovated in traditional style. Common areas include an inviting oak-paneled library, a spacious living room with a fireplace, and two porches to catch sunrise and sunset. Two candlelit dining rooms provide casually elegant dining and spectacular views (see *Dining Out*). Downstairs, there's a family-sized hot tub and Rathskeller Lounge. Rates range $96–156 per double in low season, $116–176 the rest of the year. MAP rates and a variety of package plans are also available.

🐾 ✐ **The Hilltop Inn** (603-823-5695; 1-800-770-5695; www.hilltopinn.com; nh@hilltopinn.com), 1348 Main Street, Sugar Hill 03585. Owners Mike and Meri Hern have turned their funky and fun 1895 Victorian home, located in the middle of sleepy Sugar Hill, into a most hospitable B&B. All six guest rooms include full private bath, period antiques, handmade quilts, English flannel sheets, sunsets from the deck, large country breakfasts, and afternoon snacks and tea. Rates run $90–120 per room in low season and $125–195 during summer and foliage season. Pets are welcome for $10 more, and children will be charged $35 a day as long as they sleep in the same room as their parents.

THE HILLTOP INN IN SUGAR HILL

Kim Grant

**Ledgeland Inn and Cottages** (603-823-5341), 761 Route 117, Sugar Hill 03585. Built as a rustic private home and managed by the Whipple family for more than 50 years, Ledgeland offers casual accommodations with a spectacular view of the Presidential and Franconia Ranges. The inn itself has nine rooms and is open from late June until mid-October. The 14 cottage units are open year-round and have fireplace and kitchen. Daily rates, including homemade breakfast, range $70–150 per double.

**Lovett's Inn** (603-823-7761; 1-800-356-3802; www.lovettsinn.com; lovetts@ncia.net), by Lafayette Brook, Route 18, Franconia 03580. A tradition in these parts, Lovett's was built in 1794 and is listed in the National Register of Historic Places. For the past 75 years, it has operated as an inn, securing a reputation with generations of guests for its warm hospitality, fine views, and excellent food (see *Dining Out*). New owners Jim and Jan Freitas have made sure that all five rooms in the original inn have private bath, CD player, and hair dryers; they're furnished with an eclectic mix of antiques and reproductions. Our favorite is the

Nicholas Powers room, which has great views of Cannon Mountain as well as a single whirlpool tub. An additional 14 fireplaced cottages with fairytale names are scattered around the grounds and are well appointed. Larger accommodations include the Stonyhill Suite with a double whirpool tub, and the much roomier Stonyhill Cottage with a living room, fireplace, TV, and porch. There is also an outdoor pool and spa. Most rooms are $125–175 with breakfast included and dinner an additional $35 per person. Rates increase by $40 during fall foliage season and decrease by $10 in winter. Nonsmoking.

**Sugar Hill Inn** (603-823-5621; 1-800-548-4748), Route 117, Franconia 03580. This rambling 1789 white-clapboard farmhouse, set on 16 acres of manicured lawns, gardens, and woodland, captures the essence of gracious but unpretentious New England hospitality. Barbara and Jim Quinn are easygoing hosts who combine a variety of talents. She decorated the 10 airy guest rooms and six cottage suites with stenciled walls, handmade quilts, candlewick bedspreads, and a variety of antiques. He serves guests afternoon tea, three-course breakfasts, and delicious gourmet meals. Fireplaces in several of the rooms add to the ambience, and there's a great porch to enjoy the mountain views. Rates range $90–195 including full breakfast; suites run $175–265.

**Sunset Hill House** (603-823-5522; 1-800-SUN-HILL; www.sunsethillhouse.com), Sunset Hill Road, Sugar Hill 03585. Open all year. You can see forever in two directions, the White Mountains to the east and the Green Mountains to the west, from this 1880s-era property. Located atop a 1,700-foot ridge, the inn was originally built as the annex for one of the area's grand hotels. Although the main house is now gone, this 21-room inn with its own 7-room annex remains, and has been completely renovated and remodeled. All of the traditionally furnished guest rooms come with comforters and coordinated fabrics, antique and reproduction furniture, and private baths where you'll find unique complimentary toiletries including lip balm. The exceptionally friendly owners Lon and Nancy Henderson have increased guest comfort with the addition of two 2-room Jacuzzi and fireplace suites and five other rooms with a choice of gas fireplace or Jacuzzi. All rooms have a phone, and local calls are free. Common areas include a TV room, a small bar, a heated pool, and a golf course across the street. B&B rates $100–295; MAP $35 per person. Additional golf, getaway, and holiday packages available.

**Thayer's Inn** (603-444-6469; 1-800-634-8179; www.thayersinn.com), 136 Main Street, Littleton 03561. Open year-round. Located on busy Main Street, this classic, white-pillared, Greek Revival structure has been a beacon to weary travelers since it opened in 1843. Most of the 40 rooms have private bath, TV, and telephone, and all are air-conditioned. Since each room is individually furnished, guests are invited to select their favorite on arrival. The two-bedroom suites are great for families. Don and Carolyn Lambert, innkeepers. EP $40–110; two-bedroom suites $70–90 for up to four people.

♿ **Wayside Inn** (603-869-3364; 1-800-448-9557; www.thewaysideinn.com), Route 302 at Pierce Bridge, Bethlehem 03574. This historic 18th-century inn building offers four guest rooms furnished with traditional New England country pieces. The adjacent modern motel has a dozen additional rooms with balcony, cable TV, refrigerator, air-conditioning, and either two double beds or a queen; all have private bath. You can relax on the sandy beach. Room rates $119–139 in high season, $89–99 in low season. Special package plans for golf, quilting, harvesting a Christmas tree, or gourmet packages.

**BED & BREAKFASTS** **Adair** (603-444-2600; 1-888-444-2600; www.adairinn.com), 80 Guider Lane at the junction of I-93 and Route 302, Bethlehem 03574. A grand house in the truest sense, Adair exudes serenity and good breeding. You're instantly seduced by the winding approach through rolling lawns and landscaped gardens, but ironically the estate sits minutes from I-93—though you're protected from the sounds of rushing traffic. Once at the house, the double front doors open onto a large center hall where a wide stairway leads to two floors with nine luxurious guest rooms. All have private bath (three have two-person tubs, and one has a whirlpool bath); all feature king or queen beds and are furnished with antiques or reproductions. Note the unique collection of quirky vintage hats playfully arranged on the staircase as well as the original artwork hung in rooms. Back downstairs, there are comfortable dining and living rooms with fireplaces shared with the separately owned **Tim-Bir Alley** restaurant. Across the lawn, a fully equipped private cottage provides an additional guest retreat. In the basement's granite-walled common area, there's a grand old pool table and lots of cozy couches and recliners on which to snuggle. Innkeepers Judy and Bill Whitman provide afternoon tea and a full breakfast, included in the room rate: $225–405 high season, $150–330 low season, depending on accommodations. Dining available in-season at Tim-Bir Alley (see *Dining Out*).

🐾 ✐ **The Australian Bed & Breakfast** (603-823-7788; www.australianbed-n-breakfast.com), P.O. Box 717, Franconia 03580. Marlene and Neil O'Brien offer what native Australian Neil calls "fair-dink-um" hospitality in their casual, barnlike home. Wide windows offer views along the Gale River. An octagonal stone stack, the only blast furnace still standing in New Hampshire, is on the property (see *To See—Museums and Historic Sites*). There are three guest rooms, one with a private bath; the others share. The "Down Under" game room offers billiards, darts, cable television, and a woodstove. Children and pets are welcome at no extra charge Doubles ($75–100) include a hot breakfast.

🐾 ✐ **The Balmoral** (603-869-3169; 1-800-898-8980; www.thebalmoral.com; thebalmoral@aol.com), 2533 Main Street, Bethlehem 03574. Adjacent to the Maplewood Golf Course, innkeepers Mark and Elizabeth Morrison, who trace their lineage to original Bethlehem settlers, focus on attending to their guests' needs in their Federal-period Colonial manse rather than expanding their bed count. Guests can choose among three guest rooms and one suite—all with private bath, TV/VCR, and dining table. Enjoy the company of your fellow guests at breakfast in the dining room or, if you need more privacy, have breakfast served in your room. While away a few hours with a book from the inn's extensive library or just gaze at the stunning mountain terrain outside. Animals and children are welcomed, though there is a $20 fee per day for children and a $10 flat fee for pets. Rates are $95–150, representing the range between low and high seasons.

**Bungay Jar** (603-823-7775; 1-800-421-0701; www.bungayjar.com), P.O. Box 15, Easton Valley Road, Franconia 03580. Tucked in the woods and surrounded by a brook, a lily pond, and amazing gardens, this whimsical inn—named for a wind that blows down through the mountains—makes you feel as if you've just stumbled onto a fairy-tale cottage. Actually, it's an enlarged 18th-century barn that owner Bruce Ashby has filled with a collection of furnishings and accessories that gives new meaning to the word *eclectic.* Six rooms, all with private bath, prove that opposites attract. Sleigh beds are paired with skylights; gunstock beams with Benny Goodman's old bathtub. You can feel the power of nature vibrating from every corner here. The onetime hayloft, now a two-story living room/dining room with fireplace, overlooks the Kinsman Range. So does the Garden suite on the ground floor, which boasts a double Jacuzzi tub skillfully positioned for viewing said mountain range, a king-sized bed, kitchenette, gas fireplace, and French doors leading to a private porch next to the garden. Rates—$110–145 per room in low season and $125–175 during fall foliage and holidays—include afternoon tea, homemade snacks, a full country breakfast, and access to a sauna. The Garden suite runs $195–230. Extra people are charged $25 per day for a cot, and there's a 2-night minimum stay during foliage season and weekends.

**Foxglove, A Country Inn** (603-823-8840; 1-888-343-2220), Route 117 at Lovers Lane, Sugar Hill 03585. Innkeepers John (J. R.) and Kathleen Riley took over this sweet B&B in late 2001 and have ambitious plans to keep it at the high level of service maintained by its previous owners. Rooms are carefully decorated and outfitted with period pieces handpicked by J. R., who is a well-known antiques dealer in Massachusetts—look for the actual Louis XVI mirror with settee in the corner room. You'll find black-and-white family photographs from the early 20th century lining the walls, giving the place a personal feel. Kathleen has added new comforters to all the rooms, and the former African-styled Serengeti Room will be completely overhauled to match the serene pastel decor of the other rooms. The grounds are likewise beautiful, with extensive gardens, fruit trees, hammocks, and outside terrace. A sun room (heated in winter) overlooks the backyard, where you'll most likely view wild turkeys and the occasional moose while sipping

THE BUNGAY JAR INN

Kim Grant

your morning coffee; a common room has a fireplace and lots of books. Adjacent to the main house is a carriage house warmed by gas fireplaces and handmade quilts. The two rooms here can be rented separately, but mostly occupants are couples or families traveling together. Rates during high season run $105–145, and during fall foliage $125–175. Full breakfast is included.

**The Grande Victorian Cottage** (603-869-5755; 401-333-6496; www.grandevictorian.com), 53 Berkley Street, Bethlehem 03574. This ornate turn-of-the-20th-century mansion is located on a residential street just off the main drag and within easy walking distance of tennis courts and an 18-hole golf course. There are eight lavishly decorated, period-style bedrooms, six with private bath, in the main house. Two more guest rooms and baths are in the former butler's quarters. The $75–125 rate includes a hearty country breakfast in the kitchen or dining room, and afternoon snacks on the circular porch. Designated smoking area.

**The Homestead** (603-823-5564; 1-800-823-5564; www.thehomestead1802.com), on Route 117, Sugar Hill 03585. Sitting at the confluence of Route 117 and Sunset Hill Road, the Homestead is the matriarch of Sugar Hill lodging: It's been run exclusively as an inn by the same family for seven generations, making it one of the oldest family-run inns in the United States. Your hosts, the Hayward family, offer 20 rooms, each reflecting the past with vintage furnishings as well as the slight inconvenience of shared bathrooms (each room has its own sink and mirror). Rooms in the annex, however, all have private bath. The dining room, where you're served a hearty breakfast with maple syrup from the farm, is pine paneled with old hand-hewn beams and family collections of china, glass, and silver. Antique furniture, books, and photographs fill the common rooms, making the atmosphere throughout pure nostalgia. Cross-country skiing is free, and downhill skiing packages are available. Rates: $85–150 foliage; $60–110 low season.

**The Inn at Forest Hills** (603-823-9550, 1-800-280-9550), Route 142, Franconia 03580. Close to I-93, this English Tudor–style inn has seen several incarnations since it was constructed in 1890. Originally an annex to one of the area's grand summer resorts, it later served as the home for the president of Franconia College. Seven spacious rooms spritzed with Citrus Magic air freshener, each with private bath and king- or queen-sized beds, are brightly furnished with Pottery Barn–style pieces and carefully maintained. An attic room is slated for updated additions, which may include a whirlpool tub. Some rooms have phone jacks for travelers with laptop computers, but no phones are available. Common areas include a 45-foot covered porch, a sun-filled solarium, a high-ceilinged breakfast area, and an oversized fireplace. Bostonian owners Joyce and Vladimir Petkovich have plans to install more gardens and cross-country ski trails. Rates, which include a five-course breakfast, are $110–175; higher July through October.

**Kinsman Lodge** (603-823-5686; 1-866-KINSMAN; kinsmanlodge@yahoo.com. Plain but worthwhile, this fairly recent addition to the Franconia lodging scene offers comfortable and relaxing digs while keeping the price down. Breakfast is served in bed, and the rate is $40–65. Pets and kids are graciously welcomed.

**The Mulburn Inn** (603-869-3389; 1-800-457-9440), Main Street, Bethlehem 03574. Innkeepers Christina Ferraro and Alecia Loveless purchased this stately mansion in 1998 and spent many hours renovating it to provide comfortable and affordable bed & breakfast accommodations. Built in 1908 as a summer home for a member of the Woolworth family, the house boasts imported bathroom fixtures, Italian tile fireplaces, stained-glass windows, and much hand-carved woodwork. Seven guest rooms, each with private bath, are furnished in period style. Large wraparound porches, fireplaced common rooms, and a shared Jacuzzi invite relaxing. Rates range $80–100; full breakfast included.

**MOTELS** **Gale River** (603-823-5655; 1-800-255-7989; www.galerivermotel.com; galermtl@worldpath.net), Route 18, Franconia 03580. Now run by Pat and Peter Sprague, the tidy Gale River Motel, open only in summer and fall, has 10 rooms and two cottages. Amenities include in-room coffeemaker, refrigerator, TV, and telephone, plus a heated outdoor pool, whirlpool, and hot tub. Rates for a double, $60–85. Cottages, which sleep six, are $90–110 with a 2-night minimum stay. Summer weekly cottage rental, $625–650.

**Franconia Village Hotel Resort and Conference Center** (603-823-7422; 1-888-669-6777; www.franconiavillagehotel.com), Wallace Hill Road (Exit 38 off I-93), Franconia 03580. Totally revamped in 2001, this full-service hotel caters to visitors of all stripes seeking clean, affordable accommodations with in-room amenities like microwave, refrigerator, TV, and phone (free local calls), iron and ironing board, and air-conditioning. A suite with a full kitchen keeps families on a budget happy with more space. On site, you'll find a heated indoor pool, saunas, game room, and exercise facilities as well as a family-oriented restaurant. High-season rates are $79–139; low-season, $69–129. The hotel offers a variety of ski and holiday packages.

**Stonybrook Motel** (603-823-8192; 1-800-722-3552; www.stonybrookmotel.com), 1098 Profile Road (Route 18), Franconia 03480. Debbie and Paul Yugo took over the motel in the spring of 2000 and have made many improvements. Among them is remodeling the heated indoor pool; there still is an unheated outdoor pool. Other renovations include enlarged bathrooms in two rooms with queen-sized beds; the other four queen-bedded rooms have replaced bathroom fixtures. Doubles run $52–95; upstairs rooms, with incredible mountain views and two double beds, are $75–95. The motel is closed at the end of March and reopens from mid-May until the end of October. It then reopens the day after Christmas until the end of March for ski season. Kids under 15 are free. There is a $10 charge for additional adults. Pets aren't allowed. Be sure to check out the trout pond during the summer. Feeding times are particularly entertaining as the fish clamor for food and show off their girth—the owners have decided to keep the fish around as "pets" rather then fry them up at the end of the season, hence their gargantuan size.

**Eastgate Motor Inn & Restaurant** (603-444-3971; www.eastgatemotorinn.com) off I-93 at Exit 41 on

Route 302. An easy-on/easy-off location makes this motel a good choice for those wanting to get out early in the morning to explore the region. Drive up to your standard hotel room and take advantage of the free in-room local calls. The restaurant is surprisingly good, and the prices are reasonable. Room rates during low season (January through June) are $49.70; $59.70 July through September, and $69.70 September 29 through October 14.

LODGE ✐ **Pinestead Farm Lodge** (603-823-8121), Route 116, Franconia 03580. If you're seeking unpretentious lodging at a fair price, this working farm may be right up your alley. The lodge has been offering travelers and hikers a spot to bed down since 1900. Nine rooms, in clusters of threes, share baths and fully equipped kitchens. Rooms may be rented singly, or each section may be taken as a private unit. Kids can unwind in the play yard, and folks of all ages enjoy the tennis court and other lawn games, plus easy access to fishing, hiking, and downhill and cross-country skiing. Guests are welcome to walk about to see maple sugaring, shingle cutting, and farm animals like sheep, cows, and horses all bleating, mooing, and neighing—sometimes simultaneously. The locally renowned **Pinestead Quilts,** with a retail outlet in Lincoln, are made on the premises, and can be found warming each bed. Rates for farmhouse rooms are $18–20 per person, double occupancy.

CONDOMINIUMS **Village of Maplewood** (603-869-2111; 1-800-873-2111), Main Street (Route 302), Maplewood 03574. Fifteen condo townhouse units are available for daily or weekly rental. Rates from $125 a night.

CAMPS Several **Appalachian Mountain Club High Mountain Huts** (603-466-2727; www.outdoors.org), Box 298, Gorham 03581, are located in this area. Nearest to Route 302 off Zealand Road is the **Zealand Hut** (2.8-mile hike); adjacent to I-93 in Franconia Notch are **Lonesome Lake** on the western side of the highway and **Greenleaf Hut** (2.5-mile hike) on the eastern side. Lonesome Lake is the nearest AMC hut to a road, just 1.7 miles and a mild 1-hour walk that's easy for children; there is swimming and fishing in the lake. On the trail between Greenleaf and Zealand is **Galehead.** You must hike to the huts and supply your clothes and towels; they provide meals, bunks, and blankets. The huts are open for operation from spring through early fall, and they fill up quickly; reservations are highly recommended. Some AMC programs involve guided hikes to the huts. Contact the AMC for rates and other information, and see the *AMC White Mountain Guide* for trail routes.

CAMPGROUNDS **WMNF campgrounds** are located along Route 302, east of Twin Mountain. **Sugarloaf I and II** have 62 sites, and **Zealand** has 11 sites. The Sugarloaf sites are part of the **toll-free reservation system** (1-800-280-2267; www.reserveamerica.com). (See *Hiker's Lodging* in "Mount Washington and Its Valleys—Mount Washington.")

**Lafayette Campground** (603-823-5563), a popular state park facility just off the parkway in the heart of Franconia Notch, has 97 wooded tent sites available on a first-come, first-served basis. A central lodge has showers and a small store with hiking and camping supplies. Site fees are $8–17.

**Echo Lake** in Franconia Notch also has 10 sites for RV hook-ups.

Local private campgrounds include **Fransted Campground** (603-823-5675; www.franstedcampground.com; fransted@aol.com), Route 18, Franconia, with 65 wooded tent sites and 26 trailer sites; and **Apple Hill Campground** (603-869-2238; 1-800-284-2238), Route 142 north, Bethlehem, with 45 tent sites, 20 trailer hook-ups, a store, and a bathhouse.

## ✷ Where to Eat

DINING OUT **The Flying Moose Restaurant** (603-444-2661; www.bealhouseinn.com; info@bealhouseinn.com), 2 West Main Street, Littleton. Open year-round in the **Beal House Inn.** The owner-chef's country gourmet menu emphasizes wood-grilled items, fresh seafood, rustic breads, and made-from-scratch desserts. Dinners are served Wednesday through Sunday in two intimate dining rooms. Tasty appetizers like crunchy fried coconut shrimp or wood-grilled duck breast leave the taste buds wanting more and are promptly rewarded by ambitious mains like snapper with Barbados rum and bananas, lamb shank over mashed sweet potatoes, chicken with Gorgonzola cream sauce, or seafood ravioli with curry, raisins, and apple all served with house salad, homemade bread, and oven-roasted vegetables. Desserts run the gamut from flourless chocolate cake with crème Anglaise and warm bittersweet chocolate sauces to raspberry charlotte

THE APPALACHIAN MOUNTAIN CLUB'S GREENLEAF HUT PERCHES ON THE FLANKS OF MOUNT LAFAYETTE.

Rob Burbank, AMC

and a classic French *tarte tatin* served with ice cream and warm ginger-caramel sauce. There's a good wine list with some reserve wines as well as a full bar. Appetizers range $6–8; entrées are $14–26, and desserts $5–6.

**Franconia Inn** (603-823-5542; 1-800-473-5299; www.franconiainn.com; info@franconiainn.com), 1300 Easton Road, Franconia. Breakfast 7–10 AM, dinner nightly 5:30–9 PM. Long considered *the* local restaurant for elegant dining and special occasions, the Franconia Inn's handsome candlelit dining rooms offer black-tie service and a mountain view. Cocktails are served in the cozy, paneled Rathskeller Lounge. Despite the elegant surroundings, children are warmly welcomed by the kid-oriented menu featuring a "mega-grilled" cheese sandwich and baked crispy chicken nuggets. And the kids can spend their (or your) quarters in the video game room while waiting for their meal. Typical entrées include saltimbocca, filet mignon with smoked veal breast, shrimp primavera, and veal medallions *au champagne*. Appetizer run $5–8 and entrées $11–20.

MEALTIME AT THE AMC'S GREENLEAF HUT

Rob Burbank, AMC

**Grand Depot Café** (603-444-5303), 62 Cottage Street, Littleton. Lunch is served Monday through Friday 11 AM–2 PM; dinner, 5–9 PM. Casual but gracious, this restaurant is fast becoming a favorite with locals and visitors alike. Kudos include the *Wine Spectator* Award of Excellence, and the chef trained in New York and Paris. Rack of lamb, escargots, and pâté as well as great desserts are among the grown-up specialties, but kids can order burgers or pasta from the children's menu. Entrées $16–26.

**Lovett's by Lafayette Brook** (603-823-7761; 1-800-356-3802; www.lovettsinn.com), Profile Road, Franconia. Dinner 6–9 PM; reservations suggested. Gourmands in the know have been dining here for years and appreciate the good food and fine wines. You can quaff predinner cocktails in the cozy lounge, then retire to one of three connecting open-beamed rooms to savor a memorable five-course meal. Entrées may include pan-seared rainbow trout with lemon caper butter, chicken and wild mushrooms served with a rosemary wine sauce, roast pork tenderloin finished with currant glaze, or beef tenderloin medallions drizzled with a red wine and shallot sauce. Appetizers are on the expensive side and run $12–14; entrées, $16–22.

**The Riverview Restaurant at the Wayside Inn** (603-869-3364; 1-

800-448-9557; www.thewaysideinn.com; info@thewaysideinn.com), Route 302 at Pierce Bridge, Bethlehem. Open nightly except Monday, spring through fall; Friday and Saturday in winter 6–9 PM. Victor and Kathe Hofmann, the European owners of this dining room at the Wayside Inn, emphasize Continental cuisine served on tables draped with red-checked cloth bathed in candlelight, casting a warm glow on diners. Swiss specialties are served nightly, and fondue is always popular in ski season. Kids relate to the simple meals like the grilled cheese sandwiches and spaghetti and meatballs. Appetizers $4.59–6.25, entrées $10.95–19.95.

**Sugar Hill Inn** (603-823-5621; 1-800-548-4748; www.sugarhillinn.com), Route 117, Franconia. Dinner, by reservation only, is served nightly during foliage season; seating between 6 and 8. Open the same hours on weekends and holiday periods during the rest of the year. Traditional but memorable four-course dinners range from roast duck served with cranberry-orange sauce to French-cut rack of lamb baked with fresh rosemary and wine and breast of chicken stuffed with spinach, pine nuts, garlic, and Swiss cheese. Homemade breads and desserts. $28–30.

**Sunset Hill House** (603-823-5522; 1-800-SUN-HILL; www.sunsethillhouse.com), Sunset Hill Road, Sugar Hill. Dining by reservation only, 5:30–9:30 PM; also a lighter menu served daily in the tavern. Dine bathed in the warm glow of the candlelight and warmed by the fireplace in this nicely renovated old inn. The menu rotates seasonally and may include superb grilled pork or a zesty bouillabaisse. Enjoy distinctive appetizers like savory Thai spring rolls, soups, salads, and desserts like the summer-only Bag O' Espresso—but the star of the show is the view, which envelops the entire Presidential Range. Moderate to expensive.

**Tim-Bir Alley** (603-444-6142), 80 Guider Lane at Adair Country Inn, Bethlehem. Dinner Wednesday through Sunday 5:30–9 PM, by reservation only. Chefs Timothy and Biruta Carr offer fine North Country dining at this intimate gourmet restaurant, serving an eclectic menu that changes weekly and features unique appetizers like pork-scallion dumplings with spicy peanut sauce or sautéed shrimp on noodles with pine nut pudding and plum-ginger sauce. Entrées might include garlic-and-olive-scented salmon with spinach, Brie, and pine nut pesto; tournedos of beef with grilled leeks, smoked bacon, and a Cabernet-thyme sauce; or Moroccan spiced chicken with a peach-almond chutney. End your meal with homemade desserts like mango-macadamia cheesecake with warm honey sauce or chocolate-hazelnut pâté. The chefs take great care to ensure that each meal looks as great as it tastes. Appetizers run $4.95–8.50; entrées, $17.95–23.50.

EATING OUT **The Clamshell** (603-444-6445; 603-444-6501), Dells Road, Littleton. Open weekdays 11:30 AM–4 PM and 5–9 PM, Friday and Saturday until 10 PM; Sunday noon–9 PM. Just off I-93's Exit 42, this is a popular seafood restaurant serving lobster, steaks, and prime rib; also sandwiches and a salad bar. Later hours in tavern. Lunch $4.95–13.95; dinner $8.95–18.95.

♿ **Cold Mountain Café** (603-869-2500), 2015 Main Street, Bethlehem. Open Monday through Saturday for lunch 11 AM–3:30 PM, dinner 5:30–

9:30 PM. Credit cards are not accepted. A laid-back ambience and eclectic menu attract a counterculture crowd to this tiny café wedged into a row of businesses on Bethlehem's Main Street. Run since the winter of 2000 by ex–New Yorker Jack Foley, Cold Mountain offers soups, salads, and sandwiches to eat in or take out at lunch. The menu becomes more gourmet and ambitious at dinner, with items like sun-dried tomato and mascarpone ravioli served with polenta, chicken with tamari and Thai basil, or baked salmon with tamari ginger glaze. Lunch prices run $3–6.25, dinner prices $9.95–12.95.

**Dutch Treat Restaurant** (603-823-8851), Main Street, Franconia village. Open 7 AM–9 PM. A local standby. The dining room features Italian entrées, and the adjoining Sports Lounge serves homemade pizza, and screens sporting events and classic movies on its giant TV screen.

**Franconia Village Hotel Resort and Conference Center Restaurant** (603-823-7422; 1-888-669-6777), 87 Wallace Hill Road, Franconia. Dinner is served Tuesday through Thursday 5:30–8 PM, weekends 5:30–9 PM. Closed Sunday and Monday. Breakfast is served continental-style Monday through Friday and buffet-style on weekends. For dinner, a wide variety of fish and meat entrées tempt diners, but the real draw is the Swiss night on Friday with fondues, schnitzel, and rösti on the menu. Children are well taken care of here and can choose from pizza, fried chicken, or hamburgers. Entrées $10–14. Breakfast $3–6.50. Children's menu $2–5.25.

**Franconia Village House Restaurant** (603-823-5405; fulerton@ncia.net), 651 Main Street, Franconia. Some say the best place to eat north of the notch, this locally popular restaurant and bar is open daily for dinner year-round; lunch and weekend breakfasts from July through October. Good family-style fare: soups, fish, fresh pasta, and certified Angus beef. Entrées $9.95–17.95.

**Italian Oasis Restaurant & Brewery**, 106 Main Street, Littleton. A casual, fun place, if a tad smoky for our taste, the Italian Oasis is located in a small mall right in downtown Littleton and claims to be the oldest microbrewery in New Hampshire. You'll find a wide variety of menu items, along with ales, stouts, and homemade root beer for the kids. Perhaps the menu writer quaffed a few too many when attempting humor with items called the Steak Your Claim, Man O'Cotti, and an It's Greek to Me pizza—but it's all in good fun. Kids can choose from their own menu, take-out is available, and prices are moderate: lunch $2.95–7.99; dinner $6.99–21.95. The tavern menu is served 11:30 AM–10 PM Sunday through Thursday, until 11 PM Friday and Saturday. The dinner menu is served 5–10 PM Sunday through Thursday in the dining room, until 11 PM in the tavern Friday and Saturday.

**Littleton Diner** (603-444-3994; www.littletondiner.com), 145 Main Street, Littleton. Open daily 6 AM–8 PM. This vintage-1930s parlor-car diner sits staunchly on Main Street thumbing its weathered nose at the far inferior fast-food outlets vying for patrons on the outskirts of town. Large portions of breakfasts and daily specials like meat loaf, pot roast, clam chowder, and roast pork dinner pack in fans of traditional New England cooking. Breakfast is served all day, and contrary to popular myth, the diner is entirely void of noxious cigarette smoke. Breakfast prices are $2.50–6.45 including bottomless coffee; lunch and dinner entrées run $4.95–8.95—an unbelievable value.

**Lloyd Hills** (603-869-2141), Main Street, Bethlehem. Open Saturday and Sunday 8 AM–9 PM; Monday through Friday from 11 AM. Lloyd Hills serves a wide-ranging menu featuring hefty breakfasts; soups, salads, and sandwiches at lunch, with a few pasta dishes thrown in for good measure. But the

LUPINES AND A VIEW IN SUGAR HILL

Robert Kozlow

dinner menu really allows the kitchen to shine, taking simple ingredients and whipping them into surprising meals that are for the most part French and Mediterranean in character. Chicken Piccata, scallops Valencia, and sirloin and scampi are a few examples of what you might find on the menu. And it wouldn't be a New England dining experience if you didn't finish your meal with a thick, ice cream frappe drink. FYI, Lloyd Hills was Bethlehem's original name. Lunch $2.50–9.95; entrées $8.95–18.95.

**Miller's Fare** (603-444-2146), 16 Mill Street, Littleton. Open daily for lunch except Monday. Perfect for grabbing a quick lunch after visiting the Littleton Gristmill, the Miller's Fare offers gourmet lunches and high-quality Italian coffee. During warm weather, eat on the deck while listening to the burbling Ammonoosuc River and down sandwiches dressed with the likes of sun-dried tomato and thyme dressing, lemon parsley mustard, or olive goat cheese. Sumptuous soups like roasted garlic and butternut squash or shrimp and lobster chowder are paired with upscale salads like curried couscous with tomato, capers, and currants or wild rice salad with apples, parsley, and walnuts. Vegetarians are accommodated, and the dessert and coffee menu keep you lingering longer. (The owner was formerly the pastry chef at the renowned Rabbit Hill Inn in Waterford, Vermont.) All the bread is organic and supplied by the neighboring gristmill. Soup, sandwich, and salad prices $3.50–6.95. Coffee drinks $1.50–2.25, and desserts and baked goods 85 cents–$2.25.

**Polly's Pancake Parlor** (603-823-5575; www.pollyspancakeparlor.com; pollyspp@ncia.net), Route 117, Sugar Hill. Open from the second Sunday in May through mid-October, daily 7 AM–3 PM; weekends during April, early May, late October, and November 7 AM–2 PM. This modest 1830s former carriage house overlooks the majestic Kinsman mountain range and serves standard lunch fare, but is widely known for its legendary pancakes, waffles, and French toast drizzled with the locally harvested maple syrup—the *sugar* in Sugar Hill. Thanks to Americana-themed restaurant guides and cultural detectives such as Charles Kuralt, Polly's has gained a national reputation for providing diners a glimpse into a passing era. Expect fresh food and snappy service—just don't expect to be served one minute after the restaurant closes for the afternoon (and, believe us, it sure is disappointing to find a CLOSED sign and an empty parking lot at 3:05 PM). Prices range $5–25.

**Rosa Flamingo's** (603-869-3111), Main Street, Bethlehem. Open 11:30 AM–3 PM and 4–10 PM; Friday through Sunday 11 AM–10 PM. Moderate. A peppy Italian menu makes this place popular after a day schussing down Cannon Mountain. You'll find standards like lasagna Bolognese, eggplant parmigiana, steaks, chops, and chicken. Vegetarians are also catered to with tofu and bean ravioli or penne with a tomato cream sauce. Choose from an impressive selection of beers, too (including several locally brewed ales), or from the outstanding wine list; if you smoke, hit the cigar lounge downstairs for a stogie from the Dominican Republic or Honduras. There's a children's menu featuring chicken parmigiana, barbecued ribs, chicken fingers, and ravioli. Entrées $10.95–14.95. Kid's menu $5.25–7.25.

**Topic of the Town** (603-444-6721), Main Street, Littleton. Open Monday through Wednesday for breakfast and lunch 5 AM–2 PM; Thursday 5 AM–7:30 PM; Friday and Saturday 5 AM–8 PM; and Sunday 6 AM–noon. Locals gather here to discuss the events of the day and to enjoy simple food at modest prices. Friday night hosts the famous fish fry with free second helpings.

**The Soda Fountain** (603-772-2222), 10 School Street, Lisbon. Open daily 7 AM–9 PM. Bagels, muffins, hot dogs, Belgian waffles, soups, and salads are on the menu, but chances are you'll come for the ice cream. An old family drugstore given new life.

## ✵ Selective Shopping

**Bethlehem Flower Farm** (603-869-3131), Route 302, Bethlehem. Open Wednesday through Sunday from Memorial Day through Columbus Day. More than 10,000 daylilies grow in the fields, with the best array in early August during the farm's annual festival. The gift barn offers lots of gardening accessories, as well as a café for lunch and afternoon tea.

**Franconia Marketplace,** Main Street, Franconia. Selling only products made in Franconia, this complex in the heart of town houses the **Quality Bakery** (603-823-5228), which makes whole-grain and organic breads; and **Garnet Hill** (603-823-5917), an upscale linens and housewares store.

**Harmans Cheese and Country Store** (603-823-8000), Route 117, Sugar Hill. The specialty is well-aged cheddar, but the store also stocks maple sugar products and gourmet items.

**Littleton Stamp and Coin Company** (603-444-5386), 253 Union Street, Littleton. A local business with a national reputation for selling and buying stamps and coins.

**Sugar Hill Sampler,** Route 117, Sugar Hill. A 1780s barn with a folksy pioneer museum and a large selection of candies, cheese, crafts, and antiques.

**The Village Bookstore** (603-444-5263), Main Street, Littleton. Open daily. The largest and most complete bookstore (and one of the state's best) north of the mountains.

## ✵ Special Events

*February:* **Forest Festival** (603-444-6228; www.therocks.org), the Rocks Estate, Route 302, Bethlehem. A mid-February day in the woods with logging demonstrations plus snowshoeing and cross-country skiing. **Frostbite Follies.** A weeklong series of events around Franconia includes sleigh rides, ski movies, broom hockey, ski races, community suppers.

*April:* **Maple Season Tours** (603-444-6228; www.therocks.org), the Rocks Estate, Route 302, Bethlehem. Early-April weekend features a workshop about maple trees; also learn about gathering sap and boiling it down to make maple syrup.

*June:* **Wildflower Festival** (603-444-6228; www.therocks.org), the Rocks Estate, Route 302, Bethlehem. Guided walks, workshops, demonstrations, and a children's walk on a Sunday in early June. **Fields of Lupine Festival** (603-823-5661; 1-800-237-9007), Franconia and Sugar Hill. Arts and crafts, inn tours, and concerts revolving around breathtaking hillside displays of blossoming lupine. **Open for the Season Celebration,** Bethlehem.

Old-fashioned festival that includes golf tournament, crafts fair, and ball.

*Last weekend of June:* **Old Man in the Mountains USA and Canada Rugby Matches,** Cannon Mountain House Field, Route 116, Franconia.

*July:* **North Country Chamber Players,** Sugar Hill. Classical concerts Saturday at 8 PM in the Sugar Hill Meeting House. **Hayseed Blue Grass Festival,** Dow Strip, Franconia. Bluegrass and fiddle music played outside. An eight-week season (through August) of musicals and drama is performed Monday through Saturday by Equity actors at the **Weathervane Theater** in Whitefield.

*August:* **Day Lily Festival,** Bethlehem. **Horse Show,** Mittersill Resort, Franconia.

*September:* **Franconia Scramble,** Franconia. A 6.2-mile footrace over Franconia roads. **New England Boiled Dinner,** the Town House, Franconia. Corned beef and all the fixings. **Annual Antique Show and Sale,** Sugar Hill Meeting House. Selected dealers of antiques and collectibles.

*October:* **Quilt Festival,** Franconia. **Durrell Methodist Church Bazaar,** Franconia, Saturday of Columbus Day weekend. **Crafts Fair,** elementary school, Bethlehem, Sunday of Columbus Day weekend. **The Halloween Tradition** (603-444-6228; www.therocks.org), the Rocks Estate, Route 302, Bethlehem. Ghosts and goblins haunt the estate in a program cosponsored by local Boy and Girl Scouts; also apple bobbing, pumpkin carving, and ghost stories told around the fire.

*December:* **Oh! Christmas Tree** (603-444-6228; www.therocks.org), the Rocks Estate, Route 302, Bethlehem, weekends in early December. Celebrate Christmas with wreath making, ornament making, and a haywagon tour of the Christmas tree plantation. Pick your own tree to cut. Tree sales daily in December.

# MOUNT WASHINGTON AND ITS VALLEYS

## INCLUDING MOUNT WASHINGTON GATEWAY REGION, NORTH CONWAY AREA, JACKSON AND PINKHAM NOTCH, CRAWFORD NOTCH, AND BRETTON WOODS

Literally the high point of New England, Mount Washington has been New Hampshire's top tourist attraction for more than 150 years—this despite its frequent cloud crown and temperatures more typical of a mountain three times its 6,299-foot height.

Improbably, its first recorded ascent was in June 1642 by Darby Field of Dover, assisted by Indian guides—only one of whom reluctantly accompanied him all the way to the summit. Local tribes revered the mountain as the seat of the Great Spirit.

Clearly visible from Portland, Maine (more than 60 miles to the east), Mount Washington is the central, pyramid-shaped summit in the White Mountains' Presidential Range, so called because each of its peaks is named for a different president. In 1819 legendary father-and-son innkeepers Abel and Ethan Crawford cut a bridle path (now named for the Crawford family, it's America's oldest continually used hiking trail) up the western side of the mountain, building a log cabin for patrons to rest up before venturing above tree line.

Artists and writers were among early patrons, and their work spread the mountains' fame. Dozens of mammoth hotels soon dotted the immediate area, some accommodating 500 or more guests. Hotel owners bought farms to raise their own produce, generated their own lights and power, built ponds, hiking trails, golf courses, and tennis courts, and maintained post offices. Atop Mount Washington itself a rude shelter was built soon after the bridle path opened and the first hotel, the Summit House, opened in 1852.

"We used to average 100 dinners a day . . . One noon there were representatives of 13 different nations as guests at dinner," its proprietor wrote. A rival Tip-Top House opened the next year, and in 1869 the Mount Washington Cog Railway ("the world's first mountain-climbing cog railway") began transporting travelers from the mountain's western base (by then-named Crawford Notch). Tradition has it that showman Phineas Taylor Barnum stood atop an observation tower on Mount Washington and, surveying the vista from the Canadian

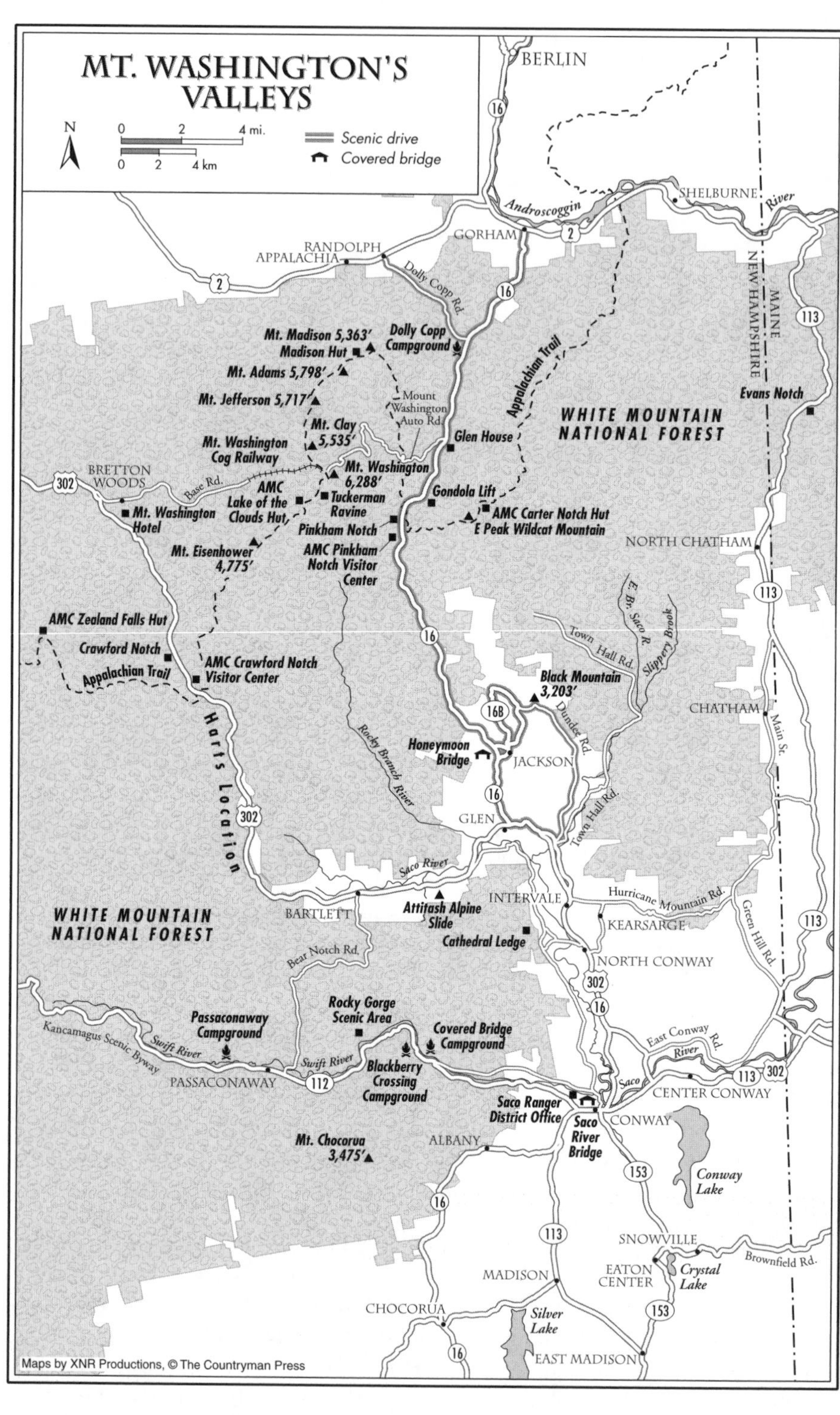
MT. WASHINGTON'S VALLEYS
N
0 2 4 mi.
0 2 4 km
Scenic drive
Covered bridge
BERLIN
SHELBURNE
Androscoggin
River
GORHAM
RANDOLPH
APPALACHIA
Dolly Copp Rd.
NEW HAMPSHIRE
MAINE
Mt. Madison 5,363′
Madison Hut
Dolly Copp Campground
Mt. Adams 5,798′
Appalachian Trail
Mt. Jefferson 5,717′
Mount Washington Auto Rd.
Evans Notch
WHITE MOUNTAIN NATIONAL FOREST
Mt. Clay 5,535′
Glen House
Mt. Washington Cog Railway
Mt. Washington 6,288′
BRETTON WOODS
Base Rd.
AMC Lake of the Clouds Hut
Tuckerman Ravine
Gondola Lift
Mt. Washington Hotel
AMC Carter Notch Hut
Pinkham Notch
E Peak Wildcat Mountain
Mt. Eisenhower 4,775′
AMC Pinkham Notch Visitor Center
NORTH CHATHAM
E. Br. Saco R.
Slippery Brook
AMC Zealand Falls Hut
Town Hall Rd.
Crawford Notch
AMC Crawford Notch Visitor Center
Appalachian Trail
Black Mountain 3,203′
Harts Location
CHATHAM
Dundee Rd.
Main St.
Honeymoon Bridge
JACKSON
Rocky Branch River
Town Hall Rd.
GLEN
Saco River
INTERVALE
Hurricane Mountain Rd.
Green Hill Rd.
BARTLETT
Attitash Alpine Slide
KEARSARGE
WHITE MOUNTAIN NATIONAL FOREST
Cathedral Ledge
Bear Notch Rd.
NORTH CONWAY
Rocky Gorge Scenic Area
Passaconaway Campground
Covered Bridge Campground
Kancamagus Scenic Byway
Swift River
Swift River
East Conway Rd.
Saco River
Blackberry Crossing Campground
PASSACONAWAY
CENTER CONWAY
Saco Ranger District Office
Saco River Bridge
CONWAY
Mt. Chocorua 3,475′
ALBANY
Conway Lake
SNOWVILLE
Brownfield Rd.
EATON CENTER
Crystal Lake
MADISON
CHOCORUA
Silver Lake
EAST MADISON
2
16
113
302
16B
112
153
Maps by XNR Productions, © The Countryman Press

border to the Atlantic, observed the view to be "the second greatest show on earth."

By 1876 it was possible to buy a 3-day $17 excursion that included a night at a hotel in Crawford Notch, a transfer to the Cog Railway to ride up Mount Washington, a night in a summit hotel, then a carriage ride down the eastern side of the mountain to connect with a stage for a trip back to the railroad line.

The year 1876 saw the founding of the Appalachian Mountain Club (the AMC), which has cut, mapped, and maintained hundreds of miles of hiking trails through the White Mountains, erecting a series of eight "high huts," each a day's hike apart in the Presidentials. While it's no longer possible to spend the night in a hotel atop Mount Washington, it is highly recommended to do so at the AMC's Mizpah Spring Hut off the Crawford Path or at the Lake of the Clouds Hut above tree line on Mount Washington (see *Hiker's Lodging* in "Mount Washington"). The AMC also maintains hiker-geared lodging in Pinkham and Crawford Notches.

Unfortunately, all but three of the area's old hotels have gone the way of the railways. Happily, the still-grand Mount Washington in Bretton Woods at the western base of its namesake mountain is now open year-round, complemented by its own major ski area as well as cross-country trails. The smaller but still elegant Wentworth and the Eagle Mountain House in Jackson are also handy to both alpine and Nordic trails. Interestingly enough, roughly the same number of visitors can be accommodated in the Mount Washington Valley today as in the 1890s.

So what and where exactly is the Mount Washington Valley? The promotional name was coined in the 1960s by a Boston PR man and the managers of its then three ski areas (Wildcat, Back, and Cranmore) specifically for the North Conway–Jackson area, which was known until then as the Eastern Slopes. It has since been expanded to apply to 28 towns surrounding Mount Washington, an area that now includes no less than seven alpine ski areas, four Nordic centers, 200 miles of snowmobiling trails, and, in summer, 12 "family attractions," eight golf courses, hundreds of miles of hiking and biking trails, 7,500 beds, and more than 70 restaurants. Within this chapter we have divided the Mount Washington Valley into five distinct sections. We begin with **Mount Washington** itself, and an overview of how to explore it. Next comes the **Mount Washington Gateway Region,** a beautiful area frequently overlooked by travelers rushing up Route 16 to North Conway, the heart of the White Mountains. The **North Conway Area** is our third and largest section. **Jackson and Pinkham Notch** describes the distinctly 19th-century-style resort village and dramatic high pass that's become a year-round center for outdoor enthusiasts at the eastern base of Mount Washington. Finally, **Crawford Notch and Bretton Woods** details sights in the magnificent mountain corridor with its grand hotel to the west of Mount Washington.

A MOUNTAIN VIEW FROM ONE OF THE AMC'S HIGH MOUNTAIN HUTS

Rob Burbank, AMC

**WHEN TO GO** The Mount Washington Valley is quieter in winter (with the exception of school vacations at Christmas and Presidents' Week) than summer, especially midweek when genuine bargains are available when combined with downhill skiing. From Memorial Day through Labor Day it's consistently busy, and you really don't want to be here in spring (Mud Season) unless you're skiing up in Tuckerman Ravine. Fall foliage season (the peak is early October) is predictably busy and expensive. November offers plenty of special promotions and incentives to do your holiday shopping here. Snow, however, rarely arrives before Christmas. March can be quite wonderful: off-season prices and plenty of snow, but check conditions before booking.

## MOUNT WASHINGTON

**HIKING GUIDANCE** **WMNF Androscoggin Ranger Station** (603-466-2713), Route 16, Gorham. Open Monday through Friday 7:30 AM–4:30 PM.

**AMC Pinkham Notch Visitors Center** (603-466-2725 for weather, trail, or general information; 603-466-2727 for overnight or workshop reservations). Serves as the information hub for hiking throughout the Presidential Range. Operates the hiker's shuttles and the system of eight huts, with two—the Lake of the Clouds and Mizpah Huts—on Mount Washington itself.

**GETTING THERE** Daily **Concord Trailways bus service** (603-228-3300; 1-800-639-3317) to Pinkham Notch Visitors Center (see above) from Boston and its Logan Airport.

**GETTING AROUND** **The AMC Hiker Shuttle** operates June through mid-October, 8 AM–4 PM. It consists of two vans, one based at the Pinkham Notch Visitors Center (see *Hiking Guidance*), the second at the Crawford Depot Visitors Center on the opposite side of Mount Washington. By changing at these transfer points, it's possible to reach all the area's major trailheads. It's suggested that you spot your car and take a van to the trailhead from which you intend to walk out.

♿ **Mount Washington State Park,** on the summit of the mountain, is open daily Memorial Day through Columbus Day. Although most of Mount Washington is part of the White Mountain National Forest, there are several other owners. One is the state of New Hampshire, which operates the **Sherman Adams Summit Building,** named for the former New Hampshire governor who was the chief of staff for President Eisenhower. This contemporary, two-story, curved building sits into the northeastern side of the mountain, offering sweeping views. Park facilities include a gift shop, snack bar, post office, rest rooms (all handicapped accessible), and a pack room for hikers. The old **Tip-Top House** (see the chapter introduction), originally built as a summit hotel in 1853, has been restored and is open daily as a reminder of the past. Free. Other summit buildings include the transmitter and generator facilities of Channel 8, WMTW-TV, which provides transmitter service for radio stations and relays for state and federal government agencies.

**Mount Washington Museum,** on the summit. Open daily when the building is open. Located one flight below the main building, the museum is operated by the

Mount Washington Observatory and offers historical exhibits and a wealth of scientific information on the meteorology, geology, botany, and biology of the mountain. A small gift shop helps support the activities of the observatory. Fee charged.

**Mount Washington Observatory** (603-356-8345), on the summit, Gorham 03518. Closed to the public, but members may tour the facility. There are, in fact, 4,000 members in 48 states and nine foreign countries. Membership costs $40 per year, $60 for a family, and gets you the thick quarterly bulletin *Windswept* and the right to participate in a winter workshop up here in subjects ranging from history and photography to geology ($375 including transport up, food, and overnight lodging). This private, nonprofit, institution occupies a section of the Sherman Adams Summit Building and is staffed all year by rotating crews of two to three people who change each week. Weather observations are taken every 3 hours, providing a lengthy record of data that extends back to the 1930s, when the institution was formed. The staff endured the highest wind ever recorded on earth, 231 miles per hour, in April 1934. The original building was the old Stage Office, a replica of which is on the summit. Various ongoing research projects study the effects of icing, aspects of atmospheric physics, and related subjects. The observatory has conducted research for a variety of commercial, institutional, and governmental organizations. Facilities include crew quarters, a weather-instrument room, a radio room, a photography darkroom, and a library. The staffers provide live morning weather reports on several area radio stations, including WMWV 93.5 FM in Conway.

## ✷ To Do

**Mount Washington Cog Railway** (603-846-5404, advance reservations recommended), off Route 302, Bretton Woods 03589. (See *To See* in "Crawford Notch and Bretton Woods.")

**Mount Washington Auto (Carriage) Road** (603-466-2222; 603-466-3988; www.mt-washington.com), Route 16. See *To See—Scenic Drives* in "Jackson and Pinkham Notch."

**HIKING** Mount Washington is crisscrossed with trails, but there are two popular routes. The **Tuckerman Ravine Trail** (4.1 miles, 4½ hours) begins at the AMC Pinkham Notch Camp on Route 16. It is nearly a graded path most of the first 2.5 miles as it approaches the ravine; then it climbs steeply up the ravine's headwall and reaches the summit cone for the final ascent to the top. The ravine area has open-sided shelters for up to 86 people, and each person has to carry up everything needed for an overnight stay. (Register at the AMC Pinkham Notch Camp; no reservations.) This is the trail used by spring skiers, and it can be walked as far as the ravine by anyone in reasonably good condition. The beginning of the trail is an easy 0.5-mile walk on a graded path to the pretty Crystal Cascade.

On the western side of Mount Washington is the **Ammonoosuc Ravine Trail** (in combination with Crawford Path, 3.86 miles, 4½ hours). It begins at the Cog Railway Base Station, located off Route 302 north of Crawford Notch. About 2.5 miles from the start is the AMC **Lake of the Clouds Hut** (see *Hiker's Lodging*), one of the best areas to view the alpine flowers, near the junction with popular Crawford Path (see the chapter introduction). This trail is 8.2 miles long and requires 6 hours to reach the summit of Mount Washington. It begins just above Crawford Notch and crosses a new, specially designed suspension bridge. After 2.7 miles comes the cutoff for the AMC **Mizpah Spring Hut** (*see Hiker's Lodging*).

In the vicinity of the AMC Pinkham Visitors Center (see *Guidance* in "Jackson and Pinkham Notch"), many short hiking trails are suitable for family groups. Ask for suggestions and directions at the camp.

A few words of caution about hiking on Mount Washington and the Presidential Range. Most of these trails end up above tree line and should be attempted only by properly equipped hikers. Winter weather conditions can occur above tree line any month of the year. Annually some 50,000 hikers safely reach the summit, many in winter, but hiking is a self-reliant activity; even fair-weather, summer hikers are warned to climb well prepared, with extra clothing and food in addition to maps and a compass. Most of the trails to the summits are 4 to 5 miles in length and require 4 or 5 hours to reach the top. Although these trails are not exceptionally long, there is an elevation gain of some 4,000 feet, a distance that becomes painfully evident to those who are not in reasonably good physical condition. Western hikers, used to the higher Rockies, soon appreciate the ruggedness and the elevation change when climbing this mountain. About 100 people have died on the slopes of the mountain, some from falls while hiking, rock or ice climbing, or skiing; but others have died in summer when they were caught unprepared by rapidly changing weather conditions. Since the weather can be most severe above tree line, cautious hikers will assess the weather conditions when reaching that point on a climb. The AMC (603-466-2725) provides daily weather information. Also call 603-466-5252 for recorded weather information.

Since AMC staffers often volunteer for mountain rescues, they are careful to give considered advice to beginning and more experienced hikers. The *AMC White Mountain Guide* has the most comprehensive trail information available for hikers, but also see Daniel Doan and Ruth Doan MacDougall's *50 Hikes in the White Mountains* (Backcountry Guides).

**SKIING** **Tuckerman Ravine** (call the Appalachian Mountain Club, 603-466-2727), off Route 16, Pinkham Notch. Spring skiing has become an annual rite for many skiers, and there is nowhere better than the steep slopes of Tuckerman Ravine. There are no lifts, so you have to walk more than 3 miles to reach the headwall of this cirque, a little valley carved out of the eastern side of Mount Washington by glaciers during the Ice Age. Winds blow snow from the mountain into the ravine, where it settles to a depth of 75 feet or more. When snow has melted from traditional ski slopes, it remains in the ravine; skiers by the thousands walk the 2.4-mile trail from the AMC Pinkham Notch Visitors Center to Hermit Lake, then on up to the floor of the bowl. The headwall is another 800 feet up. Skiing begins in early April, and we have seen some diehards skiing the small patches of snow remaining in the ravine in June.

Early in the season, when there is plenty of snow, the steep **John Sherburne Ski Trail** provides a brisk run from the ravine back to Pinkham Notch Camp. Spring sun warms the air, and many people ski in short-sleeved shirts and shorts, risking sunburn and bruises if they fall. Skiing here is for experts, since a fall on the 35- to 55-degree slopes means a long, dangerous slide to the bottom of the ravine. A volunteer ski patrol is on duty, and WMNF rangers patrol the ravine to watch for avalanches. The three-sided Hermit Lake shelters offer sleeping-bag accommodations for 86 hardy backpackers, who must carry everything up to the site for overnight stays. Winter-use-only (November through March) tent platforms are also available in the ravine. Register for shelters or tent platforms through the AMC Pinkham Notch Camp (603-466-2727, no reservations; first-come, first-served only).

SCENIC DRIVE **Mount Washington Loop.** One of the region's most popular drives is the 86-mile loop around the march of mountains named for Presidents Pierce, Eisenhower, Franklin, Monroe, Clay, Jefferson, Adams, and Madison, as well as Washington. If you begin in Glen (junction of Routes 16 and 302), your route will take you up through Pinkham Notch, past the Auto Road (see *To See—Scenic Drives* in "Jackson and Pinkham Notch") and through Gorham (see *To See—Scenic Drives* in "The Great North Woods—Northern White Mountains"), then back along Route 2 with splendid views south to the Presidentials. Follow Route 116 through "The Meadows" to Twin Mountain and south on Route 302, by the Mount Washington Cog Railroad and the Mount Washington Hotel set against the backdrop of the Mount Washington itself, on down through Crawford Notch (see "Crawford Notch and Bretton Woods") and back through Bartlett to Glen. Of course this ring around the mountains really makes no sense unless you take one (or both) routes to the summit and stop frequently along the way.

## ✷ Hiker's Lodging

**Appalachian Mountain Club** (603-466-2727; www.outdoors.org) offers a full-service year-round lodging in **Joe Dodge Lodge** (see *Lodging—Other* in "Jackson and Pinkham Notch") and at eight high huts in the Presidential Range, all accessible only by walking. Theoretically you can spend 9 days hiking from one to the next, but in practice patrons usually just spend a night at one or two. From June through mid-September all but Carter Spring Hut are "full service," meaning you supply your sheets (or sleeping bag) and towels; they provide meals, bunks, and blankets. $66 per adult, $44 per child includes the night's stay with dinner and breakfast (taxes included; less if you stay 3 days). Six huts are also open in winter on a self-serve basis ($20 per person).

We know **Mizpah Spring Hut** (see To Do—*Hiking*) better than the others, but all share the following essentials: Bunks are stacked (at Mizpah it's six to a room), equipped with three army blankets and a bare pillow. The two baths are dorm-style. Everything is immaculate, maintained by the youthful crew who also cook the gargantuan meals. Common space is attractive and well stocked with books, but the big draw here is your fellow hikers, who represent a span of ages and, usually, several European countries. It's the kind of place that draws people together. Frequently a naturalist leads an after-dinner hike. Breakfasts tend to feature fresh-baked breads and crispy bacon.

From Mizpah you can hike east to **Zealand Falls Hut** (popular with families because it's an easy hike in from Route 302), on to **Galehead Hut** on the western flank of Mount Lafyette and **Lonesome Lake Hut,** also popular with families because it's an easy hour's hike up from Franconia Notch. North of Mizpah is **Lake of the Clouds** (busy because it's right below Mount Washington's summit and favored by Boy Scout troops). Next comes **Madison Spring,** the most rugged of the huts, set above the sheer walls of Madison Gulf. **Carter Notch Hut** (open year-round on a self-service basis), the easternmost hut, lies in a sheltered divide between Wildcat Mountain and Carter Dome. We cheated by taking the Wildcat up and walking in from there. For a description of lodging at **Joe Dodge Lodge,** see *Lodging—Other* in "Jackson and Pinkham Notch." *Note:* While all three meals are open to visitors at the Pinkham Notch Visitors Center, hikers are not invited to drop in for meals at the high huts.

## ✷ Special Events

*Late June:* **Mount Washington Auto Hill Climb,** Mount Washington Auto Road, Pinkham Notch. First held in 1904, America's oldest motor-sport event: On consecutive weekends, first runners, then autos race from the Glen to the summit over the steep, winding course. For footrace details call 603-863-2537; for auto-race details, 603-466-3988.

*Mid-September:* **Mount Washington Bike Race** (603-466-3988), Mount Washington Auto Road, Pinkham Notch. This event attracts some of the top U.S. racers.

Also see *Special Events* in "Jackson and Pinkham Notch" and "Crawford Notch and Bretton Woods."

# MOUNT WASHINGTON GATEWAY REGION

***Including Tamworth, Chocorura, Madison, and Eaton Center***

Just off the beaten path, betwixt and between more high-profile destinations, this area offers an increasingly rare combination: beauty, hospitality, and peace. Flanking Route 16, just south of the Mount Washington Valley and north of Lake Winnipesaukee, this is a hilly, wooded region, spotted with small lakes—White Lake, Chocorua Lake, and Silver Lakes, not to mention Ossipee, Silver, Purity, and Crystal. Its villages include picture-perfect Tamworth, Eaton Center, and Freedom.

**GETTING THERE** Route 16 is the high road from I-95 at Portsmouth to the Mount Washington Valley. Also see Route 153 (see *To See—Scenic Drives*). Route 25 is a direct link (just 44 miles) with Portland.

## ✷ To See

**VILLAGES** **Tamworth.** Settled in 1771, the town of Tamworth (population 2,230) encompasses the villages of Wonalancet, Chocorua, Whittier, Tamworth Village, South Tamworth, Pequawket, and Bennett Corners. Tamworth Village is a compact crossroads community with the Victorian-style Tamworth Inn across from the venerable Barnstormers Summer Playhouse at its center and the Remick Country Doctor Museum (free, open year-round) on its edge. In one short block there is also a substantial library, general store (alias Remicks) and the neighboring "Another Store" (see *Eating Out*), presently selling "Women of Tamworth," a calendar featuring local maidens and matrons in artfully posed states of undress (proceeds benefit worthy causes). Inquire in the library about cross-country ski and walking trails. Head west on Cleveland Road to see Ordination Rock, north on Route 113A to Wonalancet (see *Scenic Drives*), east on 113 to Chocorua (and Route 16), and south on 113 to Whittier (named for the poet John Greenleaf Whittier, who frequented the area). The town's many distinguished second-home owners included two-term president Grover Cleveland, whose son Francis moved here to stay, founding the Barnstormers (see *Entertainment*) more than 70 years ago. In the era when the train stopped at Depot Street, this was also a winter resort with skiing (there was a rope tow) and dogsledding, based at the famous Chinook Kennels in Wonalancet. It's still as pleasant a place to come in winter (Wonalancet is a genuine snow pocket) as summer. The **Tamworth Historical Society** (603-323-8639), 24 Gregs Way in the village, is open Tuesday 7–8 PM from July 4 through August.

**Chocorua** sits astride busy Route 16. It's named for its Matterhorn-like mountain, visible from the highway, across Chocorua Lake (for more about the mountain and its own namesake, see *To Do—Hiking*). The view from Route 16 across the waterfall and its millpond is another photo op. The general store offers all the essentials and is a Trailways bus stop.

**Eaton Center.** Its population of 379 is a third what it was in the 1850s, but this remains an idyllic village with a classic 1870s white, steepled church seemingly posing by Crystal Lake. The Eaton Center Village Store (groceries and small coffee shop) serves as the source of all local information. See **Foss Mountain** under *To Do—Hiking*.

**Freedom** (population 963). Another picture-perfect village with a flagpole and a fountain. Moulton Brook flows by and behind Main Street, foxgloves bloom behind picket fences, and both the church and town hall are white with green trim. The **Freedom Historical Society** (603-367-4626) is worth checking out, depicting life in this small mill town at its most prosperous. The Freedom Village Store stocks more than staples, and the Freedom Flea Market is in operation weekends in summer on Route 25 near the Maine border.

MUSEUM AND HISTORIC HOME **Remick Country Doctor Museum and Farm** (603-323-7591; 1-800-686-6117; www.remickmuseum.org), 58 Cleveland Hill Road, Tamworth. Open year-round daily 10 AM–4 PM; also summer Saturdays and for special events. Free. On the edge of the village, this exceptional little museum depicts the life of a country doctor through the past century. Remicks have been active in Tamworth for six generations; between 1894 and 1993 two members of the family (father and son) served the medical needs of the town and outlying farms for many miles around. The. Remicks themselves farmed (their Hillsdale Farm's barn and stable are part of the museum) and lived frugally, judging from the vintage 1930s–1950s furnishing in the house, which doubled as doctor's office. The **Capt. Enoch Remick House,** also in the village and slightly grander, is also open on special occasions—which occur at least once a month, year-round: They include a farm fest and fishing derby (at the farm pond), an ox pull, a traditional tea, and so on. Just one of four surviving farms in Tamworth, this one happens to be in the middle of the village.

**GLACIAL ERRATICS** "It is a folk saying that God created the world in six days and spent the seventh throwing rocks at New Hampshire," Keith Henney wrote in *The Early Days of Eaton.* Two famous examples of these "rocks" are:

**Ordination Rock,** Cleveland Hill Road, Tamworth (a few miles west of the village). A curiosity, this cenotaph perched atop a giant boulder commemorates the ordination of Tamworth's first minister in 1792. A plaque, recalling that HE CAME INTO THE WILDERNESS AND LEFT IT A FRUITFUL FIELD, gives details of his tenure.

**Madison Boulder Natural Area,** on a side road off Route 113, Madison. Open all year, although access is limited to walking in winter. Just a big rock but amazing to see. During the Ice Age, this massive chunk was plucked off a mountaintop and carried along by a glacier until it reached this spot. Some three stories high and more than 80 feet long, it is one of the largest glacial erratics in the world and has been designated a national natural landmark. No facilities and no fees.

**SCENIC DRIVES** **The Chinook Trail.** On the late-fall morning we drove this stretch of **Route 113A,** it was magical! Turn north at the four corners in Tamworth Village, heading through woods for several miles. Note the turnoff for Hemenway State Forest (see *Green Space*) and the firehouse that's the only clue that you have entered Wonalancet. Look for the monument in front of Chinook Kennels, named for its most famous resident, born in 1917 and sire of the still-famous breed (now around 500 dogs). Chinook himself served as lead dog on Admiral Byrd's expeditions to Antarctica, but the monument is for all dogs who did so. For many years these kennels were a big attraction; dogsleds met the trains. Traveling this direction it's easy to miss the **Wonalancet Chapel,** at the bend in the road as the countryside opens up around you (look back for the best view; it's a classic chapel in the middle of nowhere, a favorite for weddings). It's a glorious 10 miles from here to Sandwich, through the tiny village of Whiteface (note the swimming hole by the bridge) and on down to North Sandwich.

**Route 153** from Wakefield through the Effinghams and Freedom to Eaton Center. This route begins in the Lake Winnipesaukee area, but we think it belongs here because you tend to be heading north on it, into the Mount Washington Valley. Frequently we begin looking for roadfood at this point, so it's good to know about the **Poor People's Pub** in Sanbornville. It's less than a mile east of Route 16 (at the junction of Routes 109 and 153), open daily for lunch and dinner, a local gathering spot that's a good bet for a sandwich or full meal. Note the cheerful **Chew-Chew Café** (good for breakfast and light lunches, open 7 AM–2 PM) by the tracks in this railroad-era village. You might also want to stop by Lovell Lake, just up Route 109, with a town beach.

**Sanbornville** is one of several villages in the town of Wakefield. Heading north up Route 153 (note **Toad Hollow,** Anita Cluett's small gem store with plenty to please crystal lovers and rockhounds), you soon come to the old town center with its impressive lineup of early-19th-century houses, including the **Museum of Childhood** (603-522-8073, open mid-May through mid-October, closed Tuesday) and the Wakefield Inn (see *Lodging—Bed and Breakfasts* in "The Lake Winnipesaukee Area"). Continue up Route 153 to Provence Lake with its narrow ribbon of sand between the road and the lake (you won't be the first to wade in) and a view of mountains to the west. Here too is the entrance to the the **Provence Lake Golf Club** (207-793-404) with 18 holes. Technically, you are in Parsonfield, Maine.

Bill Taylor in **Ye Olde Sale Shoppe** in Taylor City, South Effingham (the next village), tells you that the state line runs down the middle of his shop, every inch of which is crammed with possible purchases. Effingham Center is definitely in New Hampshire, with surprisingly substantial buildings for its size. Continuing north, your head also swivels at the sight of **Squire Lord's Mansion,** a three-story unmistakable Federal mansion with a large cupola in the middle of nowhere (please drive on; it's a private home). In Effingham Falls you cross Route 25, the high road west to Portland (44 miles) and east to Ossipee Lake (6 miles). You begin to see antiques stores (we browsed through the two floors of **Chicken Coop Antiques** and picked up a map/guide to several shops in this area).

Be sure to detour the mile or so into the village of Freedom (see *Villages*), a real beauty, with an attractive B&B (see *Lodging*). Continue on through East Madison (see the Madison Boulder under *Glacial Erratics*) to Eaton Center (see *Villages*), or turn west on Route 113 to Chocorua and Tamworth (again, described under *Villages*).

## ✷ To Do

**HIKING** **Mount Chocorua** is only 3,475 feet high, but its rugged, treeless summit makes it a popular destination, and there are many trails to its summit. The **Piper Trail** begins on Route 16 at a restaurant-campground parking lot (fee charged for parking) a few miles north of Chocorua Lake. The well-trod trail is 4.5 miles long and requires about 3½ hours hiking time. The **Liberty Trail** begins on Paugus Mill Road, which is off Route 113A, southwest of the mountain. Some 3.9 miles long, requiring about 3 hours and 20 minutes, this oldest trail on the mountain passes the Jim Liberty cabin, a mountainside cabin with bunks (there for anyone willing to use it). The **Champney Falls Trail** ascends the mountain from the Kancamagus Highway. West of Chocorua are Mounts Paugus, Passaconaway, and Whiteface, all of which can be climbed from a parking lot off Ferncroft Road, in Wonalancet on Route 113A.

**Foss Mountain.** From Eaton Center head west on Brownfield Road and right on Stuart Road, then take the first right and look for trailhead parking. Not particularly high but with a bald summit offering a 360-degree view: the full march of the Presidentials to the northwest and nearer, the Moat Mountains, Chocorua, and, to the southwest, the Ossipee Range.

**HORSEBACK RIDING** **Happiness Farm** (603-539-1702; www.happinessfarm.com), Freedom. Trail rides and riding lessons.

**Chebacco Dude Ranch** (603-522-3211), Route 153, South Effingham. Open all year. New Hampshire's only dude ranch, this 170-acre farm has access to hundreds of miles of trails. For details about staying here, see *Lodging—Dude Ranch* in "The Lake Winnipesauskee Area." Merlyn and Jim Rutherford have 11 quarter horses and offer both package and 3-hour trail rides.

LLAMA TREKKING **Fairfield Llama Farm** (603-539-2865; www.llamahikeswtmts.com), Elm Street, Freedom. Deborah Frock stresses that she is the only fully licensed llama trek outfitter in New Hampshire. Destinations vary, as do trails—1.5 to 6 miles in length. Treks take an entire day and include a "gourmet lunch." Hikers wishing to camp in remote WMNF sites might also consider using one or two of Frock's 16 llamas to transport gear. $150 for 1 to 4 people; $30 for each additional up to 12. Special rates for more than 12, and $275 for 2 days with an overnight at the Freedom House B'n'B.

SWIMMING **White Lake State Park,** Route 16, Tamworth. Open late May through mid-October. Here is a sandy beach and campground (see *Lodging—Camping*). Rental boats and good trout fishing. The 1.5-mile trail around the lake takes you through a large stand of tall pitch pines, a national natural landmark. Fee charged.

**Chocorua Lake,** Route 16, Tamworth. Just north of Chocorua village, this location offers perhaps the most photographed scene in the country: rugged Mount Chocorua viewed across its namesake lake. Most of the lakeshore has been preserved for its scenic beauty, and nary a summer cottage disturbs the pristine character of the place. At the northern end of the lake, adjacent to the highway, is a popular swimming area and a place to launch a canoe or sailboard, but public facilities are minimal.

**MOUNT CHOCORUA**

This distinctive peaked mountain gets its name from a prophet of the Pequawket Indians who refused to leave the graves of his ancestors in Tamworth when his tribe fled to Canada. He lived amicably among the settlers and left his son in the care of a local farm family while he journeyed to visit his tribesmen. When he returned, his child was dead. Chocorua refused to believe the farmer's story that the boy had mistakenly eaten poison meant for a fox. In retaliation he killed the farmer's wife and children. The husband tracked him to the summit of this mountain and shot him, but not before Chocorua laid a curse on the settlers who, according to legend, soon fell sick; then their crops died, and the settlement was abandoned. Cattle continued to die in this area, it seems, until a University of New Hampshire professor tested the local streams and discovered that they contained muriate of lime, palatable to humans but not livestock.

## ✷ Winter Sports

CROSS-COUNTRY SKIING In Tamworth inquire about the local trail along the Swift River and see Hemenway State Forest under *Green Space*.

**King Pine** (see *Downhill Skiing*) also offers a 20 km groomed trail network throughout the Purity Spring property and Hoyt Audubon Sanctuary. Lessons, rentals.

**DOWNHILL SKIING** ✐ **King Pine Ski Area** (603-367-8896; www.kingpine.com), Route 153, East Madison. Dating back to the 1930s as a ski area, operated since 1952 by the Hoyt family and part of the Purity Spring Resort complex (see *Lodging—Resort*), this is a fine family ski area with snowmaking, night skiing, nursery, ski school, equipment rentals, triple and double chairlifts, two J-bar lifts, a tubing park, and 17 trails. $29 adult on weekends, $20 junior; $22 adult midweek, $14 junior; less on certain days and with lodging packages.

**ICE SKATING** **King Pine Ski Area Skating Arena** (see *Downhill Skiing*) is open to the public (rentals) for $4.

**SLEIGH RIDES** **Happiness Farm** (603-539-1702; www.happinessfarm.com), 98 Bennett Road, Freedom. Sleigh rides are a specialty, with cider and cocoa in the warm barn after.

## ✳ Green Space

**Hemenway State Forest,** Route 113A, Tamworth. There are two trails here: a short, self-guided nature trail, and a longer trail with a spur to the Great Hill fire tower offering views of the southern White Mountains. Brochures for both trails can usually be found in the box a few yards up each trail. Note Duck Pond near the parking area, good for a dip. In winter this is a popular, dependably snowy bet for cross-country skiing.

## ✳ Lodging

**RESORT** ✐ **Purity Spring Resort** (603-367-8896; 1-800-367-8896; 1-800-373-3754; www.purityspring.com), Route 153, East Madison 03849. Open year-round. Off by itself southwest of the Conways, this low-key, affordable, 1,000-acre, family-geared resort has been run by the Hoyt family since 1870. In summer most guests stay a week, taking advantage of activities and of sports facilities that include canoes, rowboats, and waterskiing on Purity Lake as well as tennis, volleyball, and arts-and-crafts programs. The inn van delivers guests to trailheads for guided hikes, to rivers for a canoe trips, and to North Conway for a play. In winter the draw is King Pine Ski Area, also part of the resort (see *To Do—Downhill Skiing*). Some 75 country-style rooms are divided among 10 buildings, ranging from remodeled farmhouses and barns (several are suited to family groups) to four condominiums at King Pine and the sleek Mill Building, which also houses the indoor pool, hot tub, and fitness center. Summer (late May through mid-October) rates include all meals (from $95), and in fall it's MAP (from $77). Winter ski packages include skiing at King Pine Ski Area.

**INNS** ✐ **Snowvillage Inn** (603-447-2818; 1-800-447-4345; www.snowvillageinn.com), Snowville 03849. Open year-round. With rolling lawns and towering iris and lupine in spring and summer and year-round a heart-stopping view of Mount Washington and the Presidential Range set off across the valley. Built as a summer home in 1912, the 18-room inn, a lively blend of New England charm and alpine flair, is perched 1,000 feet up Foss Mountain east of Eaton Center. The guest rooms—each named for an author and all furnished with antiques—are scattered throughout three buildings: the main inn, the Carriage House, and the Chimney House. The latter provides fireplaces in the rooms, and all rooms have private bath. Each building also has a guest living room with books and games; the main inn has a large brick fireplace and spacious porch. You can cross-country ski on a 15 km groomed course, or snowshoe on Foss Mountain (see *To Do—Hiking*). Innkeeper Kevin Flynn can also provide arrangements for a gourmet lunch. A four-course candlelight dinner is served in a chaletlike dining room (see *Dining Out*). B&B rates are $109–214 per couple, depending on season and accommodations. There are also special packages, including wine-tasting weekends, available.

✐ **Rockhouse Mountain Farm Inn** (603-447-2880), off Route 153, Eaton Center 03832. Open mid-June through October. In an earlier time, farmers often took in summer boarders, usually city folks who just wanted to relax in the country, walk open fields, take a canoe trip, and enjoy ample New England cooking. That experience has been possible here since 1946 thanks to the Edge family. With 450 acres of fields and forests to roam and a variety of farm animals (peacocks, llamas, horses, Swiss cattle, ducks, geese, hens, pigs, and more), plus a private beach and boats on Crystal Lake, this is a great family spot. Guests often help with haying or feeding the animals or gathering fresh vegetables from the garden for the evening meal. There are 18 rooms, 8 with private bath; the rest share one bath for every 2 rooms. Breakfast and dinner are served daily, and the children are fed at an early first course, giving them time to play hide-and-seek, swing in the barn, or converse with the newest calf while their parents enjoy dining at a more leisurely pace. The single-entrée meals, which vary over the course of the summer, are as hearty and irresistible as Grandma used to make: roasts, homemade breads and cakes, and a variety of farm-picked vegetables and salads. Fresh eggs, milk, and cream come from the resident animals. There are weekly steak roasts, riverside picnics, and chicken barbecues. Most guests are families who stay for a week (Saturday to Saturday); some have been enjoying the Edges' easy hospitality for generations. $40 MAP per person 12 and up; reduced rates for younger children.

ↀ **The Brass Heart Inn** (603-323-7766; 1-800-833-9509; www.thebrassheartinn.com), off Route 113, Chocorua 03817. Open all year. Set in a field, seemingly a million miles from the nearest distraction, this expanded 18th-century house could be the illustration for a 19th-century children's storybook. Four huge maples flank the long front porch. Formerly known as Staffords in The Field, it has recently been renovated by Don and Joanna Harte, who have created attractive common rooms and 11 guest rooms (5 with private bath, and 6 third-floor rooms sharing hall baths). Four old-fashioned cottages with fireplaces and porches accommodate two to eight people. Walk to Chocorua Lake for swimming; there are also trails for walking or cross-country skiing. The wine-and-ochre-colored dining room is open to the public (see *Dining Out*). The big, handsome old barn can seat up to 200 people for performances and weddings. Rates: $130–180 for rooms with private bath, $70–110 for shared bath, $160–240 for cottages, breakfast included.

🐾 **The Tamworth Inn** (603-323-7721; 1-800-642-7352; www.tamworth.com), Main Street, Tamworth 03886. Open all year. In the center of the village, this rambling inn that began in 1833 backs on lawns that sweep to the Swift River. Summer guests enjoy the outdoor pool and strolling across the street to the Barnstormers summer theater (see *Entertainment*). There are 16 individually decorated rooms, including 7 suites, all with private bath, 2 with Jacuzzi tub and fireplace. Beds range from kings to twins. The inn is popular locally for dinner (see *Dining Out*), and its tavern is a good bet for supper. Innkeepers Virginia and Bob Schrader offer a full country breakfast and afternoon refreshments. The $115–235 rates also include staff gratuities. Summer theater packages include room, dinner, and tickets to the Barnstormers.

BED & BREAKFASTS **The Inn at Crystal Lake** (603-447-2120; 1-800-343-7336), Route 153, Eaton Center 03832. Open all year. This distinctive four-story, triple-porched (one on top of another) Greek Revival building overlooks Crystal Lake. Built in 1884 as a private home, it became an inn almost immediately, then a private school. Happily, it's now an inn again. Bobby Barker and Tim Ostendorf are opera and classical music buffs with a large collection of recordings and videos. They offer 11 rooms, all with private bath, phone, cable TV/VCR, and most with air-conditioning. There is ample common space plus a pub in the rear. Guests may use Crystal Lake for swimming. Rates: $79–209 including breakfast. No smoking. Children over 8 please.

**Whispering Pines Bed & Breakfast** (603-323-7337; 1-877-620-1409; www.whisperingpinesnh.com), Route 113A and Hemenway Road, Tamworth 03886. Open all year. Kim (short for Frederick) and Karen Erickson's woodland home is a friendly find. An inn back around the turn of the 20th century, it served as a summer home for Karen's grandfather for some 30 years. It's an ideal design for a B&B. The big bright country kitchen with its antique woodstove serves as a hinge between the family's living space and the guest area, a comfortable living room with a soapstone hearth stove and plenty to read. The prize guest room is Woodlands, right off the living room, but very private with its own bath. Upstairs are four more attractive guest rooms sharing two baths. Step out the back door to trails in Hemenway State Forest (see *Green Space*), great for both hiking and cross-country skiing. Out the front door is an inviting screened porch. A full breakfast is included in $70–110, depending on room and season. Children 10 and older are welcome.

**Freedom House B'n'B** (603-539-4815), 17 Old Portland Road, Freedom 03836. Open all year. Located by a millpond in a quiet country village, this 140-year-old house is decorated in country Victorian style. The inn has four rooms, sleeping two to three each and sharing two full baths. Guests are welcome to relax on two porches or in the parlor or library. Innkeeper Patrick Miele runs an antiques shop in the adjoining barn. Full country breakfast and four o'clock tea. $80 single or $95 double occupancy for larger rooms; $60–75 for smaller. A nonsmoking inn. There is a minimum 2-night stay during weekends from June through October.

**Mount Chocorua View House** (603-323-8350; 1-888-323-8350; www.mtchocorua.com), Route 16, Box 395, Chocorua 03817. Open all year. This 1845 Colonial on Route 16 is located just south of Chocorua village. Relax by the Franklin fireplace, then retire to a comfortable, carpeted room, nicely decorated by innkeepers Frank and Barb Holmes. Three guest rooms and a two-room suite have private bath; three other rooms share. Guests may use a kitchen where tea and coffee are always available. An expansive lawn out back is perfect for badminton, horseshoes, and croquet. Walk to the river. Full breakfast. From $60 for two.

**River Bend Country Inn** (603-323-7440; 1-800-628-6944; www.riverbendinn.com), Route 16, Chocorua 03817. Open all year. Set 800 feet off the highway, this 10-room inn has a private, quiet location. At this writing new owners Craig Cox and Jerry Weiss have just arrived. There are six guest rooms with private bath, four with semiprivate facilities. The common room has a fireplace and window seat; the library is stocked with books; and a deck overlooks the Chocorua River. $75–180 includes breakfast.

**CAMPING** *Note:* There are also several private campgrounds in this area.

**White Lake State Park** (603-323-7350; www.nhparks.state.nh.us), Route 16, West Ossipee. Open mid-May through Columbus Day. There are 200 campsites here, and the trick is to get one of the couple of dozen with a water view. No pets permitted. $16–22 per night for two adults and dependent children. Facilities include a camp store, showers, ice, and firewood. The lake offers swimming, canoeing, and a 2-mile walking trail. Reservations accepted after January 1: 603-271-3628.

## * Where to Eat

**DINING OUT** **Snowvillage Inn** (603-447-2818; 1-800-447-4345), Snowvillage. Open year-round. The cheery, wood-paneled and -beamed, alpine-style dining room features spectacular long views across the valley to the Presidentials—and the food is exceptional. For a detailed menu description see *Dining Out* in "North Conway Area"; we placed it there because so many North Conway innkeepers tell us that it's a place they tell their guests not to miss. Entrées $17.95–23.95. Four-course candlelight gourmet dinners with a wide choice of appetizer, salad, entrée, and dessert are available nightly at $30 per person.

**The Brass Heart Inn** (603-323-7766), off Route 113, Chocorua. Call for reservations. Under new ownership, the dining room has been redecorated in attractive wine and ocher colors. The menu is moderately priced, from $14 for farfalle duck or a roasted vegetable terrine to $20 for rack of lamb or Gorgonzola fillet of beef. Full liquor license.

**The Tamworth Inn** (603-323-7721; www.tamworth.com), Main Street, Tamworth. Open all year for dinner, nightly in summer but just Thursday through Saturday off-season. This old inn's attractive dining room includes a sun porch (overlooking the back lawn) and has a creative, ever-changing menu. A sampling: grilled ginger chicken and vegetable spring rolls with peanut soy sauce or escargots bourguignon for starters, followed by braised beef short ribs in red wine, cassoulet or bouillabaisse, topped off by poached pear tart with spiced port wine sauce or a mocha-cappuccino ice cream pie. Entrées $13.95–20.95. Lighter fare is served in the pub.

EATING OUT **The Yankee Smokehouse** (603-539-RIBS), junction of Routes 16 and 25, West Ossipee. An authentic open-pit barbecue and plenty of it. Beef and pork barbecue and other sandwiches. Full dinners, including combination plates with barbecued chicken, beef, pork, and baby back ribs. Wine and pitchers of beer.

**Katy's** (603-323-8884), Old Route 25 (posted from Route 25), Tamworth. Closed Tuesday and Wednesday, but otherwise lunch and dinner featuring German specialties: bratwurst, sauerbraten, schnitzel, and the like. Dinner entrées $9–18.

**Daley Café at The Other Store,** Tamworth Village. Open daily for breakfast and lunch, a dependable oasis with a counter, a few tables, and a seasonal deck overlooking the Swift River. There's a soup of the day, good sandwiches, pie and ice cream (paper plates and cups). Browse through the store's stationery, cards, and gifts while you wait or pick up some hardware—a large part of what this place is about. Owner Kate Thompson explains that this became known as "the other store" during the many years that it served as an annex to Remick's, as the general store was long known.

**Rosie's Restaurant** (603-323-8611), 1547 White Mountain Highway (Route 16), Tamworth. Near White Lake State Park, a local gathering spot year-round for breakfast, also open for lunch, takeout, and ice cream in warm-weather months.

**The Checquers Villa** (603-323-8686), Route 113, south of Tamworth Village. Lunch on weekends, dinners nightly. Reasonably priced pasta, pizza, soups, and salads with atmopshere.

**Jake's** (603-539-2805), Route 16, West Ossipee. Fried fish and seafood platters, pasta; a family restaurant that can be packed in summer.

**Eaton Village Store** (603-447-2403), Eaton Center. The heart of Eaton Center, a combination post office, grocery store, and coffee shop with a counter and tables for breakfast and lunch.

**Chinese Cuisine Restaurant** (603-323-9200), Route 16, Tamworth. Open year-round daily for lunch and dinner. In a small shopping center. All the standard dishes, authentically prepared and reasonably priced. It hit the spot one late-fall evening.

**Tamworth General Store.** Open daily, alias Remicks, now under the same ownership as the Chocura General Store and, at this writing, still evolving. The pizza ovens are working, however, and there's an extensive deli department—good news for hikers and picnickers.

## ✷ Entertainment

**The Barnstormers** (603-323-8500), Tamworth. Open July and August. One of the country's oldest professional summer theaters, founded more than 70 years ago by Francis Cleveland, son of the president. The theater stages outstanding plays with an Equity cast. Musicals, some popular plays, and other lesser-known offerings. Dinner-theater packages available with the Tamworth Inn (see *Lodging—Inns*).

**The Arts Council of Tamworth** (603-323-8693) presents monthly (except summer) performances—from string quartets to vaudeville in the Tamworth-Sandwich area, mainly at the Barnstormers Theater.

**Contra dances** are held Saturday night (usually 7 PM) in the Tamworth Town House. Participants are invited to come early to learn the evening's dance.

**Concerts by the River** are held every summer Sunday, 3–5 PM, on the deck beside the Swift River, at The Other Store in Tamworth Village (see *Eating Out*).

SPECIAL EVENTS *February:* Annual **dogsled races** from Sandwich to Tamworth, third Saturday.

*Fourth of July:* The **parade** in Tamworth is big.

*August*: **Old Home Days** in Freedom; **Tamworth History Day.**

Also see *Entertainment* and special events sponsored by the Remick Country Doctor Museum and Farm (www.remickmuseum.org; 1-800-686-6117) in Tamworth Village.

## NORTH CONWAY AREA

The town of Conway is composed of the villages of Conway, Intervale, and North, East, Center, and South Conway. It is North Conway, however, that dominates the community and region. A summer haven for more than 150 years and one of the country's first ski destinations, it's now a major shopping mecca, with more than 200 shops and factory outlets. It also represents the White Mountains' largest concentration of inns, motels, and restaurants.

Early in the 19th century travelers began finding their way to this sleepy farming community in the broad Saco River Valley, the obvious staging ground for "adventure travel" into New England's highest mountains, which rise dramatically just a few miles to the north. By 1825 Conway had five inns, and by the 1850s hotels were sprouting on and around Mount Washington itself. Then in the 1870s rail service reached North Conway and was extended up through Crawford Notch. The town's status as the heart of the White Mountains was secured.

North Conway's most striking building remains its ornate, twin-towered rail station, built in 1874 to serve formally dressed ladies and gentlemen arriving to pass summer weeks and months at literally dozens of local hotels.

The trains were still running in the 1930s when New Englanders "discovered" skiing. In 1938 Harvey Gibson, an enterprising North Conway businessman, designed and built the ground-hugging "Skimobile" to ferry skiers up the slopes of Mount Cranmore. A year later he brought famed Austrian instructor Hannes Schneider to town to teach folks how to ski down. Winter visitors came by ski train, found lodging in the village, and walked to the mountain.

The Skimobile is gone, but Mount Cranmore remains a popular family resort for boarding and tubing as well as skiing. North Conway's ski allure now includes extensive trails at Attitash Bear Peak a few minutes' drive (if you know the shortcut) northwest of the village. Inns are also connected by more than 60 km of cross-country trails.

Admittedly North Conway isn't what it used to be, and admittedly its popularity dipped way down for a few decades there. It's back now, though, catering to a mix of hikers and climbers, skiers and families here to see the White Mountains' attractions both natural and human-made (Storyland, Heritage New Hampshire, water slides), and, of course, to shop.

As late as the 1930s, the strip along Route 16 south of North Conway village was a dirt road; but it was the only area left for development, and business began to establish itself there. With no zoning, commercial enterprises began to line the strip, slowly at first; then in the 1980s the factory outlet craze hit, and North Conway became one of the major shopping destinations in New England. This development has worsened an already serious traffic situation on Route 16.

In summer the Conway Scenic Railroad now runs excursion trains south along the Saco to Conway and north over scary Frankenstein's Trestle into Crawford Notch. But while this is one of the few resort areas in northern New England that you can actually reach by bus (a service used chiefly by hikers from other countries), virtually everyone now arrives by car. A north–south bypass is in the works, but at this writing the West Side Road (see *To See—Scenic Drives*) is the only way we know to escape the lights and traffic on Route 16 in North Conway. On fall weekends traffic is likely to be stop-and-go for several miles north and south of the village, especially in the afternoon.

Shopping aside, North Conway is a bustling village with plenty of inns, resorts, and restaurants—also a hub for biking, climbing, canoeing, kayaking—great for families. North Conway is what you make of it.

GUIDANCE **Mount Washington Valley Chamber of Commerce & Visitors Bureau** (603-356-3171; 1-800-367-3364; www.mountwashingtonvalley.org), Box 2300, North Conway 03860-2300. Free vacation guide, visitors information, and central reservation service for more than 90 varied properties throughout the area. It maintains a walk-in information center on Route 16 (Main Street) opposite the railroad station in the middle of North Conway, open daily in summer and fall foliage season, weekends all year; the kiosk with reservations phone is open 24 hours.

**White Mountain National Forest Saco Ranger Station** (603-447-5448), on the Kancamagus Highway just west of Route 16 in Conway. Open year-round from 8 AM, until 5 PM in summer, 4:30 in winter. Pick up maps and information on activities ranging from wildlife-watching to mineral collecting.

**State of New Hampshire Information Center,** Route 16, Intervale, 3 miles north of North Conway at a "scenic vista" of Mount Washington. Rest rooms, telephones, and well-stocked brochure racks. Open all year.

**Conway Village Chamber of Commerce** (603-447-2639; www.conwaychamber.com), junction of Route 16 and West Main Street at the southern end of Conway village. Open daily in summer, weekends in winter.

See *Guidance* within each section of this chapter for other chambers of commerce.

GETTING THERE *By car:* Route 16 is the way from Boston and places south. In Conway it joins Route 302, the high road from Portland Maine (just 62 miles to the east). Also see *To See—Scenic Drives* in "Mount Washington Gateway Region" for details about Route 153, a variation on Route 16.

*By bus:* **Concord Trailways** (603-228-3300; 1-800-639-3317; www.concordtrailways.com) provides scheduled service from Boston and its Logan Airport via Manchester, Concord, and Meredith.

MEDICAL EMERGENCY **Memorial Hospital** (603-356-5461), Route 16, north of North Conway village. As you might imagine, this facility has extensive experience in treating skiing injuries!

**North Conway ambulance:** 603-356-6911. **Conway ambulance:** 603-447-5522.

## ✷ To See

MUSEUMS **Mount Washington Weather Discovery Center** (603-356-2137; 1-800-706-0432; www.mountwashington.org), 2936 Main Street (Route 16 at the North Village Commons). Open daily 10 AM–5 PM—but check, because it closes Wednesday and Thursday in slow periods. $2 adult admission. Experience what it sounded and felt like to be on top of Mount Washington when the highwest winds (231 miles per hour) were recorded through the hands-on exhibits at this, the country's only weather museum. It's the public outreach center for the world-famous summit observatory (see *Getting Around* in "Mount Washington"). Hopes are for the museum to expand and move to the base of the Mount Washington Auto Road within the life of this edition.

HISTORICAL SOCIETY **Conway Historical Society** (603-447-5551), the Eastman-Lord House, 100 Main Street, Conway. Open from Memorial Day through Labor Day, Tuesday and Thursday 6–8 PM, Wednesday 2–4 PM. The Eastman-Lord House features a Victorian parlor and 1940s kitchen, plus local memorabilia and special exhibits, including paintings by 19th-century White Mountain artist Benjamin Champney.

COVERED BRIDGES **Saco River bridge,** on Washington Street (turn west at the Route 16 lights, junction of Routes 16 and 153) in Conway village. Bear right at the fork to see this two-span bridge, originally built in 1890, rebuilt a century later. If you bear left (instead) at the fork, you come to the **Swift River bridge.** No longer used for traffic, this 144-foot, 1869 bridge has been restored (after being threatened with demolition) with picnic tables at its entrance, by the river. Covered-bridge buffs may also want to head out 9 miles east from Conway on the Kangamagus Highway and turn north at the sign to find the **Albany covered bridge** across the Swift River, dating from 1858. The **Bartlett covered bridge** on Route 302, 4.5 miles east of Bartlett village, is also the real thing despite its use as a gift shop. It has been closed to traffic since 1939.

FOR FAMILIES ✐ ♿ **Heritage New Hampshire** (603-383-9776; www.heritagenh.com), Route 16, Box 1776, Glen 03838. Open Memorial Day through Father's Day, weekends 9 AM–5 PM; through Labor Day, open daily; then weekends again from Labor Day to mid-October. Heritage New Hampshire evokes the history of this state as you travel from England on a 17th-century vessel, visit past personalities such as Daniel Webster, and reenter modern times on a train ride through Crawford Notch. Designed around an 1,800-foot walkway, which is handicapped accessible, this attraction is a 300-year review of New Hampshire history through photographs, dioramas, rides, and talking mannequins. Created long before the more technologically advanced but essentially similar attractions at Epcot, this is, nevertheless, a fine introduction to the state's past. Allow 2 hours. Adults $10, children 4–12 $4.50; under 4 free.

**Story Land** (603-383-4293; www.storylandnh.com), Route 16, Box 1776, Glen 03838. Open from Memorial Day through Labor Day, weekends 9 AM–6 PM; from Labor Day through Columbus Day, weekends 10 AM–5 PM. Created some 50 years ago and regularly expanded, Story Land is organized around well-known fairy tales and children's stories. Sixteen rides range from a pirate ship, railroad, and antique autos to an African safari, bamboo chutes flume, and Dr. Geyser's remarkable raft ride. Cinderella, the Old Woman Who Lived in a Shoe, the Three Little Pigs, and the Billy Goats Gruff are all here, along with Heidi of the Alps, farm animals to pet and feed, and dozens of other favorites. There is a restaurant, gift shop, and free parking. Admission for those 4 and up is $19, which covers all rides. Operated, along with Heritage New Hampshire next door, by the Morrill family.

**Hartmann Model Railroad and Toy Museum** (603-356-9922), Town Hall Road at Route 16/302, Intervale. An extensive American and European model-train layout, plus the Brass Caboose hobby shop. There is also a new café and crafts shop. Open daily, except the museum, which is closed Tuesday and Wednesday from January through June. Admission charged.

Also see **Santa's Village** under *To See—For Families* in "The Great North Woods—Northern White Mountains," **Wildcat Mountain Gondola Ride** (under *To Do—Aerial Lift*) and the **Mount Washington Auto Road** (under *To See—Scenic Drives*) in "Jackson and Pinkham Notch," and the **Mount Washington Cog Railway** under *To See* in "Crawford Notch and Bretton Woods."

**SCENIC DRIVES** **West Side Road,** running north from the Conway village traffic lights to River Road in North Conway, is not only a scenic road that passes two covered bridges, working farms, and mountain views but also the best and only way to avoid much of the Route 16 traffic snarl between Conway and North Conway. In Conway it begins as Washington Street, a left at the first light (junction of Routes 16 and 153). Pass the two covered bridges, and at the fork bear right (a left would lead eventually to the Albany covered bridge on the Kancamagus Highway). At the intersection with River Road, a right brings you quickly into North Conway village at the north end of Main Street. Turn left for Echo Lake State Park, Cathedral Ledge, Diana's Baths, and Humphrey's Ledge, and then continue along the Saco River to join Route 302 just east of Attitash Bear Peak ski resort in Glen.

**Hurricane Mountain Road and Evans Notch.** For a satisfying day's loop turn east off Route 16 onto Hurricane Mountain Road. It begins in Intervale, 3 miles north of North Conway (just north of the scenic vista turnout). Not for the fainthearted, the road climbs and twists across a mountain ridge to connect with north–south Green Hill Road. Turn south (right) if you want the short loop back through East Conway and Redstone to North Conway. Turn north (left) to link up with Route 113, in tiny Stow, Maine, and equally rural Chatham, New Hampshire (population 274), surrounded by the national forest. Route 113 north is not maintained in winter, but it is a smoothly graded road through Evans Notch—one of the lesser known of the White Mountain passes but featuring four campgrounds (see *Lodging—Campgrounds*), many hiking trails, and good fishing along the Wild River. In North Chatham look for the **Chester Eastman Homestead** (603-694-3388; www.cehfarm.com), site of seasonal special events—a maple sugaring day in March, spring plowing in April, a fall harvest day, a logging day in November, and ice harvesting in January—as well as hayrides by reservation. Route 113 connects with Route 2 in Gilead, Maine. Turn west (left) to head back through Shelburne and Gorham (see "The Great North Woods—Northern White Mountains") and back down through Pinkham Notch (see "Jackson and Pinkham Notch").

**Cathedral Ledge.** A winding, two-lane 1.7-mile-long road leads to the top of Cathedral Ledge with its fabulous view of the valley—an obvious place for a picnic. From the lights at the north end of North Conway village take River Road 1.4 miles to the marked turnoff.

**Bear Notch Road.** Closed to vehicles in winter, this road through the White Mountain National Forest is a popular shortcut from the Kancamagus Highway to Crawford Notch (totally avoiding North Conway). It's also a beautiful woods road, however, and a good place to spot wildlife. From Conway head west on "the Kanc" (Route 110) to the turnoff near Jigger Johnson Campground. It meets up with Route 302 in Bartlett village.

## ✷ To Do

✐ **Conway Scenic Railroad** (603-356-5251; 1-800-232-5251; www.conwayscenic.com), North Conway village. Runs weekends mid-April through Memorial Day, daily late June through the fourth Saturday in October. The splendid Victorian North Conway depot, serving passengers from 1874 through 1961, stood boarded and derelict for a dozen years, until this excursion train company restored and reopened it as a base for its two trains and three different excursions: the **Valley Train** south to Conway (11 miles, 1 hour), and north to Bartlett (21 miles, 1¼ hours), and the spectacular **North Conway** through Crawford Notch trip (50 miles, 5 hours). The latter trip traverses the most spectacular rail route in the Northeast (reservations a must). Inquire about the special foliage runs (5-plus hours) all the way through Crawford Notch to Fabyan Station. Lunch and dinner are served in a refurbished steel dining car (see *Dining Out*). The in-service rolling stock includes steam and diesel engines as well as vintage passenger cars and a parlor observation car. Historic buildings include the large turntable, roundhouse, freight house, and the old depot, which has a gift shop and exhibits. Rates are $10 for an adult coach ticket from North Conway to Conway; $20 for a first-class parlor ticket from North Conway to Bartlett; $35 to Crawford Notch; and for a dome-car trip to Fabyan Station, $54. Children's fares are less; trips with meals included cost considerably more (see *Dining Out*).

**BIKING** **Bike the Whites** (1-800-448-3534; www.bikethewhites.com). This is a self-guided inn-to-inn biking package with your luggage transported; rentals are available. The distance is 20 miles per day over back roads. The three lodging places are all among our favorites: The Forest Inn in Intervale (see *Lodging—Bed & Breakfasts*), Snowvillage Inn in Snowville, and the Tamworth Inn in Tamworth (see "Mount Washington Gateway Region" for the last two).

Mountain bike rentals are easy to come by at North Conway sports stores, and bicycle routes abound. We can recommend the ride to and around **Echo Lake State Park** and on up or down the West Side Road. At **Attitash Bear Peak,** mountain bikers are welcome on ski trails. The **Conway Town Trail** (marked in yellow) is a designated recreation trail for mountain biking, running 4 miles along the river. Begin on East Conway Road off Route 302 in Redstone. Turn right immediately after the Conway Police Station onto Meeting House Hill Road for the parking lot. Also see **Whitaker Woods** under *Green Space.*

**CANOEING AND KAYAKING** The **Saco** is a popular canoeing river. Many people like to put in where River Road crosses the river (turn west at the traffic lights at the northern edge of North Conway village), then paddle about 8 miles downstream to the Conway village covered bridge. In summer the river is wide and slow, except for light rapids between the Swift River covered bridge and the Conway (second) covered bridge. Take out after the second bridge at Davis Park.

**Saco Bound** (603-447-2177; www.sacobound.com), Route 302, Center Conway. Rentals, sales, instruction, canoe camping, shuttle service, and guided trips. They also maintain a seasonal information and canoe shop on Main Street, North Con-

THE CONWAY SCENIC RAILROAD STOPS AT THE HISTORIC CRAWFORD STATION.

Peter Randall

way. Inquire about white-water rafting and guided flatwater kayaking tours from their (seasonal) base in Errol (see "The Great North Woods—Northern White Mountains").

Rentals are also available at **Northern Extremes Canoe & Kayak** (1-877-722-6748; www.nothernextremes.com) with outlets on Main Street, North Conway (603-356-4718), and Route 302 in Glen **Saco Canoe Rental** (603-447-2737) in Conway and **Saco Valley Canoe** (603-447-2444; 1-800-447-2460) in Center Conway also offer canoe rentals.

**FISHING** Brook and brown trout, lake trout, bass, and salmon are the target fish for anglers in this area. Try your luck in the Saco, Cold, or Swift River; Conway Lake, the area's largest, is managed for landlocked salmon (the access is off Mill Street in Center Conway). Mountain Pond in Chatham (see *To See—Scenic Drives*) is favored for brook trout. Fishing licenses are required.

**North Country Angler** (603-356-6000), Route 16, North Conway village. Specialists in trout and Atlantic salmon fishing, they sell equipment and clothes and offer local fishing information, a professional fly-tying school, and multiday fly-fishing instruction programs in combination with Nereledge Inn.

**FOR FAMILIES** ✐ **Attitash Bear Peak Alpine Slide and Waterslides** (603-374-2368), Route 302, Bartlett. Open from late May through mid-June and Labor Day to early October, weekends 10 AM–5 PM; from late June through Labor Day, open daily 10 AM–6 PM. Great fun for the kids and adults too. The Alpine Slide includes a ride to the top of the mountain on the ski lift, then a slide down a curving, bowed, three-quarter-mile chute on a self-controlled sled. Then cool off in the Aquaboggin Waterslide. Other seasonal, commercial attractions include **Fun Factory Amusement Park** (603-356-6541), Route 16, North Conway. May through October; the water slide is open Memorial Day through Labor Day, the arcade all year. A mini park with miniature golf, water slides, and arcade. **Pirate's Cove Adventure Golf** (603-356-8807), Route 16, North Conway. Open May through mid-October. Eighteen-hole miniature golf with plenty of challenges for young and old.

**GOLF** **North Conway Country Club** (603-356-9391, pro shop), in the center of the village, North Conway. Eighteen holes. **The White Mountain Hotel and Country Club** (603-356-2140; www.whitemountainhotel.com), on the West Side Road, Hale's Location. A nine-hole course. You might also want to check out the **White Mountain Driving Range** (603-356-7956), Routes 16 and 16A in Intervale.

**HIKING** **Mount Kearsarge North Trail** (3.1 miles, 2¼ hours). Mount Kearsarge (elevation 3,268 feet) is just north of North Conway, and this hike has been popular since the turn of the 20th century. At Intervale, north of North Conway village, Hurricane Mountain Road diverges east. Follow this road for 1.5 miles to the trailhead. From the summit fire tower there are views across the Saco River Valley to the Moat Range and north to Mount Washington and the Presidential Range.

**Black Cap Path** (2.4 miles). The trailhead is on Hurricane Mountain Road (see

*To See—Scenic Drives*), 3.7 miles east of Route 16. The trail is through spruce and beech forests to the summit of Black Cap for views south to Conway Lake.

Also see *Green Space.*

HORSEBACK AND HORSE-DRAWN RIDES ✐ **The Stables at Farm By The River** (603-356-4855), 255 West Side Road, North Conway. Year-round horsback rides offered daily, ponies for small children. Geared to novices. $35 per hour. Also fall wagon and winter sleigh rides.

**Attitash Bear Peak** (603-374-2368) offers guided horseback tours along the Saco River in summer.

**Darby Field Inn** (see *Lodging—Inns*) offers sleigh and carriage rides.

ROCK CLIMBING **Cathedral Ledge** is famous for its many challenging routes, and from the base you can observe climbers inching up its cracks and sheer faces. For those who would like to join the climbers, **Eastern Mountain Sports Climbing School** (603-356-5433), **International Mountain Equipment Climbing School** (603-356-7064; 603-447-6700), and **Mountain Guides Alliance** (603-356-5287) offer instruction and guided climbs. **Cranmore Mountain Recreation Center** (603-356-6301) has an indoor climbing wall and offers instruction programs. If you are already an experienced climber, pick up Ed Webster's *Rock Climbs in the White Mountains of New Hampshire,* published by Mountain Imagery.

SWIMMING **Echo Lake State Park,** Old West Side Road, North Conway. Set against the backdrop of White Horse Ledge, this lovely lake offers a sandy beach, picnic area, and changing rooms. Nominal parking fee.

**Diana's Baths.** Lucy Brook cascades through a series of inviting (if chilly) granite basins below the waterfalls (swimming above is prohibited, because water there is piped into the public water supply). From North Conway follow River Road to the turnoff for Cathedral Ledge. A marked, half-mile path leads from the parking lot.

**Davis Park,** Washington Street, Conway. A great swimming beach with picnic tables next to the Saco River covered bridge, plus tennis and basketball courts.

**Conway Lake,** Center Conway. This is the area's largest lake, and the beach is public.

CATHEDRAL LEDGE IS A DESTINATION FOR ROCK CLIMBERS.

Robert Kozlow

**Saco River at Hussey Field,** River Road, North Conway. Turn onto Weston River Road at the light and park by the first bridge. This is a popular swimming hole, minutes from the middle of the village.

## ✷ Winter Sports

CROSS-COUNTRY SKIING **Mount Washington Valley Ski Touring and Snowshoe Center** (603-356-9920). More than 60 km of groomed trails through the valley, connecting inns. Rentals and information at Ragged Mountain Equipment, Route 16/302 in Intervale.

**Bear Notch Ski Touring Center** (603-374-2277; www.bearnotchski.com), Route 302, Bartlett. This is a favorite with everyone who tries it: 60 km of wooded, groomed trails with warming stations (snacks) and picnic tables; ski school, guided snowshoe and moonlight tours.

DOWNHILL SKIING AND SNOWBOARDING **Attitash Bear Peak** (603-374-2368; snow phone, 1-877-677-SNOW; lodging, 1-888-554-1900; 1-800-223-SNOW; www.attitash.com), Route 302, Bartlett. Boasting New Hampshire's most powerful snowmaking system, this two-mountain ski area has profited from a $32 million upgrade in recent years. With its 147-room Grand Summit Hotel and 60-acre Attitash Mountain Village, it offers the advantages of a reasonably priced self-contained resort within easy striking distance of both Crawford and Pinkham Notches and North Conway. *Lifts*: 12: 3 quads (2 high-speed), 3 triples, 3 doubles, 3 surface. *Trails*: 70 trails and glades: 20 percent novice, 47 percent intermediate, 33 percent advanced. *Vertical drop:* 1,750 feet at Attitash, 1,450 feet at Bear Peak. *Snowmaking:* 98 percent coverage. *Snowboarding:* Terrain garden and 500-foot half pipe. *Cross-country skiing:* Guided snowshoeing and cross-country tours; see Bear Notch Center under *Cross-Country Skiing. Facilities:* Base lodges with children's services. Three pubs and two cafeterias. Package plans include skiing, lessons, and lodging at the slope-side Grand Summit Resort Hotel and at Attitash Mountain Village with condos for 2 to 14 people, indoor pool, outdoor ice rink. *Rates:* $42 adult weekdays, $49–53 weekends and holidays.

**Cranmore Mountain Resort** (603-356-8561; slope-side lodging package information, 1-800-223-SNOW; www.cranmore.com), Skimobile Road, North Conway. A granddaddy among New England ski areas (see the chapter introduction) and still a favorite for its in-town location, sunny and moderate slopes, and night skiing. This is a great family mountain with lift-serviced snow-tubing, a relaxed place for anyone to learn to ski or snowboard. The Sports Center at the bottom is big, tubing is allotted its own space and lift, and a fast quad chair has replaced the beloved old Skimobile. Inquire about the Mountain Meister racing series, billed as the largest citizen's racing program in the country, with as many as 800 racers in 15-person teams in two runs competing against each other and against the clock. *Lifts:* 9: express quad, 1 triple, 3 doubles, 4 surface. *Trails:* 34 plus 5 glades and a Tubing Center with 8 lift-service lanes. *Vertical drop:* 1,200 feet. *Snowmaking:* 100 percent. *Snowboarding:* All trails plus a 350-foot half-pipe and terrain park. *Facilities:* Base lodges with children's center and services; Meister Hut Summit Restaurant; Cranmore Sports Center with indoor tennis courts, pool, exercise equipment, climbing wall; slope-side condos. *Rates:* In 2002 it was $32 adults, $18 juniors every day of the week. Also see Wildcat Mountain and Black Mountain in *To Do—Downhill Skiing* in "Jackson and Pinkham Notch" and Bretton Woods in "Crawford Notch and Bretton Woods."

**ICE CLIMBING** North Conway is a world-class center for ice climbing, said to offer more businesses geared to technical climbing than anywhere else in the country. Foremost is the **International Mountain Equipment Climbing School** (603-356-7064), sponsor of the annual February Ice Fest, a series of shows, demonstrations, and clinics.

**ICE SKATING** The setting and price are hard to beat: **Schouler Park** in the center of North Conway in front of the train station is free. **The Ham Ice Arena** (603-447-5886), 87 West Main Street, Conway is open year-round, featuring a 16-speaker sound system for music, rentals, and a café.

**SLEIGH RIDES** **The Darby Field Inn** (603-447-2181), off Bald Hill Road in Conway, offers sleigh rides through its high woods with views of Mount Washington.

**The Stables at The Farm By The River** (603-356-4855), West Side Road, North Conway, offer horse-drawn sleigh rides on its property along the Saco.

**The Chester Eastman Homestead** (603-694-3388), North Chatham, offers sleigh rides by reservation throughout the winter. The 12-person sled is drawn by two Percheron draft horses. Rides are 20 minutes, followed by popcorn and cocoa at the farm.

**SNOWMOBILING** **Corridor 19,** one of the state's main snowmbole corridors, crosses Route 16 right in North Conway, also accessed from Bear Notch Trails (rentals). **Northern Extremes** (603-356-4718) and **Alpine Adventures** (603-374-2344) offer guided tours geared to all abilities. **Profile RV Inc.** (603-447-5855; 1-800-638-8888) rents machines.

**SNOWSHOEING** **Snowshoe rentals** are available from **Eastern Mountain Sports** and from **Ragged Mountain Equipment** (603-356-9920). Animal Tracking Tours at **Attitash Bear Peak** depart from the conservation center at Thorn Pond; rentals available.

## ✱ Green Space

**Echo Lake State Park** (603-356-2672), off River Road, 2 miles west of Route 16 in North Conway. Open weekends beginning Memorial Day, then daily late June through Labor Day. A swimming beach with picnic tables and bathhouse plus dramatic views across the lake to White Horse (can you see the horse?) Ledge and a 1.7-mile road to the top of 1,150-foot Cathedral Ledge, good for broad views across the valley of the Saco. This is a favorite ascent for rock climbers and a nesting place for rare peregrine falcons, which can sometimes be seen soaring on the updrafts.

**Whitaker Woods,** Kearsarge Road, North Conway. North of North Conway village on the east side of Route 16/302. A wooded, town-owned conservation area with trails for walking, mountain biking, or winter cross-country skiing.

**Diana's Baths,** River Road, 2.2 miles west of North Conway. Watch for a dirt road on your left and park beside the road; it's a short walk to the stream. No swimming above the falls, since this is a public water supply. Lucy Brook has eroded and sculpted the rocks in this beautiful place. **Moat Mountain Trail** (4.2 miles, 3½ hours) leads to the summit of North Moat Mountain (elevation 3,201 feet).

**Green Hills Preserve,** North Conway. Access from Thompson Road with a designated parking area. This is a 2,822-acre preserve belonging to The Nature Conservancy, New Hampshire Chapter. It's home to several rare and endangered plants and a high-elevation stand of red pine. The half-dozen options include the **Peaked Mountain Trail** (2.1 miles, 1,739 feet) and **Middle Mountain Trail** (2 miles, 1,857 feet, with excellent views to the south, east, and west).

## ✷ Lodging

**HOTELS** *Note*: Half a dozen 20th-century-style large hotels account for about two-thirds of the lodging options in the Conway area. For the real old-timers, see **The Mount Washington Hotel** in "Crawford Notch and Bretton Woods" and the **Wentworth/Eagle Mountain House** in "Jackson and Pinkham Notch."

ꝏ ✐ ♿ **The White Mountain Hotel and Resort** (603-356-7100; 1-800-533-6301; www.whitemountainhotel.com), West Side Road at Hale's Location, Box 1828, North Conway 03860. This impressive, 1990s version of an 1890s hotel is set in expansive grounds (which include a nine-hole golf course and large condo development) off the West Side Road at the base of Cathedral and White Horse Ledges. The 80 rooms (they include 13 suites and 2 handicapped-accessible rooms) are furnished in reproduction antiques, all with air-conditioning, TV, telephone, and views off across the valley to Mount Cranmore. The dining room, open to the public, serves three meals daily (see *Dining Out*). Amenities include an inviting Irish pub and first-rate restaurant and lounge, all-season outdoor pool and Jacuzzi, sauna, fitness center, and tennis court as well as the golf course. Rates, which include a sumptuous breakfast midweek from November through mid-June, are $79–199 per couple, depending on season and accommodations; MAP, midweek, golf, and other special plans available.

✐ **Grand Summit Resort Hotel and Conference Center** (603-374-1900; 1-888-554-1900; www.attitash.com), Route 302 at Attitash Bear Peak, Bartlett 03812. Located at the base of Attitash Bear Peak, this contemporary condominium resort hotel opened in 1997 with 143 guest rooms ranging from spacious units with two queen-sized beds to complete three-bedroom suites. All have home entertainment system; most have a full kitchen and dining area. There's a health club; a 75-foot, year-round outdoor pool and whirlpool spa; an arcade; a full-service restaurant and lounge; valet parking; and on-site daycare, as well as nine conference rooms. Alpine slide, water slide, scenic chairlift, and complimentary interpretive hikes in summer; in winter you can ski in and out. Rooms range from $89–429, depending on accommodations and season.

**Red Jacket Mountain View** (1-800-RJACKET; www.redjacketmountainview.com), Route 16/302, North Conway 03860-2000. Set in 40 acres atop Sunset Hill, above the main drag, this 163-room facility has a lot going for it. The property began as a railroad baron's summer estate and has evolved into a sprawling motor-inn-style resort over the past 30 years. The 150 rooms in the main building have all the basic amenities plus the view; 12 units are two-bedroom town houses. The lounge and Champney's (named for the 19th-century artist whose painting hangs there) are at the core of the building, and the large, attractive lobby with its formal front desk is a source of information about frequent special happenings. In summer a daily children's program is offered. Year-round themed packages are a house specialty: November shopping, Christmas, mystery and Valentine's weekends, and more. Some rooms include lofts or bunks for families and others, Jacuzzis. $109–249 for rooms, $229–349 for town houses. Ask about packages.

**INNS** **The 1785 Inn** (603-356-9025; 1-800-421-1785; www.the1785inn.com), Route 16 (mailing address: Box 1785, North Conway 03860), Intervale. Open all year. The vista from the living room and many guest rooms in this genuine 1785 house are across the Saco River intervale to Mount Washington. Built by a Revolutionary War veteran when there was still plenty of space to choose from, it sits on a knoll with its dining room and guest living rooms, each with a large fireplace, facing the panorama. The inn's 17 rooms, 12 with private bath, have king-sized and double beds. Rooms are comfortably furnished, and some have two beds. Room 5 is a beauty; we also like 7 and 17. You'll definitely want a quiet room in the back of the inn as opposed to one on Route 16. The dining room is considered one of the best restaurants in the valley (see *Dining Out*). There is a swimming pool, and many trails are handy for walking in summer or cross-country skiing (the real lunch is served during ski season). Longtime innkeepers Becky and Charlie Mallar charge $69–199 per couple, including a full breakfast.

**The Darby Field Inn and Restaurant** (603-447-2181; outside New Hampshire, 1-800-426-4147; www.darbyfield.com), Bald Hill Road, Conway 03818. Open all year. Operated by Marc and Maria Donaldson since 1979, the place is named for that intrepid first climber of Mount Washington, whose summit and other high peaks can be seen from the inn. Set on a secluded hilltop—well south of North Conway, with Chase Hill Road (summer only) leading directly down to the Kancamagus Highway—the inn is surrounded by landscaped grounds and woods that include 15 km of cross-country trails. In recent years the Donaldsons have seriously upgraded to position the inn as a romantic getaway. All 14 rooms have private bath; five suites now feature Jacuzzi, gas fireplace, TV/VCR, and a balcony with views north to the Presidentials. Rooms vary, and the key factor, to our thinking, is the views: Room 11 on the third floor is small and old-fashioned but offers a great view, while Room 12 has all the bells and whistles plus view. The common room has a fireplace; there's also a small pub with a woodstove. Dinner (see *Dining Out*) is served by reservation. In summer there's a pool. B&B $120–240, MAP $170–290 (add 12 percent for service), depending on the season and accommodations. Ask about packages and midweek specials.

🐾 ✐ **Stonehurst Manor** (603-356-3113; 1-800-525-9100; www.stonehurstmanor.com), Route 16, Box 1937, North Conway 03860. Open all year. This multigabled, three-story inn, located on a 33-acre site off Route 16, features baronial stained glass, stonework, and dark oak woodwork. The 25 large rooms (all but 2 with private bath) have TVs and are well furnished, many with antiques. Beds are queens and doubles, and some rooms have two beds. Fifteen of the rooms are in the manor, and 10 are in an attached motel section. Townhouse accommodations are also available. There are tennis courts, an outdoor swimming pool and spa, and walking/cross-country trails from the door. Dinners nightly, with a Continental menu (see *Dining Out*). $96–206 plus a 7 percent service charge for two, MAP (breakfast and dinner are off the regular menu). A variety of special weekend and holiday MAP plans available.

**The New England Inn and Resort** (603-356-5541; outside NewHampshire, 1-800-826-3466; www.newenglandinn.com), Route 16A, Box 100, Intervale 03845. Open all year. This is a valley landmark, dating back in part to 1809. We found rooms in the main inn looking tired. The classic clapboard cabins with fireplaces are still attractive, but all recent energy seems to have been focused on creating The Lodge across the road, a two-story North Woods–style log structure with rooms each named for a woodland animal and each featuring a Jacuzzi. Facilities include a restaurant and **Tuckerman's Tavern,** three tennis courts, and an outdoor swimming pool. Inn rooms $59–116; cottages, cabins, and cottage suites $99–240; Lodge $150–260.

BED & BREAKFASTS ♿ **Cabernet Inn** (603-356-4704; 1-800-866-4704; www.cabernetinn.com), Route 16 (mailing address: Box 38, Intervale 03845). Begin with an 1840 house, raise it 13 feet, totally renovate and update it, and you have this striking inn just south of the intervale. Rich and Debbie Howard offer 11 guest rooms, all with queen beds, air-conditioning, private phone, and bath. Two rooms have fireplace and Jacuzzi; two with wood-burning fireplaces open onto a back deck. One, with a private entrance, is totally handicapped accessible right down to the roll-in shower. There's a formal living room on the entry levels as well as a comfortable downstairs den with a 10-foot-high hearth, TV/VCR, fridge, and board games. As with all properties on Route 16, we suggest you request a quiet back room with a view. The inn is on the valley's cross-country trail system. No children under 12, please. $85–225 includes a full breakfast featuring homemade breads.

✐ **Nereledge Inn** (603-356-2831; www.nereledgeinn.com), River Road, North Conway 03860. Open all year. Nicely old-fashioned, in a quiet setting by a swimming hole in the Saco River and with a view of Cathedral Ledge, but steps from the summer playhouse and a short walk to the village. There are 11 cheerful but unfussy guest rooms (5 with private bath, 1 with a half bath), two comfortable sitting rooms (one with a woodstove), and an English-style pub with dartboard, TV, and fireplace (BYOB). This inn appeals to active people: Many of the guests are hikers, rock climbers, and cross-country skiers. With North Country Angler, the inn hosts a fly-fishing program. Innkeepers Valerie Horn and her daughter Suzanne include a full breakfast in the rates: $64–159, children $1 per year to age 12. Add 10 percent for service. No smoking.

**The Farm by the River B&B** (603-356-2694; 1-888-414-8353; www.farmbytheriver.com), 2555 West Side Road, North Conway 03860. Open all year. Built in 1785 on a land grant from King George III, this picturesque, three-story farmhouse and barn was an active farm for most of its years. Surrounded by 65 acres with mountain views and river frontage, the onetime boardinghouse is now an inn where guests return year after year, often to the same room they had the previous season. Each of the 10 rooms, all named for former guests, is decorated in country style with antiques, quilts, and Oriental rugs. Some have king-sized bed and two-person Jacuzzi bath and fireplace, and there are a couple of two-room suites, perfect for families. Innkeepers Rick and Charlene Browne-Davis provide horseback riding all year, as well as fall foliage wagon rides and sleigh rides in winter. Snowshoes are provided for guest use on the property. Walk to the Saco River for swimming and fly-fishing. Rick is a justice of the peace and small, off-season weddings are possible. $80–170 double includes a full patio or fireside breakfast.

**The Forest Inn** (603-356-9772; 1-800-448-3534; www.forest-inn.com), Route 16A at the intervale, Box 37, Intervale 03854. Open all year. This recently renovated, antiques-furnished inn has been welcoming guests for more than a century. Its 11 rooms are decorated in country/Victorian style with queen beds, private baths, and air-conditioning; three have a fireplace. In the neighboring stone cottage three more rooms each have a fireplace and one, a whirlpool tub. Innkeepers Bill and Lisa Guppy serve a full breakfast and afternoon refreshments. There's an outdoor pool; hiking and cross-country ski trails are out the door. Packages include an inn-to-inn bicycle tour. $75–160.

**The Buttonwood Inn** (603-356-2625; 1-800-258-2625), Mount Surprise Road, Box 1817, North Conway 03860. Open all year. Innkeepers Peter and Claudia Needham have placed their outstanding B&B on the market, but we assume that it will survive this change of hands as it has the several during the time we have known it. At this writing the 10 guest rooms include 8 suites, 1 with a two-person Jacuzzi and gas fireplace, all with private bath. Just minutes from Mount Cranmore and Route 16 shopping, the 1820s farmhouse sits at the end of a road and retains its country atmosphere with wide-pine floors, Shaker furniture, quilts, and period stenciling. There are two common rooms, one downstairs with a fireplace and games, and an outdoor swimming pool surrounded by gardens. In winter you can cross-country ski from the door. Full breakfast. $95–225 for two, depending on the season and accommodations. Seasonal packages also available.

**Cranmore Inn** (603-356-5502; outside New Hampshire, 1-800-526-5502; www.cranmoreinn.com), Kearsarge Street, Box 1349, North Conway 03860. Open all year. Opened more than 130 years ago, this is the oldest continuously operating inn in the valley and looks it. Christopher and Virginia Kanzler have preserved the old-style feel in 18 rooms. Fourteen rooms have private bath; beds are mostly queens, and some rooms have two beds. There are 2 one-bedrooms and 1 two-bedroom unit with kitchens. Country decor includes matching bedspreads and curtains, stenciled wallpaper, and antique bed frames. Seasonal drinks are served in the afternoon. The common room is cozy, with a fireplace and a piano; and there is a separate TV room. You'll also find a pool and lawn games, and guests can pay a nominal fee to use the nearby Mount Cranmore Recreation Center. Just minutes from Main Street's shops and restaurants but in a quiet area. No smoking. $59–159 with full breakfast, depending on season and accommodations. Children under 4 free; for those 4 years and older, pay $1 per year to age 12.

**Victorian Harvest Inn** (603-356-3548; outside New Hampshire, 1-800-642-0749; www.victorianharvestinn.com), Locust Lane, Box 1763, North Conway 03860. Open all year. David and Judy Wooster have created a very special place to stay on a quiet side street above the clutter along Route 16/302. It's a sunny yellow inn with views across the valley from most of its eight well-furnished, air-conditioned rooms, the largest with a gas fireplace and two-person Jacuzzi tub. All rooms have private bath, four have king bed, three have queen, and one has a double bed. There's a swimming pool, a nifty library with bay window, television, films, and books. Full breakfast. No smoking. $75–220.

✐ **Cranmore Mountain Lodge** (603-356-2044; 1-800-356-3596; www.cml1.com), Kearsarge Road, North Conway 03860. Open all year. Babe Ruth's daughter once owned the place; and, if it's not taken, you can ask for the Babe's old room (Room 2, with his original furniture). The main inn has 15 rooms (some are family suites). Next door in the barn are three family suites and four loft rooms, all with antiques, private bath, air-conditioning, and TV. There's also a two-story town house that sleeps up to nine, with a full kitchen, dining room, living room, cable TV, and deck/patio. The lower section of the barn is a 22-bed dorm. Outside is a heated year-round pool and Jacuzzi, tennis, stocked trout pond, petting barn, and hard-surface basketball court. Cross-country skiing from the door. $69–240. Bunkhouse beds are $17. All rates include breakfast.

✐ **The Lavender Flower Inn** (603-447-3794; 1-800-729-0106; www.lavenderflowerinn.com), Main Street, Center Conway 03813. This 1840s house in the quiet village of Center Conway is a faded, friendly lavender. A wraparound porch with wicker chairs overlooks daylilies and daisies. There is a fireplace in the common room and cheery breakfast room. The eight guest rooms are furnished with a mix of antiques; four have private bath and three are suites, one in the rear of the house with a loft, gas fireplace, and kitchen. Conway Lake, good for boating, fishing, and swimming, is minutes away. $60–80 with shared bath, $70–90 private, $145–165 for the loft suite, a full breakfast included.

✐ **Sunny Side Inn** (603-356-6239; 1-800-600-6239; www.sunnyside-inn.com), Seavey Street, North Conway 03860. Open all year. A gabled house on a quiet street near Mount Cranmore but an easy walk to Main Street.

Nine rooms, all with private bath and air-conditioning; two have king-sized bed, one a queen, and the rest, doubles. Several rooms also have a twin, perfect for children, who are welcome here. Fireplace in the common room. Full breakfast. $60–119, depending on season and accommodations. Inquire about the five cottages, each with a gas fireplace, three with full kitchen, two with two-person Jacuzzi, $90–210.

**Mountain Valley Manner** (603-447-3988), West Side Road, Box 1649, Conway 03818. Open all year. In Conway village, this inn is just across the street from the Swift River covered bridge and only a short walk to swimming and tennis at Davis Park. Innkeepers Bob and Lynn Lein have furnished their home in the Victorian manner with lots of lace, mostly antique furniture, and pretty floral accents. The B&B has four cozy guest rooms, all with air-conditioning and private bath. Beds are king, queen, and twins. One room is a suite with a king. Ask about their antiques shop and Bob's cassette-tape-guided tours. A no-smoking inn. Full breakfast. $55–135, depending on season and accommodations.

**Covered Bridge House B&B** (603-383-9109; 1-800-232-9109; www.coveredbridge.com), Route 302, Glen 03838. Open all year. Six fresh and pretty guest rooms (four with private bath, most with in-room air-conditioning) in a Colonial Revival home on the Saco River. Two rooms share a bath and are ideal for families. Innkeepers Dan and Nancy Wanek also own the **Covered Bridge Gift Shoppe,** actually located in an 1850s-era covered bridge, next door. There's a swimming hole out back; tubing and fishing on the river; and skiing, both downhill and cross-country, just minutes away. Rates, $59–109, include a full breakfast.

**Hostelling International White Mountains** (603-447-1001), Washington Street, Conway. Reserve. Check-in is between 5 and 10 PM. A couple of blocks from the bus stop, an old farmhouse now serves as a busy hostel, accommodating 40 people (four private rooms, the remainder dorms; shared baths). The kitchen is fully equipped, and linens are provided. Clunker bikes are also available for patrons to get around and to trailheads. $19 for HI members ($22 for nonmembers) includes a continental breakfast.

CAMPGROUNDS **WMNF campgrounds,** Evans Notch. Seventy-seven wooded sites. Four of the campgrounds are open all year, and three—Hastings, Cold River, and Basin—are part of the **toll-free reservation system** (1-800-280-2267). Also see *Campgrounds* in "Jackson and Pinkham Notch" and the introduction to this White Mountain National Forest section.

## ✷ Where to Eat

DINING OUT **Bellini's** (603-356-7000; www.bellinis.com), 33 Seavey Street, North Conway. Open except Monday and Tuesday, at 5 PM. The Marcello family has more than 50 years' experience in the Italian food business, and they use all of their talents in this colorful restaurant. The pasta is imported, but everything else is freshly prepared. All the well-known southern and northern Italian specialties are offered here, including 20 different kinds of pasta and braciola (sirloin rolled and stuffed with prosciutto, stuffing, garlic, and mozzarella), along with baked minestrone soup, canneloni, and *tiramisu*. Portions are large, but there's a children's menu. Entrées range from $14 for eggplant parmigiana to $22 for drunken sirloin.

**The 1785 Inn** (603-356-9025; 1-800-421-1785), Route 16 at the intervale (mailing: Box 1785, North Conway 03860). Breakfast weekdays 8–9:30 AM; weekends and holidays 7–10 AM. Open for dinner at 5 PM nightly; also lunch during the cross-country season. Dependably outstanding. There are more appetizers (14, priced $5.85–7.85) than many restaurants have entrées. Lobster crêpe, smoked salmon ravioli, or Caesar salad for two (made at your table) could make a delightful meal by itself. But then you would miss such entrées as veal and shrimp in a rum cream sauce with artichoke hearts, sherried rabbit, raspberry duckling, and rack of lamb. The wine list includes some 200 labels. There's a fireplace and, if you request the right table, a view of the intervale and Mount Washington. Entrées $17.85–22.85.

**Snowvillage Inn** (603-447-2818; 1-800-447-4345), Snowville. Open year-round. This is in the "Mount Washington Gateway Region" section of this chapter, but it's such a dining destination from North Conway that we don't want to shortchange it with an "also see." The cheery, wood-paneled and beamed, alpine-style dining room features spectacular long views across the valley to the Presidentials—and the food is exceptional. On the October night we visited, appetizers included smoked mozzarella ravioli and grilled portobello mushroom. From nine entrées you might choose pan-seared ocean scallops, veal sautéed with sun-dried tomatoes, vodka, and cream, or a blend of tomato, basil, and saffron baked with white beans and served in a roasted bell pepper. Entrées $17.95–23.95. Four-course candlelight gourmet dinners with several choices of appetizer, salad, entrée, and dessert are available nightly at $30 per person.

**Stonehurst Manor** (603-356-3113; 1-800-525-9100), Route 16, North Conway. Breakfast 8–10 AM; dining nightly 5:30–10 PM; reservations suggested. Chefs Kirstin Johnson and Doug Gibson have each won the state's top culinary honor. They combine culinary tradition and invention in a stylish, relaxing atmosphere. Eat indoors surrounded by elaborate woodwork and stained-glass windows, or outside on the screened patio. In addition to a full menu of classic Continental favorites, offerings include gourmet pizza baked in a wood-fired stone oven and barbecue-pit-smoked aged prime rib. Entrées range $16.75–22.75, but Thursday night is special with "candlelight dinner for two"—a bargain at $19.95.

**The Darby Field Inn and Restaurant** (603-447-2181; outside New Hampshire, 1-800-426-4147; www.darbyfield.com), Bald Hill Road, Conway. Dinner served weekends 6–9 PM, midweek depending on season; reservations required. Chefs vary but the candlelight dining, pleasant dining room, and superlative view of the Presidentials in the distance are constants. The menu always includes half a dozen choices, which usually range from a vegetarian special and the fish of the day to rack of lamb ($24) and filet mignon with peppercorn sauce ($25). The White Mountain chicken is filled with a sharp cheddar and fresh apple accented stuffing, baked and finished with an apple brandy glaze ($19).

✎ **The Ledges at the White Mountain Hotel and Resort** (603-356-7100; 1-800-533-6301), West Side Road at Hale's Location, North Conway. Breakfast 7–10 AM; lunch 11:30 AM–2 PM daily except Sunday, when there's brunch 10:30 AM–2 PM; dinner is served nightly from 5:30 PM in a large, nicely tiered dining room with views across the valley to Mount Cranmore. The Friday seafood buffet is legendary, featuring a raw bar, seafood pastas, and fish fried and poached as well as the night's specials, salads, and chowders ($21.95). Sunday brunch is another event, a bargain at $14.49 adult, $6.95 for children. The dinner menu ranges from Tuscan vegetable pie to rack of lamb, veal Oscar, duckling, and filet mignon. Varied appetizers, salads, and desserts. Children's menu. Entrées ($18.95–22.95) include bread, vegetables, and salad. Pianist nightly in-season.

**Moat Mountain Smokehouse** (603-356-6381; www.moatmountain.com), 3378 White Mountain Highway (Route 16), North Conway. Open for lunch and dinner. Formerly the Scottish Lion, now a fresh, hip restaurant specializing in its own microbrew and southern fare like cornmeal-crusted catfish, St. Louis ribs, and a family-style barbecue dinner with generous platters of ribs, brisket, chicken, skillet corn bread, bowls of slaw, garlic mashed potatoes, and, naturally, black beans and rice. Of course you can also get by with a wood-grilled pizza, smokehouse sandwich, or burger, but don't pass up the brew. We lunched sumptuously in a mural-walled room with a view of Moat Mountain. Entrées $10.95–23.95.

✎ **Conway Scenic Railroad** (603-356-5251; www.conwayscenic.com), Box 1947, North Conway. Lunch (11:30 AM and 1:30 PM) and dinner (6 PM) are served weekends beginning late June, daily except Monday July 4 through September, then a reduced schedule again until foliage season (September 10 through October 20), when lunch is served daily, dinner Thursday through Saturday; obviously, it's a good idea to check. The venue is the refurbished, steel-exterior, oak-interior, 47-seat dining car *Chocorua*. The luncheon menu features soup or salad and a choice of entrées. With lunch, the fare for a 55-minute trip to Conway is $24.95 per adult; the 1¼-hour trip to Bartlett runs $32.95 per adult. "Sunset" dinner trips to Bartlett, where the dining car is transformed into a deluxe restaurant with white linens and china, include an elegant four-course meal: $47.95 per adult. Inquire about the children's menu and rates. Reservations strongly recommended for dinner. Full liquor license.

✎ **The Homestead** (603-356-5900), Route 16, south of North Conway village. Open daily for lunch and dinner 11 AM–10 PM, Sunday brunch 10 AM–2 PM. Traditional New England fare served in a restored 1793 homestead. Fish chowder, roast turkey dinner, baked stuffed haddock, steak tips, also several Italian pasta dishes and fish fries are on the menu (entrées $12.95–18.95). The bargain, when it's available, is a complete lobster dinner for $12.95. Early-bird specials from $10.95, and a Wednesday-night prime rib dinner for $12.95. Children's menu. Sandwiches, pastas, salads, and a choice of "parmigiana" entrées at lunch. Full bar. No smoking.

**The New England Inn and Resort** (603-356-5541; outside New Hampshire, 1-800-826-3466), Route 16A, Intervale. This inn's candlelit dining room serves a country-style menu. The house specialty is Shaker cranberry pot roast; other entrées include seafood imperial, rack of lamb, traditional roast turkey, and various New England favorites. Entrées $15.95–20.95; **Tuckerman's Tavern** has a pub menu, entertainment, and 25 beers on tap.

**EATING OUT** **Horsefeathers** (603-356-2687; www.horsefeathers.com), Main Street, North Conway. Open daily 11:30 AM–11:30 PM. The best-known hangout and an all-around good bet for a reasonably priced meal in an attractive setting, middle of the village. The menu is large and varied; the day's from-scratch soup may be curried crab and asparagus. Designer sandwiches like black pastrami with roasted peppers. Salads, pastas, fish-and-chips, plenty of desserts, fully licensed. Kid's menu.

**Delaney's Hole in the Wall** (603-356-7776), Route 16, just 1 mile north of North Conway village. Open 11:30 AM to 11 PM. A friendly, informal place, good for panhandle chicken, a portobello wrap, or baby back ribs. Fully licensed. Kid's menu.

**Muddy Mooose Restaurant & Pub** (603-356-7696), Route 16, North Conway, south of the village. Open for lunch and dinner. This is a zany, fun place, both in decor and in menu options like buffalo burgers (the real thing), spicy venison sausage (served with mushrooms, scallions, peppers, and penne pasta), and wild boar Marsala. You can also have a plain old burger, spareribs, or baked haddock. In summer there's a nice deck.

**Café Noche** (603-447-5050), Route 16, Conway. Open daily 11:30 AM–9 PM. The best Mexican restaurant in the North Country, plenty of atmosphere and all the classics, as hot as you like. Mexican beer and mean margaritas. Children's menu.

**Shalimar** (603-356-0123), 27 Seavey Street, North Conway. Open for lunch and dinner. Closed Monday off-season. Popular Indian restaurant featuring a wide selection of vegetarian dishes as well as chicken, lamb, beef, and shrimp dishes. There's also a children's menu that includes chicken fingers and cheese ravioli. Wine and beer served.

**A Step Above Bakeshop and Café** (603-356-2091), Main Street, North Conway village. Open daily 8 AM–3 PM, Sunday 8 AM–1 PM. Breakfast and lunch, featuring creatively prepared dishes such as Italian frittatas with lightly sautéed ingredients (broccoli, tomato, pepper, potatoes, and onions); eggs are added, then baked.

**Flatbread Company** (603-356-4470; www.flatbread.net), Eastern Slope Inn, 2760 Main Street. Open lunch through dinner. A pleasant new restaurant hidden away in the back of the hotel, featuring the distinctive pizza developed by the Vermont-based American Flatbread Company, made from 100 percent organically grown wheat and springwater, baked in a special wood-fired clay oven. Sun-dried tomatoes, fresh herbs, goat cheese, and olive oil figure in most of the toppings.

**The Red Parka Pub** (603-383-4344), Route 302, Glen. Open daily 4–10 PM. A favorite with the locals and for après-ski, this is a traditional ski tavern, with skis dating back to the 1930s adorning the walls and ceilings. Outdoor dining on the patio. Famous for hand-cut steak and prime rib, the Red Parka

Pub also features baked seafood, barbecued spareribs, and varied chicken dishes. An extensive salad bar rounds out the meal; special kids' menu.

**Glen Junction** (603-383-9660), Route 302, Glen. Open for breakfast, lunch, and dinner. Breakfast served all day from 7 AM. Designer omelets, specialty sandwiches, apple pie and ice cream. Kids (and adults) are fascinated with the two large-scale model trains that circle the dining rooms on tracks near the ceiling.

**Chinook Café** (603-447-6300), Route 16, Conway village. An inviting haven for coffee lovers, good for breakfast, some sandwiches, pastries.

**Peking Restaurant** (603-356-6976), Route 16, North Conway. Open all year, daily from 11:30 AM. Called the best Chinese restaurant in Carroll County, this place has all of your favorites to eat in or take out, including Polynesian dishes and hot and spicy Peking and Szechuan.

## ✷ Entertainment

**Arts Jubilee** (603-356-9393) offers summer musical performances, weekly afternoon children's programs, and a fall art show. Thursday-night free outdoor concerts in Schouler Park.

**Mount Washington Valley Theatre Company** (603-356-5776), Eastern Slope Playhouse, Main Street, North Conway. Season: late June through Labor Day. Curtain at 8 PM, $20 tickets, good old chestnuts like *The Music Man* and *Godpsell*. Children's theater Friday mornings at 10 and 11:30.

**M&D Theatre Productions** (603-447-1968; www.md-productions.org), Willow Place Mall, present plays and other live entertainment with proceeds benefiting local nonprofits.

**Majestic Theater** (603-447-5030), Route 16, Conway village, is a classic old movie hall with first-run movies on two screens.

**The Red Parka Pub** (see *Eating Out*) is good for après-ski and for music on summer weekends.

## ✷ Selective Shopping

Route 16 between the traffic lights in Conway village north through North Conway may be motorist's hell (with more traffic lights than the rest of northern New Hampshire combined) but it's shopper's heaven, with more than 200 specialty shops and outlets. The outlet boom hit in the 1980s, and most of the leading manufacturers have opened stores here. The largest concentration, with more than 40 stores, is the **Settlers Green Outlet Village** (Adidas, April Cornell, Banana Republic, et cetera). The **L.L. Bean Center** is, of course, anchored by its namesake store but also includes a number of others—including our favorite, Chuck Roast, featuring locally well-made Polartec fleece clothing. The **Red Barn Tangor Factory Outlet** is a other smaller complex that includes Corning Revere, Danskin, Swank, and VF stores; others are strung along Route 16 (anglers should search out the Orvis Factory Outlet near the entrance to Settlers Green). A longtime favorite is Yield House, at the southern end of the Route 16 strip, offering reproduction finished and unfinished furniture and kits. Also see *Sporting Goods* below.

ANTIQUES SHOPS **North Conway Antiques & Collectibles** (603-356-6661), Route 16, north of North Conway village (open daily 10 AM–5 PM), is a group shop with 80 dealers. Across the road the **Antiques & Collectibles Barn** (daily 10 AM–5 PM) has 25 dealers. Pick up the map/guide at either to a dozen more shops.

ARTS AND CRAFTS **League of New Hampshire Craftsmen** (603-356-2441), North Conway village. Quality handmade crafts including pottery, jewelry, clothing, and furnishings. Open all year.

**Handcrafters Barn** (603-356-8996), Route 16, North Conway. Open all year. Works by some 250 artisans as well as specialty foods, furniture, garden and bath items.

**North Wind Craftsmen** (603-356-7949), Main Street, North Conway village, offers an outstanding selection of crafted work.

GENERAL STORES **Zeb's** (603-356-9294; www.zebs.com), Main Street, North Conway village. Ye old tyme tourist-geared general store with a 67-foot-long candy counter, boasting the largest stock of New England products.

**5&10 Cents Store,** Main Street, North Conway village. This is the real thing: the local five and dime under the same family ownership since 1931. Children's books, toys, cards, stationery, and friendly old-timers at the checkout counter.

SPECIALTY SHOPS **White Birch Booksellers** (603-356-3200; www.whitebirchbooks.com), Route 16 just south of the village, is an attractive full-service independent bookstore, well stocked with everything from children's to travel books with plenty in between.

**Peter Limmer and Sons** (603-356-5378), Route 16A, Box 88, Intervale 03845. Closed Sunday. If anything is a craft item, it is a pair of handmade mountain boots created by the third generation of the Limmer family. The boots are expensive, and you may wait a year or more to have a pair custom-made to fit your feet, but we purchased a pair 25 years ago that are on their third set of soles and, after hundreds of miles of mountain trails, are still in great shape. "Limmers" have gone from Mount Washington to Mount Everest, and many hikers wouldn't enter the woods without a pair. You'll also find street and golf shoes.

SPORTING GOODS *Note:* This is New England's prime center for mountaineering equipment.

**Eastern Mountain Sports** (603-356-5433; www.emsonline.com) occupies much of the ground floor in the Eastern Slopes Inn, North Conway village, with a full line of skis plus hiking and climbing equipment. Inquire about their climbing school.

**Joe Jones Ski & Sport** (603-356-9411; www.joejonessports.com), Route 16 at the northern end of North Conway village, good for rentals as well as sales.

**Ragged Mountain Equipment, Inc.** (603-356-3042; www.raggedmountain.com), Route 14, a quarter mile north of the village. Here at the center for the town's cross-country trails you'll find cross-country and snowshoe rentals in winter, plus a full line of equipment that varies with the season. Inquire about free ski and snowshoe tours in winter, naturalist-led walks and hikes in summer.

**Wild Things** (603-447-6907; www.wildthingsgear.com), 64 Hobbs Street, Conway. Mountaineering equipment, climbing gear, backpacks, cold-weather clothing."

## ✷ Special Events

We have primarily listed annual events but not specific dates, since the exact dates change each year. Contact the Mount Washington Valley Chamber of Commerce (see *Guidance*) for details. Cranmore Recreation Center is often the host for professional tennis tournaments, and world-class skiing races are often held at valley ski areas.

*March*: **Maple Sunday** at the Chester Eastman Homestead, North Chatham (603-694-3388).

*April:* **Spring plowing** at the Chester Eastman Homestead (see above).

*July through Labor Day:* **Arts Jubilee**—free outdoor concerts in Schouler Park, at the gazebo, and at the fire station in Conway village. Sunday at 2:30 in North Conway, Tuesday next to the fire station in Conway.

*Fourth of July:* **Carnival,** North Conway. Fireworks and parade.

*Early September:* **World Mud Bowl,** North Conway. Some people enjoy this annual football game, played in knee-deep mud. At least local charities benefit from the proceeds.

*Mid-September:* **Bark in the Park Expo,** billed as New England's largest pet expo, benefits the Conway Area Humane Society.

*Late September:* **Fall on the Farm,** Chester Eastman Homestead, North Chatham (603-694-3388).

*First week in October:* **Fryeburg Fair,** Fryeburg, Maine. This is a large agricultural fair, with horse and cattle pulling, livestock exhibits and judging, midway, and pari-mutuel harness racing. Just across the border from the Mount Washington Valley, this annual fair attracts a huge crowd in the middle of foliage season.

*November:* The **Harvest to Holidays Annual Promotion** is a big deal because this is such an obvious place to shop at what otherwise is low season for local shops and restaurants. Lodging and dining bargains, shopping coupons, and special events.

# JACKSON AND PINKHAM NOTCH



Pinkham Notch is a high, steep-walled pass between the eastern slopes of the Presidential Range and neighboring mountains. Here Route 16 threads a 5,600-acre section of the White Mountain National Forest that includes Tuckerman Ravine, famous for spring skiing, adjacent Huntington Ravine, known for winter ice climbing, and the Great Gulf Wilderness, a larger glacial valley surrounded by the state's highest peaks.

Of course you see little of all this if you stick to Route 16. You shouldn't. More than any other place in New England, Pinkham Notch has become the place ordinary folk come—year-round—to tune in to and engage with New England's highest mountains in all their splendor.

Back in 1861 the 8-mile "Carriage" (now "Auto") Road, billed as "America's first man-made attraction," opened the way for anyone to ride to the summit of Mount Washington, and it remains the route that most visitors take to the top. The hiking hub of the White Mountains, the Appalachian Mountain Club (AMC)'s Pinkham Notch Visitors Center, is just down the road, a place to learn about hiking trails and outdoor skills, to hear a free lecture, or to catch the "hiker's shuttle" that circles the base of Mount Washington, stopping at trailheads. At Wildcat Mountain a four-person gondola hoists passengers to the 4,062-foot summit, from which you can walk a ridge portion of the Appalachian Trail. Great Glen Trails Outdoor Center at the base of the Auto Road offers miles of winter cross-country ski trails that turn into mountain bike trails (rentals available), as well as opportunities for novices to try their hand at fishing or paddling.

Pinkham Notch, moreover, offers year-round access to its spectacular heights. In winter SnowCoaches carry visitors (weather permitting) up the Auto Road, and

A SNOW-COVERED GAZEBO AT THE WENTWORTH HOTEL IN JACKSON

Kim Grant

the AMC Visitors Center is the venue for workshops in winter sports and skills. Wildcat Ski Area offers some of New England's longest and most satisfying trails and offers eye-level views from its slopes of spectacular Tuckerman Ravine, which becomes a ski mecca in its own right come April and May. Great Glen also draws cross-country skiers and snowshoers.

Just south of Pinkham Notch, Jackson is cradled in the high, horseshoe-shaped Wildcat River Valley. From Route 16, the first entrance to the village is through a covered bridge; beyond is a steepled church shouldering the shingled library and the imposing Wentworth Resort Hotel and its adjacent 18-hole golf course. Follow the stream uphill and you come to another nicely restored 19th-century survivor, the Eagle Mountain House. At the top of "The Loop" you'll find Whitneys Inn and Black Mountain, New England's only surviving ski hill (and there were many) to be opened behind an inn.

An incubator for alpine skiing in the 1930s (there were also rope tows behind the Wildcat Tavern and Thorn Hill), Jackson is better known today as a cross-country ski destination. The nonprofit Jackson Ski Touring Foundation, founded in 1972 when that sport too was in its infancy, presently maintains 154 km trail system.

Thanks to careful zoning and a strong community spirit, the atmosphere in Jackson is relaxing for guests and residents alike. As a group, its inns and restaurants are as nice as can be found anywhere.

GUIDANCE **Jackson Resort Association** (603-383-9356; 1-800-866-3334; www.jacksonnh.com), Box 304, Jackson village 03846. Information and reservation system.

**The Appalachian Mountain Club Pinkham Notch Visitors Center** (603-466-2721; www.outdoors.org) is a departure point for hiking and other ways of tuning in to this naturally spectacular area. Check out the daily weather information (extension 773). Also see *To Do*.

**Mount Washington Valley Chamber of Commerce and Visitors Bureau** (603-356-3171; 1-800-367-3364; www.mtwashingtonvalley.org), Box 2300, North Conway 03860. Free vacation guide and visitor information.

GETTING THERE **Concord Trailways** offers daily bus service (603-228-3300; 1-800-639-3317) from Boston and Logan Airport, with stops on Route 16 in Jackson and at the Appalachian Mountain Club's Pinkham Notch Camp.

GETTING AROUND **The AMC Hiker Shuttle** (603-466-2721) operates June through mid-October, 8 AM–4 PM, based at the Pinkham Notch Visitors Center (see *Guidance*) and serving trailheads throughout the Presidentials. For details see *Getting Around* in "Mount Washington."

## ✷ To See

SCENIC DRIVES **Mount Washington Auto Road** (603-466-3988; www.mt-washington.com), Route 16, Pinkham Notch, Box 278, Gorham 03518. Open daily, weather permitting, early May through mid-October, from 7:30 AM to 6 PM most

THE AMC HIKER SHUTTLE Robert Burbank, AMC

of the summer, with shorter hours earlier and later in the season. The Mount Washington Carriage Road opened in 1861, and for its first 50 years a 12-person wagon pulled by six horses carried passengers to the summit. The advent of the Cog Railroad (see *To See* in "Crawford Notch and Bretton Woods") cut into business, but with the advent of the motorcar its popularity revived. The first motorized ascent in 1899 was by F. O. Stanley of Stanley Steamer fame. The 8-mile, graded road climbs steadily, without steep pitches but with an average grade of 12 percent, from the Glen to the summit. Although the road is narrow in spots and skirts some steep slopes, it has a remarkable safety record and annually carries some 100,000 visitors. En route, there are many places to pull off and enjoy the view, and the road is crossed by several hiking trails. Inquire about annual foot-, bicycle, and auto races. Most (but not all) passenger cars are permitted to make the climb to the summit. A 1½-hour guided tour in chauffeur-driven vans, called stages, to keep alive a historical tradition, is also offered. A new base building, serving both the Auto Road and Great Glen Trails, includes a choice of food. Passenger-car rates: $15 for car and driver, $6 each additional passenger ($4 for children 5–12), includes an audio tour in English, French, or German. Guided tour: $22 for adults, $20 seniors, $10 for children 5–12. $8 for motorcycle and driver. In winter the SnowCoaches, a van especially designed for the ascent, transports you up the Auto Road to just above tree line, with a view down into the Great Gulf Wilderness ($35 per adult, $20 per child).

**Pinkham Notch Scenic Area,** Route 16, between Jackson and Gorham. Approaching from the Jackson end of the notch, Route 16 begins a long, gradual ascent, passing the beginnings of several hiking trails and a few pullouts adjacent to the Ellis River. Watch the ridge of the mountains on the western side, and gradually the huge Glen Boulder becomes silhouetted against the sky. This erratic was dragged to this seemingly precarious spot eons ago by a glacier. Situated at an elevation of about 2,500 feet, the boulder is a 1.5-mile, 2-hour hike from the highway, a short but steep climb to tree line. At the top of the notch, the mountainside drops steeply to the east and allows a panoramic view south down the Ellis River Valley toward Conway and Mount Chocorua. Across this valley rises the long ridge of Wildcat Mountain. Just ahead is a parking lot for Glen Ellis Falls, one of the picturesque highlights of the notch. To see the falls, cross under the highway by the short tunnel, then walk 0.2 mile down a short trail to the base of the falls.

North along Route 16, as the highway skirts along the side of Mount Washington, are the AMC Pinkham Notch Visitors Center, then Wildcat Mountain (with summer and fall mountain gondola rides) and the Mount Washington Auto Road at the Glen. Here is one of the most magnificent views in all the mountains. At left can be seen the summit of Mount Washington, although it doesn't appear to be the highest spot around. Rising clockwise above the Great Gulf—another glacial valley—are Mounts Clay, Jefferson, Adams (the state's second highest peak), and Madison. Route 16 continues north to Gorham, passing en route the WMNF Dolly Copp Campground (see *Lodging—Campgrounds*) and the entrance to Pinkham B (Dolly Copp) Road, which connects to Route 2 at Randolph. Just north of Pinkham Notch, several hiking trails head east into the Carter Range. One, the Nineteen Mile Brook Trail (3.8 miles, 2½ hours), leads to the AMC Carter Notch Hut, another full-service facility. It is also open on a self-service, caretaker basis in the winter.

**Jackson Loop.** This 5-mile circuit drive begins in Jackson village. Follow Route 16B at the schoolhouse, up the hill, and past farms and views across the valley to Whitney's; then turn left for a couple of miles to Carter Notch Road, where you turn left again, past the Eagle Mountain House and Jackson Falls, before reaching the village. For a variation on this drive, turn right at Whitney's, and right again at Black Mountain onto Dundee Road, which changes to gravel now and again as it passes abandoned farms and mountain scenery en route to Intervale at Route 16A. Turn right and pick up Thorn Hill Road to return to Jackson.

THE MOUNT WASHINGTON AUTO ROAD

Kim Grant

## ✷ To Do

**The Appalachian Mountain Club Pinkham Notch Visitors Center** (603-466-2727; www.outdoors.org). Opened in 1920 and expanded several times since, this complex (alias Pinkham Notch Camp) is the North Country headquarters for an organization of some 65,000 members (the main office is in Boston). Members receive the AMC's several publications and discounts on its many books, maps, hikes and workshops, and accommodations, which include a variety of family "camps" (inquire about **Cold River Camp** in Chatham) and **Joe Dodge Lodge** (see *Lodging—Other*) as well as at their eight high huts, each spaced a day's hike apart in the Presidentials (see *Hiker's Lodging* in "Mount Washington"). Everyone is, however, welcome to use AMC facilities and to participate in their programs. With its trained staff and large membership, the AMC is one of New England's strongest conservation voices, promoting the protection and enjoyment of the mountains, rivers, and trails throughout the Northeast.

In the Visitors Center a diorama of the Presidential Range presents an overview of the area's hiking trails. The center also sells hiking guidebooks and maps, and posts the day's weather and trail conditions. Three daily meals (see *Eating Out*) are served up in the big open-timbered dining hall, which is also the venue for year-round free evening lectures on a broad range of topics (including slide shows on exploring the world's backcountry). In the neighboring Joe Dodge Lodge you'll find year-round talks and workshops on outdoor skills, range from hiking, skiing, snowshoeing, woods crafts, and canoeing to bird study, photography, art, and writing. These vary in length from a few hours to a few days. This is also pickup point for the **Hiker Shuttle** (see *Getting Around*).

*Note:* Because AMC staffers often volunteer for mountain rescues, they are careful to give considered advice to hikers. The *AMC White Mountain Guide* has the most comprehensive trail information available for hikers, but also see Daniel Doan and Ruth Doan MacDougall's *50 Hikes in the White Mountains.*

AERIAL LIFT **Wildcat Mountain Gondola Ride** (603-466-3326; skiwildcat.com), Route 16, Pinkham Notch. During summer months Wildcat's quad chair to the summit is replaced by a gondola that hoists visitors to the summit, with a viewing platform of Mount Washington and a trail along the ridge.

GOLF **Wentworth Resort Golf Club** (603-383-9641), Jackson village. Eighteen holes, with pro shop, club and cart rentals, full lunch available. Call for tee times.

**Eagle Mountain House** (603-363-9111), Carter Notch Road, Jackson. Nine holes, full hotel facilities.

FISHING **Great Glen Outdoor Center** (603-466-2333; www.greatglentrails.com) offers an introduction, based at its pond; also guided canoe, drift boat, and wading trips to North Country waters.

HIKING Mount Washington is crisscrossed with trails, but by far the most popular is the **Tuckerman Ravine Trail** (see *To Do—Hiking* in "Mount Washington"), beginning at the AMC Pinkham Notch Camp on Route 16. We also recommend **Eagle**

**Mountain Path** (1 mile, 50 minutes) beginning behind the Eagle Mountain House (see *Lodging*) in Jackson. **Black Mountain Ski Trail** (1.7 miles, 1¾ hours) begins on Carter Notch Road, 3.7 miles from the village. It leads to a cabin and a knob that offers a fine view of Mount Washington. **North Doublehead,** via the Doublehead Ski Trail, begins on Dundee Road, 2.9 miles from the village, and follows an old ski trail to the WMNF Doublehead cabin on the wooded summit. A path leads to a good view east, and by using the Old Path and the New Path, you can make a round-trip hike from Dundee Road over both North and South Doublehead and back to the road. To North Doublehead, 1.8 miles and 1¾ hours; a round trip to both summits is about 4.3 miles and 4 hours. **Rocky Branch Trail** makes a loop from Jericho Road off Route 302 in Glen to Route 16 north of Dana Place. We suggest walking the Jericho Road end (turn off 302 in Glen and follow the road about 4.3 miles to the trailhead), which follows the brook for a couple of miles to a shelter. Allow 2 hours to make the round trip on a smooth trail. The Rocky Branch is one of the better trout-fishing brooks, and in spring it is prime wildflower country (look but don't pick!).

*Note:* The Jackson Resort Association and Mount Washington Valley Visitors Bureau both publish folders describing short walks in and around the village. Also: Although some cross-country trails are suitable for hiking, many of them are on private land and not open to the public except during the ski season.

MOUNTAIN BIKING **Great Glen Trails Outdoor Center** (603-466-2333; www.greatglentrails.com), Route 16, Pinkham Notch. In summer the 24-mile network of cross-country trails is smoothly graded, perfect for beginning to intermediate bikers and their families. Rentals include a special attachment that turns an adult bike into a tandem bike so small children can ride, too. Inquire about biking workshops.

THE APPALACHIAN MOUNTAIN CLUB'S LAKES OF THE CLOUDS HUT, ON THE SLOPES OF MOUNT WASHINGTON, CAN ONLY BE REACHED VIA HIKING TRAILS.

Robert Kozlow

**SWIMMING** There is nothing like an old swimming hole, and there are several here. The best is probably at **Jackson Falls** in Jackson village. Here the mountain-cool Wildcat River tumbles over rocky outcrops just above the village. There are several pools and picnic spots along the falls. Another favorite spot is on **Rocky Branch Brook,** just off Route 302 in Glen. Driving west, watch for Jericho Road on your right and follow it to the Rocky Branch Trailhead. Walk about 50 yards along the river back toward Route 302 for the swimming place.

## ✷ Winter Sports

**CROSS-COUNTRY SKIING** **Jackson Ski Touring Foundation** (603-383-9355; 1-800-927-6697; www.jacksonxc.org), Route 16A Jackson. This nonprofit organization promotes the sport of cross-country skiing and maintains some 154 km—that's 66 miles—of groomed (double-tracked) trails, the most extensive in the East. The trails range in elevation from 755 feet to 4,000 feet and from easy to difficult, so be sure to consult the map before heading off. The popular **Ellis River Trail** runs from the center north to Dana Place Inn and loops back through the woods. Our favorite is the **East Pasture Loop** with great views down the valley. Conditions permitting, you can link to this circuit from the Black Mountain chairlift. Expert backcountry skiers (again, conditions permitting) can also access the **Wildcat Ridge Trail,** dropping down into the valley from the top of the Wildcat quad chair to that summit. The touring foundation's center is on the golf course in the middle of the village and includes a retail and rental shop, also changing rooms with showers. It sponsors guided tours, clinics, and races. Trail fees and memberships pay for trail maintenance and improvements. $12 adult trail fee weekdays, $14 weekends. Rental pulks available to pull small children behind.

**Great Glen Trails Outdoor Center** (603-466-2333; www.greatglentrails.com), Route 16, Pinkham Notch, Gorham 03581. Open daily 8:30 AM–4:30 PM. Located near the base of the Mount Washington Auto Road, this is a four-season recreational (nonmotorized) park with ski trails used for hiking or mountain biking in warmer weather. There are 40 km of wide trails, some groomed specifically for skate skiing, diagonal stride, or snowshoeing, plus miles of backcountry trails. Heated yurts with sun decks are spaced along the trail. A new base lodge at the base of the Auto Road offers a choice of dining as well as retail, plus rentals. Lessons and guided tours are offered. Experienced snowshoers, skiers, and telemarkers inquire about taking the SnowCoaches (see the Auto Road under *To See—Scenic Drives*)4 miles up the Auto Road and skiing down. Adult ski passes are $10 on weekdays, $14 on weekends; for children 5–17 rates are $7 and $10. Seniors over 70 ski free. Mountain biking is $5 for a half day, $9 all day.

**AMC Pinkham Notch Visitors Center** (603-466-2727; www.outdoors.org). Many miles of ungroomed cross-country trails are found in Pinkham Notch. Ask advice at the AMC Visitors Center and pick up a copy of the AMC *Winter Trails* map detailing cross-country and snowshoeing trails in the area.

Also see **Bear Notch** under *Winter Sports—Cross-Country Skiing* in "North Conway Area."

**DOWNHILL SKIING** **Wildcat Mountain** (603-466-3326; lodging 1-800-255-6439;

www.skiwildcat.com), Route 16, Pinkham Notch, Jackson. North-facing Wildcat gets and holds snow, and its 2,112-foot vertical drop makes for some of the longest continuous runs in the East. It faces Mount Washington's eastern slopes across Pinkham Notch, with spectacular views of Tuckerman Ravine. Surrounded by national forest, it retains a "pure" feeling and enjoys a dedicated following. Lifts and grooming are thoroughly up to date. The Wildcat Trail, cut by the Civilian Conservation Corps in 1933, was ranked among the toughest racing trails in the United States, but Wildcat the ski area didn't open until 1957.

It was founded by a small group of former ski racers who cut fall line black diamonds. While it continues to appeal to expert skiers (many regulars know off-piste routes down), Wildcat was, however, quickly tamed by its longtime manager Stan Judge. Judge designed Polecat, a 2.75-mile run from the summit, gently canted in such a way as to nudge even the most nervous novice into step with gravity and that soaring sense of what it means to ski. It's also a favorite with telemarkers and skiers of every level. Judge designed several other intermediate trails, noteworthy for the way they curve naturally with the contours of the mountain, a rarity among modern ski trails. Wildcat can be windy and cold, but trails seem designed to maximize shelter—and come March they are glorious. *Lifts:* 1 high-speed detachable quad, 3 triple chairs. *Trails:* 44 on 225 acres, including glades, bumps, and backcountry tree skiing. *Vertical drop:* 2,112 feet. *Snowmaking:* 90 percent coverage. *Facilties:* Base lodge with ski shop, rentals, lockers, pub and snack bar, ski school, Lion's Den Kids' Ski & Snowboard School (ages 5–12), Lion Cubs ski & snow-play program (ages 3–5), Lion Cubs Nursery Sitting Service (ages 2 months–5 years). *Rates:* 1-day weekend and holiday lift ticket: $52 adult, $42 teen/senior, $25 junior. Midweek: $42 adult, $36 teen/senior, $25 junior. Multiple-day tickets cheaper. Specials: Wednesday, two ski or ride for the price of one; Thursday, $35 for women.

THE SNOW-FILLED SLOPES OF TUCKERMAN'S RAVINE LURE BACKCOUNTRY SKIERS IN SPRING.

Robert Kozlow

**Black Mountain** (603-383-4490; lodging 1-800-698-4490; www.blackmt.com), Route 16B, Jackson. A historic New Hampshire ski area, dating from the 1930s when Bill Whitney fashioned a rope tow with shovel handles. Now a haven for families in search of a small, quiet mountain. Trails off the 3,303-foot-high summit are, however, double diamond. *Lifts:* A T-bar and a double and triple lift. *Trails:* 40 trails and glades on 143 acres. *Vertical drop:* 1,100 feet. *Snowmaking:* 95 percent snowmaking. *Facilities:* Base lodge with ski and snowboard school, rentals, and a connection to Jackson's 154 km of cross-country trails. Kids' programs and child care. Dining and lodging at the base in Whitneys' Inn (see *Lodging—Inns*), also slope-side condominiums. *Rates:* $32 adult, $20 for those 18 and under on weekends; $20 adult, $15 junior midweek.

Also see: **Attitash Bear Peak Ski Area,** described under *Winter Sports—Downhill Skiing and Snowboarding* in "North Conway Area," and **Tuckerman Ravine** in "Mount Washington."

**ICE SKATING** A town-maintained ice skating rink is located in the center of the village across from the grammar school, and **Nestlenook Farm** (see below) has skating for a fee or free to guests.

**SLEIGH RIDES** **Nestlenook Farm** (603-383-9443), Dinsmore Road, Jackson village. Daily except Wednesday. Sleigh rides last 25 minutes and take you through the woods beside the Ellis River in a 25-person rustic sleigh or a smaller Austrian-built model. Oil lamps light the trails at night. Wheels are added for summer rides.

**Horse Logic** (603-383-9876) in Jackson also offers horse-drawn sleigh rides and hayrides around the village.

**WINTER WORKSHOPS** **The AMC Pinkham Notch Visitors Center** (603-466-2727; www.outdoors.org) and Joe Dodge Lodge serve as a base for midweek and weekend workshops in cross-country skiing, telemarking, snowshoeing, winter camping, ice climbing, tracking, winter photography, and more.

GUESTS ENJOY A SLEIGH RIDE AT NESTLENOOK INN.

Robert Kozlow

## ✱ Lodging

**RESORTS** ꝏ ♿ **Wentworth Resort Hotel** (603-383-9700; 1-800-637-0013; www.thewentworth.com), Jackson village 03846. Dating back to the 1860s and accommodating 400 people at its height as a self-contained summer resort (with its own farm, electric plant, greenhouse, orchestra, and golf course), the 55-room Wentworth has been reborn as a smaller, friendly, comfortable, but still-grand hotel. Over the past dozen years Swiss-born and -trained owner-manager Fritz Koeppel has been transforming rooms one by one, adding bells and whistles like Jacuzzis, hot tubs, and gas fireplaces as well as air-conditioning and discreetly hidden cable TVs, furnishing each in a different combination of reproduction antiques. Guest rooms are divided among the handsome three-story main building and several adjoining, neighboring annexes. In summer the long porch is lined with wicker rockers, decked in flowers, shaded by green-and-white-striped awnings. Guests can take a dip in the heated pool or walk to the river for a dip in the cool mountain water of the Wildcat River. The Wentworth's golf course is 18 holes; its clubhouse doubles as the winter lodge for the Jackson Ski Touring Foundation. Guests can also walk to tennis and to several lunch options "downtown." Breakfast and dinner are served in the hotel dining room, and food is very much a part of the experience here (see *Dining Out*). Rooms are $149–335, but there are special packages. At this writing $99 buys you not only Tuesday- or Wednesday-night lodging and breakfast but also two lift tickets at Wildcat. Inquire about renting one of the 14 two- and three-room condominiums that adjoin the property, overlooking the golf course.

✐ **Eagle Mountain House** (603-383-9111; 1-800-966-5779; www.eaglemt.com), Carter Notch Road, Jackson 03846. Open all year. Another among the few surviving Victorian White Mountain hotels. Although the flavor is vintage, the essentials are up to date. All 93 completely renovated rooms, including 30 suites, have private bath, phone, and cable TV. Most rooms have queen beds and are furnished in a country style. There is a nine-hole golf course, lighted tennis courts, health club, and heated pool. Winter guests can link directly with the Jackson Touring Foundation's extensive trail system. Unwind in the **Eagle Landing Lounge,** where lunch is served. Breakfast, Sunday brunch, and dinner are served in **Highfields,** the inn's dining room (see *Dining Out*). Rates: $69–179 per room, depending on season and accommodations; also B&B, MAP, and a variety of package plans, especially in ski season. Children 17 and under stay free in the same room with parents.

ꝏ 🐾 ✐ **Whitneys' Inn** (603-383-8916; 1-800-677-5737; www.whineysinn.com), Route 16B, Jackson 03846. With Black Mountain (one of the state's oldest ski areas) just behind the inn, this was one of the first ski inns, but its top-of-the-valley location is great other seasons as well. The 30 rooms vary widely. Some have sitting areas; there are also eight family suites with cable TV in a separate building (where children under 12 stay and eat free from May through August), two cottages with fireplaces, and the four-room Brookside Cottage with fireplaces. The lounge and dining room have fireplaces, and there is a separate common room for guests. The remodeled barn includes the Shovel Handle Pub, serving lunch in ski season, as well as rec rooms for teens and younger children. In summer there are lawn games, a mountain pond and heated pool for swimming, and tennis and volleyball courts. The dinner menu (see *Dining Out*) changes seasonally. Rates—$74–142 per couple, depending on season—include breakfast. Children's programs are offered in high seasons. Inquire about package plans. Pets are allowed in some rooms for a $25 fee.

**INNS** **Inn at Thorn Hill** (603-383-4242; 603-383-6448; 1-800-289-8990; www.innatthornhill.com), Thorn Hill Road, Jackson village 03846. Open all year. One of New Hampshire's most romantic inns, this 1895 mansion was designed by Stanford White and has been furnished to reflect its Victorian heritage. Of the 19 rooms (private baths go without saying), 10 are in the main house and vary in size but are luxuriously appointed, all but one with gas fireplace. There are six more in the Carriage House plus three deluxe cottages with fireplace, Jacuzzi, and outside deck and/or screened porch. The main inn has several common areas, including a pub with a fireplace, the dining room, a Victorian sitting room with TV, plus a drawing room with a view down the valley to the village and across the hills to Mount Washington. Dining nightly 6–9 (see *Dining Out*). Swim in the inn pool, relax in the outdoor hot tub, or cross-country ski from the door. The village is just a short walk down the hill. No smoking. Only children over 8. Jim and Ibby Cooper, innkeepers. MAP $190–400 (plus 15 percent service), depending on season and accommodations; various package plans. For B&B, deduct $15 per person.

**Dana Place Inn** (603-383-6822; 1-800-537-9276; www.danaplace.com), Route 16, Pinkham Notch, Jackson 03846. A combination of old and new, the main inn is an old farmhouse; additions include a heated indoor pool and Jacuzzi. Sited on 300 acres adjoining the White Mountain National Forest, it has 34 rooms, all with private bath. Facilities include tennis courts, a natural river swimming hole, hiking trails, fishing, and cross-country skiing. The dining room is open to the public (see *Dining Out*). B&B rates range $85–175; MAP $125–225.

**Wildcat Inn and Tavern** (603-383-4245), Jackson village 03846. Open all year. If you like to be in the middle of everything, try this old favorite, the 1930s home of the Jackson Ski School. Walk to cross-country skiing, shopping, golf, or tennis; the tavern offers folk music on weekends. Upstairs are 12 rooms, 10 with private bath. The rooms are cozy, with country furniture and some antiques, and most of them can be arranged as suites for families. There is also a large TV and game room and a separate living room with a fireplace, plus the tavern. Three meals are served daily in one of the area's most popular restaurants (see *Dining Out*). B&B $70–90; MAP $130–140; plus theater, tennis, and golf package plans.

**BED & BREAKFASTS** **The Blake House** (603-383-9057; www.blakehousebandb.com), Route 16, Jackson 03846. Open all year. Sarah Blake Maynard's father built this place as a ski cabin in the 1930s, and Sarah and Jeff Blake now offer four rooms with two shared baths. Set back from the highway and surrounded by white birches, this is a quiet, woodsy place frequented by hikers and skiers. One room has a king-sized bed, one has a double with a separate screened porch, others have twins. The guests' living room has cozy chairs, TV, VCR, books, games, and a fireplace, while the dining room features a huge window overlooking the forest and the rushing Sand Hill Brook. Breakfast is an expanded continental offering with fresh fruit and breads, hot and cold cereals, and egg dishes featuring eggs from Sarah's chickens. $50–90.

**Carter Notch Inn** (603-383-9630; 1-800-794-9434; www.carternotchinn.com), Carter Notch Road, Jackson 03846. Perched on a hillside overlooking the Wildcat River Valley beside Eagle Mountain House, this attractive B&B offers a wraparound front porch, a living room with a wood fire, seven air-conditioned guest rooms, and a hot tub on the back deck—not to mention plenty of old-time nostalgia. Tucker, a chocolate-colored Labrador, greets guests, but the place is owned by Lynda and Jim Dunwell. Rates are $79–159 with private bath and $59-109 with shared, and include a full country breakfast.

**Jackson House Bed & Breakfast** (603-383-4226; 1-800-338-1268; www.jacksonhousenh.com), Box 478, Jackson 03846. Set back from Route 16, this circa-1868 house was formerly an apple farm. Jane and Craig Stevenson welcome guests to share their living room with its fireplace and their sunny solarium with its bubbling hot tub. The clapboard house is bigger than it looks: 11 cheerful rooms with quilts and some homemade furniture, 4 with fireplace, 7 with private bath (4 rooms share two baths); 5 have TV. Craig is a professional chef, a graduate of Johnson and Wales; his breakfast specialty is baked walnut French toast. Hikers, skiers, children, and pets are all welcome. $59–129 for rooms, suite $149–198.

**The Inn at Jackson** (603-383-4321; 1-800-289-8600; www.innatjackson.com), Jackson village 03846. Open all year. This Stanford White–designed summer mansion overlooks the village. There are 14 large, well-furnished rooms, all with private bath; most beds are queens; 5 rooms have fireplace. You'll also find a second-floor common room, a hot tub/Jacuzzi, and a panoramic view of the village and the mountains from the breakfast sun porch. Cross-country ski from the door; walk to lunch or dinner. Full breakfast. B&B $109–179; inquire about packages.

**Ellis River House** (603-383-9339; 1-800-233-8309; www.ellisriverouse.com), Route 16, Box 656, Jackson 03846. Open all year. Situated just off the main road by its namesake river, this is a turn-of-the-20th-century farmhouse, long geared to accommodating guests. Monica and Jim Lee offer 20 antiques-furnished rooms, all with private bath. Three rooms are family suites. Fourteen have gas fireplace, eight have two-person Jacuzzi, and all are air-conditioned. A two-room cottage has a sitting room with TV, private bath and Jacuzzi, and a second-floor room with a queen bed and a fireplace. There is a heated outdoor swimming pool with adjacent sauna, and a Jacuzzi overlooking the river. You can swim or fish in the river, play volleyball, or cross-country ski from the door. A full breakfast is included in the rates, $95–205; discounts for children under 12.

**Paisley and Parsley** (603-383-0859; www.paisleyandparsely.com), Route

16B, Box 298, Jackson 03846. Open all year. Wisteria and grapevine arbors, herb and perennial rock gardens, and a spectacular view of Mount Washington lead the way to Suzanne and Bob Scolamiero's contemporary home. There are two guest rooms, each with a bath and sitting room. Only children over 12, please. A group of eight can rent the house for $50 per person. Full country breakfast and afternoon tea. $80–125.

**Nestlenook Farm** (603-383-9443; 1-800-659-9443; www.luxurymountaingetaways.com), Dinsmore Road, Jackson village 03846. Open all year. Elaborately decorated, this renovated old inn is a gingerbread "Magic Kingdom" for couples only. Painted peach and green, the house is part of a million-dollar development with extensive gardens, a gazebo, a four-season pool, and a pond ("Emerald Lake") by the Ellis River. Each of the seven "guest suites" has a private bath with a Jacuzzi. Some rooms have working fireplace or parlor stove. All have queen-sized beds, many with canopies, and separate sitting room. Guests may enjoy complimentary sleigh rides and skating, and use of the inn's snowshoes and trails, which connect to the extensive Jackson trail network. B&B $175–340.

MOTEL 🐾 ♿ **The Lodge at Jackson Village** (603-383-0999; 1-800-233-5634), Route 16, Jackson 03846. Open all year. Inspired by the area's Colonial architecture, this decade-old motel with award-winning gardens offers both charm and convenience. Thirty-two guest rooms with mountain views, air-conditioning, cable television, telephone, and refrigerator. There's a pretty pool and gardens, tennis courts, an outdoor hot tub, and an 18-hole golf course across the street. $99–229 double, depending on season.

OTHER ✐ ♿ **Appalachian Mountain Club Pinkham Notch Visitors Center** (603-466-2727; www.outdoors.org), Route 16, Pinkham Notch, Box 298, Gorham 03581. This is a full-service facility offering three all-you-can-eat meals, bunk beds, and shared baths. Knotty-pine walled bunk rooms for two, three, and four people accommodate more than 100 guests in the **Joe Dodge Lodge.** A few family rooms have a double bed and three bunks. Handicapped accessible. Geared to outdoorspeople (hikers, skiers, and such), it is cheerful (quilts, curtains, and reading lights) and comfortable, with a library and a huge fireplace in the living room and a game room with a children's corner (educational games and nature books). The main-lodge dining area is another gathering area. Free lectures nightly after dinner in July and August and Wednesday and Saturday throughout the winter. Families are encouraged. Open to AMC members and the general public. Reservations are a must. $33 per adult without meals; inquire about packages. Breakfast and lunch are $6.50 each for nonmembers, dinner $14.75. For information about the eight full-service mountain huts (only reached by walking) maintained by the AMC in the White Mountain National Forest, see *Hiker's Lodging* in "Mount Washington."

**Luxury Mountain Getaways** (603-383-9101; 1-800-472-5207; www.luxurymountaingetaways.com), Route 16, Jackson 03846. This ever-evolving resort complex is mix of condo clusters and a B&B (Nestlenook Farm) on 165 acres south of the village of Jackson. Units feature fireplace, Jacuzzi, and cooking facilities (ranging from token to full); facilities include indoor pools and four-season outdoor pools, tennis, and skiing (trails connect with the Jackson Touring Foundation system). Choose from the Victorian Village units surrounding Nestlenook Farm or Nordic Village (from $100) and Nordic Highlands (one to three bedrooms, $159–575), off in the woods. The newest development, The Chateaus at Highland Ridge, with one to four bedrooms, features 20 jet whirlpool spas, king and canopy beds ($365–1,589). Add a 10 percent "amenities fee."

🐾 **The Village House** (603-383-6666; 1-800-972-8343), Box 359, Jackson village 03846. Open all year. No longer a B&B, this old village inn caters to pet owners. Pets are accepted in all 15 rooms (all with private bath; 5 in the remodeled barn, with kitchenettes). You no longer enter through the front door, and there is no food service, but guests still have access to the swimming pool, tennis, and year-round outdoor Jacuzzi. $60–80, more during foliage season.

**CAMPGROUNDS** **WMNF Dolly Copp Campground** (603-466-3984, July through Labor Day), Route 16, Pinkham Notch, Gorham 03581. Open mid-May through mid-October. Some of the 176 sites are available through a **toll-free reservation system** (1-800-280-2267). The reservation service operates March through September (Monday through Friday noon–9 PM, weekends noon–5 PM) and costs $6 in addition to the camping fee. Reservations are accepted, but 10 days before arrival is the minimum time.

## ✱ Where to Eat

**DINING OUT** **Wentworth Resort Hotel** (603-383-9700; 1-800-637-0013), Jackson village. Dinner served 6–9 PM; reservations recommended. Four-diamond dining in a formal century-and-a-half-old hotel dining room. Chef James Davis has just the right touch. On a snowy evening we began with potato and leek soup (you could taste the roasted garlic) and dined on roast pork with crispy string potatoes and a mix of vegetables. The half-dozen options included white bean and tomato bruchetta and oven-poached lemon sole with purple potatoes, fresh fennel, and oven-dried tomatoes. Entrées $17.50–23. The wine list has earned the *Wine Spectator* Award of Excellence.

**The Thompson House** (603-383-9341), Jackson village. Lunch 11:30 AM–4 PM (mid-May through October), dinner 5:30–10 PM. Open weekends only November through Christmas, closed April through mid-May. Reservations a must. Owner-chef Larry Baima prepares a host of distinctive and imaginative combination sandwiches, soups, salads, and dinner entrées in a 1790 farmhouse. Try something Italian, Oriental, or traditional American, from pastas to seafood; it's all made fresh daily, to order, and can be prepared to suit dietary needs. We can recommend the chicken San Remo: white meat sautéed with eggplant, sweet peppers, onions, and sun-dried tomatoes in garlic-herb wine sauce. Entrées come with salad and fresh bread, $16.95–22.95. Lunch favorites include Kelly's Mexican soup and Lorenzo's Loaf (lean ground beef, spinach, mushrooms, onions, and herbs freshly baked and served open faced with mushroom gravy). Patio dining in summer and a glowing woodstove in winter make this place popular with locals, too.

**Whitneys' Inn** (603-383-8916; 1-800-677-5737), Route 16B, Jackson. Best known for its location at the base of Black Mountain, this old inn also has a pleasant, rustic dining room serving dinner 6–8:45 PM nightly. There's a lighter "Greenery Lounge" menu as well. The menu changes seasonally, but entrées ($16.95–21.95) might include baked stuffed haddock, roast duckling, veal sautéed with onions, leeks, and mushrooms, and chicken several different ways. Special dinner requests are available with advance notice; most entrées can be prepared plain, broiled, or baked.

**Wildcat Inn and Tavern** (603-383-4245), Jackson village. Open all year. Three country gourmet meals are served daily in one of the area's most popular restaurants. Dinner ranges from lasagna to lobster fettuccine, roast pheasant, and the house specialty, Tavern Steak (with béarnaise, brandy peppercorn, or garlic-herb butter). $15.95–25.95.

✐ **Dana Place Inn** (603-383-6822; 1-800-537-9276), Route 16, Pinkham Notch, Jackson. Open year-round for breakfast 7:30–9 AM and dinner 6–9 PM. Elegant à la carte dining in an old inn with a contemporary twist. Signature dishes include brandied apple chicken, duckling à l'orange, and chicken topped with spinach and portobello mushrooms wrapped in puff pastry. $18.95–21.95.

**Inn at Thorn Hill** (603-383-4242; 603-383-6448; 1-800-289-8990), Thorn Hill Road, Jackson village. Open all year. Dining by reservation nightly 6–9 PM. The menu, characterized as New England fusion cuisine, includes an award-winning wine list and changes biweekly. You might start with crabcakes with bacon and sautéed red onions followed by grilled hazelnut-dusted beef sirloin; for dessert, make room for triple chocolate raspberry domes, filled with raspberry white chocolate mousse and topped with raspberry Chambord sauce. Entrées range $21.95–26.95.

**Eagle Landing** (603-383-9111), Eagle Mountain House, Carter Notch Road, Jackson. The classic hotel dining room is surprisingly attractive with good food—entrées range from Maine coast haddock to rack of New Zealand lamb. $13.95–22.95 includes soup, salad, vegetables, and bread. The à la carte menu is a real bargain, from $9.95 for the roast turkey dinner.

Also see **Libby's Bistro,** destination dining in Gorham, in "The Great North Woods—Northern White Mountains."

**EATING OUT** **Jackson Bistro** (603-383-6633), Route 16A, Jackson village. Open for breakfast and lunch, a favorite village gathering place in the back of a general store/deli with tables overlooking the golf course. Always fresh-made soups (we can vouch for the corn chowder), blackboard sandwich menu with Boar's Head meats, Belgian waffles a specialty at breakfast.

**Wildcat Tavern** (603-383-4245), Route 16A, Jackson village. The tavern itself (as opposed to the dining room) remains the town's ever-popular après-ski spot with its overstuffed couches and easy chairs by the fire as well as the long, inviting bar area. Classics like baby back ribs and shepherd's pie, from $6.95.

**The Shannon Door & Pub Restaurant** (603-383-4211). Route 16, Jackson village. An Irish pub that's popular for après-ski in winter, open 4–9 PM for dinner, until 11 PM for pizza, burgers, and spirits weekdays, until midnight on weekends with live entertainment.

**The AMC Pinkham Notch Visitors Center** (603-466-2727), Route 16, Pinkham Notch. Check to see what the evening lecture is (nightly in summer, Wednesday and Saturday in summer). The big open-timbered dining hall with its long tables is the setting for an all-you-can-eat breakfast (6:30–8 AM), lunch (11:30 AM–1 PM) and dinner (6 PM sharp except Friday when it's a buffet, 6:30–8). Breakfast and dinner are ample and frequently outstanding, served family-style. Lunch and snacks available too.

**As You Like It** (603-383-6425), Route 16A, Jackson village. Tucked into the same white-clapboard complex that houses the Jackson Chamber of Commerce, sandwiches on fresh-baked breads, limited eat-in, great source for picnics.

**The Red Fox Pub and Restaurant** (603-383-6659), Route 16A, Jackson village. Open daily for lunch and dinner. Check out the reasonably priced Sunday breakfast buffet 7:30 AM–noon. A cheerful restaurant featuring buffalo wings, baby back ribs, baked pesto bread, and a range of soups, sandwiches, salads, and burgers, along with moderately priced entrées.

## ✷ Special Events

*Winter:* **Cross-country skiing,** Jackson village. Throughout the ski season, weekend citizens' races are held, and often special international events use the Jackson trails.

*March:* **Great Glen to Bretton Woods Adventure**—a 50 km cross-country ski race.

*Late May:* **Quacktillion and Wildquack River Festival,** Jackson village. A weekend of dancing, then cheer on one of 2,000 rubber duckies as they race down the river. Rent your own for $5.

*Early June:* **Jackson Covered Bridge 10 km,** Jackson village. One of the most demanding 10K road races in New England. **Wildflower Guided Tour and Barbecue,** Jackson village. See more than 400 wildflowers and ferns and classic 18th- and 19th-century gardens, plus a chicken barbecue.

*Mid-June:* **Bikes Only Day**—morotcycles rule on the Mount Washington Auto Road.

*Late June:* **Mount Washington Auto Hill Climb,** Mount Washington Auto Road, Pinkham Notch. First held in 1904, America's oldest motor-sport event: On consecutive weekends, first runners, then autos race from the Glen to the summit over the steep, winding course. See wwww.climbtotheclouds.com.

*Fourth of July:* **Family in the Park,** Jackson village. An old-fashioned Fourth of July celebration.

*Mid-July:* **Jackson Jazz Festival,** Black Mountain Ski Area.

*Late August:* **Mount Washington Auto Road Bicycle Hillclimb.**

*Mid-September:* **Mount Washington Bike Race** (603-466-3988), Mount Washington Auto Road, Pinkham Notch. This event attracts some of the top U.S. racers.

## CRAWFORD NOTCH AND BRETTON WOODS

Crawford is the least developed of New Hampshire's mountain passes, although historically it has been important since the 18th century when settlers followed today's Route 302 from Conway north to establish towns above the mountains. The notch was "discovered" by white men in 1770, but undoubtedly it was the location of an earlier Native American trail. It was in this narrow notch, flanked by steep mountains, that the Crawford family began taking in travelers and thus created the tourist industry that dominates the White Mountains today. At the turn of the 20th century some of the region's largest and best hotels were located just above the notch; now only the Mount Washington Hotel remains.

Although Crawford Notch itself has few attractions, there are many sights to see, including fine waterfalls and one of the best views in all the mountains.

"Look at me gentlemen, . . . for I am the poor fool who built all this!" coal baron Joseph Stickney is reported to have exclaimed on the July day in 1902 when the Mount Washington Hotel first opened. It's noted that he "laughed heartily at his own folly." By and large the 200-room hotel has been lucky. Although Stickney died in 1903, it remained in his family until World War II and was then lavishly refurbished by the U.S. government for the 1944 Bretton Woods Monetary Conference, which set the gold standard and created both the World Bank and the International Monetary Fund. During the ensuing decades it had its ups and downs until its 1991 purchase on the auction block by a group of North Country businesspeople. Thanks to their commitment to preserve this grand New England resort and the area's unsurpassed scenic beauty, the hotel, now a century young, has reclaimed its former status as the showplace of the mountains.

**GUIDANCE** **Twin Mountain/Bretton Woods Chamber of Commerce** (1-800-245-TWIN; www.twinmountain.org) produces a brochure and operates a summer information center at the junction of Routes 2 and 302.

**Appalachian Mountain Club Information Center,** Route 302, north of Crawford Notch. Open Memorial Day through foliage season in a restored 19th-century railroad depot with exhibits, rest rooms, and visitor and hiker information. Also see www.outdoors.org or contact the **AMC Pinkham Notch Visitors Center** (603-466-2727).

**The Mount Washington Valley Chamber of Commerce & Visitors Bureau** (603-356-3171; 1-800-367-3364; www.mountwashingtonvalley.org) also covers this area; for details see *Guidance* in "North Conway Area."

**GETTING AROUND** **The AMC Hiker Shuttle** operates June through mid-October, 8 AM–4 PM. It consists of two vans, one based at the Pinkham Notch Visitors Center (see *Guidance*), the second at the Crawford Depot Visitor Center on the opposite side of Mount Washington. By changing at these transfer points it's possible to reach all the area's major trailheads. It's suggested that you spot your car and take a van to the trailhead from which you intend to walk out.

For sights on the top of Mount Washington, see the "Mount Washington" section.

## ✵ To Do

**GOLF** **The Mount Washington Hotel & Resort Golf Course** (603-278-GOLF; www.mtwashington.com), Route 302, Bretton Woods. There's much to see and tee here, starting with the original nine-hole, par-35 Mount Pleasant Course, which opened in 1895. Two decades later Scotsman Donald Ross designed and supervised the construction of a second, 18-hole, par-71 course. Both have been restored and supplemented by an 18-hole putting green, full-service golf shop, and 300-yard driving range ($5 per bucket) and practice area, all with the Presidential Range as a backdrop. Plans are in the works for a new golf clubhouse with full-service, alfresco dining to complement the hotel's architecture. Meanwhile, history holds forth in the men's locker room where the vintage wooden lockers boast brass nameplates to remind you that such folks as Bobby Jones, Babe Ruth, and Thomas Edison once stepped here.

**HIKING** Many hiking trails cross and parallel the notch. One is the Appalachian Trail—follow it north to Maine or south to Georgia. Consult the *AMC White Mountain Guide* for details of the many trails. Below are some less ambitious alternatives.

**Arethusa Falls Trail** is a 1.3-mile, 1-hour, easy-to-moderate walk to New Hampshire's most impressive and highest waterfall, at its best in spring and early summer when water is high. The well-marked trail begins on the southern side of Route 302 near the eastern entrance to the park. Two more waterfalls, the Silver Cascades, can be seen from your vehicle at the top of the notch, where there is a parking lot and a scenic outlook.

**Mount Willard Trail** begins at the AMC Crawford Notch Information Center, a year-round facility with rest rooms located in a restored railroad station just above the top of the notch. It is a 1.4-mile, 1-hour walk, most of which is easy, along a former carriage road. It leads to rocky ledges with a panoramic view down through Crawford Notch. The railroad station once served the old Crawford House, one of the earliest of the old hotels. It was closed in the 1970s and finally burned.

**Saco Lake Trail** (0.4 mile, 15 minutes) is across the street from the information center. Saco Lake is the source of the river that flows through Crawford Notch, then on to Maine and the Atlantic Ocean. Behind the trail is Elephant Head, a rocky ridge shaped like a pachyderm.

**Crawford Path,** from Route 302 (opposite the Crawford House site) to Mount Washington, is the oldest hiking trail in the country, built in 1819 by the Crawford family and used as a bridle path in the 1870s. The path is a long, 8.2-mile, 6-hour walk. The **AMC Mizpah Spring Hut** (see *Hiker's Lodging* in the "Mount Washington" section) is a 2.5-mile, 2-hour walk over the well-worn trail.

**Ammonoosuc Ravine Trail.** See *To Do—Hiking* in "Mount Washington and Pinkham Notch."

Also see the "Mount Washington" section.

**HORSEBACK RIDING** **Mount Washington Hotel** (603-278-1000), Route 302, Bretton Woods. The Mount Washington Hotel's impressive Victorian-era stables offer unusually scenic trail rides, with guided group and individual trail rides for

**TO SEE**

**Mount Washington Cog Railway** (advance reservations recommended: 603-278-5404, ext. 6; 1-800-922-8825; www.thecog.com), off Route 302, Bretton Woods 03589. Runs weekends and holidays from late April to the end of May, then daily to early November, depending on weather conditions. Opened in 1869, this is the world's first mountain-climbing cog railway, and it remains one of the few places where you can observe steam locomotives at work. At one time regular trains followed a spur line to the Base Station, where passengers boarded the cog railway directly for the summit. So unique and ambitious was the plan to build the railroad that its promoter, Sylvester Marsh, was told he might as well "build a railway to the moon." The eight little engines that could, each made for the purpose by this railroad company, have boilers positioned at an angle because of the steep grade up the mountain. On the 3-hour round trip, which includes a 20-minute stop at the summit, each engine pushes a single car up, then backs down in front of the car to provide braking. Unique cog-wheels fit into slots between the rails to provide traction and braking. The average grade along the 3.25-mile track is 25 percent, but at Jacob's Ladder trestle it rises to 37.5 percent. Several switches permit ascending and descending trains to pass en route. The Base Station, a short drive on a paved road from Route 302, includes a visitors center and museum, a restaurant, a gift shop, and an RV park. When we last checked, adults were $49; seniors 65 and over, $45; children 6–12, $35—but it's best to call for up-to-date rate information.

both beginner and advanced riders. The hotel also offers a horse-drawn carriage tour of its grand grounds.

## ✷ Winter Sports

**CROSS-COUNTRY SKIING** **Bretton Woods Touring Center** (603-278-5181) at the Mount Washington Hotel, across Route 302 from the ski area. A shuttle service operates back and forth. The 100 km network is considered one of the best in New England, and it's groomed for both touring and skating techniques. There are 39 trails, all mapped and marked, divided into three linked trail systems. Some lift-serviced trails lead down from the summit of the alpine area. There are gentler options past beaver ponds and forest glades, and several rest stops, including the Nordic Café, which offers lunch, snacks, and tickets with easy access to the trails. Nordic daily trail passes are $15 for adults; $9 for those 6–12 and over 65. Skate and snow-tube rentals are also available here.

**Backcountry skiing** is popular in the **Zealand Valley,** off Route 302 between Bretton Woods and Twin Mountain. Well-equipped and -prepared skiers can schuss from Route 302 some 2.5 miles into the AMC Zealand Hut (603-466-2727), which is open all winter on a caretaker basis. Bring your own sleeping bag and

Robert Kozlow

THE MOUNT WASHINGTON COG RAILWAY, THE WORLD'S FIRST MOUNTAIN-CLIMBING COG RAILWAY, IS ONE OF THE LAST PLACES IN THE COUNTRY WHERE YOU CAN OBSERVE STEAM ENGINES AT WORK.

food; use their cabin and cooking facilities. There are telemark ski rentals available at the Bretton Woods ski resort (see below).

**DOWNHILL SKIING** **Bretton Woods Ski Area** (603-278-5000; 1-800-232-2972), Route 302, Bretton Woods. Although traditionally this ski area was considered more enjoyable than challenging, an aggressive expansion policy has added acres of expert terrain, including 30 acres of expert glade trails in recently opened Rosebrook Canyon. In 1999 Bretton Woods became the state's largest ski area and now offers 76 trails, approximately one-third each for beginner, intermediate, and advanced skiers and snowboarders. All have commanding views of the Mount Washington Range. The summit elevation is 3,100 feet; the vertical drop, just about half that at 1,500 feet. Although annual snowfall is 200 inches, snowmaking is available when needed to cover 95 percent of the terrain. Eight lifts, including two high-speed quads, handle up to 7,500 skiers per hour. The summit features a unique warming hut, once a passenger car from the Mount Washington Cog Railway. Night skiing is offered weekends and holidays, and the multitiered, post-and-beam base lodge is unusually attractive. Weekend and holiday lift rates are $53 for adults, with discounts offered for midweek or multiday packages. Seniors can ski midweek, for example, for $15; nonholiday Wednesdays are $44 for two adults.

**SNOWMOBILING** Large portions of the WMNF are off-limits to snowmobiling, trail bikes, and off-road vehicles, but there are marked trails in Crawford Notch. A popular ride is along Mount Clinton Road (begins opposite the Crawford House site on Route 302) to the Base Station Road and over the Jefferson Notch Road to Jefferson. (See *To See—Scenic Drives* in "The Great North Woods—Northern White Mountains.") For details contact the **Trails Bureau** (603-271-3254), New Hampshire Division of Parks and Recreation, Box 856, Concord 03301, or the **New Hampshire Snowmobile Association** (603-224-8906), Box 38, Concord 03301.

## ✷ Green Space

**Crawford Notch State Park.** This large state park is located in the middle of the White Mountain National Forest, some 12 miles west of Bartlett. The park headquarters is located at the Willey House Memorial, the site of an unusual mountain tragedy. In August 1826 a terrible rainstorm blew through the notch, frightening the Willey family, who operated a small inn. Hearing an avalanche sliding down the steep side of the mountain, the family and two employees ran from the inn only to be swallowed up in the debris as the avalanche split above the inn, leaving it intact. All seven people died; the avalanche scar can still be seen on the mountain. This park was established in 1911 when the state purchased the virgin spruce forest to save it from loggers' axes. Today there is a seasonal gift shop (selling New Hampshire–made craft items), a waterfowl pond, and a self-guided nature trail. Several major hiking trails begin within the park's borders.

**Eisenhower Memorial Wayside Park** is on Route 302, 2 miles west of Crawford Notch. This small park is a tribute to the former president in whose honor one of the nearby mountains in the Presidential Range was named. A short walk leads to a magnificent view of Mounts Eisenhower, Monroe, Washington, Jefferson, Adams, and Madison. The tracks of the Mount Washington Cog Railway can be seen ascending the side of Washington, and sometimes smoke from one of the engines is visible.

## ✷ Lodging

Additional lodging is available at Twin Mountain (see "The Western Whites—Franconia and North of the Notches").

**RESORTS** Lodging at the **Mount Washington Hotel and Resort** in Bretton Woods, which includes the **Bretton Arms Country Inn, Bretton Woods Motor Inn,** and **Townhomes at Bretton Woods,** is accessed by phoning 603-278-1000 or 1-800-258-0330. Special packages, such as golf or romance weekends, theme weekends, and seasonal specials, are offered throughout the year. The mailing address is Route 302, Bretton Woods 03575.

✐ **The Mount Washington Hotel,** Route 302, Bretton Woods. Open year-round. Think *Titanic:* This 200-room, 100-year-old national historic landmark rises like a white cruise ship amid a landlocked armada of blue and green peaks sweeping across the horizon. The approach, up a mile-long drive, is suitable prelude to reentering an era when elegance and leisure vied with adventure to attract vacationers to one of America's most scenic destinations. The veranda of this Spanish Renaissance Revival edifice is vast, the lobby high and columned, the dining room grand, the menu immense (see *Dining Out*). This "Grande Dame of the White Mountains" took 2 years and 250 Italian artisans to build, and its steel frame was considered state of the art when it opened in 1902. There is much history here. Winston Churchill and John Maynard Keynes were among the 700 delegates who gathered at the hotel for the Bretton Woods Monetary Conference of 1944. The roster of famous visitors, including Babe Ruth, Thomas Edison, Princess Margaret, and several U.S. presidents, takes up pages. But after nearly a century, the hotel was showing its age until 1991 when a group of northern New Hampshire entrepreneurs purchased it with a pledge to preserve and restore it to its previous grandeur. A decade later, with new carpets, windows, and plumbing, and renovations (including computer system upgrades) throughout, the hotel has resurrected its original glory. Actually, more so. The winter of 1999–2000 marked the beginning of a full four-season resort with sleigh rides, snowshoe treks, and spectacular holiday galas. Tours of this large complex (including the Gold Room where the Bretton Woods Conference documents were signed) are offered several times a day, and the public is welcome to attend various lectures on White Mountain human and natural history. Families are especially welcome here, with a number of two-room suites joined by a common bath being most popular. King of the Mountains Kids Kamp offers daily and evening programs for children 5–12, including hikes, visits with the golf pro and the chef, crafts, and various sports. Other amenities include the granite-walled Cave lounge with nightly live entertainment; gift, clothing, flower, and ice cream shops; heated indoor and out-

THE MOUNT WASHINGTON HOTEL IS SPECTACULARLY SITUATED AT THE FOOT OF THE PRESIDENTIAL RANGE.

Robert Kozlow

THE NOTCHLAND INN AT HART'S LOCATION

Kim Grant

door pools; a dozen red clay tennis courts; horseback riding; movies; guided hikes (the resort's own 1,250 acres are surrounded by 18,000 acres of White Mountain National Forest); a 27-hole golf course; and the Bretton Woods Ski Area. A health and fitness center, open all year, is adjacent to the hotel. MAP per couple (dine at any of the resort's four dining rooms) is $218 standard to $590 deluxe for a room; suites range from $425 to $949 for a three-bedroom, one-and-a-half-bath tower affair with rooftop patio and Jacuzzi. There are many special-event and weekend packages available. (See the introduction to this section for more about the hotel's history.)

**The Bretton Arms Country Inn** (603-278-1000; 1-800-258-0330; www.brettonarms.com), Route 302, Bretton Woods. A former annex of the Mount Washington Hotel, built in 1896, this is a small, restored, very attractive inn with 34 rooms, facilities for a small conference, a lounge with weekend entertainment, and dining (see *Dining Out*). A more intimate, casual, countrylike alternative to the grandeur of the main hotel. $109–249 for two per night, includes breakfast.

**Bretton Woods Motor Inn,** Route 302, Bretton Woods. The 50 rooms are all motel-style, large and pleasant with two double beds, TV, and private patio or balcony overlooking the historic Mount Washington Hotel and Presidential Range. Amenities include an indoor heated pool, Jacuzzi and sauna, and comfortable common rooms with fireplaces. The restaurant, **Darby's,** serves breakfast, lunch, and dinner (see *Eating Out*). EP $79–149 per night.

**The Townhomes at Bretton Woods,** Route 302, Bretton Woods. A variety of one- to five-bedroom condominiums with full kitchens, laundries, and fireplaced living rooms; includes access to the health and fitness center and the resort shuttle. From $169 for one-bedroom midweek accommodations to $2,479 for a five-bedroom unit for 7 days during peak season.

**INNS** **The Notchland Inn** (603-374-6131; 1-800-866-6131; www.notchland.com), Route 302, Harts Location 03812. Open all year. This granite mansion was built by pioneering Boston photographer Samuel Bemis in 1862 near the site of what most believe to be the first inn in the White Mountains, Abel Crawford's 18th-century Mt. Crawford House. Now Crawford's tavern serves as the inn's dining room, but the fireplaced front parlor, designed by Arts and Crafts pioneer Gustav Stickley, has its own historic cachet. Innkeepers Ed Butler and Les Schoof have a nonfussy, though respectful, attitude about all this, figuring they can best add to the legacy by offering handsome, up-to-date accommodations. Seven deluxe rooms and six spacious suites feature wood-burning fireplace and private bath. Some also have private deck, skylight, and Jacuzzi. There's a music room with piano and stereo, and for summer guests a sun room with wicker furniture that overlooks the pond and surrounding 100 acres where llamas and Bernese mountain dogs Coco and Abby hold court. The library is eclectic; the English perennial gardens, charming; and the five-course dinners, served nightly at 7, draw raves (see *Dining Out*). A room with breakfast (2-night minimum normally required for reservations including a Saturday) runs $180–290 depending on season and accommodations; for MAP add $30 per person; 3- to 5-night midweek packages are also available. Children over 12 are $25 extra in the same room with parents. A nonsmoking inn.

**The Bernerhof** (603-383-9132; 1-800-548-8007; www.bernerhofinn.com), Route 302, Box 240, Glen 03838. Open all year. Breakfast for guests, dinner to the public. After 4 nights at the Bernerhof, hosts Ted and Sharon Wroblewski treat guests to a complimentary champagne breakfast in bed, but even a 1-night stay is enough to convince anyone that this classic inn has a handle on both up-to-date comfort and old-fashioned hospitality. The inn, which also hosts a cooking school, has nine rooms with private bath. Four large rooms and two suites (with spa) in a recent addition are beautifully decorated, each with a Jacuzzi, air-conditioning, color cable VCR/TV, and a brass king or queen bed. Oak paneling accents the Black Bear Pub and adjacent dining room, where the creative menu demonstrates why this is regarded as one of the premier restaurants in the region (see *Dining Out*). B&B $79–175; MAP $133–208.

**The Bartlett Inn** (603-374-2353; 1-800-292-2353; www.bartlettinn.com), Route 302, Box 327, Bartlett 02812. Open all year. Just west of Bartlett village, this inn appeals to hikers, skiers, and lovers of the outdoors—folks with whom innkeeper Mark Dindorf worked when he was an AMC hutmaster. Mark, his staff, and the other guests are eager to share knowledge of backcountry hiking, white-water canoeing, mountain biking, and cross-country and telemark skiing. (Guests can ski onto the Bear Notch Ski Trail network directly from the inn.) Altogether, there are 16 rooms, 6 in the inn and 10 in cottages, 11 with private bath. Two inn rooms have fireplace, as does the living room, and there is an outside hot tub. Four cottages have fireplaces and kitchenettes. Rates, $78–175 per double, include a full breakfast. Children under 12 are free, and pets are welcome in the cottages.

**AMC HIKER'S LODGING** In fall of 2003 the **AMC Highland Center at Crawford Notch** (www.outdoors.org/highland) opens on the site of the historic Crawford House on Route 302, across from the Crawford Path. Patterned on the AMC's **Joe Dodge Lodge** at its **Pinkham Notch Visitors Center,** this is a full-service facility with meals and accommodations for up to 122. Two AMC "high huts" can also be accessed from Route 302. **Mizpah Spring Hut** (see pp. 346, 347) is sited at tree line, 2.7 miles up the Crawford Path and Zealand Hut is a more gradual 2.8 mile hike in at Zealand Road. For both huts reservations are required (603-466-2727; www.outdoors.org) and hikers must bring towels and bedding; bunks are provided and meals served.

**CAMPGROUNDS** Camping is prohibited along the roadside in Crawford Notch State Park, but there are two campgrounds. **Dry River Campground,** Route 302, Crawford Notch, is a state-owned facility open mid-May through mid-October, with 30 tent sites. No reservations. **Crawford Notch General Store and Campground** (603-374-2779), Route 302 (south of Crawford Notch), Harts Location. The store sells gas, groceries, and hiking and camping supplies and is open all year; the campground, with wooded sites, tables, fireplaces, and hot showers, is open May through October.

**WMNF Campgrounds,** just east of Twin Mountain on Route 302, includes three campgrounds with 73 sites. A **toll-free reservation system** (1-800-280-2267) operates for Sugarloaf I and II. (See *Lodging—Campgrounds* in "Jackson and Pinkham Notch.")

THE AMC'S ZEALAND FALLS HUT

Rob Burbank, AMC

## ✷ Where to Eat

DINING OUT **The Mount Washington Hotel Main Dining Room** (603-278-1000; 1-800-258-0330), Route 302, Bretton Woods. Serves breakfast and dinner daily. Lavish breakfast buffet ($18) and dinner menu that changes nightly. Prepare to dine and dress up with a capital *D* when you enter this historic room, originally designed as a circle so that no one ends up in a corner. Every night is an occasion with dancing, tuxedoed waiters, crystal chandeliers, and the full-blown elegance of another era. Prix fixe dinner, $55.

**Bretton Arms Dining Room and Parlor Lounge** (603-278-1000), Route 302, Bretton Woods. Open year-round for breakfast and dinner. Gourmet fare in a casually elegant, homelike dining room. Entrées $17–31.

♿ **The Bernerhof** (603-383-4414; 1-800-548-8007), Route 302, Glen. Open all year. Dinner 6–9 PM; the **Black Bear Pub** is open Tuesday through Sunday 5–9:30 PM. Another New Hampshire classic inn and one of the premier restaurants in the region, as well as a cooking school. Dining is American regional with European influence. Try Wiener schnitzel or pan-seared duck breast, lobster risotto, salmon BLT wrap, or gazpacho salad. A Taste of the Mountains Cooking School has been around two decades; 3-day, hands-on classes are conducted in spring and fall. A special 15-week Thursday class is taught from January through April by a variety of New England chefs. Ted and Sharon Wroblewski, owners. Daily lunch specials; dinners start at $15. The cooking school, which includes five-course gourmet lunches and dinners with suitable wines and lodging, is $459–509 per person.

**The Notchland Inn** (603-374-6131; 1-800-866-6131), Route 302, Harts Location (Bartlett). Open all year. Once the tavern at Abel Crawford's early White Mountain Hotel, this dining room was moved down the road to the Notchland Inn in the 1920s. Now diners enjoy the best of old and new with innovative cuisine in a romantic setting: The fireplaced dining room overlooks gardens and pond on one side, Mount Hope on the other. Although the chef creates a new menu nightly, there's always a choice of appetizers and soups, three entrées, and three desserts. Generally for guests, the five-course dinners are also served in a single, 7 PM seating to the public, by reservation only Tuesday through Sunday. Prix fixe is $35 for nonguests; $40 on Saturday. The rate for guests is $30 all evenings.

EATING OUT **Darby's Restaurant and Lounge** (603-278-1000; 1-800-258-0330), Route 302, Bretton Woods. Full or continental breakfast and dinner year-round. The Bretton Woods Motor Inn offers views of the Presidential Range and the Mount Washington Hotel from its 1950s–1960s diner.

**Fabyan's Station Restaurant and Lounge** (603-278-2222), Route 302 at the junction of the access road to the Cog Railway, Bretton Woods. Offers a specialized lunch and dinner menu year-round in a restored railroad station. Pub menu in the lounge.

Also see the **Red Parka Pub** and **Glen Junction,** both on Route 302 in Glen, described under *Eating Out* in "North Conway Area."

# The Great North Woods

THE NORTHERN WHITE MOUNTAINS

THE CONNECTICUT LAKES AND DIXVILLE NOTCH

Kim Grant

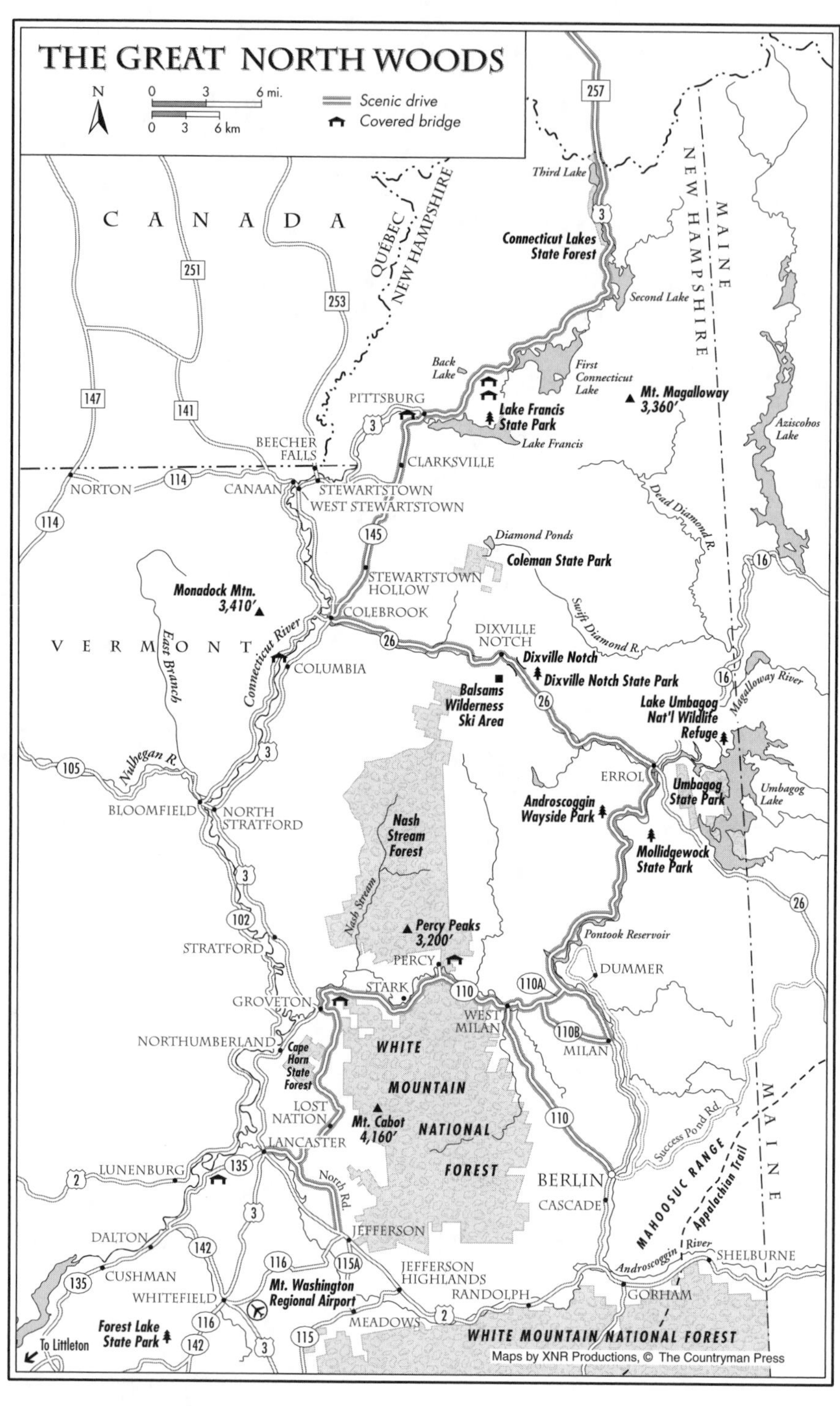

THE GREAT NORTH WOODS
N
0 3 6 mi.
0 3 6 km
Scenic drive
Covered bridge
CANADA
QUÉBEC
NEW HAMPSHIRE
MAINE
VERMONT
Third Lake
Connecticut Lakes State Forest
Second Lake
Back Lake
First Connecticut Lake
Mt. Magalloway 3,360′
PITTSBURG
Lake Francis State Park
Lake Francis
Aziscohos Lake
BEECHER FALLS
CLARKSVILLE
NORTON
CANAAN
STEWARTSTOWN
WEST STEWARTSTOWN
Dead Diamond R.
Diamond Ponds
Coleman State Park
STEWARTSTOWN HOLLOW
Monadock Mtn. 3,410′
COLEBROOK
Swift Diamond R.
DIXVILLE NOTCH
Dixville Notch
Dixville Notch State Park
East Branch
Connecticut River
COLUMBIA
Balsams Wilderness Ski Area
Magalloway River
Lake Umbagog Nat'l Wildlife Refuge
Nulhegan R.
ERROL
Umbagog State Park
Umbagog Lake
BLOOMFIELD
NORTH STRATFORD
Androscoggin Wayside Park
Nash Stream Forest
Mollidgewock State Park
Nash Stream
Percy Peaks 3,200′
Pontook Reservoir
STRATFORD
PERCY
DUMMER
STARK
GROVETON
WEST MILAN
NORTHUMBERLAND
MILAN
Cape Horn State Forest
WHITE MOUNTAIN NATIONAL FOREST
LOST NATION
Mt. Cabot 4,160′
LANCASTER
Success Pond Rd.
MAHOOSUC RANGE
Appalachian Trail
LUNENBURG
BERLIN
CASCADE
North Rd.
JEFFERSON
DALTON
Androscoggin River
SHELBURNE
CUSHMAN
JEFFERSON HIGHLANDS
WHITEFIELD
Mt. Washington Regional Airport
RANDOLPH
GORHAM
MEADOWS
Forest Lake State Park
To Littleton
WHITE MOUNTAIN NATIONAL FOREST
257
3
251
253
147
141
114
145
16
26
105
102
110
110A
110B
2
135
142
116
115A
115
Maps by XNR Productions, © The Countryman Press

# INTRODUCTION

New Hampshire's high hat, its narrow, northernmost region, is actually larger than Rhode Island. It roughly coincides with 1,855-square-mile Coos County (pronounced "co-hos"), said to be an Abenaki word meaning "crooked," perhaps referring to a river bend. The "Great North Woods" designation is relatively recent, coined to underscore the contrast between this region and the more heavily touristed sections of the White Mountains directly to its south. Towns are small and widely scattered. Attractions are natural, not human-made.

Ironically, on road maps the Great North Woods shows up as gray, in contrast to the green of the White Mountain National Forest to the south. That's because, with the exception of an 800,000-acre WMNF tract and the vast Nash Stream State Forest, it is privately owned by paper and timber-management companies. For a century these have permitted recreational use while managing the woods for a continuous yield. Although most woodland has been cut more than once, the overall impression is one of wilderness. This system of dual use is, however, now threatened by global economics. The paper companies are currently selling off their forests to finance their core business.

As we go to press a huge chunk of timber land (171,000 acres) in the Pittsburg area has just changed hands, with 146,000 of it remaining commercial timber but with conservation easements and 25,000 acres set aside to be initially managed by the New Hampshire Chapter of The Nature Conservancy. Hopefully this trend will continue.

Coos County is home to roughly 35,500 people and 5,000 moose. It's an area of broad forests, remote lakes, fast-running rivers, and rugged mountains. It's also the source of two of New England's mightiest rivers, the Connecticut and the Androscoggin. Early inhabitants are said to have traveled these rivers up to 8,500 years before the first white settlers arrived and set to chopping trees. Then, for more than a century, the rivers carried timber to mills, which were positioned at their steepest drops. Log runs on the Androscoggin continued into the 1960s.

In the 1850s railroads began exporting wood products and importing summer tourists. Local farmers were encouraged to take in guests, and huge hotels sprouted in the wilderness. By the 1950s, however, when passenger service from Portland ceased, all but a handful of the big old hotels had closed and travel patterns had shifted. In subsequent decades the interstates (I-93 on the west and I-95 on the east) steered travelers in other directions. New Hampshire's "North Country,"

**ABOUT MOOSE**

Moose are the largest animal found in the wilds of New England. They grow to be 10 feet tall and average 1,000 pounds in weight. The largest member of the deer family, they have a large, protruding upper lip and a distinctive "bell" or "dewlap" dangling from their muzzle.

"Bull" (male) moose have long been prized for their antlers, which grow to a span of up to 6 feet. They are shed in January and grow again. Female moose ("cows") do not grow antlers, and their heads are lighter in color than the bull. All moose, however, are darker in spring than summer, grayer in winter.

Front hooves are longer than the rear, as are the legs, the better to cope with deep snow and water. In summer they favor wetlands and can usually be found near ponds or watery bogs. They also like salt and so tend to create and frequent "wallows," wet areas handy to road salt (the attraction of paved roads).

Moose are vegetarians, daily consuming more than 50 pounds of leaves, grass, and other greenery when they can find it. In winter their diet consists largely of bark and twigs. Mating season is mid-September until late October. Calves are born in early spring and weigh in at 30 pounds. They grow quickly but keep close to their mothers for an entire year. At best moose live 12 years.

When under attack, moose face their attacker and stand their ground—so it's natural for them to freeze when a car approaches head-on. It's best to stop and pull to the side of the road yourself.

Moose are most numerous along roads early in the morning and again at dusk. Along "Moose Alleys" such as Route 3 north of Pittsburg and Route 16 north of Berlin, it's not unusual to see a dozen within that many miles, especially as the summer wears on and the animals become accustomed to "moose-watchers." Remember, however, that moose are wild animals. Don't try to see how close you can get.

While the area's first settlers reported seeing moose aplenty, they were hunted so aggressively (the tongue and nose were particularly prized as delicacies in 19th-century Boston) that they dwindled to a dozen or so in the entire state. The current count is around 9,500. New Hampshire's annual moose hunt is 9 days, beginning the third Saturday in October.

**WARNING**

The state records hundreds of often deadly collisions between moose and cars or trucks. The common road sign and bumper sticker reading BRAKE FOR MOOSE means just that. Be extremely wary at dusk when vision is difficult and moose are active.

as it's still commonly known, remained chiefly the preserve of serious outdoorsmen—with one high-profile exception.

Way up in Dixville Notch, the Balsams Grand Resort Hotel, dating from 1866, continues to attract thousands of guests from every corner of the country, year-round. Less well known are the nearby sporting camps and campgrounds at the very apex of the state. Similar to the rustic hunting and fishing lodges scattered widely across Maine's North Woods, here they cluster around lakes near the pristine source of the Connecticut River.

Camps and campgrounds are also gathered near the shore of beautiful Umbagog ("um-BAY-gog") Lake to the southeast. From Umbagog the Androscoggin River flows south through a long, wooded valley, beloved by canoeists and anglers. Eventually it drops through the city of Berlin and, not far below in Gorham, turns abruptly east and heads into Maine.

Logistically (if not politically) the Great North Woods divides into a northern tier—the Connecticut Lakes and Dixville Notch—and a southern tier, the Connecticut and Androscoggin River Valleys, including towns along the two roads linking them.

The Great North Woods will never be a tourist destination in the Mount Washington Valley sense—not unless a new interstate slashes across it, once more changing traffic patterns. The region is, however, reawakening as a destination for naturalists and enterprising travelers. Visitor services are increasing. This year marks the reopening of the Mountain View Grand, a big old summer hotel that languished for decades atop a ridge near Whitefield. And throughout the region B&Bs, outfitters, and restaurants are multiplying, complementing the old standbys that have hung on through thick and thin. Significantly, lodging places and restaurants can now operate year-round, thanks largely to snowmobilers.

The 19th-century hotels were all geared to summer use only and, while Berlin's Nansen Ski Club (founded in 1872) is the country's oldest ski club, this region, unlike the White Mountains to the south, was virtually unchanged by the alpine ski boom and cross-country ski boomlet. With New England's most reliable snow cover (equaled only by Maine's less accessible North Woods and Aroostook County), it is now a mecca for snowmobilers. Far fewer in number, but growing quickly, are snowshoers. Thanks to recent advances in equipment and clothing, average folks are discovering the beauty and exploring mountain trails, empty of all but animal tracks and sparkling with sun on snow.

The animal for which this region is best known is, of course, the moose. The Great North Woods is becoming known as a moose mecca. The Annual North Country Moose Festival in late August is the event of the year, and the Gorham-based Moose Tours are a big attraction.

CUT LOGS FOR LUMBER, THE GREAT NORTH WOODS

Kim Grant

# THE NORTHERN WHITE MOUNTAINS

## THE ANDROSCOGGIN AND CONNECTICUT RIVER VALLEYS AND LAKE UMBAGOG, INCLUDING GORHAM, BERLIN AND ERROL, JEFFERSON, WHITEFIELD, AND LANCASTER

Also known as "The Northern White Mountains" this easily accessible tier of the North Country is far less touristed than the landscape just to its south. Given the area's narrow girth, it's also surprisingly varied.

The New Hampshire stretch of Route 2, which both defines the area's southern boundary and serves as its prime east–west highway, measures just 36 miles, but links two very different north–south corridors carved by two major rivers, the Androscoggin and the Connecticut.

The Androscoggin rises in streams above Umbagog Lake, long a mecca for birders and anglers and now both a national wildlife refuge and a state park. Nearby Errol (population 440) serves as the hub for canoeing, fishing, and otherwise exploring both the lake and the wooded corridor along the Androscoggin as it courses south, shadowed by Route 16. At Berlin the river drops 200 feet in 3 miles, the obvious site for mills. By the 1890s Berlin boasted the world's largest paper mills, employing skilled workers representing no less than nine major ethnic groups. The Northern Forest Heritage Park on the northern fringe of town offers a sense of the rich past of the city and its woodlands, and also serves as departure point for river tours.

At Gorham, 6 miles south of Berlin, the Androscoggin River turns abruptly east. Gorham has been catering to tourists since 1851, when the Atlantic and St. Lawrence Railroad (now the Canadian National) began transporting them from Portland to the White Mountains via this direct, northern route, avoiding North Conway and more southerly White Mountains resorts. The old railroad station now houses the town historical society; the 1858 four-story Gorham House, while no longer a hotel, still marks the center of town. Gorham remains a prime crossroads (the junction of Route 2 and Route 16), and its old commercial blocks harbor some exceptional places to shop and eat.

East of Gorham, Route 2 follows the Androscoggin River 10 miles to the Maine border, passing through an impressive corridor of birch trees that the town of

**NORTHERN FOREST HERITAGE PARK**

603-752-7202; www.northernforestheritage.org, 961 Main Street, Berlin. Sited on 10 riverside acres on the northern fringe of the city, the park celebrates the story of the working forest and the multicultural heritage of the region. A three-story clapbard Brown Paper Company boardinghouse, built in 1853 to house incoming employees, serves as an information center, museum, and gift store. In the reconstructed logging camp across the street on the river, costumed interpreters reenact life in the woods circa the 1880s through the 1920s. This is also the departure point for a narrated river tour (aboard a pontoon boat), describing the way the river was used to float logs down to the mills. Just above Berlin you see large pilings, once used to anchor booms that kept the logs moving swiftly to the mills. The park's riverside amphitheater is the venue for a lively series of year-round events, including annual Great North Woods Lumberjack Championships.

Northern Forest Heritage Park

Shelburne maintains as a memorial to their war dead. Across the river is Philbrook Farm, currently operated by the fourth and fifth generations of the family who began welcoming paying visitors in 1861.

In the late 19th century New Hampshire's Board of Agriculture encouraged local farmers to take in guests. Between 1891 and 1916 it published lists of farms for sale, urging visitors to "Secure a home in New Hampshire—Where Comfort, Health and Prosperity abound."

West of Gorham, Route 2 traverses Randolph and Jefferson, century-old summer havens with exceptional panoramic views of the northern peaks of the Presidential Range. In Jefferson the memory of The Waumbec, one of the grandest of all the vanished White Mountain hotels, is preserved in its 18-hole golf course.

The imposing 146-room Mountain View Grand hotel in nearby Whitefield has been luckier. After decades of decline and then closure, the 19th-century landmark has reopened following a $20 million makeover. Its neighbor, the gracious old Spalding Inn, continues to thrive.

If Route 2 continued due west, it would run into Whitefield (Route 116 forms the link). Instead it angles north, following the Israel River to Lancaster seat of Coos ("co-hos") County, an inviting North Country town with a classic village square surrounded by shops, homes, and churches. Note the Great North Woods Welcome Center just off Main Street.

Around the turn of the 20th century, when lumbering was at its peak in this area, it was Lancaster native John Wingate Weeks who sponsored the highly controversial bill resulting in the creation of the White Mountain National Forest. Weeks's former estate atop Mount Prospect, south of Lancaster, is now a state park, well worth a stop.

A FARM IN LANCASTER

Robert Kozlow

From Lancaster, Route 3 follows the Connecticut River north. The approach to Groveton is a tableau combining North Country history and the region's prime industry: Before the Wausau paper mill stands the Groveton covered bridge, and beside it is an old logging engine dating to the days when many miles of logging railroads webbed this area. Rising high in the background are the distinctive Percy Peaks, suggesting, perhaps, that the future of this area lies in its wilderness.

To find the view pictured on the cover of this book, turn east on Route 110 from Groveton and continue 6 miles to tiny Stark village. Here the covered bridge srtands by the Union Church, both built in the 1850s. During World War II, German prisoners of war were brought to a camp here to work in the woods. To complete a loop through this region, continue east on Route 110, through White Mountain National Forest. It also accesses the 40,000 acres that now form Nash Stream State Forest.

GUIDANCE **Northern White Mountain Chamber of Commerce** (603-752-6060; 1-800-992-7480; www.northernwhitemtnchamber.org), 164 Main Street, Box 298, Berlin 03570.

**Great North Woods Welcome Center** (603-788-2530; 1-877-788-2530; www.northerngatewaychamber.org), Main Street, Lancaster 03584. Year-round welcome center, open varying days and hours.

**A New Hampshire Information Center,** Route 2 in Shelburne, with rest rooms and picnic tables, is open year-round, 9 AM–8 PM Monday through Thursday, 9 AM–9 PM Friday and Saturday.

**Umbagog Area Chamber of Commerce** (603-482-3906; www.umbagogchambercommerce.com) is a year-round source of information with a seasonal booth.

**WMNF Androscoggin Visitors Center/Ranger Station** (603-466-2713), 2.5 miles south of Gorham on Route 16. Open Monday through Friday 7:30 AM–4:30 PM, also weekends in summer. Good for year-round outdoor recreation info.

**Seasonal information booths** can be found on Main Street in **Gorham** (603-466-3103) and on the square in **Whitefield.**

GETTING THERE *By bus:* **Concord Trailways** (603-228-3300; 1-800-639-3317) provides scheduled service from Boston to Gorham. Daily service varies.

MEDICAL EMERGENCY **911** now works throughout this area.

**Androscoggin Valley Hospital** (603-752-2200), 59 Page Hill Road, Berlin. **Ambulance:** 603-752-1020.

**Weeks Medical Center** (603-788-4911), Middle Street, Lancaster 03584.

## ✷ To See

MOOSE See the "Great North Woods" introduction for a full description. The local "Moose Alley" is Route 16 north from Berlin and the length of Route 110. Organized **Moose Tours** (603-466-3103; 1-800-992-7480). From Memorial Day weekend through foliage season, nightly 2½-hour moose-viewing van tours depart from the Gorham information center, Main Street, Gorham. Call for reservations; leave about dusk from the information center.

**HISTORIC SITES AND MUSEUMS Berlin.** Pick up the leaflet walking tour guide to this "City that Trees Built." As you may suspect, judging from the steep tilt of its streets, they were laid out on a map in Boston, with no thought to the actual topography. Highlights include the Holy Resurrection Church (20 Petrograd Street) on Russian Hill—which, unfortunately, is not open on a regular basis. Cathedral-sized St. Ann's Church, serving the city's dominant French Canadian population, crowns the city's central hill. The **Berlin Public Library** (603-752-5210), Main Street, displays a collection of Native American stone implements, some dating back 7,000 years. Note the strong French-Canadian influence here, because many residents are descended from Quebec immigrants who came to work in the woods and mills. French remains a second, and sometimes the primary, language of many people.

**Weeks State Park** (603-788-4004; 603-788-3155), Route 3, 2 miles south of Lancaster. This 420-acre mountaintop park is open year-round for outdoor recreation (the gated access road is open when either the park manager or fire lookout is on duty). In winter people walk, snowshoe, and ski the access road. The 3-mile Around the Loop Trail (rated "easy walking") is well maintained, and the half-mile Nature Trail loop begins at the fire tower. The lodge/museum is usually open mid-June through Labor Day, Wednesday through Sunday, and weekends until Columbus Day.

Not recommended for RVs, the narrow access road winds for 1.5 miles up the side of Mount Prospect, through stands of white birch and with two scenic lookouts overlooking the Connecticut River Valley. At the top is the summer home of Lancaster native John Sinclair Weeks (1860–1926) who, as a Massachusetts congressman, was responsible for the 1911 bill establishing the White Mountain National Forest and all national forests in the eastern United States.

Mount Propsect is only 2,059 feet in elevaion but, true to its name, offers a spectacular 360-degree view—from the Presidentials to the Green Mountains and the Kilkenny Range. Weeks's ancestors, who farmed on this mountain, maintained a bridle path to the summit in the early 19th century, which was improved and served a hotel built on the top of the mountain in 1883. The hotel closed, but local residents continued to come to the summit. When Weeks bought much of the mountain, he upgraded the road for motor traffic and built the 87-foot-high fieldstone Mount Prospect Tower. His fanciful 1912 summer home, Mount Prospect Lodge, is pink stucco and houses his collection of local birds, as well as displays on the White Mountains and on his own fascinating life.

In summer free 7:30 PM Thursday lectures, sponsored by Friends of the Park, are offered in the Great Hall of the museum. Subjects range from nature to history, music, and art. Inquire about naturalist-led bird and flower walks.

**HISTORICAL SOCIETIES The Moffett House Museum** (603-752-4590; 603-752-7337), 119 High Street, Berlin, open Tuesday through Saturday noon–4 PM and Wednesday evenings 6–9, is a Victorian house with exhibits on the history of Berlin and Coos County.

**Gorham Historical Society** (603-466-5570), Railroad Street, Gorham. The Railroad Station Museum contains displays on local history and especially railroading, tourism, and logging.

**Wilder-Holton House** (603-788-3004), 226 Main Street, Lancaster 03584. The first two-story house built in Coos County (1780), now the museum of the Lancaster Historical Society, is open alternate Sundays from the end of June through September.

**Jefferson Historical Society** (603-586-7021) on Route 2 is open Memorial Day weekend through Columbus Day, Tuesday, Thursday, and Saturday, 11 AM–2 PM.

**Groveton's Old Meeting House** (603-636-2234), south of town on Route 3 and dating from 1799, houses exhibits of the Northumberland Historical Society. Open mid-June through mid-September 9AM–4 PM, closed Monday.

FOR FAMILIES **Santa's Village** (603-586-4445; www.santasvillage.com), Route 2, Jefferson. Open Father's Day through Labor Day, daily 9:30 AM–7 PM; until Columbus Day, weekends 9:30 AM–5 PM. Santa and his elves, along with the reindeer, make this Christmas in summer for children and adults. Ride the Yule Log Flume, the railroad, Ferris wheel, or roller coaster; watch the trained macaw show; see the new animated Twelve Days of Christmas kiosk; and, of course, sit on Santa's lap. Food and gift shops. Admission includes unlimited rides and shows. Age 4 to adult $17, seniors $15; age 3 and under with an adult free as Santa's guest.

**Six Gun City** (603-586-4592; www.sixguncity.com), Route 2, Jefferson. Open daily 9 AM–6 PM, Father's Day through Labor Day; weekends until Columbus Day. Cowboy skits and frontier shows are combined with 35 western town buildings, an outstanding horse-drawn-vehicle museum; miniature burros and horses and other animals; 11 rides; and two water slides. Food and gift shops. Admission includes unlimited rides and shows. Age 4 to adult $15.45, age 3 and under free with an adult; $10 over age 65.

**Riverside Speedway** (603-636-2005; www.riversidespeedway.com), Brown Road (just off Route 3), Groveton. Check the web site for the schedule of weekend races. Sited on flats along the Connecticut River with 20 acres of field (camping permitted) and a quarter-mile track with seating for 3,500 on the front strech and another 5,000 in the pit area.

Also see **Wildcat Mountain** (under *To Do—Aerial Lift*) and the **Mount Washington Auto Road** under *To See—Scenic Drives* in "Jackson and Pinkham Notch," and the **Mount Washington Cog Railway** under *To See* in "Crawford Notch and Bretton Woods."

THE RAILROAD STATION MUSEUM IN GORHAM

Christina Tree

COVERED BRIDGES **Mechanic Street bridge,** Lancaster, built in 1862, spans the Israel River east of Route 2/3.

**The Mount Orne bridge** crosses the Connecticut River to Lunenburg, Vermont, 5 miles southwest of Lancaster off Route 135. Built in 1911, it's more than 266 feet long.

**The Groveton bridge,** just south of the Wausau paper mill on Route 3, is open to foot traffic.

**The Stark bridge,** just off Route 110, east of Groveton, is pictured on the cover of this book.

SCENIC DRIVES **Route 16 North from Berlin to Errol.** Pinkham B Road (formerly Dolly Copp Road) is a mostly unpaved wilderness road running from Dolly Copp Campground on Route 16, past the base of Mount Madison, to Route 2. Several hiking trails begin on this road. Not winter-maintained.

Robert Kozlow

THE CAPS RIDGE TRAIL ASCENDS MOUNT JEFFERSON FROM JEFFERSON NOTCH.

**Jefferson Notch Road** is a historic route beside the western edge of the Presidential Range. Not winter-maintained, this winding gravel road reaches the highest elevation point of any public through road in New Hampshire at Jefferson Notch (3,008 feet). Drive with care, because snow and mud remain until late in spring and ice returns early in fall; it is best used in summer. The Caps Ridge Trail, at the 7-mile point on Jefferson Notch, offers the shortest route to any of the Presidential Range peaks: 2.5 miles to Mount Jefferson. From the north, Jefferson Notch Road leaves Valley Road (which connects Routes 2 and 115) in Jefferson and runs south to the Cog Railway Base Station Road. At that intersection, paved Mount Clinton Road continues on to the Crawford House site on Route 302.

Shelburne's **North Road** is a winding country byway with great views of the Presidential Range across the Androscoggin River.

**North Road** connects Lancaster with Jefferson and offers country views of the mountains, especially Mount Cabot and the Kilkenny Wilderness Area east of Lancaster. Just south of Lancaster, **Lost Nation Road** departs from North Road and runs north to Groveton. According to one tradition, this area was named by a traveling preacher who, when he could get only one person to attend church, likened the local folks to the lost tribes of Israel. **Route 110 and Route 110A/110B** from Groveton to Milan and Berlin are picturesque in any season, but also try the secondary road that runs parallel to Route 110 north of the upper Ammonoosuc River. It runs from Groveton village through Percy and Stark to rejoin Route 110 just west of the 110/110A intersection.

**Pleasant Valley Road** is a loop beginning in downtown Lancaster's Middle Street (there's only one way to turn). Take the first left (past the medical center) onto Grange Road. Follow Grange to a fork in the road and bear right onto Pleasant Valley to its junction with Garland Road. Maps are available at Lancaster Town Hall (603-788-3391).

**In Vermont:** From South Lancaster you might cross the Connecticut on the covered bridge (Route 135) into Lunenburg, a beautiful village with views east to the mountains.

Also see **Weeks State Park** under *Historic Sites and Museums.*

## ✳ To Do

**CANOEING AND KAYAKING** The **Androscoggin River** north of Berlin is one of the state's most popular canoeing waters. Paddlers are advised to check with the *AMC River Guide* or *Canoe Camping Vermont and New Hampshire Rivers* (Backcountry Publications). Pick up the AMC's new *Androcoggin River Map and Guide.*

**Saco Bound** (603-447-2177; www.sacobound.com) in Errol village has rentals, instruction, guided trips, and other canoeing information. They also coordinate flatwater kayak trips on the Magalloway River and Lake Umbagog.

**Umbagog Outfitters** (603-356-3292), Box 268, Errol 03579. Offers guided flatwater and white-water kayak tours and instruction.

The **Connecticut River** from the Columbia bridge south to Moore Dam is beautiful paddling with many put-in places. See *Connecticut River* in "What's Where."

**CRUISES** Lake Umbagog–Magalloway River cruises aboard a pontoon boat are offered by **Northern Waters Outfitters** (603-447-2177).

**FISHING** The Androscoggin River is a source of pickerel, bass, trout, and salmon. New Hampshire fishing licenses, required for adults, are sold at many stores throughout the region. Another recommended fishing spot is South Pond Recreation Area, off Route 110, West Milan. It also has a picnic and swimming area. The Peabody River and Moose Brook are also frequented by anglers. See Great Glen Outdoor Center in "Jackson and Pinkham Notch" for fly-fishing programs. Also see *To Do—Fishing* in "Connecticut Lakes and Dixville Notch." Cotes, a sporting goods store in Errol, is the source of fishing tips as well as equipment for Umbagog Lake and the upper Androscoggin (see *Selective Shopping*).

**GOLF** **Androscoggin Valley Country Club** (603-466-9468; pro shop 603-466-2641), Route 2, Gorham. Eighteen holes, bar and food service.

**The Waumbec Club** (603-586-7777), Route 2, Jefferson, is an 18-hole course overlooking the Presidential Range, built to serve one of the region's largest 19th-century resort hotels. Food and beverages, also tennis, are available.

**Mountain View Grand Country Club** (603-837-2100), Whitefield. Nine-hole course with a recently renovated clubhouse with tennis courts, a pool, and saunas, operated by the Mountain View Grand (see *Lodging—Resorts*). On a clear day the summit of Mount Washington seems but a long 2-iron shot away. Collared shirts are required.

**HIKING** *Note*: This area offers some of New England's most spectacular hikes. Indeed, hikers represent a larger percentage of visitors here than in the Mount Washington Valley. Note the establishments that cater to through-hikers on the Appalachian Trail (it crosses Route 2 east of Gorham). The following hikes just begin to suggest the quantity and quality of hikes accessible from this area in the Presidentials, as well as in the Moriah, Mahoosuc, and Kilkenny Ranges.

**Presidential Range.** The Appalachian Mountain Club's **Pinkham Notch Visitors Center** (603-466-2727; www.outdoors.org), 9 miles south of Gorham on Route 16, offers an overview of what's available on these northern and western slopes of the Presidential Range. If you are not familiar with the area, it's the place to begin. Since 1888 the AMC has also operated Madison Spring Hut, a full-service, summer-only facility at tree line between Mount Madison and mile-high Mount Adams.

For any White Mountain hiking, consult the *AMC White Mountain Guide* for details about trailheads, routes, distances, hiking time estimates, and special information. (Also see *50 Hikes in the White Mountains* or *50 More Hikes in New Hampshire,* both by Daniel Doan and Ruth Doan MacDougall, Backcountry Publications.) A map is vital here, since myriad trails interconnect on the northern side of the rugged Presidential Range peaks. There are three parking areas on Route 2 and another on Pinkham B (Dolly Copp) Road, connecting Routes 2 and 16, which are at the most popular trailheads for climbing the northern peaks of Madison, Adams, and Jefferson. Most of these trails lead above tree line and should be attempted only by properly equipped hikers. Winter weather conditions can occur above tree line any month of the year. Most of the trails to the summits are 4 to 5 miles in length and require 4 or 5 hours to reach the top. The lower portions of the trails pass through wooded areas along streams and are suitable for short walks.

**Randolph Mountain Club** (www.randolphmountainclub.org) maintains a 100-mile network of hiking trails and two cabins and two shelters for hikers high on the side of Mount Adams. Nominal overnight fees are charged. The cabins have cooking utensils and gas stoves in July and August, but hikers must supply their own food and bedding.

A less rigorous hike to Pine Mountain offers fine views of the Presidential Range. Off Pinkham B (Dolly Copp) Road (2.4 miles from Route 2 or 1.9 miles from Route 16), a private road that is open only to public foot traffic leads to the summit and connects to a loop trail. Estimated hiking time is 2 hours for a 3.4-mile round trip.

**Mahoosuc Range.** Stretching from Shelburne northeast to Grafton Notch in Maine, this rugged range offers some of the most difficult hiking on the Appalachian Trail (the mountains are not high, but the trails steeply ascend and descend the peaks). Many of the peaks—as well as rocky Mahoosuc Notch, where the ice stays in crevasses year-round—are most easily reached by Success Pond Road, a smooth logging road on the northern side of the mountains. In the middle of Berlin, turn east at the traffic lights across the river, through the log yard of the paper company, then travel up to 14 miles along the road to get to the various trailheads. Watch for logging trucks on this road. (See the *AMC White Mountain Guide* for hiking details.)

**Waumbec and Starr King Mountains,** north of Route 2 in Jefferson, are popular hikes. The climb is 3.8 miles and requires just over 3 hours to the top.

**The Kilkenny District of the White Mountain National Forest** is popular although the trails are not as well marked as in the mountains farther south. Check out Mount Cabot (4 miles, 3 hours), east of Lancaster. The Percy Peaks (2 miles, 2 hours), north of Stark, offer views across the North Country and are not likely to be crowded with other hikers. Check the *AMC White Mountain Guide* for directions to Cabot and the Percy Peaks.

**The Cohos Trail** (www.cohostrail.org) is described in the *The Cohos Trail* by Kim Nilsen (Nicolin Fields Publishing). This new trail links existing hiking paths, railbeds, and logging roads to form a continuous trail, accessible at many points along the way, running north–south through the region beginnng in Bartlett and ending at the Canadian border in Pittsburg.

Also see **Weeks State Park** under *To See—Historic Sites and Museums.*

MOUNTAIN BIKING **Moriah Sports** in Gorham (see *Selective Shopping*) rents mountain bikes and steers patrons toward innumerable trails. Moose Brook State Park in Gorham (see *Lodging—Campgrounds*) and the Nansen Ski Club Trails (see *Winter Sports—Cross-Country Skiing*) north of Berlin are popular.

SWIMMING ♿ **Forest Lake State Beach, Dalton** (603-837-9150), on a side road off Route 116 south of Whitefield. Open weekends from Memorial Day, daily late June through Labor Day. One of the original state parks dating from 1935, this 50-acre site has a 200-foot-long swimming beach, a bathhouse, and picnic sites. Handicapped accessible. Fee charged.

**Libby Pool,** Route 16, Gorham. Facilities include a bathhouse, slide, and floats, but no lifeguards. $1 admission.

**South Pond Recreation Area** in the White Mountain National Forest, off Route 110, West Milan. Open mid-June through Labor Day, this spot offers a long, sandy beach and picnic area. Fee.

WHITE-WATER RAFTING **Rapid River Rafting Inc.** (603-447-2177; www.raftdowneast.com), based in Errol, offers rafting on the Magalloway and Rapid Rivers to take advantage of timed releases, usually the last two weekends in July and first in August. The Magalloway is a beginner-level trip but the Rapid is advanced.

## ✻ Winter Sports

CROSS-COUNTRY SKIING **The Nansen Ski Club,** arguably the country's oldest ski club (in 1872, when it was founded, you had to speak Swedish to belong), maintains 23 miles (no, not km) of trails north of Berlin, on the far side of the Androscoggin River from Route 16. Trail maps are available at the clubhouse (with a woodstove) at the trailhead on the Success Loop Road off the East Milan Road (look for Nansen Ski Club signs on Route 16). To quote a local skier: "This is one of the few places that take you back to what cross-country skiing was and what it should be." $20 annual membership, donation for use; for details call Gary Coulombe: 603-752-1650.

Also see Great Glen Trails in "Jackson and Pinkham Notch" and Bretton Woods Touring Center in "Crawford Notch and Bretton Woods," both under *Winter Sports—Cross-Country Skiing.*

**SNOWSHOEING** **Moriah Sports** in Gorham (see *Selective Shopping*) rents as well as sells snowshoes, publishes a guide to local trails, and offers evening tours. *Snowshoe Hikes in the White Mountains* by Stephen Smith details excellent hikes in this area.

**SNOWMOBILING** Hundreds of miles of trails web this area, connecting with Vermont and Maine systems. New Hampshire registration is necessary (call Fish and Game: 603-271-3422). Snowmobile rentals are available at **Seven Dwarfs Motel** (846-5535) in Twin Mountain.

Contact the **New Hampshire Snowmobile Association** (603-224-8906; www.NHSA.com) and click on Coos County to contact local clubs like the Lancaster Snowdrifters.

For alpine skiing see **Wildcat Mountain** in "Jackson and Pinkham Notch"; **Bretton Woods** in "Crawford Notch and Bretton Woods"; and **The Balsams Wilderness** in "Connecticut Lakes and Dixville Notch," all under *Winter Sports—Downhill Skiing.*

**GREEN SPACE** **Lake Umbagog National Wildlife Refuge** (603-482-3415), Route 16 (5.5 miles north of Errol village), mailing address: P.O. Box 240, Errol 03579. Umbagog (pronounced "um-BAY-gog") is said to mean "clear water" in the Abenaki tongue. This 10-mile-long (with more than 50 miles of shoreline and many islands) largely undeveloped lake, with some 15,000 surrounding acres now declared a national wildlife refuge, is one of the finest wild areas in New England. It's home to nesting bald eagles, sharing the skies with ospreys, loons, and varied waterfowl. Moose amble the shorelines, and the fishing is great. The northern end of the lake is the most interesting, especially in the extensive freshwater marshes where the Androscoggin and Magalloway Rivers meet. Contact the refuge headquarters for detailed canoe and kayaking routes.

**Umbagog Lake State Park** (603-482-7795), Route 26, south of Errol, offers boat rentals, boat launch, campsites, and rental cottages (see *Lodging—Campgrounds*).

**White Mountain National Forest.** For information about the 800,000 acres in the Milan, Berlin, Gorham, and Shelburne areas, check with the WMNF Androscoggin Visitors Center/Ranger Station south of Gorham on Route 16 (see *Guidance*).

**Nash Stream State Forest** (603-788-4157) is a 40,000-acre, undeveloped wilderness located in the towns of Odell, Stratford, Columbia, and Stark. Jointly managed by conservation groups and the U.S. Forest Serice, it was rescued from sale to a developer back in 1988. It is open to day use for mountain biking, hunting, fishing, hiking, cross-country skiing, and snowmobiling. There is a seasonal, maintained gravel road off Route 110 (4 miles west of Groveton, turn north off Emerson Road).

**Nansen Wayside Park,** Route 16, 4 miles north of Berlin. The state-owned ski jump is across the street from this small park beside the Androscoggin River. Several picnic sites and a boat-launching ramp.

**The Thirteen-Mile Woods Scenic Area,** just south of Errol, is the most beautiful stretch of the river. Here the road and river curve along side by side through a wild area. At about the midpoint is the riverside Androscoggin Wayside Park, situated on a bluff overlooking the river, with picnic tables.

**Pondicherry National Wildlife Preserve,** Airport Road, Jefferson. This 1,000-acre preserve includes Big and Little Cherry Ponds as well as open bogs, one of the best places for bird-watching in the North Country.

Also see **Weeks State Park** under *To See—Historic Sites and Museums* and see Milan Hill and Mollidgewock State Parks under *Lodging—Campgrounds*.

## ✷ Lodging

**RESORTS** ⚭ ✐ ♿ **Mountain View Grand** (603-837-2100; 1-866-484-3843; www.mountainviewgrand.com), Mountain View Road, Whitefield 03598. Built originally in 1865, this was a 200-room hotel when it closed in 1986, seemingly forever. When he bought it in 1998, not everyone believed that Kevin Craffey, the owner of a Massachusetts construction company, had what it took to bring this huge place back to life. The saga of Craffey's stubborn dedication to the $20 million project is a long but successful one: As of this writing the hotel is scheduled to reopen in the summer of 2002, with 144 rooms with private baths, featherbeds, mahogany furniture, phones with Internet hook-ups, individual temperature control (hot and cold), and oversized TVs. Amenities include twice-daily housekeeping and 24-hour room service. A spa now occupies the Italian Revival–style central tower. The hotel retains 300 of its original 400 acres, including a nine-hole golf course with a clubhouse and elaborate landscaping, with waterfalls

THE MOUNTAIN VIEW GRAND HOTEL

Mountain View Grand Hotel

and flower gardens. Facilities include an Olympic-sized outdoor pool at the clubhouse, a new indoor pool in the hotel, along with a fitness center, and tennis. Dining options range from snacks in **Finn's Lobby Lounge** and light meals in the informal **Clubhouse Café and Grill** to fine dining in **Juliet's Restaurant** with nightly entertainment in the Speakeasy (see *Dining Out*). Rates range through no less than seven categories of rooms, from $89 to $239 EP. Inquire about package plans.

∞ 🐾 ✐ **The Spalding Inn** (603-837-2572; 1-800-368-8439; www.spaldinginn.com), 199 Mountain View Road, Whitefield 03598. Open mid-June through mid-October. Current owners Diane Cockrell and Michael Finder have turned this century-old resort, once known for its lawn bowling (it hosted the U.S. singles and doubles championships), into a into an appealing, less formal, country inn. Lawn bowling is still an option, and other activities include tennis, golf (next door at the Mountain View Country Club), shuffleboard, volleyball, and swimming. The rambling, brown-shingled inn offers 24 rooms (all with private bath); there are also eight family suites plus five attractive cottages (pets permitted) with one to four bedrooms, all with private bath, some with fireplace and kitchenette. There are also 12 rooms in the remodeled carriage house. All rooms have a phone and are nicely furnished. Breakfast and dinner served daily (see *Dining Out*). B&B $89–250 with breakfast. Special family plan offers reasonable rates for an adjoining room and children's meals; there is a variety of theater and golf packages.

Also see The Balsams in "Connecticut Lakes and Dixville Notch."

## BED & BREAKFASTS

*Listed east to west along Route 2*

**The Wildberry Inn** (603-466-5049; rec@moose.ncia.net), 592 Route 2, Shelburne 03581. Innkeepers Bob and Jackie Corrigan have converted a portion of their 125-year-old barn into a handsome two-story suite with cooking facilities and room for up to four people. A Palladian window offers views of the back of the property, which includes a pond and waterfall. An additional room with private bath in the main house is also attractive. The Corrigans are helpful hosts who will tune you in to all the best places to hike, ski, and dine. $75–125 per couple includes a hearty breakfast with the wildberry theme a main ingredient.

**Mt. Washington B&B** (603-466-2669; 1-877-466-2399; www.mtwashingtonbb.com), 421 Route 2, Shelburne 03581. At this classic 19th-century clapboard inn Mary Ann Mayer offers a hearty welcome and a choice of suites with whirlpool tub, along with several rooms with private bath. The decor is a mix of antique and reproduction furniture. Rates, which include breakfast, range $110–160 for the suites, $50–90 for the rooms, a very full breakast included.

**The Libby House B&B** (603-466-2272; 1-800-453-0012; www.libbyhouse.com), 55 Main Street, Box 267, Gorham 03581. At this writing we must sadly report that this fabulous find is up for sale. In the summer of 2002 only the hiker's hostel in the barn will be open ($14 for a bed and shower). Worth checking.

## INNS

✐ **The Jefferson Inn** (603-586-7998; 1-800-729-7908; www.jeffersoninn.com), Route 2 (at the junction with

Route 115A), Jefferson 03583. Mark, Cindy, and Bette Bovio bring new vigor to this fine, century-old inn. The 11 rooms, all with private bath, include bright, inviting doubles and family suites accommodating up to five. Santa's Village is just down the road (see *To See—For Families*). A trail for nearby Starr King and Waumbec Mountains leaves from the inn. Golfers will enjoy the Waumbec Country Club course, said to be the oldest in the state. Just across the street is a wonderful old stone swimming pool with a beach for children. Rates are $85–100 for rooms, $125–175 for suites, including a full breakfast.

🐾 ✐ **Applebrook B&B** (603-586-7713; 1-800-545-6504; www.applebrook.com), Route 115A, Box 178, Jefferson 03583. Open year-round. A rambling old Victorian building, this inn has 14 rooms, 8 with private bath; the others share. Two suites with their own hot tubs are $125–150. There's an outdoor hot tub and cross-country/walking trails nearby. The two large dorm rooms with three and seven beds each are great for groups. A full breakfast is included, and dinner is available to groups by advance reservation. Innkeepers Martin Kelly and Sandra Conley charge $60–100 per couple, dorm rooms $25 per person. Pets are welcome for a $10 fee, half of which goes to the Lancaster Humane Society.

✐ **The Jefferson Highlands Bed & Breakfast** (603-586-4373), Black Velvet Road, Jefferson 03583. Mary and Dick Steudle's 125-year-old home is surrounded by gardens, wide lawns, and views of the Kilkenny and Waumbec Mountains. The house itself offers three guest rooms with private bath plus a large formal dining room and a living room with a large, fieldstone fireplace. A separate housekeeping lodge with its own kitchen and stone fireplace sleeps up to eight people. There is also a room with private bath

STARK VILLAGE

Robert Kozlow

**Philbrook Farm Inn** (603-466-3831), North Road, Shelburne 03581. Open May 1 through October 31 and December 26 through March 31. Back in 1861, when Susannah and Harvey Philbrook began hosting summer boarders, "guest farms" were as common as B&Bs are today. Sited as it is above a floodplain on the Androscoggin River and circled by magnificent mountains, this one prospered.

"Every generation has added a piece," notes Connie Philbrook, a member of the fourth generation to operate the inn that's now three stories high and rambles far from its original 1830s core. In the 1890s several summer "cottages" were built, each large enough to sleep a family of eight. Resort amenities eventually came to include an outdoor pool and lawn games. Guests began returning in winter to snowshoe and then to ski at Sunday River and Wildcat Mountain (both 20-minute drives but in opposite directions).

While it's definitely not for the Jacuzzi set, this 18-room inn offers far more than firm mattresses and private baths. Guest rooms are comfortable as well as gracefully old-fashioned, curtained in organdy, papered in delicate flowers, and furnished with the kind of hand-me-downs for which most innkeepers would kill.

Parlors meander on and on, and everything in them has a story. Standing lamps in the living room turn out to be muskets (one from the War of 1812, the other from the Civil War); a closet is stuffed with jigsaw puzzles cut by grandfather Augustus. Connie recounts how people laughed when her parents paneled the large, handsome dining room in pine, considered junk wood at the time. Your hosts are Connie Leger and her sister Nancy Philbrook, along with Connie's children Ann Leger and Larry Leger. They have been told that theirs is the country's oldest inn continuously operated by the same family.

Dinner is served by reservation (6:30–7:30 PM). It's hearty New England fare, usually soup and a roast with vegetables plus a relish tray (BYOB). Breakfast is memorable for the littlest, lightest of doughnuts, baked that morning by Nancy.

Although no longer a working farm, the property is still 1,000 acres of

Philbrook Farm Inn

*HOLIDAY INN*, A WATERCOLOR PAINTING OF THE PHILBROOK FARM INN BY OWNER ANN LEGER, 1986

fields and wooded trails, surrounded by White Mountain National Forest. A time warp outside as well as in, it's a difficult place to leave.

In summer you can swim in the barnyard pool, and in winter there is snowshoeing or cross-country skiing There are two one-room and four larger cottages with kitchens and up to five bedrooms. All have a fireplace and living room. MAP rates include a full breakfast and single-entrée New England dinner with breads and pastries baked daily. Rates per couple are $125–140 MAP, $99–124 B&B; housekeeping cottages for up to eight people are $750 a week. Single rates also available. Pets are accepted in summer in the cottages.

in the barn. Guests have access to a Jacuzzi and in summer, a heated swimming pool. $55–70 per couple with breakfast; $200 per weekend or $400 per week for the lodge (no breakfast).

*Elsewhere*

**Stark Village Inn** (603-636-2644), just across the covered bridge off Route 110, west of Milan or east of Groveton (mailing address: R.F.D. 1, Box 389, Groveton 03582). Open summers, weekends, and vacation weeks. The cover of this book pictures the view from this classic New England home: the church and a covered bridge spanning the upper Ammonoosuc River. The old restored farmhouse, furnished with antiques and comfortable furniture, has three rooms—two with double beds and all with private bath. A long, rambling living room overlooks the river and is filled with books and magazines. Nearby is trout fishing, hiking, bicycling, cross-country skiing, skating on the river, or snowmobiling. For $50 a double room, $30 a single (tax included!), innkeeper Nancy Spaulding throws in a full breakfast.

**Magalloway River Inn** (603-482-9883), Route 16, Wentworth Localion, Errol 03579. Bob and Suzanne Setner's trim white, 19th-century farmhouse is a hospitable oasis offering rooms with private baths for $69.85 per couple, $91.45 for four.

**MOTELS** Gorham is home to several motels. **Town and Country Motor Inn** (603-466-3315; 1-800-325-4386), Route 2 in Shelburne just east of Gorham, has 160 air-conditioned rooms with a restaurant, health club, indoor pool, whirlpool, and steam bath. Rates are $56–78 for two.

On Route 2 in Jefferson the **Evergreen Motel** (603-586-4449; open mid-May through the Columbus Day weekend) offers 18 units, air-conditioning, TV, swimming pool, and coffee shop; it's across the street from Santa's Village.

**Lantern Motor Inn and Campground** (603-586-7151), open May through October, has 30 units with air-conditioning, TV, pool, hot tub, playground, and camping.

**Coos Motor Inn** (603-788-3079) is an attractive new 41-room motel in the middle of town. Amenities include a 24-hour Laundromat and continental breakfast; air-conditioned rooms with two double beds, phone, cable TV. Rates: $55–130 (for a two-room suite).

**Cabot Motor Inn & Restaurant** (603-788-3346), 200 Portland Street, Lancaster 03584. Located a mile east of downtown Lancaster on Route 2, a 55-room motor inn with an indoor pool, sauna, Jacuzzi, game and fitness room, and locally popular restaurant. All rooms have phone and cable TV. $45–65 in the older motel building across the road, $65–75 in the newer building.

**Lancaster Motor Inn** (603-788-4921; 1-800-834-3244), 112 Main Street, Lancaster 03584. You'll find 33 clean, comfortable, middle-of-town rooms, along with some efficiency and family units with sleep sofas. All have TV, VCR, and phone; a continental breakfast is served. The motel caters to snowmobilers in winter. $49–70.

**The Errol Motel** (603-482-3256), Route 26, Errol 03579, is open year-round and has eight rooms and three housekeeping units. Snowmobile trails from the motel connect with all local trails. Rates are $37 per person, $48 per couple, $53 for three. Housekeeping units are $7 more.

**OTHER LODGING** **Phillips Brook Backcountry Recreation Area** (1-800-872-4578; www.phillipsbrook.org). The mailing address is c/o Timberland Trails, Inc., P.O. Box 1076, Conway 03818, but the location is 3.2 miles down the Paris Road, off Route 110, 5 miles east of Stark and 12 miles east of the West Milan Store—in other words, the middle of the woods. Geared to year-round nonmotorized recreation: snowshoeing, dogsledding, and skiing in winter, mountain biking and canoeing in warm-weather months. Sited on 24,000 acres of leased land, 75 miles of marked trails (groomed once a week in winter) and 11 yurts are spaced along at distances of 0.5 to 5.5 miles apart. Guests drive drive to the lodge, located on Phillips Pond (summer canoeing and swimming). BYO food and sleeping bags. The yurts sleep six ($28 per person; $135 for the place). The lodge ($55 per person) sleeps 8 to 12 in private rooms, sharing two baths (showers), a community kitchen, and wood-fired hot tub.

**Colonial Comfort Inn** (603-466-2732; 1-800-470-4224; www.hikersparadise.com) in Gorham caters to hikers with three dorm-style rooms sharing three kitchens and baths; $14 per person.

**CAMPGROUNDS** For details on reserving sites at the the following state-operated campgrounds, see www.nhparks.state.nh.us, or check out *State Parks* in "What's Where."

**Milan Hill State Park,** Route 110B (off Route 16), Milan. A small park with 24 primitive camping sites, picnic tables, and a playground. A fire tower atop the 1,737-foot-high hill offers sweeping views of the North Country and into Canada. Camping and day-use fees charged.

**Mollidgewock State Park** (603-482-3373), Errol 03579. Open mid-May through Columbus Day. Located about 3 miles south of Errol village, in the Thirteen-Mile Woods Scenic Area. There are 42 somewhat primitive tent sites with picnic tables, fireplaces, water, and outhouses, but they are beside the river and perfect for fishing and canoeing. For reservations, call 603-271-3628.

**Umbagog Lake State Park** (603-482-7795), Route 26, Errol. Mid-May through mid-September. Formerly a private campground, this park now offers a store, boat rentals, showers, laundry facilities, housekeeping cabins, and 38 campsites as well as 30 primitive sites accessible only by boat (rentals available). Campers must bring tents and food; there are picnic tables and fireplaces. See Lake Umbagog **National Wildlife Refuge** under *Green Space.*

**Moose Brook State Park** (603-466-3860), Jimtown Road, off Route 2, Gorham. Mid-May through mid-October. This small park has a large outdoor pool (known for its cold water), a small beach, 58 tent sites, a store, and showers. Camping and day-use fees charged.

**Maidstone State Park** (802-676-3930) in the Vermont town of Brunswick. Open daily Memorial Day through Labor Day. Easily accessible from North Stratford. Five miles south of Bloomfield on Route 102, then 5 miles on a dirt road, this is a forest of maple, beech, and hemlock around a large lake, with a beach, picnic area, rental boats, picnic shelter, hiking trails, and 83 campsites, including 37 lean-tos.

Also see WMNF **Dolly Copp Campground** under *Lodging—Campgrounds* in "Jackson and Pinkham Notch." It's on Route 16 south of Gorham.

## ✱ Where to Eat

DINING OUT **Libby's Bistro** (603-466-5330), 111 Main Street, Gorham. Open Wednesday through Saturday 5:30–9 PM; also Tuesday in summer. Closed late October until Thanksgiving. Reservartions are a must. Chef-owner Liz Jackson worked for two summers as Julia Childs's prep chef before returning to her hometown and turning the vintage-1902 Gorham Savings Bank into an attractive 12-table restaurant that's drawing patrons from throughout the North Country. The half a dozen entrées change frequently, but you might dine on pan-roasted boneless breast of duck *au poivre* with shredded duck confit, red wine, orange, and sage sauce, and sweet potato cake. Entrées $16.95–20.95.

**Inn at Whitefield** (603-837-2760), Route 3, Whitefield. Open for lunch and dinner daily June through mid-October; closed Sunday night and all Monday in winter. Italian, regional, and Continental fare in pleasant surroundings conveniently located next to the Weathervane Theatre. Moderately priced.

**The Spalding Inn** (603-837-2572), Mountain View Road, Whitefield. Open mid-June through mid-October. Reservations. The menu changes daily, but the multicourse dinner usually offers of five entrées, perhaps roasted duck with brandy, chutney, and almonds, or fork-tender Yankee pot roast. Dinner is served with white napery in a sunny yellow-papered dining room. Entrées $14.95–22.95.

**Mountain View Grand** (603-837-2100), Mountain View Road, Whitefield. At this writing Juliet's, the formal restaurant at the newly renovated resort hotel, has not as yet opened, so we must leave you to judge for yourself. The space is divided into three gardenside rooms (the hotel's grand old oval dining room is now the hotel's grand ballroom).

EATING OUT

*In Gorham*

**Wilfred's** (603-466-2380), 117 Main Street. Open daily except Wednesday for lunch and dinner until 9 PM. Turkey in every conceivable form is the specialty for which the Piattoni family has been known for many years. Our turkey potpie turned out to be better than in a pot: a thick, tender mix of turkey, stuffing, and veggies with a light popover-type pastry on the side. There are other options on the menu. The **News Room Pub** in back is a local gathering spot.

**Loaf Around Bakery** (603-466-2706), 19 Exchange Street. Open 7 AM–2 PM except Tuesday and Wednesday. Unfortuantely, we arrived at 1:40 and missed what local residents assure us is the very best place to breakfast or lunch in the North Country. Soups are the specialty. The black bean and squash/pumpkin are (we hear) to die for. Breads are also highly rated. An attractive storefront, this is not a quick in-and-out place.

**Welsh's** (603-466-2206), 88 Main Street. Open daily 5:30 AM–3 PM; "all you can eat" Sunday brunch 8 AM–2 PM. Since 1898 this has been a downtown fixture, obviously expanding until it's a bit cavernous and geared to bus groups. Still, it's a good bet for a variety of omelets, a quick fish sandwich (real fish, real batter), or a grilled bacon and cheese.

**Mr. Pizza** (603-466-5573), Route 2. Open until 9 PM. This looks and feel like a chain but it isn't and, judging from the number of vehicles always parked here, it's the local hot spot. A family restaurant with a full menu ranging from burgers and pizza to surf-and-turf with a choice of salads; cocktails served.

**Yokohama Restaurant** (603-466-2501), 288 Main Street. Serves lunch and dinner; closed Monday. A longtime-popular American-Oriental eatery. Moderately priced.

### *In Berlin*

**The Northland Dairy Bar and Restaurant** (603-752-6210), Route 16. Located just north of the city and popular with canoeists and hikers, the eatery features fresh seafood, sandwiches, and its own fresh-made ice cream and pastries.

### *In Whitefield*

**Grandma's Kitchen** (603-837-2527), Route 3. Open 6 AM–9 PM. One of those great roadside places: a screened porch, a U-shaped counter, immaculate, good for homemade chowders, open-faced sandwiches, and Grape-Nut pudding.

### *In Jefferson/Lancaster*

**Lancaster SS Restaurant** (603-788-2802), 70 Main Street. Casual, family atmosphere with wooden booths, American and Chinese food. An upstairs pub has pool tables and entertainment.

**Cabot Inn** (603-788-3346), in the motel by that name, Route 2 west of downtown. Open 5 AM–8 PM. All the basics.

**Common Ground Café** (603-788-3773), 55 Main Street. Open Sunday through Thursday 9 AM–8 PM, Friday 9 AM–3 PM, closed Saturday. An adjunct to Simon the Tanner sports and shoe store (see *Selective Shopping*) operated by the Twelve Tribes. Good for soups, sandwiches, and baked goods.

**Water Wheel** (603-586-4313), Route 2, Jefferson. Open daily June through October 6 AM–2 PM, otherwise closed Tuesday and Wednesday. Breakfast and lunch.

### *North on Route 3*

**Miss GeeGee's** (603-636-6237), Route 3 North, Groveton. Opens at 5 AM. Rated by an intrepid group of locally based hikers as the best breakfast of an alleged 49 tested places in the North Country. GeeGee's omelet gets high marks, but the day's blackboard specials are usually a good bet.

**T's Diner** (603-922-3406), open from 5 AM weekdays; from 6 Saturday, and 8 Sunday. Closes at 7 PM nightly. The *T* is for Theresa, who makes the soups and pastries daily.

### *In Errol*

**The Beggin' Dawg Restaurant & Pub** (603-482-3468), junction of Routes 16 and 26. On a snowy Sunday in January we waited more than an hour to even place our order here—not because the staff weren't friendly and efficient, but because this also happens to be at the junction of two major snowmobile trails. Winter weekdays and snowmobile season aside, no problem. This is a popular local gathering place any day, with a downstairs pub.

## ✷ Entertainment

**Weathervane Theatre** (603-837-9322; www.weathervanetheatre.org), Route 3, Whitefield. Open July and August. A repertory theater (since 1966) in an old barn featuring old favorites, musicals, comedies, and mysteries.

**St. Kieran's Community Center for the Arts** (603-752-1820; 603-752-2880), 162 Madison Avenue, Berlin. Plays, concerts, and other live entertainment.

**Royal Cinema I & II,** Green Square, Route 16 north of downtown Berlin, shows first run films.

## ✷ Selective Shopping

ANTIQUES **Israel River Trading Post** (603-788-2880), 69 Main Street, Lancaster. Open Tuesday through Saturday 10 AM–4 PM. Antiques, auctions.

**Potato Barn Antiques** (603-636-2611), Route 3, Northumberland. Billed as the largest group shop in northern New Hampshire: two floors of vintage clothing, costume jewelry, china, and paper.

ART GALLERIES **Old Mill Studio** (603-837-8778), on the common, Whitefield. Open Tuesday through Sunday 11 AM–6 PM. Tucked into a corner of the common overlooking the river, representing well over 100 local artists, also offering classes.

**William Rugh Art Gallery** (603-788-5531), 18 Evergreen Drive off Route 2 east of Lancaster. Look for the yellow gallery sign. Open weekends 10 AM–4 PM. Representing a selection of well-established new Hampshire artists, including Widmayer and Thayer.

BOOKS **Wonderland Book Store** (603-466-2123), 10-A Exchange Street. Open Monday through Friday 9:30 AM–5:30 PM, Saturday 10 AM–4 PM, Sunday by chance. A first-rate independent bookstore.

CRAFTS **Northern Reflections** (603-788-4039), 81 Main Street, Berlin. Sandra Berish makes and repairs stained glass, also offers classes and supplies.

MAPLE PRODUCERS **Bisson's Maple Sugar House** (603-752-1298), 61 Cates Hill, accessible both from Gorham and Berlin. High on Cates Hill with panoramic views, this has been a family-operated business since 1921. The wood-fired evaporator is also used to make maple taffy, butter, and sugar.

**Fuller's Sugarhouse** (603-788-2719), 267 Main Street, Lancaster. Open year-round. Dave and Patti Fuller operate a sugarhouse and country store selling maple products and local specialty items.

SPORTS STORES **Moriah Sports** (603-466-5050; www.moriahsports.com), 101 Main Street, Gorham. Open Tuesday through Thursday 10 AM–6 PM, Friday until 7 PM, Saturday 9 AM–5 PM; closed Sunday and Monday in winter. Snowshoes are the specialty, some 50 different kinds! Mike McCucci also rents as well as sells mountain bikes, and sells Walden touring kayaks along with backcountry equipment. He publishes a brochure guide to local hiking and snowshoeing trails and offers nighttime snowshoe treks. Check out the bargain basement with close-out items reduced up to 70 percent.

**Gorham Hardware & Sports Center** (603-466-2312). A big, old-fashioned hardware store with plenty of things you may have forgotten if you are camping. Also a full line of sports equipment.

**Cotes** (603-482-7777), 25 Main Street, Errol. The largest establishment in town, a sporting goods selling guns, fishing tackle and flies, bows and arrows, and much more. Also rents canoes, kayaks, and snowmobiles. Needless to say, this is information central for fishermen. The neighboring hardware store (same ownership) supplies North Woods camps and campers for hundreds of surrounding miles.

OTHER **Simon the Tanner** (603-788-3773), 55 Main Street, Lancaster. Open the same hours as the Common Ground Café (see *Eating Out*), which it adjoins. An extensive and sophisticated shoe and casual clothing store operated by the Twelve Tribes.

## ✷ Special Events

*January:* **Winterfest** in Berlin/Gorham: parade, winter sports.

*First weekend in June:* **Moose Mania Weekend** (603-752-6060; 1-800-992-7480). A variety of events in Gorham and Berlin celebrate New Hampshire's largest wild animal.

*Late June:* **Old Time Fiddlers' Contest** (603-636-1325), Whitcomb Field, Stark. Bring a picnic lunch and a blanket or lawn chairs, and enjoy the music of dozens of fiddlers. Food available. Admission fee.

*July–August:* **Weathervane Theatre** (see *Entertainment*).

*July:* **Androscoggin Source to Sea**—6 days of canoeing, kayaking, and related events

*Early August:* **Old Home Days** in the tiny towns of Milan and Stewartstown.

*Labor Day weekend:* **Lancaster Fair** (603-837-2770) is a real old-fashioned country fair, highlighted by non-betting harness racing. A large midway, food, and thrill rides plus 4-H animal judging competition, grange exhibits, displays of vegetables and handcrafts, and ox and horse pulling. Admission fee; children under 12 free.

*Late September:* **Great North Woods Lumberjack Championships,** Northern Forest Heritage Park, Berlin.

# THE CONNECTICUT LAKES AND DIXVILLE NOTCH, INCLUDING COLEBROOK AND PITTSBURG

Two destinations draw travelers to the top of New Hampshire: The Connecticut Lakes in Pittsburg and the Balsams in Dixville Notch.

In all there are four Connecticut Lakes, and below them Lake Frances (created in the 1930s). Each is successively larger and lower in elevation and connected by the nascent, stream-sized Connecticut River as it begins its journey down the length of New England. The lakes are strung along some 22 miles of Route 3 between the village of Pittsburg and the Canadian border, the stem of a backwoods system of timber company roads.

This magnificent semiwilderness has been known for more than a century to anglers and hunters, sustained in recent winters by snowmobilers. Now word is spreading, thanks chiefly to its reputation as a moose mecca, promoted through the colorful North Country Moose Festival, held the last weekend in August. Visitors are discovering the area's exceptional bird life, its hiking and mountain bike trails, its wilderness cross-country and snowshoeing possibilities, and the expanses of quiet water so inviting to canoeists and kayakers. Lodging options are surprisingly varied and plentiful, ranging from classic lodges like The Glen and Tall Timber Lodge through rental camps to primitive and not-so-primitive campgrounds.

This entire Connecticut Lakes area lies within Pittsburg, New Hampshire's largest and northernmost town. With more than 300 mostly wooded and watery square miles and a population of less than 1,000, Pittsburg retains a frontier atmosphere. Many residents work in the woods and spend their spare hours hunting and fishing, often displaying a spirit of independence that goes back to 1832 when portions of this town became an independent nation called the Indian Stream Republic. The name comes from a tributary of the Connecticut River, but the nation evolved when local settlers, disgruntled by boundary squabbling between Canada and the United States, solved the problem by seceding (at a town meeting) from both countries. They created their own stamps, coins, and government, but their independence lasted only a few years before the Treaty of Washington in 1842 put the republic back in New Hampshire.

Robert Kozlow

A COLEBROOK FARM

From Pittsburg two roads (Routes 3 and 145), both exceptionally scenic, run south to bustling, friendly Colebrook, a crossroads shopping center (junction of east–west Route 26 from Errol as well as north–south Route 3 from Lancaster) for the Vermont communities of Canaan and Beecher Falls (site of Ethan Allen's huge furniture factory) as well as Columbia, Stewartstown, Errol, Pittsburg, and Dixville Notch.

Not so much a town as it is a place (since its tiny population is mostly connected with the Balsams resort), Dixville gets a moment of fame every 4 years when all 30 voters stay up past midnight to cast the first votes in the presidential election. The northernmost of New Hampshire's notches, Dixville is worth the ride just for views of this rugged, narrow pass surrounding the Balsams, the grandest of all New England's grand old hotels. It draws repeat winter- and summer-season patrons from every corner of the country, for a week at a time. It's been lucky in its ownership. In 1954, when it came up for auction, the hotel was acquired by Neil Tillotson, a descendant of Dixville Notch homesteaders. An inventor and inventive businessman, Tillotson (who died at age 102 in 2001) installed a rubber balloon factory in the former garage (still producing millions of medical exam gloves weekly). Even if you are not a registered guest here, be sure to stop. The palatial resort—its dining rooms, golf courses, and 15,000-acre property webbed with hiking, mountain biking, and cross-country ski trails—welcomes visitors.

GUIDANCE **North Country Chamber of Commerce** (603-237-8939; 1-800-698-8939; www.northcountrychamber.org), Box 1, Colebrook 03576. Open year-round weekdays, weekends in summer at this writing, the chamber serving Colebrook and Pittsburg is based at the **New Hampshire Information Center,** Route 3, 1.5 miles north of Colebrook. Other helpful web sites: www.ctrivertravel.net; www.nhconnlakes.com, and www.greatnorthwoods.org.

*Note:* Pick up a current local map at a local store. We bought *Connecticut Lakes Region Pittsburg, NH Road & Trail Guide,* printed in Colebrook, showing local woods roads (which change each year) and pinpointing landmarks like Magalloway Mountain and Garfield Falls. The ***Colebrook Chronicle*** (free) is an excellent way of tuning in to the local scene, accessible online: www.colebrookchronicle.com.

**GETTING AROUND** *Crossing the border:* The U.S. Customs and Immigration Service maintains a point-of-entry station in Pittsburg on Route 3 at the international border (819-656-2261) open 24 hours, 7 days a week.

*Note*: Throughout this area, especially above the village of Pittsburg, moose are quite common—especially at dusk when they are least visible to vehicles. Proceed slowly.

**MEDICAL EMERGENCY 911** now works throughout the region.

**Upper Connecticut Valley Hospital** (603-237-4971), Corliss Lane (off Route 145), Colebrook. This little, well-equipped hospital is the health care center for a large area of northern New Hampshire, Quebec, Vermont, and Maine. At least one doctor has a private plane and makes house calls by air.

## ✷ To See

**MOOSE** See the introduction to "The Great North Woods." The local "Moose Alley" is Route 3 north from Pittsburg to the Canadian border; also see *Scenic Drives.* The annual North Country Moose Festival, held the last weekend in August, has become the region's biggest event, usually attracting more than 3,000 people, featuring a Moose Calling Contest, street fairs and dancing, barbecues, an antique car show, and a moose stew cook-off.

**SCENIC DRIVES Route 3 north** from Pittsburg. It's 22.5 miles from the village to the border, much of it through the Connecticut Lakes State Forest, a wooded corridor along both sides of Route 3, from the northern end of the First Connecticut Lake to the Canadian border. Lake Francis comes into view in the village of Pittsburg itself. Look for the turnoff for Lake Francis State Park, a right after the left turn for Back Lake (see *To Do—Swimming* and *Fishing,* as well as *Lodging* and *Dining Out*). First Connecticut Lake is next, sprinkled with lodges and cabins off the shore along Route 3 but uninterrupted forest on the far side. Note the lakeside picnic facilities. When you next see the Connecticut River itself, just south of the Second Connecticut Lake, it is a small stream. Note the Deer Mountain Campground (see *Lodging—Campgrounds*) next on your left and finally the Third Connecticut Lake. Even in mid-August the light is northern here, and the sky seems very close. Third Lake is smaller than the others, with wooded mountains rolling away to the east and north.

**The Source.** A small sign just north of the U.S. Customs Station marks the start of the half-mile trail to the 78.1-acre watershed surrounding the pond-sized Fourth Connecticut Lake. Owned and maintained by the New Hampshire Chapter of The Nature Conservancy, it's a surprisingly rugged trail, and you should allow 2 hours to adequately enjoy the round trip. (Perhaps it seemed more of an expedition the day we attempted it because of muddy conditions and the fact that my companion was little more than 4 feet high, with her arm in a cast.) The first 15 minutes are the steepest and well worth the effort as you scramble back and forth along the ridge between Canadian and American rocks, with views into the Oz-like Quebec Valley that lies just north, a pastoral mix of farms and woods around the village of Chartierville. At 0.1 mile the Conservancy's trail turns south from the international boundary, and you follow it 0.1 mile to the north end of the lake. The 2.5-acre pond lies in a wooded hollow at 2,670 feet elevation. According to The Nature Conservancy's pamphlet guide, it's a "northern acidic mountain tarn, a remnant from the post-glacial tundra ecosystem and unusual in New Hampshire." A 0.5-mile path circles the pond, and you can step back and forth across the stream that marks the first few feet of the river's 410-mile course. The actual outlet varies, determined by resident beavers. The entire loop is 1.7 miles.

**Magnetic Hill** in Chartierville, Quebec. Continue 1 mile north of the border on Route 3, then 0.25 mile and turn around. A sign instructs you (in French) to put your vehicle in neutral and hold on while your car is pulled backward uphill. It's one of those things that are impossible to describe.

**Route 26** from Colebrook through Dixville Notch. Just east of Colebrook, Fish Hatchery Road departs Route 26 north for the Diamond Ponds and Coleman State Park. The road is paved most of the way, but several gravel side roads wind over and around the hills of East Colebrook, and one continues on to Stewartstown Hollow and Route 145 (see below). Route 26 continues to climb gradually into Dixville Notch where the castlelike Balsams Grand Hotel rises above Lake Gloriette, backed in turn by craggy Abenaki Mountain. The road continues to climb by Table Rock (see *To Do—Hiking*) and crests before spiraling down between sheer mountain walls. Note the picnic area on Flume Brook and, a bit farther west, the turnoff to the picnic area at Huntington Cascades. Route 26 continues 5 more miles to Errol, site of Umbagog Lake State Park (see "Northern White Mountains"). Route 26 south through Thirteen Mile Woods and the loop back via Route 110 to Route 3 takes you through uninterrupted timberlands (again, see "Northern White Mountains").

**Route 145** between Colebrook and Pittsburg is best driven from north to south for the sweeping view from Ben Young Hill. En route to and from Pittsburg, you will cross the 45th parallel, halfway between the North Pole and the equator. Dairy farms with red barns are impressive, dotting the hillsides and views. Beaver Brook Falls, just north of Colebrook on Route 145, is the local Niagara, with a picnic area maintained by the Kiwanis.

A WARNING SIGN AT THE BEGINNING OF "MOOSE ALLEY," ROUTE 3 NORTH OF PITTSBURG

Christina Tree

**HISTORICAL SOCIETIES** **Colebrook Area Historical Society** (603-237-4528; 603-237-4470), P.O. Box 32,

Colebrook. Open May through October, Saturday 10 AM–2 PM. Programs the second Thursday of every month. **Pittsburg Historical Society** (603-246-7233) maintains a museum in the town hall that's open for the July 4 Moose Festival, Old Home Day in August, and 1–3 PM on Saturday in July and August. In Canaan, Vermont, just over the bridge from West Stewartstown, the **Alice M. Ward Memorial Library**, open daily, houses the Canaan Historical Society's fascinating changing exhibits. The lovely yellow, Greek Revival building was built as a tavern in 1846 and said to have served for a while as the northernmost U.S. stop on the Underground Railroad. The **Poore Family Homestead Historic Farm Museum** (603-237-5500), Route 145 halfway between Colebrook and Pittsburg, is generally open June through September, weekdays 11 AM–1 PM, weekends 11 AM–4 PM, and for special events. The 1840s barn displays tools and daily household and farm equipment. The neighboring 1825 farmhouse on this 100-acre property is under restoration (suggested donation $4 per adult).

COVERED BRIDGES **The Columbia bridge** crosses the Connecticut River south of Colebrook, linking Columbia village with Lemington, Vermont. Pittsburg has three covered bridges: The **Pittsburg–Clarksville bridge,** 91 feet long, is off Route 3, 0.25 mile west of Pittsburg village; **Happy Corner bridge,** 86 feet long, is south of Route 3, 6 miles northeast of the village; **River Road bridge,** 57 feet long and one of the state's smallest covered bridges, is south of Route 3, 5.5 miles northeast of the village.

BOATERS ON LAKE GLORIETTE

Robert Kozlow

## ✷ To Do

**BOATING, INCLUDING CANOEING AND KAYAKING** Several lodges keep paddleboats moored on more than one lake for use by guests. Tall Timber Lodge rents kayaks for use on Back Lake and others. The Balsams offers kayak instruction on Lake Gloriette and guided tours on Umbagog Lake (see "Northern White Mountains").

On the **Connecticut River** paddlers put in at the Vermont end of the Canaan–West Stewartstown bridge off Route 3. The only difficult rapids (class II) in this area are below Columbia. They run for about 7.5 miles and cannot be navigated when the water is low. Paddlers are advised to check the *AMC River Guide: Vermont and New Hampshire* (AMC Books) and two free guides: *Boating on the Connecticut River,* a detailed guide available from the Connecticut River Joint Commissions (www.ctrivertravel.net), and *Canoeing on the Connecticut River.* See *Connecticut River* in "What's Where."

**FISHING** Fishing is what this area is about: Operators of most of the 14 or so lodges, motels, and campgrounds depend for their livelihoods on seekers of trout and salmon. The several Connecticut Lakes; Lake Francis; Back Lake; Hall, Indian, and Perry Streams; and the Connecticut River provide miles of shoreline and hundreds of acres of world-class fishing: trophy brook trout, giant browns, and landlocked salmon for both fly- and spin-fishermen. The 2.5-mile "Trophy Stretch" of the Connecticut River (good throughout the summer because of dam releases) is fly-fishing only. The trout season opens January 1 on streams and rivers, on the fourth Saturday in April through October 15 for lakes, but the best fishing months are May, June, and early fall. Most of the lodges provide guides, sell licenses, sell or rent tackle, rent boats, and will give fishing information. See www.colebrook-nh.com.

**Osprey Fishing Adventures** (603-922-3800; www.ospreyfishingadventures.com), P.O. Box 121, Colebrook 03576. Mid-June through Labor Day. The first fishing guide on this uppermost stretch of the Connecticut River, Ken Hastings is a biologist who teaches at Colebrook Academy in the "off-season." His 1- and 3-day fly-fishing trips use a special 14-foot, three-person MacKenzie-style drift boat and include the guide, fly-fishing instruction if requested, and lunch. Both Connecticut and Androscoggin River trips are tailored to meet clients' abilities.

**Tall Timber Lodge** (1-800-83-LODGE; www.TallTimber.com) offers boat rentals and sells a wide selection of flies. Inquire about fly-fishing school.

**Lopstick Outfitters and Guide Service** (1-800-538-6659; www.lopstick.com), First Connecticut Lake, Pittsburg. Fly-fishing shop, drift boat fishing.

**GOLF** **Panorama Golf Course** (603-255-4961), part of the Balsams Resort, Dixville Notch. This 18-hole, par-72 course, rolling over beautiful mountain slopes, was designed by Donald Ross in 1912. The lower nine-hole Coashaukee course is great for novices. Pro shop, lessons, and cart rentals; tee times are required.

**Colebrook Country Club** (603-237-5566), on Route 26, east of Colebrook village. A nine-hole, par-36 course.

PANORAMA GOLF COURSE AT THE BALSAMS

Robert Kozlow

**HIKING** See the trip to the Connecticut Lakes source under *To See—Scenic Drives*. Overlooking Colebrook from the Vermont side of the river is Monadnock Mountain, which rises steeply and offers a nice view from the summit fire tower. The trail begins in a driveway off Route 102 near the bridge between Colebrook and Lemington, Vermont. You may have to inquire at a residence to find the exact location of the trail.

**Table Rock** in Dixville Notch. Take Route 26 east 10 miles from Colebrook. There's a trailhead parking area on the right, behind the sign ENTERING DIXVILLE NOTCH STATE PARK.

**Mount Magalloway** (2 miles, 1½ hours)—at 3,360 feet, the highest peak in this neck of the woods—offers access to a fire tower. From First Connecticut Lake Dam, turn right just past Coon Brook onto a gravel road and follow LOOKOUT TOWER signs. Two trails, the Coot and the Bobcat, lead to the summit. Coot is quicker, but Bobcat is less strenuous. Bobcat is the recommended way down.

**Cohos Trail** (www.cohostrail.com). Running 159 miles north from Bartlett, the trail enters this region on Route 26 at Dixville Notch and runs due north to Pittsburg (it's possible to avoid the village entirely) and on up to the Canadian border.

**MOUNTAIN BIKING** There are miles and miles of woodland roads just right for mountain biking in this section of New Hampshire. Roads are unmarked for the most part, but inquire at **Ramblewood Cabins** (603-538-6948; see *Winter Sports—Cross-Country Skiing*) or **The Glen** (603-538-6500) for route assistance (see *Lodging—Inn*). **Tall Timber Lodge** (see *Lodging—Sporting Lodges*) rents mountain bikes.

**SWIMMING** **Back Lake.** A slide and sand beach are good for young children.

**Garfield Falls.** Definitely not for children. Ask locally about access to this beauty spot: a 40-foot drop in the East Branch of the Dead Diamond River with pools below.

## ✷ Winter Sports

**CROSS-COUNTRY SKIING** **The Balsams Grant Resort Hotel** (1-800-255-0600; in New Hampshire, 1-800-255-0800), Route 26, Dixville Notch. This 100 km network (73 km tracked) is one of New England's best-kept secrets. Elevations range from 1,820 feet at Lake Gloriette in front of the hotel to 2,686 feet at the summit of Keyser Mountain. The majority of the 35 trails generally can be skied even when far more famous White Mountain touring centers are brown or icy. Most trails are double-tracked and packed for skating, but a few remain narrow and ungroomed. Our favorite is Canal Trail, a 2 km corridor between tall balsams, following the turn-of-the-20th-century canal that still channels water from Mud Pond (where there's a warming hut) to the hotel. Rentals, lessons. Trail fee.

**Ramblewood Cabins and Campground** (603-538-6948), Route 3, Box 52, Pittsburg. Twenty-five km of groomed trails beside the First Connecticut Lake. Winter campers welcome.

*Note:* Lodging places can steer guests to miles of wilderness trails.

DOWNHILL SKIING **The Balsams Wilderness** (1-800-255-0600; in New Hampshire, 1-800-255-0800), Route 26, Dixville Notch. The most remote ski area in New Hampshire, with abundant natural snow, rare lift lines, and a country-club rather than commercial-ski-area feel. Geared to guests at the resort. *Lifts:* 4 (1 double chair, 2 T-bars, 1 surface). *Trails:* 14. *Vertical drop:* 1,000 feet. *Services:* Ski school, rentals, restaurant, child care. *Rates:* Free to inn guests, otherwise $30 per adult on weekends, $25 weekdays; $20 per junior weekends, $18 weekdays.

SNOWMOBILING More than 200 miles of groomed trails are maintained by the Pittsburg Ridge Runners alone, one of a dozen North County clubs, linking with trail systems in Maine, Vermont, and Quebec. From the Pittsburg lodges and Colebrook motels, the snowmobiler can head off after breakfast and have lunch in Maine or Canada, then return to the lodge for dinner. For maps and other information, contact the New Hampshire Snowmobile Association (603-224-8906; www.NHSA.com).

**Pathfinder Sno-Tours** (603-538-7001) offers tours with and without your own snowmboile. Rentals are also offered by **Pittsburg Motor Sports** (586-7123) and **Lopstick Snowmobile Rentals.**

## ✱ Lodging

RESORT **The Balsams Grand Resort Hotel** (1-800-255-0600; in New Hampshire, 1-800-255-0800), Route 26, Dixville Notch 03576. Open mid-May through mid-October and mid-December through March. Dating to 1866, this rambling hostelry could be a castle on the Rhine transported to the shores of Lake Gloriette. Towering beneath the jagged spires of Dixville Notch, the Balsams is one of this country's best remaining examples of the era of the grand resort. Outside, 15,000 acres of mostly wilderness celebrate nature's grandeur; inside, civilization reigns supreme. With more staff members than guests (up to 500 for 204 rooms) and a profusion of activities included in the American plan hospitality, the Balsams is a year-round destination resort for guests from throughout the country. Guests spend their days playing golf, hiking, and swimming in summer, and skiing downhill on the hotel's own 19-trail ski hill or cross-country on 95 km of high-elevation, dependably snow-covered trails in winter. With an additional 30-km-plus of snowshoeing trails, one way or another they steep themselves in the magnificence of these mountains.

All the resort's facilities are free for children with adult supervision, but there are a variety of special children's programs, including a daily summer camp and winter ski lessons. Baby-sitting is also provided for a reasonable fee.

In the evening the gentlemen don jackets and the ladies dresses. Even the children—of whom there are usually a number—seem to sense what's expected of them in this opulent world of intricately carved teak, ginger jars, potted palms, and endless carpeting. Youngsters find their way (via an ornate, vintage-1912 Otis elevator) to the library with its tiers of books and piles of puzzles. Some never make it to the pool tables, TV, or game rooms. For adults there is evening music in La Cave, off the lobby, in the Wilderness Lounge, the ballroom, and during dinner.

Dinner is the big event of the day. At 6 PM promptly, the leaded-glass doors of the dining room slide open and guests begin strolling in to eye samples of each dish on the menu—appetizers through desserts—all exhibited on a specially designed, two-tiered table topped by silver candelabra. Dishes on view might include smoked mussels with marinated lentils and basil emulsion; sautéed veal forestière with Marsala and herbed tomato sauce; diced red bliss potatoes with bacon, mushrooms, and asparagus spears; and pecan whiskey pie. The evening's entrée "for the junior gourmet" is also displayed. The public is welcome for all meals, served table d'hôte; breakfast $13, luncheon $20, dinner $38. Luncheon also is served in the Panorama Country Club, which affords a sweeping view across the Great North Woods.

Most guests come for a week, beginning with Sunday, the night that Steve Barba, president of the Balsams Corporation, welcomes guests with a talk about the evolution of the hotel: from the 25-room Dix House, opened in 1866, to an 1890s resort with a human-made lake and nine-hole golf course, to the present combination of build-

THE BALSAMS GRAND RESORT HOTEL

Kim Grant

ings—the rambling white-clapboard, green-shuttered Dixville House and the six-story, stucco Hampshire House, New Hampshire's first steel-frame and masonry multistory structure when it opened in 1918. Barba himself came to the resort when he was 13 to work as a caddie. Over the years his role has changed, but his idea of service with a personal touch remains true to what he first learned on the golf course.

Over the last few years most guest rooms have been totally renovated, from plumbing and windows to flower-patterned wallpaper, and their number has been reduced as rooms were merged to create sitting areas and new, larger bathrooms. Closets remain deep and sizable, and the windows are still curtained in organdy, the better to let in the amazing view.

In contrast to most large hotels, guest and conference seasons are strictly segregated. Rates are on a per-person, per-diem basis and range $115–250, plus tax and service, depending on day and room. Summer rates include all meals; in winter, it's breakfast and dinner. Inquire about special ski and summer week and children's rates ($10 times the age of the child).

INN 🐾 ✐ **The Glen** (603-538-6500; 1-800-455-GLEN; www.theglen.org), First Connecticut Lake, Pittsburg 03592. Open early May through mid-October. Since 1962 this former private estate (vintage 1904) has been catering to hunters, anglers, and vacationers. Novices to the Great North Woods will feel at home here, thanks to longtime innkeeper Betty Falton, who is so naturally hospitable that everyone immediately feels like family—the kind of family who appreciates the area's excellent birding ("more species of birds than anywhere else in New Hampshire") and moose-watching, mountain biking, and canoeing as well as fishing. Roughly 60 percent of the patrons are, of course, here to fish (staff will serve your catch at one of the three home-cooked meals), but there's no pressure to do anything; just tuning in to the inn's 180-acre lakeside property can absorb a week. The main lodge, with its large stone fireplace and long porch, offers six rooms with twins and doubles with private bath. Seven cabins, some accommodating up to seven people, are scattered along the lake; the two up behind the lodge also have water views. Boats and motors for rent. Rates include all three meals (lunches can be boxed): $85–100 per person, discounts for 7 days or more; children 4–16 are one-half adult rates. Pets are permitted in the cabins.

SPORTING LODGES 🐾 ✐ **Tall Timber Lodge** (603-538-6651; 1-800-835-6343; www.talltimber.com), 231 Beach Road, Back Lake, off Route 3, Pittsburg 03592. Open year-round. Founded in 1946 and owned by the Caron family since 1982, this is New Hampshire's top sporting camp. With guide services, a tackle shop, and a fly-fishing school, it's a base place for novices as well as seasoned fishers. Guests are also encouraged to try kayaking (rental kayaks), mountain biking (rental mountain bikes), and sledding (rental snowmobiles). Cross-country skiing, hiking, boating, and birding venues are researched by the staff, who all seem to have the same last name. Connie ("Mom"), Chuck, Judy, Cindy, and David Caron operate the lodge and, happily, each seems to have a different area of expertise. In the lodge itself are eight air-conditioned rooms (two with private bath) that share their own

TALL TIMBER LODGE

Christina Tree

upstairs common room with wet bar. The 18 two- to four-bedroom cabins, most lakefront, range from rustically comfortable 1940s "camps" to house-sized retreats with cathedral ceiling, stone fireplace, two-person Jacuzzi, color television, and a wall of glass overlooking the lake. Rates per room in the cottages range $70–315 per night, $685–1,360 per week. Lodge rooms are $35–75. Children under 6 are free; those 6–16 are prorated by age. **The Rainbow Grille and Tavern** (see *Dining Out*) is open nightly in-season, and breakfast is served daily. Inquire about a variety of packages.

**Lopstick Lodge and Cabins** (1-800-538-5569; www.lopstick.com), Route 3 at the First Connecticut Lake, offers 13 housekeeping cabins with one to four bedrooms, porches, and views. Some feature a stone fireplaces or gas fireplace, and a couple have Jacuzzi. One is on 6 acres beside Perry Stream. $76–235 per cabin. Also see *To Do—Fishing*.

🐾 **Timberland Lodge and Cabins** (603-538-6613; 1-800-545-6613; www.timberlandlodge.com), First Connecticut Lake, Pittsburg 03592. Up the road from The Glen, also on the lake. Several of the 25 cabins offer an unobstructed view, but the older, more reasonably priced cabins are back behind the house/office. No central dining facilties. Swimming (private beach), boating, fishing, and birdwatching. Pets are welcome. $42–76 per person; $35–64 for stays of 5 or more days.

**BED & BREAKFASTS** **Room with a View** (603-237-5106; 1-800-499-1506), Forbes Road, Colebrook 03576. Open all year. It's a ways up and about, but worth it to reach this B&B set high in a meadow with a 360-degree view of Dixville Notch and the Mohawk River Valley. Innkeepers Charles and Sonja Sheldon have furnished the seven guest rooms (two with private bath; the others share two baths) with bright contemporary quilts that Sonja made herself. The country kitchen boasts a

Tulikivi soapstone stove to warm both toes and tummies. Best of all is the outdoor hot tub on the wraparound porch where you can all but reach out and touch the stars above. Hundreds of miles of trails beckon snowmobilers and mountain bikers. No smoking. Full breakfast cooked to order. $70–75 for two, $15 for additional person in room.

**Monadnock B&B** (603-237-8216), corner of Monadnock and Bridge Streets, Colebrook 03576. Open year-round. This 1916 bungalow on a residential street in Colebrook retains its original woodwork, and innkeeper Barbara Woodard has furnished it with an eclectic mix (her collection of nutcrackers march up the front stairs). There are three guest rooms, one with a half bath; two share a full bath. A common room opens onto a balcony; guests can use a fridge, coffeemaker, and microwave. Four more guest rooms in the finished basement open off a shared room with a TV. Bicyclists, bird-watchers, and snowmobilers are especially welcome. A hearty breakfast is included in $70 per couple, $40 single.

**MOTELS** Colebrook motels include the **Northern Comfort** (603-237-4440); the **Colebrook Country Club and Motel** (603-237-5566), which also has a dining room and a lounge; and the **Colebrook House** (603-237-5521; 1-800-626-7331), a small village hotel with motel section, lounge, and dining room.

**CAMPGROUNDS** **Coleman State Park** (603-237-4560) is in Stewartstown, but it is most easily reached from Route 26 east of Colebrook. Open May through mid-October. There are 30 tent-camping sites, a recreation building, and picnic tables. Fishing is good in the Diamond Ponds and surrounding streams. No reservations. Fee charged.

**Lake Francis State Park** (603-538-6965), off Route 3 on River Road, 7 miles north of Pittsburg village. Open from mid-May through Columbus Day. This small park beside the 2,000-acre, human-made lake has 40 primitive campsites, a boat-launching ramp, and a picnic area. A popular camping site for anglers and canoeists. No reservations. Fee charged.

**Deer Mountain Campground** (603-538-6955), Route 3, 5.5 miles south of the Canadian border. State-run, no electricity, spring for water, earth toilets, 22 primitive sites.

*Note:* There are also half a dozen private campgrounds in the area.

## * Where to Eat

**DINING OUT** **The Balsams** (603-255-0800; 1-800-255-0800; www.thebalsams.com), Route 16, Dixville Notch. For nonregistered guests dinner reservations are required, along with dress appropriate for the formal dining room and for the exceptional meal ($40 prix fixe). Dishes are displayed on a central table. Appetizers might include chilled spiced crabcake with avocado mousse, followed by a vegetable barley soup, spinach salad, veal Oscar, a fruit plate, and white chocolate hazelnut pudding. The choices as well as the courses are many, and a children's menu is offered. Dinner entitles patrons to attend the night's show and dancing (reserve your table at the nightclub when you reserve dinner). Lunch ($20) is buffet-style in the dining room. Sandwiches are also available in the clubhouse at the Panorama Golf Course.

**Rainbow Grille at Tall Timber Lodge** (603-538-6651; 1-800-83-LODGE), 231 Beach Road, Back Lake, Pittsburg. Dinner 5:30–6 PM Monday and Tuesday, until 9 PM the rest of the week. A standout place to dine in a rustic-style lakeside lodge. You might begin with pheasant sausage flavored with brandy and hazelnuts. The house specialty is rainbow trout served several ways (try it pan-fried with Grand Marnier); also baby back ribs and an extensive selection of Black Angus beef. Entrées $15.95–27.50, but you can also dine on soup and a grilled chicken Caesar salad. Children's menu and full bar. Reservations suggested.

**Sutton Place** (603-237-8842), 152 Main Street, Colebrook. Open Tuesday through Saturday 5:30–8:30 PM. Here's fine, intimate dining in the front rooms of a Queen Anne–style house. Chicken cordon bleu to steak *au poivre,* with seafood, a few Italian specialties, and a light menu with smaller portions for the diet-conscious. Reservations suggested, especially on weekends. Moderately priced.

EATING OUT **Bessie's Diner** (603-266-3310), 166 Gale Street, Canaan. Open weekdays from 6 AM, Saturday from 7, and Sunday from 8; closes at 8 PM every night. Admittedly we're suckers for cheap and friendly, but Vernon and Bonnie Crawford's place is so pleasant and wholesome—ditto for the food—that we can't rave enough. On our last visit we went for the special: cabbage soup and a tuna fish casserole (real tuna with rice, beans, and onions). The menu includes burgers, 30 different kinds of sandwiches, open-faced bagel-wiches (try the Grump-Fish), subs, and wraps. Poutines (Quebec-style french fries with gravy and cheese curds) are a specialty; a wide choice of dinner choices average $6.75. Service is fast and friendly. Wine and beer. "Cow Licks," an ice cream window, operates summers.

**Happy Corner Café** (603-538-1144), Route 3 Pittsburg. Open Sunday through Thursday 6:30 AM–8 PM, until 9 PM on Friday and Saturday. Sharing the parking lot with Youngs, the big supply source for this backcountry, this is a cheerful place specializing in big breakfasts—the usual choices plus biscuits with sausage, gravy, eggs, and homefries ($4.95)—soups (always French onion), sandwiches, pastas, and chicken. Wine and beer served.

**The Spa Restaurant and The Outback Pub** (603-246-4562), West Stewartstown. Open Monday and Tuesday 3:30 AM–8 PM, Thursday until 9 PM, Friday and Saturday until 10 PM, Sunday 5 AM–8 PM This is a big, locally popular place with breakfast specialties that include homemade rolled crêpes ($3.50) and corned beef hash with a poached egg. The lunch and dinner menus are both large. Dinner runs from pizzas through king crab legs and lobster tail.

**Moriah's** (603-538-7736), Pittsfield. Open daily 6 AM–2 PM, from 6:30 AM on Sunday. A six-stool counter and a few tables in a middle-of-the-village space connected to the old general store. The basics but with homemade bread, also good for a slice of pie.

**Wilderness Restaurant** (603-237-8779), Main Street, Colebrook. Open 3:30 AM–9 PM daily. All homemade cooking; lounge and entertainment on weekends.

**Howard's Restaurant** (603-237-4025), Main Street, Colebrook. Open

5 AM–8 PM, Sunday at 6 AM, Friday night until 9 PM. A full-service restaurant with a large menu, daily specials, homemade pies and puddings.

**Colebrook Country Club** (603-237-5566), Route 26, east of Colebrook village, and the **Colebrook House** (603-237-5521), Main Street, Colebrook village, are also worth a try.

## ✷ Special Events

*February:* **Pittsburg-Colebrook Winter Carnival,** Kiwanis Club. Activities and events daily during the week of February school vacation.

*March:* **Sno-Deo** in Colebrook.

*June:* **Blessing of the Bikes,** Shrine of Our Lady of Grace, Route 3 south of Colebrook. The shrine was built some 50 years ago to serve the motoring public. The festival, held the weekend after Father's Day, attracts thousands of bicyclists and an ever-increasing number of RVs, snowmobiles, and antique cars.

*Late June:* **Family Fly-Fishing Weekend,** Coleman State Park (603-237-4560), Stewartstown.

*Fourth of July:* **Fourth of July celebrations.** Fireworks at dusk at Murphy Dam, Lake Francis, also barbecue, live music, airplane rides. Parade and barbecue in Colebook.

*Late July:* **Logfest** in Stewartstown (www.logfest.com).

*Third Sunday of August:* **Annual Pittsburg Guides' Show** (603-538-6984), on Back Lake, Pittsburg. The area's working guides show off their skills in log rolling, canoe and kayak competition, and fly-casting. Admission.

*Last week of August:* **Annual North Country Moose Festival** (603-237-8939), Pittsburg, Colebrook, and Errol, New Hampshire, and Canaan, Vermont. Regionwide celebration of the popular moose with parades, barbecues, dances, auto shows, arts and crafts exhibits, and sales. Also see *To See—Moose.*

# INDEX

## D

## E



## F

## G

## M

## N

## O



## P

## Q



## R

## S

## T

## U



## V



## W

## Y



## Z